Cisco ISE for BYOD and Secure Unified Access

Second Edition

Aaron T. Woland, CCIE No. 20113

Jamey Heary, CCIE No. 7680

Cisco Press

800 East 96th Street

Indianapolis, Indiana 46240 USA

Cisco ISE for BYOD and Secure Unified Access
Second Edition

Aaron T. Woland

Jamey Heary

Copyright© 2017 Cisco Systems, Inc.

Published by:
Cisco Press
800 East 96th Street
Indianapolis, IN 46240 USA

Printed in the United States of America

1   17

Library of Congress Control Number: 2017938614

ISBN-13: 978-1-58714-473-8

ISBN-10: 1-58714-473-5

Warning and Disclaimer

This book is designed to provide information about Cisco Identity Services Engine, Cisco TrustSec, and Secure Network Access. Every effort has been made to make this book as complete and as accurate as possible, but no warranty or fitness is implied.

The information is provided on an "as is" basis. The authors, Cisco Press, and Cisco Systems, Inc. shall have neither liability nor responsibility to any person or entity with respect to any loss or damages arising from the information contained in this book or from the use of the discs or programs that may accompany it.

The opinions expressed in this book belong to the author and are not necessarily those of Cisco Systems, Inc.

Trademark Acknowledgments

All terms mentioned in this book that are known to be trademarks or service marks have been appropriately capitalized. Cisco Press or Cisco Systems, Inc., cannot attest to the accuracy of this information. Use of a term in this book should not be regarded as affecting the validity of any trademark or service mark.

Special Sales

For information about buying this title in bulk quantities, or for special sales opportunities (which may include electronic versions; custom cover designs; and content particular to your business, training goals, marketing focus, or branding interests), please contact our corporate sales department at corpsales@pearsoned.com or (800) 382-3419.

For government sales inquiries, please contact governmentsales@pearsoned.com.

For questions about sales outside the U.S., please contact intlcs@pearson.com.

Feedback Information

At Cisco Press, our goal is to create in-depth technical books of the highest quality and value. Each book is crafted with care and precision, undergoing rigorous development that involves the unique expertise of members from the professional technical community.

Readers' feedback is a natural continuation of this process. If you have any comments regarding how we could improve the quality of this book, or otherwise alter it to better suit your needs, you can contact us through email at feedback@ciscopress.com. Please make sure to include the book title and ISBN in your message.

We greatly appreciate your assistance.

Editor-in-Chief: Mark Taub

Alliances Manager, Cisco Press: Ron Fligge

Executive Editor: Mary Beth Ray

Managing Editor: Sandra Schroeder

Development Editor: Christopher Cleveland

Senior Project Editor: Tonya Simpson

Copy Editor: Bill McManus

Technical Editor: Pete Karelis

Editorial Assistant: Vanessa Evans

Cover Designer: Chuti Prasertsith

Composition: codeMantra

Indexer: Erika Millen

Proofreader: Sasirekha Durairajan

Americas Headquarters
Cisco Systems, Inc.
San Jose, CA

Asia Pacific Headquarters
Cisco Systems (USA) Pte. Ltd.
Singapore

Europe Headquarters
Cisco Systems International BV Amsterdam,
The Netherlands

Cisco has more than 200 offices worldwide. Addresses, phone numbers, and fax numbers are listed on the Cisco Website at **www.cisco.com/go/offices.**

Cisco and the Cisco logo are trademarks or registered trademarks of Cisco and/or its affiliates in the U.S. and other countries. To view a list of Cisco trademarks, go to this URL: www.cisco.com/go/trademarks. Third party trademarks mentioned are the property of their respective owners. The use of the word partner does not imply a partnership relationship between Cisco and any other company. (1110R)

About the Authors

Aaron Woland, CCIE No. 20113, is a Principal Engineer in Cisco's Security Group and works with Cisco's largest customers all over the world. His primary job responsibilities include Secure Access and Identity deployments with ISE, solution enhancements, standards development, Advanced Threat Security and solution futures. Aaron joined Cisco in 2005 and is currently a member of numerous security advisory boards and standards body working groups. Prior to joining Cisco, Aaron spent 12 years as a consultant and technical trainer. His areas of expertise include network and host security architecture and implementation, regulatory compliance, and route-switch and wireless.

Aaron is the author of many Cisco white papers and design guides and is co-author of *CCNP Security SISAS 300-208 Official Cert Guide*; *Cisco Next-Generation Security Solutions: All-in-one Cisco ASA Firepower Services, NGIPS, and AMP*; and *CCNA Security 210-260 Complete Video Course*.

Aaron is one of only five inaugural members of the Hall of Fame Elite for Distinguished Speakers at Cisco Live, and is a security columnist for *Network World*, where he blogs on all things related to secure network access. His other certifications include GHIC, GSEC, Certified Ethical Hacker, MCSE, VCP, CCSP, CCNP, CCDP, and many other industry certifications. You can follow Aaron on Twitter: @aaronwoland.

Jamey Heary, CCIE No. 7680, is a Distinguished Systems Engineer at Cisco Systems, where he leads the Global Security Architecture Team, GSAT. Jamey and his GSAT team work as trusted security advisors and architects to Cisco's largest customers worldwide. Jamey sits on the PCI Security Standards Council's Board of Advisors, where he provides strategic and technical guidance for future PCI standards. Jamey is the author of *Cisco NAC Appliance: Enforcing Host Security with Clean Access*. He also has a patent on a new DDoS mitigation and firewall IP reputation technique. Jamey blogged for many years on *Network World* on security topics and is a Cisco Live Distinguished Speaker. Jamey sits on numerous security advisory boards for Cisco Systems and was a founding member of several Cisco security customer user groups across the United States. His other certifications include CISSP, and he is a Certified HIPAA Security Professional. He has been working in the IT field for 24 years and in IT security for 20 years. You can contact Jamey at jheary@appledreams.com.

About the Technical Reviewer

Epaminondas "Pete" Karelis, CCIE Emeritus #8068, is the director of enterprise architecture for Venable LLP, an AmLaw 100 law firm, and has been in IT for more than 20 years. He views himself as a technologist, and has a strong focus on the integration of systems, storage, security, virtualization, and networking. In addition to the Cisco certifications (CCNA, CCDA, CCNP, CCIE R&S) he has held Microsoft (MCSE, MCT) and Checkpoint (CCSE) certifications. Coupled with his strong scripting, programming, and API integration skills, as well as his storage and virtualization experience, he is uniquely enabled to create tightly integrated solutions that incorporate the network with the application and server infrastructure. The ISE Anycast solution mentioned in this book is one of his examples of integrating network awareness with application and service delivery to allow for high availability without the use of load balancers. In his spare time, Pete enjoys spending time with his wife and two beautiful children, as well as reading tech blogs and keeping up to date on future technologies and open-source developments.

Dedications

From Aaron: First and foremost, this book is dedicated to my amazing best friend, fellow adventurer, and wife, Suzanne. This book would surely not exist without your continued support, encouragement, and patience, as well as the sheer number of nights you took care of our newborn twins so I could write. Thank you for putting up with all the long nights and weekends I had to be writing. You are beyond amazing.

To Mom and Pop: You have always believed in me and supported me in absolutely everything I've ever pursued; showed pride in my accomplishments, no matter how small; encouraged me to never stop learning; engrained in me the value of hard work; and inspired me to strive for a career in a field that I love. I hope I can continue to fill your lives with pride and happiness, and if I succeed it will still only be a fraction of what you deserve.

To my four incredible daughters, Eden, Nyah, Netanya, and Cassandra: You girls are my inspiration, my pride and joy, and continue to make me want to be a better man. Eden, when I look at you and your accomplishments over your 18 years of life, I swell with pride. You are so intelligent, kind, and hard working. You will make a brilliant engineer one day, or if you change your mind, I know you will be brilliant in whatever career you find yourself pursuing (perhaps a dolphin trainer). Nyah, you are my morning star, my princess. You have the biggest heart, the kindest soul, and a brilliant mind. You excel at everything you put your mind to, and I look forward to watching you grow and use that power to change the world. Maybe you will follow in my footsteps. I can't wait to see it for myself. Natty and Cassie: You are only 12 weeks old as I write this, yet you have already filled my life with so much joy that I cannot describe it! It is bewildering and addicting to watch you every day and see your growth, wondering what you will be like as you grow up in this limitless world.

To my brother, Dr. Bradley Woland: Thank you for being so ambitious, so driven. It forced my competitive nature to always want more. As I stated when I rambled on in the 12-minute wedding speech, you do not only succeed at everything you try, you crush it! If you were a bum, I would never have pushed myself to the levels that I have. To his beautiful wife, Claire: I am so happy that you are a member of my family now; your kindness, intelligence, and wit certainly keep my brother in check and keep us all smiling.

To my sister, Anna: If I hadn't always had to compete with you for our parents' attention and to keep my things during our "garage sales," I would probably have grown up very naive and vulnerable. You drove me to think outside the box and find new ways to accomplish the things I wanted to do. Seeing you succeed in life and in school truly had a profound effect on my life. Thank you for marrying Eddie, my brilliant brother-in-law. Eddie convinced me that I could actually have a career in this technology stuff, and without his influence, I would probably be in law enforcement or under the hood of car.

To my grandparents, Jack, Lola, Herb, and Ida: You have taught me what it means to be alive and the true definition of courage, survival, perseverance, hard work, and never giving up.

Monty Shafer: the world lost a great man this year, and I lost a brother. You started out as my student, but you've taught me so much in this world. I know that you're up there, watching over Kiersten, Haley, and Devin and all of us whom you loved.

Finally, to Sash Altus, who is undoubtedly rockin' out in heaven with Monty and Dan while my grandparents are complaining about the noise.

From Jamey: This book is dedicated to my beautiful, supportive, and amazing wife, Becca, and our two incredible sons, Liam and Conor, without whose support and sacrifice this book would not have been possible. Becca, you continue to amaze me with your ability to motivate me in life and support my endeavors even when they make life harder for you. Thanks for putting up with the late nights and weekends I had to spend behind the keyboard instead of playing games, Legos, football, or some other fun family activity. You are all the greatest, and I couldn't have done this without you!

Thanks to my parents for their sacrifices and providing me with every opportunity to succeed in life as I was growing up. Dad, you got me my first job in technology that kicked off this whole rewarding career. Know that I cherish greatly the continuous love and support you've both provided throughout my life.

Acknowledgments

From Aaron:

There are so many people to acknowledge. This feels like a speech at the Academy Awards, and I'm afraid I will leave out too many people.

Thomas Howard and Allan Bolding, for their continued support, encouragement, and guidance. Most importantly, for believing in me even though I can be difficult at times. I could not have done any of it without you.

Craig Hyps, Principal Technical Marketing Engineer at Cisco: You are a machine. You possess such deep technical knowledge on absolutely everything (not just pop culture). Your constant references to pop culture keep me laughing, and your influence can be found on content all throughout the book and this industry. *"Can you dig it?"*

Christopher Heffner, Security Architect at Cisco and my "brother from another mother," for convincing me to step up and take a swing at being an author, and for twisting my arm to put "pen to paper" again.

Jonny Rabinowitz and Christopher Murray: You guys continue to set an incredibly high bar, and somehow move that bar higher all the time. You have a fight in you to never lose, never give up, and always do the right thing, and that fight is completely infectious. Your constant enthusiasm, energy, brilliance, and expertise have impressed me and inspired me.

I am honored to work with so many brilliant and talented people every day. Among them: Jesse Dubois, Vivek Santuka, Doug Gash, Chad Mitchell, Jamie Sanbower, Moses Hernandez, Andrew Benhase, Avinash Kumar, Victor Ashe, Jeff Fanelli, Louis Roggo, Kyle King, Tim Snow, Andrew Ossipov, Mike Storm, Jason Frazier, Amit Tropper, and Shai Michelson. You guys truly amaze me, seriously.

To ISE's world-class TME team: Hosuk Won, Tim Abbott, Hsing-Tsu Lai, Imran Bashir, Hari Holla, Ziad Sarieddine, John Eppich, Fay-Ann Lee, Jason Kunst, Krishnan Thiruvengadam, and Paul Carco. *World-class* is not a strong enough adjective to describe this team. You are beyond inspirational, and I am proud to be a member of this team.

Darrin Miller, Nancy Cam-Winget, and Jamey Heary, Distinguished Engineers who set the bar so incredibly high. You are truly inspirational; people to look up to and aspire to be like, and I appreciate all the guidance you have given me.

Max Pritkin, I think you have forgotten more about certificates and PKI than most experts will ever know (if you ever forgot anything, that is). You have taught me so much, and I look forward to learning more from your vast knowledge and unique way of making complex technology seem easy.

To the world's greatest Engineering Team, and of course I mean the people who spend their days writing and testing the code that makes up Cisco ISE. You guys continue to show the world what it means to be "world-class."

To our technical editor, Epaminondas (Pete) Karelis: Thank you for agreeing to take this project on, and for making us look so good! You are a wealth of knowledge, and you did an amazing job catching all of my blunders in this book. I value your leadership almost as much as your friendship.

John Herbert, from movingpackets.net, I learned so much from you in such a short time span. Your brilliance is only superseded by your wit! I hope to be listening to recordings of you harassing the *"Your computer has been hacked and we need to protect it"* scammers for many years to come.

My colleagues: Naasief Edross, Russell Rice, Dalton Hamilton, Tom Foucha, Matt Robertson, Randy Rivera, Brian Ford, Paul Russell, Brendan O'Connell, Jeremy Hyman, Kevin Sullivan, Mason Harris, David Anderson, Luc Billot, Dave White Jr., Nevin Absher, Ned Zaldivar, Mark Kassem, Greg Tillett, Chuck Parker, Shelly Cadora, Ralph Schmieder, Corey Elinburg, Scott Kenewell, Larry Boggis, Chad Sullivan, Dave Klein, Nelson Figueroa, Kevin Redmon, Konrad Reszka, Steven Grimes, Jay Cedrone, Peter Marchand, Eric Howard, Marty Roesch, and so many more! The contributions you make to this industry inspire me every day.

Last, but not least: to all those at Cisco Press, especially Mary Beth Ray and Chris Cleveland. I thank you and your team of editors for making Jamey and me look so good. Apparently, it takes an army of folks to do so. I'm sorry for all the times you had to correct our grammar.

From Jamey:

The cool thing about going second in the acknowledgements section is I can just say, I echo Aaron's sentiments! So many people have made it possible for this book to exist, and for that matter, for the most excellent ISE solution to exist to write about in the first place. "Great job!" to the policy and access business unit; your tireless efforts are bearing fruit. Thank you.

Thank you to Aaron Woland, for pushing the idea of our writing this second edition of the book and making it real. Your technical kung fu is impressive, as is your ability to put pen to paper so others can understand and follow along. It was yet another fun ride!

Thank you to our most awesome tech editor, Pete Karelis. Your attention to detail helped make this book great! Special thanks to Chris Cleveland and Mary Beth Ray and the whole Cisco Press team. As Aaron stated, your contributions and tireless efforts are supremely appreciated. Thanks for this opportunity.

I know I must have forgotten some people; so many have helped me along this journey. Thank you!

Contents at a Glance

Contents

Reader Services

Register your copy at www.ciscopress.com/title/9781587144738 for convenient access to downloads, updates, and corrections as they become available. To start the registration process, go to www.ciscopress.com/register and log in or create an account*. Enter the product ISBN 9781587144738 and click Submit. When the process is complete, you will find any available bonus content under Registered Products.

*Be sure to check the box that you would like to hear from us to receive exclusive discounts on future editions of this product.

Command Syntax Conventions

The conventions used to present command syntax in this book are the same conventions used in the IOS Command Reference. The Command Reference describes these conventions as follows:

- **Boldface** indicates commands and keywords that are entered literally as shown. In actual configuration examples and output (not general command syntax), boldface indicates commands that are manually input by the user (such as a **show** command).

- *Italic* indicates arguments for which you supply actual values.

- Vertical bars (|) separate alternative, mutually exclusive elements.

- Square brackets ([ ]) indicate an optional element.

- Braces ({ }) indicate a required choice.

- Braces within brackets ([{ }]) indicate a required choice within an optional element.

Introduction

Today's networks have evolved into a system without well-defined borders/perimeters that contain data access from both trusted and untrusted devices. Cisco broadly calls this trend *borderless networking*. The Cisco Secure Access architecture and Cisco Identity Services Engine (ISE) were developed to provide organizations with a solution to secure and regain control of borderless networks in a Bring Your Own Device (BYOD) world.

A few basic truths become apparent when trying to secure a borderless network. First, you can no longer trust internal data traffic. There are just too many ingress points into the network and too many untrusted devices/users inside the network to be able to trust it implicitly. Second, given the lack of internal trust, it becomes necessary to authenticate and authorize all users into the network regardless of their connection type: wired, wireless, or VPN. Third, because of the proliferation of untrusted and unmanaged devices connecting to your internal network, device control and posture assessment become critical. Each device must be checked for security compliance before it is allowed access to your network resources. These checks vary according to your security policy, but usually involve checking the device type, location, management status, and operating-system patch level, and ensuring that antimalware software is running and up to date.

This book addresses the complete lifecycle of protecting a modern borderless network using Cisco Secure Access and ISE solutions. Secure access and ISE design, implementation, and troubleshooting are covered in depth. This book explains the many details of the solution and how it can be used to secure borderless networks. At its heart, this solution allows organizations to identify and apply network security policies based on user identity, device type, device behavior, and other attributes, such as security posture. Technologies such as 802.1X, profiling, guest access, network admission control, RADIUS, device administration, TACACS+, and TrustSec are covered in depth.

The goal is to boil down and simplify the architectural details and present them in one reference without trying to replace the existing design, installation, and configuration guides already available from Cisco.

Who Should Read This Book?

This book is targeted primarily to a technical audience involved in architecting, deploying, and delivering secure networks and enabling mobile services. It can help them make informed choices, and enable them to have an engaging discussion with their organization, on how they can achieve their security and availability goals, while reaping the benefits of a secure access solution.

This book is helpful to those looking to deploy Cisco ISE to secure your wired, wireless, and VPN access. It is also useful for those moving to a BYOD IT model.

How This Book Is Organized

This book is organized into 31 chapters distributed across 7 different parts, each based on a main theme. As a bonus, four appendixes are included as Part VIII to provide added value to readers. Although this book can be read cover to cover, readers can move between chapters and parts, covering only the content that interests them. The seven parts of the book are described first:

Part I, "Identity-Enabled Network: Unite!": Examines the evolution of identity-enabled networks. It provides an overview of security issues facing today's networks and what has been the history of trying to combat this problem. This part covers a foundation-building review of AAA, 802.1X, the NAC framework, NAC appliance, the evolution into Secure Access, and the creation of Cisco ISE. It discusses the issues faced with the consumerization of information technology, the mass influx of personal devices, ensuring only the correct users, correct devices, with the correct software are allowed to access the corporate network unfettered.

Part II, "The Blueprint, Designing an ISE-Enabled Network": Covers the high-level design phase of a secure network access project. Solution diagrams are included. This part covers the different ISE functions available, how to distribute these functions, and the solution taxonomy. It discusses the enforcement devices that are part of this solution and ones that are not. Change of Authorization (CoA) is introduced. All these concepts are clarified and reinforced throughout the other parts.

Part III, "The Foundation, Building a Context-Aware Security Policy": Describes how to create a context-aware security policy for the network and devices. This is often the hardest part of a secure network access project. This part covers the departments that need to be involved, the policies to be considered, and best practices. Coverage includes some lessons learned and landmines to watch out for. Screenshots and flow diagrams are included in this part to aid in the readers' understanding of the process, how communication occurs and in what order, and how to configure the miscellaneous device supplicants.

Part IV, "Let's Configure!": Details the step-by-step configuration of ISE, the network access devices (NAD), and supplicants. The goal of this part is to have the entire infrastructure and policy management configured and ready to begin the actual deployment. Technology and complex topics are explained along with the configuration steps, aiding in the understanding of the configuration steps by tying them together with the technological explanation.

Part V, "Advanced Secure Access Features": Dives into some of the more advanced solution features that truly differentiate the ISE secure access system. This part covers advanced configurations of the ISE profiling engine, Cisco TrustSec, high availability, backups, passive identity capabilities, EasyConnect, and context sharing with the Platform eXchange Grid (pxGrid).

Part VI, "Monitoring, Maintenance, and Troubleshooting for Network Access AAA": Examines the maintenance of ISE, backups, and upgrades. It covers how to troubleshoot not only ISE, but the entire secure access system, and how to use the tools provided in the ISE product. Common monitoring and maintenance tasks, as well as troubleshooting tools, are explained from a help-desk support technician's point of view.

Part VII, "Device Administration": All new material for this second edition, this part covers the principles of device administration AAA and TACACS+, how to design it with ISE, and the step-by-step configuration of key Cisco network devices: Catalyst switches, Wireless LAN Controllers, and Nexus data center switches.

Here is an overview of each of the 31 chapters:

- **Chapter 1, "Regain Control of Your IT Security":** This chapter introduces the concepts that brought us to the current evolutionary stage of network access security. It discusses the explosion of mobility, virtualization, social networking, and ubiquitous network access coupled with the consumerization of information technology.

- **Chapter 2, "Fundamentals of AAA":** This chapter reviews the critical security concept of authentication, authorization, and accounting (AAA); compares and contrasts the two main AAA types of network access and device administration; and dives into the foundations of RADIUS and TACACS+.

- **Chapter 3, "Introducing Cisco Identity Services Engine":** Cisco ISE makes up the backbone of Cisco's next-generation, context-aware, identity-based security policy solution. This chapter introduces this revolutionary product and provides an overview of its functions and capabilities.

- **Chapter 4, "The Building Blocks in an Identity Services Engine Design":** This chapter covers the components of the secure access solution, including ISE personas, licensing model, and the policy structure.

- **Chapter 5, "Making Sense of the ISE Deployment Design Options":** This chapter examines all the available personas in ISE and design options with the combination of those personas.

- **Chapter 6, "Quick Setup of an ISE Proof of Concept":** This chapter provides a high-level overview of the ISE personas, walks you through the initial configuration (called bootstrapping) of ISE itself, and introduces role-based access control (RBAC).

- **Chapter 7, "Building a Cisco ISE Network Access Security Policy":** This chapter guides you through the process of creating a comprehensive network access security policy (NASP) that you can use in an environment that is safeguarded by Cisco ISE.

- **Chapter 8, "Building a Device Security Policy":** This chapter explores ISE device profiling and Threat-Centric NAC features in some detail. The goal is to disclose the different ways in which ISE can identify device types and other contextual information about devices for use in an ISE policy.

- **Chapter 9, "Building an ISE Accounting and Auditing Policy":** This chapter covers why you need accounting and auditing for ISE; using PCI DSS as your ISE auditing framework; and Cisco ISE user accounting. Understanding and keeping track of what is happening inside the network and inside of ISE is critical to achieving a successful ISE deployment.

- **Chapter 10, "Profiling Basics and Visibility"**: This chapter introduces the concepts of profiling and configuration choices needed to create a foundation to build upon. It examines the different profiling mechanisms and the pros and cons related to each, discussing best practices and configuration details.

- **Chapter 11, "Bootstrapping Network Access Devices"**: This key chapter examines the configuration of the NADs themselves and focuses on best practices to ensure a successful ongoing deployment.

- **Chapter 12, "Network Authorization Policy Elements"**: This chapter examines the logical roles within an organization and how to create authorization results to assign the correct level of access based on that role.

- **Chapter 13, "Authentication and Authorization Policies"**: This chapter explains the distinct and important difference between authentication and authorization policies, presents the pieces that make up the policies, and provides examples of how to create a policy in ISE that enforces the logical policies created in Chapter 12.

- **Chapter 14, "Guest Lifecycle Management"**: Guest access has become an expected resource at companies in today's world. This chapter explains the full secure guest lifecycle management, from Web Authentication (WebAuth) to sponsored guest access and self-registration options.

- **Chapter 15, "Client Posture Assessment"**: This chapter examines endpoint posture assessment and remediation actions, the configuration of the extensive checks and requirements, and how to tie them into an authorization policy.

- **Chapter 16, "Supplicant Configuration"**: This chapter looks at configuration examples of the most popular supplicants.

- **Chapter 17, "BYOD: Self-Service Onboarding and Registration"**: This critical chapter goes through a detailed examination of BYOD concepts, policies, and flows. Both the user and administrative experiences are detailed, as well as the integration between ISE and third-party MDM vendors and ISE's internal certificate authority (CA).

- **Chapter 18, "Setting Up and Maintaining a Distributed ISE Deployment"**: Cisco ISE can be deployed in a scalable distributed model or as a standalone device. This chapter examines how ISE can be deployed in this distributed model, and the caveats associated. It also details high availability (HA) with technologies such as load balancing.

- **Chapter 19, "Remote Access VPN and Cisco ISE"**: This chapter details the integration of ISE with remote access VPNs using the Cisco ASA.

- **Chapter 20, "Deployment Phases"**: This chapter explains the best practices related to phasing in a secure network access deployment. The chapter goes through the phases of Monitor Mode, Low-Impact Mode, and Closed Mode deployments.

- **Chapter 21, "Advanced Profiling Configuration"**: This chapter builds on what was learned and configured in Chapter 10, examining how to profile unknown endpoints and looking deeper into the profiling policies themselves.

- **Chapter 22, "Cisco TrustSec AKA Security Group Access"**: This chapter introduces the next-generation policy model known as Cisco TrustSec and Security Group Tags.

- **Chapter 23, "Passive Identities, ISE-PIC, and EasyConnect"**: Brand new for this second edition, this chapter compares and contrasts active versus passive identities, and the EasyConnect method of network access control.

- **Chapter 24, "ISE Ecosystems: The Platform eXchange Grid (pxGrid)"**: Also brand new for this edition, this chapter discusses the use of ISE as the center of a security ecosystem, the importance of context sharing, and the best practices for deploying the Platform eXchange Grid (pxGrid).

- **Chapter 25, "Understanding Monitoring, Reporting, and Alerting"**: This chapter explains the extensive and redesigned monitoring, reporting, and alerting mechanisms built into the ISE solution.

- **Chapter 26, "Troubleshooting"**: This chapter aids the reader when having to troubleshoot the ISE identity-enabled network and its many moving parts.

- **Chapter 27, "Upgrading ISE"**: This chapter focuses on the upgrading of ISE nodes using both the graphical tool and the command line, with a heavy focus on the secondary PAN first (SPF) method of upgrade.

- **Chapter 28, "Device Administration Fundamentals"**: This chapter details the integration of device administration AAA and TACACS+ into the ISE solution and the design options for deploying it in parallel or in conjunction with network access AAA.

- **Chapter 29, "Configuring Device Admin AAA with Cisco IOS"**: Building on Chapter 29, this chapter details the configuration of ISE and Cisco IOS–based Catalyst switches for the purposes of device administration AAA with TACACS+.

- **Chapter 30, "Configuring Device Admin AAA with Cisco WLC**: This chapter details the configuration of ISE and Cisco Wireless LAN Controllers for the purposes of device administration AAA with TACACS+.

- **Chapter 31, "Configuring Device Admin AAA with Cisco Nexus Switches"**: This chapter details the configuration of ISE and Cisco Wireless LAN Controllers for the purposes of device administration AAA with TACACS+.

Chapter 1

Regain Control of Your IT Security

This chapter covers the following topics:

- The weakest-link security problem

- Introduction to Cisco ISE

- Introduction to identity and context

The explosion of mobility, virtualization, social networking, and ubiquitous network access coupled with the consumerization of information technology brings new security challenges to organizations, including:

- Insufficient security controls for non-corporate-owned devices, especially consumer-class devices such as the iPhone and iPad. This is known as the Bring Your Own Device (BYOD) phenomenon.

- An increased potential for the loss of sensitive data, which can cause an array of problems for your business, customers, and partners.

- Dissolution of network security boundaries (borderless networks), resulting in an increased number of entry points to your network and, therefore, an increased risk to your business.

- Increased complexity in maintaining compliance with security and privacy regulations, laws, and other enforced standards such as Payment Card Industry Data Security Standard (PCI-DSS).

IT network and security policies, budgets, and resources are not keeping pace with the rapid innovations happening in our business models, workplace, and technology. With today's security challenges and threats growing more sophisticated and broad, traditional network security approaches are no longer sufficient without augmentation. Organizations require security systems that can provide more actionable intelligence, that are pervasively deployed, and that are more tightly integrated with other installed networking and security tools than they have been in the past.

The threat landscape has also evolved dramatically in the last couple years. Attackers are now using social-engineering techniques to gain trusted credentials on your network and services. Social engineering, essentially hacking people, is the fastest-growing attack vector today. Many of the recent breaches can be traced back to attackers obtaining trusted credentials that allowed them to pivot throughout the breached networks just like any other user would. This raises serious concerns, such as how do you protect against an attacker that has admin credentials on your Microsoft Active Directory (AD) domain? One way is to ensure that each user connecting into the network is dynamically limited to access to only those services that they require. We call this dynamic network segmentation, or micro-segmentation.

The purpose of this chapter is to define the major focus areas that need to be considered to take back, and continue to maintain, control of your IT security. This must be accomplished in the face of recent technology trends while still enabling businesses to function efficiently. The secret lies in centralized, pervasive security policy control.

Security: Still a Weakest-Link Problem

The bad guys are always looking for the path of least resistance to their targets. Why waste effort attacking a hardened target system directly when you can get there by quickly compromising something weaker and using its privileges to exploit your target? This is the basic principle of the weakest-link problem. The information you are trying to protect is only as secure as the weakest entry point (link) to that information. This has always been true in IT security. The big change is in the increase of the sum total of links, or entry points, that must be dealt with. Additionally, the use of social engineering is on the rise due to its high success rate.

Never before have networks and their data been more accessible by external untrusted individuals. Also, the number of devices in today's typical network has grown dramatically over time with the addition of network-capable nodes such as IP phones, IP video-conferencing systems, and mobile devices such as cell phones and tablets. Most recently, the phenomenon of the Internet of Things (IoT) is causing an explosion in the number of network devices. These devices range from IP cameras, home automation devices, appliances, cars, smart watches, and so many more. Just think about all the devices you have that are connected to your home network. Now extrapolate that number to your company. It's an amazing number of devices, each with its own operating system, vulnerabilities, and security concerns.

Today's networks allow access from literally anywhere on the globe via a combination of wireless, wired, and virtual private networks (VPNs), guest portals, cloud services, consumer devices, mobile devices, business-to-business (B2B) connections…and the list goes on.

Back in the day, prior to the expansion of cost-effective mobile computing and network-able handheld devices, networks were composed of stationary corporate-owned desktop PCs, each of which often had only one employee assigned to it for dedicated usage. Now each employee has numerous network-attached devices, most or all of which are highly mobile. For example, on his home network one of this book's authors has an iPhone, an iPad, an Apple Watch, a Windows 7 PC, a MacBook Air, a Verizon MiFi device, a Wi-Fi corporate IP Phone, a Cisco telepresence system, and a desk IP Phone. And those are just the devices he uses for work! It doesn't include his home devices or cloud services, which easily triples the number. Some of these are personal devices, while others are corporate-owned assets. But all have a risk profile to his company.

No organizations today are closed entities with well-defined network security perimeters. This leads us to the concepts of ubiquitous access and borderless networks. Gone are the days of a nicely defined network security perimeter made up of a firewall that guards against unauthorized access from the outside. Security architecture is changing from a point defense perimeter approach to a defense-in-depth network security architecture that is policy-driven and threat-focused.

Here are some fundamental shifts created by today's environment:

- You can no longer simply trust the packets on your internal networks.

- The network must require identity- and context-aware access control at all attachment points—wired, wireless, and VPN (internal and external).

- Security policies must become identity- and context-aware, as well as centrally managed.

- Security and network systems must work together seamlessly to create an architecture that works effectively.

- Integrated and automated threat defense is now a requirement. Static defenses are too easily bypassed and manual policy change and remediation is too slow to defend against the threats.

Today, networks are most secure at their traditional network perimeter, namely the Internet-facing access points. However, the security of the internal networks, especially wired networks, behind those impressive perimeter fortress walls is sorely lacking. By and large, once a user gains access to the internal networks, they are given free and unrestricted network access. In addition, the pervasiveness of mobility has thrown the concept of internal vs. external out the window. Mobile devices roam between both internal and external networks while sometimes connecting to both simultane-ously. Never before has the average employee been so connected in so many ways in so many places. Effectively dealing with the security risks that spring forth from this new networking reality by using the Cisco Identity Services Engine (ISE) and Cisco Secure Access are the focus of this book.

Cisco Identity Services Engine

Cisco describes its Identity Services Engine solution in this way:

> A different approach is required to both manage and secure the evolving mobile enterprise. With superior user and device visibility, Cisco ISE simplifies the mobility

experience for enterprises. It also shares vital contextual data with integrated technology partner solutions. With the integration, consolidation, and automation that Cisco ISE provides, you can identify, contain, and remediate threats faster. The Cisco Identity Services Engine is a next-generation identity and access control policy platform that enables enterprises to facilitate new business services, enhance infrastructure security, enforce compliance, and streamline service operations. Its unique architecture allows enterprises to gather real-time contextual information from networks, users, and devices to make proactive governance decisions by enforcing policy across the network infrastructure—wired, wireless, and VPN.

At a high level, the Cisco ISE and Secure Access solution provide the following services:

- Gain awareness of everything hitting your network.

- Control network access securely, consistently, and efficiently.

- Relieve the stress of a complex access management environment.

Some of the key capabilities that ISE will provide are:

- User identity awareness and control.

- Network, user, and device context awareness. Examples of context include operating system patch level, AD group member, antivirus client installed and up to date, device type such as printer, physical location of device, risk profile of device, and more.

- A centralized security policy across wired, wireless, and VPN access for simpler corporate governance.

- Centralized guest access management that is both feature-rich and easy to use.

- System-wide visibility into who, where, and what is on a network.

- Authentication, authorization, and accounting (AAA), device profiling, device posture, mobile device onboarding, and guest services in a single solution to simplify deployments and cut operational costs via ISE.

- Automated device profiling/identification using ISE-based traffic probes, Cisco IOS device sensors included in Cisco switches, and active endpoint scanning.

- Simplified BYOD onboarding through self-service device registration and provisioning. Significantly reduces the burden on IT without sacrificing security.

- TACACS+ device AAA.

- Cisco TrustSec policy management and enforcement using security group tagging.

- Built-in certificate authority (CA) specifically designed to make it simple to use.

- Ability to share the information and context inside of ISE with other devices, such as next-generation firewalls (NGFW) and using Cisco Platform Exchange Grid (pxGrid).

To summarize, the Cisco ISE solution allows you to connect any user on any device to any segment of your network more easily, reliably, and securely. The rich policy-based nature of the ISE solution provides you with identity- and context-based access differentiation.

Sources for Providing Identity and Context Awareness

Having *identity awareness* in the network simply means that you are able to determine and authenticate the individuality of the user or group of users trying to gain access to your network. To establish individuality, combine both a username (or equivalent) and any other available user attributes. For example, Jamey Heary successfully authenticated onto the network using his AD account JHeary. JHeary is a member of both the Users and Contractors groups. There is now an identity for the user JHeary that can be utilized to determine which network policy ISE should assign to the network.

ISE can obtain identity information and validate its authenticity using several methods and sources, including AD. This identity information can be user-based, endpoint-based, or both. Here are the most common methods ISE uses to obtain identity information:

- **802.1X:** 802.1X is an IEEE standard for Layer 2 access control to wired and wireless networks. As an example, WPA2 Enterprise uses 802.1X plus Extensible Authentication Protocol (EAP) for authentication. 802.1X can use either user identity or machine identity, or it can use both. 802.1X offers the capability to permit or deny Layer 2 network connectivity, assign a VLAN, and apply various other traffic- and network-related policies.

- **Redirect to web portal:** A user's web browser is automatically redirected to a user authentication web page (in other words, a web authentication) where they can input their identity via a customized web form.

- **Guest access:** Users are identified as guest users in various ways. Common methods are no authentication, temporary credentials, temporary event key, and social network credentials like Facebook. Guest access can also be defined based on connection information. For example, anyone who connects to the public-net wireless service set identifier (SSID) is considered a guest user.

- **VPN authentication:** Users enter their credentials into their VPN client before a VPN tunnel or a Secure Sockets Layer (SSL) VPN is allowed to pass traffic.

- **Easy Connect:** ISE policy allows users to log on to Active Directory from their domain-joined PC. ISE then applies an updated network policy based on their AD credentials and groups.

- **MAC address authentication bypass:** ISE uses the endpoint's hardware MAC address from its network interface card to gain access to the network. This is called MAC Authentication Bypass (MAB). Because of the ease of MAC forgery, it is recommended to use additional methods such as device-profiling information to ensure authenticity.

Now that identity awareness has been established, you need to gather real-time contextual information from networks, users, and devices. Cisco ISE has several ways of collecting and using contextual information. Here are some of the more common context sources:

■ User authorization attributes from identity sources such as Lightweight Directory Access Protocol (LDAP), AD, RADIUS, or the internal ISE user database.

■ Device attributes from LDAP using a machine account lookup.

■ An integrated device profiling engine that actively and/or passively scans a device or monitors its network behavior to determine what kind of device it is. For example, if a device has a MAC address owned by Apple and its browser user-agent string includes the words "Apple iPad," then the profiling engine will classify it as an Apple iPad.

■ Location information such as physical location, network access type (wired, wireless, VPN), GPS location, and switch port location.

■ Device posture, which gathers posture information from the host. Posture information reported to ISE can include OS type and version, OS patches, service pack level, security software, application inventory, running processes, registry keys, digital certificates, and many others.

■ Context information gathered from other network and security solutions such as Cisco Advanced Malware Protection (AMP), Cisco Stealthwatch, Cisco NGFW, a Qualys vulnerability scanner, and many others. Context examples include vulnerability data found on host, malware running on host, host connecting to malicious content, and other threat-centric contexts.

Unleash the Power of Centralized Policy

The final step is putting identity and context information to work via ISE's policy framework. Cisco ISE provides a centralized view from which you can administrate the policy of up to 500,000 endpoints enterprise-wide regardless of their network access type—wired, wireless, or VPN. Cisco ISE also supports network devices from multiple vendors. The policies you create will monitor and enforce users' compliance with any written security policy and other corporate governance regulations your organization has in place. Additionally, ISE can automate the quarantine and remediation of users/hosts based on live threat data. For example, if Cisco AMP finds malware on a host, it can tell ISE to quarantine that host on the network. ISE is capable of performing simple or complex, yet elegant, policy rules that are both identity- and context-aware. Once a policy rule is matched, its permissions are applied to the network and/or device. It is in this way that ISE's centralized policy structure is able to greatly simplify and restore your visibility, control, and governance of the network.

The kinds of permissions that ISE can grant once a policy match is obtained are extensive. Here are a few of the popular ones:

- Deny any network access

- Permit all network access

- Restrict network access by downloading an access control list (ACL) to the access device (switch, wireless controller, VPN headend)

- Change the assigned VLAN on a switch port or wireless connection

- Redirect client for web authentication

- Auto-provision the device's 802.1X supplicant or client

- Assign a Security Group Tag (SGT) to all data frames

- Execute an Auto Smartports macro on a Cisco switch

Figure 1-1 depicts some of the permissions that are available using Cisco ISE. In the following chapters of this book, we will explore permissions and the other topics of this chapter in more detail.

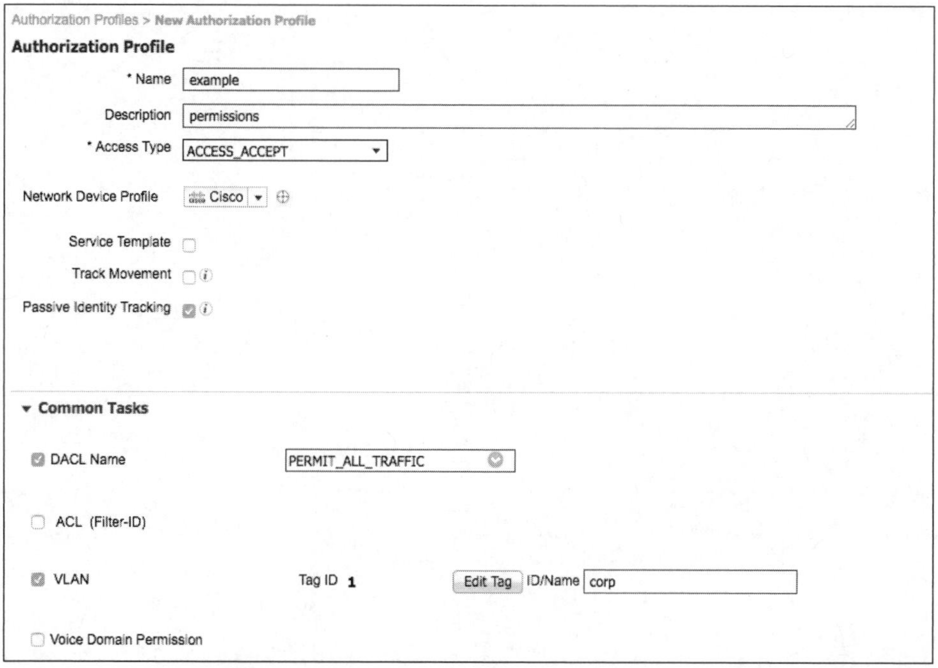

Figure 1-1   *Cisco ISE Permission Authorization Profile Example*

Summary

This chapter examined the increasing security risks, threats, and corporate governance challenges being faced in our borderless networks that are filled with highly mobile corporate-owned and personally owned devices. This chapter focused on network security as a weakest-link problem in an environment where the number of links is exponentially expanding due to mobility, virtualization, IoT, and the consumerization of IT. Cisco Identity Services Engine and Cisco Secure Access were introduced as solutions to help alleviate these risks and challenges. The secret to efficiently tackling these tasks is pervasive and centralized policy control of all devices and network access methods. In this book, we will explore the topics of this chapter in much more detail.

Chapter 2

Fundamentals of AAA

This chapter covers the following topics:

- Authentication, authorization, and accounting (AAA)
- Terminal Access Controller Access-Control System Plus (TACACS+)
- Remote Authentication Dial-In User Service (RADIUS)

In the world of security, we can only be as secure as our controls permit us to be. There are laws in the United States defining what a passenger of an airplane is permitted to bring onboard. If the TSA agents weren't operating the metal detectors and X-ray machines (and all the other things that slow us down when trying to reach our airplanes), then how would the FAA ever really enforce those policies?

With technology, we are faced with the same challenges. We need to have controls in place to ensure that only the correct entities are using our technological "gadgets." The same security concepts from the airport can be applied to many use cases, including human interaction with a computer, a computer's interaction with a network, and even an application's interaction with data.

This security principle is known as authentication, authorization, and accounting (AAA), often referred to as *Triple-A*.

Before allowing someone or something to perform an action, you must ensure you know who that entity actually is (authentication) and if the entity is permitted, what level of access should be granted (authorization). Additionally, you need to ensure that accurate records are maintained showing that the action has occurred, so you keep a security log of the events (accounting).

The concepts of AAA can be applied to many different aspects of a technology lifecycle. However, this book will focus on the two main aspects of AAA related to network security:

■ **Device administration AAA:** Controlling access to who can log in to a network device console, Telnet session, Secure Shell (SSH) session, or other method is one form of AAA that you should be aware of. This is AAA for device administration, and although it can often seem similar to network access AAA, it has a completely different purpose and requires different policy constructs.

■ **Network access AAA:** Securing network access can provide the identity of the end-point, device, or user before permitting the entity to communicate with the network. This is AAA for network access and is the type of AAA that is most focused on in this book.

Triple-A

Authentication, simply put, is the validation of an identity, also known as a *credential*. It is a very important step in the process of performing any sort of secure access control, regardless of what you are controlling. Forget about information technology for a second, and consider paying for groceries with a credit card. As a credit card owner, you have the choice to sign the back of the card or to write "check ID" on the back. The more secure method is to force the validation of the credential (the ID) of the person using that card and ensure that credential matches the name on the front of the credit card.

Having a cashier check the identity of the card user to ensure the person in front of them matches the person shown on the ID itself is *authentication*. Ensuring that the identity matches the name printed on the credit card is *authorization*. Think about this scenario: Jamey Heary goes into a retail store and hands the cashier a credit card to pay for the $10,000 of electronics he is purchasing. He passes his driver's license to the cashier, who verifies that the picture matches Jamey. It is certainly his identity; however, the name printed on the credit card is Aaron Woland. Should the credit card transaction go through? Of course not (and he better not try).

Jamey's attempt to use Aaron's credit card is now in the log files of the point of sale system, the video monitoring system of the store, and other systems. This is the accounting portion of AAA. It's a critical piece that is required for reporting, audits, and more.

It will become paramount for you as a security professional to understand the difference and purpose of all three A's in the Triple-A security principal.

Compare and Select AAA Options

As previously described in this chapter, there are two uses of AAA that you will focus on in this book—device administration and network access.

Device Administration

AAA for device administration is a method of AAA for controlling access to a network device console, Telnet session, SSH session, or other method of accessing the device operating system itself where configuration of the device occurs. For example, imagine your company has an Active Directory group named Cisco Administrators, which should have full access (privilege level 15) to the Cisco switches in the company's network. Members of Cisco Administrators should therefore be able to make changes to virtual local-area networks (VLANs), see the entire running configuration of the device, and more.

There could be another group named Cisco Operators who should only be allowed to view the output of **show** commands, and not be allowed to configure anything in the device. Device administration AAA provides this capability.

However, device administration AAA can get much more granular. Cisco Identity Services Engine (ISE) has a capability to provide command sets, which are listings of commands that are permitted or denied to be executed by an authenticated user. In other words, a user can authenticate to the Cisco IOS shell, and ISE can permit or deny the user's execution of individual commands, if you choose.

Figure 2-1 illustrates device administration.

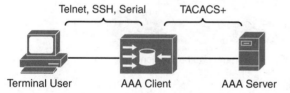

Figure 2-1   *Device Administration AAA*

Administering devices can be very interactive in nature, with the need to authenticate once but authorize many times during a single administrative session in the command line of a device. As such, it lends itself well to using the Terminal Access Controller Access-Control System (TACACS) client/server protocol, more so than Remote Authentication Dial-In User Service (RADIUS). As the name describes, TACACS was designed for device administration AAA to authenticate and authorize users into mainframe and Unix terminals and other terminals or consoles.

Both the TACACS and RADIUS protocols will be discussed in more depth within this chapter; however, because TACACS separates out the authorization portion of AAA, allowing for a single authentication and multiple authorizations within the same session, it lends itself to device administration more than RADIUS. RADIUS does not provide the capability to control which commands can be executed.

Network Access

Secure network access is essentially all about learning the identity of the user or end-point before permitting that entity to communicate within the network. This type of AAA is the main focus in this book. Network access AAA really took a strong hold back in the day of modems and dial-up networking with plain old telephone service (POTS). Companies provided network access to workers from outside the physical boundaries of the company's buildings with the use of modems. People gained Internet access by using dial-up to an Internet service provider (ISP) over their modems, as well. Basically, all that was needed was a modem and a phone line.

Of course, allowing anyone to dial in to the company network just by dialing the modem's phone number was not a secure practice. The user needed to be authenticated and authorized before being allowed to connect. That is where RADIUS came into play originally, as is evident in the name of the protocol (Remote Authentication *Dial-In* User Service). RADIUS was used between the network access device (NAD) and the authentication server. The authentication was normally Password Authentication Protocol (PAP), Challenge Handshake Authentication Protocol (CHAP), or Microsoft CHAP (MS-CHAP).

Figure 2-2 illustrates dial-up remote access.

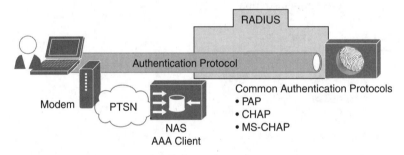

Figure 2-2   *Dial-Up Remote Access*

As technology continued to evolve and direct dial-in to a company was replaced by remote-access virtual private networks (VPN), Wi-Fi became prevalent, and the IEEE standardized on a method to use Extensible Authentication Protocol (EAP) over local-area networks (IEEE 802.1X), RADIUS was used as the protocol of choice to carry the authentication traffic. In fact, IEEE 802.1X cannot use TACACS. It must use RADIUS.

Note   There is another protocol similar to RADIUS, known as DIAMETER, that may also be used with 802.1X. However, it is mostly found in the service provider space and is out of scope for this book.

In today's world, RADIUS is the protocol used almost exclusively with network access AAA and is the main control plane in use between Cisco ISE and the network devices themselves.

TACACS+

As previously introduced, TACACS is a protocol set created and intended for controlling access to mainframe and Unix terminals. Cisco created a new protocol called TACACS+, which was released as an open standard in the early 1990s. TACACS+ may be derived from TACACS, but it is a completely separate and non-backward-compatible protocol designed for AAA. Although TACACS+ is mainly used for device administration AAA, it can also be used for some types of network access AAA.

TACACS+ became a supported protocol with Cisco ISE in version 2.0. Prior to ISE 2.0, the Cisco Secure Access Control Server (ACS) was Cisco's primary AAA server product for enterprises that needed to use TACACS+ for device administration AAA. However, starting with ISE 2.0, ISE has replaced ACS as Cisco's enterprise flagship AAA server for both RADIUS and TACACS+.

> **Note**   Other Cisco products support TACACS+, such as the Cisco Access Registrar solution. However, those solutions are geared toward service providers and are not germane to this book.

TACACS+ uses Transmission Control Protocol (TCP) port 49 to communicate between the TACACS+ client and the TACACS+ server. An example is a Cisco switch authenticating and authorizing administrative access to the switch's IOS CLI. The switch is the TACACS+ client, and Cisco ISE is the server, as illustrated in Figure 2-3.

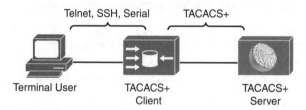

Telnet, SSH, Serial   TACACS+

Terminal User   TACACS+   TACACS+
                        Client   Server

Figure 2-3   *TACACS+ Client–Server Communication*

One of the key differentiators of TACACS+ is its capability to separate authentication, authorization, and accounting as separate and independent functions. This is why TACACS+ is so commonly used for device administration, even though RADIUS is still certainly capable of providing device administration AAA.

Device administration can be very interactive in nature, with the need to authenticate once but authorize many times during a single administrative session in the command line of a device. A router or switch may need to authorize a user's activity on a per-command basis. TACACS+ is designed to accommodate that type of authorization need. As the name describes, TACACS+ was designed for device administration AAA to authenticate and authorize users into mainframe and Unix terminals and other terminals or consoles.

TACACS+ communication between the client and server uses different message types depending on the function. In other words, different messages may be used for authentication than are used for authorization and accounting. Another very interesting point to know is that TACACS+ communication will encrypt the entire body of the packet to assure privacy of any credentials being transported and that any messages transported over the session will not be not modified in transit.

TACACS+ Authentication Messages

When using TACACS+ for authentication, only three types of packets are exchanged between the client (the network device) and the server:

- **START:** This packet is used to begin the authentication request between the AAA client and the AAA server.

- **REPLY:** Messages sent from the AAA server to the AAA client.

- **CONTINUE:** Messages from the AAA client used to respond to the AAA server requests for username and password.

The following paragraphs describe the authentication flow process and the messages used.

When an authentication request is sent from the client to the server, it begins with a START message from the network device to the server. The START message tells the server that an authentication request is coming. All messages from the server to the network device (client) will be a REPLY during authentication. The server sends a REPLY message asking for the client to retrieve the username. The username is sent to the server within a CONTINUE message.

After the server receives the username, it sends a REPLY message back to the client requesting the password, which is sent back to the server in a CONTINUE message. The server then sends a final REPLY message with the pass or fail status of the authentication request.

The possible values returned from the AAA server to the AAA client within the final REPLY message are:

- **ACCEPT:** The user authentication succeeded and the authorization process may begin, if the AAA client is configured for authorization.

- **REJECT:** The user authentication has failed. The login will be denied or the end user will be prompted to try again, depending on the configuration of the AAA client.

- **ERROR:** An error occurred at some point during the authentication. AAA clients will typically attempt to authenticate the user again or attempt a different method of authenticating the user.

- **CONTINUE:** The user is prompted for additional information. This is not to be confused with the CONTINUE message sent from the AAA client to the AAA server. This value is sent from the AAA server within a REPLY message, indicating that more information is required. CONTINUE is also used for generating additional prompts to gather more information during the logon process. This is used for items such as changing a password or requesting a second authentication (such as username, password, and secure token).

Figure 2-4 illustrates the authentication messages between the client and server.

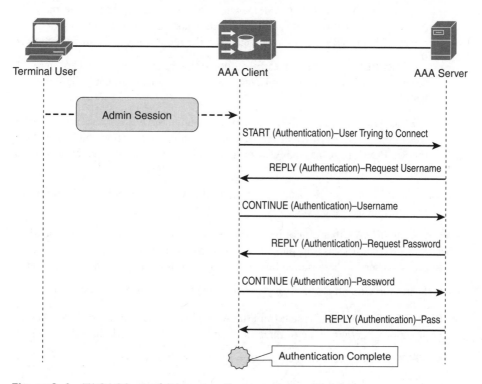

Figure 2-4 *TACACS+ Authentication Communication Flows*

TACACS+ Authorization and Accounting Messages

When using TACACS+ for authorization, only two messages are used between the AAA client and the AAA server:

- **REQUEST:** This message is sent from the AAA client to the AAA server to request an authorization. The authorization may be related to access to a CLI shell or possibly to authorize a specific command. The protocol doesn't distinguish between a request for shell access or a request for a CLI command authorization. The function requested is known as a *service*. For example, the service would be *shell* for CLI access to a device running Cisco IOS. Each service may be communicated with attribute-value (AV) pairs. You can find more about specific TACACS+ AV pairs at http://bit.ly/1mF27aT.

■ **RESPONSE:** This message is sent from the AAA server back to the AAA client with the result of the authorization request, including specific details such as the privilege level assigned to the end user. RESPONSE messages may contain one of five replies:

■ **FAIL:** Indicates the user should be denied access to the requested service.

■ **PASS_ADD:** Indicates a successful authorization and that the information contained within the RESPONSE message should be used in addition to the requested information. If no additional arguments are returned by the AAA server within the RESPONSE message, then the request is simply authorized as is.

■ **PASS_REPL:** Indicates a successful authorization but the server has chosen to ignore the REQUEST and is replacing it with the information sent back in the RESPONSE.

■ **FOLLOW:** Indicates that the AAA server wants the AAA client to send the authorization request to a different server. The new server information will be listed in the RESPONSE packet. The AAA client can either use that new server or treat the response as a FAIL.

■ **ERROR:** Indicates a problem occurring on the AAA server and that further troubleshooting needs to occur.

A key function of AAA that cannot be overlooked is accounting. It is crucial to security to have a record of what has transpired. In addition to the authorization request being sent to the AAA server, there should be accounting records of the activities of the user.

Much like authorization messages, only two message types are used in accounting:

■ **REQUEST:** This message is sent from the AAA client to the AAA server to indicate a notification of activity. One of three values may be included with the REQUEST:

■ **START:** A start record indicates that a service has begun.

■ **STOP:** The stop record indicates that the service has ended.

■ **CONTINUE:** The continue record, also sometimes referred to as a Watchdog or UPDATE record, is sent when a service has already started and is in progress but there is updated information to provide in relation to the service.

■ **RESPONSE:** This message is sent from the AAA server back to the AAA client with the result of the accounting REQUEST and may contain one of three replies:

■ **SUCCESS:** Indicates that the server received the record from the client.

■ **ERROR:** Indicates an error on the server and that the record was not stored.

■ **FOLLOW:** Indicates that the server wants the client to send the record to a different AAA server and includes that server's information in the RESPONSE.

Figure 2-5 illustrates an end user being authorized to access the IOS exec CLI. The figure is a direct continuation of the authentication sequence shown in Figure 2-4. In this illustration, the end user gets authorized to enter the IOS exec and is authorized to run the **show run** command.

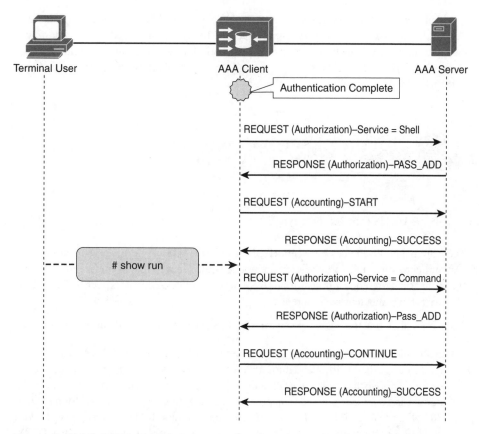

Figure 2-5 *TACACS+ Authorization and Accounting Communication Flows*

We cover TACACS+ in much more detail in Part VII, "Device Administration."

RADIUS

RADIUS is an IETF standard for AAA. As with TACACS+, it follows a client/server model in which the client initiates the requests to the server. RADIUS is the protocol of choice for network access AAA, and it's time to get very familiar with RADIUS. If you connect to a secure wireless network regularly, RADIUS is most likely being used between the wireless device and the AAA server. Why? Because RADIUS is the transport protocol for EAP, along with many other authentication protocols.

Originally, RADIUS was used to extend the authentications from the Layer 2 Point-to-Point Protocol (PPP) used between the end user and the network access server (NAS) and carry that authentication traffic from the NAS to the AAA server performing the authentication. This enabled a Layer 2 authentication protocol to be extended across Layer 3 boundaries to a centralized authentication server.

As described previously in this chapter, RADIUS has evolved far beyond just the dial-up networking use cases it was originally created for. Today it is still used in the same way, carrying the authentication traffic from the network device to the authentication server. With IEEE 802.1X, RADIUS is used to extend the Layer 2 EAP from the end user to the authentication server, as illustrated in Figure 2-6.

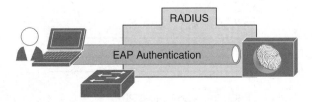

Figure 2-6   *RADIUS Carries the Layer 2 EAP Communication*

There are many differences between RADIUS and TACACS+. One such difference is that authentication and authorization are not separated in a RADIUS transaction. When the authentication request is sent to an AAA server, the AAA client expects to have the authorization result sent back in reply.

There are only a few message types with RADIUS authentication and authorization:

■ **Access-Request:** This message is sent from the AAA client to the AAA server to request an authentication and authorization. The request could be for network access or for device shell access—RADIUS does not discriminate. The function requested is known as a *service type*. For example, the service type may be *framed* for an IEEE 802.1X authentication. Table 2-1 outlines some common RADIUS service types. You can find a more complete listing of RADIUS service types at http://bit.ly/1CGDE8Y.

Table 2-1   *Common RADIUS Service Types*

Value	Service Type Name	Commonly Used For
1	Login	Login request; often used with web authentications with non-Cisco network equipment
2	Framed	IEEE 802.1X
5	Outbound	Local web authentication
10	Call-Check	MAC Authentication Bypass (MAB)

■ **Access-Accept:** Sent from the AAA server to the AAA client signaling a passed authentication. The authorization result will be included as AV pairs, which may include items such as the assigned VLAN, a downloadable access control list (dACL), a Security Group Tag (SGT), and much more.

■ **Access-Reject:** Sent from the AAA server to the AAA client signaling the authentication failure. The failed authentication also signifies that no authorization has been
granted.

■ **Access-Challenge:** This optional message may be sent from the AAA server to the
AAA client when additional information is needed, such as a second password for
two-factor authentications.

Figure 2-7 illustrates a sample RADIUS flow.

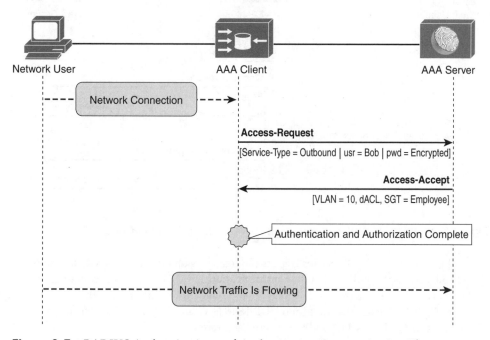

Figure 2-7   *RADIUS Authentication and Authorization Communication Flows*

When looking at Figure 2-7, keep in mind that authentication and authorization are
combined with RADIUS. The Access-Accept message includes the AV pairs defining
what the user is authorized to do.

A key function of AAA that cannot be overlooked is accounting. It is crucial to security
to have a record of what has transpired. In addition to the authorization request being
sent to the AAA server, there should be accounting records of the activities of the user.

Only two message types are used in accounting:

■ **Accounting-Request:** This message is sent by the AAA client to the AAA server.
It may include time, packets, Dynamic Host Configuration Protocol (DHCP)
information, Cisco Discovery Protocol (CDP) information, and so on. The message
may be a START message indicating that service has begun or a STOP message
indicating the service has ended.

■ **Accounting-Response:** This message acts like an acknowledgement of receipt, so the AAA client knows the accounting message was received by the AAA server.

Figure 2-8 illustrates a sample RADIUS accounting flow. The figure is a direct continuation of Figure 2-7 where the authentication and authorization occurred.

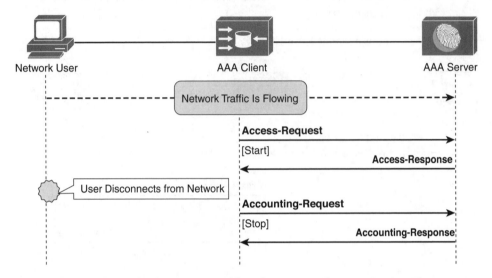

Figure 2-8 *RADIUS Authentication and Authorization Communication Flows*

Unlike TACACS+, RADIUS uses UDP as the transmission protocol. The standard ports used by RADIUS are UDP 1812 for authentication and UDP 1813 for accounting. However, Cisco supported RADIUS before the standard was ratified and the ports used were UDP 1645 (authentication) and UDP 1646 (accounting). Most Cisco devices will support using either set of ports to ensure backward compatibility.

AV Pairs

As you noticed, attribute-value pairs (AV pairs) are referenced all through the TACACS+ and RADIUS sections. When communicating with an AAA protocol, there are many attributes that can be referenced to clearly dictate answers or results. The RADIUS server may be assigning an attribute to the authentication session like a VLAN, for example. The VLAN placeholder is the attribute, and the actual assigned VLAN number is the value for that placeholder. The placeholder and its assigned value are paired together and are referred to as attribute-value pairs (AV pairs).

Change of Authorization

Because RADIUS was always defined to be a client/server architecture, with the client always initiating the conversation, it became challenging for the AAA server to take action. As RADIUS was defined, the AAA server could only assign an authorization as a result of an authentication request.

As technology advanced, many new demands appeared, including the capability for the network to kick out misbehaving clients, to quarantine them, or basically to just change their access.

How can that happen when the network access is using a RADIUS control plane and the AAA client must always initiate the RADIUS conversations? That is where RFC 3576 and its successor RFC 5176 come in. These RFCs define a new enhancement to RADIUS known as Dynamic Authorization Extensions to RADIUS or, as it is more commonly called, Change of Authorization (CoA).

CoA is what allows a RADIUS server to initiate a conversation to the network device and disconnect a user's session, bounce the port (perform a shut/no-shut), or even tell the device to reauthenticate the user. As you learn more about Cisco ISE and the advanced functionality it brings to network access AAA, you will also see how critically important CoA is.

Comparing RADIUS and TACACS+

Table 2-2 summarizes the two main AAA protocols: RADIUS and TACACS+.

Table 2-2   *Comparison of RADIUS and TACACS+*

	RADIUS	**TACACS+**
Protocol and Port(s) Used	UDP: 1812 and 1813 or UDP: 1645 and 1646	TCP: 49
Encryption	Encrypts only the Password field	Encrypts the entire payload
Authentication and Authorization	Combines authentication and authorization	Separates authentication and authorization
Primary Use	Network access	Device administration

Summary

This chapter examined the security principal of authentication, authorization, and accounting (AAA) and its importance in the security world. It introduced the different types of AAA relevant to networks, network access AAA and device administration AAA. This chapter compared and contrasted the two most common AAA protocols, RADIUS and TACACS+, revealing that TACACS+ is best suited for device administration while RADIUS is best suited for network access.

Chapter 3

Introducing Cisco Identity Services Engine

This chapter covers the following topics:

- Architecture approach to centralized and dynamic network security policy enforcement

- ISE features and benefits

- ISE policy construct

Cisco Secure Access is the term Cisco uses to describe its network access control system. It is an all-encompassing term that generally relates to the Cisco Secure architecture with all its components, hosts, and devices, working together to secure an organization's hosts and network access. At a high level, Cisco Secure Access is the architecture that allows you to set policy for who can gain access to your network and what they can do while they are there. This might include a host connecting to a switch port, a wireless network, or a VPN. Cisco Secure Access enables you to granularly control initial, and ongoing, access to the network and all its services using policies. It controls where users and devices can go on a network and what they can do. This architecture covers all the network access methods including wired, wireless, and VPN.

Cisco Identity Services Engine (ISE) is the central policy engine for the Cisco Secure Access architecture. It is the heart and soul, the backbone, of Secure Access. Without ISE, Cisco Secure Access cannot exist. As a policy engine solution, ISE lets you gain awareness of everything hitting your network, provides access control consistently and efficiently, and relieves the stress of complex network access management.

Architecture Approach to Centralized and Dynamic Network Security Policy Enforcement

A bit of history is required to understand how the Network Access Control (NAC) and authentication, authorization, and accounting (AAA) server markets have evolved to date. This will set the stage for a discussion of the architecture approach that Cisco ISE now implements. Prior to 2004, Cisco developed a NAC solution called Cisco NAC Framework. It was heavily based on 802.1X and integration with network services. Unfortunately, it was ahead of its time and never widely deployed. It can be argued that it was the right approach to security, but back then, the clients, devices, switches, operating systems, and just about everything else in the network weren't capable or ready for an 802.1X-based integrated solution.

In response to the slow adoption of the NAC Framework, Cisco acquired Perfigo, and in 2004 released the Cisco NAC Appliance solution that was based on the Perfigo technology. Cisco NAC Appliance provided an overlay NAC solution that did not require, nor use, 802.1X or an architecture approach. It was a pure overlay technology using Simple Network Management Protocol (SNMP) and inline NAC appliances to get the job done. Over the years, this solution gained traction and quickly became the most deployed and highest rated NAC solution on the market. As the maturation and proliferation of support for 802.1X grew over the years, it became clear to Cisco that it was time to reintroduce a next-generation NAC solution that was based on 802.1X and embraced an architecture approach instead of an overlay design.

In 2011, Cisco released Cisco ISE to provide its customers with an 802.1X-based NAC solution. ISE was a new, built from the ground up, security policy control system. Since 2011, Cisco has continued to aggressively evolve and innovate on the ISE solution and the Cisco Secure Access architecture. Figure 3-1 depicts the concept of how Cisco ISE operates.

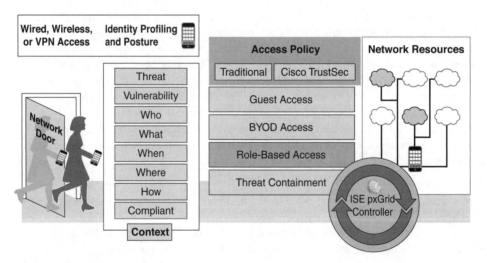

Figure 3-1   *Cisco ISE Centralized Policy Control Operation*

So many capabilities that used to require separate systems, vendors, and training can now be collapsed into a single solution, ISE. New capabilities that we only dreamed of in 2011 have been added. Let's examine the business and IT benefits of deploying and operationalizing the capabilities of ISE:

- **Centralize network access control** based on business role and security policy to provide a consistent network access policy for end users whether they connect through wired, wireless, or VPN. All this can be done from a centralized ISE console that then distributes enforcement across the entire network and security infrastructure.

- **Simplify security audit and compliance** using ISE's single management console for simpler policy creation, visibility, and reporting across all company networks. IT can easily validate compliance for audits, regulatory requirements, and mandated federal guidelines.

- **Secure business- and context-based access** per your company policies. ISE can match users, endpoints, and each endpoint's security posture plus other attributes such as time, location, and access method, thus creating an all-encompassing contextual identity. With this identity, IT administrators can apply precise network security policy controls.

- **Gain greater network visibility** and more accurate host/node identification with ISE profiling and profile feed service capabilities. This functionality provides detailed real-time and historical visibility of all the devices on the network.

- **Simplify the guest experience** using the robust capabilities that ISE provides for allowing guests to quickly and easily connect to your network. Guests can use a coffee-shop hotspot, self-service registration, or sponsored access to get to specific resources. ISE includes fully customizable, branded guest portals, created in minutes with dynamic visual workflows that let you easily manage the guest policy and experience.

- **Accelerate bring-your-own-device (BYOD) and enterprise mobility** with simple out-of-the-box setup, self-service device onboarding and management, internal device certificate management, and integration with enterprise mobility management (EMM) partners. This allows an organization to quickly and easily move to the more secure EAP-TLS wireless for the enterprise and/or allow BYOD devices to connect without sacrificing corporate security. Users can manage devices according to the business policies defined by IT administrators. The IT staff can get the automated device provisioning, profiling, and posturing it needs to comply with security policies. At the same time, employees can get their own devices onto the network without requiring IT assistance.

- **Dynamically construct a software-defined segmentation policy** that segments users, devices, and nodes on your network based on security policy. ISE uses Cisco TrustSec technology to define context-based access control policies using Security Group Tags (SGT). This policy is then pushed to TrustSec-capable network devices for enforcement. When used in a security group ACL (SGACL), SGTs allow you to dynamically segment the network without the complexity and overhead of traditional segmentation methods such as VLANs and ACLs. Additionally, security devices can alert ISE to live host threat activity such that ISE can change a user/host SGT value dynamically. The new SGT value typically quarantines the host from doing additional damage on the network, kind of like turning on your deflector shields.

- **Share user, device, and other contextual data** within the Cisco Secure Access architecture as well as with Cisco partner solutions. ISE uses Cisco Platform Exchange Grid (pxGrid) technology to share rich contextual data between products. This technology improves threat visibility and accelerates the capabilities to detect, investigate, mitigate, and remediate security threats. pxGrid improves a system's overall contextual awareness and thus decreases time to containment of network threats.

- **Automatically contain threats** through Cisco pxGrid technology or ISE APIs. ISE automates the defense of your network based on live threat data from multiple security systems. ISE can quarantine systems, change their SGT, disconnect nodes from the network, apply new access lists, and perform many other remediation actions.

- **Network device administration access control and auditing** using TACACS+. Cisco ISE supports full TACACS+ to provide you with AAA services to all your network and security devices. Cisco even has a Cisco ACS-to-ISE migration tool to speed the transfer of your ACS policies to ISE.

Cisco Identity Services Engine Features and Benefits

ISE has a lot of features and benefits. To help you get quickly up to speed on the major features, Table 3-1 lists them and describes the benefits each offers.

Table 3-1   *Cisco ISE Features and Benefits*

ISE Feature	Benefits
Centralized management	Helps administrators centrally configure and manage profiler, posture, guest, authentication, and authorization services in a single web-based GUI console.
	Simplifies administration by providing integrated management services from a single pane of glass.
Business-policy enforcement	Provides a rule-based, attribute-driven policy model for flexible and business-relevant access control policies. Also provides the ability to create fine-grained policies by pulling attributes from predefined dictionaries.
	Includes attributes such as user and endpoint identity, posture validation, authentication protocols, profiling identity, and other external attribute sources. These can be created dynamically and saved for later use.
	Integrates with multiple external identity repositories such as Microsoft Active Directory, Lightweight Directory Access Protocol (LDAP), RADIUS, RSA one-time password (OTP), certificate authorities for both authentication and authorization, and support for Open Database Connectivity (ODBC).

ISE Feature	Benefits
Access control	Provides a range of access control options, including downloadable access control lists (dACLs), VLAN assignments, URL redirections, named ACLs, and SGTs using the advanced capabilities of network devices enabled with Cisco TrustSec technology.
Secure supplicant-less network access with Easy Connect	Provides the ability to swiftly roll out highly secure network access without configuring endpoints for authentication and authorization. Derives authentication and authorization from login information across application layers, allowing user access without requiring an 802.1X supplicant to exist on the endpoint.
Source-Group Tag Exchange Protocol (SXP) support	Acts as an SXP speaker or listener as defined in SXP draft and as the network's source of truth for SGT information. Bridges over the segments that are not compliant with Cisco TrustSec policies to make sure that differentiated role-based access is provided across the entire network.
Guest lifecycle management	Provides a streamlined experience for implementing and customizing guest network access. Creates corporate-branded guest experiences, with advertisements and promotions, in minutes. Support is built in for hotspot, sponsored, self-service, and numerous other access workflows. Provides the administration with real-time visual flows that bring the effects of the guest flow design to life. Tracks access across your network for security and compliance demands and full guest auditing. Time limits, account expirations, and Short Message Service (SMS) verification offer additional security controls.
Streamlined device onboarding	Offers automatic supplicant provisioning and certificate enrollment for standard PC and mobile computing platforms. This reduces IT help desk cases along with providing more secure access and a better experience to users. Enables end users to add and manage their devices with self-service portals and supports Security Assertion Markup Language (SAML) 2.0 for web portals. Integrates with mobile device management (MDM)/EMM vendors to enroll mobile devices and help ensure that they are compliant with access policy.

ISE Feature	Benefits
Built-in AAA services	Uses standard RADIUS protocol for authentication, authorization, and accounting (AAA).
	Supports a wide range of authentication protocols, including, but not limited to, Password Authentication Protocol (PAP), Microsoft Challenge Handshake Authentication Protocol (MS-CHAP), Extensible Authentication Protocol MD5 (EAP-MD5), Protected EAP (PEAP), EAP Flexible Authentication via Secure Tunneling (EAP-FAST), EAP Transport Layer Security (EAP-TLS), and EAP Tunneled Transport Layer Security (EAP-TTLS). Note: Cisco ISE is the only RADIUS server to support EAP chaining of machine and user credentials.
Device administration access control and auditing	Supports TACACS+ protocol to authenticate, authorize, and audit users when they access devices that support the TACACS+ protocol, such as network devices and servers.
	Grants users access to commands on every device based on their credentials, the group they belong to, where they connect from, and what action they are trying to take on the device.
	Provides access to device configuration on a need-to-know and need-to-act basis while keeping audit trails for every change in the network.
Internal certificate authority	Offers an easy-to-deploy internal certificate authority (CA) to simplify certificate management for devices. There is no need to add the significant complexity of an external CA application.
	Provides a single console to manage endpoints and their certificates. Certificate status is checked through the standards-based Online Certificate Status Protocol (OCSP). Certificate revocation is automatic.
	Supports standalone deployments and subordinate ones (that is, ones in which the CA is integrated with your existing enterprise public key infrastructure, or PKI).
	Facilitates the manual creation of bulk or single certificates and key pairs to connect these devices to the network with a high degree of security.
Device profiling	Ships with predefined device templates for many types of endpoints, such as IP phones, printers, IP cameras, smartphones, and tablets.
	Creates custom device templates to automatically detect, classify, and associate custom-defined identities when endpoints connect to the network.
	Helps to create endpoint-specific authorization policies based on device type.
	Collects endpoint attribute data with active scanning and passive network monitoring and telemetry.

ISE Feature	Benefits
Device-profile feed service	Delivers automatic updates of Cisco's validated device profiles for various IP-enabled devices from multiple vendors. It detects all the newest devices and simplifies the task of keeping up with them.
	Offers a mechanism where partners and customers can share their customized profile information to be vetted by Cisco and redistributed.
Endpoint posture service	Performs endpoint posture assessment on PCs and mobile devices connecting to the network.
	Works through a persistent client-based agent, a temporal agent, or a query to an external MDM/EMM vendor's system to validate that an endpoint conforms to appropriate compliance policies.
	Provides the ability to create powerful policies that include, but are not limited to, checks for the latest OS patches, antivirus and anti-spyware packages with current definition file variables (version, date, etc.), antimalware packages, registry settings (key, value, etc.), patch management, disk encryption, mobile PIN-lock or rooted or jailbroken status, application presence, USB attached media, and so on.
	Supports the automatic remediation of PC clients as well as periodic reassessments alongside leading enterprise patch-management systems to make sure the endpoint is not in violation of company policies.
	Requires the AnyConnect 4.x agent for posture assessment on these OS platforms: Microsoft Windows 7, 8, or 10 (32-bit or 64-bit) and Mac OS X 10.7, 10.8, 10.9, or 10.11.
Extensive multi-forest Active Directory support	Provides comprehensive authentication and authorization against multi-forest Microsoft Active Directory domains.
	Groups multiple disjointed domains into logical groups. Configurations of complex Active Directory topologies are simplified to support ever-changing business environments.
	Includes flexible identity rewriting rules to smooth the solution's transition and integration.
	Supports Microsoft Active Directory 2003, 2008, 2008R2, 2012, 2012R2, and 2016.
Cisco Rapid Threat Containment	Takes network mitigation and investigation actions in response to security events.
	Integrates Cisco ISE and Cisco security technology partner solutions in a broad variety of technology areas.
	Uses Cisco pxGrid as a highly scalable IT clearinghouse for multiple security tools to communicate with each other in real time, automatically.

ISE Feature	Benefits
Monitoring and troubleshooting	Offers a built-in web console for monitoring, reporting, and troubleshooting to assist help desk and network operators in quickly identifying and resolving issues.
	Provides robust historical and real-time reporting for all services. Logs all activities and offers real-time dashboard metrics of all users and endpoints connecting to the network.
Government Certifications	Meets the requirements of Federal Information Processing Standard (FIPS) 140-2, Common Criteria, ISO 27001, and Unified Capabilities Approved Product List. Also IPv6, ready.
	Note: Certifications may not be available on all releases, or they may be in varying states of approval. Current certifications and releases can be found at http://www.cisco.com/web/strategy/government/sec_cert.html.

ISE Platform Support and Compatibility

ISE is available as a physical or virtual appliance. Both physical and virtual form factors can be used to create ISE clusters to serve larger organizations and provide the scale, redundancy, and failover required of a critical enterprise system.

ISE virtual appliances are supported on VMware ESXi 5.x and 6.x or Kernel-based Virtual Machine (KVM) on Red Hat 7.x. A production deployment should be run on hardware that equals or exceeds the configurations of the current physical ISE platforms. For lab or testing environments that provide no product services, the solution can be run on virtual targets that have at least 4 GB of memory and at least 200 GB of hard drive space available.

For physical platform support of ISE, please refer to the Cisco Secure Network Server Data Sheet on Cisco.com.

Cisco Identity Services Engine Policy Construct

The Cisco ISE product line was first introduced to provide network access control using RADIUS and 802.1X. Cisco created it to provide businesses with an integrated architecture approach to their network access and policy requirements. The ISE solution now provides many more capabilities, including consolidated and comprehensive network and threat visibility using identity and contextual awareness. This includes the who, what, where, when, and how of network access. Figure 3-2 illustrates the high-level components of an ISE policy. Figure 3-2 is not meant to be all encompassing, but rather an example.

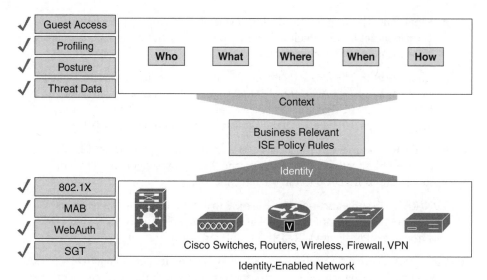

Figure 3-2 *Cisco ISE Policy Construct*

Let's break down the information found in Figure 3-2 into its constituent parts. The two main parts are Context and Identity. *Identity* provides knowledge of the user or device; this gives us the who. *Context* extends the amount of information we have about an identity to provide additional information such as what, where, when, and how. The consolidation of identity and context allows the creation of business-relevant policies. Here is a good example of what this would look like: Jamey Heary (who) logged in to the network in building 4 (where) using Cisco AnyConnect (what) today at 9 p.m. (when) using his iPhone (how). ISE, working with a Cisco Mobility Services Engine, can even determine a wireless node's actual location within 3 meters and change its ISE policy based on location.

Now that you know what information you want to include in your ISE policies, you need to figure out how to gather that data. A major strength of Cisco ISE is its ability to support all access methods—wired, wireless, and VPN—into a single policy table. To do this, ISE relies on network systems for both the collection of identity and context and the enforcement of policy. The left side of Figure 3-2 provides some examples of how identity and context information can be collected by the ISE architecture. This is not a comprehensive list. Let's take a look at each of these in some detail, starting with identity.

Identity can be gathered in multiple ways using the ISE solution. The following methods are available, in order of preference:

- **802.1X:** IEEE 802.1X is the standard for port-based network access control. The protocol uses Extensible Authentication Protocol (EAP), a flexible authentication framework defined in RFC 3748. The protocol defines three components in the authentication process:

■ **Supplicant:** The agent on the device/PC that is used to access the network. The supplicant is either built in or added onto the operating system. It requests authentication by the authenticator.

■ **Authenticator:** The device that controls the status of a link; typically a wired switch or Wireless LAN Controller (WLC). EAP data is first encapsulated in EAP over LAN (EAPoL) frames between the supplicant and authenticator, then re-encapsulated between the authenticator and ISE using RADIUS.

■ **Authentication server:** A backend server that authenticates the credentials provided by supplicants. For example, the WLC passes credentials from the supplicant via RADIUS to ISE for authentication.

■ **VPN/RADIUS authentication:** By using ISE to authenticate your VPN clients, ISE then knows the identity of your VPN users. For example, Cisco ASA sends credentials from the VPN client via RADIUS to ISE for authentication.

■ **Cisco ASA identity firewall:** Cisco ASA supports identity firewalling (IDFW). ASA can use ISE as an authentication server for this purpose. In this way, ISE learns the identity of all users passing through the IDFW-enabled Cisco ASA.

■ **Web authentication:** Provides authentication via web page, usually via a URL redirect of the user's browser. The built-in Guest Server functionality of ISE provides this web portal service. For example, a user attaches to a wireless network without authentication—that is, open mode. The user's browser is then redirected to the login page hosted by ISE. ISE collects the credentials and performs the authentication.

■ **MAC Authentication Bypass (MAB):** MAB relies on a MAC address for authentication. A MAC address is a globally unique identifier that is assigned to all network-attached devices, and therefore it is often referred to as a *hardware* or *physical address*. Because it is a globally unique identifier, it can be used in authentication. However, the ability to assign your own MAC address to your device means that, by itself, a MAC address is not a strong form of authentication. Later on, you will read about how ISE Profiler functionality with MAB provides you with a much more secure alternative to just MAB.

Let's look at a MAB example. A printer that does not support 802.1X attaches to the wired network. 802.1X authentication times out and MAB takes over. The switch sends the printer's MAC address to ISE. ISE then verifies the MAC address is allowed using its MAC address database or some external database containing a list of approved MAC addresses.

Caution   MAB by itself is not an authentication mechanism. MAB, as its name implies, bypasses authentication.

■ **TrustSec Security Group Tags:** ISE can use Security Group Tags for authentication and authorization as well. An SGT is a value that is inserted into the client's data frames by a network device, such as a switch. This tag can be read by another network device receiving the data frame. It is then used to apply a security policy. For example, data frames with a guest_user tag are allowed to communicate only with nodes that have a guest_internet tag. ISE can statically map an IP address to an SGT. ISE collects and can distribute all of the IP-to-SGT mapping tables to the network nodes to enforce policy against.

■ **Unauthenticated/authenticated guest access:** ISE includes a Guest Server functionality that provides a guest user splash page and, optionally, a user agreement page and/or a page that asks for information from the user such as their email address, name, company, and so forth. Guests are allowed access without providing identity information, which is usually termed *unauthenticated guest access*. This is what you would find at your local café that provides free Internet access. Guests are not authenticated by ISE, but, instead, any actions or information they provide are cataloged. In contrast, authenticated guest access allows Internet access to guests using temporary credentials that expire after a set time period. Guests are provided with these credentials through SMS, a printed handout, or other means. In almost all cases, the network access that a guest receives is severely restricted in comparison to what an authenticated employee receives, and usually allows only Internet access.

The most secure methods, which we recommend that you implement in your network, are 802.1X, VPN authentication, and ASA Identity Firewall logins. All of these techniques provide a robust and seamless user experience. If these are not available for use in specific scenarios within your own network, then employ MAB with ISE Profiler, use web authentication through a browser-based web portal page, or offer an unauthenticated or authenticated guest access option.

ISE Authorization Rules

After authentication is complete, ISE performs its policy enforcement, also known as *authorization*. ISE can utilize dozens of policy attributes to each policy rule in a consolidated policy rule table for authorization. Here is a sampling of some of the more popular policy attributes available for use in ISE:

■ Posture assessment results

■ Active Directory group membership

■ Active Directory user-based attributes (company name, department, address, job title, and so on)

■ Location

■ Access method (MAB, 802.1X, wired, wireless, and so on)

■ Time and date

- Profiler match for device type

- If device has been registered with ISE or enrolled with an MDM

- Digital certificate information (commonly used to determine corporate vs. noncorporate assets)

- Hundreds of RADIUS attributes and values

The ISE policy rule table can be evaluated on a first-match basis (most common) or multiple-match basis. If there are no matches, then a default catch-all rule is enforced. Figure 3-3 shows an example ISE authorization policy.

Status	Rule Name		Conditions (identity groups and other conditions)		Permissions
✓	Medical Devices Class D	if	Medical-Devices-Type-D	then	Medical_Class_D
✓	Cisco_IP_Phone	if	Cisco-IP-Phone	then	Cisco_IP_Phones AND SJC19_Cisco_IPPhones
✓	SJCM_Guest _Wired_Com pliant	if	(Wired_MAB AND Session:PostureStatus EQUALS Compliant)	then	CWA-Access AND SJC19_Wired_Guest_devices
✓	SJCM_Guest _Unsupporte d_Access	if	(Wired_MAB AND EndPoints:LogicalProfile EQUALS Unsupported)	then	CWA-Access AND SJC19_Wired_Unsupported
✓	SJCM_Guest _Wired_unkn own	if	Wired_MAB	then	CWA-Redirect_Wired

Figure 3-3   *Cisco ISE Authorization Policy Example*

Summary

Cisco ISE has revolutionized the way we protect our networks. The Cisco Secure Access architecture with ISE allows IT to seamlessly deploy a network access control and visibility solution across the entire network architecture using a robust centralized policy framework. ISE uses several innovative capabilities to ensure that the solution is as simple as possible to deploy and operationalize, and the solution is dynamic and can change your protection profile in real time based on live threats. A new approach is needed to regain control of and actively defend modern network access. ISE, with all of its many capabilities, provides that new approach.

Chapter 4

The Building Blocks in an Identity Services Engine Design

This chapter covers the following topics:

- ISE solution components
- ISE personas
- ISE licensing, requirements, and performance guidance
- ISE policy-based structure

Knowing how to properly design security solutions is what separates the professional from the amateur. Without a proper design, the eventual implementation will most likely be a disaster. One of the keys to success when designing a security solution is to first understand all of the pieces, or building blocks, you have to work with. After you understand the building blocks, you need to become skilled at manipulating them in ways that best fit your environment. This chapter focuses on the building blocks that are available with the ISE solution and architecture. The purpose and function of each building block are covered in this chapter. Chapter 5, "Making Sense of the ISE Deployment Design Options," discusses your options for manipulating these building blocks.

ISE Solution Components Explained

At a high level, the following are the three solution component groups that make up the ISE architecture:

- Infrastructure components
- Policy components
- Endpoint components

Each group has a distinct role to play in the ISE solution. Let's examine the roles and functions of these groups in more detail.

Infrastructure Components

Infrastructure components are those devices that ISE will work with to create the secure access architecture. These are devices such as wireless controllers, switches, VPN concentrators, next-generation firewalls, authentication services such as Active Directory, and many others. The exact components you require will vary based on your ISE use cases and business objectives. Infrastructure components supported by Cisco ISE are numerous, with more added regularly. These network infrastructure devices include both Cisco-branded devices and non-Cisco devices. Full ISE functionality can be achieved with non-Cisco branded devices starting in ISE 2.0; however, the Cisco-branded devices, predictably, provide more functionality with better integration into the ISE solution. Pay particular attention to the recommended code versions of the components to ensure the best experience.

Note   For the latest support list of infrastructure components, refer to the most recent release of *Cisco Identity Services Engine Network Component Compatibility* at http://www.cisco.com/en/US/products/ps11640/products_device_support_tables_list.html.

ISE will interact with infrastructure devices, such as switches, to perform various features. Unfortunately, not all infrastructure devices support the functionality necessary for a given ISE feature to work. Therefore, it is necessary to understand the most common functionality to look for support for on your devices. The following list contains the functionality that you want to ensure a device supports when you evaluate it:

- **MAC Authentication Bypass (MAB):** Using the MAC address of an endpoint that cannot authenticate itself to the network.

- **802.1X:** The IEEE standard for communicating identity credentials using Extensible Authentication Protocol (EAP) over LAN.

- **Web Authentication:** Authenticating users attempting network access via a web page. Web Authentication has two deployment modes:

  - **Central Web Authentication (CWA):** The most popular option, controlled by ISE.

  - **Local Web Authentication (LWA):** Performed by the switch or Wireless LAN Controller (WLC) and cannot perform CoA (described next), modify the port virtual LAN (VLAN), or support session ID.

- **Change of Authorization (CoA):** RADIUS attribute that ISE issues to an access device to force the session to be reauthenticated. CoA forms the backbone of the 802.1X ISE solution.

- **VLAN:** The Layer 2 broadcast domain that might be assigned to incoming devices.

- **Downloadable ACL (dACL):** An access control list that is sent from ISE to the access device to restrict the session.

- **Security Group Tag (SGT):** SGTs are the main component in the Cisco TrustSec architecture. ISE serves as the main policy engine for a TrustSec architecture and, as such, can assign and manipulate SGTs. ISE uses the various policy rules and context it has gathered to determine the appropriate SGT for a particular host and user. This tag is then sent to a network device, which can then insert the SGT into the host's frames/packets or make enforcement decisions based on SGT-to-IP mappings.

- **Cisco IOS Device Sensor:** Enables profiling functionality built into the Cisco IOS Catalyst Switch or Cisco WLC hardware. This allows profiling to occur locally at the access device instead of centrally at an ISE node.

Now that you know the functionalities to look for in a network device, Table 4-1 maps them to ISE features. This gives you a better idea of what device functionality is required to enable a given ISE feature.

Table 4-1 *Feature to Functionality Mapping*

Feature	Functionality
AAA	802.1X, MAB, VLAN assignment, dACL
Profiling	RADIUS CoA and profiling probes
BYOD	RADIUS CoA, URL redirection + SessionID
Guest	RADIUS CoA, URL redirection + SessionID, Local Web Auth
Posture	RADIUS CoA, URL redirection + SessionID
MDM	RADIUS CoA, URL redirection + SessionID
TrustSec	SGT classification

Table 4-2 shows a partial mapping of ISE supported devices to ISE features. It also provides recommended minimum OS levels for the device to be used with ISE.

Table 4-2 *ISE Supported Infrastructure Components—Partial List*

Device	Recommended OS[1] Minimum OS[3]	AAA	Profiling	BYOD	Guest	Posture	MDM	TrustSec[2]
Cisco Access Switches								
IE 2000	IOS 15.2(2) E4	✓	✓	✓	✓	✓	✓	✓
IE 3000	IOS 15.0(2) EB	✓	✓	✓	✓	✓	✓	✓
CGS 2520	IOS 15.2(3)E3	✓	✓	✓	✓	✓	✓	✓
	IOS 15.2(3)E3	✓	✓	✓	✓	✓	✓	✓

Device	Recommended OS[1] Minimum OS[3]	AAA	Profiling	BYOD	Guest	Posture	MDM	TrustSec[2]
Catalyst 2960 LAN Base	IOS 12.2.55-SE10	✓	✓	✓	✓	✓	✓	X
	IOS v12.2.(55)SE5	✓	✓	✓	✓	✓	✓	X
Catalyst 2960-C	IOS 15.2(2)E4	✓	✓	✓	✓	✓	✓	✓
Catalyst 3560-C	IOS 12.2.(55) EX3	✓	✓	✓	✓	✓	✓	✓
Catalyst 2960-Plus	IOS 15.2(2)E4	✓	✓	✓	✓	✓	✓	✓
Catalyst 2960-SF	IOS 15.0(2)SE7	✓	✓	✓	✓	✓	✓	X
Catalyst 2960-S	IOS 15.2(2)E4	✓	✓	✓	✓	✓	✓	✓
	IOS 12.2.(55)SE5	✓	✓	✓	✓	✓	✓	X
Catalyst 2960–XR	IOS 15.2(2)E4	✓	✓	✓	✓	✓	✓	✓
Catalyst 2960–X	IOS 15.0.2A-EX5	✓	✓	✓	✓	✓	✓	X
Catalyst 2960-CX	IOS 15.2(3)E1	✓	✓	✓	✓	✓	✓	✓
Catalyst 3560-CX	IOS 15.2(3)E	✓	✓	✓	✓	✓	✓	✓
Catalyst 3560G	IOS 12.2.(55)SE10	✓	✓	✓	✓	✓	✓	✓
Catalyst 3750G	IOS 12.2.(55)SE5	✓	✓	✓	✓	✓	✓	✓
Catalyst 3560V2	IOS 12.2.(55)SE10	✓	✓	✓	✓	✓	✓	✓
Catalyst 3750V2	IOS 12.2.(55)SE5	✓	✓	✓	✓	✓	✓	✓
Catalyst 3560-E	IOS 12.2.(55)SE10	✓	✓	✓	✓	✓	✓	✓
Catalyst 3750-E	IOS 12.2.(55)SE5	✓	✓	✓	✓	✓	✓	✓
Catalyst 3560-X	IOS 15.2(2)E4	✓	✓	✓	✓	✓	✓	✓
Catalyst 3750-X	IOS 12.2.(55)SE5	✓	✓	✓	✓	✓	✓	✓
Catalyst 3850	IOS-XE 3.6.4	✓	✓	✓	✓	✓	✓	✓
Catalyst 3650	IOS-XE 3.3.5.E	✓	✓	✓	✓	✓	✓	✓
Catalyst 4500-X	IOS-XE 3.6.4	✓	✓	✓	✓	✓	✓	✓
	IOS-XE 3.4.4 SG	✓	✓	✓	✓	✓	✓	✓
Catalyst 4500 Supervisor 7-E, 7L-E	IOS-XE 3.6.4	✓	✓	✓	✓	✓	✓	✓
	IOS-XE 3.4.4 SG	✓	✓	✓	✓	✓	✓	✓
Catalyst 4500 Supervisor 6-E, 6L-E	IOS 15.2(2)E4	✓	✓	✓	✓	✓	✓	✓
	IOS 15.2(2)E	✓	✓	✓	✓	✓	✓	✓

Device	Recommended OS[1] / Minimum OS[3]	AAA	Profiling	BYOD	Guest	Posture	MDM	TrustSec[2]
Catalyst 4500 Supervisor 8-E	IOS-XE 3.6.4	✓	✓	✓	✓	✓	✓	✓
	IOS-XE 3.3.2 XO	✓	✓	✓	✓	✓	✓	✓
Catalyst 6500-E (Supervisor 32)	IOS 12.2(33)SXJ10	✓	✓	✓	✓	✓	✓	✓
	IOS 12.2(33)SXI6	✓	✓	✓	✓	✓	✓	✓
Catalyst 6500-E (Supervisor 720)	IOS 15.1(2)SY7	✓	✓	✓	✓	✓	✓	✓
	IOS v12.2(33)SXI6	✓	✓	✓	✓	✓	✓	✓
Catalyst 6500-E (VS-S2T-10G)	IOS 152-1.SY1a	✓	✓	✓	✓	✓	✓	✓
	IOS 15.0(1)SY1	✓	✓	✓	✓	✓	✓	✓
Catalyst 6807-XL	IOS 152-1.SY1a	✓	✓	✓	✓	✓	✓	✓
Catalyst 6880-X (VS-S2T-10G)	IOS 15.0(1)SY1	✓	✓	✓	✓	✓	✓	✓
Cat 6848ia	IOS 152-1.SY1a	✓	✓	✓	✓	✓	✓	✓
	IOS 15.1(2) SY+	✓	✓	✓	✓	✓	✓	✓
Meraki MS Platforms	Latest Version	✓	✓	X	!	X	X	X
	Latest Version	✓	✓	X	!	X	X	X
Third-Party Access Switches								
Avaya ERS 2526T	4.4	✓	!	X	X	X	X	X
	4.4	✓	!	X	X	X	X	X
Brocade ICX 6610	8.0.20	✓	✓	X	X	X	X	X
	8.0.20	✓	✓	X	X	X	X	X
HP H3C	5.20.99	✓	!	X	X	X	X	X
HP ProCurve	5.20.99	✓	!	X	X	X	X	X
HP ProCurve 2900	WB.15.18.0007	✓	✓	✓	✓	✓	✓	X
	WB.15.18.0007	✓	✓	✓	✓	✓	✓	X
Juniper EX3200	12.3R6.6	✓	!	X	X	X	X	X
	12.3R6.6	✓	!	X	X	X	X	X
Cisco Wireless LAN Controllers[4]								
WLC 2100	AirOS 7.0.252.0	!	✓	X	!	X	X	X
	AirOS 7.0.116.0	!	✓	X	!	X	X	X

Device	Recommended OS[1] / Minimum OS[3]	AAA	Profiling	BYOD	Guest	Posture	MDM	TrustSec[2]
WLC 4400	AirOS 7.0.252.0	!	✓	X	!	X	X	X
	AirOS 7.0.116.0	!	✓	X	!	X	X	X
WLC 2500	AirOS 8.0.135.0	✓	✓	✓	✓	✓	✓	✓
	AirOS 7.2.103.0	!	✓	✓	✓	✓	✓	X
WLC 5508	AirOS 8.0.135.0	✓	✓	✓	✓	✓	✓	✓
	AirOS 7.0.116.0	!	✓	X	!	X	X	✓
WLC 5520	AirOS 8.1.131.0	✓	✓	✓	✓	✓	✓	✓
	AirOS 8.1.122.0	✓	✓	✓	✓	✓	✓	✓
WLC 7500	AirOS 8.0.135.0	✓	✓	✓	✓	✓	✓	X
	AirOS 7.2.103.0	!	✓	X	X	X	X	X
WLC 8510	AirOS 8.0.135.0	✓	✓	✓	✓	✓	✓	X
	AirOS 7.4.121.0	✓	✓	X	X	X	✓	X
WLC 8540	AirOS 8.1.131.0	✓	✓	✓	✓	✓	✓	X
	AirOS 8.1.122.0	✓	✓	✓	✓	✓	✓	X
vWLC	AirOS 8.0.135.0	✓	✓	✓	✓	✓	✓	X
	AirOS 7.4.121.0	✓	✓	✓	✓	✓	✓	X
WiSM1 6500	AirOS 7.0.252.0	!	✓	X	!	X	X	X
	AirOS 7.0.116.0	!	✓	X	!	X	X	X
WiSM2 6500	AirOS 8.0.135.0	✓	✓	✓	✓	✓	✓	✓
	AirOS 7.2.103.0	!	✓	✓	✓	✓	✓	✓
WLC 5760	IOS-XE 3.6.4	✓	✓	✓	✓	✓	✓	✓
	IOS-XE 3.3	✓	✓	✓	✓	✓	✓	✓
WLC for ISR (ISR2 ISM, SRE700, and SRE900)	AirOS 7.0.116.0	!	✓	X	!	X	X	X
	AirOS 7.0.116.0	!	✓	X	!	X	X	X
Meraki MR Platforms	Public Beta	✓	✓	✓	✓	✓	✓	X
	Latest Version	✓	!	X	!	X	X	X
Third-Party Wireless LAN Controllers								
Aruba 3200XM	6.4	✓	✓	✓	✓	✓	✓	X
Aruba 650	6.4	✓	✓	✓	✓	✓	✓	X

Device	Recommended OS[1] Minimum OS[3]	AAA	Profiling	BYOD	Guest	Posture	MDM	TrustSec[2]
Motorola RFS 4000	5.5	✓	✓	✓	✓	✓	✓	X
	5.5	✓	✓	✓	✓	✓	✓	X
HP 830	35073P5	✓	✓	✓	✓	✓	✓	X
	35073P5	✓	✓	✓	✓	✓	✓	X
Ruckus ZD1200	9.9.0.0	✓	✓	X	X	X	X	X
	9.9.0.0	✓	✓	X	X	X	X	X

✓—Fully supported

X—Not supported

!—Limited support, some functionalities are not supported

1. Recommended OS is the version tested for compatibility and stability.

2. For a complete ISE Compatibility list, see http://www.cisco.com/c/en/us/support/security/identity-services-engine/products-device-support-tables-list.html.

3. Minimum OS is the version in which the features were introduced.

4. Cisco WLCs and Wireless Service Modules (WiSMs) do not support dACLs but support named ACLs. Autonomous AP deployments do not support endpoint posturing. Profiling services are supported for 802.1X-authenticated WLANs starting from WLC release 7.0.116.0 and for MAB-authenticated WLANs starting from WLC 7.2.110.0. FlexConnect, previously known as Hybrid Remote Edge Access Point (HREAP) mode, is supported with central authentication configuration deployment starting from WLC 7.2.110.0. For additional details regarding FlexConnect support, refer to the release notes for the applicable wireless controller platform.

Table 4-3 lists the most capable and recommended infrastructure components for each category (at the time of writing).

Table 4-3   *Recommended Infrastructure Components*

Access Switches	Campus Core Switches	Wireless Controllers	Routers	Firewall
Catalyst 2960-plus	Catalyst 6500/6800 Supervisor VS-S2T-10G	WLC 5520	ISR 4000 Models	ASA 9.5+
Catalyst 3850/3650	Catalyst 4500 Supervisor 8-E	WLC 5760	ASR 1000 Models	Firepower NGFW 6.2+
Catalyst 4500x		WiSM 2 for Catalyst 6500	ISR Models 15.3.2T+	

Policy Components

The Cisco ISE solution provides wired, wireless, and VPN context-aware access control management in the following areas:

- Cisco ISE determines whether users are accessing the network on an authorized, policy-compliant device.

- Cisco ISE establishes user identity, location, and access history, which can be used for compliance and reporting.

- Cisco ISE assigns policy and services based on the host and user context. Examples are assigned user role, AD group, location, device type, etc.

- Cisco ISE grants authenticated users access to specific segments of the network, or specific applications and services, or both, based on authorization results.

Cisco ISE comprises the one and only policy component in the ISE solution. Having a single centralized policy engine signifies the power inherent in the ISE solution. Cisco ISE provides a flexible attribute-based access control solution that combines on a single platform authentication, authorization, and accounting (AAA); TACACS+; RADIUS; posture; profiling; certificate authority (CA) server; and guest management services. Administrators can centrally create and manage access control policies for users and endpoints in a consistent fashion, and gain end-to-end visibility into everything that is connected to the network. Cisco ISE automatically discovers and classifies endpoints, provides the right level of access based on identity and context, and provides the ability to enforce endpoint compliance by checking a device's posture. Cisco ISE also provides advanced enforcement capabilities, including TrustSec through the use of SGTs, Security Group Firewalls such as the Cisco ASA, and Security Group ACLs (SGACL). Finally, ISE provides a dynamic quarantine service that any outside device can use to tell ISE to quarantine a host on the network. ISE will instantiate the policy change, which is then enforced by a network access device such as a Wireless LAN Controller. The most popular use case is FirePOWER next-generation firewall/IPS (NGFW/NGIPS) telling ISE to quarantine a host it has an indication of compromise for.

Endpoint Components

The network endpoints play an integral role in the total ISE solution. It is the endpoint that authenticates to ISE using 802.1X, MAB, EasyConnect, or web authentication. It is also from the endpoint that ISE gathers posture information to ensure a host is in compliance with security policies. Here are the recommended endpoint components (these are recommended, not required):

- **802.1X supplicant/agent:** A supplicant is basically just software that understands how to communicate via Extensible Authentication Protocol over LAN (EAPoL). There are many supplicants available for use. A supplicant is built into Windows and

Mac OS X that is good enough for most ISE deployments. An open source Linux supplicant is also available. Supplicants are also available via Cisco AnyConnect and other third-party supplicant software agents. Cisco IP Phones, video equipment, printers, and many other devices now come with built-in supplicants. Additionally, nearly any device that is able to use Wi-Fi will have a native supplicant.

■ **Cisco AnyConnect Compliance Module:** For Windows, Mac OS X, and Linux. Provides host posture information to ISE. This includes information such as whether antivirus is installed, running, and up to date, whether the operating system is fully patched, whether certain registry keys are present, and many more.

In many cases, you will have wired devices on your network that are not capable of performing 802.1X. This is typically the case with wired printers, IP Phones, badge readers, HVAC, and other industrial or biomedical endpoints. It is for this reason that ISE has a profiler service that can automate the process of properly identifying and authorizing devices that can't do it by themselves.

ISE Personas

The ISE architecture has many personas to help it scale to large networks and large numbers of users and devices. Cisco ISE has a highly available and scalable architecture that supports standalone and distributed deployments. ISE standalone mode means that all the personas are on a single ISE appliance or a pair of ISE appliances. ISE distributed mode means that the personas are spread out and dedicated to just particular ISE appliances. ISE has three main personas. The persona or personas of an ISE node determine the services it provides. An ISE node can assume any or all of the following personas:

■ **Administration:** Allows you to perform all administrative operations in a standalone or distributed Cisco ISE deployment. The Administration node provides a single pane of glass for management. It handles all system-related and policy-based configuration. In a distributed ISE deployment, you can have a single or a high-availability (HA) pair of nodes running the Administration persona. An HA pair is highly recommended. An ISE node dedicated to the administration persona is known as a Policy Administration Node (PAN).

■ **Policy Service:** Provides network access, posture, guest access, client provisioning, web portals, and profiling services. This persona evaluates the policies and makes all the decisions. You can have more than one node assume this persona. When a node is dedicated to the Policy Service persona, it is referred to as a Policy Service Node (PSN). Typically, a distributed deployment would have more than one PSN, and they might be geographically separated from each other.

■ **Monitoring:** Enables Cisco ISE to function as the log collector and store log messages from all the Administration and Policy Service Nodes in your network. This persona provides advanced monitoring and troubleshooting tools that you can use to manage your network and resources effectively. A node with this persona aggregates and correlates the data that it collects to provide you with meaningful information in the form of reports. Cisco ISE allows you to have a maximum of two nodes with this persona, both of which can take on primary or secondary roles for high availability. Both the primary and secondary Monitoring nodes collect log messages. If the primary Monitoring node goes down, the secondary Monitoring node automatically becomes the primary Monitoring node. When an ISE node is dedicated to the Monitoring persona, it is referred to as a Monitoring & Troubleshooting Node (MnT).

- **pxGrid:** Cisco pxGrid is used to share the context-sensitive information from Cisco ISE session directory to other policy network systems such as Cisco NGFW or Stealthwatch. The pxGrid framework can also be used to exchange policy and configuration settings between nodes.

Note   Due to the high performance requirements of the Monitoring persona, in midsize to large deployments, it is recommended that you dedicate a node to specifically run this persona.

ISE also has two node types that determine the node's functions:

- ISE node
- Inline Posture Node (IPN)

Note   The Inline Posture Node type has been deprecated in ISE 2.0+. It is described here for completeness but is no longer a recommended or viable deployment option. Use a Cisco ASA instead of an IPN.

Only the ISE node type can be configured with one or more of the previously discussed personas. The IPN must be a dedicated node and cannot assume any of the personas. As an IPN, it is logically or physically inline in the network. Typically, this means it is behind a VPN headend device or behind a non-Cisco WLC that cannot support CoA or another required feature. While inline, this node type can block traffic and apply other network policies as per the ISE policy rule table.

Figure 4-1 provides an idea of how these personas and node types look logically. Only the primary connections are shown, for simplicity.

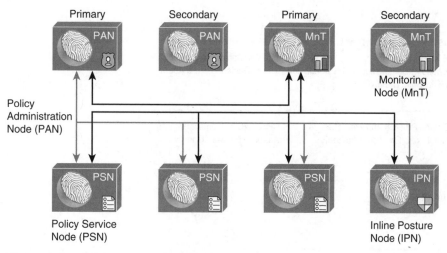

Figure 4-1 *ISE Persona and Node Types*

ISE Licensing, Requirements, and Performance

This section discusses the centralized ISE licensing model, hardware and virtual machine requirements, and the published performance of an ISE node.

ISE Licensing

Identity Services Engine licensing is fairly straightforward. To maximize flexibility for customers, licensing in Cisco ISE is supplied in different packages as Base, Plus, Apex, Device Administration, and AnyConnect Apex. Start with the Base license, then deploy other licenses on top as needed.

Cisco ISE allows the total number of Plus and Apex licenses to be equal to or less than the total number of Base licenses. Apex and Plus licenses can be installed independently without any restriction on the number of Apex versus Plus licenses. Cisco ISE licenses are based on the number of concurrent endpoints with active network connections, whereas AnyConnect Apex licenses are on a per-user basis. The AnyConnect Apex license count can exceed the Cisco ISE Base license count.

Figure 4-2 depicts the ISE license types and functionalities.

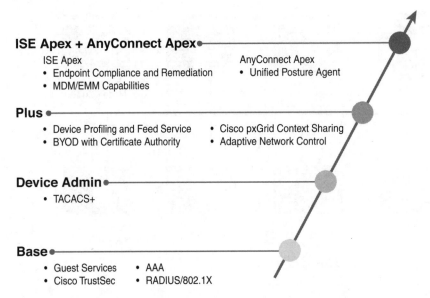

ISE Apex + AnyConnect Apex

ISE Apex
- Endpoint Compliance and Remediation
- MDM/EMM Capabilities

AnyConnect Apex
- Unified Posture Agent

Plus
- Device Profiling and Feed Service
- BYOD with Certificate Authority
- Cisco pxGrid Context Sharing
- Adaptive Network Control

Device Admin
- TACACS+

Base
- Guest Services
- Cisco TrustSec
- AAA
- RADIUS/802.1X

Figure 4-2 *ISE Licensing*

The licenses shown in Figure 4-2 would additionally include a user count and term. For example, L-ISE-PLUS3Y-100= means a 100-user advanced license that is valid for 3 years. To assist you in understanding what licenses you may need for your deployment, refer to Figure 4-3.

Benefit	Use case	RADIUS / 802.1x	AAA	TrustSec security group tagging	Guest services	TACACS+	Rapid threat containment	ANC/EPS	Device profiling and feed service	BYOD with CA	pxGrid context sharing	MDM / EMM	Threat-Centric NAC	Posture (endpoint compliance and remediation)
Control all access from one place	**Guest** — Provide unique guest permissions to visitors	●	●		●									
	Secure access — Control user access and ensure device authentication	●	●	●										
	Device Admin — Differentiate access for device administrators					●								
	BYOD — Seamlessly onboard devices with the right access	●	●	●					●	●				
See and share rich user and device details	**Visibility** — See when, where, and why users are on your network	●	●	●					●					
	Integration — Share information with other products	●	●	●					●		●			
	Compliance — Ensure that endpoints meet network standards	●	●	●					●				●	●
Stop threats from getting in and spreading	**Segmentation** — Limit exposure with pre-defined access segmentation	●	●	●										
	Containment — Reduce risk with rapid threat containment	●	●	●			●	●	●					
	Prevention — Prevent breaches at the endpoint level	●	●										●	

Figure 4-3 *ISE Licensing Use Case Mapping: Features Included by License Type*

ISE Requirements

Cisco ISE comes in two form factors: physical appliance and virtual appliance. The physical appliance comes with the server hardware. The virtual appliance comes as a

VMware virtual appliance package that you can load onto a VMware ESX server. ISE virtual is also available as a KVM appliance package. At the time of writing, the physical appliance comes in two form factors: small and large.

Given that the physical appliances will be upgraded once or twice a year by Cisco, be sure to check Cisco.com for the latest specifications.

For the virtual appliance, the specifications for the virtual machine (VM) host should be sized at or above the specifications for the physical appliance you are trying to match. For example, if you want to have performance similar to that of a Medium physical appliance, then you would build a VM with the specifications of a Medium appliance. Hard drives with 10-K or higher RPM are highly recommended for ISE VM. VMware VMotion and cloning are only supported in ISE version 1.2 or later. It is possible to decrease the HD requirements in certain situations. Here are the ISE persona minimum disk space requirements for production VM deployments:

- Standalone ISE: 600 GB

- Administration: 200 GB

- Monitoring: 600 GB

- Administration and Monitoring: 600 GB

- Administration, Monitoring, and Policy Service: 600 GB

- Policy Service: 100 GB (200 GB strongly recommended)

Note   Do not use Intel Hyper-Threading Technology for the ISE VM. Ensure that the correct number of cores are allocated per VM; it is the cores that matter in the configuration.

Note   ISE version 1.2 (and later) moved to a 64-bit OS, thus enabling it to address more than 4 GB of RAM memory.

ISE Performance

ISE performance is dependent on several factors and, unfortunately, is not a straightforward or precise calculation. It is dependent on the node type, persona(s), policy complexity, bandwidth requirements, and several other variables. Figure 4-4 and Figure 4-5 dissect the different performance specs for ISE. Use typical design guidance when using performance metrics: never exceed 80 percent of stated capacity, and design for 50 percent or less out of the gate. This allows you to build growth into the architecture and ensures that you have a healthy buffer in case your environment doesn't mirror the performance metrics tested and documented by Cisco.

Deployment Model	Platform	Max Active Sessions per Deployment	Max # Dedicated PSNs
Standalone (all personas on same node) (2 nodes redundant)	3415	5,000	0
	3495	10,000	0
	3515	7,500	0
	3595	20,000	0
Admin + MnT on same node; Dedicated PSN (Minimum 4 nodes redundant)	3415 as Admin+MNT	5,000	5
	3495 as Admin+MNT	10,000	5
	3515 as Admin+MNT	7,500	5
	3595 as Admin+MNT	20,000	5
Dedicated Admin and MnT nodes (Minimum 6 nodes redundant)	3495 as Admin and MNT	250,000	40
	3595 as Admin and MNT	500,000	50
Max Active Sessions != Max Endpoints; ISE 2.1 supports 1.5M Endpoints in DB			

Figure 4-4   *ISE 2.1 Max Active Session Counts by Deployment Model and Platform*

Scaling per PSN	Platform	Max Concurrent Sessions per PSN
Dedicated Policy nodes (Max Sessions Gated by Deployment Maximums)	SNS-3415	5,000
	SNS-3495	20,000
	SNS-3515	7,500
	SNS-3595	40,000

Figure 4-5   *ISE 2.1 Max Concurrent Session Counts by Platform*

ISE 2.1 adds increased scalability. Here are the new specs:

- Max concurrent active sessions per deployment = **500k** (up from 250k)

  Requires PAN and MnT nodes to be 3595 or VM equivalent

- Max internal endpoints = **1.5M** (up from 1M)

- Max internal users = **300k** (up from 25k)

- Max network access devices = **100k** (up from 30k)

- Max PSNs per deployment = **50** (up from 40)

ISE Policy-Based Structure Explained

The Identity Services Engine solution relies on a policy-driven rule set to make its decisions. ISE has several different policy types that are all consolidated into a policy set. A *policy set* is a grouping of several different policy rules from both authentication and authorization policies. You can then have multiple policy sets that are processed in order, top down. Finally, you can have global exception rules across the entire ISE deployment. The following policy rule types can be called within an ISE policy set:

- Authentication policy

- Authorization policy

- Profiling policy

- Device posture policy

- Client provisioning policy

- Security group access policy

- Guest policy

Each policy type will be explained in the configuration section of this book. To enable the policy set view, choose **Administration > System > Settings > Policy** and select **Policy Set**. Given the power of policy sets, it is a best practice to enable this feature.

For now, just realize that, as part of preparing for your ISE deployment, you have these policy types at your disposal. Figure 4-6 shows a simple example of a policy set.

Figure 4-6 *ISE Policy Set Example*

In the left pane of Figure 4-6, you can see the policy sets. These policy sets are processed from the top down, beginning with the Global Exceptions policy set. Within each set you will see authentication policies and authorization policies that make up the set. These policy rules are also processed from the top down, thus making the ordering of rules very important. Always put the most used rules at the top.

Summary

This chapter provided a baseline to understand all of the building blocks you have to work with inside of ISE. With this knowledge, you can begin to understand your ISE options for the following:

- ISE solution components

- ISE personas

- ISE licensing, requirements, and performance

- ISE policy structure

Next, Chapter 5 explores all of the details of the various deployment options for ISE.

Chapter 5

Making Sense of the ISE Deployment Design Options

This chapter covers the following topics:

■ Centralized versus distributed deployment

Cisco Identity Services Engine supports two different design and deployment options. This chapter explains the options with the goal of helping you to select the best one for your environment. The deployment options are broken down into two main topics to consider: centralized and distributed. This chapter examines these and other ISE design options.

Chapter 4, "The Building Blocks in an Identity Services Engine Design," already discussed the operation of ISE standalone mode versus distributed mode. For standalone mode, the design of the deployment is very simple: you locate the standalone node at the best network location for its job. This is typically in a data center but at a minimum needs to be somewhere that has reliable environmental conditions and reliable connectivity to the network access devices (NAD), external identity servers, and other critical services. A failed ISE standalone node is something to be avoided at all costs. As discussed in Chapter 4, all ISE node types, such as Administration, Monitoring, and Policy Service, can be made highly available. It is highly recommended to always deploy your standalone node and distributed nodes using high availability. When ISE is deployed in standalone mode, with all node types running on one ISE appliance, you can deploy a secondary standalone ISE node to act as a backup to the original primary server and all of its running services/nodes. The node types are broken out from standalone mode to distributed mode when scaling beyond 20,000 simultaneous endpoints on a Cisco SNS 3595 appliance (less when on smaller appliance models).

When deploying Cisco ISE in a distributed deployment with high availability, it is important to know how to configure each node persona's high availability. Both the Admin and Monitoring nodes work in a primary/standby configuration whereby one active node does all of the work until it fails, at which time the other, backup node, takes over. The Policy Service Node (PSN) is different in that it is made resilient either by load balancing between several PSNs or by configuring your NADs with a list of available PSNs to choose from. In the latter case, if the NAD detects a failure of a PSN, it will choose the next one in its list.

Centralized Versus Distributed Deployment

A *centralized deployment* is one in which all of your ISE nodes are physically located in one location, usually adjacent to each other at Layer 2. All local and any remote sites connect to the centrally deployed ISE nodes.

A *distributed deployment* is one in which your ISE PSNs are physically and strategically dispersed in multiple locations. Your Administration and Monitoring nodes remain at your most robust central network location, and only your PSNs are distributed.

In either deployment mode, your configuration, monitoring, and all ISE admin functions have a consolidated, single-pane-of-glass look and feel for the administrators. Also, both deployment methods support the ISE maximum number of concurrent endpoints in a single ISE deployment, which in version 2.2 is 500,000 endpoints.

Note   The final deployment configuration doesn't need to be determined at the outset of your ISE deployment. In almost all cases, you should do your initial ISE deployment, also known as a proof of concept, in centralized mode.

Whenever you have two or more PSNs that are Layer 2 adjacent, you should use the Node Group function in ISE, which enables you to not only load-balance between multiple PSNs within the same group but also detect a failure of a PSN within the group. It is recommended that you do not exceed a maximum of four PSNs per node group. All PSNs in a group exchange multicast update packets to detect a failure of a server within the group. If a PSN fails, then the group sends a Change of Authorization (CoA) to the NAD for any sessions in the pending state. A session is in the pending state if it has been authorized but posture assessment is not yet complete. The CoA forces the client to reauthenticate to a new available ISE PSN.

Node groups and high availability are both covered in greater detail in Chapter 18, "Setting Up a Distributed ISE Deployment."

Centralized Deployment

Centralized deployment is the most popular method with which to start an ISE deployment. In a centralized deployment, all ISE nodes are located in the same physical location, with LAN-like bandwidth and latency expected between all ISE nodes. Centralized deployment should be used for small, medium-sized, or large deployments that have a single campus location and/or small remote sites. Centralized deployment mode also works best if you have remote sites that already connect to a common central site for the vast majority of their services. Figure 5-1 shows an example diagram of a centralized ISE deployment.

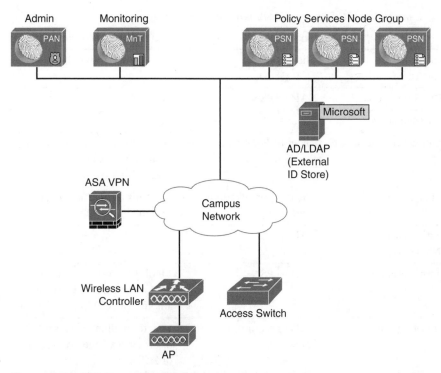

Figure 5-1   *ISE Centralized Deployment*

Deploying ISE in a campus or other area where all clients and ISE nodes are connected via LAN transport is the ideal situation for a centralized ISE deployment. However, this doesn't exclude you from using this method when you have remote sites that are not using a LAN-like transport, especially if those sites have a small number of clients at each. The following are things to consider for centralized deployment with remote sites and clients:

- Number of clients at the remote sites

- Bandwidth available between the client NADs and the ISE PSN

- Reliability of WAN links/circuits between client NADs and ISE nodes

- Resiliency requirements if the WAN goes down between the client NADs and ISE

- Whether quality of service (QoS) is deployed on the networks between the client NADs and ISE

Calculating exact ISE bandwidth requirements is not a simple or straightforward exercise. There are just too many variables in the mix for that to be the case. However, there are some general guidelines available for estimating your bandwidth needs. The minimum bandwidth required between a client and its PSN with posture assessment enabled is 128 bps per endpoint. You can, and should, use QoS to ensure the ISE traffic is prioritized appropriately over the WAN. Table 5-1 provides some general guidance on bandwidth requirements.

Table 5-1 *Centralized ISE Deployment Bandwidth Guidance*

Process	Flow	Bandwidth Guidance
Min. BW client to PSN with posture	Client to PSN	128 bps per endpoint
AAA RADIUS functions	NAD to PSN	Very low
Posture no remediation	Client to PSN	Low
Web Authentication/Guest Services	Client to PSN	Low (be sure to keep any custom web page graphics to small sizes)
Posture remediation	Client to remediation sources	Depends on size and location of remediation files
Profiling with DHCP, SNMP, DNS, HTTP	NAD to PSN	Low
Profiling with NetFlow, SPAN[1]	NAD to PSN	Medium to very high depending on the capture filters and amount of NetFlow traffic
Syslog monitoring traffic	NAD to monitoring node	Low to medium when set to informational and no logging of ACLs
NAC client install or upgrade	Client to PSN	Medium (client software is approx. 30 Mb in size); use QoS to rate-limit

1.   SPAN = Switched Port Analyzer.

For centralized deployment to work over a WAN, you must have highly reliable WAN links. To ensure your critical ISE communication is successful end to end every time, use QoS. At a minimum, you should use QoS to prioritize all RADIUS and TACACS+ communications between NADs and ISE PSNs such that other traffic will not saturate the links to the point that ISE traffic is delayed or dropped, causing authentication and posturing issues for those active clients.

Centralized mode depends on the availability of communications between clients, NADs, and ISE nodes at all times. If this communication is broken temporarily, Cisco ISE does have some resiliency features that can ensure a working solution during the failure. Having robust WAN redundancy in your network greatly reduces the risk of this problem. During an outage, your currently connected clients typically are not impacted, but new clients coming on are impacted. It is up to the local NAD (switch or WLC) to determine how to treat new devices connecting during an ISE outage. Catalyst switches support several failure scenario solutions: fail open, fail closed, or fail to a specific VLAN or local authentication service. This is covered in more detail in Chapter 11, "Bootstrapping Network Access Devices."

Distributed Deployment

Even though the centralized deployment method is generally recommended, there are some use cases where a distributed deployment works better. Here are some examples:

- You have remote sites with unreliable or low-bandwidth WAN circuits.

- You have a local authentication service at your remote sites, such as a local Active Directory server.

- You have sizable or critical remote sites. You need to improve remote site resiliency against a WAN outage.

- You have regional or geographically disperse data centers that aggregate WAN connections.

- You want to increase ISE resiliency by distributing ISE nodes across two data centers.

- You need the ISE PSN profiler to be local to the clients it is serving. This is typically for cases in which you are forced to use SPAN or NetFlow probes to profile clients. Deploying a PSN remotely eliminates the potentially large WAN bandwidth requirements.

Note   You must use ISE version 1.2 or greater for a distributed deployment. ISE version 2.1 or later is recommended.

Typically, in a distributed ISE deployment, the Admin and Monitoring nodes are both centralized, while the PSNs are geographically dispersed. Also popular is to split your Admin and PSNs between two data centers/sites. This allows you to survive a data center outage at a single site.

Note   The nodes in an Admin HA pair or Monitoring HA pair do not need to be Layer 2 adjacent; they can be multiple Layer 3 hops away from each other. However, resilient, low-latency, high-bandwidth links must be available between the primary and secondary nodes.

Note   For ISE 2.1 and later, the maximum latency between the Admin node and any other ISE node, including secondary Admin, MnT, and PSN, is 300 ms. Maximum latency is 200 ms for ISE 2.0 or earlier. Low latency is most critical between PSNs and the primary Policy Administration Node (PAN).

In this model, you are placing your PSNs closer to both your NADs and your clients. This results in better performance and a more scalable ISE deployment, especially when working with high-latency, bandwidth-constrained, or unreliable WAN connections. Figure 5-2 depicts an example ISE distributed deployment model.

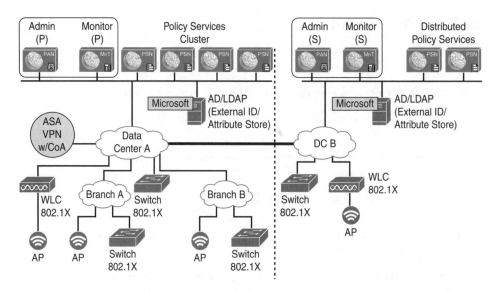

Figure 5-2 *ISE Distributed Deployment*

In a distributed deployment such as the one shown in Figure 5-2, the databases between all of the ISE nodes are automatically synchronized. The primary Admin node is the source of all database replication traffic. Its job is to replicate the database to all other ISE nodes, including monitoring, policy services, and a secondary Admin node. Upon registering a secondary node (that is, as any node that is not the Admin primary) with the primary Admin node, a database sync connection is automatically set up between the two nodes. A full copy of the database is kept up to date in near real time on all nodes by the primary Admin node. This includes configuration changes. You can view the status of replication from the Deployment pages of the ISE Administrative user interface.

In a distributed deployment, having adequate bandwidth is most critical between

■ PSNs and Primary PAN (database replication)

■ PSNs and MnT (audit logging)

Database synchronization also happens in a centralized deployment, but because these nodes have LAN connectivity, you don't need to worry about bandwidth. Over a WAN, however, you do need to consider the ramifications of database replications, especially as they pertain to latency and bandwidth requirements. To this end, Cisco has developed a bandwidth and latency calculator to help you determine the correct specifications required. Bandwidth required for RADIUS traffic is not included. The calculator is focused on inter-ISE node bandwidth requirements. The calculator can be accessed at https://communities.cisco.com/docs/DOC-64317. In lieu of the calculator, Table 5-2 provides some general guidance.

Table 5-2   *Minimum Bandwidth Requirements*

Description	Requirement
Minimum bandwidth between Monitoring and Policy Service nodes	1 Mbps
Minimum bandwidth between Monitoring and Admin nodes	256 Kbps
Minimum bandwidth between Client and Policy Service node with posture	128 bps per endpoint
Minimum bandwidth between Monitoring and Monitoring nodes (redundant)	256 Kbps
Minimum bandwidth between Admin and Policy Service nodes (redundant admin)	256 Kbps

Table 5-2 lists the absolute minimum, so be sure to scale up as required. Additionally, all database sync and replication traffic should be given QoS priority just below RADIUS, voice, and video but above normal traffic types.

A partial database replication is triggered whenever a PSN sends a database update to the primary Admin node. The primary Admin node then initiates an update replication to all other ISE nodes. When deploying ISE distributed PSNs, note that AAA/RADIUS and posture-assessment features cause very minimal database replication traffic. ISE profiling and Guest Services, however, can cause lots of database replication traffic due to their frequent database writes and updates. As a result, lower latency and higher bandwidth WAN links are necessary when using these services within your ISE deployment.

Note   NetFlow and SPAN-based collection methods are *not* supported for distributed deployments due to the potentially high volume of data replication required by these methods.

In the event of a loss of connectivity to the Admin node, distributed PSNs will continue to provide full authentication and authorization services to their local NADs and endpoints. This assumes that the cut-off PSN still has access to its AAA resources. Note that the following disruptions occur on the PSN until the Admin node is brought back online:

- Cannot authenticate new sponsored or self-service Guest user accounts.

- Cannot profile new endpoints.

- Logging is interrupted if connectivity between the PSN and Monitoring node is also lost.

- Automatic client provisioning services will not function.

Summary

This chapter examined the centralized deployment mode and the distributed deployment mode. It suggested that in most cases, the centralized mode should be used. However, it also presented use cases in which the distributed mode is preferable. See Chapter 18 for details on the configuration when distributing the ISE personas.

Chapter 6

Quick Setup of an ISE Proof of Concept

This chapter covers the following topics:

- Deploy ISE for wireless in 15 minutes
- Deploy ISE to gain visibility in 15 minutes

Many of us tech geeks learn best by doing and experiencing things hands-on. The barrier to this is usually time and effort to set everything up. Well, that barrier has been drastically lowered for you with ISE 2.2+. Starting with version 2.2, ISE includes some very powerful configuration wizards that enable you to set up an ISE proof of value in your development environment in just a couple hours. The idea is to be able to set up ISE quickly and easily, run through its functionality, and prove out ISE's value for your organization in a real environment. This chapter steps you through how to get ISE up and running from scratch for a few common use cases very quickly. The Cisco ISE team has been working to make the deployment of ISE quicker and easier release to release so look for even more enhancements in future versions.

Deploy ISE for Wireless in 15 Minutes

ISE 2.2 added a new setup wizard called *Wireless Setup*. The wizard can configure both the Identity Services Engine and a Cisco Wireless LAN Controller (WLC) plus connect ISE to Active Directory. This section walks you through using the Wireless Setup Wizard to quickly deploy ISE with the following services configured:

- **Guest wireless access:** This functionality provides the full guest wireless portal experience, including creating customized portal pages. Guest self-registration is the configuration demonstrated in this section, but you can also select a hotspot or sponsored guest configuration instead using the wizard. Self-registration enables your guests to fill out a simple information form and create their own accounts. You control how long those accounts remain active; the default is 24 hours. The wizard sets up both ISE and the Cisco WLC.

■ **Secure wireless access with WPA2, 802.1X, and PEAP authentication:** This functionality provides wireless access to your corporate users. The most popular wireless settings for a typical business protected Wi-Fi network will be utilized, including WPA2, 802.1X, PEAP, and Active Directory authentication of users. The wizard sets up ISE and the Cisco WLC and connects ISE to Active Directory for user authentication.

■ **Bring Your Own Device (BYOD) wireless access:** This functionality provides your employees with the option to securely provision and use their own wireless devices on either your corporate network or a specific BYOD network you specify. The employees will be able to enroll and remove their own devices from a customized device portal.

Wireless Setup Wizard Configuration

Once you have the ISE appliance bootstrapped and on the network, log in to the ISE GUI at https://<*ISE IP*>/admin. If this is your first time logging in, you will be presented with the option to run the Wireless Setup Wizard; select it. If this is not your first time logging in, you can find the wizard in the upper-right corner of the GUI under the **Play** icon, as shown in Figure 6-1.

Figure 6-1   *Wireless Setup Wizard Startup*

After you launch the wizard, you are presented with the three major configuration options. See Figure 6-2 for details. You can choose to run one, two, or all three of these in any order.

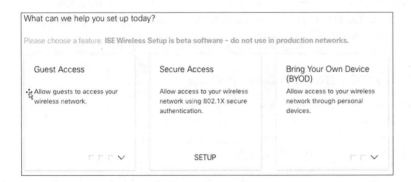

Figure 6-2   *Wireless Setup Wizard Home Page*

Note   At the time of writing, this wizard is in beta. By the time you read this, it likely won't still be in beta. Regardless, heed the warnings and disclaimers in your version of the ISE wizard.

As illustrated in Figure 6-3, the Guest Access tile has three different suboptions to choose from: Self Registration, Hotspot, and Sponsored. For purposes of this example, choose **Self Registration**.

Note   All examples in this chapter assume that your WLC is not already configured with wireless settings. If your WLC does have SSIDs, VLANs, and so forth already configured, that is okay too. The wizard will display your existing values for selection or allow you to create new ones.

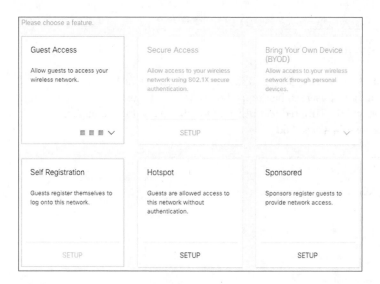

Figure 6-3   *Wireless Setup Wizard Guest Types*

Guest Self-Registration Wizard

These steps show you how to configure the guest self-registration service. This enables guests to register themselves, via a web portal, to log in to a network.

Step 1.   Enter the information for your wireless controller, as shown in Figure 6-4. Best practice for shared secrets is to use at least a 16-character password. Click **Register**.

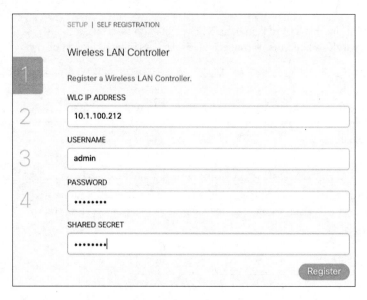

Figure 6-4   *Self-Registration Step 1*

Step 2.   Configure the wireless SSID and the network interface or VLAN that you want your guest users to be dropped onto. Next configure the account duration and the URL redirect behavior for after guest login completes (see Figure 6-5). Click **Add.**

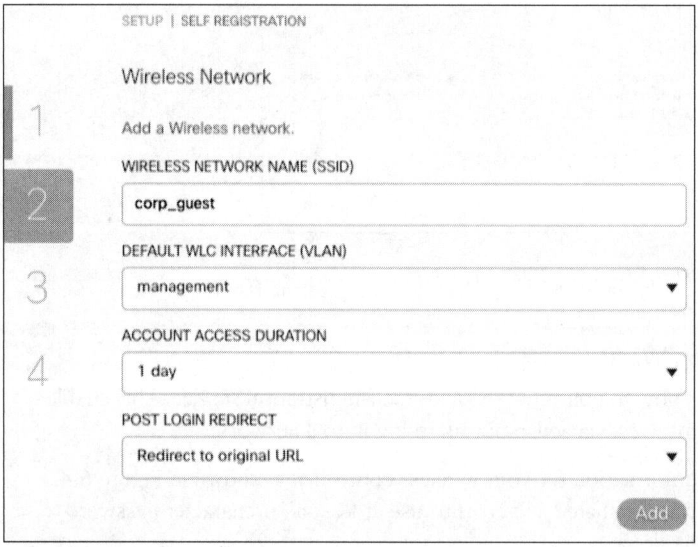

SETUP | SELF REGISTRATION

Wireless Network

Add a Wireless network.

WIRELESS NETWORK NAME (SSID)

corp_guest

DEFAULT WLC INTERFACE (VLAN)

management

ACCOUNT ACCESS DURATION

1 day

POST LOGIN REDIRECT

Redirect to original URL

Add

Figure 6-5   *Self-Registration Step 2*

Step 3.   Customize the guest portal pages. From the screen displayed in Figure 6-6, click the pencil icon to edit your portal pages.

Figure 6-6   *Self-Registration Step 3*

This takes you to the portal editor, in which you customize three pages, as shown in Figure 6-7. You need to go through each page to ensure it looks the way you want it. Each page has similar steps, so only the Login Page steps are shown.

Figure 6-7   *Self-Registration Portal Pages*

Step 4.   From the drop-down list, choose **Login Page**. Figure 6-8 shows a partially customized page. Everywhere you see the pencil icon indicates an area you can customize. You can upload your own background and icon images, you can and should change the terms and conditions, and you can add additional text fields. To add a new text field, drag the text field from the left column onto the login page.

Figure 6-8   *Self-Registration Portal Customization*

The icons in the upper-right corner are preview buttons for different types of devices. Click one to see what your page would look like on that device type.

Step 5.   Customize your notifications by clicking the **Notifications** menu in the lower-left area of the page. This enables you to tell the system how you want to send credentials to guests for the new accounts they create. It also allows you to customize the text in the message to the guest. Figure 6-9 depicts the various options available.

Figure 6-9   *Self-Registration Portal Notifications*

Step 6.   Click the **Commit** button when you are satisfied with your customizations.

Step 7.   Click the **Test Portal** button to launch the real portal from ISE so that you can check your work. If you need to make changes, just click the pencil icon again and continue editing your portal. Click **Next** to proceed to step 4 of the wizard, as shown in Figure 6-10.

Figure 6-10   *Self-Registration Portal Go Live*

Step 8.   Check your work and click the **Go Live** button to finish the setup. Your guests can now log in via wireless to your network.

Secure Access Wizard

This wizard guides you through the steps to configure Active Directory user authentication on your wireless network using ISE. Go to the Wireless Setup Wizard and select **Setup** under Secure Access (refer to Figure 6-2).

Step 1.   From the screen shown in Figure 6-11, select the WLC that you want to set up and click **Commit**.

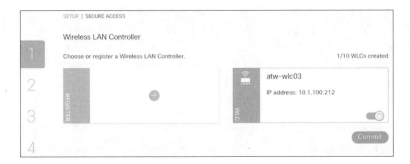

Figure 6-11   *Secure Access Step 1*

Step 2.   From the screen shown in Figure 6-12, choose the wireless network from the list of networks already configured on your WLC or click **+** to create a new one. The default WLC interface is the wired interface or VLAN that authorized users will drop onto from wireless. Click **Add**.

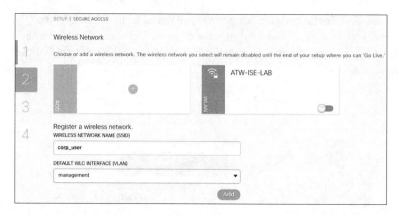

Figure 6-12   *Secure Access Step 2*

Step 3.   From the screen shown in Figure 6-13, set up your AD by entering your domain name and a user/pwd for an AD services account for ISE to use. Click **Join**.

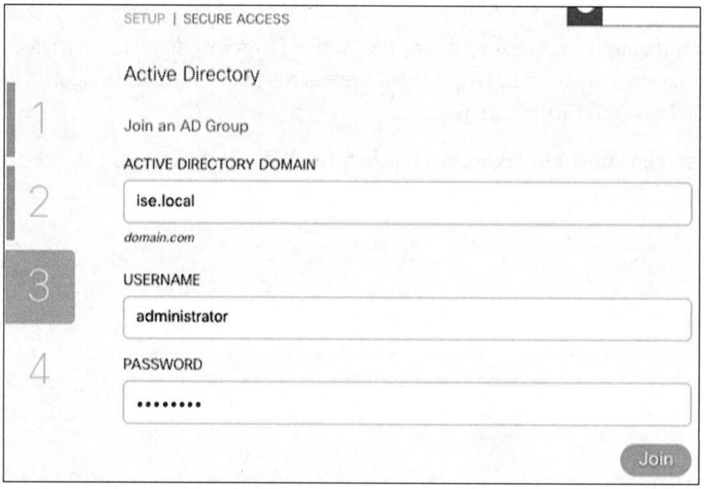

Figure 6-13   *Secure Access Step 3*

Once joined, you may want to set up AD user groups that should drop onto a different wired interface or VLAN (see Figure 6-14).

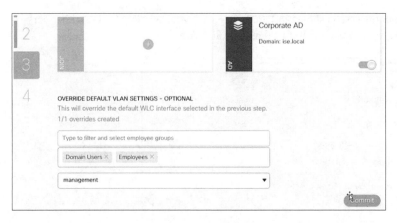

Figure 6-14   *Secure Access Override Default VLAN Settings*

Step 4.   Click **Commit**, and then on step 4 click the **Go Live** button. Your AD users can now log in to your wireless network securely.

Bring Your Own Device (BYOD) Wizard

The BYOD wizard will configure ISE to allow access to your wireless networks using registered and compliant personal or corporate devices. From the Wireless Setup Wizard, click **Bring Your Own Device**, select either **Single** or **Dual** SSID, and then click **Setup**. This example shows setup of Single SSID.

Step 1.   From the screen shown in Figure 6-15, select your WLC or add a new one. Click **Commit**.

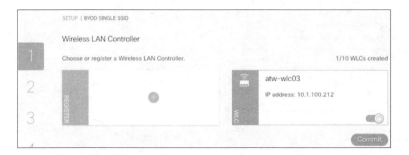

Figure 6-15   *BYOD Step 1*

Step 2.   From the screen shown in Figure 6-16, add your wireless SSID and network
you want to use for BYOD devices. Click **Add**.

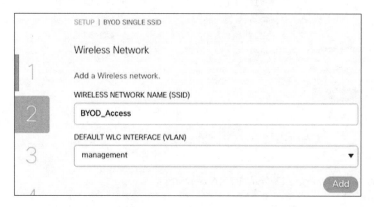

Figure 6-16   *BYOD Step 2*

Step 3.   Select your AD controller and, optionally, configure Override Default VLAN
Settings. This enables you to change the default WLC interface that a particular user group drops onto after authorization. (see Figure 6-17).

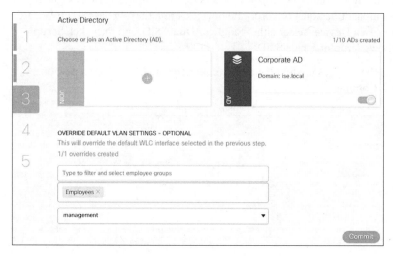

Figure 6-17   *BYOD Step 3*

Step 4.   You should customize both the BYOD portal and the My Devices portal. The
customization works just like the Guest portal customization we reviewed
previously. Enter a custom URL for your portal so employees can remember
it easily (see Figure 6-18). Add this domain into your DNS server and point it
to ISE. Be sure to preview your portals before you go to step 5 of the wizard.
Once done, click **Next**. Check your work and then click the **Go Live** button.

Your employees can now register, enroll, and remove their BYOD devices securely on your wireless network.

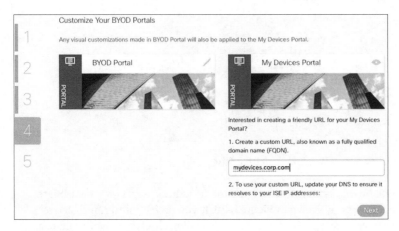

Figure 6-18   *BYOD Step 4*

You have now completed all of the functions in the Wireless Setup Wizard. To get back to the ISE dashboard, click the **Back to ISE** link in the upper-right corner of the screen.

Deploy ISE to Gain Visibility in 15 Minutes

Gaining visibility into what is on your network is a key first step to deploying ISE. Starting in ISE 2.1, the ISE Visibility Setup Wizard is available to help you quickly set up ISE Profiler, NMAP, and other features that show you what types of devices are connecting to your network. It even polls Active Directory for host OS information. The Visibility Setup Wizard configures ISE to be ready for network switches, WLCs, and firewalls to send profiling data to it. After the wizard is completed, you will start to see contextual data from hosts; however, you should then take the next step and manually configure key network devices to send profiling data to ISE. This will greatly enhance your ISE contextual and visibility data.

Visibility Setup Wizard

Log in to the ISE GUI. Open the Visibility Setup Wizard by clicking the **Play** icon in the upper-right corner of the ISE GUI and choosing the **Visibility Setup** link. This launches the wizard's Welcome page, shown in Figure 6-19. Click **Next** and complete the following steps. After each step, click **Next** to move on to the next step.

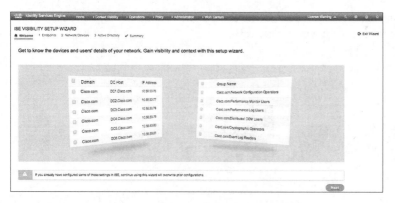

Figure 6-19   *Visibility Setup Wizard Welcome Page*

Step 1.   The first wizard step is to configure the IP address ranges you want ISE to scan for hosts, as shown in Figure 6-20. If you prefer not to run an active NMAP scan, then uncheck the Active Scanning check box. Not running an active scan decreases the amount of context ISE is able to gather.

Figure 6-20   *Visibility Setup Wizard Step 1*

Step 2.   The second wizard step is to add your network devices into ISE so that it can discover them and the hosts connected to them. This also allows ISE, via SNMP, to receive host connectivity and port information. Figure 6-21 depicts the devices that are added, while Figure 6-22 shows an example of adding a device. To add a device, click **Add**.

Figure 6-21 *Visibility Setup Wizard Step 2*

Edit Network Device   ✕

Name *	Cisco_switch
IP Address *	192.168.254.1
Location	Denver
Device Type	switch
Description	3750X

SNMP Settings

SNMP Version *	2c
RO Community *	●●●●●●●●●●●● Show

Cancel   Save

Figure 6-22 *Visibility Setup Wizard Step 2: Adding a Device*

The Location and Device Type fields are free-form fields you should use to logically organize your devices. Location could be a city or it could be a closet on the third floor; whatever works best for your organization. Click **Save**.

Step 3.   Step three of the wizard is where you connect to Active Directory. ISE will pull host OS information and other attributes from AD. If you have already configured AD in ISE, you can click the **Skip** link. If not, see Figure 6-23 for configuration details.

♠ Welcome   1 Endpoints   2 Network Devices   3 **Active Directory**   ✓ Summary

Connect to Active Directory (AD)

Connect Active Directory server to get user identity information. You can add one or more Active Directories.

Display Name *	ise.local
Domain FQDN *	ise.local
ISE Node *	atw-ise231.securitydemo.net
Username *	administrator
Password *	....
Organization Unit	CN=COMPUTERS,DC=CISCO,DC=COM

e.g. CN=COMPUTERS,DC=CISCO,DC=COM

Test Connection

☑ Successfully Connected.

Figure 6-23 *Visibility Setup Wizard Step 3*

Step 4.   The final step, four, is just a summary screen of all your previous steps. From here, you can click the **Edit** button and go back to a previous step. To complete, click **Test Connection** on AD one last time. If successful, you can click **Exit Wizard**. You're done! ISE is now profiling your network, collecting context and visibility data. Let it run for at least an hour and then check the page at **Context Visibility > Endpoints > Endpoint Classification**, as shown in Figure 6-24.

Figure 6-24 *Endpoint Classification Page*

Notice at the bottom of the page the list of all the devices and their contextual information. By checking a row, you can then issue actions on that host, such as those listed in Figure 6-25.

Figure 6-25   *Endpoint Classification Page Actions*

The most common profiling data probes for ISE are the RADIUS, SNMPQUERY, DHCP, Network Scan (NMAP), and Active Directory probes. The probes are sent from the Policy Service Nodes in an ISE deployment. The Visibility Setup Wizard discussed previously has already configured all of these profiler probes.

To verify the probes' configuration or make changes, go to **Administration > System > Deployment**. Click your ISE PSN node. On the General Settings tab, ensure that the profiling service, under the policy service, is checked.

Next, click the **Profiling Configuration** tab. Verify that all of the probes checked in Figure 6-26 are enabled.

Figure 6-26   *Profiling Probes Configuration*

Configuring Cisco Switches to Send ISE Profiling Data

The most common profiling probes used with Cisco switches are SNMPQUERY, RADIUS, and DHCP.

SNMPQUERY Probe

The SNMPQUERY probe is used by ISE to send SNMP Get requests to access devices, such as switches, to collect relevant endpoint data stored in their SNMP MIBs. There are two types of SNMP queries that the ISE PSN performs: System Query (Polled) and Interface Query (Triggered). This probe also collects Cisco Discovery Protocol (CDP) information.

Step 1.   Configure all of your switches with a read-only community string such as **snmp-server community ciscoro RO 10, access-list 10 permit 1.1.1.1**. For better security, always configure an ACL when you configure community strings.

Step 2.   CDP is usually enabled by default on switches. To verify, ensure that the global command **cdp run** and the switch port command **cdp enable** are configured.

RADIUS Probe

For RADIUS, you just need to add the device to ISE for standard RADIUS communications and configure RADIUS AAA on the switches.

Configure all of your switches with RADIUS AAA using the following IOS commands:

```
aaa authentication dot1x default group radius
aaa authorization network default group radius
aaa accounting dot1x default start-stop group radius
ip radius source-interface <Interface>
radius-server attribute 6 on-for-login-auth
radius-server attribute 8 include-in-access-req
radius-server attribute 25 access-request include
radius-server host <ISE_PSN_Address> auth-port 1812 acct-port 1813 key xxx
radius-server vsa send accounting
radius-server vsa send authentication
```

DHCP Probe

This probe collects attributes from within the DHCP client request. It uses the DHCP helper or relay commands on switches or routers.

From the CLI of your Cisco switches or routers that are currently acting as DHCP relays, add a second relay or helper statement to send a copy of the DHCP request to your ISE PSN.

Under each routed interface relaying DHCP for hosts, add the following IOS command:

```
ip helper-address ISE_PSN_address
```

Or NX-OS command

```
ip dhcp relay ISE_PSN_address
```

The address specified should be to the PSN interface with the DHCP probe enabled. For redundancy, you can add more IP Helper statements to relay DHCP to other PSNs. However, doing so adds additional load on your PSNs, so use this sparingly.

Summary

This chapter has shown you how to get ISE up and running and providing value very quickly. At this point you have secure wireless for guests, employees, and employee BYOD devices. You also have ISE authenticating with Active Directory and collecting context and visibility profiling data from your network. The multiple profiler probes you configured will show you who, what, and where devices and users are on your network. That is a nice start to your ISE deployment—well done!

Chapter 7

Building a Cisco ISE Network Access Security Policy

This chapter covers the following topics:

- Components of a Cisco ISE network access security policy

- Determining the high-level goals for network access security

- Defining the security domains

- Understanding and defining ISE authorization rules

- Establishing acceptable use policies

- Host security posture assessment rules to consider

- Defining dynamic network access privileges

In order for any network-centric security solution to be successful, a solid network access security policy (NASP) must first be in place. Once a policy is in place, ISE will enforce the policy network-wide. A NASP defines, in as much detail as is practical, the type of network access that will be given to users and device types. Because network and device security threats are constantly changing, a NASP must also be a living, changeable document. This book does not attempt to assemble an all-encompassing NASP, but instead focuses on showing you how to build policies that are relevant to the Cisco ISE solution. Thus, this chapter guides you through the process of creating a comprehensive NASP that you can use in an environment that is safeguarded by Cisco ISE. Building a NASP is not always straightforward, and can be frustrating at times, but stick with it; your hard work will be rewarded in the end. The key to a successful ISE deployment is *not* to try to accomplish everything in the first phase. Start with the easy and quick approach, like what was shown in Chapter 6.

Components of a Cisco ISE Network Access Security Policy

One of the hardest things about writing a comprehensive network access security policy is figuring out what should be included. This chapter guides you through the parts and pieces that, at a minimum, should be included in any NASP written for the Cisco ISE solution. For your ISE solution to be most effective, you must first determine exactly what an acceptable network access security posture is under different circumstances and contexts. After you do so, you can then translate your NASP into the proper checks, rules, and security requirements that ISE will use to determine the correct policy to apply to the network and/or device. For example, if the device is not a corporate asset and is connected to the corporate wireless network, then a strict NASP should be enforced. However, if a registered corporate asset of the same device type connects to corporate wireless, a less strict NASP should be enforced. You also need to determine what the NASP should be for different types of devices and their security posture. For example, if a contractor logs in to your network using a Windows 10 laptop, the security policy would differ from the same user logging in with a Mac OS X laptop.

An ISE NASP is made up of several different policy types. When combined inside ISE, these policy types provide you with the ultimate in flexibility for achieving a truly context-aware network access decision. The following are main policy types for which ISE will obtain contextual information it can then use to build such policies:

- **Authentication Policy:** Verifies the user's and/or device's identity or provides unauthenticated guest access. For example: Authenticate all wireless users against the corporate Active Directory (AD).

- **Authorization Policy:** Describes both the contextual attributes used for authorization of the user and/or device and the enforcement method triggered once a policy rule is matched. For example: Users who are members of the AD group *Employees* and are using an approved company-owned device are allowed to use the wireless SSID corp. All of your dynamic segmentation policies, including TrustSec policies, will be configured here.

- **Host Posture Assessment Policy:** Deals with the security level of the host itself. Different operating systems and device types offer different levels of posture assessment capability. ISE can also integrate with a third-party Mobile Device Management (MDM) system to gather posture information from mobile devices such as iPhones and iPads. An example policy: All Windows 10 PCs must have all corporate patches and be running an approved up-to-date antimalware software package such as Cisco AMP.

- **Device Profiling Policy:** Allows you to set policy based on the type of device trying to access your network. Profiling is an agentless method of passively watching the device's behavior and/or responses to determine what type it is. For example: If a user connects with an iPhone, do not allow them access to any data center or HR resources.

The preceding list is not comprehensive but showcases the most popular policy types typically included in a comprehensive network access security policy. A BYOD policy would be made up of the different listed policies combined into a specific BYOD policy and, as such, is not included as its own policy type in this chapter. However, you may choose to, and likely will, have a separate BYOD policy within your NASP that ISE will enforce.

Network Access Security Policy Checklist

The following is a checklist of the most common steps considered necessary to create an ISE network access security policy. Each checklist item will be explained in detail in the subsequent sections of this chapter. Use this checklist, along with the detailed explanations, to get a head start in the creation of your own unique NASP.

- ☐ Obtain senior management sponsors that will support you through the creation of the NASP and the deployment of the ISE solution.

- ☐ Determine which people and departments need to be involved in the creation of the NASP. Make sure they are included right from the start of the project.

- ☐ Determine what your high-level goals for network access security are.

- ☐ Break up your organization into security domains. The requirements of the NASP can then be customized for each security domain as necessary.

- ☐ Define authorization rules that are relevant for your organization.

- ☐ Establish an acceptable use policy (AUP) for your network.

- ☐ Define the ISE network access security checks, rules, and requirements for each authorization rule.

- ☐ Define the network access privileges that should be granted to each authorization rule.

- ☐ Establish a Network Access Security Policy life-cycle process that ensures the regular updating and changing of the NASP's checks, rules, and requirements.

Involving the Right People in the Creation of the Network Access Security Policy

At the very beginning of the planning for an ISE deployment or purchase, it is extremely important to obtain project sponsorship from senior-level management. Given that ISE will force a change on the user community's behavior and network access, this is a mandatory step. Without senior-level sponsorship, a few activist users who are not happy with or willing to accept the new policy changes could derail your ISE deployment. Having the endorsement of senior management grants you the power to push back on those users in a constructive way.

Too often the security group spends the time to develop sound security policies and practices only to be told that they are overly restrictive and need to be changed. This can be avoided by making sure that you keep your sponsors involved and up to date on the progress and content of your NASP. It is also critical that you have your final version approved by your sponsorship committee prior to releasing it to the user community. Try to anticipate the type of reaction, resistance, and questions the user community will have. Be ready with solid rebuttals, facts, and collateral to combat their arguments, answer their questions, and make them feel more comfortable that the new NASP is the correct one and best for the business.

One of the first steps in the creation of any NASP is the formation of the network access security policy committee. This committee should be made up of the principal persons whose group or users will be most affected by or have some ownership in the new policy. It is a best practice to keep the committee small in the beginning phases of the policy creation. Once this core team has a clear policy direction, some substance, and some content, then the NASP committee should be expanded to include more key persons.

When the NASP reaches a completed draft format, the NASP committee should again be expanded. This time the expansion is to include those principal persons who do not have any direct ownership or responsibility for the creation of the NASP but do have a sizeable user community that will be directly affected by the policy's proposed changes. This last group serves to scrutinize the policies in your NASP draft to make sure the policies do not inhibit business practices or workflow, are practical, and have achieved the proper balance of risk mitigation versus ease of network access for the organization.

Once a final NASP version has been created, the entire committee must agree to present a united front when the new policy begins to be enforced inside the organization. A nonunited, or splintered, NASP committee almost always will result in the splintering or haphazard adoption of the NASP within the organization.

The following is a list of the most common principal persons that should be a part of the creation of a NASP. Additionally, the CSO and CIO must be sponsors or core committee members. You should modify this list for your environment.

- Sponsors should include the following:

    - At least one executive-level sponsor other than the CSO/CIO.

    - At least one company board member. If this is too inconvenient for your organization to arrange, then settle for a presentation to the board of your ISE project, its goals, and its business relevance.

    - An attorney from the legal department, to review your AUP and legal disclaimers, at a minimum.

- Core NASP committee members should include key persons from the following groups:

  - Security group

  - Networking group

  - Server group

  - Desktop support group

  - Operations group

  - Security incident response team

- Extended NASP committee members should include key persons from the following groups:

  - Human resources group

  - Legal group

  - Audit/compliance group

- Final NASP committee members should include key persons from the following groups:

  - Managers of large end-user groups within the organization (such as division heads, department heads, and so on).

  - The end-user community, for feedback and impact analysis. Be sure to select at least one "newbie" end user.

This list should be used as a guideline and is not meant to be all-inclusive. The goal of committee member selection is to ensure that the committee has adequate representation from all key stakeholders, budget holders, management, legal counsel, and technical staff. Some of the groups listed might not be included if your ISE deployment will be limited in scope or functionality. Each group will have a slightly different role to fulfill on the committee. Make sure that you communicate up front what their roles will be. Try to keep your core group to less than ten people so that it can operate efficiently.

Determining the High-Level Goals for Network Access Security

Determining what your high-level goals are for network access security is a critical step toward the completion of a comprehensive network access security policy. These high-level goals will serve as your benchmarks and guides throughout the NASP creation process. The final NASP document should represent a detailed plan that achieves these high-level goals. It is important to periodically refer to these high-level goals to ensure your NASP remains focused and on target to meet your stated security goals.

Among the references for creating a security policy, one that has stood the test of time is RFC 2196, "Site Security Handbook." The following is an excerpt:

Your goals will be largely determined by the following key tradeoffs:

1. services offered versus security provided –

Each service offered to users carries its own security risks. For some services the risk outweighs the benefit of the service and the administrator may choose to eliminate the service rather than try to secure it.

2. ease of use versus security –

The easiest system to use would allow access to any user and require no passwords; that is, there would be no security. Requiring passwords makes the system a little less convenient, but more secure. Requiring device-generated one-time passwords makes the system even more difficult to use, but much more secure.

3. cost of security versus risk of loss –

There are many different costs to security: monetary (i.e., the cost of purchasing security hardware and software like firewalls and one-time password generators), performance (i.e., encryption and decryption take time), and ease of use (as mentioned above). There are also many levels of risk: loss of privacy (i.e., the reading of information by unauthorized individuals), loss of data (i.e., the corruption or erasure of information), and the loss of service (e.g., the filling of data storage space, usage of computational resources, and denial of network access). Each type of cost must be weighed against each type of loss.

Note   For more detailed information about the creation of network access security goals and security policies in general, reference IETF RFC 2196 at http://www.ietf.org/rfc/rfc2196.txt.

Your final high-level network access security goals will be the result of establishing a fine balance among the preceding trade-offs. The result of each trade-off will be different for each organization or division within an organization.

Common High-Level Network Access Security Goals

Here are some examples of network access security goals that are frequently instituted in organizations that deploy an ISE solution. These examples are meant to be a sampling and not a comprehensive list.

■ Enforce a consistent context-based dynamic segmentation security policy across the infrastructure.

■ Obtain system-wide visibility showing who, what, how, and where a user or device is on the wired, wireless, or VPN network.

- Protect the network from unauthorized access, both internal and external, at all network access points.

- Authenticate all users attempting to gain access to the network.

- Authorize all users, based on risk, attempting to gain access to the network.

- Assign a TrustSec Security Group Tag (SGT) to all wired, wireless, and VPN users after network authorization.

- Provide differentiated network access based on user and device attributes, risk profile, and role.

- All non-guest mobile devices must be enrolled in the corporate mobile device management (MDM) system.

- All users must periodically acknowledge an acceptable use policy before being granted network access.

- All PCs and Macs must be running an approved antimalware and personal firewall program that is continuously up to date.

- All non-guest devices must be running an approved operating system version that is up to date.

- Any device that is found to be running banned software applications will be denied network access.

- All guest devices must be segmented from non-guest devices and other guest devices and provided only regulated Internet access.

- Compromised users or endpoints must be alerted and quarantined on the network to limit the scope of the breach.

It is common for an organization to modify its network access security goals based on a specific network location or access type. For example, an organization might have a policy that states that all devices connecting through wireless in the Denver data center must be corporate-owned in order to gain network access.

Many organizations choose to deploy an ISE solution gradually by enforcing their network access security policies incrementally. The following is a list of common best practice policy enforcement phases:

Note Deploying ISE to protect wireless networks is by far the easiest solution to build and maintain. Among the various reasons for this, the primary reason is that the protocols used for wireless client AAA are robust and easy to deploy. Thus, the list that follows includes wireless deployments first. Wireless is the low-hanging fruit for an ISE deployment. The different wired deployment modes in the list that follows will be covered in detail in subsequent chapters.

- Deploy wireless guest access security policies.

- Deploy wireless authentication and lightweight authorization access control policies.

- Deploy policies for wired and wireless network visibility profiling of users and devices.

- If applicable, deploy mobile device provisioning and enrollment into an MDM system.

- Deploy wired 802.1X and MAC Authentication Bypass (MAB) for AAA in Monitor Mode.

- Deploy wired 802.1X for AAA in Low-Impact Mode.

- Deploy wired 802.1X for AAA in Closed Mode.

Then, as the adoption of the ISE solution grows, the network access security policy enforcement can be spread ubiquitously throughout the organization.

Network Access Security Policy Decision Matrix

Figure 7-1 summarizes the process for determining the exact network access security policy that will be enforced for a given user, for a given device, or in a given network location.

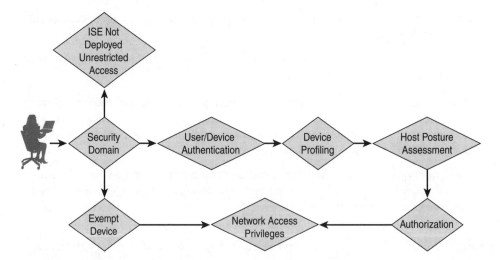

Figure 7-1   *Network Access Security Policy Decision Matrix*

The following list explains the device security policy decision steps shown in Figure 7-1. Following this list are several sections that describe these decision steps in greater detail.

1. The device connects to a location on the network.

2. The device is determined to be a member of a certain security domain. The NASP must define what the security domains are for the organization. The NASP must define one of three choices for each unique security domain:

- The security domain does not have ISE deployed, thus allowing unrestricted network access. The NASP for this security domain states that no network access security policies are to be enforced in this domain.

- The security domain has ISE deployed but exempts specific devices from ISE access control when they are seen on the network.

- The security domain has ISE deployed and forces all devices to comply fully with the ISE NASP.

3. If the device is a member of the exempt list, then it flows directly to the network access privileges. The remaining steps are bypassed. The NASP must define exactly what the network access privileges will be for each type of exempt device. It is possible to have different network access security policies for different types of exempt devices. For example, you can have an exempt network access security policy that allows IP phones to access the network unrestricted.

4. If the device is part of a security domain that requires full compliance with the ISE policy, then the user/device is forced to authenticate. The NASP should determine exactly how the user and/or device is authenticated and verified.

5. After successfully authenticating, the device is then profiled to figure out what kind of device it is.

6. The posture of the device is checked to determine whether the host is in compliance. The NASP should define what the security requirements are.

7. If the host is in compliance with the security requirements, it is authorized. The authorization rules are parsed and the first rule matched is executed upon.

8. The network access policies assigned to the matched authorization rule are enforced. The NASP should define the type of network access that should be granted to clients. The access requirements are produced from a combination of authentication, authorization, profiler, and posture rules combined.

Defining the Security Domains

A security domain is used to group things together that have a common risk profile, under a common network access security policy. These things could be a combination of user groups, locations, network types, device types, and/or business function. Security domains allow you to break your security policy into manageable sections. For example, you might have a Guest Wireless security domain or a Corporate Wireless security domain. Figure 7-2 shows an example of security domains.

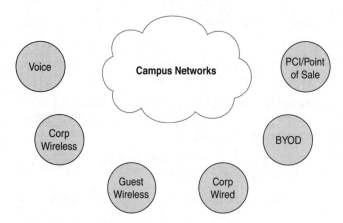

Figure 7-2   *Sample Security Domains*

Most organizations need to define the security domains that are depicted in Figure 7-2. Each one of these groups usually requires its own unique network access security policy and thus should be its own security domain. (A few other common security domains that are not depicted are Data Center and Internet of Things [IoT] security domains.) Separating these areas into unique security domains allows you to create unique network access security polices for each. The more compartmentalized your NASP is, the more granular and targeted it can be while at the same time keeping things manageable and realistic. This results in a more locked-down network access security policy for your organization that can be operationalized. Using security domains is optional, of course, but makes a great way to segment your NASP. Above all, try to keep your NASP short and concise; the keep it short and simple (KISS) principle applies here.

Here are some commonly used security domains:

■ **Remote Access:** This domain includes any device that is accessing the network remotely via VPN and/or dial-up modem.

■ **OOB Management:** This domain includes any device that resides on the out-of-band network management network. This is typically a highly secured domain.

■ **Internet Access:** This domain includes any device that accesses the Internet. An example policy for this domain could be: Before a device is allowed to access the Internet, its operating system and antivirus software must be up to date.

■ **Guest:** This domain includes any device that is a guest on the network. This domain typically is segmented into access types as well (for example, guest wireless, guest VPN, and guest LAN domains). This allows for the creation of very granular network access security policies for guests.

■ **Wired:** This domain includes any device that connects to the network via a wired switch port. It is very common to separate security domains by VLAN or location at the LAN level. This allows the NASP to have policies for specific VLANs and locations instead of having one generic policy for all wired devices.

■ **Wireless:** This domain includes any device that uses wireless to access the network. It is common for the wireless domain to be separated out by VLAN or location (for example, a guest wireless security domain or a Denver campus wireless security domain).

This list is by no means comprehensive, but it should serve to give you a good start in the creation of your own security domains.

Understanding and Defining ISE Authorization Rules

The effective use of authorization rules is a key component to any successful ISE deployment. ISE is very much rule-based. An authorization rule defines the network access security policies that will be required for its members. ISE evaluates authorization rules top down and first match, just like a router ACL. Because of this, the rule order is important in ISE. Additionally, your most-often-hit rules should be at the top for efficiency of the system. The concept of authorization rules is the backbone of ISE.

The login information is used to gather attributes from an external identity server such as LDAP, AD, or RADIUS.

Tip   It is a best practice to map attributes from an external authentication server (such as AD, LDAP, or RADIUS) to an authorization rule in ISE. A common attribute used is MemberOf in Windows AD. This allows authorization rules to be based on existing AD groups within your organization. For example, an LDAP user *Conor* is a MemberOf AD group *employee*.

ISE authorization rules have policies that determine which ISE functions will be performed on clients. All clients that match the authorization rule will be subjected to its security permissions. The common permissions that can be controlled by authorization rules are as follows:

■ Access Type (Accept/Reject)

■ Apply a TrustSec Security Group Tag to the client traffic

■ Downloadable ACLs

■ VLAN Assignment

■ Airespace ACL Name—Assigns ACL in Cisco WLC to client traffic

■ Voice Domain Permission

■ Initiate Web Authentication

■ Execute Switch Auto Smartports macro

■ Apply an Interface Template

- Periodically assess host vulnerabilities

- Filter-ID—Sends ACL via RADIUS filter attribute

- Reauthentication—Decide if you want to maintain connectivity during reauthentication

- MACsec Policy—Sets 802.1ae link-by-link encryption to must-secure, should-secure, or must-not-secure

- Network Edge Authentication Topology (NEAT)—Allows you to authenticate network devices (such as switches) to other network devices via 802.1X

- ASA VPN attributes

- Client posture assessment

- Network Scanner—NMAP

- Acceptable Use Policy

As you can see, authorization rules have a number of common permission controls available. ISE also has numerous advanced permissions via advanced attribute settings when defining your permissions.

Commonly Configured Rules and Their Purpose

This section focuses mostly on the rules that are commonly found in the network access security policies of organizations that use the ISE solution. The goal is to present you with a solid starting point from which to determine the authorization rule needs of your organization's network access security policy.

Let's explore some of the most commonly used rules. Remember, a rule defines the rights and privileges a client will have once they pass authentication, authorization, and posture assessment. All organizations must have their own customized rules. The number and purpose of these rules will vary according to your environment. Each of the rules you build should have a separate policy definition section in your NASP document. Here are some of the most commonly configured rules:

- Guest/visitor Rule

- Employee Rule

- Corporate Authorization Rule

- Contractor/Temp Rule

- Student Rule

- Faculty Rule

- Rules based on network location, such as Denver Authorization Rule

- Admin Rule

- Staff Rule

- Wireless Authorization Rule

- VPN Authorization Rule

- Printers and other non-802.1X devices rule(s)

The non-802.1X-capable device rules, coupled with the ISE profiler, can be used to segment and limit access to/from the noninteractive network devices, such as some printers, faxes, IP Phones, and so on. This enables you to create very strict network access policies for these devices. These policies should allow them to communicate only by using protocols that match the services they provide.

Establishing Acceptable Use Policies

A network acceptable use policy (AUP) is a clear and concise document that defines what users can and cannot do on a network. However, the primary focus of the AUP is to communicate to users what they cannot do. It also lays out the penalties for noncompliance and provides support contact information. Ideally, all users must accept the organization's AUP the first time they attempt to access the network and must periodically re-acknowledge the AUP thereafter. The problem has always been enforcing this requirement. Without some kind of network access control system, ubiquitous enforcement is not possible. The ISE solution supports the enforcement and auditing of network acceptable use policies.

Before creating your AUP for ISE users and guests, determine who needs to be involved and what the approval process for a final policy will look like. Create an AUP committee that includes, at a minimum, persons from the legal and IT departments. Draft a flow chart of the expected approval process the AUP will have to go through. Next, determine which documents the committee needs to produce to successfully complete the AUP. For example, to have an AUP approved in the education space, it is customary to require the following documents:

- **Justification and purpose for creating an AUP:** This typically needs to be presented to the school board and must be approved in the beginning to allow for the creation of the AUP committee.

- **A high-level AUP specifically created for or by the school board to establish the framework from which the final detailed AUP will be crafted:** It establishes the major security goals and network use guidelines. This must be approved by the school board.

- **A parent letter and permission form informing them of the AUP and the use of ISE to enforce this AUP:** This must be approved by the school board.

- **The final Acceptable Use Policy document:** Typically, this is created by the committee and presented to the school board for approval. This is the document that will be used by the ISE solution.

In general, an acceptable use policy will include these parts or sections:

- **AUP Overview or Purpose:** Serves as an introduction to the AUP.

- **AUP Scope or Coverage:** Defines who must comply with this acceptable use policy.

- **Acceptable Network Use Guidelines:** Conveys the appropriate use of the network.

- **Unacceptable or Prohibited Network Uses:** This section may have several sub-sections, such as a subsection for email, copyrighted material, viruses and worms, unauthorized access, illegal activity, and so forth.

- **Violation or Enforcement Policy:** Communicates the penalties and/or legal action that could be taken against AUP violators.

- **Privacy Disclaimer:** Indicates that the organization assumes no responsibility or liability for a user's privacy while using the network.

- **Definitions:** Fully defines all acronyms and terms used in the document.

- **Legal Disclaimer:** Purpose is to release the organization from any and all legal liabilities resulting from the AUP itself or network use. Let the lawyers define this one.

- **Right to Modification:** A disclaimer communicating your ability to modify this policy at any time without notice.

- **Contact Information:** Provides users with a point of contact for additional information, questions, or complaints.

Your AUP may include more or fewer sections than those listed. The preceding list of sections should give you a general idea of what to include in your AUP.

Tip   To find additional information about AUPs, such as "How To" guides and examples, search Google using the keywords **network acceptable use policy**. For AUP samples, check out the SANS policy site at https://www.sans.org/security-resources/policies/.

The ISE solution has two methods for enforcing an AUP:

- **Via a guest portal login:** Used only by users that log in via web authentication.

- **Via the Cisco AnyConnect w/ISE Posture Module Agent:** Used only by users that have the Agent installed.

Both methods can, and typically do, use and enforce the same AUP. Both methods enforce the policy by denying users network access until they acknowledge or accept the network AUP. Once they accept the policy, they are granted network access.

The enforcement of an AUP is an optional feature. Enforcement can be selectively enabled as well. Enforcement can be turned on or off based on the client's identity group. Additionally, it can be enabled and disabled based on the use of web login or the NAC agent. For example, you might want to enable AUP enforcement just for guest clients. ISE can also support enforcement of periodic AUP acceptance.

Host Security Posture Assessment Rules to Consider

This section covers the process of how to include host posture criteria into an organization's network access security policy document. One of the powerful features of ISE when using the Cisco AnyConnect Posture Agent is its ability to perform very granular device security posture assessments and remediation on Windows and Mac devices. Therefore, your NASP should contain the checks, rules, and requirements that ISE will use. This includes the discovery, enforcement, and remediation polices that ISE will employ on Windows and Mac devices. Because the agent is loaded on the device, it has the ability to read into the device's registry, applications, services, and file system. The Cisco AnyConnect Posture Agent can be installed directly onto the client or brought down as a temporary agent via a browser. The main difference between the two methods is that the temporary web agent doesn't have the rights to perform remediation actions for the user.

The full agent offers robust remediation capabilities for a device that fails a security requirement, such as antivirus software that is not up to date. The remediation capabilities include file distribution, link distribution, delivery of instructions, and, most notably, an auto-update mechanism for antivirus, antispyware, Windows OS patches, and client firewall rules. The NASP should include the details on how devices will be remediated under different circumstances.

All posture assessment and remediation configuration is done using the ISE GUI. It is here that you define the posture policy by configuring rules based on operating system and/or other conditions that will satisfy the policies contained in your corporate NASP document. Before you create your NASP for ISE, it is important to understand the ISE process for posture assessment. This process uses a combination of policy checks, rules, and requirements. The ISE posture service checks the health (posture) of the clients for compliance with your corporate network security policies before the host gains privileged network access. The ISE Client Provisioning service deploys the AnyConnect Posture Agent to any hosts that don't have it installed and set up.

Rules like the one shown in Figure 7-3 are configured at the ISE Admin node.

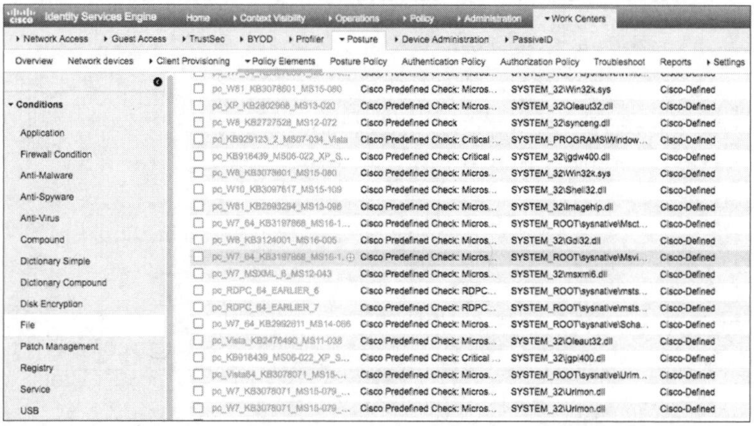

Figure 7-3 *File Condition Check Examples*

ISE file condition checks, such as the ones shown in Figure 7-3, are the Cisco predefined checks that are downloaded from Cisco every two hours. Checks can be groups of several checks combined together using Boolean operators. They can also be operating-system-specific.

ISE then allows you to create posture rules that combine multiple checks into a compound condition. Figure 7-4 shows a sampling of the Cisco predefined rules in ISE.

Figure 7-4 *Compound Condition Rules Example*

ISE requirements, like the ones shown in Figure 7-5, define what remediation action is offered to any noncompliant users. In this example, the Windows System Center Configuration Manager (SCCM) service is being turned on to ensure that all SCCM-enforced updates are installed on the PC.

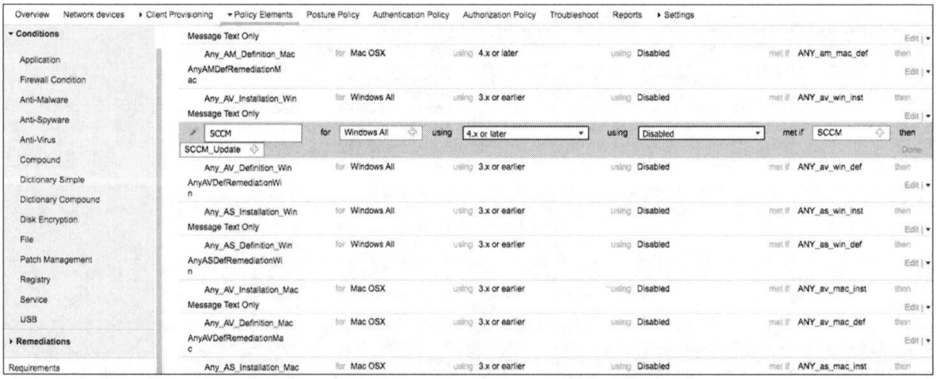

Figure 7-5 *Requirement Examples*

If all matching requirement rules are passed, then the client is marked as posture-compliant. Otherwise, the client is marked posture-noncompliant. This overall status can then be used in authorization rules to properly adapt network access privileges. Figure 7-6 shows an example of restricting a noncompliant host using a downloadable ACL (dACL) that only allows hosts to get to remediation resources.

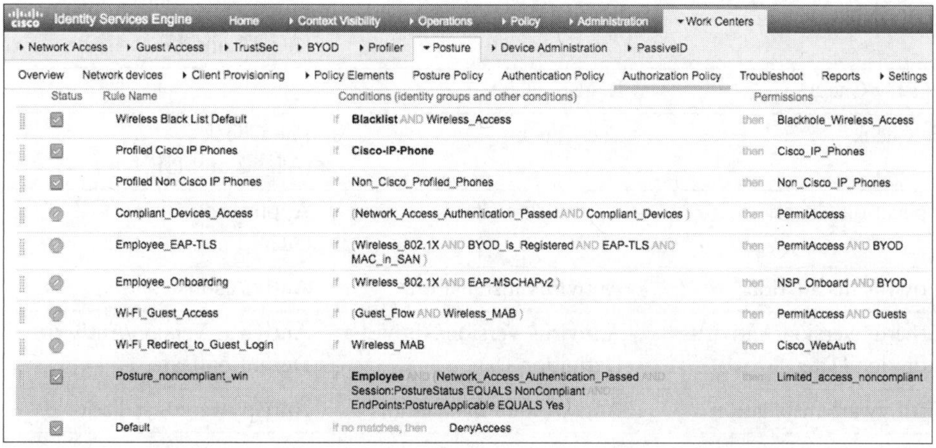

Figure 7-6 *Posture-Aware Authorization Rule Example*

Here is a summary of the rules and requirements structure in ISE:

- Rules are made up of one or more checks that can be combined into an expression using the Boolean operators and "&", or "|", not "!", and evaluation priority parentheses "()". If the result is true, then the client passes the rule.

- Requirements are made up of one or more rules. A requirement can specify that a device must pass any selected rule, all selected rules, or no selected rules in order for the device to pass the requirement.

- Requirements also define the mechanism to use and the instructions that will allow the client to remediate any failed rules. For example: Distribute a file or link with the instructions "Click the link and download, install, and run the XYZVirus cleaning tool."

- Requirements are mapped to authorization rules and/or operating system types.

Table 7-1 shows the posture assessment options available in ISE when using the various Cisco AnyConnect Posture Agent software versions. You can see that the Windows AnyConnect Posture Agent has the most functionality of the three types.

Table 7-1   *Posture Assessment Options*

ISE Posture Agent for Windows	Web Agent for Windows	ISE Posture Agent for Mac OS X
Operating System/Service Packs/Hotfixes	Operating System/Service Packs/Hotfixes	—
Service Check	Service Check	Service Check (AC 4.1 and ISE 1.4)
Registry Check	Registry Check	—
File Check	File Check	File Check (AC 4.1 and ISE 1.4)
Application Check	Application Check	Application Check (AC 4.1 and ISE 1.4)
Antivirus Installation	Antivirus Installation	Antivirus Installation
Antivirus Version/Antivirus Definition Date	Antivirus Version/Antivirus Definition Date	Antivirus Version/Antivirus Definition Date
Antispyware Installation	Antispyware Installation	Antispyware Installation
Antispyware Version/ Antispyware Definition Date	Antispyware Version/ Antispyware Definition Date	Antispyware Version/ Antispyware Definition Date
Patch Management Check (AC 4.1 and ISE 1.4)	—	Patch Management Check (AC 4.1 and ISE 1.4)
Windows Update Running	Windows Update Running	—
Windows Update Configuration	Windows Update Configuration	—
WSUS Compliance Settings	WSUS Compliance Settings	—

Table 7-2 displays all of the different remediation actions that the various AnyConnect Posture Agents can perform. Again, the Windows AnyConnect Posture Agent has the most functionality. These actions can be done for the user transparently or user interaction can be implemented.

Table 7-2 *Posture Remediation Options*

ISE Posture Agent for Windows	Web Agent for Windows	ISE Posture Agent for Mac OS X
Message Text (Local Check)	Message Text (Local Check)	Message Text (Local Check)
URL Link (Link Distribution)	URL Link (Link Distribution)	URL Link (Link Distribution)
File Distribution	File Distribution	—
Launch Program	—	—
Antivirus Definition Update	—	Antivirus Live Update
Antispyware Definition Update	—	Antispyware Live Update
Patch Management Remediation (AC 4.1 and ISE 1.4)	—	—
Windows Update	—	—
WSUS	—	—

Now that we have explored all of the posture variables and features, let's take a look at a final summary flow of posture assessment in ISE. Figure 7-7 illustrates the order of operations ISE takes from checks to the final posture policy evaluation.

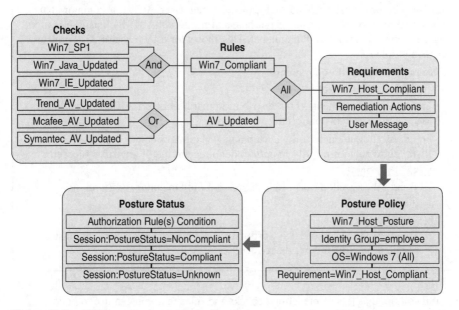

Figure 7-7 *ISE Posture Assessment Process*

Sample NASP Format for Documenting ISE Posture Requirements

As discussed, ISE uses several mechanisms to define what it should look for, or posture assess, on a given device. It also has several mechanisms for the proper remediation of any failed security requirements. Ultimately, the network access security privileges a client receives are based on the posture status result (for example, compliant) of a matched policy rule, which in turn is used as an authorization rule condition that the client matches. With this in mind, your NASP should have sections for each posture policy rule, and under each you should have the checks, rules, and requirements that pertain to clients of that posture policy rule. Here is a nice example of a NASP formatted in this way:

Employee Posture Policy

Table of Contents for Employee Posture Policy:

 I. **Identity Group Criteria**—Any user that is a member of the employees group in Active Directory.

 II. **Acceptable Use Policy**—Reference which AUP, if any, is to be enforced by ISE. For example, you might reference an AUP called Trusted_User_AUP. It is common that only a reference to an AUP name is put here and the actual AUP document lives in its own section within the NASP document. This allows for easy reuse of AUP policies across multiple roles.

 III. **Windows 7 Security Requirements**
   1. Approved AV Installed & Up to Date

   Trend_AV_Requirement—Link distribution that points to the Trend client download page on the corporate antivirus server.

   Trend_AV_Requirement to Rule Mapping—Map requirement *Trend_AV_Installed* to rule *Trend_AV_Installed*. Requirement met if any rules succeed.

   a. Security Rules –
   Trend_AV_Installed rule—Rule expression only includes the Trend_AV_Installed check.

   b. Security Checks –
   Trend_AV_Installed check—Corporate Trend Micro antivirus client must be installed on all Windows devices.

The ISE solution has lots of predefined checks and rules that you can use to build your posture rules. All of the built-in checks have a pc_ preceding their name, such as pc_AutoUpdateCheck. All of the built-in rules have a pr_ preceding their name, such as pr_AutoUpdateCheck. These checks and rules are constantly updated by Cisco and are automatically downloaded by ISE. Also, ISE has auto-update support for Microsoft Windows, numerous antivirus vendors, and antispyware vendors out of the box. This means that ISE keeps up to date with the latest versions, .dat files, and hotfixes available for each of the supported vendors automatically. Keep this in mind when creating your ISE network access security policy.

Common Checks, Rules, and Requirements

The following are some of the most common checks, rules, and requirements implemented by administrators of the ISE solution. All of the examples shown have corresponding Cisco predefined checks and rules and are auto-updated by ISE.

- An antivirus program must be installed, running, and up to date. Most organizations specify specific AV programs for certain posture policy rules. For example, the employee posture rule may state that clients must use corporate Trend Micro AV, whereas the guest posture rule may state that clients are allowed to use any of the numerous ISE-supported AV vendors.

- An antispyware program must be installed, running, and up to date. Most organizations specify specific AS programs for certain authorization rules. For example, the employee posture rule may state that clients must use the corporate Webroot AS client, whereas the guest policy rule may state that clients are allowed to use any of the ISE-supported AS vendors.

- All Windows 7 clients must be running Service Pack 1. The built-in registry check is called pc_W7_SP1.

- All Windows clients must have the Windows auto-update service running. By default, ISE looks to make sure the wuauserv service is running. The built-in check is called pc_AutoUpdateCheck. The built-in rule is called pr_AutoUpdateCheck_Rule.

- All 64-bit Windows 7 and 8 hosts must have installed the latest critical Microsoft security hotfixes as defined by the ISE rule pr_Win7_64_Hotfixes and pr_Win8_64_Hotfixes, respectively. These rules, and their corresponding checks, are continuously updated by Cisco. They include the most critical security hotfixes for Windows 7 and Windows 8 operating systems. They do not, however, include every security update that Microsoft has ever released for each operating system. If you require additional hotfixes, you can duplicate the relevant pr_Win_64_Hotfixes predefined rule to include them.

- All requirements dealing with the updating of antivirus and antispyware programs will use the built-in AV Definition Update type. These rules are preconfigured to map to the matrix of AV and AS vendors and products supported by ISE. These rules do not require you to configure any checks and are continuously updated by Cisco. If the user fails these requirements, the user can be presented with an Update button. When clicked, this Update button auto-launches the update program for the AV or AS program that failed the policy.

Method for Adding Posture Policy Rules

Many organizations do not have a process in place to determine if, when, and how a security update should be added to their network access security policy document. Organizations that lack this type of process, or method, are in greater danger of making bad decisions about the security updates they choose to install. For this reason, it is important for organizations to establish and follow a formal method for adding and updating their posture policy rules. This section deals with this topic as it pertains to the initial creation and subsequent revisions of the NASP document. Knowing which host security patches to enforce using ISE is a big job. The goal is to provide the information necessary for you to set up your own method, or process, for determining which posture rules you want to include in your initial NASP for ISE. A secondary goal is to provide the information necessary for you to set up your own method, or process, for determining when to add, change, and delete the checks, rules, and requirements that make up your host posture policy rules in ISE.

Research and Information

The ISE solution comes with many preconfigured checks and rules, such as the ones described previously. Simply implementing these built-in policies will go a long way toward increasing the security posture of most organizations' devices and networks. However, these are by no means the only security checks and rules that are available. In many cases, your organization may choose to implement checks, rules, and requirements that are beyond the scope of the predefined ones. When this occurs, it is vital that you are able to find the information and research needed to make the most informed decision possible. Regardless of whether or not the security fixes you put in place use the built-in policies, custom policies, or a combination of both, it is vital that you understand the purpose of the fixes, their impact, and their severity level. It is also necessary to remain informed about the emergence of new vulnerabilities, exploits, and viruses. Obtaining this information is not always trivial. Following are some of the commonly used security websites, blogs, and resources available online. Most are free but some also offer a paid service.

- **SecurityFocus** (http://www.securityfocus.com): Famous for its Bugtraq list. This is one of the best places for obtaining the latest vulnerability information.

- **SecLists.Org Mailing Lists** (http://seclists.org): This site is a mashup of the best security sites. It is your one-stop shop for staying in the know on the latest security news.

- **Microsoft TechNet Security Center** (https://technet.microsoft.com/en-us/security/): This web portal serves as a good jumping-off point for investigating any Microsoft security vulnerabilities, updates, and exploits.

- **Microsoft Security Bulletin** (https://technet.microsoft.com/en-us/security/bulletins): This website has a nice search engine for Microsoft security bulletins. The site also has a link to sign up to receive security bulletins via email or RSS. The search engine allows you to search for vulnerabilities based on severity level and operating system type and version.

- **National Cyber Awareness System** (https://www.us-cert.gov/ncas/): The U.S. Computer Emergency Readiness Team (US-CERT) created this website to ensure that you have access to timely information about security topics and threats. You can sign up to receive alerts from US-CERT.

- Government sites such as the **National Vulnerability Database** (https://nvd.nist.gov) and **U.S. Computer readiness team** (https://www.us-cert.gov) are filled with timely security alert information and are vendor-agnostic.

- **Metasploit** (https://www.metasploit.com/): This site does not offer any security information but does provide a very easy-to-use security tool that will help you test the security of your devices.

- **Cisco Security** (https://tools.cisco.com/security/center/home.x): This website serves as a security portal to find information regarding security bulletins from all the major application and operating system vendors. It also provides a wealth of cybersecurity reports and response bulletins.

These websites and others like them can be found throughout the Internet. They can be powerful tools for gathering the security information needed to make an informed decision on which security patches ISE should enforce.

Establishing Criteria to Determine the Validity of a Security Posture Check, Rule, or Requirement in Your Organization

Your organization's network access security policy should have a section that documents the criteria to be used to decide if a proposed security check, rule, or requirement needs to be added to ISE. The establishment of set criteria will serve to improve the accuracy of the decision process. The criteria used should be tailored for your specific environment and should refrain from using generalities whenever possible. The more fine-grained the criteria used, the more informed the decision process will be.

For every proposed and existing security fix in the NASP, and subsequently in ISE, you should be familiar with, or know where to obtain, the following information regarding a security vulnerability:

- What products, applications, and versions are affected?

- What is the severity level or Common Vulnerability Scoring System (CVSS) score? See https://www.first.org/cvss for more information on CVSS.

- What is the potential impact or risk to the organization if the vulnerability is exploited? This point should be explored in detail, noting a best- and worst-case scenario.

- Can the vulnerability be exploited remotely?

- Are exploits publicly available?

- Is the use of the affected software widespread in your organization?

- Are the ports, protocols, and devices in question being blocked using a firewall, IPS, personal firewall, or ISE already? If so, to what extent does this mitigate the exploit risk?

- Is a patch available for the vulnerability?

- If a patch is available, is it possible to test the patch to make sure it works as advertised?

- If no testing can be done, is the risk of deploying a faulty patch less than the risk of the vulnerability?

- If no patch is available, is it possible to use any of the security features in ISE to help mitigate this feature? If no, is it possible to use any other security products to do so?

Before taking action, it is important to understand what the expected overhead on the IT staff might be if the new patch or fix is implemented. This should be explored in detail, noting a best- and worst-case scenario. Here are some of the topics for consideration:

- How stable is the new patch?

- Is additional helpdesk load necessary?

- Is additional IT staff load necessary?

- What is required of the end-user community?

- Was additional network load created due to deployment of new patches?

- If deploying patches over the WAN, what is the potential impact?

- Who will perform any testing needed? What resources are required to perform the testing?

- What is needed to set up the deployment method for distributing the patch or update?

- What is the expected impact on and reactions from the user community if the fix for the vulnerability is rolled out?

Method for Determining What Posture Policy Rules a Particular Security Requirement Should Be Applied To

Once you have decided that a security fix or patch should be deployed in your environment, the next step is to decide which posture rules should receive the fix or if you should create a new rule. Additionally, it is important to determine whether the fix should be mandatory or optional. This might vary based on posture rule. It is a best practice to deploy new security requirements as optional first and then, after a set amount of time, make them mandatory. This results in the least impact possible on the user community. However, if a vulnerability poses significant risk to the organization, then the new security requirement should be rolled out as mandatory initially.

Here are some things to consider when deciding which posture rules should receive a new security requirement:

- Do all identity groups run the affected software?

- Do any of the identity groups pose a greater risk than others if the patch causes adverse affects on clients? In other words, do certain posture rules contain clients that, if debilitated due to a bad patch, would significantly affect the organization? If so, would starting with less-risky rules first to further assess the robustness of the patch make sense?

- Do any posture rules have an elevated exposure to the vulnerability in question? If so, does this elevated exposure warrant mandatory enforcement of the new security requirement?

- Does the security requirement apply to the guest posture rule, if one exists?

Method for Deploying and Enforcing Security Requirements

Once you have decided that a security requirement should be added to the NASP and ISE, you need to come up with a deployment strategy. As previously discussed in Table 7-2, a requirement remediation has the following options: file distribution, link distribution, launch executable, message only, AV definition update, AS definition update, and Windows update.

The easiest options to deploy are the update types because they use the built-in deployment and updating mechanisms already configured on the local device. For example, the requirement type of Windows update uses the Windows Update service already present on and configured for the client that needs the updates.

Regardless of the requirement type chosen, the following deployment questions should be considered:

- Should the deployment method be the same for all posture rules?

- Which deployment method would be the most efficient at reaching the posture rules in question?

- Should the enforcement of the new security requirement be optional, audit, or mandatory in the beginning? Does this vary by posture rule or identity group?

- If optional, should the requirement be made mandatory at some point in time? If so, define the time period between optional and mandatory. Does this vary by posture rule?

- If audit only, what is the goal of the audit? What will be done with the data collected?

- Will it ensure clients in quarantine have privileges to access the proposed remediation resources? For example, if you use a link to www.fixme.com as your deployment method, you need to ensure that access to this URL is not restricted.

Defining Dynamic Network Access Privileges

The ISE solution has several methods available to dynamically grant and restrict the network access privileges of clients. Most of these methods are defined per authorization rule. A network access security policy for ISE should include details on which network access privileges should be given to which authorization rules and devices. The authorization rules should take into consideration the posture status of a device (unknown, compliant, noncompliant) to determine the access privileges given.

Here is an example that uses access control rules in ISE: A client in the contractor authorization rule should be granted access to the Internet only on TCP ports 80 and 443, and should be denied access all other network access. The following common and easily understandable syntax can be used for documenting ISE access control policies in the NASP. Typically, these rules are found under their corresponding authorization rule section in the NASP.

```
<line #> Permit|Deny <protocol> from <device(s) | network(s)> to <device(s) |
network(s)> equaling | not equaling port(s) <list of port numbers or names>
Description: <explanation of rule>
```

The previous example would be written in the NASP under the contractor authorization rule/traffic control subsection as follows:

```
10 Deny IP from any to any internal network
Description:  Block IP traffic from anyone to any internal subnet or device.
20 Permit tcp from guest authorization rule to any equaling ports 53,80 & 443
Description:  Allow web traffic from clients in the guest authorization rule to
the internet
30 Deny IP from guest authorization rule to any
Description:  Block everything else
```

Formatting the rules in this way not only makes them unambiguous but allows them to be easily translated into the traffic control rules configured in the ISE Manager.

Enforcement Methods Available with ISE

ISE supports numerous types of permissions that can be applied to an authorization rule result. Not all enforce methods supported by ISE are supported in all modes of operation. This issue applies mostly to limitations of the hardware the client is connected to. For example, to support security group tagging, the wired switch or wireless controller has to support it. Table 7-3 lists the different network access control permission methods available and provides a brief description for each.

Table 7-3 *ISE Authorization Rule Permissions*

Enforcement or Control Method	Description
Access control rules	The equivalent of network ACLs. They permit and deny traffic like a stateless firewall would.
VLAN segmentation	Dynamically changing the Layer 2 VLAN based on the authorization rule matched by the connected client.
Smartport Macro	Ability to run the macro that can affect just about anything on that switch port, including QoS settings.
Reauthentication	The timer serves as an absolute time limit for a client in a given authorization rule. Once the timer is expired, the client is reauthenticated.
Security Group Tag	Cisco TrustSec tag applied by the network to every frame sent from the client. Requires switch or WLC support.
MACsec encryption	Wire-speed Layer 2 encryption via 802.1ae. Requires switch or WLC support.
Web authentication	Forces a URL redirect to a web authentication page.
Cisco RADIUS AV pair values	Almost any Cisco or other vendor AV pair can be manipulated with ISE as part of authorization permissions.

Commonly Used Network Access Policies

In short, a network access policy defines what a user and device can and cannot do on the network. Although the exact rules that make up any network access policy will be customized for a particular environment, there are some commonalities shared between organizations. This section focuses on those common elements. Your NASP typically covers all of the enforcement methods ISE supports (see Table 7-3). Access control lists are almost always tied to an authorization rule in ISE. Some authorization rules (such as guest) usually have very restrictive network access policies, while others typically are wide open (such as employee). Also, it is always a best practice to lock down the network access rule on any noncompliant posture authorization rule.

Here are some popular or mandatory authorization rules shown with a common example of their associated NASP. This is formatted for an ISE NASP. You can choose to use this NASP format or develop your own. It is important to ensure that your NASP is well documented. Note that these pick up where the earlier sample NASP left off, at section IV. (See the section "Sample NASP Format for Documenting ISE Posture Requirements.")

Employee Authorization Rule

Table of Contents for Employee Security Policy:

IV. **Network Access Permissions**

    1. VLAN Segmentation – Yes

      a. Noncompliant Posture VLAN = quarantine-vlan/100

      b. Access VLAN Name/ID = employees/10

    2. Access Control List – Yes

      a. Compliant ACL = permit All IP

      b. Noncompliant ACL =

```
5  Permit TCP from any to "AUP web server" equaling 80
Description:  Allow anyone to access the acceptable use policy link
10 Permit TCP from any to "Link based remediation resources" equaling
   80 & 443
Description:  Allow web traffic to the appropriate remediation resources
20 Permit TCP from any to "file based remediation" equaling 80 & 443
Description:  Allow web traffic to the cam for remediation file
   distribution
30 Permit UDP from any to "dmz DNS Server" equaling DNS
Description:  Allow DNS only to the dmz dns server
40 Deny IP from any to any
Description:  Block everything else
```

    3. Auto Smartports Macro – no

    4. SGT number – 10

The subsequent partial example does not show the full NASP format. Only the sections relevant to the network access permissions are shown.

Guest Authorization Rule

1. VLAN Segmentation – Yes
   a. Noncompliant Posture VLAN = None, no posture required
   b. Access VLAN Name/ID = guest/20

2. Access Control List –

   ```
   10 Permit UDP from any to "dmz DNS Server" equaling DNS
   Description:  Allow DNS but only to the dmz dns server
   20 Deny IP from any to any internal network
   Description:  Block IP traffic from guests to any internal subnet or
     device.
   30 permit IP from host to any external IP subnet
   Description:  Allow everything not internal
   ```

3. Auto Smartports Macro – no
4. SGT number – 20

Summary

This chapter examined the intricacies of creating a network access security policy for a Cisco ISE deployment. It included the following recommendations:

- Create and follow a NASP checklist.

- Make sure to obtain executive buy-in for the creation and subsequent enforcement of a NASP.

- Create a NASP committee. Be sure to involve the right people.

- Determine your organization's high-level network access security goals. Use these as guides when creating the detailed network access security policy.

- Break up your organization into security domains.

- Determine and create the authorization rules necessary for your organization.

- Create one or more acceptable use policies.

- Determine if host posture checks will be used. If so, decide what checks, rules, and requirements will be enforced for each posture rule.

■ Establish and follow a method for adds, moves, and changes to authorization rules and posture rule checks, rules, and requirements.

■ Determine a method for deploying the AnyConnect Posture Agent and/or remediation resources.

■ Determine which network access permissions should be assigned to each authorization rule.

■ Either use the NASP document formatting shown throughout this chapter or pick your own formatting. It is important to document your NASP in a concise and easily understood manner.

Chapter 8

Building a Device Security Policy

This chapter covers the following topics:

- ISE device profiling
- Threat-Centric NAC

Cisco Identity Services Engine takes into account the security of the individual devices when determining which network access control policy to invoke. Chapter 7, "Building a Cisco ISE Network Access Security Policy," discussed the creation of a network access security policy (NASP), part of which took into account the device's security posture. Device posture assessment is one of several tools that Cisco ISE can use to determine the actual security of a network-connected device. ISE can also use the following features to determine the device security policy to implement:

- Device profiling
- Threat-Centric NAC

This chapter explores these features in some detail. The goal is to disclose the different ways in which ISE can identify device types and other contextual information about devices for use in an ISE policy.

ISE Device Profiling

ISE includes a built-in device profiling function. ISE device profiling is one of the most useful and easy-to-deploy ISE features. All ISE deployments should include profiling in their setup. ISE profiling collects both passive and active device data, including device behavior, to determine what kind of device it is seeing. Profiling is capable of showing you all the devices that are connected to your network, their type, their behavior, and the logged-in user.

Cisco ISE includes hundreds of built-in profiling rules and device profiler conditions. These are updated dynamically using the profiler feed service. ISE profiling gathers information from multiple data sources to make a device type determination. This information is matched against the ISE profiler conditions until a best match is made. That condition is then used to match a profiler policy rule. Once a profiler policy rule is matched, the result can then be used as an ISE authorization rule condition. It is in this way that ISE can provide different network privileges based on a device profile. Figure 8-1 shows a sampling of the visibility you have with ISE profiler.

Figure 8-1   *ISE Profiler Endpoint Context Visibility*

Figure 8-2 depicts a sampling of the ISE profiler conditions that come preinstalled with ISE. ISE will also receive updated and new profiles through its profiler feed service. The feed service connects to Cisco.com to see if any new profile data is available for download. If so, it will download and update its profiling database accordingly.

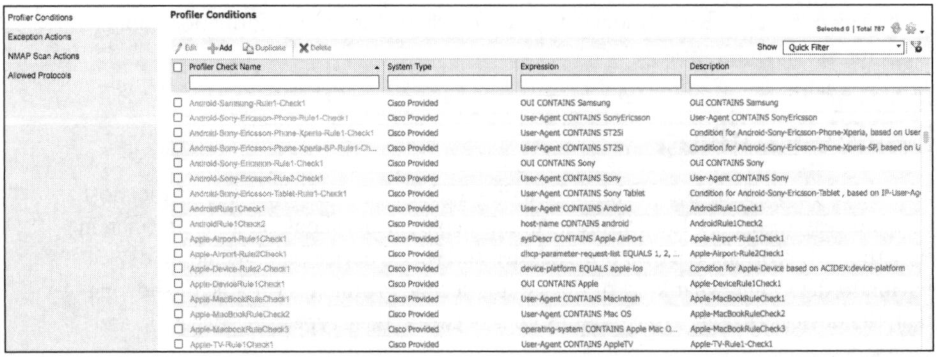

Figure 8-2   *ISE Profiler Conditions*

Each condition shown in Figure 8-2 contains logic that defines how the condition is met. As you can see, many of the conditions have multiple rules or multiple checks for the same device type. The Apple iPad conditions are a good example of this. Figure 8-3 shows just one of four checks that are used to determine if a device is an Apple iPad.

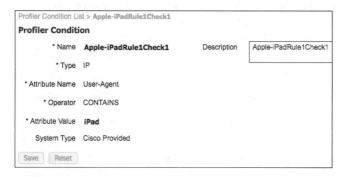

Figure 8-3 *ISE Apple iPad Profiler Conditions*

The example condition shown in Figure 8-3 matches the *user-agent string* from a web browser.

ISE Profiling Policies

The Cisco ISE conditions just discussed are used to create your ISE device profile policies. Sticking with the Apple iPad profile example, Figure 8-4 shows the profiler policy that uses the iPad condition shown in Figure 8-3.

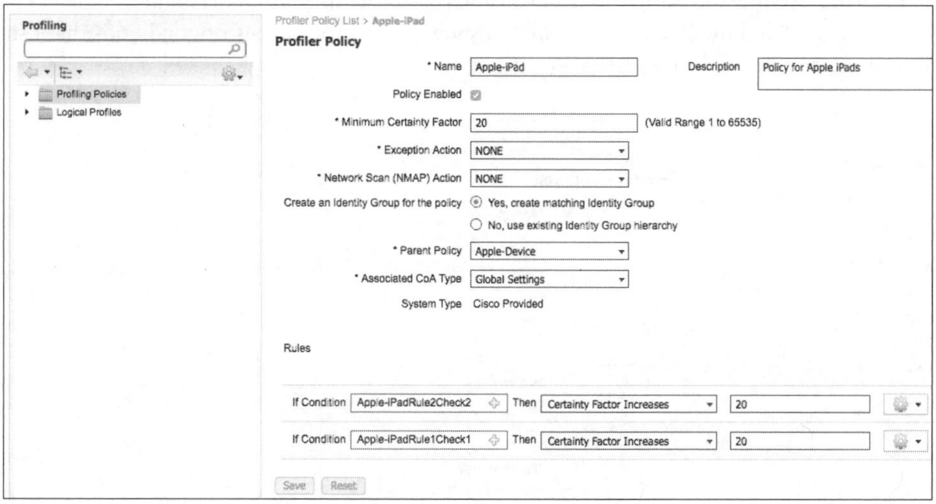

Figure 8-4 *ISE Apple iPad Profiler Policy*

The policy shown in Figure 8-4 uses two rules. Both rules, if matched, will raise the certainty factor by 20 points. This profiler policy defines that the minimum certainty factor for this policy to be matched is 20. It is also important to note that in order for this policy to even be processed by ISE, the defined parent policy must have been matched first by the device being profiled. The parent policy in this Apple iPad policy is shown to be *Apple-Device*.

When you are creating your device security policy for Cisco ISE, be sure to include the logic that is used by ISE profiler in that policy. A profile is made up of two mandatory components, conditions (as shown in Figure 8-3) and policy rules (as shown in Figure 8-4), and one optional component, Logical Profiles. The policy should include the following for any custom-created profiles needed:

- **Device Profile Condition(s) Definition:** Match criteria needed (that is, user-agent string, MAC OUI, DHCP hostname, etc.).

- **Device Profile Policy:**

  - Rules definition of policy and amount to raise the certainty factor. Rules use the conditions above.

  - Define the minimum certainty factor for the policy.

  - Define any parent policies.

  - If you want to use this in an authorization policy, then check Yes, Create Matching Identity Group.

- **Device Logical Profile (optional):** A grouping of multiple profile policies into a single logical profile rule.

ISE Profiler Data Sources

To create a profiler condition to match against, you first need to understand what match criteria is offered by Cisco ISE. Figure 8-5 shows the various types of conditions that can be used to match a device's behavior against.

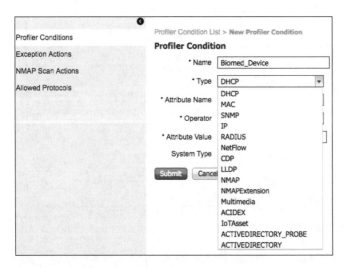

Figure 8-5 *ISE Profiler Condition Types*

Each of these 15+ condition types has several subtypes to choose from as well. This allows you to create very specific conditions on which to match against. For example, the IP type can match against a specific browser user-agent string.

Note   In an ISE distributed deployment, the Profiler Service runs as a part of the Policy Service node but the profiler configuration is done from the Admin node.

Using Device Profiles in Authorization Rules

Once you have your profiler policies in place and matching correctly on devices, you now need to configure ISE authorization rules to use your profiles. Figure 8-6 depicts an example of a rule that matches on Apple iPad devices that are accessing the network using wireless. The resulting permissions are to restrict iPads to only Internet access.

Standard				
Status	Rule Name	Conditions (identity groups and other conditions)		Permissions
☑	Wireless Black List Default	If **Blacklist** AND Wireless_Access	then	Blackhole_Wireless_Access
☑	Profiled Cisco IP Phones	If **Cisco-IP-Phone**	then	Cisco_IP_Phones
☑	Restrict Apple iPads	**Apple-iPad** AND Wireless_Access	then	Internet_Only

Figure 8-6   *ISE Apple iPad Authorization Policy*

Threat-Centric NAC

Threat-Centric Network Access Control (TC-NAC) was added to ISE in 2.1 and expanded in subsequent releases. TC-NAC enables ISE to collect threat and vulnerability data from many third-party threat and vulnerability scanners and software. This gives ISE a threat and risk view into the hosts it is controlling access rights for. TC-NAC enables you to have visibility into any vulnerable hosts on your network and to take dynamic network quarantine actions when required. ISE can create authorization policies based on vulnerability attributes, such as Common Vulnerability Scoring System (CVSS) scores, received from your third-party threat and vulnerability assessment software. Threat severity levels and vulnerability assessment results can be used to dynamically control the access level of an endpoint or a user.

You can configure the external vulnerability and threat software to send high-fidelity Indications of Compromise (IoC), Threat Detected events, and CVSS scores to Cisco ISE. This data can then be used in ISE TC-NAC authorization policies to dynamically or manually change an endpoint's network access privileges accordingly.

You should write ISE TC-NAC policies and rules into your NASP device security policy just like you did for ISE profiler in Chapter 7. You should determine which vendors should be added to ISE, at which CVSS score thresholds action should be taken, and which action ISE should take based on a threat or VA issue. These and other policy considerations are discussed in this section.

As of version 2.2, Cisco ISE supports the following adapters, as shown in Figure 8-7:

■ Cisco Advanced Malware Protection (AMP) for Endpoints

■ Cisco Cognitive Threat Analytics (CTA)

■ Qualys

■ Rapid7 Nexpose

■ Tenable Security Center

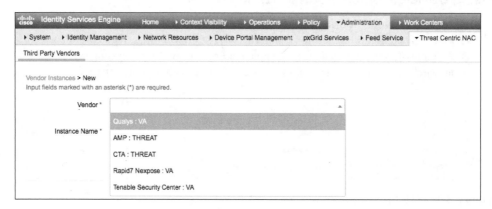

Figure 8-7 *ISE TC-NAC Software Support*

Figure 8-7 also shows that some of the supported vendors send threat data to ISE (designated as THREAT) while others send Vulnerability Assessment (VA) data to ISE.

When a vulnerability event is received for an endpoint, Cisco ISE can automatically trigger a Change of Authorization (CoA) for that endpoint. However, a CoA is not triggered automatically when a threat event is received and must be done manually.

To take action on a host with a threat event, go the **Context Visibility > Endpoints > Compromised Endpoints** page and select the endpoint(s). Next, click **ANC** (Adaptive Network Control) and select **Assign a Policy**. Select the policy, such as Quarantine, to assign to the endpoint(s). Now Cisco ISE triggers a CoA for that endpoint(s) and applies the corresponding ANC policy. If an ANC policy is not available, Cisco ISE triggers a CoA for that endpoint and applies the original authorization policy. You can use the Clear Threat and Vulnerabilities option on the Compromised Endpoints page to clear the threat and vulnerabilities ISE associated with an endpoint.

The following ISE dictionary attributes can be used in creating ISE authorization conditions:

■ CTA-Course_Of_Action (values can be Internal Blocking, Eradication, or Monitoring)

■ Qualys-CVSS_Base_Score

- Qualys-CVSS_Temporal_Score

- Rapid7 Nexpose-CVSS_Base_Score

- Tenable Security Center-CVSS_Base_Score

- Tenable Security Center-CVSS_Temporal_Score

The valid CVSS range is from 0 to 10 for both Base Score and Temporal Score attributes. Zero is benign while a score of nine to ten is usually considered critical. For more information on CVSS scoring, see https://www.first.org/cvss.

You can create an authorization policy by using the vulnerability CVSS score or the CTA result to dynamically quarantine or change the access permissions of a host. Figure 8-8 shows a couple sample authorization rules. As you can see, all of the authorization attributes, such as User ID, in ISE can be added to a threat exception rule.

Figure 8-8 *ISE TC-NAC Authorization Exception Rule*

Note The Threat-Centric NAC service requires an ISE Apex license.

Using TC-NAC as Part of Your Incident Response Process

You should consider adding some TC-NAC procedures to your security Incident Response (IR) policy. This section reviews the various ISE TC-NAC screens that are good to consult during a live IR investigation. Let's start with the TC-NAC Live Log screen, which displays the incident type, adapter name, matching authorization rule, and authorization profiles (old and new) for an endpoint. You can also view the detailed information for an event. To access the TC-NAC Live Log screen go to **Operations > Threat-Centric NAC Live Logs.**

Even more powerful is the **Context visibility > Endpoints** page. Here you can view and sort based on all sorts of contextual information, such as Authentication, Compromised Endpoints and Vulnerable Endpoints. Figure 8-9 shows the full list of submenu choices for Endpoints in Context Visibility. You can use the filters in each of these submenus to quickly find the endpoint(s) under investigation.

Figure 8-9   *ISE TC-NAC Incident Response Pages*

You can view the vulnerability information for endpoints on the Vulnerable Endpoints page. Figures 8-10 and 8-11 show how you can quickly filter based on whatever incident information you have available to find much more context about the hosts in the incident under investigation. Figure 8-10 shows using just an IP address to filter on. Immediately, you have all sorts of other useful information.

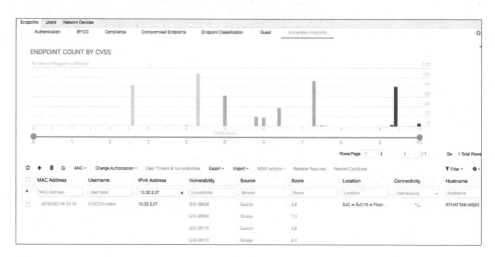

Figure 8-10   *ISE TC-NAC Vulnerable Endpoints*

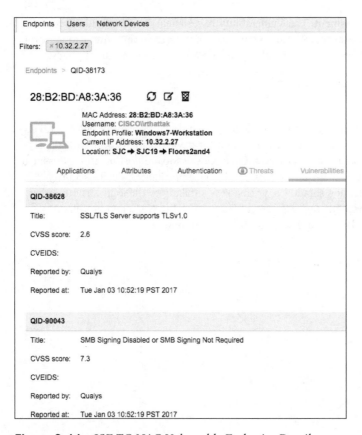

Figure 8-11 *ISE TC-NAC Vulnerable Endpoint Detail*

From that one IP address, ISE is able to tell you who is logged into the host, the location and switch port the host is connected to, hostname, OS, vulnerabilities, active threats, applications running, and much more. Having this type of information at your fingertips can greatly speed up your incident response investigation.

For TC-NAC specific reports go to **Operations > Reports > Threat Centric NAC.** The following reports are available for the Threat-Centric NAC service:

- **Adapter Status:** The Status report displays the status of the threat and vulnerability external software connection.

- **COA Events:** When a vulnerability event is received for an endpoint, Cisco ISE triggers a CoA for that endpoint. The CoA Events report displays the status of these CoA events. It also displays the old and new authorization rules and the profile details for these endpoints.

- **Threat Events:** The Threat Events report provides a list of all the threat events that Cisco ISE receives from the various adapters that you have configured. Vulnerability Assessment events are not included in this report.

- **Vulnerability Assessment:** The Vulnerability Assessment report provides information about the assessments that are happening for your endpoints. You can view this report to check if the assessment is happening based on the configured policy.

Summary

This chapter covered the features and functionality that Cisco ISE has for enforcing a device security policy and providing you with great device visibility and posture awareness. The three main features Cisco ISE has for this job are host posture assessment (covered in Chapter 7), Threat-Centric NAC, and device profiling. A device security policy for your organization should be written very similarly to the logic structure that Cisco ISE uses for device posture assessment, Threat-Centric NAC, and profiling. This will ease the translation from written policy to ISE policy.

Chapter 9

Building an ISE Accounting and Auditing Policy

This chapter covers the following topics:

- Why you need accounting and auditing for ISE

- Using PCI DSS as your ISE auditing framework

- Cisco ISE user accounting

Keeping track of what is happening inside the network and inside of ISE is critical to understanding how the ISE solution is behaving. It is also critical for compliance and internal audit reasons. For example, auditing the changes that each ISE administrator makes to the configuration is extremely important. ISE Accounting is the mechanism that absorbs the RADIUS accounting packets from network devices such as switches, Wireless LAN Controllers, and ASA VPN headends. ISE Auditing is the logging and reporting of everything that happens internal to ISE. This includes administrator configuration changes, ISE system health, processing of ISE rules, and full logging of authentication and authorization activities.

Note In a distributed ISE deployment, the Policy Administration Node (PAN) handles all system-related configuration and configurations auditing. The Policy Service Node (PSN) handles all of the network access device (NAD) RADIUS accounting packets. All of the relevant information is also sent from the other nodes to the Monitoring & Troubleshooting Node (MnT) for purposes of creating accounting and auditing reports.

Why You Need Accounting and Auditing for ISE

Logging mechanisms, such as RADIUS accounting and ISE configuration auditing, provide the ability to track user and administrator activities. This is critical in preventing, detecting, or minimizing the impact of a security compromise. This information can also speed along an incident response investigation. The presence of these logs in all environments allows thorough tracking, alerting, and analysis when something does go wrong. Determining the cause of a compromise or just a configuration mistake is very difficult, if not impossible, without accounting and auditing records.

Creating a comprehensive ISE audit trail is necessary for passing many of your compliance audits. The Payment Card Industry Data Security Standard (PCI DSS), a standard for the protection of credit card data, provides a robust framework for auditing requirements. It is highly likely that if you follow the auditing recommendations in the PCI DSS standard, you will pass most other types of logging audits. It is for that reason that we are reusing much of the PCI DSS framework for the ISE accounting and auditing policy recommendations in this chapter.

Using PCI DSS as Your ISE Auditing Framework

PCI DSS Requirement 10, "Track and monitor all access to network resources and cardholder data," and its subrequirements lay out a nice framework you can use to build your own auditing policy for Cisco ISE. Table 9-1 depicts the relevant section from the PCI DSS 3.2 standard (available at https://www.pcisecuritystandards.org/document_library). The left column describes the requirement and the right column describes how you could audit that requirement to ensure it is being met. The Cisco ISE solution is capable of meeting all of PCI Requirement 10.

Table 9-1   *PCI DSS 3.2 Requirement 10*

PCI DSS Requirements	Testing Procedures
10.1 Implement audit trails to link all access to system components to each individual user.	**10.1** Verify, through observation and interviewing the system administrator, that: ■ Audit trails are enabled and active for system components. ■ Access to system components is linked to individual users.
10.2 Implement automated audit trails for all system components to reconstruct the following events:	**10.2** Through interviews of responsible personnel, observation of audit logs, and examination of audit log settings, perform the following:
10.2.1 All individual user accesses to cardholder data	**10.2.1** Verify all individual access to cardholder data is logged.
10.2.2 All actions taken by any individual with root or administrative privileges	**10.2.2** Verify all actions taken by any individual with root or administrative privileges are logged.

PCI DSS Requirements	Testing Procedures
10.2.3 Access to all audit trails	**10.2.3** Verify access to all audit trails is logged.
10.2.4 Invalid logical access attempts	**10.2.4** Verify invalid logical access attempts are logged.
10.2.5 Use of and changes to identification and authentication mechanisms—including but not limited to creation of new accounts and elevation of privileges—and all changes, additions, or deletions to accounts with root or administrative privileges	**10.2.5.a** Verify use of identification and authentication mechanisms is logged. **10.2.5.b** Verify all elevation of privileges is logged. **10.2.5.c** Verify all changes, additions, or deletions to any account with root or administrative privileges are logged.
10.2.6 Initialization, stopping, or pausing of the audit logs	Verify the following are logged: ■ Initialization of audit logs. ■ Stopping or pausing of audit logs.
10.2.7 Creation and deletion of system-level objects	**10.2.7** Verify creation and deletion of system level objects are logged.
10.3 Record at least the following audit trail entries for all system components for each event:	**10.3** Through interviews and observation of audit logs, for each auditable event (from 10.2), perform the following:
10.3.1 User identification	**10.3.1** Verify user identification is included in log entries.
10.3.2 Type of event	**10.3.2** Verify type of event is included in log entries.
10.3.3 Date and time	**10.3.3** Verify date and time stamp is included in log entries.
10.3.4 Success or failure indication	**10.3.4** Verify success or failure indication is included in log entries.
10.3.5 Origination of event	**10.3.5** Verify origination of event is included in log entries.
10.3.6 Identity or name of affected data, system component, or resource	**10.3.6** Verify identity or name of affected data, system component, or resources is included in log entries.

PCI DSS Requirements	Testing Procedures
10.4 Using time synchronization technology, synchronize all critical system clocks and times and ensure that the following is implemented for acquiring, distributing, and storing time. **Note:** One example of time synchronization technology is Network Time Protocol (NTP).	**10.4** Examine configuration standards and processes to verify that time synchronization technology is implemented and kept current per PCI DSS Requirements 6.1 and 6.2.
10.4.1 Critical systems have the correct and consistent time.	**10.4.1.a** Examine the process for acquiring, distributing and storing the correct time within the organization to verify that: ■ Only the designated central time server(s) receives time signals from external sources, and time signals from external sources are based on International Atomic Time or UTC. ■ Where there is more than one designated time server, the time servers peer with one another to keep accurate time. ■ Systems receive time information only from designated central time server(s).
	10.4.1.b Observe the time-related system-parameter settings for a sample of system components to verify: ■ Only the designated central time server(s) receives time signals from external sources, and time signals from external sources are based on International Atomic Time or UTC.

PCI DSS Requirements	Testing Procedures
	■ Where there is more than one designated time server, the designated central time server(s) peer with one another to keep accurate time. ■ Systems receive time only from designated central time server(s).
10.4.2 Time data is protected.	**10.4.2.a** Examine system configurations and time synchronization settings to verify that access to time data is restricted to only personnel with a business need to access time data.
	10.4.2.b Examine system configurations, time synchronization settings and logs, and processes to verify that any changes to time settings on critical systems are logged, monitored, and reviewed.
10.4.3 Time settings are received from industry-accepted time sources.	**10.4.3** Examine systems configurations to verify that the time server(s) accept time updates from specific, industry-accepted external sources (to prevent a malicious individual from changing the clock). Optionally, those updates can be encrypted with a symmetric key, and access control lists can be created that specify the IP addresses of client machines that will be provided with the time updates (to prevent unauthorized use of internal time servers).
10.5 Secure audit trails so they cannot be altered.	**10.5** Interview system administrators and examine system configurations and permissions to verify that audit trails are secured so that they cannot be altered as follows:

PCI DSS Requirements	Testing Procedures
10.5.1 Limit viewing of audit trails to those with a job-related need.	**10.5.1** Only individuals who have a job-related need can view audit trail files.
10.5.2 Protect audit trail files from unauthorized modifications.	**10.5.2** Current audit trail files are protected from unauthorized modifications via access control mechanisms, physical segregation, and/or network segregation.
10.5.3 Promptly back up audit trail files to a centralized log server or media that is difficult to alter.	**10.5.3** Current audit trail files are promptly backed up to a centralized log server or media that is difficult to alter.
10.5.4 Write logs for external-facing technologies onto a secure, centralized, internal log server or media device.	**10.5.4** Logs for external-facing technologies (for example, wireless, firewalls, DNS, mail) are written onto a secure, centralized, internal log server or media.
10.5.5 Use file-integrity monitoring or change-detection software on logs to ensure that existing log data cannot be changed without generating alerts (although new data being added should not cause an alert).	**10.5.5** Examine system settings, monitored files, and results from monitoring activities to verify the use of file-integrity monitoring or change-detection software on logs.
10.6 Review logs and security events for all system components to identify anomalies or suspicious activity. **Note:** Log harvesting, parsing, and alerting tools may be used to meet this Requirement.	**10.6** Perform the following:
10.6.1 Review the following at least daily: ■ All security events ■ Logs of all system components that store, process, or transmit CHD and/or SAD ■ Logs of all critical system components	**10.6.1.a** Examine security policies and procedures to verify that procedures are defined for reviewing the following at least daily, either manually or via log tools: ■ All security events ■ Logs of all system components that store, process, or transmit CHD and/or SAD

PCI DSS Requirements	Testing Procedures
■ Logs of all servers and system components that perform security functions (for example, firewalls, intrusion-detection systems/intrusion-prevention systems (IDS/IPS), authentication servers, e-commerce redirection servers, etc.).	■ Logs of all critical system components ■ Logs of all servers and system components that perform security functions (for example, firewalls, intrusion-detection systems/intrusion-prevention systems (IDS/IPS), authentication servers, e-commerce redirection servers, etc.)
	10.6.1.b Observe processes and interview personnel to verify that the following are reviewed at least daily: ■ All security events ■ Logs of all system components that store, process, or transmit CHD and/or SAD ■ Logs of all critical system components ■ Logs of all servers and system components that perform security functions (for example, firewalls, intrusion-detection systems/intrusion-prevention systems (IDS/IPS), authentication servers, e-commerce redirection servers, etc.).
10.6.2 Review logs of all other system components periodically based on the organization's policies and risk management strategy, as determined by the organization's annual risk assessment.	**10.6.2.a** Examine security policies and procedures to verify that procedures are defined for reviewing logs of all other system components periodically—either manually or via log tools—based on the organization's policies and risk management strategy.

PCI DSS Requirements	Testing Procedures
	10.6.2.b Examine the organization's risk-assessment documentation and interview personnel to verify that reviews are performed in accordance with organization's policies and risk management strategy.
10.6.3 Follow up exceptions and anomalies identified during the review process.	**10.6.3.a** Examine security policies and procedures to verify that procedures are defined for following up on exceptions and anomalies identified during the review process.
	10.6.3.b Observe processes and interview personnel to verify that follow-up to exceptions and anomalies is performed.
10.7 Retain audit trail history for at least one year, with a minimum of three months immediately available for analysis (for example, online, archived, or restorable from backup).	**10.7.a** Examine security policies and procedures to verify that they define the following: ■ Audit log retention policies ■ Procedures for retaining audit logs for at least one year, with a minimum of three months immediately available online
	10.7.b Interview personnel and examine audit logs to verify that audit logs are retained for at least one year.
	10.7.c Interview personnel and observe processes to verify that at least the last three months' logs are immediately available for analysis.
10.8 Additional requirement for service providers only: Implement a process for the timely detection and reporting of failures of critical security control systems, including but not limited to failure of:	**10.8.a** Examine documented policies and procedures to verify that processes are defined for the timely detection and reporting of failures of critical security control systems, including but not limited to failure of:

PCI DSS Requirements	Testing Procedures
<ul><li>Firewalls</li><li>IDS/IPS</li><li>FIM</li><li>Anti-virus</li><li>Physical access controls</li><li>Logical access controls</li><li>Audit logging mechanisms</li><li>Segmentation controls (if used)</li></ul>**Note:** This requirement is a best practice until January 31, 2018, after which it becomes a requirement.	<ul><li>Firewalls</li><li>IDS/IPS</li><li>FIM</li><li>Anti-virus</li><li>Physical access controls</li><li>Logical access controls</li><li>Audit logging mechanisms</li><li>Segmentation controls (if used)</li></ul>
	10.8.b Examine detection and alerting processes and interview personnel to verify that processes are implemented for all critical security controls, and that failure of a critical security control results in the generation of an alert.
10.8.1 Additional requirement for service providers only: Respond to failures of any critical security controls in a timely manner. Processes for responding to failures in security controls must include:<ul><li>Restoring security functions</li><li>Identifying and documenting the duration (date and time start to end) of the security failure</li><li>Identifying and documenting cause(s) of failure, including root cause, and documenting remediation required to address root cause</li><li>Identifying and addressing any security issues that arose during the failure</li></ul>	**10.8.1.a** Examine documented policies and procedures and interview personnel to verify processes are defined and implemented to respond to a security control failure, and include:<ul><li>Restoring security functions</li><li>Identifying and documenting the duration (date and time start to end) of the security failure</li><li>Identifying and documenting cause(s) of failure, including root cause, and documenting remediation required to address root cause</li><li>Identifying and addressing any security issues that arose during the failure</li></ul>

PCI DSS Requirements	Testing Procedures
■ Performing a risk assessment to determine whether further actions are required as a result of the security failure	■ Performing a risk assessment to determine whether further actions are required as a result of the security failure
■ Implementing controls to prevent cause of failure from reoccurring	■ Implementing controls to prevent cause of failure from reoccurring
■ Resuming monitoring of security controls	■ Resuming monitoring of security controls
Note: This requirement is a best practice until January 31, 2018, after which it becomes a requirement.	
	10.8.1.b Examine records to verify that security control failures are documented to include:
	■ Identification of cause(s) of the failure, including root cause
	■ Duration (date and time start and end) of the security failure
	■ Details of the remediation required to address the root cause
10.9 Ensure that security policies and operational procedures for monitoring all access to network resources and cardholder data are documented, in use, and known to all affected parties.	**10.9** Examine documentation and interview personnel to verify that security policies and operational procedures for monitoring all access to network resources and cardholder data are:
	■ Documented
	■ In use
	■ Known to all affected parties

The following sections depict some examples of how to configure ISE to meet a sampling of the requirements in Requirement 10.

ISE Policy for PCI 10.1: Ensuring Unique Usernames and Passwords

To ensure that each administrator of Cisco ISE has a unique username and password for auditing purposes, you must utilize RBAC for administrator users. Figure 9-1 shows an example of creating a local ISE super administrator account.

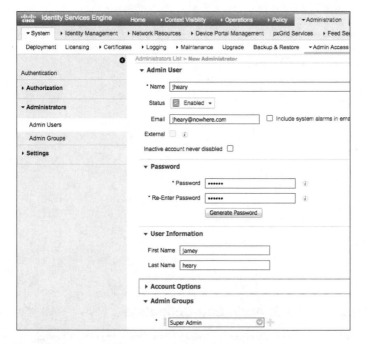

Figure 9-1   *Creating a Local ISE Administrator*

Each administrator should have their own account with the proper level of privileges required for them to do their job. Always exercise the concept of least privilege when assigning administrators a privilege level. You want them to have only the bare minimum privileges they require. You can use the built-in administrator authorization permissions or create your own inside of ISE. The authorization permissions are broken down into two types: Menu Access and Data Access. Menu Access permissions determine which menus the administrator can see. Data Access permissions allow you to grant full or no access to the following data in the Cisco ISE interface: Admin Groups, User Identity Groups, Endpoint Identity Groups, Locations, and Device Types.

Figure 9-2 depicts the Menu Access permissions screen (located at **Administration > System > Admin Access**) showing the help desk menu permissions. You can see that access to some menus is allowed and is blocked to others.

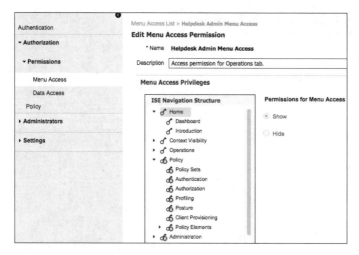

Figure 9-2 *Menu Access Permissions*

ISE Policy for PCI 10.2 and 10.3: Audit Log Collection

PCI Requirement 10.2 and its multiple subrequirements explain the types of audit logs that should be enabled on a system like ISE to ensure proper audit trails are created. Cisco ISE includes robust auditing controls and configuration options you can use to comply with PCI DSS 10.2 requirements. The requirements of PCI DSS 10.3 are met by the internals of the way ISE logs events and occur without your having to do any additional configuration.

The audit logs that ISE can create are broken into logging categories, as shown in Figure 9-3 (navigate to **Administration > System > Logging > Logging Categories**). As a best practice, all of these categories should be enabled for local logging level (as shown in the Local Log Level column).

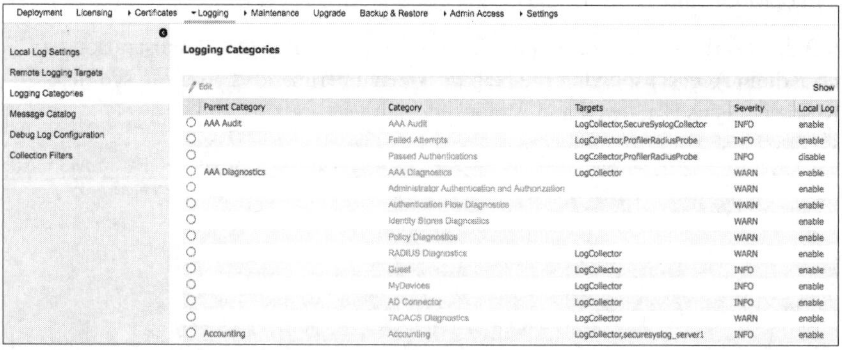

Figure 9-3 *ISE Audit/Logging Categories*

The Targets column indicates to which logging servers the messages will be sent for logging and storage. Targets are typically UDP syslog servers or secure syslog servers, as explained next.

ISE Policy for PCI 10.5.3, 10.5.4, and 10.7: Ensure the Integrity and Confidentiality of Audit Log Data

To ensure the integrity and confidentiality of audit log data, copying the logs to a non-ISE logging server is recommended. This ensures that in the event of an ISE compromise, administrator error, or system failure, the audit trail logs are not lost. You can also apply file integrity checking tools on the external log server data store for additional protection. Figure 9-4 illustrates the configuration options for configuring remote logging targets.

	Name	IP Address	Port	Type	Description	Status
○	LogCollector	127.0.0.1	20514	UDP SysLog	Syslog Target for Log Collector	Enabled
○	ProfilerRadiusProbe	127.0.0.1	30514	Profiler SysLog	Syslog Target for Profiler RADIUS Probe	Enabled
○	SecureSyslogCollector	127.0.0.1	6514	Secure SysLog	Secure Syslog Collector	Enabled
○	TCPLogCollector	127.0.0.1	1468	TCP SysLog	TCP SysLog collector	Disabled
○	securesyslog_server1	4.4.4.4	6514	Secure SysLog		Enabled

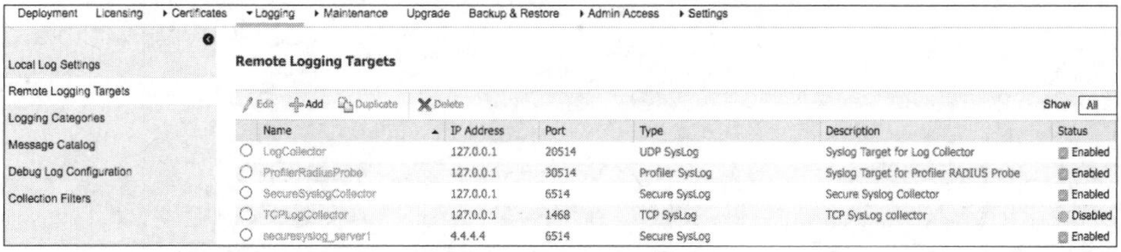

Figure 9-4   *Configuring ISE Remote Logging Targets*

The type of log server targets supported include UDP syslog, TCP syslog, and secure syslog.

PCI Requirement 10.7 requires you to keep audit logs for a period of one year, with at least 90 days' worth of logs kept readily available. The ISE default is only 1 day. To comply with 10.7, it is recommended that you configure ISE to keep 90 days of local audit logs, as shown in Figure 9-5, and use your external logging target servers for the long-term, one-year storage. This allows Cisco ISE to operate without the burden of a large audit log data store. If 90 days' worth of audit data is too large to be stored locally on ISE, then use the external logging servers and reduce the number of days' worth of logs the ISE local log stores. ISE will auto-prune the oldest logs first if it runs out of space.

Figure 9-5   *ISE Local Log Data Retention Policy*

ISE Policy for PCI 10.6: Review Audit Data Regularly

Now that you have Cisco ISE set up to produce the proper audit trails, you need to review that data regularly. PCI requires that you review the logs of AAA servers such as Cisco ISE on a daily basis, which is a great practice to follow but a fairly tall order for today's overworked administrators. Luckily, Cisco ISE has built-in reports and scheduled reports that can be created and, if desired, emailed to you daily. The Internal Administrator Summary report, shown in Figure 9-6 and located at **Operations > Reports > Audit**, is a good place to go to review all of the different administrator activity reports for ISE administrators.

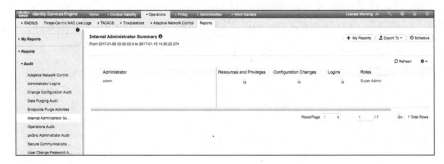

Figure 9-6   *ISE Internal Administrator Summary Report*

Clicking any of the document magnifying-glass icons in the different columns will open and run a report for that column. Clicking any of the hyperlinks in the report will spawn another audit report with more detail of the event. Figure 9-7 depicts an example of an ISE administrator configuration detail change report.

Configuration Audit Detail ❶

From 2017-01-08 00:00:00.0 to 2017-01-15 14:39:05.701
Generated At: 2017-01-15 14:39:05.05

Details

Logged At	2017-01-15 12:56:00.682
Server Time	2017-01-15 12:56:00.682 -8:00
Administrator	admin
Object Type	UPSLogTarget
Object Name	securesyslog_server1
Event	Added configuration
IP Address	10.1.100.231
Interface	GUI
ISE Server	All
Source ISE Server	atw-ise231

Modified Properties
Modified Properties
Object created: Port = 6514\Facility Code = LOCAL6\Length = 1024\Description = \Include Alarms = FALSE\status = ENABLED\Buffer Message = TRUE\

Figure 9-7   *ISE Administrator Change Configuration Audit Report*

Any ISE report that you run can be saved as a scheduled report or added to My Reports (shown at the top of the navigation pane in Figure 9-6). Before you create a scheduled report, you first have to set up a data repository in which to store the reports. Go to **Administration > System > Maintenance > Repository** to create one. For scheduled reports, you can input the relevant data, as shown in Figure 9-8, such as an email address to send the report to, frequency, and so forth.

Figure 9-8   *Scheduled Admin Change Configuration Report*

Cisco ISE User Accounting

In addition to auditing the administrators of ISE, it is also important to be able to audit the users authenticated via ISE. For this function, Cisco ISE offers the same user reporting structure that was just reviewed for administrators. It is found in the **Operations > Reports > Endpoints and Users** section of the ISE GUI. The Authentications Summary report shown in Figure 9-9 is a good example of a user audit report.

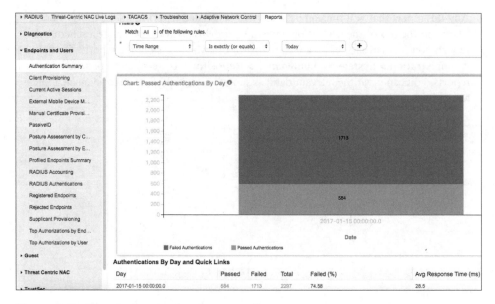

Figure 9-9   *User Authentication Summary Report*

As you can see in Figure 9-9, many user and device detailed reports are available in the Endpoints and Users section under Reports. Figure 9-10 depicts one of them, the Top Authorizations by User report.

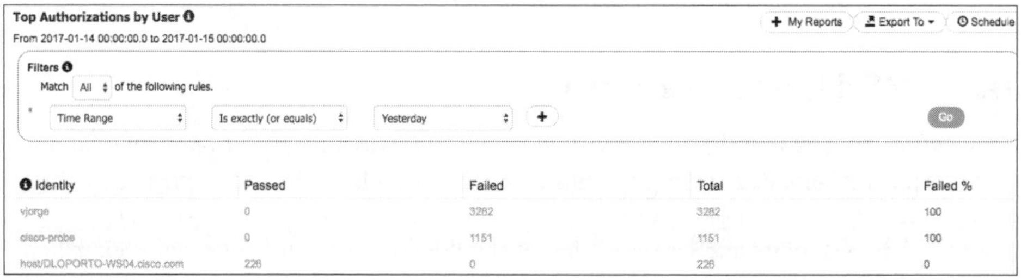

Figure 9-10   *Top User Authorizations Report*

Summary

Proper auditing and accounting is instrumental in operating the ISE solution. It assists with troubleshooting tasks, compliance reporting, and finding configuration errors and security compromises. By using PCI Requirement 10 as your guide, you will likely be able to pass audits against other security standards, including your own internal audit. Having said that, it is not a panacea, so be sure to check the regulations you will be audited against to ensure you configure Cisco ISE appropriately.

Chapter 10

Profiling Basics and Visibility

This chapter covers the following topics:

- Understanding profiling concepts

- Infrastructure configuration

- Profiling policies

- ISE Profiler and CoA

- Profiles in authorization policies

- Verifying profiling

- Triggered NetFlow: A Woland-Santuka pro tip

In this chapter we will examine profiling concepts and why profiling is so important to the context-aware policies necessary in today's business environment. We will dive into the manner in which profiling has evolved from a Band-Aid for deploying 802.1X deployments to the inventory and visibility tool that it is today. You will learn about the multitude of ways that Cisco Identity Services Engine (ISE) can glean the profiling data (probes) and you will learn how to configure the infrastructure to efficiently use the ISE profiling probes, including when ISE is within a VMware virtual environment.

Understanding Profiling Concepts

The term *profiling* has been used a lot in today's society and can often have negative connotations. Police and security professionals may use a series of attributes about a human being, such as hair and eye color, the way they are dressed, and the way they behave to help profile them quickly as being a threat or a non-threat. However, this is ultimately guesswork that (hopefully) becomes more accurate with experience and practice.

Profiling as it relates to network access is very similar. However, the term should be thought of in a positive light as it relates to the Cisco TrustSec system and the Cisco ISE solution.

The Cisco ISE Profiler is the component of the Cisco ISE platform that is responsible for endpoint detection and classification. It does so by using a probe or series of probes that collect attributes about an endpoint. The Profiler then compares the collected attributes to predefined device profiles (such as a set of signatures) to locate a match.

Why would profiling be an important technology for a company rolling out an identity solution? In the early days of identity-based networks and 802.1X, countless man-hours were spent identifying all the devices that did not have supplicants—in other words, the devices that could not authenticate to the network using 802.1X, such as printers and fax machines. You had to identity all the switch ports that were connected to the printer and configure those ports to either

- Not use 802.1X

- Use MAC Authentication Bypass (MAB)

MAB is an extension to 802.1X that allows the switch to send the device's MAC address to the authentication server. If that MAC address is in the approved list of devices, then the authentication server sends back an *accept* result, thereby allowing specific MAC addresses to skip authentication.

Imagine just how many-man hours were spent collecting and maintaining this list of MAC addresses. An onboarding process was required so that when a new printer was added to the network, its MAC address was added to the approved list, and so forth. Obviously, some enhancements to this onboarding process were required. There had to be some way to build this list more dynamically and save all those man-hours of prep and maintenance.

This is where profiling technology enters the picture. It allows you to collect attributes about devices from a multitude of sources such as DHCP, NetFlow, HTTP user-agent strings, NMAP scans, and more. Those collected attributes are then compared to a set of signatures, similar to the way an intrusion prevention system (IPS) works. These signatures are more commonly referred to as *profiles*.

Following is an example of how profiling technology works:

1. The Profiler collects a MAC address that belongs to Epson, Inc.

2. The Profiler does an NMAP scan on the IP address and sees that common printer ports are open.

3. Based on those two attributes, the system assigns that device to the profile "Epson Printer."

Profiling technology has evolved to the point that now your authentication server has the capability to use that profiling data for much more than just building the list of MAC addresses permitted to use MAB.

Cisco ISE uses the resulting collection and classification data from the Profiler as conditions in the authorization policy. Now you can build an authorization policy that looks at much more than your identity credentials. You can combine a user's identity with the classification result and invoke specific authorization results.

Figures 10-1 and 10-2 provide an example of a differentiated authorization policy based on profiling.

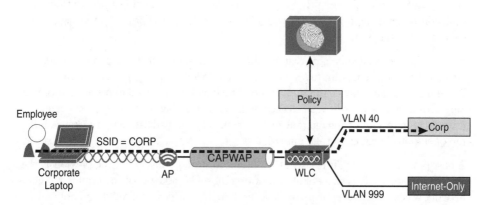

Figure 10-1 *Employee Using Corporate Laptop to Gain Full Access*

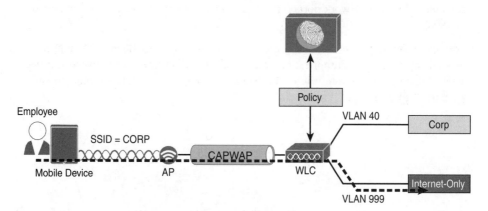

Figure 10-2 *Same Employee Credentials on a Mobile Device Gets Limited Access*

Users connecting to the same wireless SSID and using the same credentials can be associated to different wired VLAN interfaces based on the device profile, such as the following:

- Employees using corporate laptops with their Active Directory user ID are assigned to the corporate VLAN and given full access to the network.

- Employees using mobile devices with their same Active Directory user ID are assigned to a GUEST VLAN and provided Internet access only.

Although it may be quite intuitive to visualize the types of network access policies you will be able to create based on the device's profile, the design of where and how the Profiler collects the data about the endpoints requires thought and planning.

One of the first questions a security team may ask when discovering profiling with any network access control solutions is, "Can we use this as an anti-spoofing solution?" Remember that MAC Authentication Bypass is a very limited replacement for a strong authentication. It would be fairly easy for a malicious user to unplug a printer from the wall, configure her laptop to use the same MAC address as the printer (spoofing), and gain access to the network.

You should always keep in mind that profiling is a technology that compares collected attributes about an endpoint to a set of signatures called *profiling policies* to make the best guess of what a device is. Can this type of technology be used to prevent spoofing? Sure. However, it is very difficult to accomplish anti-spoofing with this type of technology. It would require a lot of tuning, trial and error, and constant adjustment, which makes it too operationally expensive and untenable.

A best-practice approach is to use a least-privilege strategy instead. If the previously mentioned malicious user is successful in spoofing the MAC address of the printer and gains network access, what level of network access should that device have? In other words, the authorization policy for printers should not provide full network access, but provide a limited subset of access instead. For example, a printer should only be permitted to communicate using network ports critical to printer operations (such as TCP port 9100 or 9600).

Profiling technology and the value it provides continue to evolve beyond MAB lists, beyond attributes in an authorization policy, and toward inventory of network-attached assets. Figure 10-3 illustrates this evolution of profiling, which will be evident in many aspects of ISE version 2.1 and beyond.

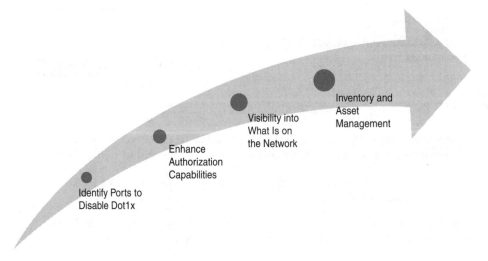

Figure 10-3   *Profiling Technology Evolution*

ISE Profiler Work Center

Beginning with ISE 2.0, the administrative experience within the ISE GUI has been shifting to the use of Work Centers. As the name implies, an ISE Work Center is designed to provide a single location where all tasks associated with the specific process can be accomplished. In this case, the Profiler Work Center is designed to provide you, the ISE admin, with a single section of the GUI to accomplish all the tasks related to profiling.

The Profiler Work Center is intuitively located under **Work Centers > Profiler**, as shown in Figure 10-4. As with all Work Centers in the ISE GUI, you can pretty much get everything configured if you just follow the steps from left to right.

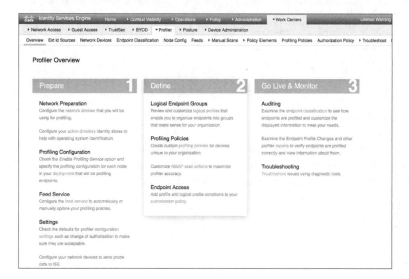

Figure 10-4 *Profiler Overview Screen*

ISE Profiling Probes

As described, the Cisco ISE solution is capable of providing access policies where the decisions may be made based on who, what, where, when, how, and other factors. Profiling is focused on the "what" elements of the policy. For the policy engine to know what the device is, you must first collect that data.

The Cisco ISE solution uses a number of collection mechanisms known as probes. Each probe is software designed to collect data to be used in a profiling decision. An example of this would be the HTTP probe, which captures HTTP traffic and enables the Profiler to examine attributes from the traffic, such as HTTP user-agent strings. Without the probe enabled on the policy server, the data would never be collected. The good news is that, starting in ISE version 1.3, profiling and a default set of probes are enabled by default.

Probe Configuration

You enable the probes on each Policy Service Node (PSN) where appropriate. In the Administration GUI of the Policy Administration Node (PAN), navigate to **Work Centers > Profiler > Node Config**. The same screen may also be found under **Administration > System > Deployment**. From here, select the PSN that you are configuring the probes for. You will repeat these steps for each PSN in your deployment.

Step 1. Select one of the Policy Services Nodes, as shown in Figure 10-5. In this case, the node is still standalone, which means that it is a single node running all personas (Administration, Monitoring, and Policy Service).

Figure 10-5 *ISE Deployment Screen*

Step 2. On the General Settings tab, note that the Enable Profiling Service check box is selected, as shown in Figure 10-6. This service is enabled by default on all PSNs, and is not configurable when in standalone mode.

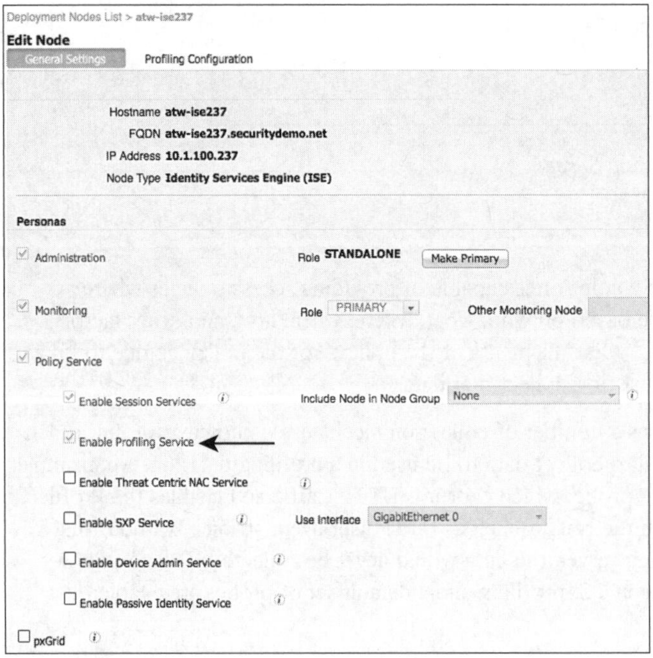

Deployment Nodes List > atw-ise237

Edit Node

General Settings   Profiling Configuration

Hostname **atw-ise237**
FQDN **atw-ise237.securitydemo.net**
IP Address **10.1.100.237**
Node Type **Identity Services Engine (ISE)**

Personas

☑ Administration   Role **STANDALONE**   [Make Primary]

☑ Monitoring   Role [PRIMARY ▼]   Other Monitoring Node

☑ Policy Service

    ☑ Enable Session Services ⓘ   Include Node in Node Group [None ▼] ⓘ

    ☑ Enable Profiling Service ←

    ☐ Enable Threat Centric NAC Service ⓘ

    ☐ Enable SXP Service ⓘ   Use Interface [GigabitEthernet 0 ▼]

    ☐ Enable Device Admin Service ⓘ

    ☐ Enable Passive Identity Service ⓘ

☐ pxGrid ⓘ

Figure 10-6 *General Settings*

Step 3.   Select the **Profiling Configuration** tab, as shown in Figure 10-7.

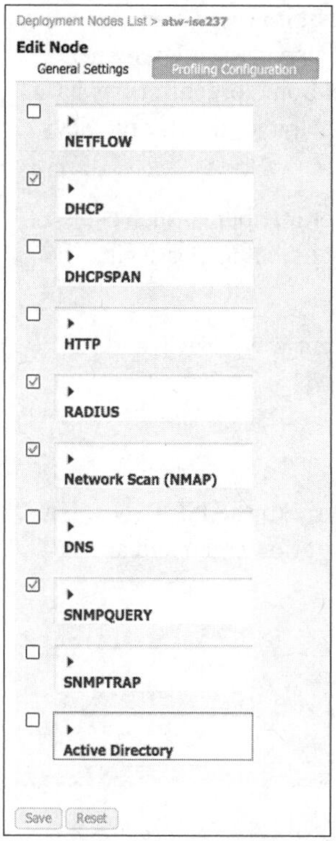

Figure 10-7   *Profiling Configuration*

The following ten probes are available on each Policy Services Node, as shown in Figure 10-7:

- NETFLOW
- DHCP
- DHCPSPAN
- HTTP
- RADIUS
- Network Scan (NMAP)
- DNS
- SNMPQUERY
- SNMPTRAP
- Active Directory

Next we examine each probe in detail (but not in the preceding order).

DHCP and DHCPSPAN Probes

DHCP can be one of the most useful data sources for an endpoint device. A primary use of DHCP in profiling is to capture the device MAC address; however, there are many other uses for the data. Much like HTTP, DHCP requests will also carry a User-Agent field that helps to identify the operating system of the device. Some organizations have been known to use a custom DHCP user-agent string, which helps to identify the device as a corporate asset.

Not only the populated fields from the DHCP Client, but other attributes, such as requested DHCP Options and DHCP Host-Name, can be very useful in classifying the device.

There are two DHCP probes, each working in a slightly different way: DHCP and DHCPSPAN.

DHCP Probe

The DHCP probe requires the DHCP requests to be sent directly to the ISE PSN(s). This is often done by using the **ip helper-address** interface configuration command and is illustrated in Figure 10-8.

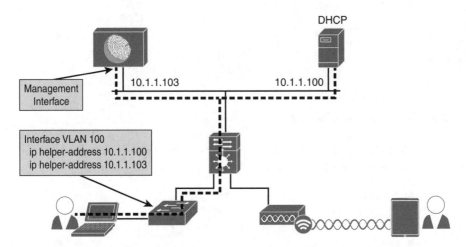

Figure 10-8   *DHCP with* **ip helper-address** *Logical Design*

The **ip helper-address** command on a Layer 3 interface will convert a DHCP broadcast (which is a Layer 2 broadcast) to a unicast or directed broadcast (which sends the broadcast to all hosts on a specific subnet). Simply add the IP address of your PSN(s) to the list of helper addresses, and it will be copied on all DHCP requests.

DHCPSPAN Probe

Another way for ISE to glean the DHCP requests and even the DHCP responses is the use of a Switched Port Analyzer (SPAN) session in true promiscuous mode. A SPAN session copies all traffic to/from a source interface on a switch to the destination interface, which would be one of ISE's interfaces assigned to the DHCPSPAN probe. Figure 10-9 illustrates the logical design of using SPAN.

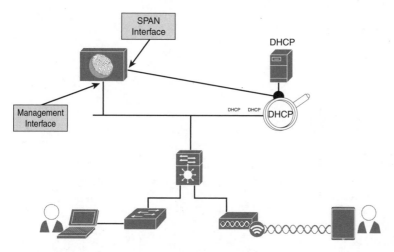

Figure 10-9 *DHCP SPAN Logical Design*

When using the SPAN method, you will need to consider where the best location is to create the SPAN session and gather the data. One recommended location is the DHCP server, where the DHCP probe will see both ends of the conversation (request and response). However, there are caveats to this method, such as, "What if the organization uses distributed DHCP servers?" This is why the non-SPAN method tends to be the most commonly deployed.

Considerations with the Cisco WLC

Regardless of the SPAN or "helper-address" methods of using the DHCP probe(s), when using a Cisco Wireless LAN Controller (WLC), the WLC has a default configuration of acting as a RADIUS proxy, which is its own form of a "helper-address" where the WLC acts as a middleman for all DHCP transactions. Unfortunately, this behavior has a negative effect on the DHCP probe and must be disabled on the WLC. Upon doing so, the DHCP requests from wireless endpoints appear as broadcast messages on the VLAN, and an IP helper-address statement should be configured on the Layer-3 interface of that VLAN (the switch or router).

Probe Configuration

Minimal configuration is required on the ISE side to enable the DHCP probe(s). From the Profiling Configuration tab displayed in Figure 10-7:

Step 1. Notice that DHCP is enabled by default. This default setting has existed since ISE 1.3.

Step 2. GigabitEthernet 0 is the default interface. You can choose a different interface or all interfaces. You can't choose multiple interfaces individually. The choice is a single interface or all interfaces.

Figure 10-10 shows the DHCP probes. You should never need to enable both probes for the same interface. That would cause double processing of DHCP packets and be wasteful of system resources.

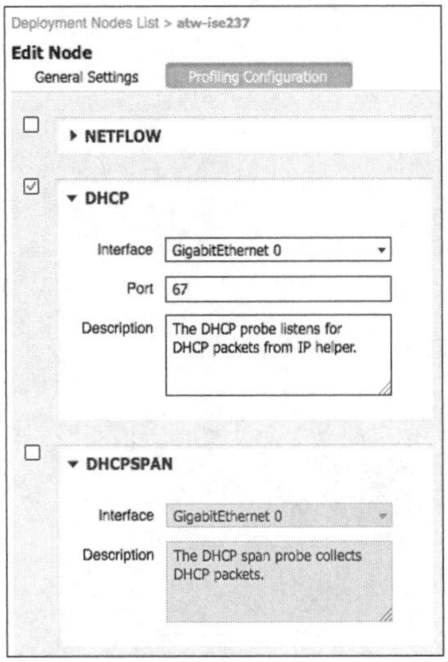

Figure 10-10 *DHCP Probes*

Note If you are using only device-sensor capable infrastructure, neither DHCP probe needs to be enabled.

RADIUS Probe

RADIUS is the primary communication mechanism from a network access device (NAD) to the authentication server (ISE). RADIUS packets contain useful data to help classify a device that exists within RADIUS communication.

Originally, the focus was on the MAC address and IP address of the device. By having this data conveyed in the RADIUS packet, ISE can build the all-important MAC-to-IP address bindings. Because the endpoint database uses MAC addresses as the unique identifier for all endpoints, these bindings are absolutely critical. Without them, the Layer 3 probes, such as HTTP and NMAP scanning, would never work correctly.

The Calling-Station-ID field in the RADIUS packet provides the endpoint's MAC address, and the Framed-IP-Address field provides its IP address in the RADIUS accounting packet.

Additionally, the RADIUS probe can trigger the SNMPQUERY probe to poll the NAD (see the SNMP probe information later in the chapter).

Most importantly, with the proliferation of device-sensor capable switches and wireless controllers, the RADIUS probe becomes even more critical. Device-sensor is a feature in the switch or controller that collects endpoint attributes locally and then sends those attributes to ISE within RADIUS accounting packets.

By allowing the network device to proactively send the profiling data to ISE, the architecture has placed the collection agents as close to the endpoint as possible, at the point of access to the network. Additionally, it has eliminated the need to send the **ip helper-address** information to ISE and the need to reactively query the switches for CDP/LLDP information (see the later discussion of the SNMPQUERY probe).

Considerations with RADIUS Probe

All NADs in the Secure Unified Access deployment should be configured to send RADIUS accounting packets. It is also important to note that the Cisco switch must learn the endpoint's IP address via DHCP snooping or IP Device Tracking to fill in the Framed-IP-Address field.

It is possible for a network device to send too much information, or to send accounting packets too often.

Probe Configuration

The RADIUS probe has been enabled by default since ISE version 1.3. There is minimal configuration available on the ISE side to enable or configure the RADIUS probe. From the Profiling Configuration tab displayed in Figure 10-11, click the check box next to the RADIUS probe to enable it.

Although there is not really any configuration possible with this probe, it is one of the most useful probes, especially when combined with Device Sensor.

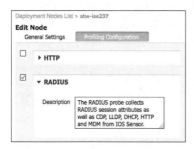

Figure 10-11 *RADIUS Probe*

Network Scan (NMAP) Probe

A welcome improvement to ISE version 1.1 was the addition of the Endpoint Scanning (NMAP) probe, which is now called the Network Scan (NMAP) probe in version 2.1. NMAP is a tool that uses port scans, SNMP, and other mechanisms to identity a device's Operating System, or other attributes of the device. The NMAP probe may be manually run against a single IP-Address or subnet. More importantly, the profiler engine can be configured to react to a profiling event with a reactive NMAP probe.

For example, when an endpoint is discovered to be an Apple-Device, ISE automatically launches an NMAP OS-Scan against that endpoint to determine if it is running macOS or iOS. From the results of that scan, ISE further classifies the device as a Mac or a mobile device.

ISE version 2.1 enhances that NMAP probe even further by leveraging the Server Message Block (SMB) protocol for probing Windows devices, leveraging McAfee ePolicy Orchestrator (ePO) ports to recognize corporate assets, and allowing custom ports to be configured to help identify custom devices.

Considerations with the NMAP Probe

The NMAP probe is executed against an IP address or range of IP addresses. However, it is absolutely crucial to keep in mind that the endpoint database uses a MAC address as the unique identifier of any endpoint. As such, the Policy Services Node relies on the MAC address-to-IP-address binding to update an endpoint's attributes with the results of the NMAP scan. Therefore, it is critical that the PSN receive valid information from the other probes.

The NMAP probe can be manually run against a single IP address or subnet, or (more commonly) an NMAP scan can be triggered as an action of a profile.

Probe Configuration

As with the other probes discussed thus far, only minimal configuration is needed for the NMAP probe. From the Profiling Configuration tab, displayed in Figure 10-12 (ISE 1.2) and 10-13 (ISE 2.1), click the check box next to the Network Scan (NMAP) probe to enable it. Figure 10-12 shows the NMAP probe configuration that exists in ISE 1.2 through ISE version 2.0, offering the option to run a manual scan against a single node or an entire network. Figure 10-13 shows the same NMAP probe configuration in ISE 2.1. The manual scan option has been relocated and enhanced.

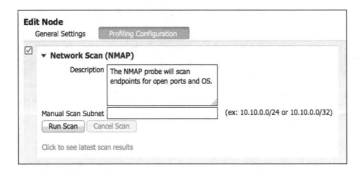

Figure 10-12   *Network Scan (NMAP) Probe in ISE 1.4*

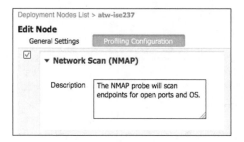

Figure 10-13 *Network Scan (NMAP) Probe in ISE 2.1*

Beginning in ISE 2.1, the NMAP manual scan option is located at **Work Centers > Profiler > Manual Scans**, as shown in Figure 10-14. This is a brilliant enhancement because it provides a lot more control and visibility from a single place. The following steps cover the options:

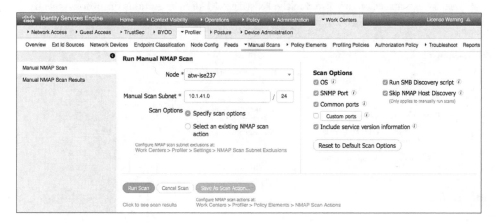

Figure 10-14 *Manual NMAP Scan*

Step 1.   Select which node in the deployment to run the scan from. This is important, because certain nodes may be closer to the target network, or certain nodes may not be able to reach some networks.

Step 2.   Provide a subnet or host address (/32) to scan from that host.

Step 3.   Choose either **Specify Scan Options**, as shown in Figure 10-15, or **Select an Existing NMAP Scan Action**, as shown in Figure 10-16.

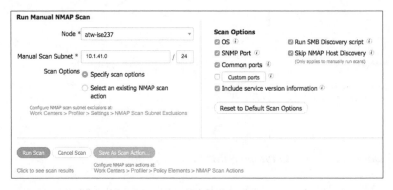

Figure 10-15   *Specify Scan Options*

If you choose Specify Scan Options, you can click Save As Scan Action to store the new action and add it to the library of available scan actions. Those available scan actions are listed in the Existing NMAP Scan Actions drop-down menu (see Figure 10-16) when you choose Select an Existing NMAP Scan Action.

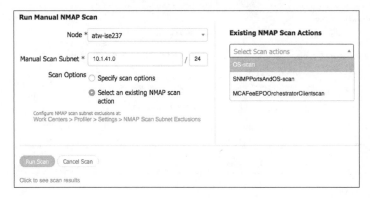

Figure 10-16   *Select an Existing NMAP Scan Action*

Step 4.   For purposes of demonstration, choose **Specify Scan Options**. The following are the scan options that are available on the right side of the screen:

■ **OS:** This option leverages the NMAP capability to attempt OS detection by examining TCP/IP fingerprints; in other words, it tries to detect what the OS is by the window size and other default settings in the TCP/IP stack.

■ **SNMP Port:** The scan checks whether SNMP is listening on the discovered host. If it is, the SNMP probe can be used to perform an SNMP walk of the device.

■ **Common Ports:** NMAP scans a predefined set of TCP and UDP ports.

■ **Custom Ports:** Often, an organization has devices that are unique to the environment, especially when Internet of Things (IoT) devices are in use. This option is used to define specific ports that would help identify those devices.

- **Include Service Version Information:** The NMAP scan captures any detailed information that the vendor displays in banners associated with different services. This setting requires Common Ports or Custom Ports to be enabled as a prerequisite.

- **Run SMB Discovery Script:** SMB is used mainly by Microsoft operating systems. This option can be used to try to determine the OS, computer name, domain name, NetBIOS computer name, NetBIOS domain name, workgroup, time zone, and more.

- **Skip NMAP Host Discovery:** NMAP host discovery is used to probe to ensure an endpoint exists before performing deeper scans. The host discovery mechanism provides better performance by not wasting cycles trying to scan endpoints that do not exist. Enabling this bypass option ensures that the deeper scans are always attempted on each IP address in the scan range. This setting only applies to manual scans. When an NMAP scan action is triggered, the host discovery is always skipped and the endpoint is deep scanned.

Step 5.   Click **Run Scan** to run the manual scan.

The NMAP probe will be explored in more detail in Chapter 20, "Deployment Phases."

DNS Probe

The DNS probe is used to collect the fully qualified domain name (FQDN) of an endpoint using a reverse lookup for the static or dynamic DNS registration of that endpoint. It is quite useful when looking for a specific DNS name format of corporate assets (Active Directory members).

A reverse DNS lookup will be completed only when an endpoint is detected by one of the DHCP, RADIUS, HTTP, or SNMP probes.

To enable the DNS probe, click the check box next to the DNS probe to enable it, as shown in Figure 10-17. This probe uses the name-server configuration from the Identity Services Engine node itself.

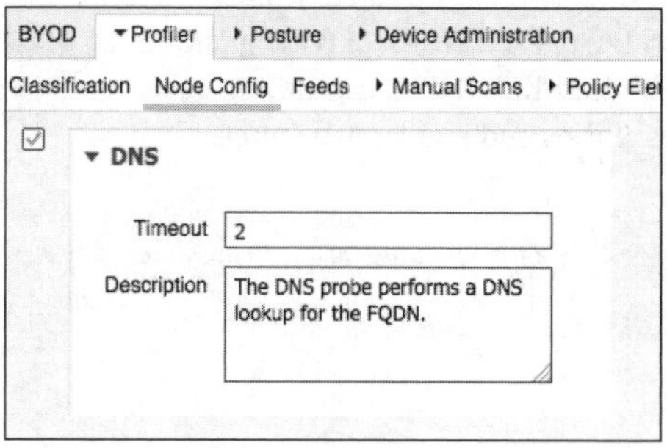

Figure 10-17   *DNS Probe*

SNMPQUERY and SNMPTRAP Probes

SNMP is used to query NADs that do not yet support the Cisco Device Sensor. After enabling the SNMPQUERY probe, ISE polls all of the SNMP-enabled NADs at the configured polling interval.

> **Note**   It is recommended to remove SNMP settings from NADs that support Device Sensor, to avoid double work and wasted processing.

There are two SNMP probes: SNMPTRAP and SNMPQUERY.

SNMPTRAP Probe

The SNMPTRAP probe receives information from the configured NAD(s) that support MAC notification, linkup, linkdown, and informs. The purpose of this probe is two-fold: it is used to trigger the SNMPQUERY probe and it is used as a toggle switch to allow the SNMPQUERY probe to reactively query a NAD instead of waiting for the periodic polling interval. Therefore, for the SNMPTRAP probe to be functional, you must also enable the SNMPQUERY probe.

The SNMPTRAP probe receives information from the specific NAD(s) when the MAC address table changes or when link state changes on a switch port. To make this feature functional, you must configure the NAD to send SNMP traps or informs.

SNMPQUERY Probe

The SNMPQUERY probe does the bulk of the work. There are actually three different kinds of SNMPQUERY probes:

- **System probe:** Polls all NADs that are configured for SNMP at the configured interval.

- **Interface probe:** Occurs in response to an SNMPTRAP or RADIUS accounting start packet (only if the SNMPTRAP probe is enabled).

- **Network Scan (NMAP) probe:** Triggers the SNMP walk of an endpoint.

When querying a NAD, ISE looks for interface data (which interface, which VLAN), session data (if the interface is Ethernet), Cisco Discovery Protocol (CDP), and Link Layer Discovery Protocol (LLDP) data. The CDP and LLDP data can be very useful in identifying a device type by its registered capabilities and similar attributes.

> **Note**   For distributed deployments, NAD polling is distributed among all Policy Services Nodes enabled for SNMPQUERY probes.

Probe Configuration

Although there is a bit of configuration to these probes, such as the trap types to examine and the SNMP port, it is recommended that you leave these at their default settings unless directed otherwise by Cisco TAC.

Step 1. Click the check box next to the SNMPQUERY and SNMPTRAP probes to enable them.

Step 2. For the SNMPTRAP probe, select either the GigabitEthernet 0 interface or all interfaces. You can't choose multiple interfaces individually. The choice is a single interface or all interfaces.

Figure 10-18 shows the enabled SNMP probes and their default settings.

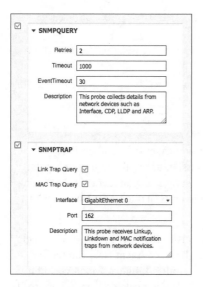

Figure 10-18 *SNMP Probes*

Active Directory Probe

Added to ISE 2.1, the Active Directory (AD) probe is designed to help answer the question, "Is this endpoint a corporate asset?" This probe leverages what is known as the Active Directory Run Time (ADRT) connector, which is the powerful Active Directory connector introduced back in ISE 1.3. After a computer hostname is learned from either the DHCP probe or DNS probe, the AD probe will search in AD for attributes and allow the following attributes to be used in profiler policy creation:

■ **AD-Host-Exists:** If the endpoint exists in AD, then it helps identify that it could be a corporate system.

■ **AD-Join-Point:** Defines the AD domain where the host was located.

■ **AD-Operating-System:** The OS type version of the endpoint.

■ **AD-OS-Version:** The version of that endpoint's OS.

■ **AD-Service-Pack:** The service pack version of the endpoint.

As this list of attributes demonstrates, this probe provides customers some decent flexibility to identify systems and glean inventory of those systems. Figure 10-19 shows the Active Directory probe configuration. The configuration is limited to enabling (or disabling) the probe and configuring the number of days before rescanning for attributes.

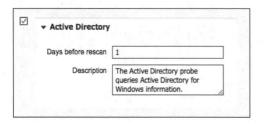

Figure 10-19   *Active Directory Probe Configuration*

HTTP Probe

When applications use HTTP, such as a web browser or even software like Microsoft Outlook and Windows Update, it typically identifies itself, its application type, operating system, software vendor, and software revision by submitting an identification string to its operating peer. This information is transmitted in an HTTP Request-Header field called the User-Agent field.

Cisco ISE uses the information in HTTP packets, especially the User-Agent field, to help match signatures of what profile a device belongs in. The User-Agent field can tell ISE the difference between the various Windows versions, Android, Linux, Mac OS, and iOS device types, sometimes delivering OS and version details not available from other profile attributes. Example 10-1 shows the user-agent string for Mac OS.

Example 10-1   *User Agent for Mac OS X 10.11 (El Capitan)*

```
Mozilla/5.0 (Macintosh; Intel Mac OS X 10_11) AppleWebKit/601.1.27 (KHTML, like
  Gecko)
Version/8.1 Safari/601.1.27
```

Example 10-2 shows the User Agent for Windows 8.1.

Example 10-2   *User Agent for Windows 8.1*

```
Mozilla/5.0Mozilla/5.0 (Windows NT 6.3; WOW64; Trident/7.0; Touch; rv:11.0) like
  Geckos
```

As you can see, HTTP packet inspection is a key element to profiling effectively. Figure 10-20 illustrates the logical design of ISE examining the HTTP packets.

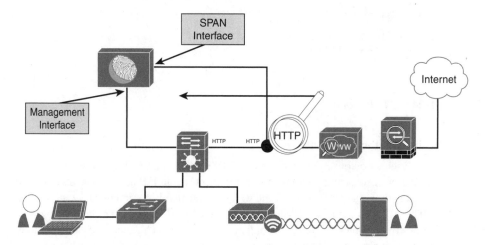

Figure 10-20   *HTTP SPAN Logical Design*

There are two primary mechanisms for the HTTP probe to collect the HTTP traffic:

- **Use a SPAN session in true promiscuous mode:** When using the SPAN method, consider the best location to create the SPAN session and gather the data. One recommended location is the Internet edge, where a network organization typically deploys a Cisco IronPort Web Security Appliance.

- **Use a SPAN session in conjunction with a filter to limit the traffic visible to ISE:** Another option to use with the SPAN design is the use of VLAN ACL (VACL) captures on a Catalyst 6500 or ACL-based SPAN sessions on a Nexus 7000. These options allow you to build an ACL that defines exactly what traffic you want to capture and send along to ISE, instead of a pure promiscuous SPAN, where the ISE interface will see all traffic. This is a better way to manage the resource utilization on your ISE server when available.

As you can see, there are multiple ways to use the HTTP probe, and you should consider what works best for your environment and then deploy with that approach. In many environments, it is best to not use SPAN at all, but instead leverage ISE's own portals to capture the user-agent strings.

To configure the HTTP probe, click the check box next to the HTTP probe to enable it, as shown in Figure 10-21. Select either the GigabitEthernet 0 interface or all interfaces.

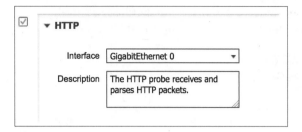

Figure 10-21   *HTTP Probe*

HTTP Profiling Without Probes

ISE deployments do not require the use of SPAN sessions or VACL captures to receive the HTTP user-agent strings. The Web Portal system within ISE itself has been outfitted to collect the user-agent details from the web browser that is communicating with an ISE portal. This occurs regardless of whether profiling is enabled. The user-agent string is used to determine which OS is connecting and therefore which agent or client to send to the endpoint (in the cases of client provisioning and native supplicant provisioning).

When any portal collects that user-agent string, it is automatically passed over to the profiling engine within ISE, without requiring the HTTP probe to be enabled. It is a simple and efficient way to get the extremely valuable user-agent string without having to rely on the computationally expensive SPAN methods.

NetFlow Probe

NetFlow is an incredibly useful and undervalued security tool. Essentially, it is similar to a phone bill. A phone bill does not include transcripts of all the conversations you have had; instead, it is a summary record of all calls sent and received, including the duration of the call. Cisco routers and switches support NetFlow, sending a "record" of each packet that has been routed, including the ports and other very usable information.

Just enabling NetFlow in your infrastructure and forwarding all its data to ISE can quickly oversubscribe your Policy Services Node. If you are planning to use the NetFlow probe, it is highly recommended that you have a robust solution, such as Cisco Stealthwatch (from Cisco's acquisition of Lancope), to filter out any unnecessary data and send only what you truly need to ISE. For that reason, this book does not focus on the NetFlow. It is recommended that you perform extensive planning prior to its use.

Configuring the NetFlow probe is limited to enabling the check box next to the NetFlow probe and selecting either the GigabitEthernet 0 interface or all interfaces. Figure 10-22 shows the enabled NetFlow probe.

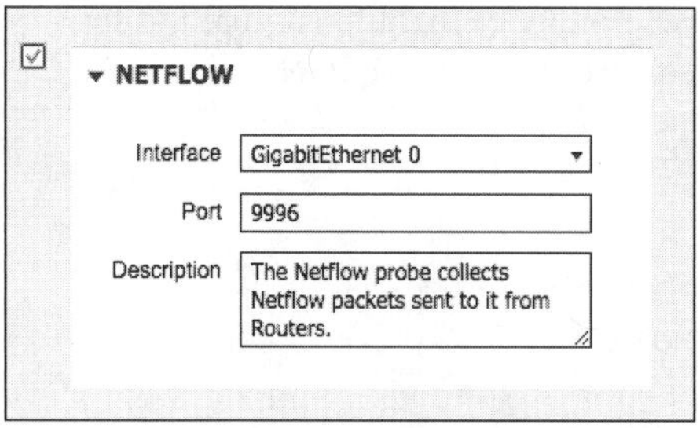

Figure 10-22 *NetFlow Probe*

Infrastructure Configuration

As an overall best practice, it is recommended to examine the cost-benefit analysis of using processor-intensive probes or probe designs. For example, it is often recommended to use DHCP Helper instead of configuring a SPAN session and examining a multitude of traffic that may or may not be relevant.

Let's use HTTP traffic as an example. HTTP traffic is extremely useful for identifying the OS on a client endpoint; however, HTTP SPAN can consume a large amount of system resources on the Policy Services Node. Additionally, it may not be critical to have full visibility into the user-agent strings of all devices, such as corporate-managed Windows devices.

Some deployments use VACL captures, which can limit what traffic is sent via the capture interface. Other deployments use the authorization policy in ISE to send unknown devices to an ISE portal, allowing the portal to update the profiling data (see the "HTTP Profiling Without Probes" section).

Craig Hyps is a Principal Technical Marketing Engineer with the ISE team and has presented a brilliant session at Cisco Live events many times related to designing ISE for scale and high availability. The session number may change depending on the year and location, but you can find the sessions, including video-on-demand recordings, by visiting http://www.ciscolive.com, navigating to **Learn Online > On-demand Library**, and then searching the Sessions category for "ISE for Scale and High Availability" or searching the Speakers category for the name "Hyps." That session is fantastic and highly recommended for additional learning on this topic.

DHCP Helper

As shown earlier in Figure 10-8, the **ip helper-address** commands are configured on the default gateway for each of the access-layer VLANs. To configure the destination address to copy DHCP requests to, enter interface configuration mode of the Layer 3 address for the VLAN and enter the **ip helper-address** [*ip-address*] command. One method is to add the DHCP server and all applicable ISE Policy Service Nodes to the list of helper-address destinations.

Figure 10-23 shows example output from a Layer 3 interface that is configured to send DHCP requests to the DHCP server in addition to two different ISE PSNs.

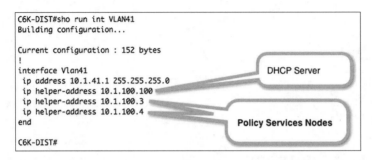

```
C6K-DIST#sho run int VLAN41
Building configuration...

Current configuration : 152 bytes
!
interface Vlan41
 ip address 10.1.41.1 255.255.255.0
 ip helper-address 10.1.100.100
 ip helper-address 10.1.100.3
 ip helper-address 10.1.100.4
end

C6K-DIST#
```

Figure 10-23   ip helper-address *Settings*

Copying all the DHCP requests to all the PSNs can have undesirable results, especially in large deployments. It will cause all PSNs that receive the DHCP packet to believe they should be owners of the endpoint data and therefore cause excess data replication. To alleviate that, it is often much more desirable to keep the DHCP traffic going to a specific PSN that is designated for profiling. Redundancy can be provided by leveraging techniques such as Anycast between two PSNs, possibly between PSNs located in different data centers.

Figure 10-24 illustrates the DHCP traffic reaching the DHCP server but also all three PSNs in the network. In such a scenario, all three PSNs would claim ownership of the endpoint record and data replication between them would ensue. Whichever PSN ends up owning the RADIUS session would be the ultimate owner of the endpoint record and the data would replicate once more to it.

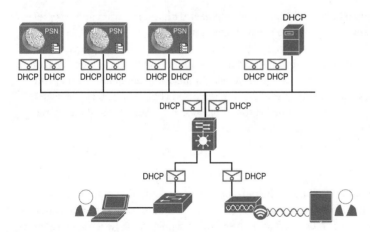

Figure 10-24   ip helper *Sending DHCP to All Nodes*

Figure 10-25 illustrates using two data centers with Anycast, where the same IP address exists in both data centers and routing is used to determine which one receives the DHCP packets. This provides redundancy for profiling while limiting how many replications must occur. See Chapter 18, "Setting Up a Distributed ISE Deployment," for more information on Anycast.

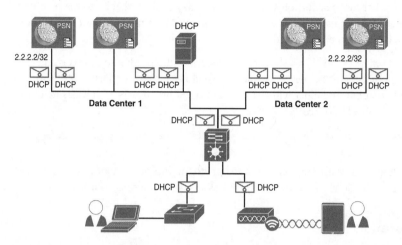

Figure 10-25 ip helper *Sending DHCP to Anycast Address in Two Data Centers*

Figure 10-26 illustrates using two data centers with load balancers in each data center. The load balancers are configured with a single virtual IP (VIP) each, and in this case the same IP address exists on both VIPs (Anycast), with routing used to determine which one receives the DHCP packets. This provides redundancy for profiling, provides redundancy for RADIUS, and permits linear scaling by adding more PSNs behind each VIP, all while limiting how many replications must occur. (Chapter 18 also provides more information on load balancers.)

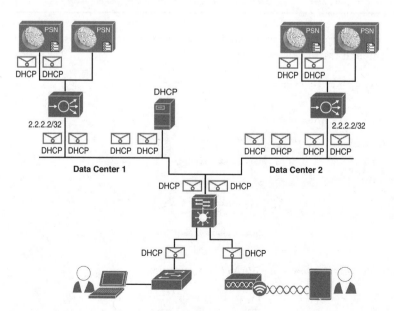

Figure 10-26 ip helper *Sending DHCP to VIPs Using Anycast in Two Data Centers*

These figures are examples of design choices for profiling that provide redundancy. These are just examples—you can imagine how many different variations and configuration alternatives exist. For more details on scaling and high availability, check out the recorded VoDs of the legendary Craig Hyps's Cisco Live presentations at http://www.ciscolive.com (using the search methods previously described).

As the technical editor of this book, E. Pete Karelis, so kindly pointed out, this is a good place to mention that the **ip helper** command will send more than just DHCP traffic to the destination. Enabling IP helper will also forward other broadcasts as unicasts in addition to BOOTPC/BOOTPS(DHCP):

```
Time (37), DNS (53), TACACS (49), NetBIOS Name (137), NetBIOS Datagram (138),
  TFTP (69)
```

They can be filtered out with the **no ip forward protocol udp** *port-number* command. Generally, it's good hygiene to not forward unnecessary traffic across your network.

SPAN Configuration

A monitor session is configured in global-configuration mode, and can be local (SPAN) or remote (RSPAN). Example 10-3 shows a SPAN configuration where an Internet-facing VLAN is the source of the session and an interface on the Policy Services Node is the destination. For more on SPAN configuration, see: http://www.cisco.com/c/en/us/support/docs/switches/catalyst-6500-series-switches/10570-41.html.

Example 10-3   monitor session *Command Input*

```
DC-4948(config)# monitor session [1-4] source [interface | vlan] [rx | tx]
DC-4948(config)# monitor session [1-4] destination interface [interface_name]
```

Figure 10-27 shows the output of the **show monitor** command, where you can see the source and destination of the session.

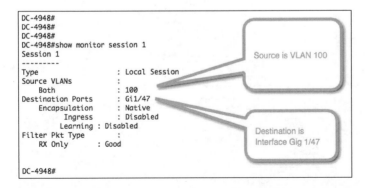

Figure 10-27   *Example Monitor Session (SPAN) Configuration*

VLAN ACL Captures

VACL capture configuration is a multistep process, as demonstrated in the following example:

Step 1.   Build an access list to classify the traffic you want to capture:

```
C6K-DIST(config)# ip access-list extended HTTP_TRAFFIC
C6K-DIST(config-ext-nacl)# permit tcp any any eq www
```

Step 2.   Build an access list for all the rest of the traffic:

```
C6K-DIST(config)# ip access-list extended ALL_TRAFFIC
C6K-DIST(config-ext-nacl)# permit ip any any
```

Step 3.   Create a VLAN access-map sequence to "capture" HTTP traffic:

```
C6K-DIST(config)# vlan access-map HTTP_MAP 10
C6K-DIST(config-access-map)# match ip address HTTP_TRAFFIC
C6K-DIST(config-access-map)# action forward capture
```

Step 4.   Add a new sequence to the access map to forward all other traffic:

```
C6K-DIST(config)# vlan access-map HTTP_MAP 20
C6K-DIST(config-access-map)# match ip address ALL_TRAFFIC
C6K-DIST(config-access-map)# action forward
```

Step 5.   Apply the VLAN access map to the VLAN list:

```
C6K-DIST(config)# vlan filter HTTP_MAP vlan-list 41,42
```

Step 6.   Configure the "destination" port for the PSN's SPAN interface:

```
C6K-DIST(config-if)# switchport capture allowed vlan 41
C6K-DIST(config-if)# switchport capture allowed vlan add 42
C6K-DIST(config-if)# switchport capture
```

Device Sensor

As described in the "RADIUS Probe" section, Device Sensor is a feature in the switch or wireless controller that collects endpoint attributes locally and then sends those attributes to ISE within RADIUS accounting packets. By allowing the network device to proactively send the profiling data to ISE, it can create a very elegant and distributed profiling architecture by placing the collection agents as close to the endpoint as possible. It also eliminates a lot of the redundancy considerations discussed in the "DHCP and DHCPSPAN Probes" section as well as the need to reactively query the switches for CDP/LLDP information. This greatly increases the scalability and performance of profiling by proactively sending the information to the correct ISE PSN automatically and removing any requirement for ISE to reactively reach out for the data.

Device Sensor made its way into Cisco switches in IOS 15.0(1) and IOS-XE 3.3.0. The Cisco WLC added Device Sensor capabilities in AireOS version 7.3.

Device Sensor requires a multipart configuration. The first portion is to configure the Device Sensor *filter lists*. These lists inform Device Sensor of which items to consider important for each of the different protocols.

Device Sensor supports three protocols: DHCP, CDP, and LLDP. Therefore, you must create one list for each protocol, as follows:

Step 1.   Create a list for DHCP.

You need to configure three options for ISE: **host-name**, **class-identifier**, and **client-identifier**:

```
C3750X(config)# device-sensor filter-list dhcp list dhcp_list_name
C3750X(config-sensor-dhcplist)# option name host-name
C3750X(config-sensor-dhcplist)# option name class-identifier
C3750X(config-sensor-dhcplist)# option name client-identifier
```

Step 2.   Create a list for CDP.

You need to configure two CDP options for ISE: **device-name** and **platform-type**:

```
C3750X(config)# device-sensor filter-list cdp list cdp_list_name
C3750X(config-sensor-cdplist)# tlv name device-name
C3750X(config-sensor-cdplist)# tlv name platform-type
```

Step 3.   Create a list for LLDP.

You need to configure three LLDP options for ISE: **port-id**, **system-name**, and **system-description**:

```
C3750X(config)# device-sensor filter-list lldp list lldp_list_name
C3750X(config-sensor-lldplist)# tlv name port-id
C3750X(config-sensor-lldplist)# tlv name system-name
C3750X(config-sensor-lldplist)# tlv name system-description
```

Step 4.   Include the lists created in Steps 1–3 in the Device Sensor.

In the preceding steps, you defined what options that Device Sensor should store. At this point, configure Device Sensor to use those lists:

```
C3750X(config)# device-sensor filter-spec dhcp include list
  dhcp_list_name

C3750X(config)# device-sensor filter-spec lldp include
  list cdp_list_name

C3750X(config)# device-sensor filter-spec cdp include list
  lldp_list_name
```

Step 5.   Enable Device Sensor.

Device Sensor is now configured. Enable the device-sensor service to run on the switch, and configure when it will send its updates:

```
C3750X(config)# device-sensor accounting
C3750X(config)# device-sensor notify all-changes
```

VMware Configurations to Allow Promiscuous Mode

As shown in Figure 10-28, a VMware vSwitch rejects promiscuous mode by default. To use SPAN type probes with ISE, you configure the vSwitch to allow promiscuous connections.

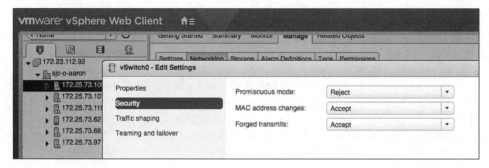

Figure 10-28 *Default vSwitch Configuration*

To modify the configuration and enable promiscuous traffic, follow these steps:

Step 1.   Highlight the vSwitch and click **Edit Settings**.

Step 2.   In the Edit Settings dialog box, click **Security** in the navigation menu.

Step 3.   Change the Promiscuous Mode drop-down to **Accept**, as shown in Figure 10-29.

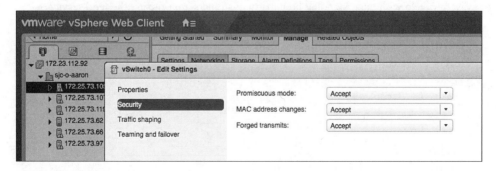

Figure 10-29 *Promiscuous vSwitch Setting*

Profiling Policies

Collecting the data for profiling is only part of the solution. The other aspects are to have endpoint signatures and a policy engine to compare the collected attributes to those signatures, which will lead to the assignment of the endpoint profile.

The profiling engine is a policy engine that works a lot like an intrusion detection system (IDS) that compares traffic to a set of signatures to identify suspicious activity. The profiling engine has hundreds of built-in signatures, called *profiles*, that are designed to match when certain attributes exist. Additionally, much like an IDS system, an update service enables the engine to download new signatures.

Profiler Feed Service

Although ISE comes with a very large and comprehensive list of signatures to classify endpoints (profiles), there are so many more devices that are produced almost daily (think of the next smartphone or version of the phone's OS); and there is a constant stream of new profiles created by Cisco that should be shared to the ISE deployments of the world. That's why Cisco created a profiler feed service. When a new device is released to market, Cisco creates a profile for it. New profiles are created from Cisco partners and device manufacturers. Cisco also has a team that focuses on profile creation. The ISE profiler feed service is used to distribute these new profiles after the Quality Assurance (QA) team has approved them.

Configuring the Profiler Feed Service

Configuring the feed service is straightforward. Once enabled, it reaches out to Cisco.com at the set time interval and downloads any published profiles. Among its many features, it offers an option to send an email alert to the administrator when an update occurs, an Undo Latest button for reversing the latest update, a Test Feed Service Connection button to ensure the feed service is reachable and working, a link to view a report on the latest updates, and an option to send your information anonymously to Cisco to help with understanding how many customers are utilizing the feed service.

Figure 10-30 shows a configured Profiler Feed Service Configuration screen, which is located under both **Administration > Feed Service > Profiler** and **Work Centers > Profiler > Feeds.**

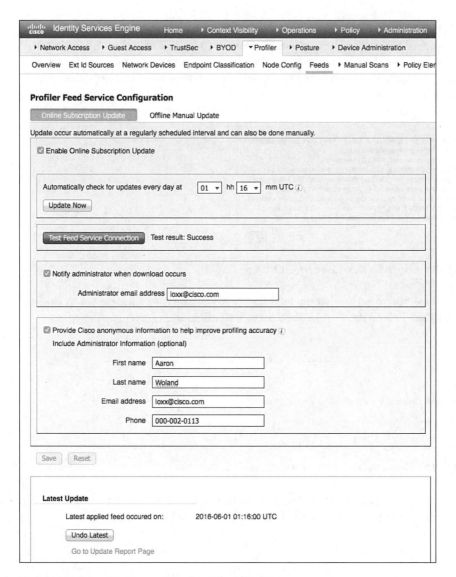

Figure 10-30 *Configured Profiler Feed Service*

If you don't want to wait for a configured interval for the feed service to run, you can click the **Update Now** button. Be cautious with manually updating the profiles during a production workday. When the profiles are updated, it causes all endpoints in the endpoint database to be compared against the new list of profiles. In other words, a complete re-profiling of endpoints occurs and that can be very processor-intensive.

Verifying the Profiler Feed Service

The Test Feed Service Connection button in Figure 10-30 was added in ISE version 1.4. The test verifies not only reachability of the feed server, but also that the connection is successful. Figure 10-31 shows an example of a failure message when a proxy server is required but none is configured.

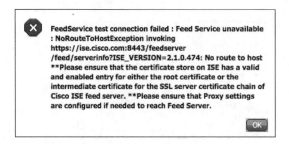

Figure 10-31   *Feed Service Connection Failure*

Another method to verify that the feed service is working is to click the **Go to Update Report Page** link on the Profiler Feed Service Configuration screen, as shown in Figure 10-32.

Figure 10-32   *Go to Update Report Page Link*

Clicking that link opens another window with the Change Configuration Audit report prefiltered for the feed service–related entries, as shown in Figure 10-33.

Change Configuration Audit

Time Range: From 01/05/2015 08:06:01.000 PM to 01/11/2015 06:33:46.000 PM
Administrator: FeedService
Generated At: 2015-01-11 15:37:44.918

Logged At	Administrator	Server	Interface	Object Type	Object Name	Event
2015-01-06 01:06:42.725	FeedService	atw-cp-ise02	GUI	FeedEndpointPoli	RICOH-Aficio-MP-	Changed configuration
2015-01-06 01:06:42.231	FeedService	atw-cp-ise02	GUI	EndpointPolicy	RICOH-Aficio-MP-	Added configuration
2015-01-06 01:06:41.885	FeedService	atw-cp-ise02	GUI	Rule	RICOH-Aficio-MP-	Added configuration
2015-01-06 01:06:41.804	FeedService	atw-cp-ise02	GUI	Check	RICOH-Aficio-MP-	Added configuration
2015-01-06 01:06:41.738	FeedService	atw-cp-ise02	GUI	FeedEndpointPoli	RICOH-Aficio-MP-	Changed configuration
2015-01-06 01:06:41.243	FeedService	atw-cp-ise02	GUI	EndpointPolicy	RICOH-Aficio-MP-	Added configuration
2015-01-06 01:06:40.893	FeedService	atw-cp-ise02	GUI	Rule	RICOH-Aficio-MP-	Added configuration
2015-01-06 01:06:40.813	FeedService	atw-cp-ise02	GUI	Check	RICOH-Aficio-MP-	Added configuration
2015-01-06 01:06:40.745	FeedService	atw-cp-ise02	GUI	FeedEndpointPoli	RICOH-Aficio-MP-	Changed configuration
2015-01-06 01:06:40.253	FeedService	atw-cp-ise02	GUI	EndpointPolicy	RICOH-Aficio-MP-	Added configuration
2015-01-06 01:06:39.898	FeedService	atw-cp-ise02	GUI	Rule	RICOH-Aficio-MP-	Added configuration
2015-01-06 01:06:39.816	FeedService	atw-cp-ise02	GUI	Check	RICOH-Aficio-MP-	Added configuration
2015-01-06 01:06:39.737	FeedService	atw-cp-ise02	GUI	FeedEndpointPoli	RICOH-Aficio-MP-	Changed configuration
2015-01-06 01:06:39.247	FeedService	atw-cp-ise02	GUI	EndpointPolicy	RICOH-Aficio-MP-	Added configuration
2015-01-06 01:06:38.878	FeedService	atw-cp-ise02	GUI	Rule	RICOH-Aficio-MP-	Added configuration

Figure 10-33 *Change Configuration Audit for Feed Service*

Because ISE must be able to reach Cisco.com for the profiler feed service to function, you may need to configure ISE to use a proxy server to reach the Internet. This optional configuration is located at **Administration > System > Settings > Proxy**, as shown in Figure 10-34.

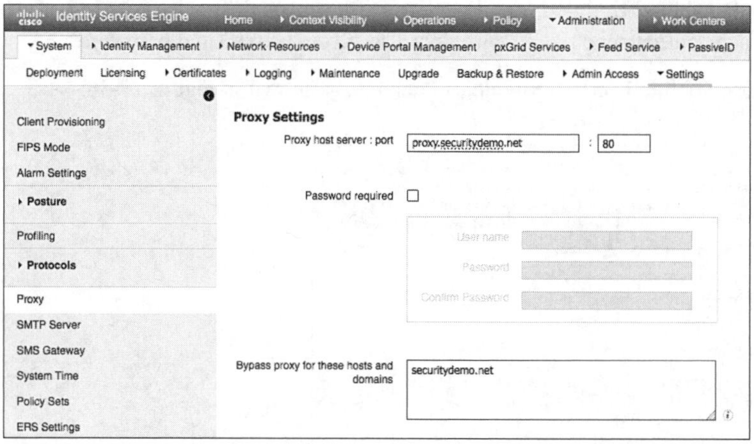

Figure 10-34 *Proxy Setting*

Offline Manual Update

Not all organizations are permitted to allow ISE to communicate outbound to the feed service. Many are deployed in air-gapped networks. For those environments, an offline manual update was added in ISE version 2.1.

To use the offline feed update, follow these steps:

Step 1.   Navigate to the offline feed service page via either **Administration > Feed Service > Profiler > Offline Manual Update**, as shown in Figure 10-35, or **Work Centers > Profiler > Feeds > Offline Manual Update**.

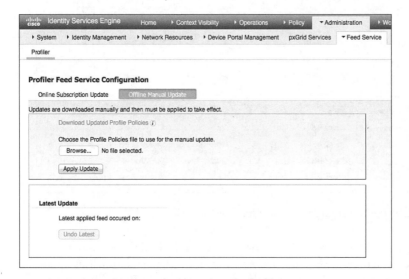

Figure 10-35   *Offline Manual Update Tab*

Step 2.   Click **Download Updated Profile Policies**. This opens the feed service at http://ise.cisco.com/partner. Log in with your Cisco.com user ID and password.

Step 3.   Choose **Offline Feed > Download Package**, as shown in Figure 10-36.

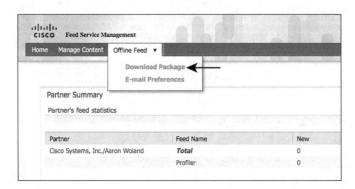

Figure 10-36   *Download Package Option*

Step 4.   Click **Generate Package**, as shown in Figure 10-37.

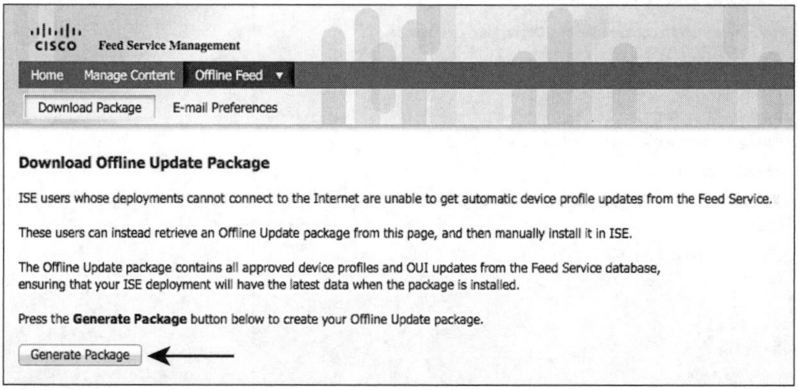

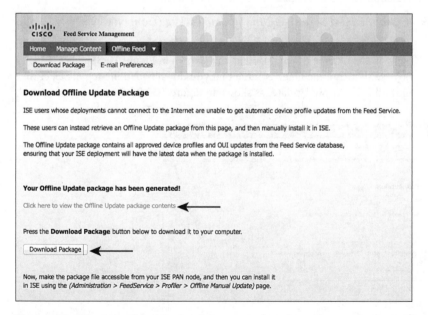

Figure 10-37   *Generate Package Button*

Step 5.   Click **Download Package**, as shown in Figure 10-38, and save the resulting
tar.gz.gpg file.

Figure 10-38   *Download Package Button and Link to View Package Contents*

Step 6.   To see the contents of the Offline Update package, click the **Click Here to
View the Offline Update Package Contents** link shown in Figure 10-38, which
launches another window that displays the contents, as shown in Figure 10-39.

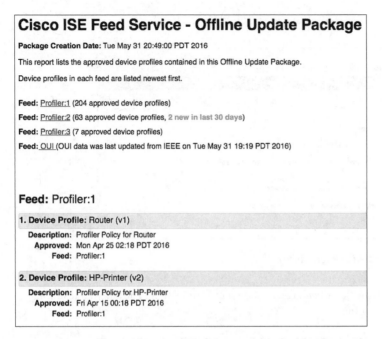

Figure 10-39 *Cisco ISE Feed Service Offline Update Package Contents*

Step 7.   Back on the Offline Manual Update tab (shown in Figure 10-35), click
Browse to locate the tar.gz.gpg file that you downloaded in Step 6. Select the
file and click **Apply Update**, as shown in Figure 10-40.

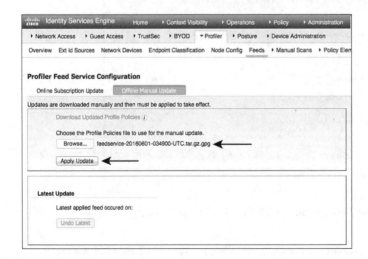

Figure 10-40 *Apply Update Button*

Endpoint Profile Policies

As previously described, the profiler probes collect attributes of endpoints. The endpoint profiler policies are similar to signatures, because they define the endpoint profiles themselves. For example, to match an Apple-Device profile, the endpoint must have a MAC address beginning with an Apple OUI.

Each endpoint profile policy defines a set of attributes that must be matched for a device to be classified as that endpoint type. ISE has a large number of predefined profile policies, and you can use the feed service to update those policies and provide new ones.

You can view the endpoint profile policies by navigating to **Policy > Profiling** or, as seen in Figure 10-41, **Work Centers > Profiler > Profiling Policies**.

Figure 10-41 *Profiling Policies Screen*

Each profile is listed as Cisco Provided or Administrator Modified. This classification ensures that the feed service will not override a profile that has been changed by the administrator.

Profiles are hierarchical and inclusive in nature, and you may pick any level to use within your authorization policies, enabling you to be very specific or broad in your rules. Figure 10-42 shows a parent policy named Android with a child policy named Android HTC, which in turn has another child policy named Android HTC-Phone (**Android > Android-HTC > Android-HTC-Phone**).

Figure 10-42   *Android Profile Hierarchy Example*

When building an authorization policy, you can choose to use the profile at any point in that chain. If you were to select Android, it would apply to all devices classified as Android as well as anything classified as a child profile of Android. For example, it would include Android-Sony-Ericsson-Tablet.

Figure 10-43 displays how a profile hierarchy is built within ISE.

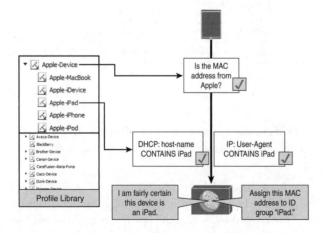

Figure 10-43   *Profiling Hierarchy Illustrated*

To serve as further examples of the hierarchy, there is a predefined authorization rule named Profiled Cisco IP Phones. This rule permits full access to the network and assigns permission to join the Voice VLAN—for all devices that are profiled as a Cisco-IP-Phone parent profile and any of the child profiles. Figure 10-44 shows this rule.

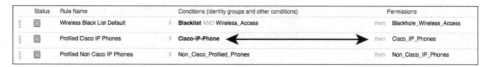

Figure 10-44   *Default Profiled Cisco IP Phones Rule*

Continuing to examine policy hierarchy and how it works, you will dig into a specific example in the next section, drilling into the endpoint details.

Context Visibility

In ISE 2.0 and earlier, the endpoints were hidden away under **Administration > Identity Management > Identities > Endpoints**. Beginning with ISE 2.1, the endpoints have been brought front and center with a major presence on the main dashboard, a full Profiler Work Center, and a new GUI area known as Context Visibility.

In the example network in the figures, there is a Cisco 7970 IP Phone, and that phone has been granted access from the Profiled Cisco IP Phones default authorization rule that you examined in Figure 10-44, which permits all endpoints matching a Cisco-IP-Phone profiler identity group.

Start by examining the endpoint attributes and comparing them to the profiling policies:

Step 1.   Navigate to **Context Visibility > Endpoints**.

Step 2.   Click **Endpoint Classification,** as shown in Figure 10-45.

Figure 10-45   *Endpoint Classification*

Step 3.   In the Endpoints dashlet in the upper left, click **ip-phones**. This begins to filter the list, as pointed out in Figure 10-46.

Figure 10-46   *Endpoint Classification, Filtered for ip-phones*

Step 4.   Click the MAC Address, **00:13:C3:07:F2:C8**, to display the endpoint details, shown in Figure 10-47.

Figure 10-47   *Endpoint Details: 00:13:C3:07:F2:C8*

Step 5.   Notice that the Endpoint Policy (the profile of the device) is Cisco-IP-Phone-7970 and the Identity Group Assignment is Cisco-IP-Phone, as you can see in Figure 10-48.

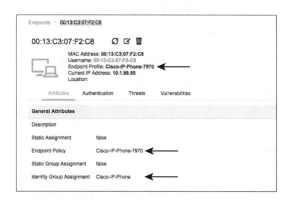

Figure 10-48   *Endpoint Policy and Identity Group Assignment*

Step 6.   Scroll down the endpoint details to see much more information. The database stores copious details about an endpoint to aid you in identification, classification, asset management, and visibility. Additionally, under the Other Attributes section, shown in Figure 10-49, you see that AuthorizationPolicyMatchedRule is Profiled Cisco IP Phones, which means the correct authorization rule is being matched.

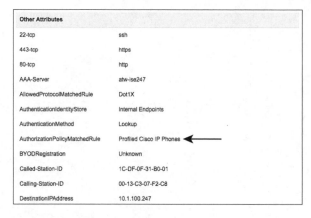

Figure 10-49   *Endpoint Details: AuthorizationPolicyMatchedRule*

Step 7.   Scroll further down in the endpoint details to see that the EndPointSource is the RADIUS probe, as shown in Figure 10-50. That means the RADIUS probe provided the most information needed to classify this device (which must have arrived from Device Sensor on the NAD).

DeviceRegistrationStatus	NotRegistered
ElapsedDays	1
EndPointMACAddress	00-13-C3-07-F2-C8
EndPointPolicy	Cisco-IP-Phone-7970
EndPointProfilerServer	atw-ise247.securitydemo.net
EndPointSource	RADIUS Probe
FailureReason	12514 EAP-TLS failed SSL/TLS handshake because of an unknown CA in the client certificates chain
IdentityGroup	Cisco-IP-Phone
InactiveDays	0
IsThirdPartyDeviceFlow	false
LastNmapScanTime	2016-Jun-01 20:48:31 UTC
Location	Location#All Locations#NorthAmerica#SJC
MACAddress	00:13:C3:07:F2:C8
MatchedPolicy	Cisco-IP-Phone-7970
MessageCode	3001

Figure 10-50   *Endpoint Details: EndPointSource*

Step 8.   Continue scrolling down the list of attributes and notice the CDP cached data from the switch that was sent to ISE via the RADIUS probe, as shown in Figure 10-51.

Total Certainty Factor	205
UseCase	Host Lookup
User-Name	00-13-C3-07-F2-C8
UserType	Host
allowEasyWiredSession	false
cdpCacheCapabilities	H;P;M
cdpCacheDeviceId	SEP0013C307F2C8
cdpCachePlatform	Cisco IP Phone 7970
cdpCacheVersion	SCCP70.9-1-1SR1S
dhcp-class-identifier	Cisco Systems, Inc. IP Phone CP-7970G
dhcp-client-identifier	01:00:13:c3:07:f2:c8
dhcp-parameter-request-list	1, 66, 6, 3, 15, 150, 35
dhcp-requested-address	10.1.99.50
host-name	SEP0013C307F2C8
ip	10.1.99.50
operating-system	Cisco IP Phone 7941, 7961, 7965G, or 7975
operating-system-result	Cisco IP Phone 7941, 7961, 7965G, or 7975

Figure 10-51   *Endpoint Details: CDP Data*

You can see these attributes of the endpoint, but how is that used within the profiling policy? To answer that question, examine the profiling policy hierarchy for the endpoint.

Step 9.   Navigate to either **Work Centers > Profiler > Profiling Policies > Cisco-Device** or **Policy > Profiling > Cisco-Device**. Cisco-Device is the top level of the profiling hierarchy for this endpoint. Clicking that will open the Cisco-Device profile, as displayed in Figure 10-52.

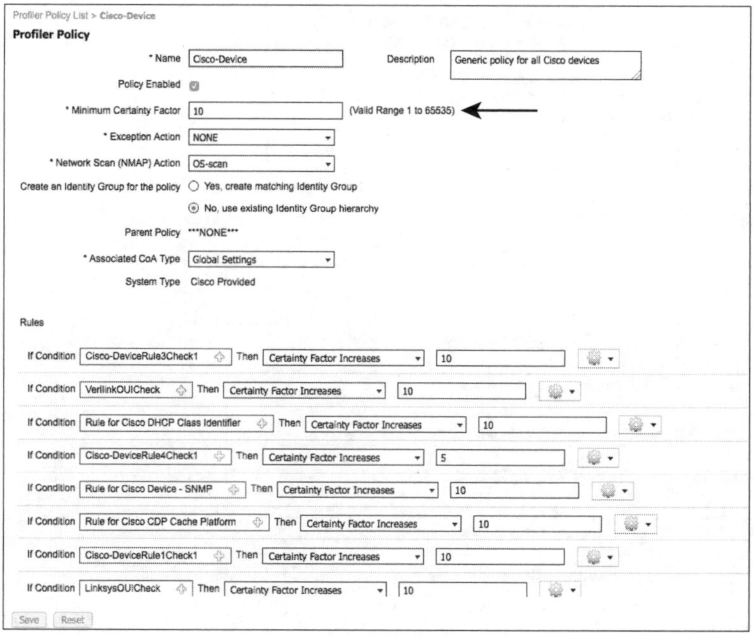

Figure 10-52   *Cisco-Device Profiling Policy*

Using Figure 10-52 as a reference point, note the following details:

- The Minimum Certainty Factor of this profile is 10. Certainty factor is an aggregate value between 1 and 65535. Each of the conditions at the bottom of the policy that are matched will add up to equal the endpoint's certainty value. The higher the value, the more certain the ISE Profiler is that an endpoint matches the specific profile.

- The OUI is Cisco Systems, Inc, as shown in Figure 10-53, and that matches the condition for Cisco-Device, as shown in Figure 10-54. This is one possible mapping that meets the minimum certainty value and should match the endpoint to this parent policy.

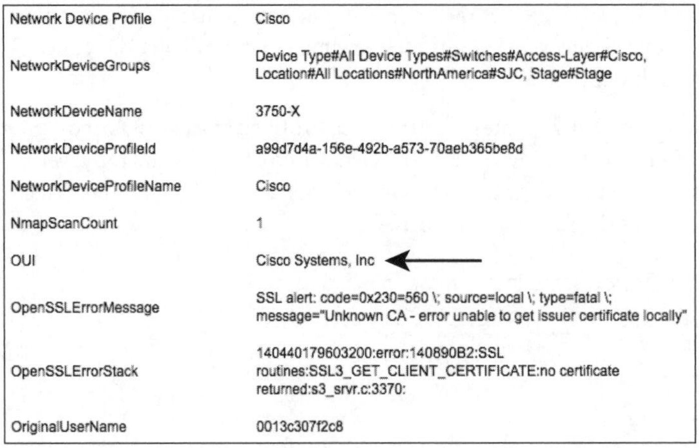

Network Device Profile	Cisco
NetworkDeviceGroups	Device Type#All Device Types#Switches#Access-Layer#Cisco, Location#All Locations#NorthAmerica#SJC, Stage#Stage
NetworkDeviceName	3750-X
NetworkDeviceProfileId	a99d7d4a-156e-492b-a573-70aeb365be8d
NetworkDeviceProfileName	Cisco
NmapScanCount	1
OUI	Cisco Systems, Inc
OpenSSLErrorMessage	SSL alert: code=0x230=560 \; source=local \; type=fatal \; message="Unknown CA - error unable to get issuer certificate locally"
OpenSSLErrorStack	140440179603200:error:140890B2:SSL routines:SSL3_GET_CLIENT_CERTIFICATE:no certificate returned:s3_srvr.c:3370:
OriginalUserName	0013c307f2c8

Figure 10-53 *OUI of the Endpoint*

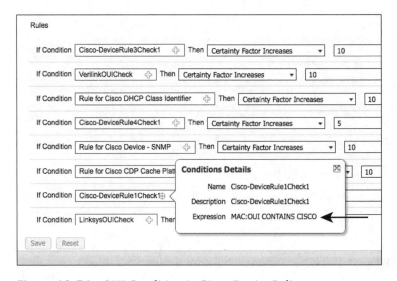

Figure 10-54 *OUI Condition in Cisco-Device Policy*

■ There is a Network Scan (NMAP) Action set to OS-Scan. For this action to occur, there must be a condition in the profile that has a result to trigger the network scan. Figure 10-55 displays this mapping of the condition to the action.

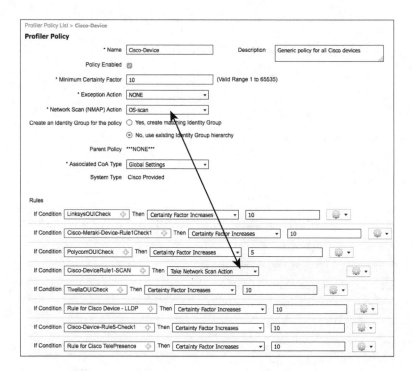

Figure 10-55 *Network Scan Action and Condition with Scan Result*

■ This profiling policy has a tremendous number of conditions, most of which add a certainty value of 5 or 10. The certainty value only needs to be a minimum of 10 to match the profile, so matching any one of these conditions will most likely equal a match.

Step 10. Continuing down the tree of the profiling policy, navigate to **Work Centers > Profiler > Profiling Policies > Cisco Device > Cisco-IP-Phone**, as shown in Figure 10-56, to examine the conditions that are used for this policy.

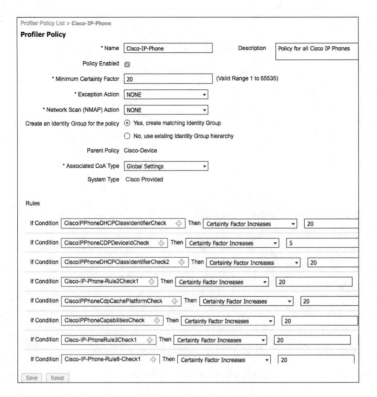

Figure 10-56   *Cisco-IP-Phone Profiling Policy*

Using this profile as a reference point, note the following details:

■ To be compared to this profiling policy, the device must first match its parent policy. In this case, the device has to match the Cisco-Device policy before these conditions will ever be examined.

■ The Minimum Certainty Factor of this profile is 20, as shown in Figure 10-56. Certainty factor is an aggregate value between 1 and 65535. Each of the conditions at the bottom of the policy may add more certainty to this profile, if they are matched.

■ The CDP Cache, shown in Figure 10-51, shows that the cdpCachePlatform attribute was sent as Cisco IP Phone 7970.

■ Figure 10-57 shows the Cisco-IP-Phone profile policy uses a condition looking for the cdpCachePlatform value to contain Cisco IP Phone and increase the certainty by 20.

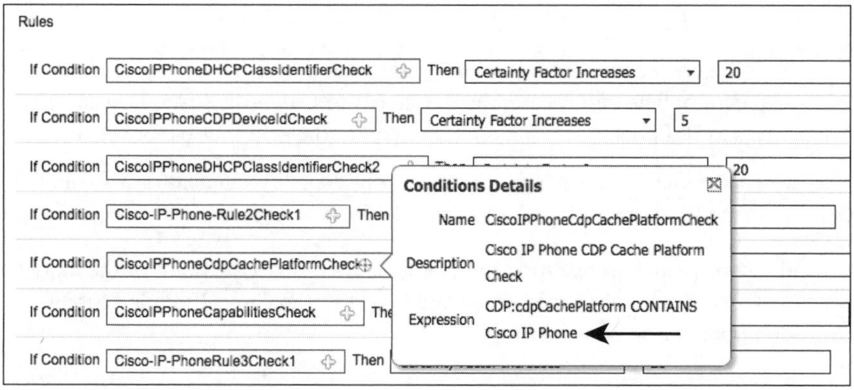

Rules

If Condition	CiscoIPPhoneDHCPClassIdentifierCheck	Then	Certainty Factor Increases ▾	20
If Condition	CiscoIPPhoneCDPDeviceIdCheck	Then	Certainty Factor Increases ▾	5
If Condition	CiscoIPPhoneDHCPClassIdentifierCheck2			20
If Condition	Cisco-IP-Phone-Rule2Check1	Then		
If Condition	CiscoIPPhoneCdpCachePlatformCheck			
If Condition	CiscoIPPhoneCapabilitiesCheck	The		
If Condition	Cisco-IP-PhoneRule3Check1	Then		

Conditions Details

Name   CiscoIPPhoneCdpCachePlatformCheck

Description   Cisco IP Phone CDP Cache Platform Check

Expression   CDP:cdpCachePlatform CONTAINS Cisco IP Phone ◄——

Figure 10-57   *cdpCachePlatform Condition*

This step examined Cisco-IP-Phone, but what does it take to get one step further—to reach the final Cisco-IP-Phone-7970 profile?

Step 11. Navigate to **Work Centers > Profiler > Profiling Policies > Cisco Device > Cisco-IP-Phone > Cisco-IP-Phone-7970** to examine conditions used in this policy, as shown Figure 10-58.

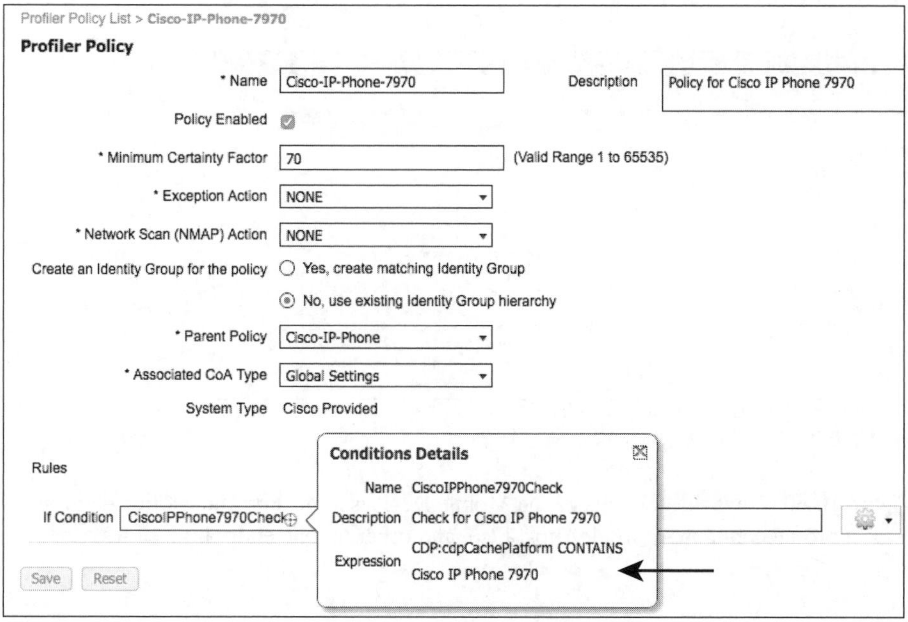

Profiler Policy List > Cisco-IP-Phone-7970

Profiler Policy

| * Name | Cisco-IP-Phone-7970 | Description | Policy for Cisco IP Phone 7970 |

Policy Enabled ☑

* Minimum Certainty Factor 70   (Valid Range 1 to 65535)

* Exception Action NONE ▾

* Network Scan (NMAP) Action NONE ▾

Create an Identity Group for the policy ◯ Yes, create matching Identity Group

◉ No, use existing Identity Group hierarchy

* Parent Policy Cisco-IP-Phone ▾

* Associated CoA Type Global Settings ▾

System Type Cisco Provided

Conditions Details

Name   CiscoIPPhone7970Check

Description   Check for Cisco IP Phone 7970

Expression   CDP:cdpCachePlatform CONTAINS Cisco IP Phone 7970 ◄——

Rules

| If Condition | CiscoIPPhone7970Check | | | ⚙ ▾ |

Save   Reset

Figure 10-58   *Cisco-IP-Phone-7970 Profile*

Using Figure 10-58 as a reference, note the following details:

- To be compared to this profiling policy, the device must first match its parent policy. In this case, the device has to match the Cisco-Device and Cisco-IP-Phone policy before these conditions will ever be looked at.

- The profile itself has only one condition: the cdpCachePlatform attribute is Cisco IP Phone 7970, which Figure 10-51 has confirmed.

Rarely would you build an authorization policy that is specific to the point of the model number of the Cisco IP Phone; instead, you would just use the Cisco-IP-Phone parent policy in your authorization policies.

Logical Profiles

After ISE 1.0 was first released, many customers quickly requested the capability to group profiles that are not hierarchical—for example, to create a profile group named IP-Phones that contains all the individual profiles of IP phones, Cisco and non-Cisco alike. Cisco answered that request in ISE 1.2 by introducing the concept of *logical profiles*, which are groupings of profiles. ISE version 2.1 adds more logical profiles, such as Cameras, Gaming Devices, Home Network Devices, Medical Devices, and more.

To examine the logical profiles in ISE, navigate to **Work Centers > Profiler > Profiling Policies > Logical Profiles**, as shown in Figure 10-59.

Figure 10-59 *Logical Profiles*

Figure 10-60 shows the contents of the Mobile Devices logical profile. Notice that the logical profile contains Android, Apple-iPad, and other mobile endpoint profiles.

Logical Profiles List > **Mobile Devices**

Logical Profile

* Name Mobile Devices   Description Default logical profile for mobile devices.

* Policy Assignment

Available Policies:

2Wire-Device
3Com-Device
Aastra-Device
Aastra-IP-Phone
Aerohive-Access-Point
Aerohive-Device
American-Power-Conversion-Device
Android-Amazon

Assigned Policies:

Android
Apple-iPad
Apple-iPhone
Apple-iPod
BlackBerry
HP-TouchPad-Tablet
HTC-Device
Microsoft-Surface-Tablet

Save   Reset

▼ **Logical Profile**

Endpoints in Logical Profile

Show

Endpoint policy	▲ MAC Address	IP Address
Android-Samsung	D0:87:E2:12:B2:04	10.1.41.101

Figure 10-60 *Mobile Devices Logical Profile*

Logical profiles are not limited to only those defined by Cisco. You can also create your own.

ISE Profiler and CoA

When using an endpoint profile as an attribute within your authorization policy, you will be providing differentiated results for specific profiles. However, there is often a "chicken and the egg" phenomenon happening simultaneously. You cannot provide the right access to a device without knowing what that device is, yet you cannot find out what the device is without providing some level of access so the endpoint will be active on the network and ISE can identify the endpoint profile.

Enter the concept of change of authorization (CoA). Without CoA, the only time a policy server such as ISE is permitted to send a command to the NAD is during a response to an authentication request. This created numerous issues because there would not be a way to disconnect a bad actor from the network or change the level of access an endpoint is permitted to have based on a newer data element that has been learned by the profiling engine. The current authorization to the network would have to sustain until the next time the endpoint has to authenticate.

Because the authorization policy can be configured to send different results for an endpoint before it is profiled, and then send another level of authorization after the endpoint profile becomes more solidified, and the final result after the endpoint profile is definitely known, you cannot wait for the next authentication request each time. Instead, the profiling engine can use CoA to change the level for each state the endpoint goes through. Stated a bit more succinctly, because ISE learns more about endpoints at random time intervals, ISE can send a CoA to the network access device to have a different level of access applied to the session.

There are two main areas for configuring CoA with profiling. A global setting enables CoA for profiling in the ISE deployment, and a CoA can be configured on a per-profile basis.

Global CoA

To enable CoA for profiling in the ISE cube, and to configure the CoA type used by pro-filing globally, navigate to either **Administration > System > Settings > Profiler** or **Work Centers > Profiler > Settings** (as shown in Figure 10-61).

Figure 10-61 *Profiler Global Settings*

As shown in Figure 10-61, the default setting is No CoA. Click the drop-down list, as shown in Figure 10-62, to see the other choices: Port Bounce and Reauth.

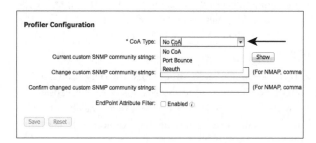

Figure 10-62 *Profiler CoA Types*

The Port Bounce CoA performs a **shutdown** on the switch port and then perform a **no shutdown** to reenable it. This causes the link state to change, simulating the unplug-ging and plugging in of network cable. The benefit to this type of CoA is that many devices will try to renew their DHCP assigned IP addresses when the link state changes. Additionally, there is a built-in failsafe to never send a Port Bounce when more than one MAC address is seen on the switch port. That failsafe is in place to ensure there is no negative impact on IP telephony. When more than one MAC address exists on the switch port, a Reauth will be sent instead.

The Reauth CoA instructs the NAD to initiate a new authentication to the endpoint, sending another EAPoL Start message to trigger the supplicant to send the credentials again, or (in the case of MAB) the NAD will resend a RADIUS authentication with the endpoint MAC address as the identity credential. Either way, there is a new authentication, but that authentication maintains the same authentication session ID. By maintaining the session ID, ISE is able to tie together the multiple states of the endpoint.

Regardless of the CoA type used, ISE has now forced a new authentication attempt so that a different authorization result can be sent to the NAD, providing the correct level of network access with the latest profiling information being used. However, setting a global CoA type to Port Bounce is not recommended. The safer bet is to use the Reauth option.

After the profiler CoA is enabled globally, a CoA is automatically sent for any endpoint that transitions from unknown to any known profile.

Per-Profile CoA

ISE 1.2 added a setting to profiles that enables an administrator to control her own destiny with CoA. This came about with the need to send a Port Bounce CoA for certain devices only, while using the global Reauth CoA for the remaining endpoints. This is known as the *per-profile CoA*. When a CoA type is configured for a profile, it is used when an endpoint is classified as that profile type. Figure 10-63 shows this setting.

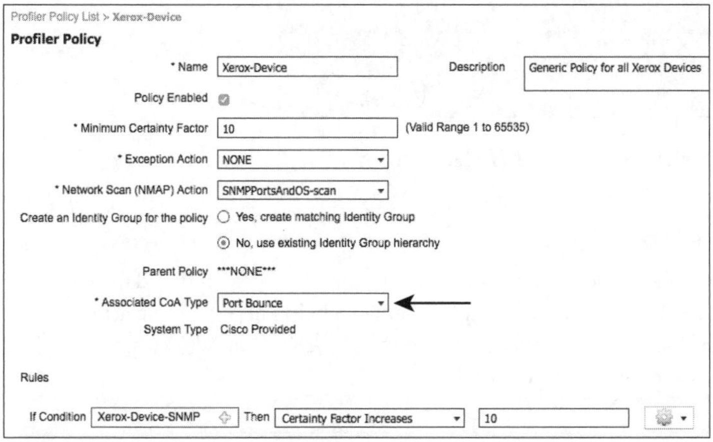

Figure 10-63   *Per-Profile CoA*

As shown in Figure 10-63, a device that is profiled as a Xerox-Device now triggers a Port Bounce CoA, causing the link to go down and back up again, which in turn triggers the endpoint to request a new IP address from the DHCP server. This is very useful when a device is using MAB and needs to be assigned to a different VLAN.

Global Profiler Settings

Additional settings related to profiling are set at the global (system-wide) level, not just the global CoA type. These include the SNMP community strings for NMAP SNMP walks and the enable setting for endpoint attribute filtering.

Configure SNMP Settings for Probes

The SNMPQUERY probe uses the SNMP community strings that are defined as part of the NAD entry under **Administration > Network Resources > Network Devices**. Theoretically, each NAD could have a different community string.

As described in the "Network Scan (NMAP)" section, NMAP uses SNMP to examine endpoints. For this to function, the ISE Profiler must know what SNMP community strings to use. The community strings to use are configured within **Work Centers > Profiler > Settings** by listing each community string one-by-one with a comma separating each value. After they are saved, the two text boxes are erased, and you must click the **Show** button to see the configured strings, as shown in Figure 10-64.

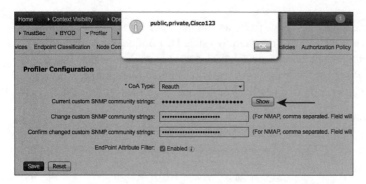

Figure 10-64 *Global SNMP Settings for NMAP Probe*

Endpoint Attribute Filtering

Profiler can and does collect a lot of data about endpoints. It stores all that data and replicates it to the other ISE nodes in the deployment. To help keep the replication traffic down, ISE has the EndPoint Attribute Filter, which you enable at **Work Centers > Profiler > Settings**, as shown in Figure 10-65.

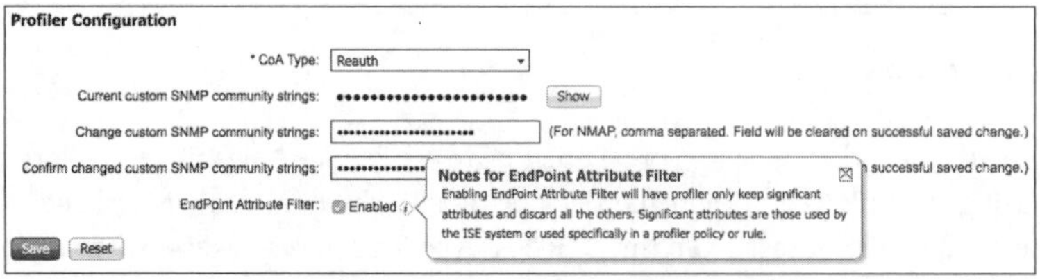

Figure 10-65 *Enabling EndPoint Attribute Filter*

When the filtering is enabled, Profiler will build a whitelist of attributes that are used in the existing profiler policies. In other words, Profiler examines every policy that is enabled and creates a list of attributes that are needed for all those policies. Only those attributes will now be collected and stored in the endpoint database.

Use of the EndPoint Attribute Filter is highly recommended but only after a deployment has been up and running properly for an extended period of time. If you use it right away, you run the risk of not profiling all of your initial devices, because it is theoretically possible to ignore attributes that will be needed to uniquely identify the endpoint type.

NMAP Scan Subnet Exclusions

Another global setting for the Profiler service is NMAP Scan Subnet Exclusions, shown in Figure 10-66. Many organizations have special devices that do not like to be scanned, or that can be negatively impacted if you scan them, and therefore the organization prohibits it, such as medical devices or manufacturing equipment. This setting enables administrators to exclude those networks from being scanned by the NMAP engine.

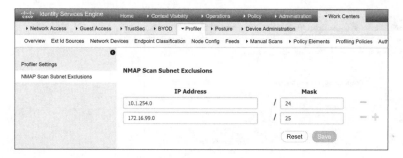

Figure 10-66   *NMAP Scan Subnet Exclusions*

Profiles in Authorization Policies

As you saw with the profiled Cisco-IP-Phone authorization rule earlier in this chapter, the profile can be used as a condition of an authorization policy rule in the form of an Identity Group. Originally, ISE required an Identity Group in order to use any of the profiling policies in the rule; however, it has evolved into the ability to use the profile directly (called the EndPointPolicy).

Endpoint Identity Groups

Local identities within the ISE database may be in the form of user identities or endpoint identities. Identity Groups may contain multiple identities, although an identity (user or endpoint) can be a member of only one Identity Group at a time.

To create an Identity Group based on the profile, select the **Yes, Create Matching Identity Group** option on the profile, as displayed in Figure 10-67.

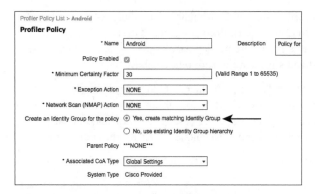

Figure 10-67 *Create Matching Identity Group*

If that option is selected, the matching Identity Group can be found under **Administration > Identity Management > Groups > Endpoint Identity Groups** (as shown in Figure 10-68).

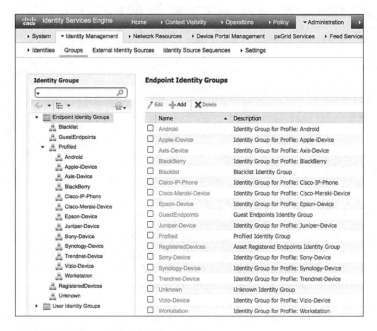

Figure 10-68 *Endpoint Identity Groups*

In ISE 1.0, using endpoint Identity Groups was the only way to include profiles in authorization policies. The use of these Identity Groups for profiling has been deprecated in favor of using the actual endpoint profile or logical profiles directly in the authorization policy. It is a lot more flexible and less operationally expensive.

Therefore, starting with ISE 1.2, endpoint Identity Groups are used for a different purpose. They are used for more of a MAC address management (MAM) model, where you can create a static list of MAC addresses to be authorized specifically. For example, you could create a list of all Apple iPads that are owned by the company so they can be differentiated from personally owned iPads.

The Blacklist Identity Group is a perfect example of Identity Group usage in this manner. If a user's personal device is stolen, he can log in to the My Devices Portal and identify the device as Stolen, as shown in Figure 10-69. This immediately adds the endpoint to the Blacklist group, as shown in Figure 10-70. The device is now denied network access by default, as shown in Figure 10-71.

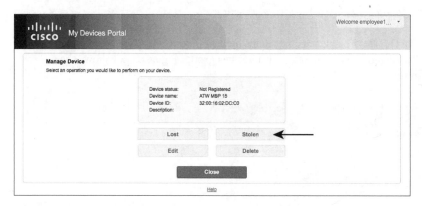

Figure 10-69 *Identifying an Endpoint as Stolen*

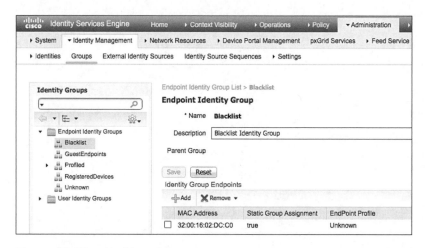

Figure 10-70 *Blacklisted Devices*

Figure 10-71 *Default Blacklist Authorization Rule*

From the My Devices Portal, selecting Reinstate (see Figure 10-72) moves the device from the Blacklist group to the RegisteredDevices group. Figure 10-73 shows the empty Blacklist group.

Figure 10-72 *Reinstating the Endpoint*

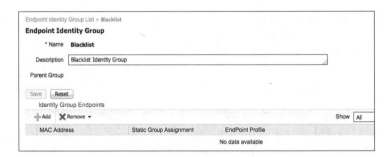

Figure 10-73 *Empty Blacklist Endpoint Identity Group*

EndPointPolicy

Beginning with ISE 1.2, Identity Groups are no longer the way to apply policy based on the endpoint's profile. Policy is now built with the actual profile through the use of the Endpoints:EndPointPolicy attribute.

To see the use of the profile in a policy, you will duplicate the existing onboarding authorization rule and then modify that new rule to use the Android profile, which does not have a corresponding Identity Group.

From the ISE GUI, do the following:

Step 1.   Navigate to **Policy > Authorization.**

Step 2.   **Duplicate** the default Employee_Onboarding rule.

Step 3.   Name the rule **Employee_Onboarding_Android.**

Step 4.   Add a new condition to the existing Wireless_802.1X and MSCHAP conditions of **Endpoints > EndPointPolicy.**

Step 5.   Choose **Android** from the list of endpoint policies.

Figure 10-74 shows the resulting authorization rule.

	Status	Rule Name		Conditions (identity groups and other conditions)		Permissions
	☑	Wireless Black List Default	If	**Blacklist** AND Wireless_Access	then	Blackhole_Wireless_Access
	☑	Profiled Cisco IP Phones	If	**Cisco-IP-Phone**	then	Cisco_IP_Phones
	☑	Profiled Non Cisco IP Phones	If	Non_Cisco_Profiled_Phones	then	Non_Cisco_IP_Phones
	☑	Compliant_Devices_Access	If	(Network_Access_Authentication_Passed AND Compliant_Devices)	then	PermitAccess
	☑	Employee_EAP-TLS	If	(Wireless_802.1X AND BYOD_Is_Registered AND EAP-TLS AND MAC_in_SAN)	then	PermitAccess AND BYOD
	☑	Employee_Onboarding_Android	If	(Wireless_802.1X AND EAP-MSCHAPv2 AND EndPoints:EndPointPolicy EQUALS Android)	then	NSP_Onboard AND BYOD ◄—
	☑	Employee_Onboarding	If	(Wireless_802.1X AND EAP-MSCHAPv2)	then	NSP_Onboard AND BYOD
	☑	Unknown Endpoint	If	**Unknown** AND Network_Access_Authentication_Passed	then	Limited Access AND CollectData
	☑	Basic_Authenticated_Access	If	Network_Access_Authentication_Passed	then	PermitAccess
	☑	Default	if no matches, then	DenyAccess		

Figure 10-74   *Authorization Rule Using EndPointPolicy Condition*

Throughout all of this, always keep in mind the simplicity of using logical profiles to streamline your authorization policies, and limit the number of individual EndPointPolicies that you need to add to your authorization rules.

Importing Profiles

As you have read, you can create profiles as the ISE administrator or have them downloaded via the profiler feed service. They can also be exported and imported with ISE. This is extremely useful for value-add from Cisco partners; or even the ability to import specific profiles for your individual business vertical.

For example, Craig Hyps, introduced earlier (Principal TME for ISE), has devised an entire medical industry package that contains over 250 medical device profiles. In this case, if you are an ISE administrator focused on the healthcare vertical, you could download this medical NAC package and import all 250+ profiles. Customers who are not in the medical industry would not need to waste any profiling CPU cycles looking for endpoints that are not relevant for their environment.

This approach to profile distribution is similar to that used to distribute signature packs with IDSs. Signature packs are a way to ensure the IDS keeps the important signature types in memory and does not install the unimportant ones. Figure 10-75 shows the medical NAC profile package being selected for import in the GUI at **Work Centers > Profiler > Profiling Policies > Import**. The import could be a single profile or a combined package of many profiles. The profile or series of profiles will be in a single XML file.

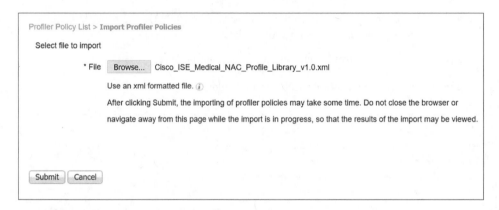

Figure 10-75   *Importing a Profile or Profile Package*

After clicking Submit, the import begins and a status bar appears, as shown in Figure 10-76. After the import is complete, all the imported profiles are now part of the profile policies and all endpoints in the database undergo a re-profiling process.

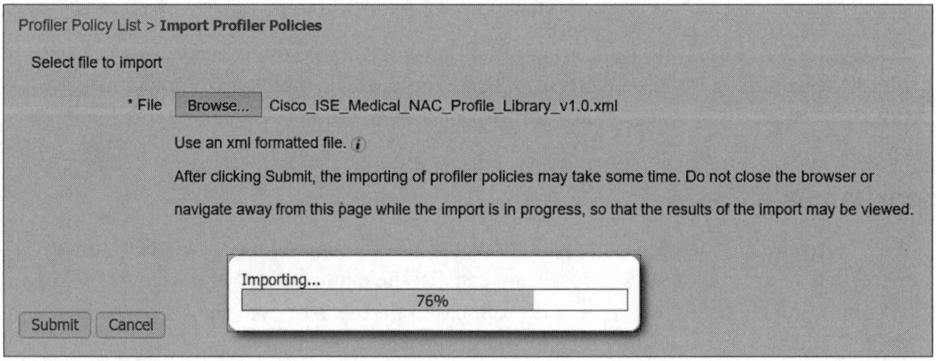

Profiler Policy List > **Import Profiler Policies**

Select file to import

* File   Browse...   Cisco_ISE_Medical_NAC_Profile_Library_v1.0.xml

Use an xml formatted file. ⓘ

After clicking Submit, the importing of profiler policies may take some time. Do not close the browser or navigate away from this page while the import is in progress, so that the results of the import may be viewed.

Importing...
76%

Submit   Cancel

Figure 10-76   *Importing Status*

Verifying Profiling

There are a few key places to check to verify profiling operation: within the ISE GUI and by examining the network device itself.

The Dashboard

The dashboard is always the first screen you see when you log in to the ISE GUI. The dashboard has two places to look to see if profiling is working, as shown in Figure 10-77:

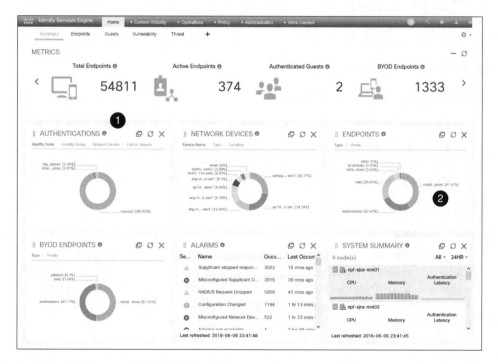

Figure 10-77   *Cisco ISE Dashboard*

1. **Total Endpoints counter:** Shows the number of endpoints that are currently in the endpoint database. Clicking it launches an endpoints-focused dashboard.

2. **Endpoints widget:** Shows the breakdown of the known endpoints and their profiles.

Endpoints Dashboard

From the ISE Home screen, several dashboards are available, such as Summary, Endpoints, and Guests. Selecting the Endpoints Dashboard displays a screen similar to what you see in Figure 10-78. This dashboard is focused solely on displaying information about endpoints.

Figure 10-78   *Endpoints Dashboard*

Examining Figure 10-78, the following two areas of the dashboard are called out:

1. **Endpoints widget:** Shows the breakdown of the known endpoints and their profiles.

2. **Endpoint Categories widget:** Shows the categorization of the endpoints, sorted by Identity Group, or even by operating system. Clicking one of the categories launches another window into the Context Visibility tooling, prefiltered on the category that you clicked.

Context Visibility

Context Visibility is a fancy label for "asset inventory on steroids." Beginning with ISE 2.1, it is the go-to method of examining the endpoints on the network and drilling into the data available in the system about those endpoints. Navigating to **Context Visibility > Endpoints > Endpoints Classification** is a great way to examine the profiling activity in your environment and what endpoints have been identified and classified. Figure 10-79 shows the Endpoints Classification dashboard within Context Visibility.

Figure 10-79   *Context Visibility > Endpoints > Endpoint Classification*

Examining Figure 10-79, the following three areas of the dashboard are called out:

1. **Endpoints widget:** Shows the breakdown of the known endpoints and their profiles.

2. **Endpoint Categories widget:** Shows the categorization of the endpoints, sorted by Identity Group, or even by operating system. Clicking on one of the categories will filter the Endpoints list at the bottom.

3. **Endpoints List:** A filterable and exportable list of endpoints and their context data that is available within the database.

Device Sensor Show Commands

In addition to the ISE GUI, Cisco network devices can aid in verifying that profiling is happening correctly. With Cisco switches that run device-sensor, there is a **show** command specifically for the device-sensor capability in the switch: **show device-sensor cache [all | mac]**. Example 10-4 shows the output of the **show** command. Although the values may not make a lot of sense to a human being, they show that the device-sensor is collecting and caching profiling data.

Example 10-4   show device-sensor cache all *Command Output*

```
3750-X# show device-sensor cache all
Device: 0050.5687.0004 on port GigabitEthernet1/0/2
-------------------------------------------------
Proto Type:Name                   Len Value
dhcp    43:vendor-encapsulated-optio    5 2B 03 DC 01 00
dhcp    55:parameter-request-list      14 37 0C 01 0F 03 06 2C 2E 2F 1F 21 F9 2B FC
dhcp    60:class-identifier            10 3C 08 4D 53 46 54 20 35 2E 30
dhcp    12:host-name                   12 0C 0A 58 59 5A 2D 42 69 6F 4D 65 64
dhcp    61:client-identifier            9 3D 07 01 00 50 56 87 00 04
dhcp    77:user-class-id               13 4D 0B 73 79 6D 75 6E 75 73 2D 62 69 6F
```

Triggered NetFlow: A Woland-Santuka Pro Tip

Vivek Santuka, CCIE No. 17621, is a Consulting Systems Engineer at Cisco Systems who focuses on ISE for Cisco's largest customers around the world. Aaron Woland and Vivek devised the methodology discussed in this section, which they like to call "Triggered NetFlow."

As you read in the "NetFlow Probe" section, the challenge with using NetFlow is that it requires de-duplication capabilities, scalable flow collection, and so forth. However, it is incredibly useful for identifying general-use compute platforms that are used in environment-specific ways, such as medical devices based on the Windows operating system. It's also very useful in identifying IoT devices that are otherwise unknown.

The best way to help identify these devices that are unique to an organization's environment is to examine the traffic patterns. For example, it's possible that a hospital's IV pump may only be uniquely identified by seeing the destination systems that it communicates to within the hospital data center.

In those cases, NetFlow is the perfect identification tool because it will match on the traffic flow instead of endpoint attributes. However, that does not mean it's operationally feasible to enable NetFlow in the entire organization and risk overwhelming ISE with all those flows.

Triggered NetFlow is a deployment methodology designed to flip NetFlow on only when and where it is needed, and turn it back off immediately afterward. It is not a new technology, but a combination of existing technologies within ISE and the Cisco switching infrastructure. The overall concept follows the flow illustrated in Figure 10-80. With any successful authentication where the endpoint profile is unknown, the authorization result will include a Security Group Tag (let's just call the SGT "CollectData"). When that SGT is received by the switch, an Embedded Event Manager (EEM) script is executed that enables NetFlow on that switch port.

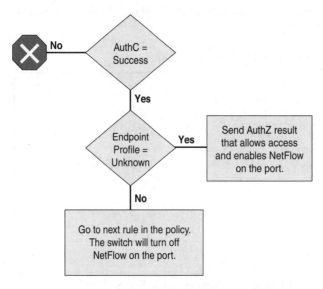

Figure 10-80 *Logical Flow for Triggered NetFlow*

The use of this solution requires that you have an understanding of how ISE authentications and authorizations work, how to use the EEM, and how to configure NetFlow within Cisco IOS. Knowledge of how TrustSec (aka Security Group Tags) functions is not required, but it can't hurt.

There are many different ways to accomplish this same task. The method outlined and tested by Aaron and Vivek is just one such example. If you have experience using the switch features and want to deviate from this specific prescribed solution, go right ahead! Please do, and perhaps post on the ISE forums (http://cs.co/ise-community/) so others may benefit from your tweaks. With that in mind, Example 10-5 shows the EEM script that Aaron and Vivek used, while Example 10-6 shows the example NetFlow configuration.

Example 10-5 *Sample EEM Script for Triggered NetFlow*

```
event manager applet CaptureData
 event syslog pattern "Authorization succeeded for client"
 action 1.0 regexp "Interface (.*) AuditSessionID" "$_syslog_msg" match intname
 action 1.1 cli command "enable"
 action 1.2 cli command "show auth sess int $intname | i SGT"
 action 1.3 set sgttag "0000-0"
 action 1.4 regexp "000C-0" "$sgttag"
 action 1.5 regexp "SGT:  (.*)" "$_cli_result" match sgttag
 action 1.6 regexp "000C-0" "$sgttag"
 action 1.7 if $_regexp_result eq "1"
 action 1.8  cli command "conf t"
 action 1.9  cli command "int $intname"
 action 2.0  cli command "ip flow ingress"
 action 2.1 else
 action 2.2  cli command "conf t"
 action 2.3  cli command "int $intname"
 action 2.4  cli command "no ip flow ingress"
 action 2.5 end
```

Example 10-6 *Sample NetFlow Configuration*

```
flow record ise-flows
 description export only flows needed by ise
 match datalink mac source-address
 match ipv4 protocol
 match ipv4 source address
 match ipv4 destination address
 match transport source-port
 match transport destination-port
 match transport tcp flags
!
flow exporter ISE
 description Export to ISE PSN1
 destination 10.1.100.234
 source TenGigabitEthernet1/1/1
 transport udp 9996
!
flow exporter ISE-flows
!
flow monitor ISE-Flows
 description Used for ISE Profiler
 record ise-flows
 exporter ISE
```

```
 cache timeout active 60
!
flow monitor CaptureData
 record ise-flows
!
flow monitor test
```

Figure 10-81 shows the SGT that was created to trigger the NetFlow application on the port.

Figure 10-81   *CollectData Security Group Tag*

Figure 10-82 shows the authorization rule for the unknown endpoints, which permits a limited network access and includes the CollectData SGT.

Figure 10-82   *Unknown Endpoint Authorization Rule*

We hope you found this pro tip useful, even if it was just to help you consider how to leverage existing technologies to enable a better ISE deployment for your specific needs for your organization.

Summary

This chapter introduced the importance of device profiling for any network environment where identity is being enforced. It also introduced the new Context Visibility tooling within ISE 2.1, the probe deployment options, logical profiles, importing profiles, and feed service usage.

There are many probes that Cisco ISE can use, and the value of each probe is specific to your environment and needs. There is a direct correlation between the difficulty in deploying a probe and its inherent value to your Secure Access deployment, so ensure that you are using what is best for your organization.

Chapter 11

Bootstrapping Network Access Devices

This chapter covers the following topics:

- Cisco Catalyst Switches
- Cisco Wireless LAN Controllers

I don't know about you, but when I go to put on my boots, I have to grab the bootstraps to pull the boots onto my feet. I can't wear them, or even begin to lace them up, without first pulling them on. So, "bootstrapping" is a critical step for me to be successful in wearing my chosen boots. This is where the metaphor "bootstrapping" came from. In the context of this chapter, it refers to configuring a device to work with Cisco ISE secure network access. Before end users attempt to connect their devices to the network and have them be authenticated, the network access device (NAD) must be configured to authenticate those devices.

Two NAD types are the focus of this chapter, Cisco Catalyst Switches and Cisco Wireless LAN Controllers (WLC). For both NAD types, the focus is on establishing a predictable, repeatable configuration that follows Cisco best practices for most situations.

Cisco Catalyst Switches

Cisco started as a networking company, taking the lead in the world for multiprotocol routers and very shortly thereafter leading the world in network switching. Cisco now has the vast majority of the market share for switching infrastructure. Because of that long-standing market leadership position, some people might not expect Cisco to continue to innovate its switching technology. Of course, that's not Cisco's style. Even though Cisco has more ports configured for 802.1X in the world than any other vendor, it continues working to make the authentication experience even better and more feature-rich. With that continuous innovation of switching products comes a bit of confusion as to which versions support which new features. This section is intended to clear up any confusion you might have.

The following list classifies the switch capabilities into a few unofficial groupings intended to simplify the evolution of Cisco switches and facilitate their discussion in this chapter:

- **Classic IOS:** This grouping includes IOS 12.2(55)SE versions. Compared to non-Cisco switches, these switches are considered to be rock-solid workhorses, very stable and feature rich—but still missing some of the newer advances in network authentication, profiling, and TrustSec. These are still the most common switches encountered in the field during Secure Access deployments—they are tried and true and die-hard. Because they don't have the advanced profiling capabilities, such as Device Sensor, they are configured for SNMP polling from ISE instead.

- **IOS 15.x:** This grouping includes the IOS 15.x flavors and their IOS-XE counterparts. These platforms add some incredible features and functions, such as the IOS Device Sensor described in detail in Chapter 10, "Profiling Basics and Visibility." With the Device Sensor capabilities, the switch collects profiling attributes locally and sends them to ISE in a RADIUS accounting packet. With this capability, the switch should not be configured for SNMP polling; instead, it must be configured to collect the profiling attributes. Overall, the configuration style on these switches is the same as that for the classic IOS switches, but some differences exist due to the more advanced capabilities.

- **C3PL:** The newer 15.2.x and IOS-XE 3.6.x switches follow the Cisco Common Classification Policy Language (C3PL) style of configuration. This provides some intriguing and advanced authentication features, as well as a very different configuration style that has powerful options, but it can be confusing when learning how to use it. However, many administrators who start to use this configuration style end up loving it and rarely want to go back to the classic methods of configuration. At the time of writing, this is the least common type of deployment in the field, but it is gaining in popularity.

Global Configuration Settings for Classic IOS and IOS 15.x Switches

This section covers the global configuration of all the non-C3PL switches participating in the Secure Access System. In other words, this section focuses on the configuration of both the classic IOS and IOS 15.x switches. C3PL switches are covered later in the chapter, in the section "Common Classification Policy Language (C3PL) Switches."

Configure Certificates on a Switch

Within the Cisco Secure Access system, the switch performs the URL redirection for web authentication and the redirection of the discovery traffic from the posture to the Policy Service Node.

Performing URL redirection at the Layer 2 access (edge) device is a vast improvement over previous NAC solutions that require an appliance to capture web traffic and perform redirection to a web authentication page. This simplifies the deployment for both web authentication and the posture agent discovery process. The switch needs to be configured to redirect nonencrypted HTTP traffic and encrypted HTTP traffic (HTTPS).

From global configuration mode on the switch, perform the following steps:

Step 1. Set the DNS domain name on the switch.

Cisco IOS does not allow for certificates, or even self-generated keys, to be created and installed without first defining a DNS domain name on the device.

Type **ip domain-name** *domain-name* at the global configuration prompt.

Step 2. Generate keys to be used for HTTPS.

Type **crypto key generate rsa general-keys modulus 2048** at the global configuration prompt.

Enable the Switch HTTP/HTTPS Server

The embedded HTTP/S server in Cisco IOS Software is used to grab HTTP traffic from the user and redirect that user's browser to the Centralized Web Authentication (CWA) portal, a device registration portal, or even to the Mobile Device Management (MDM) onboarding portal. This same function is used for redirecting the Posture Agent's traffic to the Policy Service Node.

To enable the HTTP server, follow these steps:

Step 1. Enable the HTTP server in global configuration mode.

Type **ip http server** at the global configuration prompt.

Step 2. Enable the HTTP Secure (HTTPS) server.

Type **ip http secure-server** at the global configuration prompt.

Many organizations want to ensure that this redirection process using the switch's internal HTTP server is decoupled from the management of the switch itself. If you are not using HTTP for management, then decoupling the HTTP server is highly encouraged. You can accomplish this by following the next two steps.

Step 3. Type **ip http active-session-modules none** in global configuration mode.

Step 4. Type **ip http secure-active-session-modules none** in global configuration mode.

Global AAA Commands

The following steps walk you through the commands to enable and configure authentication, authorization, and accounting (AAA) from global configuration mode. Each step includes a description of why you type the command and what it does.

Step 1.   Enable AAA on the access switch(es).

By default, the AAA subsystem of the Cisco switch is disabled. Prior to enabling the AAA subsystem, none of the required commands are available in the configuration. Enable AAA as follows:

```
C3560X(config)# aaa new-model
```

> **Note**   An interesting tidbit of history is that the command **aaa new-model** got its name because the AAA subsystem was replaced back in the 9.x days of Cisco IOS. The original AAA subsystem was deprecated and eventually removed from IOS, and now the "new model" is the only available subsystem. Thanks to Pete Karelis for that fun bit of trivia.

Step 2.   Create an authentication method for 802.1X.

An authentication method is required to instruct the switch to use a particular group of RADIUS servers for 802.1X authentication requests. Create the authentication method as follows:

```
C3560X(config)# aaa authentication dot1x default group radius
```

Step 3.   Create an authorization method for 802.1X.

The method created in Step 2 enables the user/device identity (username/password or certificate) to be validated by the RADIUS Server. However, simply having valid credentials is not enough. An authorization is also required. The authorization is what defines that the user or device is actually allowed to access the network, and what level of access is actually permitted. Create the authorization method as follows:

```
C3560X(config)# aaa authorization network default group radius
```

Step 4.   Create an accounting method for 802.1X.

RADIUS accounting packets are extremely useful, and in many cases are required. These types of packets ensure that the RADIUS server (Cisco ISE) knows the exact state of the switch port and endpoint. Without the accounting packets, Cisco ISE would have knowledge only of the authentication and authorization communication. Accounting packets provide information on when to terminate a live session, as well as local decisions made by the switch (such as AuthFail VLAN assignment, etc.).

If the switch supports Device Sensor, the sensor data will be sent to ISE using the RADIUS accounting configuration. Create the accounting method as follows:

```
C3560X(config)# aaa accounting dot1x default start-stop group radius
```

Step 5.   Configure periodic RADIUS accounting updates.

Periodic RADIUS accounting packets allow Cisco ISE to track which sessions are still active on the network. The following command configures periodic updates to be sent whenever there is new information, as well as a periodic update once per 24 hours (1440 minutes) to show ISE that the session is still alive:

```
C3560X(config)# aaa accounting update newinfo periodic 1440
```

Global RADIUS Commands

In the case of global RADIUS commands, a small difference exists between the classic IOS switches and the IOS 15.x switches. The reason for this difference is that IOS 15.x is gaining support for IPv6 infrastructure and classic IOS is limited to IPv4.

Classic IOS

You can configure a proactive method to check the availability of the RADIUS server. With this practice, the switch sends periodic test authentication messages to the RADIUS server (Cisco ISE). It is looking for a RADIUS response from the server. A success message is not necessary—a failed authentication will suffice, because it shows that the server is alive.

The following steps walk you through adding the RADIUS server to your configuration and enabling the proactive RADIUS server health checks:

Step 1.   Within global configuration mode, add a username and password for the RADIUS keepalive, which is proactively checking the online status of the RADIUS server.

The username you create here will be added to the local user database in Cisco ISE at a later step. This account will be used in a later step where you define the RADIUS server.

```
C3560X(config)# username radius-test password password
```

Step 2.   Add the Cisco ISE servers to the RADIUS group.

In this step you add each Cisco ISE Policy Service Node (PSN) to the switch configuration, using the test account you created previously. The server is proactively checked for responses one time per hour, in addition to any authentications or authorizations occurring through normal processes. Repeat this configuration for each PSN:

```
C3560X(config)# radius-server host ise_ip_address auth-port 1812
  acct-port 1813 test username radius-test key shared_secret
```

Step 3.   Set the dead criteria.

The switch has been configured to proactively check the Cisco ISE server for
RADIUS responses. Now configure the counters on the switch to determine
if the server is alive or dead. The following configuration settings are set to
wait 5 seconds for a response from the RADIUS server and to attempt the test
three times before marking the server dead. If a Cisco ISE server doesn't have
a valid response within 15 seconds, it is marked as dead. Also set the value of
how long the server will be marked dead, which is set to 15 minutes in the following example.

```
C3560X(config)# radius-server dead-criteria time 5 tries 3
C3560X(config)# radius-server deadtime 15
```

Step 4.   Enable Change of Authorization (CoA).

Previously, you defined the IP address of a RADIUS server that the switch
will send RADIUS messages to. However, you define the servers that are
allowed to perform Change of Authorization (RFC 3576) operations in a different listing, also within global configuration mode:

```
C3560X(config)# aaa server radius dynamic-author
C3560X(config-locsvr-da-radius)# client ise_ip_address server-key
  shared_secret
```

Repeat the command for each of the PSNs and the Monitoring (MNT) nodes
of the ISE cube (deployment).

Step 5.   Configure the switch to use the Cisco vendor-specific attributes (VSA).

Here you configure the switch to send any defined VSAs to Cisco ISE PSNs
during authentication requests and accounting updates:

```
C3560X(config)# radius-server vsa send authentication
C3560X(config)# radius-server vsa send accounting
```

Step 6.   Enable the VSAs:

These VSAs are used to ensure the service-type, framed-ip-address, and class
attributes are sent in the RADIUS communications to ISE.

```
C3560X(config)# radius-server attribute 6 on-for-login-auth
C3560X(config)# radius-server attribute 8 include-in-access-req
C3560X(config)# radius-server attribute 25 access-request include
```

Step 7.   Ensure that the switch always sends traffic from the correct interface.

Switches may often have multiple IP addresses associated to them. Therefore,
it is a best practice to always force any management communications to occur
through a specific interface. This interface IP address must match the IP
address defined in the Cisco ISE Network Device object.

```
C3560X(config)# ip radius source-interface interface_name
C3560X(config)# snmp-server trap-source interface_name
C3560X(config)# snmp-server source-interface informs interface_name
```

IOS 15.x Switches

As with the classic IOS switches, you can configure a proactive method to check the availability of the RADIUS server. With this practice, the switch sends periodic test authentication messages to the RADIUS server (Cisco ISE). It is looking for a RADIUS response from the server. A success message is not necessary—a failed authentication will suffice, because it shows that the server is alive.

The following steps walk you through adding the RADIUS server to your configuration and enabling the proactive RADIUS server health checks:

Step 1.   Within global configuration mode, add a username and password for the RADIUS keepalive.

The username you create here will be added to the local user database in Cisco ISE at a later step. This account will be used in a later step where you define the RADIUS server.

```
Cat4503(config)# username radius-test password password
```

Step 2.   Add the Cisco ISE PSNs as RADIUS servers.

This is where the configuration differs quite a bit from the classic IOS configuration. You create an object for the RADIUS server and then apply configuration to that object:

```
Cat4503(config)# radius server server-name
Cat4503(config-radius-server)#  address ipv4 address auth-port 1812
  acct-port 1813
Cat4503(config-radius-server)# key Shared-Secret
Cat4503(config-radius-server)# automate-tester username radius-test
  probe-on
```

Step 3.   Set the dead criteria.

The switch has been configured to proactively check the Cisco ISE server for RADIUS responses. Now configure the counters on the switch to determine if the server is alive or dead. The following configuration settings are set to wait 5 seconds for a response from the RADIUS server and to attempt the test three times before marking the server dead. If a Cisco ISE server doesn't have a valid response within 15 seconds, it is marked as dead. We also set the value of how long the server will be marked dead, which is set to 15 minutes in the following example.

```
Cat4503(config)# radius-server dead-criteria time 5 tries 3
Cat4503(config)# radius-server deadtime 15
```

Step 4.   Enable Change of Authorization (CoA).

Previously you defined the IP address of a RADIUS server that the switch will send RADIUS messages to. However, you define the servers that are allowed to perform Change of Authorization (RFC 3576) operations in a different listing, also within global configuration mode:

```
Cat4503(config)# aaa server radius dynamic-author
Cat4503(config-locsvr-da-radius)# client ise_ip_address server-key
  shared_secret
```

Repeat the command for each of the PSNs and the MNT nodes of the ISE cube (deployment).

Step 5.   Configure the switch to use the Cisco vendor-specific attributes.

Here you configure the switch to send any defined VSAs to Cisco ISE PSNs during authentication requests and accounting updates:

```
Cat4503(config)# radius-server vsa send authentication
Cat4503(config)# radius-server vsa send accounting
```

Step 6.   Enable the VSAs:

These VSAs are used to ensure the service-type, framed-ip-address, and class attributes are sent in the RADIUS communications to ISE.

```
Cat4503(config)# radius-server attribute 6 on-for-login-auth
Cat4503(config)# radius-server attribute 8 include-in-access-req
Cat4503(config)# radius-server attribute 25 access-request include
```

Step 7.   Ensure that the switch always sends traffic from the correct interface.

Switches may often have multiple IP addresses associated to them. Therefore, it is a best practice to always force any management communications to occur through a specific interface. This interface IP address must match the IP address defined in the Cisco ISE Network Device object.

```
Cat4503(config)# ip radius source-interface interface_name
Cat4503(config)# snmp-server trap-source interface_name
Cat4503(config)# snmp-server source-interface informs interface_name
```

Create Local Access Control Lists for Classic IOS and IOS 15.x

Certain functions on the switch require the use of locally configured access control lists (ACL), such as URL redirection. Some of these ACLs that are created are used immediately, and some may not be used until a much later phase of your deployment. The goal of this section is to prepare the switches for all possible deployment models at one time, and limit the operational expense of repeated switch configuration.

You create these local ACLs in the following steps:

Step 1. Add the following ACL to be used on switch ports in Monitor Mode:

```
C3560X(config)# ip access-list extended ACL-ALLOW
C3560X(config-ext-nacl)# permit ip any any
```

Step 2. Add the following ACL to be used on switch ports in Low-Impact Mode:

```
C3560X(config)# ip access-list ext ACL-DEFAULT
C3560X(config-ext-nacl)# remark DHCP
C3560X(config-ext-nacl)# permit udp any eq bootpc any eq bootps
C3560X(config-ext-nacl)# remark DNS
C3560X(config-ext-nacl)# permit udp any any eq domain
C3560X(config-ext-nacl)# remark Ping
C3560X(config-ext-nacl)# permit icmp any any
C3560X(config-ext-nacl)# remark PXE / TFTP
C3560X(config-ext-nacl)# permit udp any any eq tftp
C3560X(config-ext-nacl)# remark Drop all the rest
C3560X(config-ext-nacl)# deny ip any any log
```

Step 3. Add the following ACL to be used for URL redirection with web authentication:

```
C3560X(config)# ip access-list extended ACL-WEBAUTH-REDIRECT
C3560X(config-ext-nacl)# remark explicitly deny DNS from being
  redirected to address a bug
C3560X(config-ext-nacl)# deny udp any any eq 53
C3560X(config-ext-nacl)# remark redirect all applicable traffic to the
  ISE Server
C3560X(config-ext-nacl)# permit tcp any any eq 80
C3560X(config-ext-nacl)# permit tcp any any eq 443
C3560X(config-ext-nacl)# remark all other traffic will be implicitly
  denied from the redirection
```

Step 4. Add the following ACL to be used for URL redirection with the Posture Agent:

```
C3560X(config)# ip access-list extended ACL-AGENT-REDIRECT
C3560X(config-ext-nacl)# remark explicitly deny DNS and DHCP from being
  redirected
C3560X(config-ext-nacl)# deny udp any any eq 53 bootps
C3560X(config-ext-nacl)# remark redirect HTTP traffic only
C3560X(config-ext-nacl)# permit tcp any any eq 80
C3560X(config-ext-nacl)# remark all other traffic will be implicitly
  denied from the redirection
```

Global 802.1X Commands

The following steps walk you through the commands to enable and configure 802.1X from global configuration mode. Each step includes a description of why you type the command and what it does.

Step 1.   Enable 802.1X globally on the switch.

Enabling 802.1X globally on the switch does not actually enable authentication on any of the switch ports. Authentication is configured, but it is not enabled until the later sections where you configure Monitor Mode.

```
C3560X(config)# dot1x system-auth-control
```

Step 2.   Enable downloadable ACLs (dACL) to function.

dACLs are a very common enforcement mechanism in a Cisco TrustSec deployment. For dACLs to function properly on a switch, IP device tracking must be enabled globally:

```
C3560X(config)# ip device tracking
```

Global Logging Commands (Optional)

The following steps walk you through the commands to enable and configure logging from global configuration mode. Each step includes a description of why you type the command and what it does.

Step 1.   Enable syslog on the switch.

Syslog may be generated on Cisco IOS Software in many events. Some of the syslog messages can be sent to the ISE MNT node to be used for troubleshooting purposes. Enabling this across all NADs all the time is not recommended; instead, enable it only when beginning your project and when troubleshooting.

To ensure Cisco ISE is able to compile appropriate syslog messages from the switch, use the following commands.

```
C3560X(config)# logging monitor informational
C3560X(config)# logging origin-id ip
C3560X(config)# logging source-interface interface_id
C3560X(config)# logging host ISE_MNT_PERSONA_IP_Address_x transport udp
   port 20514
```

Step 2.   Set up standard logging functions on the switch to support possible troubleshooting/recording for Cisco ISE functions.

Enterprise Policy Manager (EPM) is a part of the Cisco IOS Software module that is responsible for features such as web authentication and dACLs. Enabling EPM logging generates a syslog related to dACL authorization, and part of the log can be correlated inside Cisco ISE when such logs are sent to Cisco ISE.

```
C3560X(config)# epm logging
```

Only the following NAD syslog messages are actually collected and used by Cisco ISE:

- AP-6-AUTH_PROXY_AUDIT_START
- AP-6-AUTH_PROXY_AUDIT_STOP
- AP-1-AUTH_PROXY_DOS_ATTACK
- AP-1-AUTH_PROXY_RETRIES_EXCEEDED
- AP-1-AUTH_PROXY_FALLBACK_REQ
- AP-1-AUTH_PROXY_AAA_DOWN
- AUTHMGR-5-MACMOVE
- AUTHMGR-5-MACREPLACE
- MKA-5-SESSION_START
- MKA-5-SESSION_STOP
- MKA-5-SESSION_REAUTH
- MKA-5-SESSION_UNSECURED
- MKA-5-SESSION_SECURED
- MKA-5-KEEPALIVE_TIMEOUT
- DOT1X-5-SUCCESS / FAIL
- MAB-5-SUCCESS / FAIL
- AUTHMGR-5-START / SUCCESS / FAIL
- AUTHMGR-SP-5-VLANASSIGN / VLANASSIGNERR
- EPM-6-POLICY_REQ
- EPM-6-POLICY_APP_SUCCESS / FAILURE
- EPM-6-IPEVENT
- DOT1X_SWITCH-5-ERR_VLAN_NOT_FOUND
- RADIUS-4-RADIUS_DEAD

Global Profiling Commands

This section separates the configuration of devices that support Device Sensor and the configuration of devices that must rely on SNMP for profiling.

Cisco IOS 15.x Switches with Device Sensor Capabilities

Cisco IOS Device Sensor requires a multipart configuration. The first part is to configure the device-sensor filter lists, which inform Device Sensor of which items to care about for the different protocols.

Device Sensor supports three protocols: Dynamic Host Configuration Protocol (DHCP), Cisco Discovery Protocol (CDP), and Link Layer Discovery Protocol (LLDP). Create one list for each protocol by following these steps:

Step 1.   Create a list for DHCP.

You need to configure three options for ISE—**host-name**, **class-identifier**, and **client-identifier**:

```
C3560X(config)# device-sensor filter-list dhcp list dhcp_list_name
C3560X(config-sensor-dhcplist)# option name host-name
C3560X(config-sensor-dhcplist)# option name class-identifier
C3560X(config-sensor-dhcplist)# option name client-identifier
```

Step 2.   Create a list for CDP.

You need to configure two CDP options for ISE—**device-name** and **platform-type**:

```
C3560X(config)# device-sensor filter-list cdp list cdp_list_name
C3560X(config-sensor-cdplist)# tlv name device-name
C3560X(config-sensor-cdplist)# tlv name platform-type
```

Step 3.   Create a list for LLDP.

You need to configure three LLDP options for ISE—**port-id**, **system-name**, and **system-description**:

```
C3560X(config)# device-sensor filter-list lldp list lldp_list_name
C3560X(config-sensor-lldplist)# tlv name port-id
C3560X(config-sensor-lldplist)# tlv name system-name
C3560X(config-sensor-lldplist)# tlv name system-description
```

Step 4.   Include the lists created in Steps 1–3 in the Device Sensor.

In the first three steps, you defined which options Device Sensor should store. Now configure Device Sensor to use those lists:

```
C3560X(config)# device-sensor filter-spec dhcp include list
  dhcp_list_name
C3560X(config)# device-sensor filter-spec cdp include list cdp_list_name
C3560X(config)# device-sensor filter-spec lldp include list lldp_list_name
```

Step 5.   Enable Device Sensor.

Device Sensor is now configured but needs to be enabled. Enable Device Sensor to run on the switch and configure when it will send its updates:

```
C3560X(config)# device-sensor accounting
C3560X(config)# device-sensor notify all-changes
```

Classic IOS Switches Without Device Sensor Capability

The ISE Policy Service Node uses SNMP to query the switch for certain attributes to help identify the devices that are connected to the switch. As such, you need to configure SNMP communities for Cisco ISE to query, as well as SNMP traps to be sent to Cisco ISE.

Step 1.   Configure a read-only SNMP community.

ISE only requires read-only SNMP access. Ensure that this community string matches the one configured in the Network Device object in Cisco ISE:

```
C3560X(config)# snmp-server community community_string RO
```

Step 2.   Configure the switch to send traps.

Now enable an SNMP trap to be sent with changes to the MAC address table. A trap that includes the device MAC address and interface identifier is sent to Cisco ISE whenever a new address is inserted, removed, or moved in the address table.

```
C3560X(config)# snmp-server enable traps mac-notification change move
  threshold
```

Step 3.   Add Cisco ISE as an SNMP trap receiver (optional).

If you will be using the SNMPTRAP probe, add a server as a trap receiver for the configured MAC notification. This is not needed in most cases, and you don't want to send traps and use the RADIUS probe together because both trigger the SNMPQUERY probe.

```
C3560X(config)# snmp-server host ise_ip_address version 2c
  community_string mac-notification
```

Sample configurations are provided in Appendix C, "Sample Switch Configurations."

Interface Configuration Settings for Classic IOS and IOS 15.x Switches

You have just completed the global configuration settings of the access layer switches, including RADIUS, SNMP, profiling, and AAA methods.

This section focuses on building a single port configuration that can be used across your entire Secure Unified Access deployment, regardless of the switch type, the deployment stage, or which deployment model you choose.

Configure Interfaces as Switch Ports

One of the first things to do before configuring any of the authentication settings on the switch port is to ensure that the switch port is configured as a Layer 2 port, not a Layer 3 port. This command is a simple, one-word command that you run, and from that point the other commands you run will all take effect.

Step 1.   Enter interface configuration mode for the switch port range:

```
C3560X(config)# interface range first_interface - last_interface
```

Step 2.   Ensure that the ports are Layer 2 switch ports:

```
C3560X(config-if-range)# switchport
```

Step 3.   Configure the port for Layer 2 edge, using the **host** macro.

The **host** macro automatically runs three commands for you. It configures the port to be an access port (nontrunk), disables channel groups, and configures spanning tree to be in portfast mode.

```
C3560X(config-if-range)# switchport host
switchport mode will be set to access
spanning-tree portfast will be enabled
channel group will be disabled
```

Configure Flexible Authentication and High Availability

The default behavior of 802.1X is to deny access to the network when an authentication fails. In many of the early customer deployments of 802.1X, this behavior was discovered to be undesirable because it does not allow for guest access and does not allow employees to remediate their computer systems and gain full network access.

The next phase in handling 802.1X authentication failures was to provide an "Auth-Fail VLAN" to allow a device/user that failed authentication to be granted access to a VLAN that provided limited resources. This was a step in the right direction, but it was still missing some practicality, especially in environments that must use MAC Authentication Bypass (MAB) for all the printers and other nonauthenticating devices. With the default behavior of 802.1X, an administrator has to configure ports for printers and other devices that do not have supplicants differently from the ports where they plan to do authentication.

In response to these issues, Cisco created Flexible Authentication (Flex-Auth). Flex-Auth enables a network administrator to set an authentication order and priority on the switch port, thereby allowing the port to attempt, in order, 802.1X, MAB, and then WebAuth. All of these functions are provided while maintaining the same configuration on all access ports, thereby providing a much simpler operational model for customers than is provided by traditional 802.1X deployments.

As mentioned previously, there are multiple methods of authentication on a switch port: 802.1X (dot1x), MAB, and WebAuth. With 802.1X authentication, the switch sends an identity request (EAP-Identity-Request) periodically after the link state has changed to up (see the "Configure Authentication Timers" section for recommended timer changes). Additionally, the endpoint supplicant should send a periodic EAP over LAN Start (EAPoL-Start) message into the switch port to speed up authentication. If a device is not able to authenticate, it merely waits until the dot1x timeout occurs, and then MAB occurs. Assuming the device MAC address is in the correct database, it is then authorized to access the network. Figure 11-1 illustrates this concept.

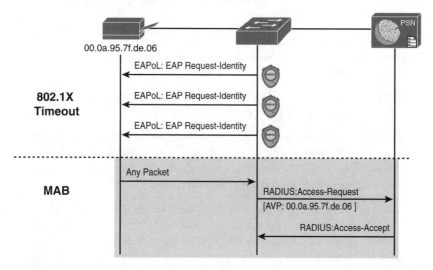

Figure 11-1 *Flexible Authentication*

The following steps walk you through the configuration of Flex-Auth and the configurable actions for authentication high availability:

Step 1. Configure the authentication method priority on the switch ports.

The best practice is to always prefer the stronger authentication method, dot1x, which is also the default of all Cisco switches:

```
C3560X(config-if-range)# authentication priority dot1x mab
```

Step 2. Configure the authentication method order on the switch ports.

There are certain deployment methods where MAB should occur before 802.1X authentication. For those corner cases, Cisco switches allow a network administrator to set a user-definable authentication order. However, the best practice is to maintain the order of dot1x and then MAB:

```
C3560X(config-if-range)# authentication order dot1x mab
```

Step 3. Configure the port to use Flex-Auth:

```
C3560X(config-if-range)# authentication event fail action next-method
```

Step 4. Configure the port to use a local VLAN for voice and data when the RADIUS server is "dead" (when it stops responding).

In the "Global RADIUS Commands" section, you configured the RADIUS server entry to use a test account that proactively alerts the switch when Cisco ISE has stopped responding to RADIUS requests. Now you will configure the switch port to locally authorize the port when that server is found to be dead, and reinitialize authentication when the server becomes alive again:

```
C3560X(config-if-range)# authentication event server dead action
  authorize vlan vlan-id
C3560X(config-if-range)# authentication event server dead action
  authorize voice
C3560X(config-if-range)# authentication event server alive action
  reinitialize
```

Step 5. Configure the port to use a local VLAN when the RADIUS server is "dead" and to allow existing and new hosts.

This feature was introduced to resolve problems with multiple authenticating hosts on a single port when a portion of them have already been authenticated while the RADIUS server was operational, and others (new hosts) are trying to authenticate when the RADIUS server is down.

Prior to the introduction of this new feature, all authenticated hosts (when the RADIUS server is up) get full access to network and the others (the new hosts) do not get access to the network. With this new feature/CLI configuration, when new hosts try to access the network and the RADIUS server is down, that port is reinitialized immediately and all hosts (in this port) get the same VLAN.

```
C3560X(config-if-range)# authentication event server dead action
  reinitialize vlan vlan-id
```

Step 6. Set the host mode of the port.

The default behavior of an 802.1X-enabled port is to authorize only a single MAC address per port. There are other options, most notably Multi-Domain Authentication (MDA) and Multiple Authentication (Multi-Auth) modes. During the initial phases of any Cisco TrustSec deployment, it is best practice to use Multi-Auth mode to ensure that there is no denial of service while deploying 802.1X.

Note   Port Security is not compatible with 802.1X, because 802.1X handles this function natively.

Multi-Auth mode allows virtually unlimited MAC addresses per switch port, and requires an authenticated session for every MAC address. When the deployment moves into the late stages of the authenticated phase, or into the enforcement phase, it is then recommended that you use MDA mode, which allows a single MAC address in the Data domain and a single MAC address in the Voice domain per port. Set the host mode of the port as follows:

```
C3560X(config-if-range)# authentication host-mode multi-auth
```

Step 7.   Configure the violation action.

When an authentication violation occurs, such as more MAC addresses than are allowed on the port, the default action is to put the port into an err-disabled state. Although this behavior may seem to be a nice, secure behavior, it can create an accidental denial of service, especially during the initial phases of deployment. Therefore, set the action to be **restrict**, as follows. This mode of operation allows the first authenticated device to continue with its authorization, and denies any additional devices.

```
C3560X(config-if-range)# authentication violation restrict
```

Configure Authentication Settings

802.1X is designed to be binary by default. Successful authentication means the user is authorized to access the network. Unsuccessful authentication means the user has no access to the network. This paradigm does not lend itself very well to a modern organization. Most organizations need to do workstation imaging with Preboot Execution Environments (PXE), or may have some thin clients that have to boot with DHCP and don't have any way to run a supplicant.

Additionally, when early adopters of 802.1X deployed authentication companywide, there were repercussions. Many issues arose. For example, supplicants were misconfigured; there were unknown devices that could not authenticate because of a lack of supplicant, and other reasons.

Cisco created Open Authentication to aid with deployments. Open Authentication allows all traffic to flow through the switch port, even without the port being authorized. This feature permits authentication to be configured across the entire organization, but does not deny access to any device.

Figure 11-2 depicts the difference between a port with the default behavior of 802.1X versus a port with Open Authentication configured. This is a key feature that enables the phased approach to deploying authentication.

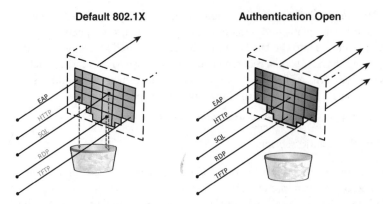

Figure 11-2 *Default 802.1X Authentication Versus Open Authentication*

Perform the following steps to configure authentication:

Step 1. Set the port for Open Authentication:

```
C3560X(config-if-range)# authentication open
```

Step 2. Enable MAC Authentication Bypass on the port:

```
C3560X(config-if-range)# mab
```

Step 3. Enable the port to perform IEEE 802.1X authentication:

```
C3560X(config-if-range)# dot1x pae authenticator
```

Configure Authentication Timers

Many timers can be modified as needed in a deployment. Unless you are experiencing a specific problem where adjusting the timer may correct unwanted behavior, it is recommended that you leave all timers at their default values except for the 802.1X Transmit (tx-period) timer. The tx-period timer defaults to a value of 30 seconds. Leaving this value at 30 seconds provides a default wait of 90 seconds (3 × tx-period) before a switch port begins the next method of authentication, and activates the MAB process for nonauthenticating devices.

Based on numerous deployments, we recommend that you set the tx-period value to 10 seconds to provide the most optimal time for MAB devices. Setting the value to less than 10 seconds may result in unwanted behavior; setting the value greater than 10 seconds may result in DHCP timeouts. To configure the tx-period timer to 10 seconds, enter the following command:

```
C3560X(config-if-range)# dot1x timeout tx-period 10
```

Apply the Initial ACL to the Port and Enable Authentication

The following steps prepare the port for Monitor Mode, in which a default ACL is applied on the port without denying any traffic:

Step 1.   Apply the initial ACL (ACL-ALLOW):

```
C3560X(config-if-range)# ip access-group ACL-ALLOW in
```

Step 2.   (Optional) Enable authentication.

If you wish to enable authentication now, you may do so as follows. However, we recommend that you wait until after you configure your policies for Monitor Mode. See Chapter 20, "Deploying in Phases," for more details on Monitor Mode.

```
C3560X(config-if-range)# authentication port-control auto
```

Note   The preceding command is required to enable authentication (802.1X, MAB, WebAuth). Without this command, everything appears to be working, but no authentication is sent to the RADIUS server.

Configuration Settings for C3PL Switches

This section reviews configuration for the newer 15.2.x and IOS-XE 3.6.x switches that follow the Cisco Common Classification Policy Language (C3PL) style of configuration. An interesting side note is that these types of switches still accept the old style of commands. In fact, that is the default, and you must enable the C3PL style of commands with the global configuration command **authentication display new-style**.

That command is a little misleading, because it changes much more than just the display. It completely changes the way that you, the administrator, interact with the switch and changes the available features. To change back to the classic model of configuring authentication and the classic features, use the **authentication display legacy** command.

It's very important to note that after you start configuring the C3PL policies themselves, you cannot revert to the legacy mode. You can switch back only if you haven't configured C3PL yet; otherwise, you have to erase the switch configuration and reload or restore an older backup configuration.

Why Use C3PL?

This new syntax offers many benefits, most of which are located under the hood and not noticeable to the end user. For example, C3PL allows the configuration to exist in memory once and be invoked multiple times. This is a processor- and memory-efficiency enhancement. Among the administrator-facing differences, the most notable benefits are:

- 802.1X and MAB can run simultaneously without having to sequence the two distinctive authentication processes, whereby 802.1X authentication has to be failed for MAB to start.

- The use of service templates to control preconfigured ACL on the interface in the event of RADIUS not being available.

With the classic platforms, the sequencing of 802.1X and MAB can result in certain MAB endpoints not being able to get IP addresses in a timely manner. By processing 802.1X and MAB simultaneously, the endpoints can receive a DHCP-assigned IP address in a timely manner. Additionally, with classic platforms, a static ACL is often applied to interfaces in order to restrict network access for devices that have not authenticated yet. In those cases, the ACL remains applied to devices attempting to connect while the RADIUS server is unavailable, resulting in denial of service until the RADIUS server is reachable. This may seem desirable in theory, but it actually makes life more difficult for the policy server administrator, and is not recommended.

Now that you've just been let down, let's build you back up. The new C3PL style does provide some very useful enhancements such as service templates. With the introduction of service templates, another ACL that would permit network access can be applied to the interface when a certain condition matches, such as when the RADIUS server is not reachable. This is known as the *Critical ACL* functionality.

C3PL also has a feature known as *differentiated authentication*, which enables you to authenticate different methods with different servers. For example, you can send MAB to ServerA and 802.1X authentications to ServerB. Although this is a neat concept, it does not apply to Secure Access deployments with ISE because it does not maintain state with a single policy server, which defeats the point of having a solution like ISE.

There is also a pretty cool feature in C3PL known as *Critical MAB*. This allows the switch to use a locally defined list of MAC addresses in the event that the centralized RADIUS server is unavailable.

Basically, the use of C3PL is recommended in a Secure Access deployment with ISE only in cases where you require the use of Critical ACL, Critical MAB, or interface templates. Otherwise, just continue to use the classic method of authentication configuration and keep your configurations across all platforms similar.

Figure 11-3 illustrates the traditional method, where each interface has its own configuration associated to it.

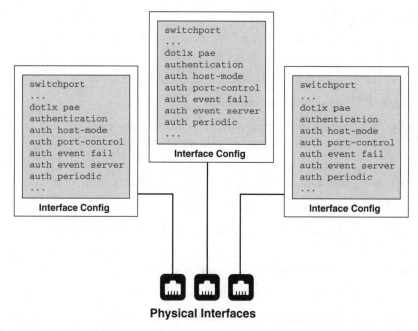

Figure 11-3 *Classic Configuration*

In contrast, Figure 11-4 illustrates the C3PL method, which offers much more flexibility to configure what is applied to the interface and when.

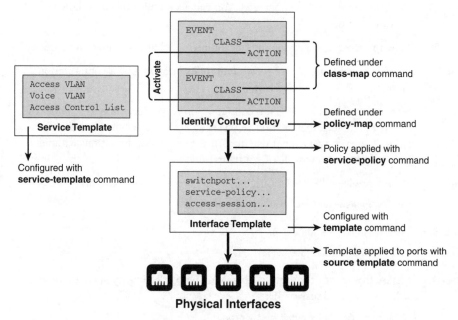

Figure 11-4 *C3PL Configuration*

Global Configuration for C3PL

As with the Classic IOS and IOS 15.x switches, you need to configure certificates for URL redirection.

From global configuration mode on the switch, perform the following steps:

Step 1.   Set the DNS domain name on the switch.

Cisco IOS does not allow for certificates, or even self-generated keys, to be created and installed without first defining a DNS domain name on the device.

Type **ip domain-name** *domain-name* at the global configuration prompt.

Step 2.   Generate self-signed keys to be used for HTTPS.

Type **crypto key generate rsa general-keys mod 2048** at the global configuration prompt.

Step 3.   Enable the HTTP server in global configuration mode.

Type **ip http server** at the global configuration prompt.

Step 4.   Enable the HTTP Secure server in global configuration mode.

Type **ip http secure-server** at the global configuration prompt.

Many organizations want to ensure that this redirection process using the switch's internal HTTP server is decoupled from the management of the switch itself. If you are not using HTTP for management, then decoupling the HTTP server is highly encouraged. You can accomplish this by following the next two steps.

Step 5.   Type **ip http active-session-modules none** in global configuration mode.

Step 6.   Type **ip http secure-active-session-modules none** in global configuration mode.

Now you will enable the C3PL configuration style. Remember that under the covers the same authentication engine is at work and IOS is doing the translation; however, you cannot use the C3PL-specific configurations without switching to the new style of configuration.

Step 7.   Within privileged EXEC mode, enable the new style of configuration:

```
C3850# authentication display new-style
```

Step 8.   Enable the AAA subsystem:

```
C3850(config)# aaa new-model
```

Step 9.   Ensure that any of the services that AAA network security services provide will use the same session ID:

```
C3850(config)# aaa session-id common
```

Step 10.   Create an authentication method for 802.1X.

An authentication method is required to instruct the switch to use a particular group of RADIUS servers for 802.1X authentication requests. Create the authentication method as follows:

```
C3850(config)# aaa authentication dot1x default group radius
```

Step 11.   Create an authorization method for 802.1X.

The authorization is what defines that the user or device is actually allowed to access the network, and what level of access is actually permitted. Create the authorization method as follows:

```
C3850(config)# aaa authorization network default group radius
```

Step 12.   Create an accounting method for 802.1X.

RADIUS accounting packets are extremely useful, and in many cases are required. These types of packets ensure that the RADIUS server (Cisco ISE) knows the exact state of the switch port and endpoint. Without the accounting packets, Cisco ISE would have knowledge only of the authentication and authorization communication. Accounting packets provide information on when to terminate a live session, as well as local decisions made by the switch (such as AuthFail VLAN assignment, etc.). Create the accounting method as follows:

```
C3850(config)# aaa accounting dot1x default start-stop group radius
```

Step 13.   Configure periodic RADIUS accounting updates.

Periodic RADIUS accounting packets allow Cisco ISE to track which sessions are still active on the network. The following command configures periodic updates to be sent whenever there is new information, as well as a periodic update once per 24 hours (1440 minutes) to show ISE that the session is still alive:

```
C3850(config)# aaa accounting update newinfo periodic 1440
```

Global RADIUS Commands for C3PL

As with the classic IOS and IOS 15.x switches, you can configure a proactive method to check the availability of the RADIUS server. With this practice, the switch sends periodic test authentication messages to the RADIUS server (Cisco ISE). It is looking for a RADIUS response from the server. A success message is not necessary—a failed authentication will suffice, because it shows that the server is alive.

The following steps walk you through adding the RADIUS server to your configuration and enabling the proactive RADIUS server health checks:

Step 1.   Within global configuration mode, add a username and password for the RADIUS keepalive.

The username you create here will be added to the local user database in Cisco ISE at a later step. This account will be used in a later step where you define the RADIUS server.

```
C3850(config)# username radius-test password password
```

Step 2.   Add the Cisco ISE PSNs as RADIUS servers.

This is where the configuration differs quite a bit from the classic IOS configuration. You create an object for the RADIUS server and then apply configuration to that object:

```
C3850(config)# radius server server-name
C3850(config-radius-server)# address ipv4 address auth-port 1812
  acct-port 1813
C3850(config-radius-server)# key Shared-Secret
C3850(config-radius-server)# automate-tester username radius-test probe-on
```

Step 3.   Set the dead criteria.

The switch has been configured to proactively check the Cisco ISE server for RADIUS responses. Now configure the counters on the switch to determine if the server is alive or dead. The following configuration settings are to wait 5 seconds for a response from the RADIUS server and to attempt the test three times before marking the server dead. If a Cisco ISE server doesn't have a valid response within 15 seconds, it is marked as dead. The following configuration also sets the value of how long the server will be marked dead to 15 minutes. High availability is covered in more detail in Chapter 18, "Setting Up a Distributed ISE Deployment."

```
C3850(config)# radius-server dead-criteria time 5 tries 3
C3850(config)# radius-server deadtime 15
```

Step 4.   Enable Change of Authorization (CoA).

Previously, you defined the IP address of a RADIUS server that the switch will send RADIUS messages to. However, you define the servers that are allowed to perform Change of Authorization (RFC 3576) operations in a different listing, also within global configuration mode:

```
C3850(config)# aaa server radius dynamic-author
C3850(config-locsvr-da-radius)# client ise_ip_address server-key
  shared_secret
```

Repeat the client command for each PSN and MNT node.

Step 5.   Configure the switch to use the Cisco vendor-specific attributes (VSA).

Here you configure the switch to send any defined VSAs to Cisco ISE PSNs during authentication requests and accounting updates:

```
C3850(config)# radius-server vsa send authentication
C3850(config)# radius-server vsa send accounting
```

Step 6.   Enable the VSAs.

Enabling the VSAs requires two additional entries compared to enabling them on non-C3PL switches. In the newer IOS-XE based devices, attribute 31 (calling-station-id) is no longer on by default:

```
C3850(config)# radius-server attribute 6 on-for-login-auth
C3850(config)# radius-server attribute 8 include-in-access-req
C3850(config)# radius-server attribute 25 access-request include
C3850(config)# radius-server attribute 31 mac format ietf upper-case
C3850(config)# radius-server attribute 31 send nas-port-detail mac-only
```

Step 7.   Ensure that the switch always sends traffic from the correct interface.

Switches may often have multiple IP addresses associated to them. Therefore, it is a best practice to always force any management communications to occur through a specific interface. This interface IP address must match the IP address defined in the Cisco ISE Network Device object.

```
Cat4503(config)# ip radius source-interface interface_name
Cat4503(config)# snmp-server trap-source interface_name
Cat4503(config)# snmp-server source-interface informs interface_name
```

Configure Local ACLs and Local Service Templates

As with the other switch type classifications, certain functions on C3PL switches require the use of locally configured ACLs, such as URL redirection. Some of these ACLs that are created are used immediately, and some may not be used until a much later phase of your deployment. The goal of this section is to prepare the switches for all possible deployment models at one time, and limit the operational expense of repeated switch configuration.

Step 1.   Add the following ACL to be used on switch ports in Monitor Mode:

```
C3850(config)# ip access-list extended ACL-ALLOW
C3850(config-ext-nacl)# permit ip any any
```

Step 2.   Add the following ACL to be used on switch ports in Low-Impact Mode:

```
C3850(config)# ip access-list extended ACL-DEFAULT
C3850(config-ext-nacl)# remark DHCP
C3850(config-ext-nacl)# permit udp any eq bootpc any eq bootps
C3850(config-ext-nacl)# remark DNS
C3850(config-ext-nacl)# permit udp any any eq domain
C3850(config-ext-nacl)# remark Ping
C3850(config-ext-nacl)# permit icmp any any
C3850(config-ext-nacl)# remark PXE / TFTP
C3850(config-ext-nacl)# permit udp any any eq tftp
C3850(config-ext-nacl)# remark Drop all the rest
C3850(config-ext-nacl)# deny ip any any log
```

Step 3.   Add the following ACL to be used for URL redirection with web authentication:

```
C3850(config)# ip access-list extended ACL-WEBAUTH-REDIRECT
C3850(config-ext-nacl)# remark explicitly deny DNS from being
  redirected to address a bug
C3850(config-ext-nacl)# deny udp any any eq 53
C3850(config-ext-nacl)# remark redirect all applicable traffic to the
  ISE Server
C3850(config-ext-nacl)# permit tcp any any eq 80
C3850(config-ext-nacl)# permit tcp any any eq 443
C3850(config-ext-nacl)# remark all other traffic will be implicitly
  denied from the redirection
```

Step 4.   Add the following ACL to be used for URL redirection with the Posture Agent:

```
C3850(config)# ip access-list extended ACL-AGENT-REDIRECT
C3850(config-ext-nacl)# remark explicitly deny DNS and DHCP from being
  redirected
C3850(config-ext-nacl)# deny udp any any eq 53 bootps
C3850(config-ext-nacl)# remark redirect HTTP traffic only
C3850(config-ext-nacl)# permit tcp any any eq 80
C3850(config-ext-nacl)# remark all other traffic will be implicitly
  denied from the redirection
```

Service templates are new to C3PL switches. A service template is similar to an ISE authorization profile but can be locally present on the switch. A service template is a collection of VLAN, Named ACL, Timer, and URL Redirect string that can be applied based on the C3PL event. Just like dACLs, service templates can be centrally located on ISE and be downloaded during authorization. However, here you are going to create a service template local to the switch to apply when none of the configured RADIUS servers (ISE PSNs) are reachable to process 802.1X or MAB requests (known as the *critical-auth* state).

Add the following service template named CRITICAL to be used when no RADIUS servers are available, also known as the critical-auth state:

```
C3850(config)# service-template CRITICAL
C3850(config-service-template)# description Apply for Critical Auth
C3850(config-service-template)# access-group ACL-ALLOW
```

Global 802.1X Commands

The following steps walk you through the commands to enable and configure 802.1X from global configuration mode. Each step includes a description of why you type the command and what it does.

Step 1.   Enable 802.1X globally on the switch.

Enabling 802.1X globally on the switch does not actually enable authentication on any of the switch ports. Authentication will be configured, but it is not enabled at this point.

```
C3560X(config)# dot1x system-auth-control
```

Step 2.   Enable downloadable ACLs to function.

dACLs are a very common enforcement mechanism in a Cisco TrustSec deployment. For dACLs to function properly on a switch, IP device tracking must be enabled globally:

```
C3560X(config)# ip device tracking
```

Note In some uncommon cases, Windows 7 and some other devices do not respond to ARPs. Windows displays "Duplicate IP Address Detected: 0.0.0.0." In such instances, you might need to use the command **ip device tracking use SVI**.

C3PL Fundamentals

The Cisco Common Classification Policy Language is used across a variety of Cisco solutions, including Catalyst switches, Cisco routers, Cisco ASA firewalls, and more. With these C3PL devices, the configuration is made up of building blocks. Policies contain one or more events, events contain one or more classes, and classes contain one or more conditions to be matched. Figure 11-5 illustrates this concept.

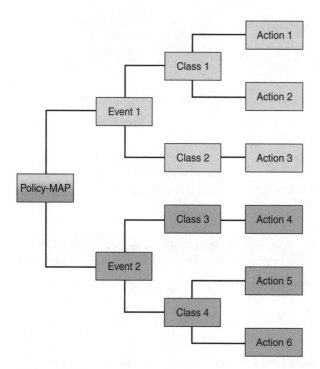

Figure 11-5 *C3PL Hierarchy*

Configure the C3PL Policies

The class is the base-level object and the first item that you configure for the C3PL policy. After you create the class, you create a policy with an event. That event calls the class that you created previously. Figure 11-6 illustrates the relationship of an event to classes and the relationships of the classes to actions. This illustration was created by a truly gifted Technical Marketing Engineer at Cisco named Hariprasad ("Hari") Holla. Hari has presented on this topic many times at Cisco Live, and you can even watch VoD recordings of those sessions for free at http://www.ciscolive.com; navigate to **Learn Online > On-demand Library > Speakers** and enter **Hariprasad Holla** as the search string.

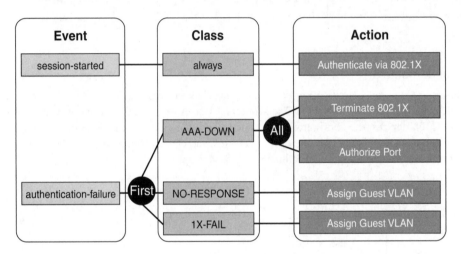

Figure 11-6 *Event, Class, and Action Relationships (Courtesy Hariprasad Holla)*

Configure Control Classes

A control class defines the conditions under which the actions of a control policy are executed. You define whether all, any, or none of the conditions must evaluate to true to execute the actions of the control policy. Control classes are evaluated based on the event specified in the control policy.

Note   If this is first time C3PL-type commands are being used on this switch, it will present a warning that it cannot revert to legacy mode unless the switch configuration is cleared.

Step 1.   Configure a control class for when none of the RADIUS servers are available (the critical-auth state):

```
C3850(config)# class-map type control subscriber match-any AAA-DOWN
C3850(config-filter-control-classmap)# match result-type aaa-timeout
```

Step 2.   Configure a control class for when 802.1X authentication fails for the session:

```
C3850(config)# class-map type control subscriber match-all DOT1X-FAILED
C3850(config-filter-control-classmap)# match method dot1x
C3850(config-filter-control-classmap)# match result-type method dot1x
  authoritative
```

Configure Control Policies

Control policies are used to dictate which actions should be taken in response to the specified events. The policy contains one or more rules that associate a control class with one or more actions. The actions that you can configure in a rule are specific to the event itself. In other words, you wouldn't have a MAB action apply to a dot1x event. Control policies typically control the authentication of the end user or endpoint and the applying services to the authentication session, or even to a physical interface. Figure 11-6 shows this hierarchy and the relationship between the components of the policy.

In the following steps, you create a control policy leveraging the control classes you created in the previous section and then apply the policy to a range of interfaces on the switch:

Step 1.   Configure a control policy that will be applied to all 802.1X/MAB-enabled interfaces.

```
C3850(config)# policy-map type control subscriber DOT1X-DEFAULT
```

Step 2.   Configure actions for when the session starts.

The following configuration enables 802.1X and MAB to run simultaneously, assigning a higher priority for 802.1X over MAB. This practice is not recommended for production environments; it is presented here just to illustrate that MAB and 802.1X can be run at the same time.

```
C3850(config-event-control-policymap)# event session-started match-all
C3850(config-class-control-policymap)# 10 class always do-all
C3850(config-action-control-policymap)# 10 authenticate using dot1x
  priority 10
C3850(config-action-control-policymap)# 20 authenticate using mab
  priority 20
```

Step 3.   Configure actions for policy violations:

```
C3850(config-action-control-policymap)# event violation match-all
C3850(config-class-control-policymap)# 10 class always do-all
C3850(config-action-control-policymap)# 10 restrict
```

Step 4.   Configure the switch to attempt to authenticate the endpoint using 802.1X when a supplicant is detected on the endpoint:

```
C3850(config-action-control-policymap)# event agent-found match-all
C3850(config-class-control-policymap)# 10 class always do-all
C3850(config-action-control-policymap)# 10 authenticate using dot1x
```

Step 5. Configure the action for 802.1X authentication failures, or when there is a lack of ISE PSNs (RADIUS servers) available:

```
C3850(config-action-control-policymap)# event authentication-failure
  match-all
C3850(config-class-control-policymap)# 10 class AAA-DOWN do-all
C3850(config-action-control-policymap)# 10 authorize
C3850(config-action-control-policymap)# 20 activate service-template
  CRITICAL
C3850(config-action-control-policymap)# 30 terminate dot1x
C3850(config-action-control-policymap)# 40 terminate mab
C3850(config-action-control-policymap)# 20 class DOT1X-FAILED do-all
C3850(config-action-control-policymap)# 10 authenticate using mab
```

Note Because we will be using Centralized WebAuth (CWA), which sends ACCESS-ACCEPT even for unknown MAC addresses, there will be no failure for MAB, thus a failure event for MAB is not defined in the preceding configuration.

Apply the Control Policy to the Interfaces

Now that the policy is created, it needs to be applied to the access-layer interfaces with the **service-policy** command. Not all aspects of the 802.1X configuration are completed in C3PL, so some configuration items will occur at the interfaces separately.

Step 1. Apply the control policy to the interface range:

```
C3850(config)# interface range GigabitEthernet 1/0/1 - 24
C3850(config-if-range)# description Dot1X Enabled Ports
C3850(config-if-range)# switchport host
C3850(config-if-range)# service-policy type control subscriber
  DOT1X-DEFAULT
```

Step 2. Apply the remaining interface configuration:

```
C3850(config-if-range)# authentication periodic
C3850(config-if-range)# authentication timer reauthenticate server
C3850(config-if-range)# mab
C3850(config-if-range)# ip access-group DEFAULT-ACL in
C3850(config-if-range)# access-session host-mode multi-auth
C3850(config-if-range)# no access-session closed
C3850(config-if-range)# dot1x timeout tx-period 10
C3850(config-if-range)# access-session port-control auto
C3850(config-if-range)# no shutdown
```

Cisco Wireless LAN Controllers

This section reviews the configuration for the Cisco Wireless LAN Controller. The focus is on version 8.3, which includes many nice enhancements to the WLC, such as the integrated Device Sensor technology, URL-based ACLs, and support for FlexConnect access points. WLC Version 8.3 also adds the very desirable feature of being able to secure your guest network with pre-shared keys instead of leaving it open and unencrypted.

If you ever have any questions or concerns about which version of the WLC is best, the most stable, and the most recommended, check out this website: https://supportforums.cisco.com/document/12481821/tac-recommended-aireos. That is where a team made up of Wireless TAC and ISE TAC give their joint recommendations based on their experiences.

AireOS Features and Version History

Much like any other product decision, your choice of WLC version needs to be based on examining which features you want or need for your environment and weighing the benefit of those features against the older versions that might not have them, but are more of a known and proven entity. To help you with your version decision, Table 11-1 identifies some ISE-related features that have been added to the WLC since version 7.0.

Table 11-1 *AireOS Features and Version History*

Cisco WLC Version	Secure Access Features Added
AireOS 7.0	URL redirection, CoA, and ISE-NAC features are limited to 802.1X-enabled networks only.
	Open SSIDs must use Local WebAuth (LWA) without posture or onboarding capabilities.
AireOS 7.2	URL redirection, CoA, and ISE-NAC features are enabled on open and dot1x-enabled WLANs.
	Device Sensor functionality added.
AireOS 7.3	FlexConnect support for the ISE-NAC features added.
	CLI support for DNS snooping and URL-based ACLs.
	TrustSec support with SGT Exchange Protocol (SXP).
AireOS 7.4	mDNS snooping.
	Application Visibility and Control (AVC).
	NetFlow support.
AireOS 7.6	GUI configuration of DNS snooping and URL-based ACLs introduced.

Cisco WLC Version	Secure Access Features Added
AireOS 8.0	HTTPS redirection support added.
	Application Visibility and Control (AVC).
AireOS 8.1	
AireOS 8.2	
AireOS 8.3	True URL filtering provided.
	RADIUS-NAC renamed to ISE-NAC, RFC 3576 renamed to "Support for CoA."

Now that you've examined the different versions, it is time to begin the configuration of the Wireless LAN Controller.

As with the previous section covering configuration of Cisco Catalyst Switches, this section assumes that you have established basic connectivity with the NAD and are now ready to bootstrap the WLC for use with ISE.

Configure the AAA Servers

The first step in bootstrapping the WLC is to add the ISE Policy Service Nodes to the WLC as RADIUS authentication and accounting servers.

Add the RADIUS Authentication Servers

In the following steps, you add the ISE PSNs as RADIUS authentication servers in the WLC.

From the WLC GUI, perform the following steps:

Step 1.   Navigate to **Security > RADIUS > Authentication**.

Step 2.   Ensure that MAC Delimiter is set to **Hyphen**.

This ensures that the format of the MAC address is aa-bb-cc-dd-ee-ff, which is the way ISE expects it to be. Figure 11-7 shows the MAC Delimiter setting.

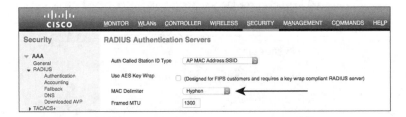

Figure 11-7   *Security > RADIUS > Authentication > MAC Delimiter*

Step 3.   Click **New** to add the ISE Policy Service Node.

Step 4. In the Server IP Address field, enter the IP address of the PSN (or the virtual IP address, if using a load balancer).

Step 5. In the Shared Secret field, enter the shared secret. This *must* match what is configured in ISE for the Network Device object.

Step 6. In the Port Number field, enter **1812** for authentication.

Step 7. From the Server Status drop-down list, choose **Enabled.**

Step 8. From the Support for CoA drop-down list, choose **Enabled** (in older WLC version, this field is labeled Support for RFC 3576).

Step 9. In the Server Timeout field, change the default setting to 5 seconds, which should work nicely.

Step 10. For Network User, check the **Enable** check box. This simply indicates that the RADIUS server may be used for network authentications.

Step 11. Click **Apply** in the upper-right corner.

Step 12. Click **Save Configuration** at the top of the screen.

Figure 11-8 shows a completed server configuration.

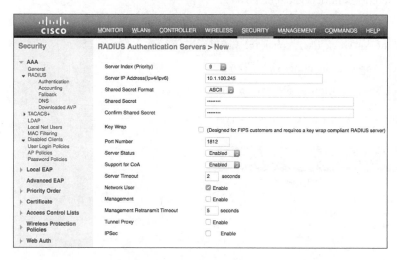

Figure 11-8 *RADIUS Authentication Server Configuration*

Repeat these steps for each Policy Service Node that you need to add.

Add the RADIUS Accounting Servers

Now that you have defined the ISE PSNs for authentication, you need to define them again for accounting.

From the WLC GUI, perform the following steps:

Step 1.   Navigate to **Security > RADIUS > Accounting**.

Step 2.   From the MAC Delimiter drop-down list, choose **Hyphen**, as shown in Figure 11-9.

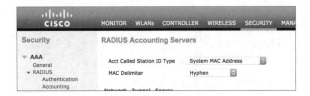

Figure 11-9   *Security > RADIUS > Accounting > MAC Delimiter*

Step 3.   Click **New** to add the ISE Policy Service Node.

Step 4.   In the Server IP Address field, add the IP address of the PSN.

Step 5.   In the Shared Secret field, enter the shared secret to match what is configured on ISE.

Step 6.   In the Port Number field, enter **1813**.

Step 7.   From the Server Status drop-down list, choose **Enabled.**

Step 8.   For the **Network User**, check the **Enable** check box.

Step 9.   Click **Apply** in the upper-right corner.

Step 10. Click **Save Configuration** at the top of the screen.

Figure 11-10 shows a completed server entry.

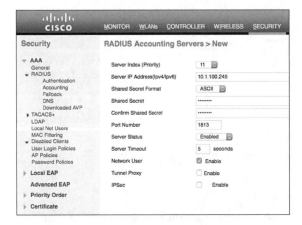

Figure 11-10   *RADIUS Accounting Server Configuration*

Repeat these steps for each Policy Service Node that you need to add.

Configure RADIUS Fallback (High Availability)

The primary RADIUS server (the server with the lowest server index) is assumed to be the most preferable server for the Cisco WLC. If the primary server becomes unresponsive, the controller switches to the next active server (the server with the next lowest server index). The controller continues to use this backup server, unless you configure the controller either to fall back to the primary RADIUS server when it recovers and becomes responsive or to switch to a more preferable server from the available backup servers.

From the WLC GUI, perform the following steps:

Step 1. Navigate to **Security > AAA > RADIUS > Fallback**.

Step 2. From the Fallback Mode drop-down list, choose **Active**.

Selecting Active causes the Cisco WLC to revert to a server with a lower priority from the available backup servers by using RADIUS probe messages to proactively determine whether a server that has been marked inactive is back online.

Step 3. In the Username field, enter the name to be sent in the inactive server probes.

We have been using radius-test as the username so far in the book. Technically, you do not need to enter a password for this test user account, because the system simply looks for a response from the RADIUS server; pass or fail does not matter.

Step 4. In the Interval in Sec field, enter a value. The interval states the inactive time in passive mode and probe interval in active mode. The valid range is 180 to 3600 seconds, and the default value is 300 seconds.

Figure 11-11 shows the fallback settings for RADIUS.

Figure 11-11 *Fallback Parameters*

Configure the Airespace ACLs

Earlier in the chapter, you pre-staged the Cisco Catalyst Switches with local ACLs. Similarly, pre-stage the WLC with a Web Authentication ACL named **ACL_WEBAUTH_REDIRECT**. This ACL name is used specifically because it matches the preconfigured setting in ISE, which may make your job a little easier if this is a brand-new (aka greenfield) deployment. Beginning with ISE 2.0, there are some smart-default configurations that ship with ISE to make unboxing ISE and setting it up very fast and easy.

The smart-default configurations for Guest and BYOD include the use of the redirect ACL with this specific name.

Naturally, you can use whatever name you wish, and simply change the configuration built in to ISE. However, for the purposes of this book, we will keep the same ACL name.

Create the Web Authentication Redirection ACL

As with the Cisco Catalyst Switches, you need a local ACL on the WLC to redirect web traffic to the Centralized Web Authentication portal. However, with the Catalyst Switch, a **permit** statement means that the traffic should be redirected, and a **deny** statement describes traffic that should not be redirected. With the switch, you need two ACLs: one to define what gets redirected, and a second one to filter traffic (permit or deny traffic flow).

The WLC has a single ACL, and it pulls double-duty. It permits and denies traffic flow, but at the same time it redirects the traffic that is denied to the Centralized Web Authentication portal.

From the WLC GUI, perform the following steps:

Step 1.   Navigate to **Security > Access Control Lists > Access Control Lists**, as shown in Figure 11-12.

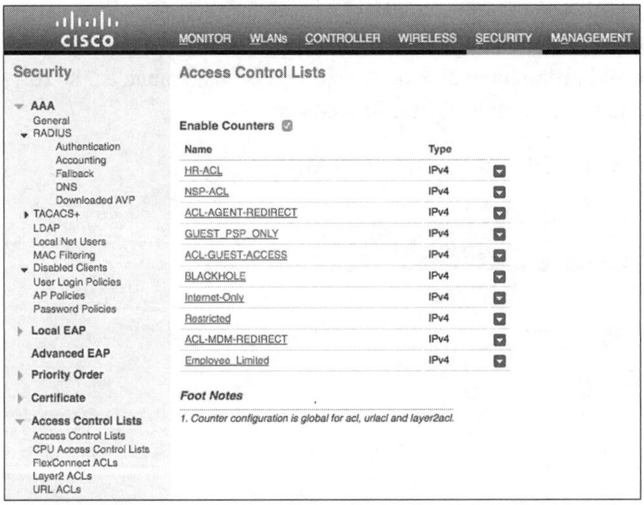

Figure 11-12   *Security > Access Control Lists > Access Control Lists*

Step 2.   Click **New** to add a new ACL.

Step 3.   In the Access Control List Name field, fill in the name **ACL_WEBAUTH_ REDIRECT**.

Step 4.   Click **Apply**.

Step 5.   When you return to the main Access Control Lists screen, click the new entry: **ACL_WEBAUTH_REDIRECT**.

Step 6.   Click **Add New Rule** in the upper-right corner.

A rule in the WLC is the equivalent of an access control entry (ACE) in the switch. It is a line in the ACL.

Step 7.   Create a set of rules for this ACL that does the following:

- Permits all traffic outbound (toward the client).

- Permits DNS.

- Permits TCP port 8443 to the ISE servers. For simplicity, you may want to permit all traffic to the ISE nodes. It also allows you to reuse the same ACL for most use cases.

- Denies all other traffic—which will redirect all denied web traffic.

Figure 11-13 shows an example of a completed ACL.

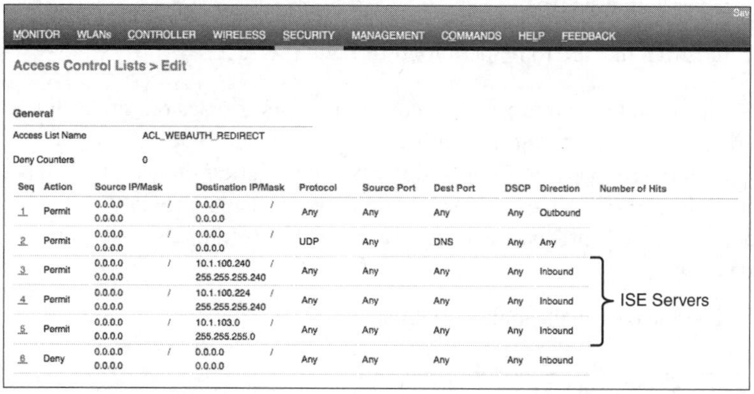

Figure 11-13   *ACL_WEBAUTH_REDIRECT Example*

Add Google URLs for ACL Bypass

When Android endpoints go through the BYOD onboarding process, they must have access to the Google Play Store to download the Network Setup Assistant app. However, allowing that access through your network is not as simple as just entering an IP address in the ACL—hundreds of addresses may resolve to the DNS names needed for the Google Play Store. Beginning with WLC version 7.6, Airespace ACLs include the capability to use DNS-based ACLs in the form of URL lists.

To add Google URLs for ACL bypass, follow these steps:

Step 1.   Navigate to **Security > Access Control Lists > Access Control Lists.**

Step 2.   Hover your mouse pointer over the blue-and-white drop-down arrow icon to the right of the ACL_WEBAUTH_REDIRECT ACL that you created in the previous section.

Step 3.   Click **Add-Remove URL**, as shown in Figure 11-14.

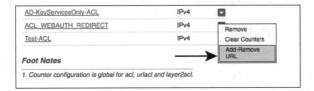

Figure 11-14   *Hovering Over Add-Remove URL Option*

You are now brought to the URL List. The URLs that you enter here are configured with an implicit wildcard in the first portion. In other words, entering google.com matches *.google.com. Any matches to these URL entries will be permitted through the ACL.

Step 4.   Enter the URLs that are to be permitted through the ACL.

In the United States, entering google.com and clients.google.com typically does the trick. In other countries, other URLs may need to be entered for the smooth operation of Android endpoints. One solution that has worked is to add .*.* for the domain extensions. In other words, enter google.*.* instead of google.com and enter android.clients.google.*.* instead of android.clients. google.com.

Figure 11-15 shows an example URL list.

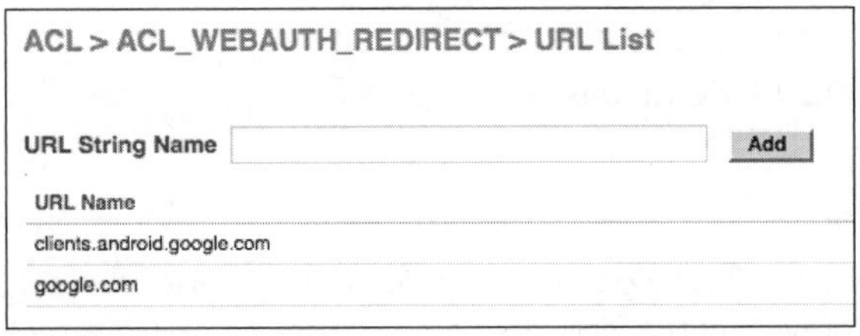

ACL > ACL_WEBAUTH_REDIRECT > URL List

URL String Name [   ]   Add

URL Name

clients.android.google.com

google.com

Figure 11-15   *URL List*

Create the Dynamic Interfaces for the Client VLANs

When you want to assign a user or device to a VLAN on a Catalyst Switch, just assign the VLAN to the port, and the entire switch port will now be assigned to that particular VLAN.

The WLC has only a few physical connections to the wired network, and it must bridge all wireless users from their RF network (Wi-Fi) to the physical wired network. The WLC must also have the ability to assign a different VLAN per authenticated session (if necessary). If you are thinking that the WLC just needs to be connected with a trunk, you are correct.

The WLC is configured to use 802.1Q to tag traffic for a specific VLAN as that traffic exits the controller. However, the controller calls this a *dynamic interface* because the WLC can either assign a physical interface to traffic or assign an 802.1Q tag to traffic.

In this section, you will create two dynamic interfaces: one for employee traffic and one for guest traffic.

Create the Employee Dynamic Interface

This interface will be used for all successful authentications to the Corporate WLAN, providing full access to the entire network.

From the WLC GUI, perform the following steps:

Step 1.   Choose **Controller > Interfaces**.

Step 2.   Click **New**.

Step 3.   Name your interface. Use the name **employee** for purposes of this example.

Step 4.   In the VLAN Identifier field, enter the VLAN ID to be used in the 802.1Q tag (**41** in this example).

Step 5.   Click **Apply**.

Step 6.   Click the new interface named **employee**.

You most likely will not need to change any settings until you reach the Physical Information section.

Step 7.   In the Interface Address section, provide an IP address, netmask, and gateway for the VLAN in the respective fields.

Step 8.   In the DHCP Information section, in the Primary DHCP Server field, enter the DHCP server address.

Step 9.   Click **Apply**.

Figure 11-16 shows an example employee dynamic interface configuration.

Interfaces > Edit

General Information

Interface Name	employee
MAC Address	d0:d0:fd:91:e2:65

Configuration

Guest Lan	☐
Quarantine	☐
Quarantine Vlan Id	0
NAS-ID	none

Physical Information

Port Number	2
Backup Port	0
Active Port	2
Enable Dynamic AP Management	☐

Interface Address

VLAN Identifier	41
IP Address	10.1.41.2
Netmask	255.255.255.0
Gateway	10.1.41.1
IPv6 Address	::
Prefix Length	128
IPv6 Gateway	::
Link Local IPv6 Address	fe80::d2d0:fdff:fe91:e260/64

DHCP Information

Primary DHCP Server	10.10.100.100
Secondary DHCP Server	
DHCP Proxy Mode	Global
Enable DHCP Option 82	☐

Figure 11-16   *Example Employee Dynamic Interface Configuration*

Create the Guest Dynamic Interface

The guest dynamic interface is used for all devices connecting to the Guest WLAN, as well as for unsuccessful or unauthorized authentications to the Corporate WLAN. This interface has Internet access only.

From the WLC GUI, perform the following steps:

Step 1.   Choose **Controller > Interfaces.**

Step 2.   Click **New.**

Step 3.   Name your interface. Use the name **Guest** for purposes of this example.

Step 4.   In the VLAN Identifier field, enter the VLAN ID to be used in the 802.1Q tag (**42** in the example).

Step 5.   Click **Apply.**

Step 6.   Click the new interface named **Guest**.

You most likely will not need to change any settings until you reach the Physical Information section. In the Configuration section, do *not* enable the Guest LAN check box. This is not for guest WLANs; it is for providing guest access to directly connected wired LANs.

Step 7.   In the Interface Address section, provide an IP address, netmask, and gateway for the VLAN in the respective fields.

Step 8.   In the DHCP Information section, in the Primary DHCP Server field, enter the DHCP server address.

Step 9.   Click **Apply**.

Figure 11-17 shows an example guest dynamic interface configuration.

Figure 11-17   *Example Dynamic Guest Interface Configuration*

Create the Wireless LANs

Now that the RADIUS servers, ACLs, and dynamic interfaces are all created and configured, we will move on to creating two WLANs: one for guests (Guest) and one for corporate users (Corporate). The Guest WLAN will be an "open" WLAN, while the Corporate WLAN will be configured to use 802.1X to authenticate devices. With the WLC version 8.3 and newer, the Guest network can also be configured to use WPA/WPA2 with a pre-shared key.

Create the Guest WLAN

The Guest WLAN will be created as an open SSID, but it will send the endpoint MAC addresses to ISE over RADIUS for MAB, just like the wired networks.

From the WLC GUI, perform the following steps:

Step 1.   Click the **WLANs** menu.

Step 2.   Click **Create New**.

Step 3.   Click **Go**.

Step 4.   From the Type drop-down list, choose **WLAN**.

Step 5.   In the Profile Name field, enter the WLAN profile name; use **ISE-Guest** for purposes of this example, as shown in Figure 11-18.

Figure 11-18 _Example Guest WLAN Creation_

Step 6.   In the SSID field, enter an SSID name; use **ISE-Guest** in this example.

Step 7.   Click **Apply**.

The Edit 'ISE-Guest' screen opens with the General tab displayed, as shown in Figure 11-19, which is where you can enable and disable the WLAN and configure other general options.

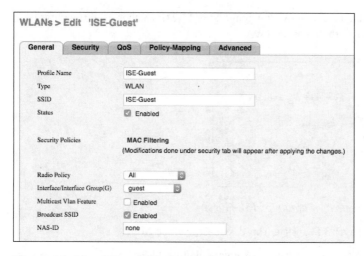

Figure 11-19   *General Tab for ISE-Guest*

Step 8. If you are ready to work with this SSID, check the **Enabled** check box to the right of Status.

Step 9. From the Interface/Interface Group(G) drop-down list, choose the **Guest** interface that you created previously.

Step 10. Check the **Enabled** check box to the right of Broadcast SSID if you want to broadcast the SSID, which is the general practice for open guest networks.

Step 11. Click the **Security** tab, shown in Figure 11-20 with the Layer 2 subtab displayed (the default).

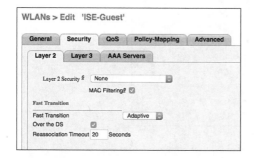

Figure 11-20   *Layer 2 Security Subtab for ISE-Guest*

Step 12. From the Layer 2 Security drop-down list, change from the default (WPA+WPA2) to **None**.

Step 13. Check the **MAC Filtering** check box (which is wireless MAB).

Step 14. Click the **Layer 3** subtab, shown in Figure 11-21, which is used to configure Local Web Authentication (LWA).

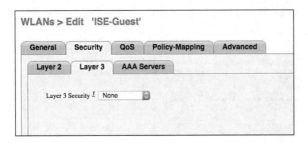

Figure 11-21 *Layer 3 Security Subtab for ISE-Guest*

Step 15. From the Layer 3 Security drop-down list, choose **None**.

Step 16. Click the **AAA Servers** subtab, shown in Figure 11-22.

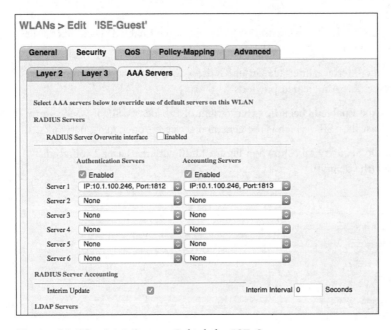

Figure 11-22 *AAA Servers Subtab for ISE-Guest*

The Cisco WLC enables administrators to specify different authentication and accounting servers. However, this configuration is incompatible with an ISE RADIUS server. ISE provides session services that are tied together from the session ID in the authentication packet and the session ID in the accounting packet.

Step 17. Check the **Enabled** check box under both Authentication Servers and Accounting Servers and select your respective ISE Policy Service Node(s) in the columns.

Step 18. In the RADIUS Server Accounting section, check the **Enabled** check box to the right of Interim Update.

Step 19. Set the Interim Interval to **0** seconds.

Note For WLC versions 7.6 and earlier, the recommendation is to disable interim updates (leave the corresponding Enabled check box unchecked). For version 8.0 and later, interim updates should be enabled with an interval of 0 seconds, as specified in Step 19. With this setting, an accounting update is sent only when the client IP address changes. Device Sensor updates are not impacted.

Step 20. Click **Apply**.

Step 21. Click the **Advanced** tab, the top portion of which is shown in Figure 11-23.

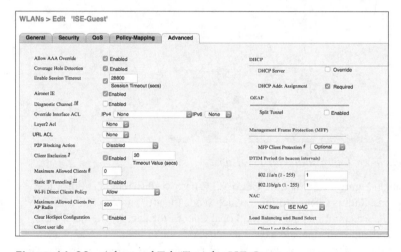

Figure 11-23 *Advanced Tab (Top) for ISE-Guest*

Step 22. Check the **Enabled** check box for Allow AAA Override.

This enables ISE to assign a VLAN and ACL that are different from those configured on the WLAN and interface by default.

Step 23. Check the **Enabled** check box for Enable Session Timeout, and set the Session Timeout to **28800** seconds.

The default value of 1800 has been known to be too short in many environments.

Step 24. In the NAC section, from the NAC State drop-down list, choose **ISE NAC**.

In versions earlier than 8.3, this setting is named Radius NAC instead of ISE NAC. Regardless of the name, this setting is critical for URL Redirection, Centralized Web Authentication (CWA), Posture Assessment, Native Supplicant Provisioning, MDM redirections, and more.

Step 25.   Check the **Enabled** check box for Client Exclusion and change the Timeout Value to **30** seconds.

Step 26.   In the DHCP section on the right side of the screen, check the **Required** check box for DHCP Addr. Assignment.

This setting is required for the DHCP Device Sensor built in to the WLC.

Step 27.   Scroll down to the middle of the Advanced tab and, under Radius Client Profiling, check both the **DHCP Profiling** and **HTTP Profiling** options, as shown in Figure 11-24.

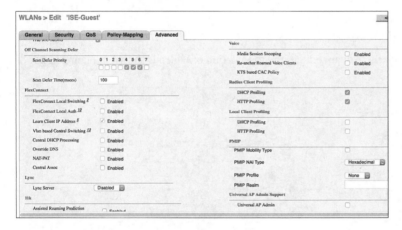

Figure 11-24   *Advanced Tab (Middle) for ISE-Guest*

Note in Figure 11-24 that the Cisco WLC has two different client profiling options: Radius Client Profiling, which sends the attributes to ISE within RADIUS accounting packets, and Local Client Profiling, where the WLC keeps the information and uses it locally. Although the interface appears to offer the option to enable both types of profiling, they are mutually exclusive and cannot be enabled at the same time.

Step 28.   Click **Apply** in the upper-right corner.

Step 29.   Click **Save Configuration** at the top of the screen.

Create the Corporate SSID

The Corporate WLAN is created as a closed SSID and requires 802.1X authentication for an endpoint to associate to the WLAN. Unlike wired networks, wireless networks have the added benefit of truly rejecting all access without a successful authentication. Users are attuned to the requirement of configuring software in order to connect to a wireless network. The same is not true when it comes to wired networks.

From the WLC GUI, perform the following steps:

Step 1.   Click the **WLANs** menu.

Step 2.   Click **Create New**.

Step 3.   Click **Go**.

Step 4.   From the Type drop-down list, choose **WLAN**.

Step 5.   In the Profile Name field, enter the WLAN profile name; use **ISE** for purposes of this example, as shown in Figure 11-25.

Figure 11-25   *Example Corporate WLAN Creation*

Step 6.   In the SSID field, enter an SSID name; use **ISE** in this example.

In this example, the SSID name ISE is used because it is the SSID name that is preconfigured in the smart-default for ISE 2.0 and later prebuilt native supplicant profile. Using this SSID name will help speed up your installation and demo-ability, just like using the ACL_WEBAUTH_REDIRECT name for the Airespace ACL.

Step 7.   Click **Apply**.

The Edit 'ISE' screen opens with the General tab displayed, as shown in Figure 11-26.

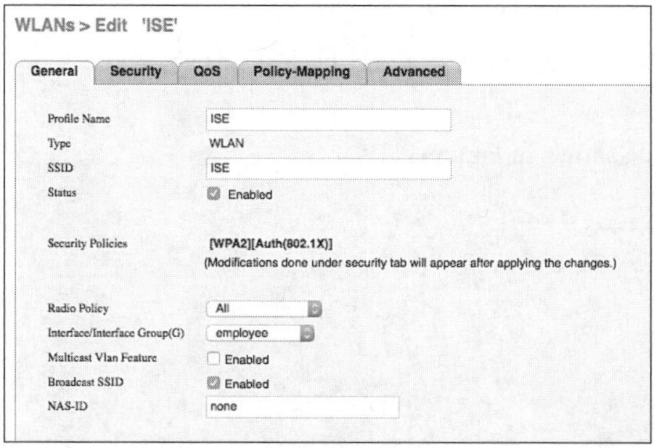

Figure 11-26   *General Tab for ISE Corporate WLAN*

Step 8.   If you are ready to work with this SSID, check the **Enabled** check box to the right of Status.

Step 9.   From the Interface/Interface Group(G) drop-down list, choose the **Employee** interface that you created previously.

Step 10.   Click the **Security** tab, shown in Figure 11-27 with the Layer 2 subtab displayed (the default).

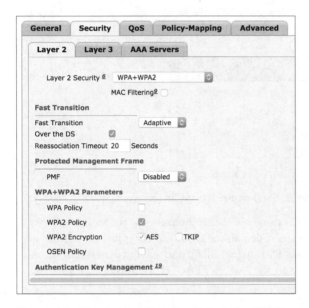

Figure 11-27   *Layer 2 Security Subtab for ISE Corporate WLAN*

Step 11.   In the Layer 2 Security field, the default setting of **WPA+WPA2** is correct for this sample configuration.

Step 12.   Do *not* check the MAC Filtering check box.

Step 13.   In the Authentication Key Management section, check the **Enabled** check box for 802.1X.

Step 14.   Click the **Layer 3** subtab, shown in Figure 11-28.

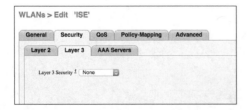

Figure 11-28   *Layer 3 Security Subtab for ISE Corporate WLAN*

Step 15. From the Layer 3 Security drop-down list, choose **None**.

Step 16. Click the **AAA Servers** subtab, shown in Figure 11-29.

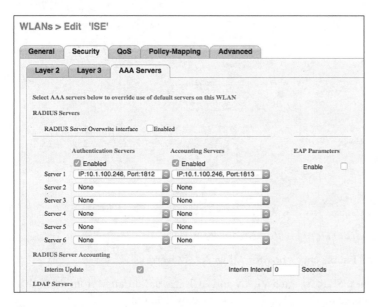

Figure 11-29 *AAA Servers Subtab for ISE Corporate WLAN*

The Cisco WLC enables administrators to specify different authentication and accounting servers. However, this configuration is incompatible with an ISE RADIUS server. ISE provides session services that are tied together from the session ID in the authentication packet and the session ID in the accounting packet.

Step 17. Check the **Enabled** check box under both Authentication Servers and Accounting Servers and select your respective ISE Policy Service Node(s) in the columns.

Step 18. In the RADIUS Server Accounting section, check the **Enabled** check box to the right of Interim Update.

Step 19. Set the Interim Interval to **0** seconds.

Note For WLC versions 7.6 and earlier, the recommendation is to disable interim updates (leave the corresponding Enabled check box unchecked). For version 8.0 and later, interim updates should be enabled with an interval of 0 seconds, as specified in Step 19. With this setting, an accounting update is sent only when the client IP address changes. Device Sensor updates are not impacted.

Step 20. Click **Apply**.

Step 21.   Click the **Advanced** tab, the top portion of which is shown in Figure 11-30.

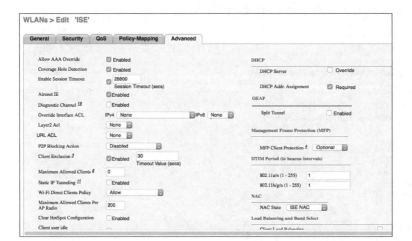

Figure 11-30   *Advanced Tab (Top) for ISE Corporate WLAN*

Step 22.   Check the **Enable** check box for Allow AAA Override.

This enables ISE to assign a VLAN and ACL that are different from those that are configured on the WLAN and interface by default.

Step 23.   Check the **Enabled** check box for Enable Session Timeout and set the Session Timeout to **28800** seconds.

The default value of 1800 has been known to be too short in many environments.

Step 24.   In the NAC section, from the NAC State drop-down list, choose **ISE NAC**.

In versions earlier than 8.3, this setting is named Radius NAC instead of ISE NAC. Regardless of the name, this setting is critical for URL Redirection, Centralized Web Authentication (CWA), Posture Assessment, Native Supplicant Provisioning, MDM redirections, and more.

Step 25.   Check the **Enabled** check box for Client Exclusion and change the Timeout Value to **30** seconds.

Step 26.   In the DHCP section on the right side of the screen, check the **Required** check box for **DHCP Addr. Assignment**.

This setting is required for the DHCP Device Sensor built into the WLC.

Step 27.   Scroll down to the middle of the Advanced tab and, under Radius Client Profiling, check both the **DHCP Profiling** and **HTTP Profiling** options, as shown in Figure 11-31.

Note in Figure 11-31 that the Cisco WLC has two different client profiling options: Radius Client Profiling, which sends the attributes to ISE within RADIUS accounting packets, and Local Client Profiling, where the WLC keeps the information and uses it locally. Although the interface appears to offer the option to enable both types of profiling, they are mutually exclusive and cannot be enabled at the same time.

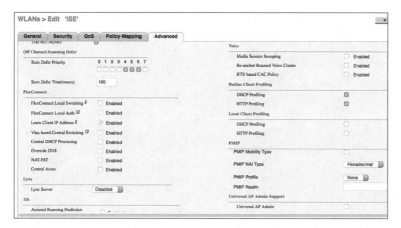

Figure 11-31   *Advanced Tab (Middle) for ISE Corporate WLAN*

Step 28.   Click **Apply** in the upper-right corner.

Step 29.   Click **Save Configuration** at the top of the screen.

Summary

This chapter reviewed the best practice configurations for Cisco Catalyst Switches and Cisco Wireless LAN Controllers. It walked you through the configuration of these network access devices for use in all scenarios and all deployment phases of the Secure Unified Access system.

An identity system like this one is so much more than just the Policy Server. The NADs themselves along with their advanced capabilities are absolutely critical to having a successful system. That is why the NAD configurations provided in this chapter are absolutely mission critical to the success of your project.

Chapter 12

Network Authorization Policy Elements

This chapter covers the following topics:

■ ISE network authorization policy elements

■ Authorization results

This chapter focuses on exploring network authorization policy elements, with an emphasis on the authorization results policy elements. Cisco ISE network authorization policies are used to define and control a user's or device's access on the network. These policies apply for all access methods: wired, wireless, and VPN.

ISE Authorization Policy Elements

An ISE authorization policy is made up of user-defined policy rules. A policy typically has more than one rule, but this is not required. ISE provides two policy execution options:

■ First matched rules apply

■ Multiple matched rule applies

The default, *first matched rules apply*, is by far the most commonly used option in deployments. It works like a firewall ACL in that once a rule is matched, execution stops and no further rule processing occurs. With *multiple matched rule applies*, ISE evaluates all rules and combines the permissions for all matched rules.

If ISE had only a single policy table for everything, it would get unwieldy fairly quickly. Therefore, ISE has policy sets. Using policy sets enables you, as the administrator, to break up your authentication and authorization policies in multiple separate policies for a specific use case. Together, this is called a *policy set*. Policy sets can be combined to create a full policy or can be used individually for a specific use case. Policy sets are disabled by default, but it is highly recommended that you enable them in **Administration > System > Settings > Policy Sets**. Figure 12-1 depicts policy sets.

Figure 12-1 *ISE Policy Sets*

Within an ISE authorization policy, there are three policy types. Each policy has a section at the top for Exceptions, a section for Standard Policies, and a rule at the bottom of the Standard Policies section for Default. The following is a brief explanation of each policy type. Figure 12-2 shows an example of these rule types.

- **Exception Policies:** These policy rules are used to override standard and default policy rules. Exception policy rules are evaluated first and, if matched, take precedence over standard and default rules in the policy. This rule type is usually used when you need to make a temporary change to ISE policy quickly. They are also great for making permanent exceptions for specialized groups, device types, locations, and so on.

Figure 12-2 *ISE Policy Rule Types*

■ **Standard Policies:** These policy rules are the regular/typical rules that you would spend most of your time writing. They are the core of ISE functionality.

■ **Default Rule:** The catch-all rule at the bottom of every authorization policy is the default rule type. If none of the exception or standard policy rules match, then the action specified in the default rule is matched and executed. This rule is typically defined as a simple deny access or permit access but can have any permissions you need instead.

ISE authorization policy rules are made by combining policy elements. Each policy rule within a policy has at least four elements: rule status, rule name, identity groups and conditions, and permissions. This makes up the basic structure of a policy rule. Figure 12-3 shows a generic rule template and the elements within.

Figure 12-3 *ISE Policy Rule Elements*

ISE policy rule elements are defined by ISE conditions. Cisco ISE allows you to create conditions as individual and reusable policy elements that can be referred from other rule-based policies. There are two types of conditions:

■ **Simple condition:** A simple condition consists of an operand (attribute), an operator (equal to, not equal to, greater than, and so on), and a value. You can save simple conditions and reuse them in other rule-based policies. Simple condition takes the form A *operand* B, where A can be any attribute from the Cisco ISE dictionary and B is the value(s) that the attribute A can take. For example, Device Type Equals Switch.

■ **Compound condition:** A compound condition consists of one or more simple conditions that are connected by the AND or OR operator. Compound conditions are built on top of simple conditions. You can save and reuse compound conditions in other rule-based policies. For example, ((A = B) AND (C = D)), such as ((Device Type = Switch) AND (AD Group = Employees)).

The elements and attributes that you use to create your conditions and policies are stored in the ISE Policy Elements database (**Policy > Policy Elements**). Cisco ISE policy elements are objects that are used in an authorization policy. Cisco ISE policy elements are broken up into three high-level groups:

■ **Dictionaries:** The dictionaries contain objects that are used throughout ISE to define conditions, policies, profiles, and more. A dictionary object's purpose is to "teach" ISE how to categorize external data that it either receives (syslog, SNMP trap, RADIUS, and so on) or asks for (polling, AD query, RADIUS, and so on). ISE predefines hundreds of system dictionary objects for you. System-defined dictionaries are read-only. You cannot create, edit, or delete any system-defined attribute in a system dictionary. For example, ISE includes a predefined CERTIFICATE dictionary, which contains many predefined CERTIFICATE attributes, as shown on the left in Figure 12-4 with the Issuer-Common Name attribute selected. The values and mapping to ISE internal names are shown on the right in Figure 12-4. ISE also allows you to create your own custom dictionary and custom dictionary attributes.

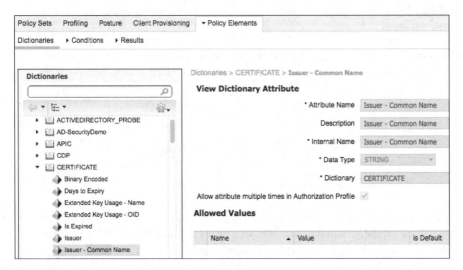

Figure 12-4   *ISE Dictionary Policy Element*

- **Conditions:** Conditions are policy elements that define a simple or compound expression to match against. Authorization Condition policy elements are Dictionary objects used to define a simple or compound expression to match against. Conditions are used in authorization policies as explained previously. Figure 12-5 shows an example of a condition that matches when the value in dictionary element Network Access:EapAuthentication equals EAP-MSCHAPv2. Other common conditions include things such as Active Directory group membership, time of day, and much more. ISE includes some default conditions to speed deployment.

Figure 12-5   *ISE Condition Policy Element*

- **Results:** Results are policy elements that define a group of network access control privileges. Authorization policy element *Results* are used to define and group authorization permissions. These are then referenced in an ISE authorization Policy Rule permissions column. Authorization results are broken into two groups: Authorization Profiles and Downloadable ACLs. Results elements are explained in detail in this chapter.

Authorization Results

Authorization results define the permissions that are allowed when an authorization policy rule is matched. They are, in general, the RADIUS attributes that will be sent to the network access devices (NAD) to control some aspect of access control for the session. As discussed, authorization results are broken into two groups: authorization profiles and downloadable ACLs. Authorization profiles act like permission templates and, as such, define all of the different access control permissions you want to apply to a matched policy rule. For example, suppose you want to change a matched user's VLAN to contractors and permit them network access. To do this, you would create an authorization profile that includes Access Type set to Access_Accept and VLAN name set to Contractors. Authorization profiles can include lots of different permissions and permission types. One popular permission is a downloadable access control list (dACL). This section explores dACLs and the other permission controls available in ISE. The basic idea is that you define authorization profiles that contain various permissions and then assign those permissions to an authorization policy rule in a policy set. See Figure 12-6 for an example authorization policy rule showing permissions set to an authorization profile.

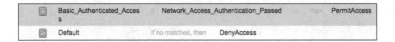

Figure 12-6 *ISE Authorization Policy Rule with Permissions*

Configuring Authorization Downloadable ACLs

An ACL is like a firewall policy. It contains a list of access control entries (ACE). dACLs, previously mentioned, are ACLs that can be dynamically downloaded on-demand from ISE to Cisco switches. Once you create a dACL on ISE, the dACL is then added to an authorization profile. Each ACE defines a traffic control rule to permit or deny packets. The syntax for writing ACEs in ISE is just like the syntax you would use to write them on the switch that you are sending them to.

ACEs use the following attributes:

- **Source and destination protocols:** Authentication Header Protocol (**ahp**), Enhanced Interior Gateway Routing Protocol (**eigrp**), Encapsulation Security Payload (**esp**), generic routing encapsulation (**gre**), Internet Control Message Protocol (**icmp**), Internet Group Management Protocol (**igmp**), any Interior Protocol (**ip**), IP in IP tunneling (**ipinip**), KA9Q NOS-compatible IP over IP tunneling (**nos**), Open Shortest Path First routing (**ospf**), Payload Compression Protocol (**pcp**), Protocol-Independent Multicast (**pim**), Transmission Control Protocol (**tcp**), or User Datagram Protocol (**udp**).

■ **Source and destination IP address:** The source IP address must always be **any**. The NAD will replace **any** with the source IP address of the connected device. dACLs are only supported on switches; the Cisco Wireless LAN Controller (WLC) uses a different mechanism called Airspace ACLs.

■ **Protocol source and destination ports:** Available ports are from 0 to 65535 for TCP and UDP.

■ **Remark:** ACL comments.

■ **Cisco syntax for a TCP ACL: access-list** *access-list-number* {deny | permit} **tcp** *source source-wildcard* [*operator port*] *destination destination-wildcard* [*operator port*] [**established**] [**precedence** *precedence*] [**tos** *tos*] [**fragments**] [**log**] [**log-input**] [**time-range** *time-range-name*] [**dscp** *dscp*] [*flag*].

■ All ACL have an implicit **deny** at the end of them.

■ If you use the **time-range** feature, you must manually configure the time range on the switch. ISE can then call the time-range in the ACL. Be sure to check that the naming matches exactly.

Note The **log** keyword should be used sparingly because logging is done in software on the switch. Also, the first packet that triggers the ACL causes a logging message right away, and subsequent packets are collected over 5-minute intervals before they appear as logged. The logging message includes the access list number, whether the packet was permitted or denied, the source IP address of the packet, and the number of packets from that source permitted or denied in the prior 5-minute interval. The **smartlog** keyword at the end of an ACE uses NetFlow records export and therefore may be more efficient on the switch. The ISE syntax checker as of version 2.2 doesn't think it is valid, but it is.

To configure a dACL, go to **Policy > Policy Elements > Results > Authorization > Downloadable ACLs** and click **Add**. You can also duplicate an existing ACL and edit the duplicate.

Figure 12-7 shows an example of an ISE dACL configuration. As you can see, ACL error checking is built into ISE to ensure your syntax is correct.

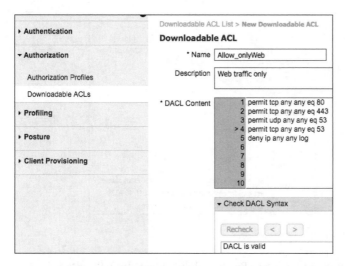

Figure 12-7 *ISE dACL Example*

Cisco ISE includes a basic dACL syntax checker to help to ensure your ACE statements are correct. If you enter malformed syntax and click the Recheck button, the syntax checker will show you the error along with some assistance. The help is very similar to what you would receive at the command-line interface (CLI) of the switch itself.

The dACL syntax checker is able to check for basic ACL fields but does not support all the ACL commands that a particular Cisco switch might support. Therefore, the syntax checker may report an error even if your syntax is correct. The dACL is a free-text field and ISE will send whatever it contains to the device regardless of the syntax checker results. At that point, it is up to you to ensure that your syntax is correct without the help of the syntax checker. If correct, the dACL will work just fine, regardless of the error shown in the syntax checker.

Configuring Authorization Profiles

An authorization profile acts as a container in which a number of specific permissions allow access to a set of network services. The authorization profile defines a set of permissions to be granted for a network access request. The authorization profile attributes are delivered via RADIUS. The RADIUS code is configured in the profile along with one or more attribute-value pairs (AVP). Figure 12-8 shows one example. The most common permission settings are Access_Accept/Access Reject, dACL name, Airespace ACL Name, VLAN, and Reauthentication timers.

Figure 12-8   *Authorization Profile Permissions*

To configure an authorization profile, go to **Policy > Policy Elements > Results > Authorization > Authorization Profiles** and click **Add.** You can also duplicate an existing profile and then edit it. Figure 12-9 shows an example profile.

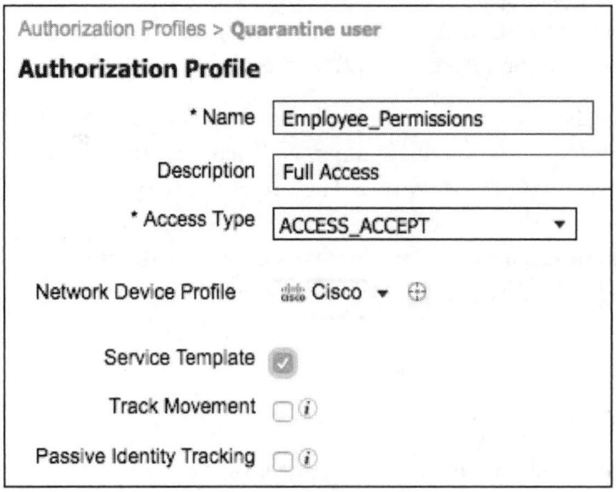

Figure 12-9   *Authorization Profile Example*

Figure 12-9 displays the following authorization profile fields:

■ **Name:** Enter a descriptive name; spaces are allowed here, as are ! # $ % & ' ( ) * + , - . / ; = ? @ _ {.

■ **Description:** Enter an explanatory description.

■ **Access Type:** The only two options are Access_Accept and Access_Reject. If you use Access_Reject, the user is unconditionally denied access to all requested network resources.

■ **Service Template:** Checking this check box tells ISE to use the profile name as the SA-NET profile name. SA-NET profiles are configured on newer Cisco switches. Ensure the naming matches exactly between ISE and the switch. Cisco ISE sends the name of the service template to the device, and the device downloads the content (RADIUS attributes) of the template if it does not already have a cached or statically defined version of it. In addition, Cisco ISE sends Change of Authorization (CoA) notifications to the device if a RADIUS attribute was added, removed, or changed in the service template.

■ **Track Movement:** ISE can integrate with the Cisco Mobility Services Engine (MSE) to enable device tracking based on physical location. This physical location can then be used in ISE authorization rules to change permissions based on a device's physical location. A device's location is reported by MSE once, upon ISE session establishment. However, if you would like to track a device's movement every 5 minutes, then check this check box. Note that Track Movement could impact the performance of ISE if not used judiciously, so use it sparingly in your policy.

■ **Passive Identity Tracking:** If you are using ISE EasyConnect, then you must enable this feature. This enables the EasyConnect process to run and for ISE to issue CoAs. Chapter 6, "Quick Setup of an ISE Proof of Concept," covers EasyConnect in more detail.

The final section in the authorization profile is called *Common Tasks*. This is a collection of the commonly used permissions. They are presented in plain-English format to make it easy for the administrator to configure. In the background, they are translated into RADIUS attributes and AV pairs. Figure 12-10 depicts the Common Tasks list in a profile.

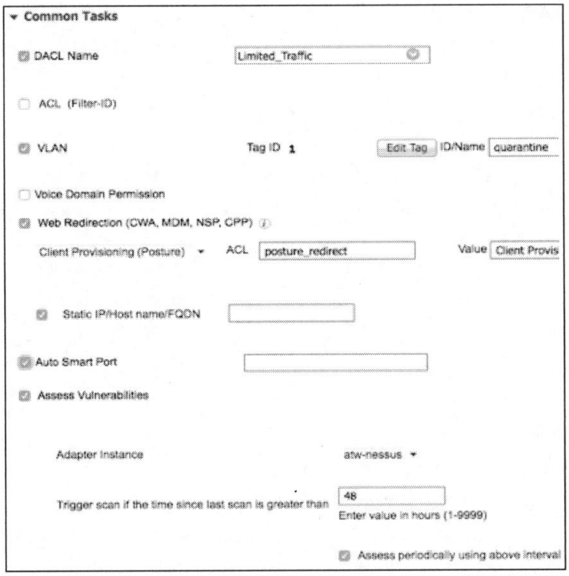

Figure 12-10 *Authorization Profile Common Tasks Partial List*

Summary

ISE authorization is made up of several different elements that work together to create an authorization policy set. These policy sets are then matched against to create a permissions list for an ISE user or device session.

Authorization profiles hold the permissions list returned to a network access device when a RADIUS request is accepted. Cisco ISE provides a mechanism that enables you to configure common tasks to support commonly used permissions and attributes.

Policy elements are components used to define the authorization policy. The policy elements are as follows:

- Dictionaries
- Condition(s)
- Results

These policy elements are referenced when you create policy rules, and your choice of conditions and attributes can create specific types of authorization profiles. A firm understanding of the ISE authorization policy structure and elements is key to a successful ISE deployment.

Chapter 13

Authentication and Authorization Policies

This chapter covers the following topics:

- Relationship between authentication and authorization
- Authentication policies
- Authorization policies
- Saving attributes for reuse

The previous chapter focused on the levels of authorization you should provide for users and devices based on your logical security policy. You will build policies in ISE that employ network authorization results, such as downloadable access control lists (dACL) and authorization profiles to accommodate the enforcement of that "paper policy."

These authorization profiles are the end result: the final decision of a login session or a particular stage of a login session.

This chapter examines how to build the authentication and authorization policies that will eventually assign those results that were created in Chapter 11, "Bootstrapping Network Access Devices." These policies can be equated to the rules in a firewall and are constructed in a similar fashion.

Relationship Between Authentication and Authorization

Many IT professionals, especially those with backgrounds in wireless technologies, tend to confuse the terms authentication and authorization and what they actually do. Wireless is used as an example here because it has experienced such tremendous growth over the past few years, and with that growth, security capabilities have increased tremendously. Wireless was the most prevalent use case of 802.1X authentication, and in the vast majority of wireless environments, a user was given full network access as long as her username and password were correct (meaning that authentication was successful).

An authentication is, simply put, "validating credentials." If you go into a bank and request a withdrawal from an account, the bank teller asks for ID. You pass your driver's license to the bank teller, and the teller inspects the driver's license, going through a checklist of sorts:

- Does the picture on the license look like the person in front of the teller's window?

- Is the license from a recognized authority (i.e., one of the U.S. states or territories)?

Let's say, for conversation's sake, that you handed the teller a valid ID (authentication was successful); does that mean you are *entitled* to the money you asked for?

The next step of the bank teller is to check the account and ensure that the person requesting the withdrawal is entitled to complete that transaction. Perhaps you are allowed to withdraw up to $1,000, but no more. This is the process of authorization. Just having a successful authentication does not prove entitlement.

This is why most of the time working within a product like ISE is spent setting up and tuning the authorization policy. Authorization is where the bulk of the final decisions are made.

Enable Policy Sets

An authentication policy leads to an authorization policy. This makes sense, because you cannot authorize someone if you don't know who they are first, right? The ISE user interface is built this way, with the authentication and authorization policies being separate.

However, having just a single authentication policy and a single authorization policy that have to work for all the many different use cases gets to be very cumbersome, hard to navigate, and difficult to troubleshoot.

That is where policy sets come into play. A *policy set* is a separate pair of authentication and authorization rules. Back in the ACS 5.x days, we called it "service selection rules." Policy sets were introduced in ISE version 1.2. Many of us who have a lot of experience deploying 802.1X in networks have said that policy sets were the only way to deploy successfully.

For instance, let's assume there is a wireless LAN (WLAN) named WOLAND-GUEST for all guest users to use, and a completely different WLAN named WOLAND-CORP for employees to use. Those two distinct networks will have completely different policies assigned to them. Different authentication types would be expected on the guest network, as well as different authorizations assigned to the users who join those networks.

By leveraging policy sets, we can organize our policies so that the guest policies are completely separate from the employee policies in the ISE GUI. This helps us keep logical separation in our own management of the solution, but also enables easier troubleshooting as well.

By changing the ISE GUI to start using policy sets, we are following Cisco TAC and TME best practices, and we are simultaneously helping this book along by adding in the illustration of the relationship between authentications and authorizations.

From the ISE GUI, navigate to **Administration > System > Settings > Policy Sets**, click **Enabled**, as shown in Figure 13-1, and then click **Save**. When you click **Save**, you will be logged out of the GUI so that the GUI framework may be reinitialized with the correct policy set model. This is not a reboot of the appliance, just a log-off and re-login instead.

Figure 13-1   *Enabling Policy Sets*

Log back into ISE and you will see Policy Sets under the Policy menu, as well as any of the Work Centers where the authentication and authorization polices are applicable.

Navigate to **Work Centers > Network Access > Policy Sets**, or **Policy > Policy Sets** as shown in Figure 13-2. As you see in Figure 13-2, there is a summary of all the policy sets that exist in the main window on the right side, while you can add, move, and create new policy sets on the left side.

Figure 13-2 *Policy Sets Overview*

Click the **Default** policy set on the left side to see the authentication and authorization policies expand on the right side, as shown in Figure 13-3.

Figure 13-3 *Default Policy Set*

Notice the flow in Figure 13-3. An incoming RADIUS request matches a top-level rule, where the policy set is determined. The next step is to process the authentication followed by the authorization. Figure 13-4 illustrates that flow.

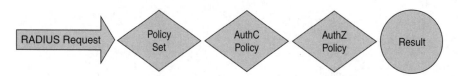

Figure 13-4 *Overview of Policy Sets Flow*

The incoming network access request will be processed by the designated authentication policy, which leads to the authorization policy. It is the authorization result that dictates if access is granted and, if so, what is allowed and what is not.

Authentication Policy Goals

Authentication policies have the following goals, but the ultimate end goal of an authentication policy is to determine if the identity credential is valid or not:

1. Drop incoming requests that aren't allowed and prevent them from taking up any more processing power.

2. Route authentication requests to the correct identity store (sometimes called a policy information point [PIP]).

3. Validate the identity.

4. Pass successful authentications through to the authorization policy.

Accept Only Allowed Protocols

By default, ISE allows nearly all supported authentication protocols. However, it would behoove the organization to lock this down to only the ones that are expected and supported. This serves a few purposes: keep the load on the PSNs down and use the authentication protocol to help choose the right identity store.

Route to the Correct Identity Store

Once the authentication request is accepted, ISE makes a routing decision. The identity store that should be checked is based on the incoming authentication request. Obviously, if a certificate is being presented, ISE should not try and validate that certificate against the internal user database.

If your company has multiple lines of business, it may also have more than one Active Directory domain or more than one LDAP store. Using attributes in the authentication request, you can pick the correct domain or LDAP store.

Validate the Identity

After the correct identity store has been identified, ISE confirms the credentials are valid. If it's a username and password, ISE checks whether they match what is in the directory store. If it's a certificate, ISE checks whether it trusts the certificate signer and whether the certificate has been revoked.

Pass the Request to the Authorization Policy

If the authentication failed, the policy can reject the request without wasting the CPU cycles required to compare the request to the authorization policy. Also, if the request did not match any of the configured rules, should a reject message be sent? However, when the request passes authentication, it is now time for the hand-off to the authorization policy.

Understanding Authentication Policies

Now that you understand the four main responsibilities of the authentication policy, it will be easier to understand why you are doing the things that are introduced in this section.

Something we like to call "smart defaults" were added to the product beginning with Cisco ISE 1.4 and enhanced further in each release. These settings are designed to make it very quick and easy to start using ISE immediately after the install completes. In fact, with ISE 2.0, the authors of this book can have the entire system set up all the way through BYOD onboarding in less than 20 minutes thanks to these smart default settings.

To help you understand authentication policies and smart defaults in more depth, this section examines some of the default policies and takes a deeper look at the out-of-the-box settings.

From the ISE GUI, navigate to **Work Centers > Network Access > Policy Sets > Default**, or **Policy > Policy Sets**, as displayed previously in Figure 13-3.

Basic authentication policy rules are logically organized in this manor:

> **IF** *conditions* **THEN ALLOW PROTOCOLS IN** *AllowedProtocolList*
>
> **AND CHECK THE IDENTITY STORE IN LIST** *IdentityStore*

Rules are processed in a top-down, first-match order, just like a firewall policy or an access list. So, if the conditions do not match, the authentication is compared to the next rule in the policy.

As shown in the upper-right quadrant of Figure 13-3, ISE is preconfigured with a default rule for MAC Authentication Bypass (MAB). Use this rule to dig into authentication rules and how they work. If you have a live ISE system, it may help to follow along with the text.

Figure 13-5 demonstrates the MAB rule in flowchart format.

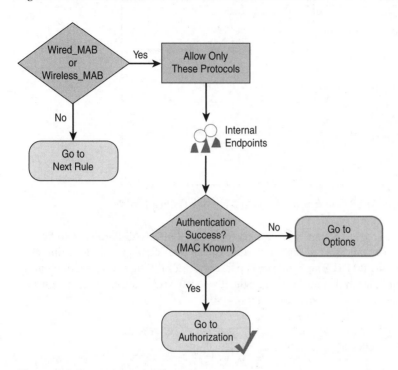

Figure 13-5   *MAB Rule Flow Chart*

Conditions

As Figures 13-4 and 13-5 indicate, the conditions of this MAB rule state, "If the authentication request is Wired_MAB or Wireless_MAB, it matches this rule." You can expand these conditions by hovering your mouse pointer over the conditions in ISE and clicking the target icon that appears or by looking directly at the authentication conditions shown in the following steps:

Step 1.   Navigate to **Work Centers > Network Access > Policy Elements > Conditions > Authentication Compound Conditions**.

Step 2.   Select **Wired_MAB**.

As you can see in Figure 13-6, the Wired_MAB condition is mapped to different dictionary attributes per network device vendor.

Figure 13-6 *Wired_MAB Condition for Cisco Network Device Profile*

For Cisco, the condition is looking for the RADIUS NAS-Port-Type to be Ethernet and Service-Type to be Call Check. This combination of attributes from the RADIUS authentication packet notifies ISE that it is a MAB request from a switch. Figure 13-7 highlights these key attributes in a packet capture of the MAB authentication request.

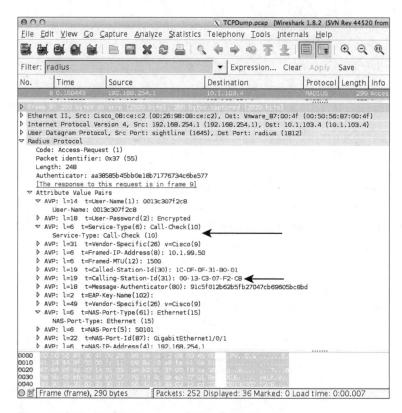

Figure 13-7 *Packet Capture of Wired MAB*

It's important to note that different vendors will use different attributes. The same compound condition will get mapped to different attributes so it may be leveraged by different network vendors without requiring separate policies. Figure 13-8 shows the settings after clicking BrocadeWired. Brocade switches send MAB requests using a Service-Type of Framed, which is the same Service-Type that many vendors use for 802.1X authentications.

Note   The RADIUS Service-Type attribute is supposed to define the type of RADIUS request, and a unique one would be used for each authentication request type. However, MAB is not a standard and therefore there is no set attribute to use.

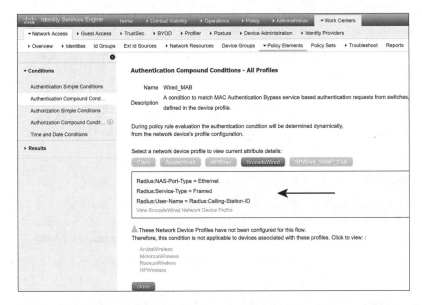

Figure 13-8   *Wired_MAB Condition for BrocadeWired Network Device Profile*

To see the different vendor mappings, click the network device vendor name; however, the main focus of this book is on the Cisco network devices.

Step 3.   Navigate to **Work Centers > Network Access > Policy Elements > Conditions > Authentication Compound Conditions**.

Step 4.   Select **Wireless_MAB**.

As shown in Figure 13-9, Wireless_MAB is similar to Wired_MAB; however, it uses a NAS-Port-Type of Wireless - IEEE 802.11. This combination of attributes from the RADIUS authentication packet tells ISE that it is a MAB request from a wireless device.

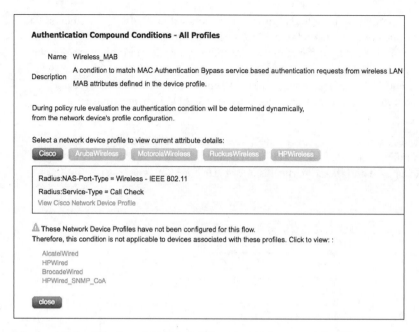

Authentication Compound Conditions - All Profiles

Name   Wireless_MAB

Description   A condition to match MAC Authentication Bypass service based authentication requests from wireless LAN MAB attributes defined in the device profile.

During policy rule evaluation the authentication condition will be determined dynamically, from the network device's profile configuration.

Select a network device profile to view current attribute details:

Cisco   ArubaWireless   MotorolaWireless   RuckusWireless   HPWireless

Radius:NAS-Port-Type = Wireless - IEEE 802.11

Radius:Service-Type = Call Check

View Cisco Network Device Profile

⚠ These Network Device Profiles have not been configured for this flow.
Therefore, this condition is not applicable to devices associated with these profiles. Click to view: :

AlcatelWired
HPWired
BrocadeWired
HPWired_SNMP_CoA

close

Figure 13-9 *Wireless_MAB Condition for Cisco Network Device Profile*

Allowed Protocols

After the conditions are matched, the rule now dictates what authentication protocols are permitted. Looking at the predefined MAB rule, this rule uses the Default Network Access list of allowed protocols (which is almost every supported authentication protocol).

Let's examine the default allowed protocols. From the ISE GUI, perform the following steps:

Step 1.   Navigate to **Work Centers > Network Access > Policy Elements > Results > Allowed Protocols**.

Step 2.   Select **Default Network Access**.

As you can see in Figure 13-10, the list of supported protocols and their options is extensive. This default list is inclusive with the intention of making deployments work easily for customers, but security best practice is to lock this down to only the protocols needed for that rule.

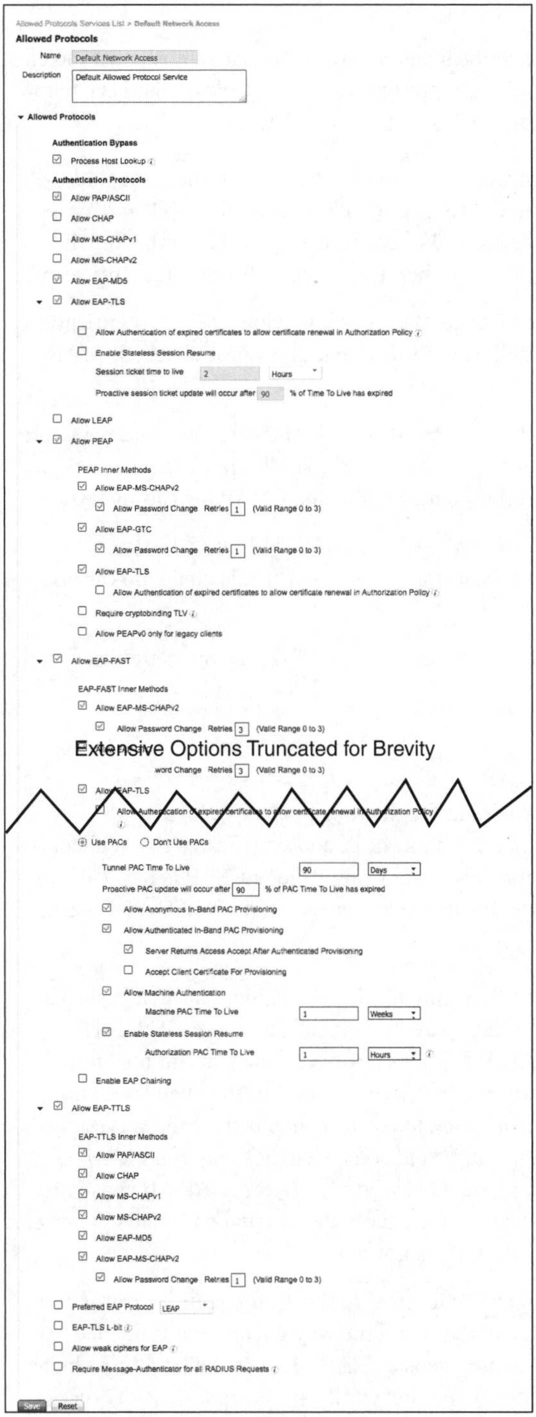

Figure 13-10 *Default Network Access*

Authentication Protocol Primer

This section examines the most common authentication protocols seen in most environments, so you can create a more specific list of allowed protocols for your deployment. Let's follow the Allowed Protocols list shown in Figure 13-10, from the top down:

- **PAP:** Password Authentication Protocol. The username is sent in the clear, and the password is optionally encrypted. PAP is normally used with MAB, and some devices use PAP for web authentications. We recommend you enable this for the MAB rule only and disable PAP for any authentication rules for real authentications.

  Checking the check box for Detect PAP as Host Lookup allows PAP authentications to access the internal endpoints database. If this check box is not checked, MAB does not work.

- **CHAP:** Challenge Handshake Authentication Protocol. The username and password are encrypted using a challenge sent from the server. CHAP is not often used with network access; however, some vendors send MAB using CHAP instead of PAP.

  Checking the check box for Detect CHAP as Host Lookup allows CHAP authentications to access the internal endpoints database. If this check box is not checked, MAB does not work.

- **EAP:** Extensible Authentication Protocol has a host of flavors, which are discussed in the sections that follow.

Extensible Authentication Protocol (EAP) Types

EAP is an authentication framework providing for the transport and usage of identity credentials. EAP encapsulates the usernames, passwords, and certificates that a client is sending for purposes of authentication. There are many different EAP types, each of which has its own benefit and downside. As an interesting side note, 802.1X defines EAP over LAN (EAPoL).

- **EAP-MD5:** Uses a Message Digest algorithm to hide the credentials in a hash. The hash is sent to the server, where it is compared to a local hash to see if the credentials are accurate. However, EAP-MD5 does not have a mechanism for mutual authentication. That means the server validates the client, but the client does not authenticate the server (i.e., does not check to see if it should trust the server). EAP-MD5 is common on some IP phones, and some switches may send MAB requests within EAP-MD5. Checking the check box for Detect EAP-MD5 as Host Lookup allows EAP-MD5 authentications to access the internal endpoints database. Without this check box checked, MAB does not work.

- **EAP-TLS:** Uses Transport Layer Security to provide the secure identity transaction. This is similar to Secure Sockets Layer (SSL) and the way encryption is formed between your web browser and a secure website. EAP-TLS has the benefit of being an open IETF standard, and it is considered universally supported. EAP-TLS uses X.509 certificates and provides the ability to support mutual authentication, where the client must trust the server's certificate, and vice versa. It is considered among the most secure EAP types, because password capture is not an option; the endpoint must still have the private key. EAP-TLS has solidified itself as the EAP type of choice when supporting BYOD in the enterprise.

Tunneled EAP Types

The EAP types previously described transmit their credentials immediately. These next three EAP types form encrypted tunnels first and then transmit the credentials within the tunnel (see Figure 13-11):

- **PEAP:** Protected EAP. Originally proposed by Microsoft, this EAP tunnel type has quickly become the most popular and widely deployed EAP method in the world. PEAP forms a potentially encrypted TLS tunnel between the client and server, using the X.509 certificate on the server in much the same way the SSL tunnel is established between a web browser and a secure website. After the tunnel is formed, PEAP uses one of the EAP types listed next as an inner method, authenticating the client using EAP within the outer tunnel:

  - **EAP-MS-CHAPv2:** When using this inner method, the client's credentials are sent to the server encrypted within an MS-CHAPv2 session. This is the most common inner method, as it allows for simple transmission of username and password, or even computer name and computer passwords, to the RADIUS server, which in turn authenticates them to Active Directory.

  - **EAP-GTC:** EAP-Generic Token Card. This inner method created by Cisco as an alternative to MS-CHAPv2 allows generic authentications to virtually any identity store, including one-time password (OTP) token servers, LDAP, NetIQ eDirectory (formerly Novell), and more.

  - **EAP-TLS:** Although rarely used and not widely known, PEAP is capable of using EAP-TLS as an inner method.

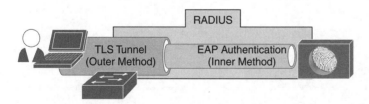

Figure 13-11 *Tunneled EAP Types (PEAP and FAST)*

- **EAP-FAST:** EAP Flexible Authentication via Secure Tunnel. This is similar to PEAP. FAST was created by Cisco as an alternative to PEAP that allows for faster reauthentications and supports faster wireless roaming. Just like PEAP, FAST forms a TLS outer tunnel and then transmits the client credentials within that TLS tunnel. Where FAST differs from PEAP is the ability to use Protected Access Credentials (PAC). A PAC can be thought of like a secure cookie, stored locally on the host as "proof" of a successful authentication.

■ **EAP-MS-CHAPv2:** When using this inner method, the client's credentials are sent to the server encrypted within an MS-CHAPv2 session. This is the most common inner method, as it allows for simple transmission of username and password, or even computer name and computer passwords, to the RADIUS server, which in turn authenticates them to Active Directory.

■ **EAP-GTC:** EAP-Generic Token Card. This inner method was created by Cisco as an alternative to MS-CHAPv2 that allows generic authentications to virtually any identity store, including OTP token servers, LDAP, NetIQ eDirectory, and more.

■ **EAP-TLS:** EAP-FAST is capable of using EAP-TLS as an inner method. This became popular with EAP chaining.

■ **EAP Chaining with EAP-FASTv2:** As an enhancement to EAP-FAST, a differentiation was made to have a user PAC and a machine PAC. After a successful machine authentication, ISE issues a machine PAC to the client. Then, when processing a user authentication, ISE requests the machine PAC to prove that the machine was successfully authenticated, too. This is the first time in 802.1X history that multiple credentials have been able to be authenticated within a single EAP transaction, and it is known as *EAP chaining*. The IETF is creating a new open standard based on EAP-FASTv2 and, at the time of writing, is to be referred to as EAP-TEAP (tunneled EAP), which should eventually be supported by all major vendors.

■ **EAP-TTLS:** EAP Tunneled Transport Layer Security. This is also similar to PEAP and EAP-FAST, as it too establishes an outer TLS tunnel to then pass the identity credentials securely within that tunnel. While EAP-FAST is most often credited as a Cisco EAP type, and PEAP is often credited to Microsoft, EAP-TTLS is always credited to Funk Software, which was acquired by Juniper. EAP-TTLS is most often found in Juniper UAC deployments and sometimes in European education networks that use a solution called eduroam (education roaming). As with all tunneled EAP types, numerous inner methods can be used within the tunnel, such as:

■ PAP/ASCII

■ CHAP

■ MS-CHAPv1

■ MS-CHAPv2

■ EAP-MD5

■ EAP-MS-CHAPv2

Certificate Renewal for EAP-TLS

Whether using EAP-TLS by itself or as an inner method, one fact holds true: user certificates can and do expire. In that case, a user or computer needs to request a new certificate. When the computer is managed by an endpoint manager, such as Active Directory, it typically takes care of the renewal of certificates. However, when the certificate is issued via a BYOD onboarding mechanism, there is nothing within the authentication protocol (PEAP or EAP-TLS) that handles renewing the certificate. Instead, the user must be run through the BYOD onboarding process another time and issued another certificate.

Part of certificate validation during an authentication is to ensure the certificate is valid. If a certificate has expired, it is no longer considered valid. That poses a chicken-and-egg problem for an ISE administrator. The endpoint may have to allow the certificate to expire before allowing it to be renewed, yet an expired certificate will fail authentication and therefore shouldn't be permitted for use with network access.

To address this problem, there is a setting under all EAP-TLS methods in the Allowed Protocols list to allow authentication of expired certificates to allow certificate renewal in the authorization policy, as shown in Figure 13-12. Checking this check box instructs ISE to still permit access with an expired certificate to enable the end user to go through the onboarding process again.

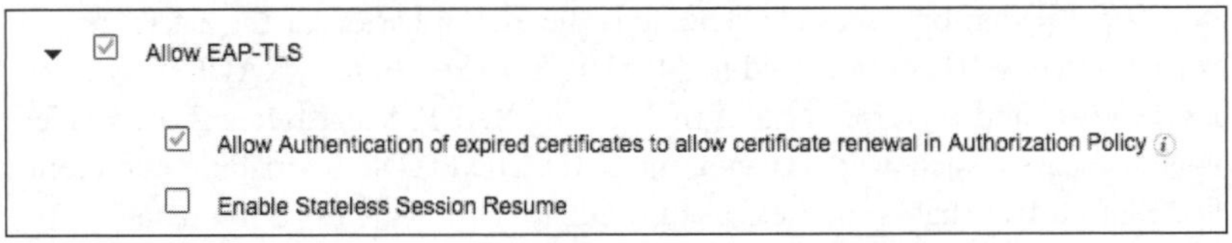

Figure 13-12 *Allowing Authentication of Expired Certificates*

Identity Store

After processing the allowed protocols, the authentication request is then authenticated against the chosen identity store, or in this case of MAB, it is compared to the internal endpoints database (list of MAC addresses stored locally on ISE).

If the MAC address is known, it is considered to be a successful MAB (notice it was not termed successful *authentication*). MAB is exactly that, bypassing authentication, and it is not considered a secure authentication.

The selected identity source may also be an identity source sequence, which attempts a series of identity stores in order.

Options

Every authentication rule has a set of options stored with the identity store selection. These options tell ISE what to do if an authentication fails, if the user/device is unknown, or if the process fails. The options are Reject, Continue, and Drop:

- **Reject:** Send Access-Reject back to the NAD.

- **Continue:** Continue to the authorization policy regardless of authentication pass/fail. (Used with web authentication.)

- **Drop:** Do not respond to the NAD; NAD will treat as if RADIUS server is dead.

Common Authentication Policy Examples

This section considers a few quick examples of authentication policies, based on common use cases or simply because they are interesting.

Using the Wireless SSID

One of the most common authentication policy requests that the authors get is to treat authentications differently based on the SSID of the wireless network. Creating the policy is not difficult; what becomes challenging is the identification of the attribute to use, because Source-SSID is not a field in a RADIUS packet. In fact, RADIUS was designed before Wi-Fi and therefore one of the existing RADIUS attributes is overloaded with additional use cases, such as identifying the SSID. The RADIUS attribute commonly used is Called-Station-ID. That is the field used to identify the wireless SSID name.

Beginning with ISE version 2.1, a new authentication dictionary was added to ISE, called *normalized RADIUS*. Cisco created this dictionary to make the creation of policies like this one easier, across the gamut of network devices, because different network device vendors may use different attributes to identify the SSID. Now, by using the Normalized RADIUS > SSID dictionary object, you can create one rule that looks for a specific SSID, and have that rule match for Cisco, Aruba, Ruckus…you name it. The translation is done in the background to match whatever is defined in the network device profile for the vendor.

For this example, let's build a rule for an SSID named CiscoPress. This rule will be configured to

- Only match authentications coming from that SSID

- Allow only EAP-FAST authentications

- Utilize EAP chaining

- Authenticate against Active Directory

From the ISE GUI, perform the following steps:

Step 1. Navigate to **Work Centers > Network Access > Policy Sets.**

Step 2. Select the **Default** policy set.

Step 3. In the Authentication Policy section, insert a new rule above the preconfigured Dot1X rule.

Step 4. Provide a name for the rule. For purposes of this example, name it **CiscoPress SSID.**

Step 5. For the condition, choose **Normalized RADIUS > SSID.**

Step 6. Select **Contains** from the middle drop-down under Description.

Step 7. Type the SSID name in the text box. Figure 13-13 shows the condition.

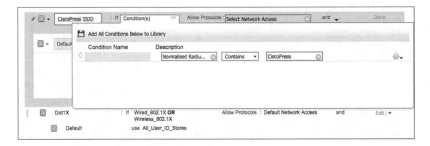

Figure 13-13   *SSID Contains CiscoPress*

Step 8. Create a new allowed protocol object that only allows EAP-FAST, as shown in Figure 13-14. Select the drop-down for Allowed Protocols.

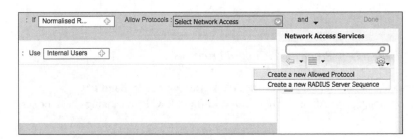

Figure 13-14   *Creating a New Allowed Protocol*

Step 9. Click the cog icon and choose **Create a New Allowed Protocol.**

Step 10. In the Name text box, enter a name of the new allowed protocol (**EAP-FAST Only** for purposes of this example).

Step 11. (Optional) Provide a description.

Step 12. Working top-down, ensure that all the check boxes are unchecked until you reach Allow EAP-FAST.

Step 13. Check the **Allow EAP-FAST** check box (if it isn't already checked).

Step 14. For ease of use, enable EAP-MS-CHAPv2, EAP-GTC, and EAP-TLS for inner methods by checking the corresponding check boxes under EAP-FAST Inner Methods.

Step 15. Click the **Use PACs** radio button for faster session re-establishment, and to allow EAP chaining.

Figure 13-15 shows the EAP-FAST settings for the new Allowed Protocols definition.

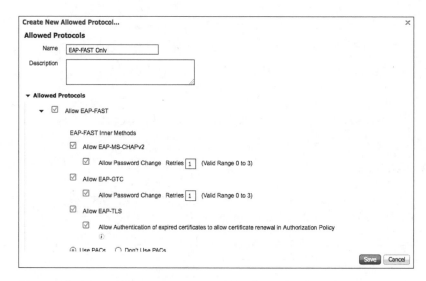

Figure 13-15 *Adding a New Protocol to Allowed Protocols*

Step 16. For ease of deployment, check the **Allow Anonymous In-Band PAC Provisioning** and **Allow Authenticated In-Band PAC Provisioning** check boxes.

Step 17.   Check the boxes for **Server Returns Access-Accept After Authenticated Provisioning** and **Accept Client Certificate For Provisioning**.

Step 18.   Check the **Allow Machine Authentication** check box.

Step 19.   Check the **Enable Stateless Session Resume** check box.

Step 20.   Check the **Enable EAP Chaining** check box, as shown in Figure 13-16.

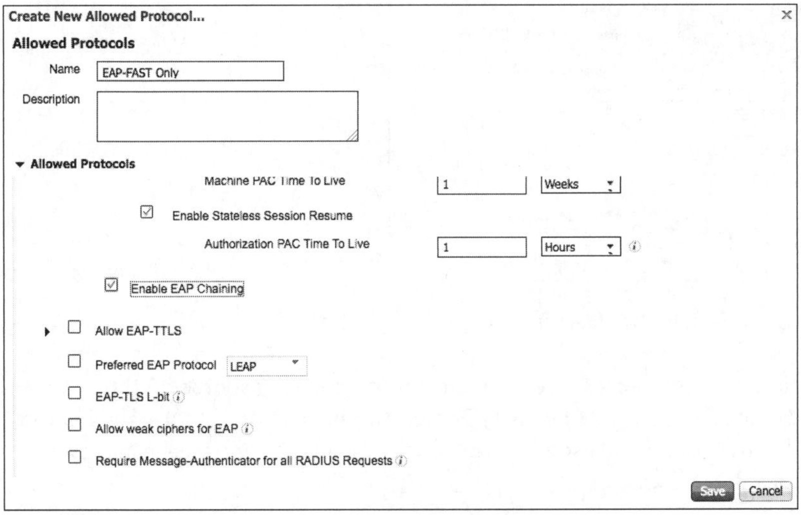

Figure 13-16   *Adding a New Protocol to Allowed Protocols, Continued*

Step 21.   Because you are only allowing one protocol, there is no need to set a preferred EAP protocol, so leave the Preferred EAP Protocol check box unchecked.

Step 22.   Click **Save**.

Step 23.   Click the drop-down arrow for the Identity Source field (currently set to Internal Users), as shown in Figure 13-17.

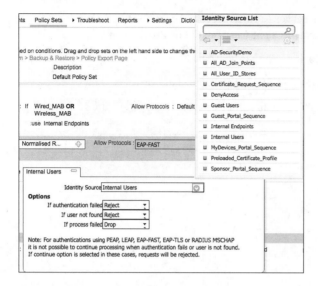

Figure 13-17 *Selecting the AD Identity Source*

Step 24. In the list of choices, choose your Active Directory source. In this example, choose **AD-SecurityDemo**. Another option is to use the built-in All_AD_Join_Points source, which will systematically try each and every joined AD domain.

Step 25. Under Options, leave the default settings for what action to take if authentication fails, the user is not found, or the process fails.

Step 26. Click **Done**.

Step 27. Click **Save**.

Figure 13-18 shows the completed authentication rule.

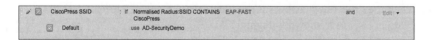

Figure 13-18 *Completed CiscoPress SSID Authentication Rule*

This completes the creation of the authentication rule. The authorization policy is what determines which actions to take for the authentications that passed.

Remote-Access VPN

Very often, authentications for a remote-access VPN connection get routed to an OTP server, such as an RSA SecureID server. For this example, let's build a rule for remote-access VPN authentications and configure it to do the following:

■ Only match authentications coming from the VPN device

■ Route that authentication to the OTP server

From the ISE GUI, perform the following steps:

Step 1. Navigate to **Work Centers > Network Access > Policy Sets > Default**.

Step 2. In the Authentication Policy section, insert a new rule above the preconfigured Dot1X rule.

Step 3. Provide a name for the rule. For purposes of this example, name it **RA VPN**.

Step 4. For the condition, choose **DEVICE:Device Type**.

Step 5. Set the operator to **Equals**.

Step 6. Choose the Network Device Group VPN.

Figure 13-19 shows the selection of the conditions.

Figure 13-19 *Device Type Equals VPN*

Step 7. For this example, set the Allow Protocols field to **Default Network Access**.

Step 8. For the identity store, the OTP server was selected that was previously configured in **Administration > Identity Management > External Identity Sources > RADIUS Token (ATWOTP)**.

Step 9. Leave the default options.

Step 10. Click **Done**.

Step 11. Click **Save**.

Figure 13-20 shows the completed RA VPN rule.

Figure 13-20 *Completed RA VPN Authentication Rule*

Alternative ID Stores Based on EAP Type

In this modern day of BYOD and mobility, it is common to have multiple user and device types connecting to the same wireless SSID. In scenarios like this, often times, the corporate users with corporate laptops authenticate using EAP-FAST with EAP chaining while BYOD-type devices need to use certificates and EAP-TLS. Anyone authenticating with PEAP is recognized as a non-corporate and non-registered asset and sent to a device registration portal instead of being permitted network access.

For this example, let's modify the preconfigured Dot1X rule by creating subrules for each EAP type. This rule will be configured to

- Match wired or wireless 802.1X

- Route EAP-TLS authentications to a Certificate Authentication Profile (CAP)

- Route PEAP authentications to an LDAP server

- Route EAP-FAST to Active Directory

- Route EAP-MD5 to internal endpoints for host-lookup as a MAB request

From the ISE GUI, perform the following steps:

Step 1.   Navigate to **Work Centers > Network Access > Policy Sets > Default.**

Step 2.   Click **Edit** to edit the preconfigured Dot1X rule.

Step 3.   Create a new allowed protocol object that only allows EAP authentications. Select the drop-down for allowed protocols.

Step 4.   Click the cog icon in the upper-right corner and choose **Create a New Allowed Protocol.**

Step 5.   Provide a name. For purposes of this example, name it **All EAP Types.**

Step 6.   (Optional) Provide a description.

Step 7.   Working top-down in the Allowed Protocols list, ensure that all EAP types are enabled (checked), except for LEAP (unless you need LEAP for backward compatibility).

Step 8.   Check the **EAP Chaining** check box, as you did previously in the wireless SSID exercise.

Step 9.   Click **Save.**

Step 10. Insert a new subrule above the Default identity store subrule and name it **EAP-TLS.**

Step 11. For the condition, choose **Network Access > EapAuthentication EQUALS EAP-TLS** (as shown in Figure 13-21).

Figure 13-21 *Condition Set to Network Access:EapAuthentication EQUALS EAP-TLS*

Step 12. For the identity source, choose the preconfigured Certificate Authentication Profile (CAP) named **Preloaded_Certificate_Profile**.

Step 13. Insert a new row above the EAP-TLS row to insert EAP-FAST. You place EAP-FAST above EAP-TLS because EAP-TLS may be used as an inner method of EAP-FAST.

Step 14. Choose **Network Access > EapTunnel EQUALS EAP-FAST** for the condition.

Step 15. Select the Active Directory object for the identity source.

Figure 13-22 shows the rules so far.

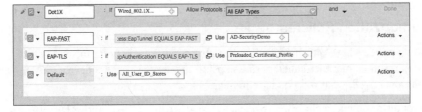

Figure 13-22 *Condition Set to Network Access:EapTunnel EQUALS EAP-FAST*

Step 16. Insert a new row above the EAP-TLS row to insert PEAP.

Step 17. Choose **Network Access > EapTunnel EQUALS PEAP** for the condition.

Step 18. Select the LDAP object for the identity source.

Step 19. Insert a new row below the EAP-TLS row to insert EAP-MD5.

Step 20. Choose **Network Access > EapAuthentication EQUALS EAP-MD5** for the condition.

Step 21. Select internal endpoints for the identity source.

Step 22. Change the default identity store (bottom row) to **Deny Access**.

Step 23. Click **Done**.

Step 24. Click **Save**.

Figure 13-23 shows the completed rule and subrules.

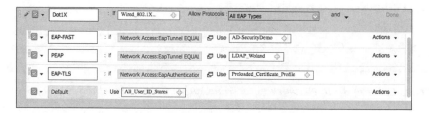

Figure 13-23   *Completed Authentication Rule and Subrules*

This completes the authentication section of this chapter. The next section takes an in-depth look at authorization policies and common authorization rules.

Authorization Policies

The ultimate goal of an authentication policy is to determine if the identity credential is valid or not; however, success or failure in the authentication policy may not necessarily determine whether the user or device is actually permitted access to the network. The authorization rules make that determination.

Goals of Authorization Policies

Authorization policies have one main goal: to examine conditions in order to send an authorization result (sometimes called permissions) to the network access device (NAD). What conditions? Well, what did you have in mind?

Common conditions could include internal and external attributes, like Active Directory group membership or internal group membership within ISE. Policies can be built using attributes like location, time, if a device was registered, whether a mobile device has been jail-broken…nearly any attribute imaginable. Even the authentication is an attribute: was authentication successful; which authentication protocol was used; and what is the content of specific fields of the certificate that was used?

The authorization policy compares these conditions with the explicit goal of providing an authorization result. The result may be a standard RADIUS Access-Accept or Access-Reject message, but it can also include more advanced items, like VLAN assignment, dACLs, Security Group Tag (SGT), URL redirection, and more.

The result allows or denies access to the network, and when it is allowed, it can include any and all restrictions for limiting network access for the user or endpoint.

Understanding Authorization Policies

Now that you understand the fundamental responsibilities of the authorization policy, it will be easier to understand the exercises in this section. To understand authorization policies even more, let's examine a few.

Basic authorization policy rules are logically organized in this manner:

IF *conditions* THEN *AssignThesePermissions*

Just like the authentication policy, authorization policy rules are processed in a top-down, first-match order. So, if the conditions do not match, the authentication is compared to the next rule in the policy.

As previously mentioned, ISE is preconfigured with rules that we call smart defaults. There is a rule for blacklisted devices, named Wireless Black List Default, another for Profiled Cisco IP Phones, and yet another for Profiled Non Cisco IP Phones. There are also some preconfigured rules that are disabled out of the box but can be used for BYOD onboarding and guest access. We will examine those rules in the relevant chapters for those topics.

Let's examine the Cisco IP Phone and Wireless Black List Default rules in order to dig into authorization rules and how they work. If you have a live ISE system, it may help to follow along with the text.

From the ISE GUI, perform the following steps:

Step 1.   Navigate to **Work Centers > Network Access > Policy Sets > Default**.

In the Authorization Policy section, you should notice an immediate difference between the authorization policy and the authentication policy examined earlier in this chapter. The authorization policy attempts to display the rule logic in plain English. The bold text designates an identity group, while the standard font is a normal attribute. The operator is always AND when both identity group and other conditions are used in the same rule.

Figure 13-24 displays the default authorization policy.

	Status	Rule Name		Conditions (identity groups and other conditions)		Permissions
	☑	Wireless Black List Default	if	**Blacklist** AND Wireless_Access	then	Blackhole_Wireless_Access
	☑	Profiled Cisco IP Phones	if	**Cisco-IP-Phone**	then	Cisco_IP_Phones
	☑	Profiled Non Cisco IP Phones	if	Non_Cisco_Profiled_Phones	then	Non_Cisco_IP_Phones
	⊘	Compliant_Devices_Access	if	(Network_Access_Authentication_Passed AND Compliant_Devices)	then	PermitAccess
	⊘	Employee_EAP-TLS	if	(Wireless_802.1X AND BYOD_is_Registered AND EAP-TLS AND MAC_in_SAN)	then	PermitAccess AND BYOD
	⊘	Employee_Onboarding	if	(Wireless_802.1X AND EAP-MSCHAPv2)	then	NSP_Onboard AND BYOD
	⊘	Wi-Fi_Guest_Access	if	(Guest_Flow AND Wireless_MAB)	then	PermitAccess AND Guests
	⊘	Wi-Fi_Redirect_to_Guest_Login	if	Wireless_MAB	then	Cisco_WebAuth
	☑	Basic_Authenticated_Access	if	Network_Access_Authentication_Passed	then	PermitAccess
	☑	Default		If no matches, then		DenyAccess

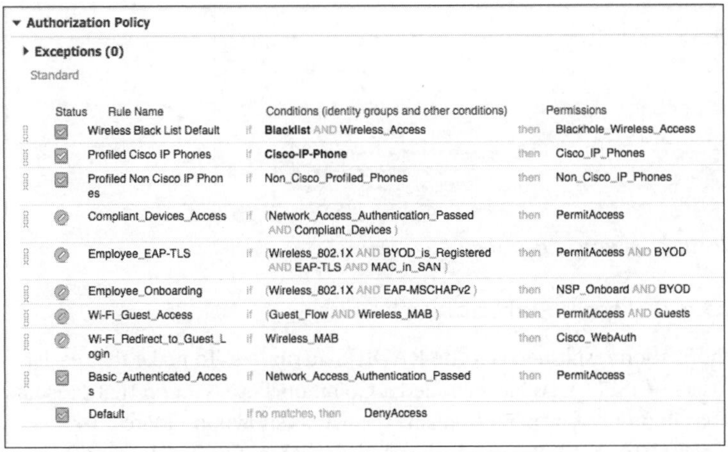

Figure 13-24   *Default Authorization Policy*

Step 2.   Click **Edit** to edit the rule named Profiled Cisco IP Phones.

Notice the identity group is a separate list than the other conditions. In this rule, there is an identity group named Cisco-IP-Phone. The next field is where other conditions are selected.

This particular rule is a prebuilt rule that permits any device that was profiled as a Cisco IP Phone, sending an Access-Accept that also sends an attribute-value pair (AVP) that permits the phone into the voice VLAN. Figure 13-25 shows an identity group of Cisco-IP-Phone.

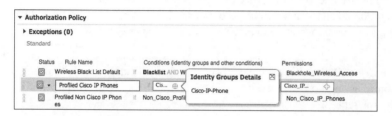

Figure 13-25   *Profiled Cisco IP Phones Rule*

Step 3.   Examine the permissions (result) that is sent. Navigate to **Work Centers > Network Access > Policy Elements > Results > Authorization Profiles**.

An authorization profile is a set of authorization results that should be sent together. Figure 13-26 displays the default authorization profiles.

Figure 13-26   *Default Authorization Profiles*

Step 4.   Click **Cisco_IP_Phones Authorization Profiles**.

The authorization result needs to be RADIUS attributes. To make that easier for the users of ISE, Cisco has included a Common Tasks section that presents the options in more of a "plain English" format, as shown in Figure 13-27 for the default Cisco_IP_Phones authorization profile. Further down, the Attributes Details section, shown in Figure 13-28, displays the raw RADIUS result that is sent.

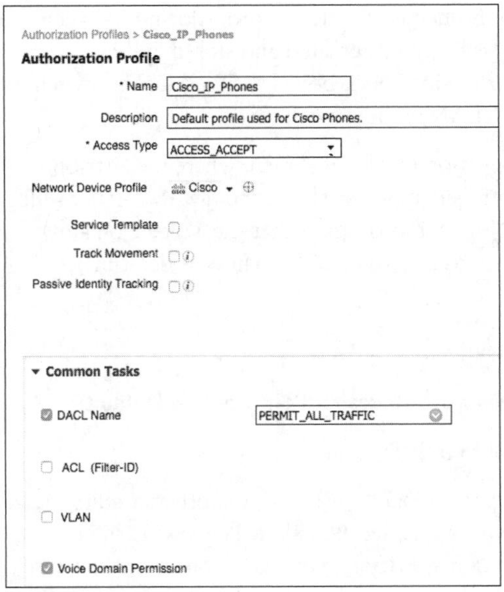

Authorization Profiles > **Cisco_IP_Phones**
Authorization Profile

* Name   Cisco_IP_Phones

Description   Default profile used for Cisco Phones.

* Access Type ACCESS_ACCEPT ▾

Network Device Profile   ⟐ Cisco ▾ ⊕

Service Template ☐

Track Movement ☐ ⓘ

Passive Identity Tracking ☐ ⓘ

▾ **Common Tasks**

☑ DACL Name   PERMIT_ALL_TRAFFIC   ⊘

☐ ACL (Filter-ID)

☐ VLAN

☑ Voice Domain Permission

Figure 13-27 *Cisco_IP_Phones Authorization Profile*

▾ **Common Tasks**

☑ DACL Name   PERMIT_ALL_TRAFFIC   ⊘

☐ ACL (Filter-ID)

☐ VLAN

☑ Voice Domain Permission

▾ **Advanced Attributes Settings**

Select an item   ⊘ =   ⊘ ━ ╋

▾ **Attributes Details**

Access Type = ACCESS_ACCEPT
DACL = PERMIT_ALL_TRAFFIC
cisco-av-pair = device-traffic-class=voice

Save   Reset

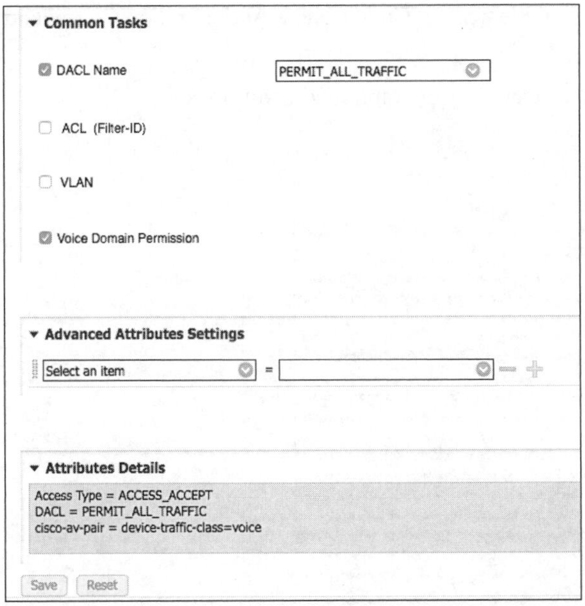

Figure 13-28 *Cisco_IP_Phones Authorization Profile Attributes Details*

In Figure 13-27, note the DACL Name task includes a drop-down box where you select a downloadable access list that is created and stored in ISE. Checking the Voice Domain Permission check box is required for the switch to allow the phone into the voice VLAN on the switch.

Figure 13-28 shows the lower portion of the UI screen, where the Attributes Details section previously mentioned appears. This is the raw RADIUS result that will be sent to the NAD. Notice in this figure that the Voice Domain Permission check box actually translates to cisco-av-pair = device-traffic-class=voice.

Next, examine the Wireless Black List Default rule:

Step 1. Navigate to **Work Centers > Network Access > Policy Sets > Default**.

Step 2. Edit the rule named Wireless Black List Default.

Again, notice the identity group is a separate list from the other conditions. In this rule, there is an identity group named **Blacklist**. The next field is populated with a prebuilt condition specifying wireless connections. This particular rule is built to prevent devices that have been marked lost or stolen from accessing the network.

Step 3. Examine the authorization condition being used. Navigate to **Work Centers > Network Access > Policy Elements > Conditions > Authorization Compound Conditions**.

Figure 13-29 shows the default list of compound conditions.

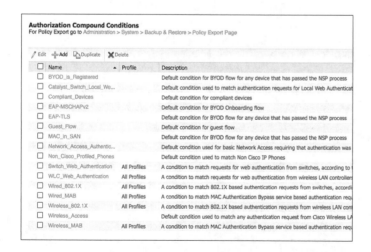

Figure 13-29 *Prebuilt Authorization Compound Conditions*

Step 4. Click on **Wireless_Access**.

As shown in Figure 13-30, the Wireless_Access compound condition references the RADIUS attribute of NAS-Port-Type Equals Wireless–IEEE 802.11.

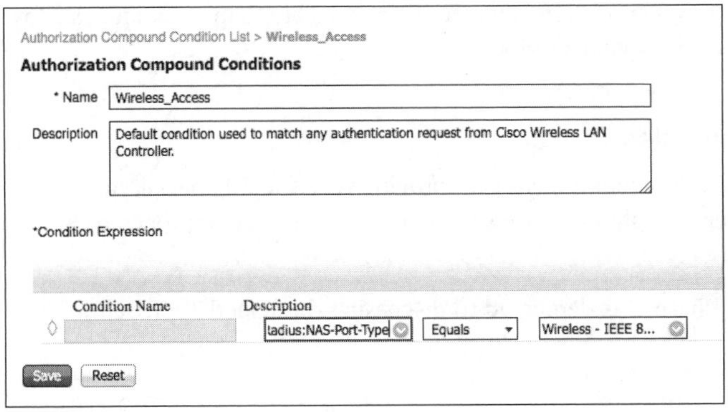

Figure 13-30 *Wireless_Access Compound Condition*

Step 5. Examine the authorization result that is being sent for this authorization rule. Navigate to **Work Centers > Network Access > Policy Elements > Results > Authorization Profiles.**

Step 6. Select **Blackhole_Wireless_Access.**

As shown in the composite image Figure 13-31, the Blackhole_Wireless_Access authorization profile does not use any of the common tasks. Instead, it employs the Advanced Attribute Settings fields to send a URL-Redirect and URL-Redirect-ACL result to the WLC, along with an Access-Accept. So, this result allows the devices onto the network, but forces all traffic to redirect to a web page describing that the device is blacklisted.

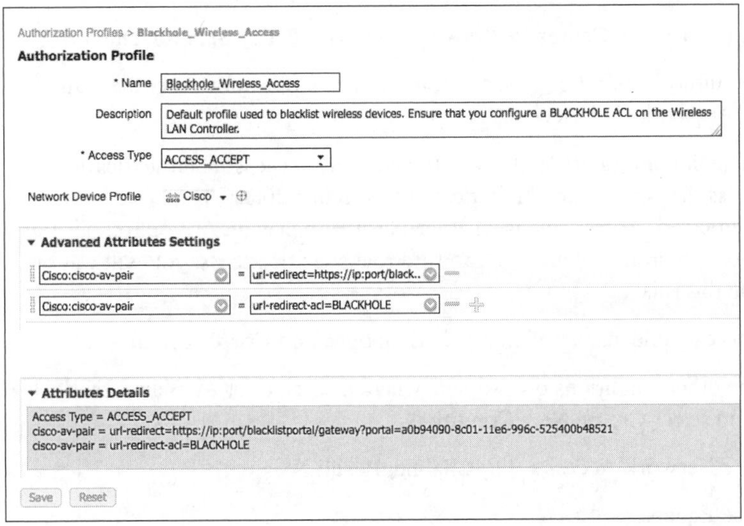

Figure 13-31 *Blackhole_Wireless_Access Authorization Profile*

These two authorization rules demonstrate a variety of rules. This chapter examines a few common authorization policies in later sections.

Role-Specific Authorization Rules

The end goal of a Secure Access deployment is to provide very specific permissions to any authorization. However, that should always be handled in a staged approach to limit the impact to the end users.

Chapter 20, "Deployment Phases," is dedicated to discussing the staged approach for authorizations.

Authorization Policy Example

This section provides an example of an authorization policy made up of numerous rules based on a common use case. This use case was selected to show multiple aspects of the authorization policy and help to solidify your working knowledge of the parts of an authorization policy and the workflows associated with creating the policy.

For this example, let's configure three authorization rules: one that assigns full access to an employee that authenticated successfully with EAP chaining; one that assigns more limited access to the same employee authenticating with a non-corporate machine; and one that assigns Internet-only access to the same employee authenticating on a mobile device.

Employee and Corporate Machine Full-Access Rule

In this rule, assign full-access permissions to an employee who is authenticating from a valid corporate asset. From the ISE GUI, perform the following steps:

Step 1.   Navigate to **Work Centers > Network Access > Policy Sets > Default**.

Step 2.   In the Authorization Policy section, insert a new rule above the rule named Basic_Authenticated_Access.

The default configuration of ISE is to allow any successful authentication to access the network, making it easier to install and test. The Basic_ Authenticated_Access rule is what enables that behavior. As you roll out ISE into your environment and look toward role-specific access, you will want to disable this rule.

Step 3.   For this example, name the new rule **Employee and CorpMachine**.

Step 4.   For the other conditions drop-down, where it says Select Attribute, click the **+** sign and select **Create New Condition**.

Step 5.   Choose **Network Access > EapChainingResult**.

Step 6.   Choose **Equals**.

Step 7.   Select **User and Machine Both Succeeded.**

Step 8.   Click the cog icon on the right side and choose **Add Attribute/Value.**

Step 9.   Select **AD1 > External Groups Equals "Employees"** (or another AD group of your choosing).

Step 10.   For the AuthZ Profiles, click the **+** sign.

Step 11.   Click the cog icon in the upper-right corner and choose **Add New Standard Profile.**

Step 12.   In the Name text box, name the new authorization profile **Employee Full Access.**

Step 13.   (Optional) Add a description.

Step 14.   From the Access Type drop-down list, choose **ACCESS_ACCEPT.**

Step 15.   Check the **DACL Name** check box and choose **PERMIT_ALL_TRAFFIC** from the drop-down list.

Figure 13-32 shows the Employee Full Access authorization profile.

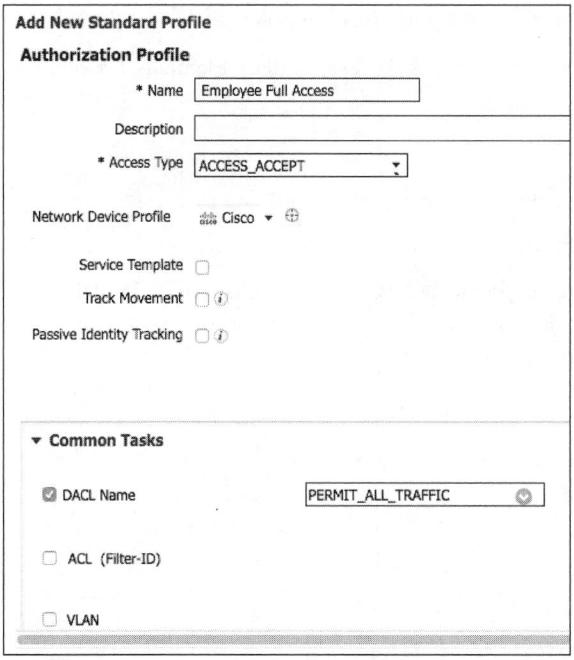

Figure 13-32 *Employee Full Access Authorization Profile*

Step 16.   Click **Save**.

Step 17.   Click **Done** to finish editing the rule.

Step 18.   Click **Save** to save the authorization policy.

Figure 13-33 shows the completed authorization rule.

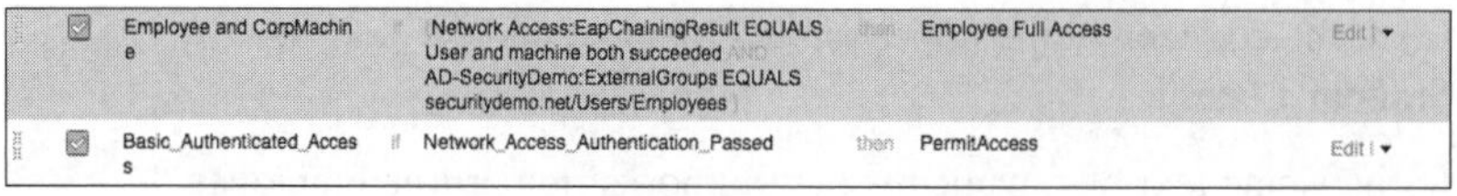

| | | Employee and CorpMachine | Network Access:EapChainingResult EQUALS User and machine both succeeded AND AD-SecurityDemo:ExternalGroups EQUALS securitydemo.net/Users/Employees | Employee Full Access | Edit \| ▼ |
| | | Basic_Authenticated_Access | if Network_Access_Authentication_Passed | then PermitAccess | Edit \| ▼ |

Figure 13-33   *Completed Employee and CorpMachine Rule*

Internet Only for Mobile Devices

Now that the rule for employees with corporate devices has been created, you need to create the rule below it that provides Internet access only to employee authentications on mobile devices.

To begin this rule, first create a new DACL that is applied to switches, create the authorization result, and then go back into the authorization policy and build the rule:

Step 1.   Navigate to **Work Centers > Network Access > Policy Elements > Results > Downloadable ACLs**.

Step 2.   Click **Add**.

Step 3.   In the Name text field, name the ACL **Internet-Only**.

Step 4.   (Optional) Provide a description.

Step 5.   In the DACL Content pane, provide an ACL that permits required traffic for Internet access and denies traffic destined to the corporate network. Figure 13-34 shows an example.

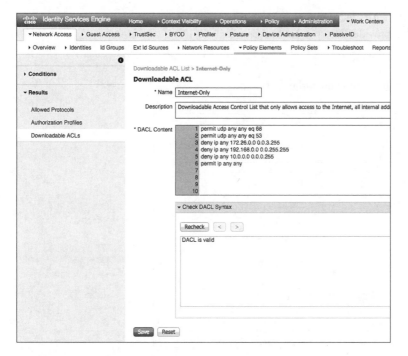

Figure 13-34 *Internet-Only DACL*

Step 6.   Click **Submit**.

Now that the DACL is created, it's time to create the authorization profile:

Step 1.   Navigate to **Work Centers > Network Access > Policy Elements > Results > Authorization Profiles**.

Step 2.   Click **Add**.

Step 3.   In the Name field, name the authorization profile **Internet Only**.

Step 4.   (Optional) Provide a description.

Step 5.   From the Access Type drop-down list, choose **ACCESS_ACCEPT**.

Step 6.   Check the **DACL Name** check box and choose **Internet-Only** from the drop-down list.

Step 7.   (Optional) Check the **VLAN** check box and provide a guest VLAN.

Keep in mind this VLAN Name or ID is used for both wired and wireless devices. An alternative is to create separate rules for wired and wireless, so the user is assigned VLAN on wireless but not wired.

Step 8.   Select **Airspace ACL Name** and fill in the name of the ACL on the controller that provides Internet-only access.

Step 9.   Click **Submit**.

Figure 13-35 shows the completed authorization profile.

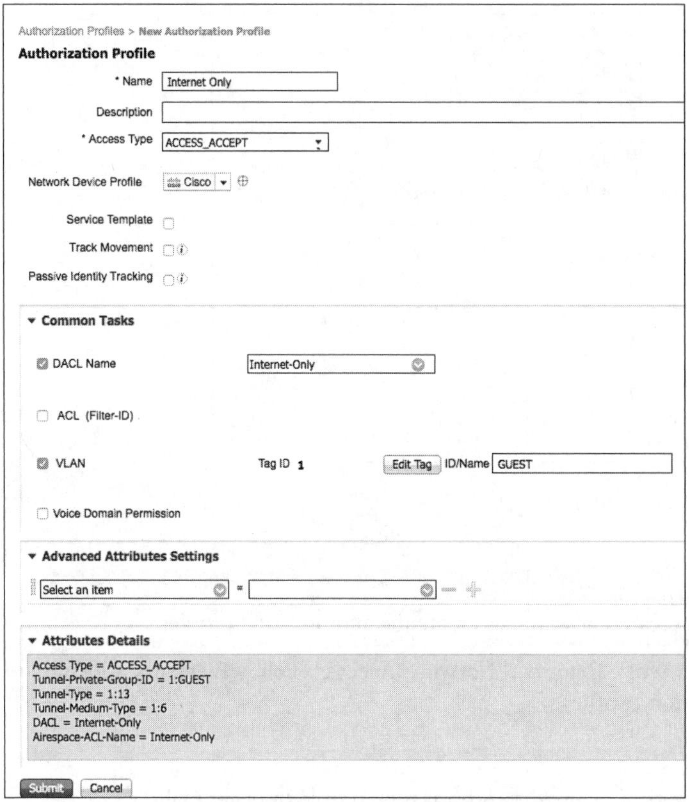

Figure 13-35   *Internet Only Authorization Profile*

Before you build the authorization policy, take a look at a pre-existing logical profile that is designed to encompass all mobile devices out of the box. We will leverage this in your authorization policy, as it makes the policy building much easier and provides a reusable policy object:

Step 1.   Navigate to **Work Centers > Profiler > Profiling Policies > Logical Profiles**. Figure 13-36 shows the pre-existing logical profiles.

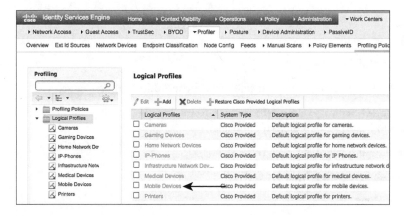

Figure 13-36 *Logical Profiles*

Step 2.   Examine the Mobile Devices logical profile by clicking its name (not its check box). This grouping of profiles, shown in Figure 13-37, consists of endpoint profiles such as Apple-iPad, Android, Samsung-Phone, and others.

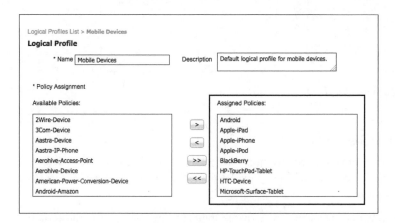

Figure 13-37 *Mobile Devices Logical Profile*

Finally, it is now time to create the authorization rule:

Step 1.   Navigate to **Work Centers > Network Access > Policy Sets > Default**.

Step 2.   In the Authorization Policy section, insert a new rule above the Basic_Authenticated_Access rule.

Step 3.   Name the rule **Employee Mobile Devices**.

Step 4. Click the **+** sign for conditions, and choose **Endpoints > LogicalProfile**.

Step 5. Choose **Equals**.

Step 6. Select **Mobile Devices**.

Step 7. Click the cog icon on the right side and choose **Add Attribute/Value**.

Step 8. Select **AD-SecurityDemo > External Groups Equals "Employees"** (or another AD group of your choosing).

Step 9. For the AuthZ Profiles, click the **+** sign.

Step 10. Choose **Standard > Internet Only**.

Step 11. Click **Done**.

Step 12. Click **Save**.

The completed authorization rule is displayed in Figure 13-38.

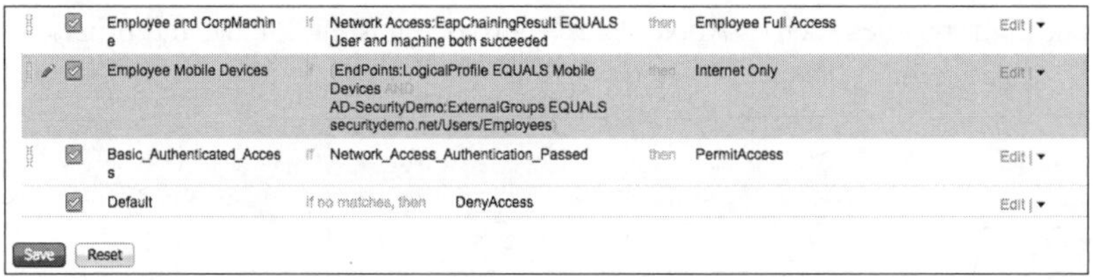

		Employee and CorpMachine	if	Network Access:EapChainingResult EQUALS User and machine both succeeded	then	Employee Full Access	Edit | ▾
	☑	Employee Mobile Devices		EndPoints:LogicalProfile EQUALS Mobile Devices AD-SecurityDemo:ExternalGroups EQUALS securitydemo.net/Users/Employees	then	Internet Only	Edit | ▾
	☑	Basic_Authenticated_Access	if	Network_Access_Authentication_Passed	then	PermitAccess	Edit | ▾
	☑	Default		if no matches, then		DenyAccess	Edit | ▾

Save **Reset**

Figure 13-38 *Employee Mobile Devices Authorization Rule*

Employee Limited Access Rule

Now that the rule for employees connecting with mobile devices has been created, you need to create the rule below it that only provides limited access to employee authentications on any other device.

To begin this rule, first create a new DACL that is applied to switches, create the authorization result, and then go back into the authorization policy and build the rule:

Step 1. Navigate to **Work Centers > Network Access > Policy Elements > Results > Downloadable ACLs**.

Step 2. Click **Add**.

Step 3. In the name text box, name the ACL **EmployeeLimited**.

Step 4. (Optional) Provide a description.

Step 5. In the DACL Content pane, provide an ACL that permits required traffic and denies traffic destined to the corporate network. For this example, allow traffic to reach your virtual desktop infrastructure and essential services, like DNS only.

Figure 13-39 shows the example EmployeeLimited DACL.

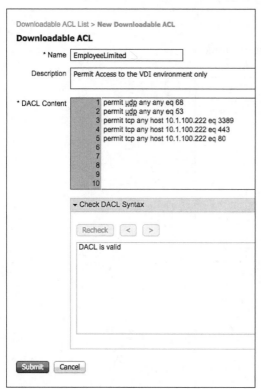

Figure 13-39 *EmployeeLimited DACL*

Step 6. Click **Submit**.

Now that the DACL is created, build the authorization policy to permit network access and apply that DACL:

Step 1. Navigate to **Work Centers > Network Access > Policy Elements > Results > Authorization Profiles**.

Step 2. Click **Add**.

Step 3. In the Name text box, name the authorization profile **Employee Limited**.

Step 4. (Optional) Provide a description.

Step 5. From the Access Type drop-down list, choose **ACCESS_ACCEPT**.

Step 6. Check the **DACL Name** check box and choose **EmployeeLimited** from the drop-down list.

Step 7. Do not assign a different VLAN for this authorization.

Step 8.   Select **Airespace-ACL-Name** and fill in the name of the ACL on the controller that provides Internet-only access.

Step 9.   Click **Submit**.

Figure 13-40 shows the completed authorization profile.

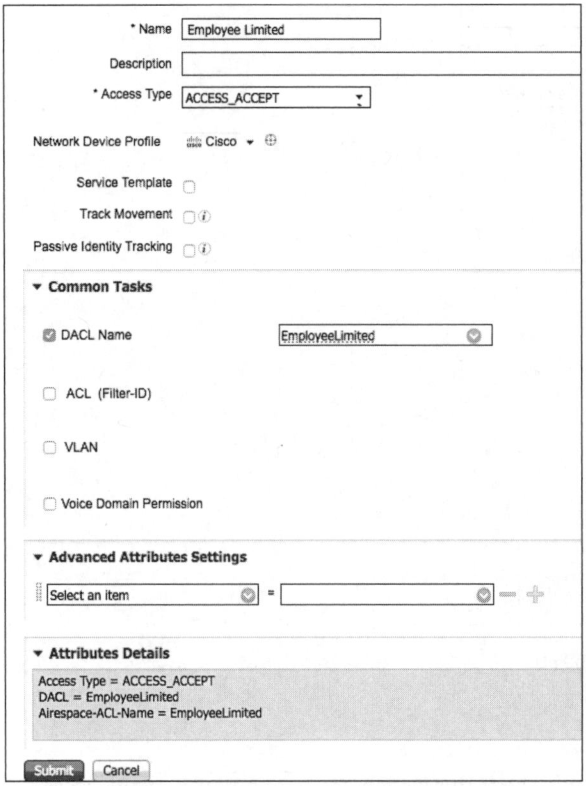

Figure 13-40   *Employee Limited Authorization Profile*

Now, create the authorization policy rule to assign that authorization profile:

Step 1.   Navigate to **Work Centers > Network Access > Policy Sets > Default**.

Step 2.   In the Authorization Policy section, insert a new rule above the Basic_Authenticated_Access rule.

Step 3.   Name the Rule **Employee VDI Only**.

Step 4.   Click the **+** sign for conditions.

Step 5.   Select **AD-SecurityDemo > External Groups Equals "Employees"** (or another AD group of your choosing).

Step 6.   For the AuthZ Profiles, click the **+** sign.

Step 7.   Choose **Standard > Employee Limited**.

Step 8.   Click **Done**.

Step 9.   Click **Save**.

Figure 13-41 shows the completed Employee VDI Only authorization rule.

		Employee and CorpMachin e	If	Network Access:EapChainingResult EQUALS User and machine both succeeded	then	Employee Full Access	Edit | ▾
		Employee Mobile Devices	If	(EndPoints:LogicalProfile EQUALS Mobile Devices AND AD-SecurityDemo:ExternalGroups EQUALS securitydemo.net/Users/Employees)	then	Internet Only	Edit | ▾
		Employee VDI Only		AD-SecurityDemo:ExternalGroups EQUALS securitydemo.net/Users/Employees	then	Employee Limited	Edit | ▾

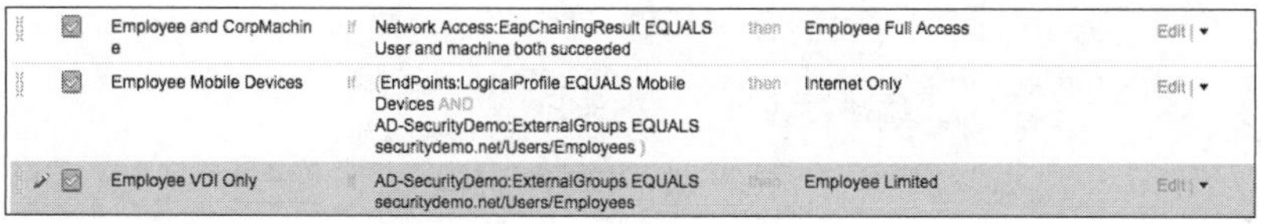

Figure 13-41   *Employee VDI Only Authorization Rule*

Note   The ordering of rules is very important. They are processed in a top-down manner. Therefore, you must always ensure that the most-specific rules are above the less-specific rules. In the example shown in Figure 13-41, if the Employee VDI Only rule were above the Employee Mobile Devices rule, then mobile devices would also be limited to VDI only, which is not the intended result.

Saving Attributes for Reuse

ISE offers the ability to save conditions to the library to make it much easier to reuse them in other policies. To show this, let's go back into your example authorization policy and save a few of the conditions.

From the ISE GUI, perform the following steps:

Step 1.   Navigate to **Work Centers > Network Access > Policy Sets > Default**.

Step 2.   In the Authorization Policy section, **Edit** the Employee and CorpMachine rule.

Step 3.   Expand the conditions by clicking the **+** sign.

Step 4.   Click **Add All Conditions Below to Library**, as shown in Figure 13-42. This adds the full set of conditions, including the AND operator.

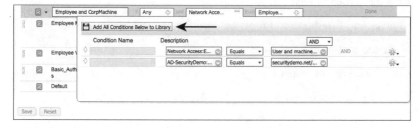

Figure 13-42   *Add All Conditions Below to Library*

Step 5. Provide a name for this new saved condition, such as **EmployeeFullEAPChain** for this example.

Step 6. Click the green check mark, as shown in Figure 13-43, and finish editing the rule.

Employee and CorpMachine
Any
Network Acce...
Employe...
EmployeeFullEAPChain
Internet Only
Condition Name
Description
AND
Network Access:E...
Equals
User and machine...
AND
Employee Limited
AD-SecurityDemo:...
Equals
securitydemo.net/...
PermitAccess

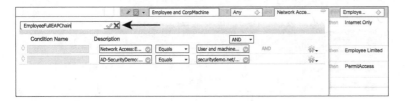

Figure 13-43 *Add All Conditions Below to Library Check Mark*

Step 7. Click **Save**.

As shown in Figure 13-44, the authorization policy text is simplified now with the name of the saved compound condition instead of the raw attributes.

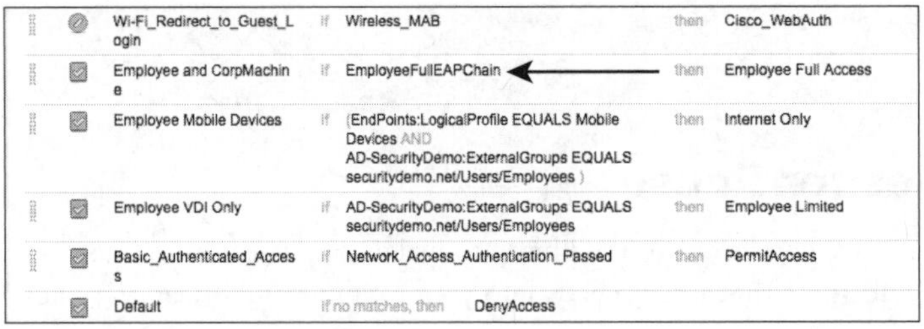

Wi-Fi_Redirect_to_Guest_Login
if Wireless_MAB
then Cisco_WebAuth
Employee and CorpMachine
if EmployeeFullEAPChain
then Employee Full Access
Employee Mobile Devices
if (EndPoints:LogicalProfile EQUALS Mobile Devices AND AD-SecurityDemo:ExternalGroups EQUALS securitydemo.net/Users/Employees)
then Internet Only
Employee VDI Only
if AD-SecurityDemo:ExternalGroups EQUALS securitydemo.net/Users/Employees
then Employee Limited
Basic_Authenticated_Access
if Network_Access_Authentication_Passed
then PermitAccess
Default
if no matches, then DenyAccess

Figure 13-44 *Authorization Policy After Saving Conditions to Library*

Next, save the Employees group for AD as a condition:

Step 1. Navigate to **Work Centers > Network Access > Policy Sets > Default.**

Step 2. In the Authorization Policy section, click **Edit** to edit the Employee Mobile Devices rule.

Step 3. Expand the conditions by clicking the **+** sign.

Step 4. Click the cog icon on the right side of the line where the Employee Active Directory group is used.

Step 5. Choose **Add Condition to Library.**

Step 6. Name the condition **Employees.**

Step 7. Click the green check mark.

Figure 13-45 displays the saving of Employees to the Conditions library.

Figure 13-45 *Saving Employees to Library*

Step 8. Click **Done** to finish editing the rule.

Step 9. Click **Save**.

Figure 13-46 shows the final authorization policy.

Figure 13-46 *Final Authorization Policy*

Summary

This chapter examined the relationship between authentication and authorization and how to build policies for each. It described a few common authentication policies and authorization policies to help solidify your knowledge of how to work with these policy constructs. Chapter 20 will focus on specific configurations of these policies to help in the actual deployment of ISE and the Secure Access solution.

Chapter 14, "Guest Lifecycle Management," examines web authentication, guest access, and the full lifecycle management of guest users.

Guest Lifecycle Management

This chapter covers the following topics:

- Overview of guest services

  - Hotspot guest portal configuration

  - Sponsored guest portal configuration

  - Authentication and authorization guest policies

  - Guest sponsor portal configuration

  - Guest sponsor portal usage

- Configuration of network devices for guest CWA

Cisco Identity Services Engine provides a complete solution for guest network access. A *guest* is defined as someone who needs temporary and restricted access to your network. This is usually a visitor or temporary contractor. The access provided to guests is usually limited to Internet access. But, as you will learn in this chapter, this can be opened up or closed down as you see fit. *Guest sponsors*, employees who have the rights to create guest accounts, typically create and distribute guest usernames/passwords to their visitors. This is a common function of the front-desk receptionist who already has the job of checking in visitors. As visitors arrive, the receptionist checks them in and provides them with guest access, if required, while they are on the premises.

To configure ISE guest services quickly, read Chapter 6, "Quick Setup of an ISE Proof of Concept," to learn about the Wireless Setup Wizard. This chapter guides you through the non-wizard steps to set up ISE guest service in its many shapes and colors. ISE guest services support both wired and wireless access methods. Guest authentication takes two general forms: non-authenticated guest and authenticated guest. Non-authenticated guest provides just a web redirect to a guest portal page and allows the guest to click through to gain access. Authenticated guest requires the guest to enter unique credentials on the guest portal page before being allowed access to the network. Regardless, guest services are provided via a web authentication (auth) method that requires the guest to use a browser to connect. ISE has two deployment modes available, Central Web Authorization (CWA) and Local Web Authorization (LWA). Table 14-1 shows the differences.

Table 14-1   *Central Versus Local Web Authentication*

Local Web Auth (LWA)	Central Web Auth (CWA)
Web pages are delivered by the network device.	Web pages are redirected to ISE and delivered by ISE centrally.
Guest authentication is performed by the network device.	Guest authentication is handled by ISE.
Does not allow/support Change of Authorization.	Allows/supports CoA. This allows posture and profiling services for guests. It also allows VLAN enforcement.
Authorization enforcement uses ACLs only.	Authorization enforcement uses ACLs and VLANs.
Requires complete local web auth configuration on each NAD (switch or WLC).	Configuration for web auth is performed in ISE.
Each device has its own web portal files, web server, customization, etc.	Web portals and portal customization are performed inside of ISE centrally.

As you have probably already deduced, Central Web Auth is by far the most popular and easiest method. In almost all cases, you will want to deploy CWA. As a result, most of this chapter focuses on CWA, with limited LWA discussion. Check the ISE release notes on Cisco.com for the latest versions required.

Figure 14-1 shows the Local Web Authentication flow.

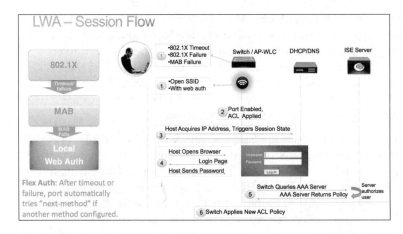

Figure 14-1   *Local Web Auth Flow*

Figure 14-2 shows the flow for Central Web Authentication

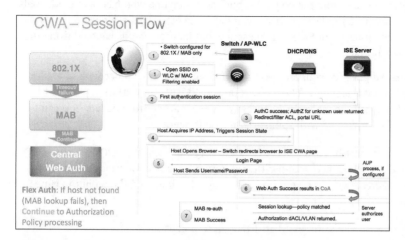

Figure 14-2   *Central Web Auth Flow*

The ISE guest services are available using the ISE Base license. If you decide to use posture or profiling for guests, then additional licensing applies. The ISE Policy Service Node (PSN) persona runs the guest services and web portal services.

Cisco ISE provides several methods of guest access. There are non-authenticated guest and authenticated guest options. Non-authenticated guest access is useful when you just want to provide your visitors with a hassle-free way to obtain access to the Internet. It typically involves a custom guest portal page that shows your acceptable use policy (AUP) and provides a button to click to get on the network.

Authenticated guest access requires all guests to have a username and password to gain access. These credentials are created by a guest sponsor who is typically an employee or receptionist of the company. The sponsor can select the access rights, time duration, and several other authorization guest privileges when creating the guest account. Cisco ISE also supports the creation of mass numbers of guest accounts quickly. This is useful for conferences, large meetings, and so on.

Overview of ISE Guest Services

Cisco ISE provides the following three types of guest end-user services that you can customize. These options run on the ISE PSNs in your network.

- **Hotspot guest portal:** All visitors are redirected to a Welcome web page. They usually have to click an Accept button for an AUP to proceed, but that is configurable. ISE supports the creation of multiple customized guest portals that are selected based on criteria you specify. For example, you can create a portal for long-term contractors that is different from a visitor guest portal. Hotspot is the most popular guest portal method in use.

■ **Sponsor guest portal:** Sponsored guests obtain their credentials from a sponsor. This is typically someone from the company, but can be anyone who has valid credentials to the sponsor portal in ISE. Sponsors can deliver guest account details to their visitors via email, printing, or SMS. All guest account management is handled using the sponsor web portal.

■ **Self-registered guest portal:** This portal allows guests to obtain network access by creating their own accounts. The guest is presented with a registration page to fill out, which typically includes an AUP that they must accept to proceed. You can combine self-registration with sponsor approval if needed.

Each guest account must be associated with a guest type. Guest types allow a sponsor to assign different levels of access and different network connection times to a guest account. You can create your own guest types or use the following three built-in types that ISE includes:

■ **Daily:** Short-term guests of less than 1 day up to 5 days

■ **Weekly:** Guests of one to two weeks

■ **Contractor:** Long-term guests of up to a year

Guest credentials can take many forms in ISE. The hotspot type doesn't require any credentials from guests. For the other portal types, you can choose from the following options:

■ **Username/password:** Provided either by a sponsor or using self-registration. The username and password requirements are defined in the ISE guest username and guest password policies.

■ **Access code:** A single shared code typically given to a group of visitors for temporary guest access. The access code can be written on the whiteboard of a classroom or handed out in printed form. Access codes can be used within all three portal types, including hotspot.

■ **Registration code:** Similar to an access code except the code is for use during guest self-registration. A guest must enter a correct code to complete registration. If you want to collect some information from your guests but not allow them to self-register without some kind of credential, this method comes in handy.

Hotspot Guest Portal Configuration

The ISE hotspot guest is the easiest method to configure and the easiest for your guest users to navigate. Hotspot guest portals do not require any user authentication; they use open mode on Wi-Fi and usually present the guest with an AUP. Here are the general steps to configure a hotspot guest portal:

Step 1. **Configure the hotspot portal:** ISE defaults are usually sufficient, with the exception of the customization necessary for the AUP and the support information page. To configure the portal, go to **Work Centers > Guest Access > Portals & Components > Guest Portals > Hotspot Guest Portal > Edit.**

Step 2. **Configure the authorization profile:** Configure a profile for web redirection to your newly created portal. Go to **Work Centers > Guest Access > Policy Elements > Results > Authorization Profiles** and click **Add**. See Figure 14-3 for an example.

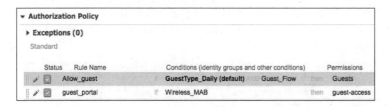

Figure 14-3 *Hotspot Authorization Profile*

Step 3. **Configure the authorization rule in your policy sets:** You need to create two rules to activate the hotspot. The first rule matches after a user successfully goes through the guest portal process. The second rule triggers the guest portal process. See Figure 14-4 for an example of the rules you need to create.

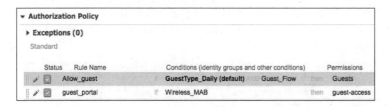

Figure 14-4 *Guest Hotspot Authorization Rules*

Note For information on how to configure the Cisco Wireless LAN Controller (WLC) to use ISE for guest access, see "Configure ISE Wireless CWA and Hotspot Flows with AireOS and Next Generation WLCs," at http://www.cisco.com/c/en/us/support/docs/security/identity-services-engine-21/200565-Configure-ISE-Wireless-CWA-and-Hotspot-F. html.

Sponsored Guest Portal Configuration

The first step in configuring ISE for sponsored guest services is to define how ISE authenticates users. ISE guest services includes two special kinds of user accounts: sponsors and guests. Sponsors are employees or ISE users who have the rights to create guest accounts for visitors. You define the access method, privileges, and feature support for sponsors inside of ISE but can use an external identity source such as Active Directory. Sponsors authenticate to the sponsor portal to create guest accounts. ISE supports multiple types of authentication methods. The sections that follow outline the procedures to set up your guest sponsor portal:

■ Create an Active Directory identity store

■ Create ISE guest types

■ Create guest sponsor groups

Create an Active Directory Identity Store

If it has not already been created, create an Active Directory identity store. AD is the most popular ID store for sponsors, but you can skip this step and use RADIUS or internal ISE users instead.

Step 1. Go to **Administration > Identity Management > External Identity Sources > Active Directory**.

Step 2. Configure and join ISE to your Active Directory. See Chapter 6 for details on joining AD.

Step 3. Choose or create a group in AD that will be used to specify who is a sponsor. For example, create a group called ISE Guest Sponsors and add the members who you want to be sponsors. Select and add that group to ISE as shown in Figure 14-5.

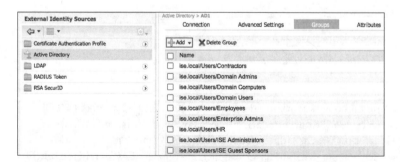

Figure 14-5 *AD Group for Sponsors*

Step 4. Configure an Identity Source Sequence that includes AD. Go to **Administration > Identity Management > Identity Source Sequences**. Note the built-in group called Sponsor_Portal_Sequence, as shown at the bottom of the list in Figure 14-6. Edit that group. Figure 14-7 depicts making AD the first choice in the list followed by local ISE users.

Figure 14-6 *Sponsor Portal Sequence List*

Figure 14-7 *Sponsor Portal Sequence Edit*

Step 5.   Apply the ID sequence as your sponsor authentication source. Go to **Administration > Web Portal Management > Settings > Sponsor > Authentication Source**. Select your sequence.

Create ISE Guest Types

You need to create guest types before you create your sponsor groups because the guest types are used in the sponsor groups. Guest types provide different levels of access to different guest accounts. Sponsors must assign a guest type to a guest when creating an account, but they cannot make changes to the profiles themselves. An ISE administrator does that.

To add a custom guest type, navigate to **Work Centers > Guest Access > Portals & Components > Guest Types** and click **Create** or **Duplicate**. Fill out the information as appropriate for your needs. Figures 14-8 through 14-10 show an example of creating a daily guest type profile.

As shown in the Maximum Access Time section of Figure 14-8, you can apply restrictions to both the account duration and the time period and days of week during which access is allowed. These settings can help you to ensure that visitors assigned to this basic guest type cannot use their credentials after hours or on weekends. Many businesses set the times to match their reception desk hours.

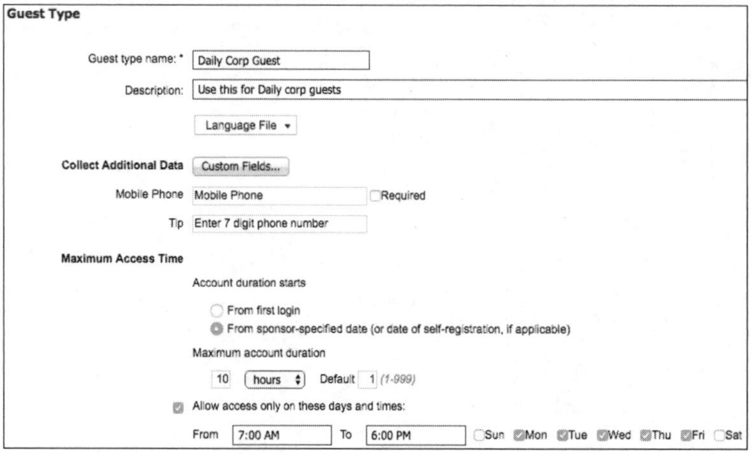

Figure 14-8   *Guest Type Customization: Maximum Access Time*

Figure 14-9 shows your login options, such as the maximum number of simultaneous logins and the maximum number of guest devices that can be registered. In Figure 14-9, both options are set to two. You also set the endpoint identity group to which guest devices should be added after they have registered. The default GuestEndpoints group is used in the example.

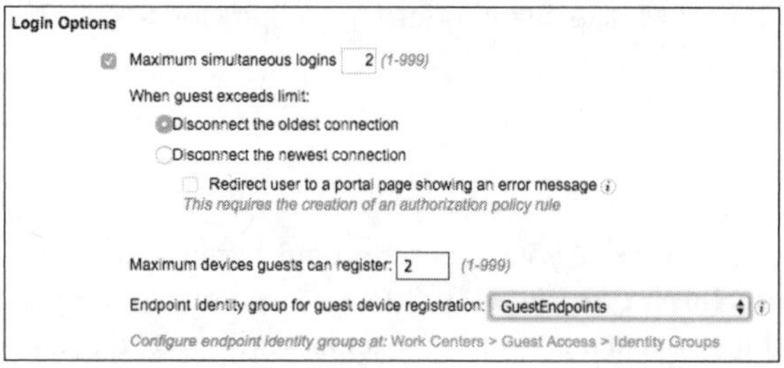

Figure 14-9   *Guest Type Customization: Login Options*

Figure 14-10 shows the settings available to you for notifying your guests that their account is going to expire soon. These settings are useful for weekly or long-term guest accounts. Because the present example is for creating a guest type for daily guests, there is no need to set up any notifications. Figure 14-10 also shows you the sponsor accounts that are authorized to use this guest type.

Figure 14-10   *Guest Type Customization: Expiration Notification and Sponsor Groups Assignment*

Create Guest Sponsor Groups

Now that you have created or customized the guest types, you can create sponsor groups. A sponsor is assigned the permissions from all of the groups they are members of.

ISE uses the following logic for multiple matching of sponsor groups (essentially, it adds the permissions together and defaults to the least restrictive permissions when a conflict is detected):

1. An individual permission such as "Delete guests' accounts" is granted if it is enabled in any of the matching groups.

2. The sponsor can create guests using the guest types in any of the matching groups.

3. The sponsor can create guests at the locations in any of the matching groups.

4. For a numeric value such as a batch size limit, the largest value from the matching groups is used.

Guest sponsor configuration is accomplished in two parts: create the sponsor groups, and then create the sponsor group policies.

The following three built-in sponsor groups are available, as illustrated in Figure 14-11:

- **ALL_ACCOUNTS:** This is the super-admin group equivalent for sponsors. It allows a sponsor in this group to manage all guest accounts in the ISE network.

- **GROUP_ACCOUNTS:** Sponsors can manage guest accounts from other sponsors in the same sponsor group.

- **OWN_ACCOUNTS:** Sponsors can manage only the guest accounts that they have created.

Figure 14-11 *Guest Sponsor Group Defaults*

To create a new sponsor group, follow these steps from the ISE GUI:

Step 1.   Navigate to **Work Centers > Guest Access > Portals & Components > Sponsor Groups** and click **Create** or **Duplicate**.

Step 2.   Enter a descriptive name and description. Click **OK**. Enter the match criteria for this group. A sponsor must belong to at least one of the match criteria member groups. It is common to use an Active Directory group here. Figure 14-12 shows an example of using an AD group named Employees. Optionally, you can add other conditions to the match criteria. This allows you to match just about any ISE criteria available.

Figure 14-12 *Guest Sponsor Group: Match Criteria*

Step 3. In the Sponsor Permissions section, shown in Figure 14-13, select the actions that members of the sponsor group are authorized to perform. This list represents the options that are available to the sponsor when they create a guest account.

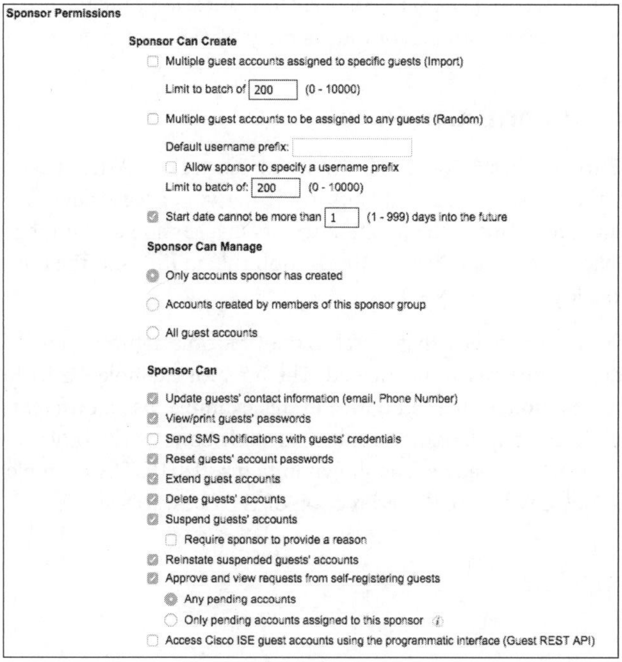

Figure 14-13 *Guest Sponsor Group: Authorization Levels*

Step 4. Assign the guest types for which members of the sponsor group can create guest accounts. These roles can then be used in ISE authorization rules to determine guest privileges on the network. Figure 14-14 shows that Daily and Weekly guest types are available to sponsors who match this group.

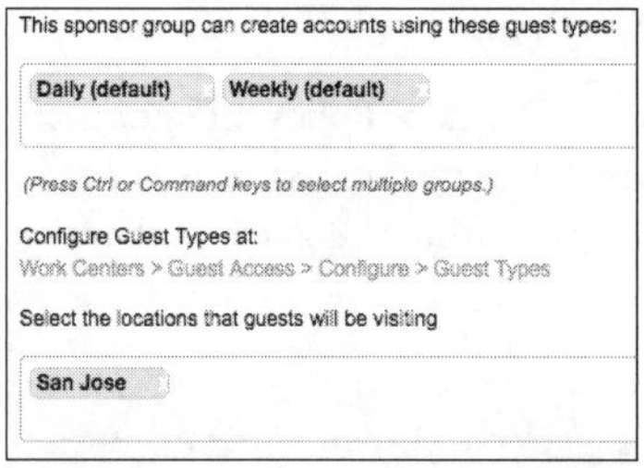

Figure 14-14 *Guest Sponsor Group: Guest Types*

Step 5. Click **Save** when done.

Authentication and Authorization Guest Policies

You now need to set up ISE for guest authentication and authorization policies. Just like in the hotspot guest configuration described previously, you need to configure ISE to trigger the guest process. Go to **Policy > Policy Sets** and select your policy. You should see a default MAC Authentication Bypass (MAB) rule in the authentication policy. The default MAB rule doesn't need any modifications for the majority of ISE customers.

Guest Pre-Authentication Authorization Policy

If needed, refer to Figure 14-2 for a refresher on the Central Web Auth flow. After successful web authentication by the guest, ISE sends a CoA to the network access device. The endpoint is then re-authenticated. This authentication results in a session lookup that now matches a policy. That policy is matched in an authorization rule in ISE, and the configured permissions are then deployed to the NAD.

You need to configure an authorization policy that matches the first time a guest connects to the network and before the guest is authenticated. The hotspot example earlier in the chapter showed how to create a policy rule to do this; in this example, use a different variation that uses the catch-all Default authorization rule instead. If none of the other rules is matched, then the Default rule is matched, as shown in Figure 14-15. The example Default rule configuration initiates CWA via URL redirection of the guest to the ISE guest portal.

Figure 14-15   *Default Authorization Policy: Guest Web Auth*

The group Cisco_WebAuth shown in Figure 14-15 is a default ISE authorization profile. It is recommended that you modify this default by adding an ACL to it. This restricts guests' network access to only what is needed while they sign in.

For wired guests, create a downloadable ACL (dACL). Go to **Policy > Policy Elements > Results > Authorization > Downloadable ACLs**. Click **Add**. Create a pre-auth ACL, as shown in Example 14-1, to limit network traffic that can flow during the guest authentication process. Click **Submit**.

Note   Downloadable ACLs are not supported on Cisco WLC. Configure an Airspace ACL name instead and preposition/preconfigure the ACL in Example 14-1 on the WLC.

Example 14-1 *dACL for Wired Guests*

```
permit udp any any eq bootps
permit udp any any eq domain
permit tcp any any eq domain
remark ping for troubleshooting
permit icmp any any echo
permit icmp any any echo-reply
remark allow web traffic to the ISE PSN 10.1.100.232
permit tcp any 10.1.100.232 eq 80
permit tcp any 10.1.100.232 eq 443
remark allow internet-only web traffic to kick off redirect
deny tcp any <Internal networks> eq 80
deny tcp any <Internal networks> eq 443
permit tcp any any eq 80
permit tcp any any eq 443
remark 10.1.100.232 is the ISE PSN for Guest Portal
permit tcp any host 10.1.100.232 eq 8443
permit tcp any host 10.1.100.232 eq 8905
permit tcp any host 10.1.100.232 eq 8909
permit udp any host 10.1.100.232 range 8905 8906
permit udp any host 10.1.100.232 eq 8909
deny ip any any
```

Port 8443 is used by the ISE guest portal by default. Ports 8905 and 8906 are used by the NAC Agent SWISS protocol. Port 8909 is used for client provisioning activity.

If deploying for wireless guests, be sure you enable the Airespace ACL name as part of your policy. ISE will call the ACL that is configured on the WLC. It does not download the ACL. The following are the steps to create an Authorization Policy.

Step 1. Go to **Policy > Policy Elements > Results > Authorization > Authorization Policies.** Edit the default Cisco_WebAuth policy.

Step 2. Under Common Tasks, select your dACL name. The dACL will be downloaded to the NAD by ISE. If this is for wireless guests, then instead populate the Airespace ACL field with the name of the ACL you configured on the WLC.

Step 3. The default Cisco_WebAuth policy references the web-redirect ACL name of ACL-WEBAUTH-REDIRECT. You need to pre-position this ACL on the switch or WLC. For wired switches, the contents of ACL-WEBAUTH-REDIRECT should include the following (10.1.100.232=ISE PSN):

```
ip access-list extended ACL-WEBAUTH-REDIRECT
    deny ip any host 10.1.100.232
    permit tcp any any eq www
    permit tcp any any eq 443
    permit tcp any any eq 8443
```

```
remark be sure to include any proxy ports you have enabled
    permit tcp any any eq 8080
```

On a switch, any ACL statement with a **permit** will force a URL redirect. This ACL does *not* permit and deny traffic; it only defines what ports kick off a URL redirect. For wireless, **deny** rules force a URL redirect. Rewrite the preceding wired ACL as necessary.

Step 4. Add your newly created authorization profile to the default authorization policy rule. Go to **Policy > Policy Sets > Authorization**. Click **Edit** on the last rule in the list called Default. Select your Cisco_WebAuth policy, as shown previously in Figure 14-15. Click **Done** and then **Save**.

Guest Post-Authentication Authorization Policy

Once the guest successfully authenticates using their guest account credentials, ISE issues a Change of Authorization (CoA) request to the NAD. This time, the MAB session lookup matches. You need to configure an authorization policy in ISE to set the guest network permissions you want to allow. Go to **Policy > Policy Sets** and select your policy. Under Authorization Policy, click the down-arrow icon on the left side and follow these steps:

Step 1. Enter a descriptive rule name, such as Allow Guest.

Step 2. Select the identity groups that you want to match on. Common examples are GuestEndPoints, GuestType_Daily, and GuestType_Weekly. Remember that each identity group must match the guest type that the sponsor assigned to the guest account upon its creation. If you have multiple guest roles, then you need to create multiple authorization rules. Each rule provides different permissions to the guest.

Step 3. Assign the permissions, such as guest Internet only web. You can pick from your list of authorization profiles or create a new one by clicking the gear icon and selecting **Add New Standard Profile**. The most common permission elements are dACL, Airespace ACL, Security Group Tag, and VLAN. Figure 14-16 shows an example.

Figure 14-16 *Guest Authorization Rule*

Remember that authorization rules, by default, are processed from the top down until the first match. Be sure your guest rules are in the appropriate order. Your authenticated guest access rule needs to precede the WebAuth redirection rule.

Guest Sponsor Portal Configuration

Sponsors are responsible for creating guest accounts for authorized visitors who need limited network or Internet-only connectivity while onsite. Typically, sponsors are allowed to create, send, and manage guest accounts. You need to configure the sponsor portal to allow sponsors to create guest accounts. ISE includes a default sponsor portal for you to use as well.

Set up the method you will use to authenticate your sponsors. This was covered previously in the "Create an Active Directory Identity Store" section but is mentioned here for a refresher. In most cases, Active Directory is used. Go to **Work Centers > Guest Access > Identities > Identity Source Sequences**. The built-in sequence is called Sponsor_Portal_Sequence and includes the identity stores Internal Users and All_AD_Join_Points. You can use this sequence or create your own.

Guest Portal Interface and IP Configuration

It is a best practice to configure your guest portal on its own ISE physical interface with its own IP address. This drastically reduces the security risk of an ISE compromise. Separating the admin portal from the guest portal provides some of this added security. You can specify the port used for each web portal, allowing you to use different ports for the end-user portals, such as Sponsor, Guest (also Client Provisioning), My Devices, and Blacklist. The Blacklist portal should be kept all alone on its own interface with its own IP address. This is also true for the admin configuration portal, which always uses Ethernet0 and a default port of HTTPS/443. To configure a sponsor portal or edit the default, go to **Work Centers > Guest Access > Portals & Components > Sponsor Portals**.

Sponsor and Guest Portal Customization

The ISE sponsor portal can be completely customized to fit your organization's needs. Every button, label, icon, and text can be customized. ISE lets you customize the sponsor portal in just about any way you can dream up. Also covered in this section is "Guest Portal Behavior and Flow Settings," "Guest Portal Page Customization," and "Creating Multiple Guest Portals. The Sponsor Settings and Customization configuration screen located at **Work Centers > Guest Access > Portals & Components > Sponsor Portals** has two pages:

- Portal Behavior and Flow Settings
- Portal Page Customization

Sponsor Portal Behavior and Flow Settings

The Portal Behavior and Flow Settings page has a bunch of settings you can configure. Figure 14-17 depicts the various sections available. The most commonly used sections are Portal Settings, Login Settings, and AUP Page Settings.

Under Portal Settings, it is typical to input a vanity URL in the Fully Qualified Domain Names (FQDN) and Host Names field. This makes it easier for your employees/sponsors to remember where they go to register guests. Be sure to configure the DNS server so that it resolves the FQDN to the sponsor portal IP address. Figure 14-17 shows it populated with sponsors.acme.com.

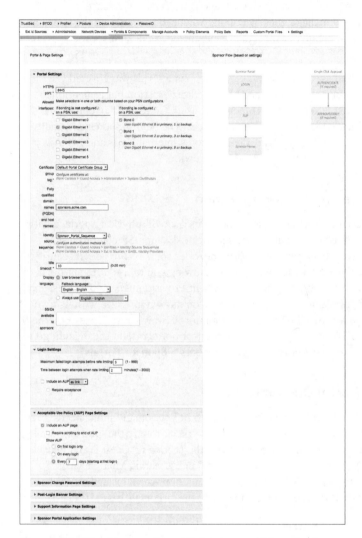

Figure 14-17   *Sponsor Portal Behavior and Flow Settings*

Note the Sponsor Flow diagram to the right of the Portal Settings section. The diagram changes as you change your settings.

> **Note**   Ensure that any ISE PSN certificates that you have also include the vanity URL FQDN in their Subject Alternative Name. This prevents certificate mismatch warnings from popping up on the sponsor's browser.

Sponsor Portal Page Customization

On the Portal Page Customization page, you can customize all aspects of the portal, including its text, color, theme, graphics, button, and so forth, as shown in Figure 14-18. This page also allows you to customize the Acceptable Usage Policy (AUP) and guest notification messages, such as emails, SMS, and printed credentials. Typically, customizing the sponsor portal experience to your business requires that you spend some time here.

Figure 14-18   *Sponsor Portal Page Customization*

Once you click **Save**, the PSN automatically applies the changes so that they take effect immediately. However, the PSN continues its other services uninterrupted.

Guest Portal Behavior and Flow Settings

The customization for the sponsored guest portal is very similar to the customization for the sponsor portal. Go to **Work Centers > Guest Access > Portals & Components > Guest Portals**. Select and edit the default Sponsored Guest Portal or create a new one. Figure 14-19 shows the Portal Behavior and Flow Settings page with the most commonly modified sections expanded so you can see the settings. Configure the settings to meet your needs.

Figure 14-19 *Sponsored Guest Portal Behavior and Flow Settings*

Guest Portal Page Customization

Like the sponsor portal page, you can customize the guest portal pages. It is very common to customize these pages so that the guest portal is branded to your business. The Portal Theme selection sets the colors, fonts, graphics, and so forth for all of the portal pages. Figure 14-20 shows the various options available.

Figure 14-20   *Sponsored Guest Portal Page Customization*

As shown in Figure 14-20, you can upload your own logos and images from your local PC. All saved changes take effect immediately. To view your changes before you save, click the **Desktop Preview** hyperlink. This opens your browser to the portal so that you can see what it looks like.

Here are some of the tips for getting your theme right:

■ Upload a .jpeg, .gif, or .png image file to use as the logo on the portal Login page for the Guest, Sponsor, and My Devices portals.

■ When you upload an image, it is automatically resized to fit an image size required for that area. (See ISE help for details on image sizes.) To avoid distortion, resize your image to fit these dimensions:

- Login logo and banner logo image size of 86 pixels (width) by 45 pixels (height).

- Login background image size is 533 pixels (width) by 325 pixels (height).

- Banner background image size is 133 pixels (height). The width is not controlled, and the banner background color displays to fill the remaining area.

- The post-login banner displays for 15 seconds.

Creating Multiple Guest Portals

In some cases, you might want to create multiple portals for different uses. For example, you might have different business groups that each need their own name on the guest portal. Configuring multiple portals is fairly straightforward. Here are the steps required:

Step 1. Create one or more guest portals at **Work Centers > Guest Access > Portals & Components > Guest Portals**, as previously described.

Step 2. Create an authorization profile for each portal (**Work Centers > Guest Access > Policy Elements > Results > Authorization Profiles > Add**). For each element, select the Web Redirection value under Common Tasks to equal the portal name you created. Repeat this for each portal.

Step 3. Use the portal in an authorization policy rule. Go to **Policy > Policy Sets**. Select your policy and scroll down to the Authorization section. Add a new rule at the bottom, right above the Default rule. Specify the conditions for which you want this particular guest portal to be selected. You should also include a condition for endpoint=unknown. Then, add other conditions to specify where you want the portal to be used. Figure 14-21 shows an example using location of the NAD.

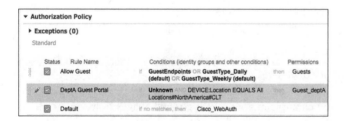

Figure 14-21 *Multi-Portal Authorization Rule*

Guest Sponsor Portal Usage

This section explains the usage of the sponsor portal. The main topics addressed are

- Portal layout

- Creating guest accounts

- Managing guest accounts

Sponsor Portal Layout

To access the ISE sponsor portal, open your browser to the vanity URL you configured, such as sponsors.acme.com, or go to https://<IP address of ISE PSN with portal>:8443/sponsorportal/. You will see the Sponsor Portal login page, along with any customization you have made to the portal. Figure 14-22 shows an example Sponsor Portal login page.

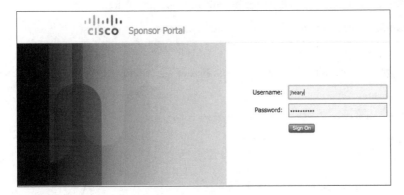

Figure 14-22   *Sponsor Portal Login*

At the bottom of the page is a link to help (not shown).

Once logged in, you see a page similar to Figure 14-23. The options on your screen vary depending on the sponsor privileges you have. Figure 14-23 depicts an account with restricted sponsor privileges.

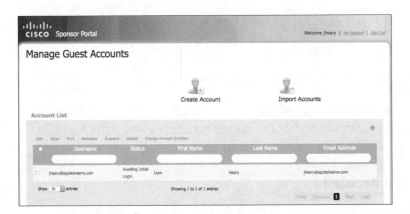

Figure 14-23   *Sponsor Portal Home Page*

The first thing you should do is review/update your sponsor settings. Click **My Settings** in the top-right corner. Set up your email address as a minimum.

Creating Guest Accounts

From the sponsor portal home page, there are three ways to create guest accounts:

- **Create Account:** Creates a single guest account

- **Import Accounts:** Uses an Excel spreadsheet to import multiple accounts. The spreadsheet template is available for download from this option.

- **Create Random Accounts:** Allows you to quickly generate a lot of guest accounts at once

To perform one of these options, just click its icon. Figure 14-24 shows the form for Create Account.

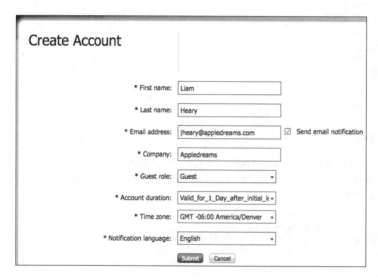

Figure 14-24   *Sponsor Portal: Guest Account Creation*

Fill out the required fields and click **Submit**. The credentials are emailed to the guest. If you would like to print the credentials, go back to the sponsor portal home page, select the account, and click **Print**.

Managing Guest Accounts

Your ability to manage guest accounts depends on the privileges of your sponsor account. You can perform the following actions on an existing guest account:

- Edit

- Notify (email, text, print)

- Reinstate (activates a previously suspended account)

- Suspend

- Delete

- Change account duration

To perform one of the actions, select an account and click the action (refer to Figure 14-23).

Configuration of Network Devices for Guest CWA

With ISE ready to serve as your Central Web Auth source, the next step is to configure your switches and WLCs. This process is straightforward and simple.

Wired Switches

This configuration assumes that you already have the switch configured to communicate with ISE. If not, see Chapter 11, "Bootstrapping Network Access Devices," for details. This example demonstrates using an ACL that is configured directly on the switch instead of using a dACL from ISE, as was shown previously in this chapter. The most common method deployed for wired is dACL, so this example is presented here for completeness of your options.

There are three steps to enabling CWA on your switches:

Step 1.   Configure a pre-authentication ACL on the switch. This determines what traffic is allowed to flow before authentication happens. Here is an example ACL:

```
ip access-list extended webauth
permit udp any any eq bootps
permit udp any any eq domain
permit tcp any any eq domain
remark ping for troubleshooting
permit icmp any any echo
permit icmp any any echo-reply
remark allow web traffic to kick off redirect
permit tcp any any eq www
permit tcp any any eq 443
remark 10.1.100.232 is the ISE PSN for Guest Portal
permit tcp any host 10.1.100.232 eq 8443
permit tcp any host 10.1.100.232 eq 8905
permit tcp any host 10.1.100.232 eq 8909
permit udp any host 10.1.100.232 range 8905 8906
permit udp any host 10.1.100.232 eq 8909
```

Step 2.   Configure a redirect ACL on the switch. Any traffic that matches a **permit** statement is redirected to the guest URL. Here is a sample ACL:

```
ip access-list extended ACL-WEBAUTH-REDIRECT
    deny ip any host 10.1.100.232
    permit tcp any any eq www
    permit tcp any any eq 443
    permit tcp any any eq 8443
remark be sure to include any proxy ports you have enabled
    permit tcp any any eq 8080
```

Step 3.   Configure your switch for HTTP and ports for MAB and apply ACLs:

```
ip http server
ip http secure-server
interface GigabitEthernet1/0/12
    description ISE1 - dot1x clients - UCS Eth0
    switchport access vlan 100
    switchport mode access
    ip access-group webauth in
    authentication order mab
    authentication priority mab
    authentication port-control auto
    mab
    spanning-tree portfast
```

You can use the **show auth sess int gi1/12** switch command to see the session info.

Wireless LAN Controllers

Configuring the Cisco WLC for CWA is a three-step process. These steps assume that you already have the basic WLC to ISE configuration completed. If not, see Chapter 11 for more details. Follow these steps to get up and running:

Step 1.   Ensure that the RADIUS server has Support for CoA set to Enabled, which is the default, as shown in Figure 14-25.

Figure 14-25 *Support for CoA*

Step 2.   Select or create your guest WLAN and SSID. Edit the WLAN and go to
Security > Layer 2. Enable **MAC Filtering,** as shown in Figure 14-26.

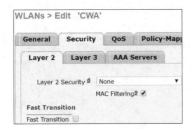

Figure 14-26 *WLC MAC Filtering*

Step 3.   Go to **Security > Layer 3.** From the Layer 3 Security drop-down list, choose
None as shown in Figure 14-27.

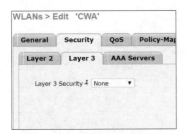

Figure 14-27 *WLC Layer 3*

Step 4.   Go to **Security > AAA Servers**. Add ISE AAA, as shown in Figure 14-28. When deploying ISE in your wireless network, do not configure a primary and secondary ISE server. Instead, configure high availability (HA) between the two ISE servers. Having a primary and secondary ISE setup requires a posture validation to happen before the client moves to the RUN state. If HA is configured, the client is automatically moved to the RUN state in the fallback ISE server.

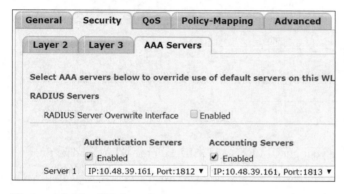

Figure 14-28   *WLC AAA Servers*

Step 5.   Click the **Advanced** tab. Enable the settings shown highlighted in Figure 14-29.

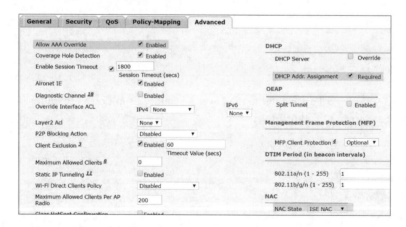

Figure 14-29   *WLC Advanced Tab*

Step 6.   Create the web-redirection ALC. Be sure to use the same name as you used in the ISE configuration authorization profile web-redirect ACL. This ACL is referenced in the Access-Accept of the ISE and defines what traffic should be redirected (denied by the ACL) and what traffic should not be redirected (permitted by the ACL). Here, you just prevent from redirection traffic toward the ISE. You might want to be more specific and only prevent traffic to/from the ISE on port 8443 (guest portal), but still redirect if a user tries to access the ISE on port 80/443. Go to **Security > Access Control Lists > Access Control Lists.** Figure 14-30 shows an example, where 10.48.39.161 is the IP of ISE.

Seq	Action	Source IP/Mask	Destination IP/Mask	Protocol	Source Port	Dest Port	DSCP	Direction	Number of Hits
1	Permit	0.0.0.0 / 0.0.0.0	0.0.0.0 / 0.0.0.0	UDP	DNS	Any	Any	Any	836
2	Permit	0.0.0.0 / 0.0.0.0	0.0.0.0 / 0.0.0.0	UDP	Any	DNS	Any	Any	2072
3	Permit	0.0.0.0 / 0.0.0.0	10.48.39.161 / 255.255.255.255	Any	Any	Any	Any	Any	4895
4	Permit	10.48.39.161 / 255.255.255.255	0.0.0.0 / 0.0.0.0	Any	Any	Any	Any	Any	7160
5	Deny	0.0.0.0 / 0.0.0.0	0.0.0.0 / 0.0.0.0	Any	Any	Any	Any	Any	6587

General — Access List Name: cwa_redirect — Deny Counters: 0

Figure 14-30 *WLC ACL*

Step 7.   Click Save.

Summary

This chapter focused on creating a robust guest user environment. It covered everything from basic setup to full portal customization. The majority use case covered was Central Web Authentication with the sponsored guest type. Topics explored in this chapter include guest portals, sponsor portals, sponsor lifecycle, configuration of wired and wireless devices, guest authentication, and portal customization.

Chapter 15

Client Posture Assessment

This chapter covers the following topics:

- ISE posture assessment flow
- Configure global posture and client provisioning settings
- Configure the AnyConnect and NAC client provisioning rules
- Configure the Client Provisioning Portal
- Configure posture elements
- Configure posture policy
- Configure host application visibility and context collection (optional)
- Enable posture client provisioning and assessment in your ISE authorization policies
- Posture reports and troubleshooting
- Enable posture assessment in the network

In short, this chapter shows you how to use ISE to answer, "Are my clients compliant with the company's client/host security policy?"

Wouldn't it be great if you could always be confident that all of your hosts are running up-to-date software with all the right patches and running up-to-date antivirus and anti-malware software? Cisco ISE posture assessment helps you to ensure that your clients are in compliance with your host security policy. Posture assessment allows you to check the security health of your PC and Mac clients. This includes checking for the installation, running state, and last update for security software such as antivirus, antimalware, personal firewall, and so forth. It also includes checking to ensure that the hosts' operating systems are patched appropriately. In addition, ISE posture policies can check for additional custom attributes such as files, processes, registry settings, and applications, just to name a few. Taken together, these features enable ISE to determine the security health of a client that is trying to access your network. ISE uses posture policies to determine the access rights and remediation options that should be provided to clients.

> **Note**   ISE posture functionality requires an ISE Apex license.

To ease the configuration process, ISE has a Work Center specifically for Posture. As shown in Figure 15-1, the steps for configuring posture are broken down into three categories: Prepare, Define, and Go Live & Monitor.

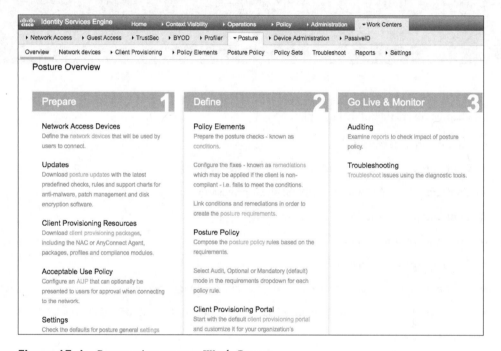

Figure 15-1   *Posture Assessment Work Center*

Here are the high-level steps, in the order I prefer, that are required to set up the ISE posture assessment feature:

1. Configure global posture and client provisioning settings:

    a. Download to ISE the latest posture updates and the client provisioning packages.

    b. Verify the default global posture settings meet your needs.

2. Configure the posture client provisioning policy.

3. Configure the Client Provisioning Portal.

4. Configure posture elements:

    a. Configure posture conditions.

    b. Configure posture remediation.

    c. Configure posture requirements.

5. Configure posture policy.

6. Optionally, configure host application visibility and context collection.

7. Enable posture client provisioning and assessment in your ISE authorization policies.

8. Enable posture assessment on the network devices.

ISE Posture Assessment Flow

It is important to understand where posture fits in the overall system flow of ISE. Figure 15-2 illustrates the flow that ISE goes through when posture assessment is enabled.

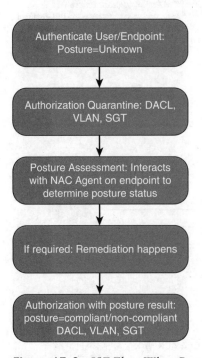

Figure 15-2 *ISE Flow When Poster Assessment Is Enabled*

Figures 15-3 and 15-4 depict the flow ISE goes through for an 802.1X end user with posture assessment.

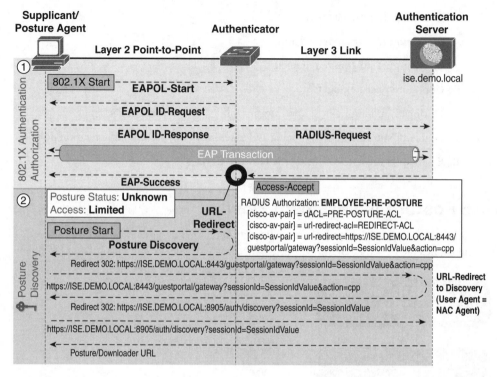

Figure 15-3 *Posture Assessment 802.1X Flow Steps 1–2*

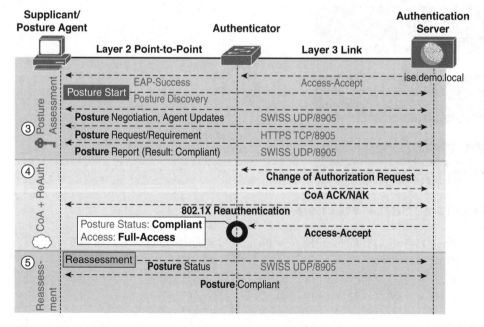

Figure 15-4 *Posture Assessment 802.1X Flow Steps 3–5*

Here is a brief description of what is happening at each step (1–5) shown in Figures 15-2 and 15-3:

1. The client 802.1X supplicant talks to the access switch to start 802.1X. The EAP transaction takes place with the switch acting as the proxy between the client and ISE. If the authentication is successful, the posture status is set to Unknown.

2. ISE instructs the switch to redirect the client to an ISE URL for downloading the posture NAC Agent software or the dissolvable NAC Web Agent, depending on policy.

3. Now that the client has a NAC Agent, posture assessment proceeds through its flow. The NAC Agent uses the SWISS protocol to communicate with ISE. (SWISS is a proprietary UDP protocol created by Cisco.) At the end, a posture result is created.

4. ISE sends a Change of Authorization (CoA) request to the switch. This triggers an 802.1X reauthentication. A new authorization rule is matched given the new posture status of the client (compliant, noncompliant). The new access rights of the match authorization rule are downloaded to the switch.

5. If periodic reassessment is enabled, the client periodically goes through posture assessment to check for any changes. This happens without affecting the client communication. If the status changes, then a CoA is issued and the steps begin anew.

Configure Global Posture and Client Provisioning Settings

In this section, you will enable the global settings required to turn on posture assessment. There are two parts: client provisioning setup and posture setup. Client provisioning deals with the NAC Agent software, its delivery, and other such settings. Posture setup deals with downloading the posture condition database and clients, keeping it up to date, posture reassessment, and other general settings.

Posture Client Provisioning Global Setup

To begin client provisioning setup, you need to enable and download your posture resources. ISE posture assessment requires an agent to run. There are three major types of ISE posture agents for posture assessment, each of which supports Windows and macOS operating systems:

- Cisco AnyConnect with the compliance module
- Cisco NAC Agent
- NAC Web Agent

The NAC web agent is on-demand and dissolvable, meaning it is downloaded via the ISE Central Web Authentication page based on policy. It temporarily runs via the client's web browser as an ActiveX or Java applet. The NAC Web Agent is not permanent like the other NAC Agents are, and deletes itself once posture is complete. The AnyConnect and NAC Agents install permanently like any other agent software would.

Here is a list of all the client provisioning resource types:

- Persistent and temporal posture agents:

  - Windows and Mac OS X Cisco AnyConnect Agents with the ISE compliance module installed

  - Windows and Mac OS X Cisco NAC Agents

  - Cisco NAC Web Agent

- Agent compliance modules

- Agent customization packages

The following resources are also available but are not used for ISE posture assessment. They are used for the provisioning of the clients' 802.1X supplicant and are covered in Chapter 16, "Supplicant Configuration."

- Native supplicant profiles

- Native supplicant provisioning/installation wizards

To enable and download the posture resources, go to **Administration > System > Settings > Client Provisioning**. Figure 15-5 shows the various settings available here, as described in the following list. Before you make any changes, ensure that you have your ISE proxy settings configured, if required for your environment.

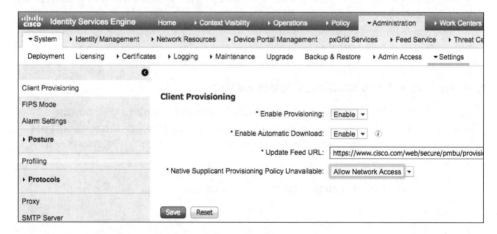

Figure 15-5 *Global Client Provisioning Settings*

Step 1. Enable client provisioning.

Step 2a. (Optional) Enable automatic download. This downloads any and all client files from Cisco.com. Select the exact files you want, as covered following this list.

Step 2b. If you choose to enable automatic download, use the default feed URL or set up your own client repository site. As of ISE version 2.2, the default URL is https://www.cisco.com/web/secure/pmbu/provisioning-update.xml.

Step 3. In most cases, keep the default setting of **Allow Network Access** for the Native Supplicant Provisioning Policy Unavailable.

Step 4. Click **Save**. Expect to wait a few minutes while ISE downloads the client files if you enabled automatic download.

To select just the client files you need for your environment, go to **Policy > Policy Elements > Results > Client Provisioning > Resources**, as shown in Figure 15-6. (You can also get there via **Work Centers > Posture > Client Provisioning > Resources**.) This screen shows you all of the agents and other ISE resources you have downloaded already. To add more, click **Add** and choose either to add them from Cisco.com or to add them from your local PC. If you choose to add them from Cisco.com, you will see a list of available agents and software. Select what you want and click **Save**. The software is downloaded, which can take several minutes. Figure 15-7 shows the Cisco.com software select screen. To see the complete Description field, grab the column separator and drag it larger, similar to what you would do in Excel to make a column wider.

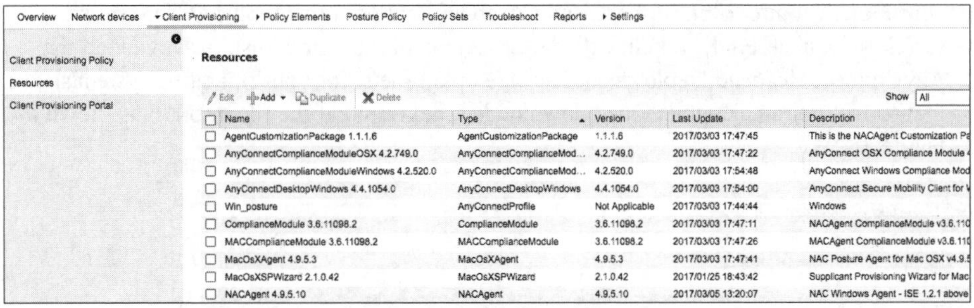

Figure 15-6 *Client Provisioning Resources*

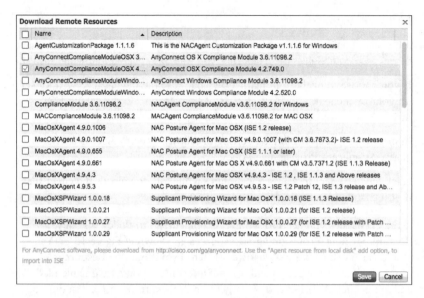

Figure 15-7 *Adding Client Provisioning Resources from Cisco.com*

The note at the bottom of Figure 15-7 tells you that, as of ISE version 2.2, you cannot download the full AnyConnect Agent through ISE. You can, however, download the AnyConnect compliance module that fits inside the full AnyConnect client. To obtain the full AnyConnect Agent, you must download it from Cisco.com/go/AnyConnect; hover your mouse pointer over Support, enter **AnyConnect Secure Mobility Client** in the search field, click **Find**, and click the latest version in the search results. Download the AnyConnect Headend Deployment Package (.pkg) file(s) for your operating system(s). See Figure 15-8 for an example. Once downloaded, next upload the file into ISE as shown in Figure 15-9.

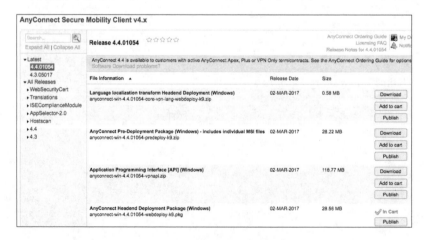

Figure 15-8 *AnyConnect Agent Package Files*

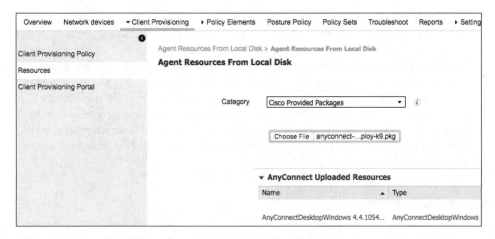

Figure 15-9 *Add AnyConnect to ISE*

Posture Global Setup

This section steps you through how to set up the global settings for ISE posture assessment. The various timer settings should be adjusted to meet the needs of your organization.

Posture General Settings

To begin, ensure that the basic posture settings are correct for your environment. Go to **Administration > System > Settings > Posture > General Settings**, or go to **Work Centers > Posture > Settings > Posture General Settings**. Figure 15-10 shows the settings.

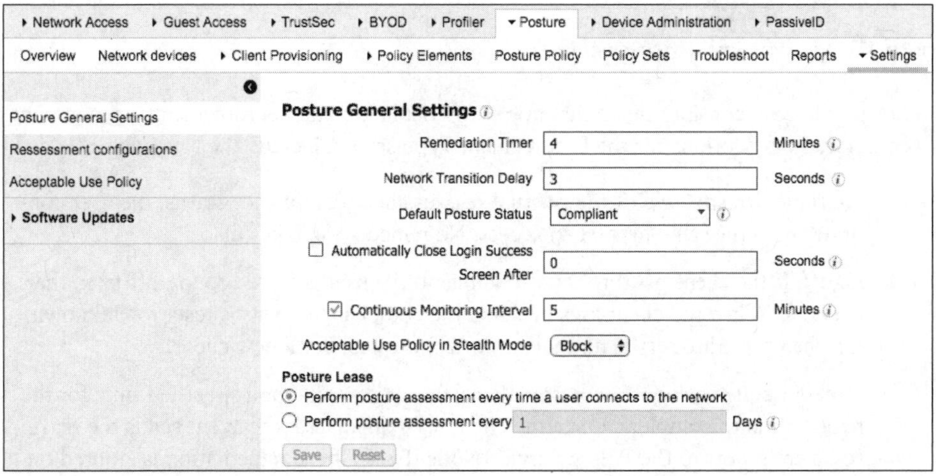

Figure 15-10 *Posture General Settings*

These global settings take effect only if there is not a more specific posture profile in effect. The Default Posture Status field provides posture status for non-Agent devices (for example, Linux-based operating systems) and endpoints for which no NAC Agent installation policy applies. It is a best practice to enable **Automatically Close Login Success Screen After** and set it to **0** seconds. This disables display of the login success screen, which enhances the end-user experience in most organizations. You can also set the Posture Lease behavior of ISE. The option to perform posture assessment based on the number of days since the last posture scan is a great new feature; however, it only works with the Cisco AnyConnect compliance module and not with the NAC Agent or Web Agent.

Posture Reassessments

If you would like to periodically recheck the posture of your endpoints, you can enable it via **Posture > Settings > Reassessment Configurations**. It works on a per-user identity group basis or is enabled for all. Figure 15-11 shows the reassessment settings.

Figure 15-11   *Posture Reassessment*

Ensure that you consider the ramifications of enabling certain enforcement types in your configurations. Options for the Enforcement Type setting include the following:

■ **continue:** Irrespective of the posture reassessment compliance status, the user continues with the same privileged access. No remediation takes place.

■ **logoff:** If the client posture is not compliant, the user is forced to log off from the network. When the client logs in again, the compliance status is reset to Unknown. ISE then runs through its normal authorization steps for a new client.

■ **remediate:** If the client is not compliant, the agent waits for a specified time for the remediation to complete. Once the client has remediated, the agent sends the reassessment report to the Policy Service Node (PSN). If the remediation is ignored on the client, then the agent sends a logoff request to the PSN to force the client to log off from the network.

As you can see from Figure 15-11, ISE uses the following group selection rules:

1. Each configuration must have a unique group or a unique combination of groups.

2. No two configurations may have any group in common.

3. If a config already exists with a group of 'Any', then no other configs can be created unless

   a. the existing config with a group of 'Any' is updated to reflect a group (or groups) other than 'Any', or

   b. the existing config with a group of 'Any' is deleted

4. If a config with a group of 'Any' must be created, delete all other configs first.

Posture Updates

Cisco provides a posture update service to ensure that ISE has the latest information regarding posture check information. It is a best practice to set up auto-updates for posture. To do this, navigate to **Work Centers > Posture > Settings > Software Updates > Posture Updates,** as shown in Figure 15-12. Configure ISE to retrieve posture updates either from Cisco.com or from an internal server you maintain. In almost all cases, you should enable **Automatically Check for Updates.** Enter the start time in 24-hour format, such as 4:30:00; the repeat time is in hours, such as 2. Ensure that you have configured any necessary proxy settings in ISE before attempting an update. If this is your first time updating, click the **Update Now** button and ensure that it completes successfully.

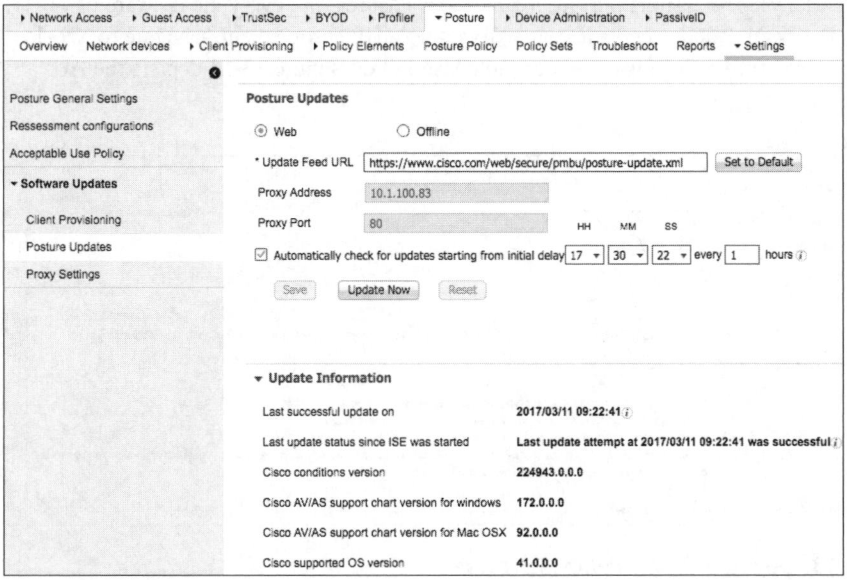

Figure 15-12 *Posture Updates*

Acceptable Use Policy Enforcement

ISE provides the ability to enforce the acceptance of an acceptable use policy (AUP) after a successful login and compliant posture assessment completes. After login and successful posture assessment of clients, the client agent displays a temporary network access screen that contains a link to an AUP. To proceed, users must click the link, which redirects them to a page that displays the AUP, where they must acknowledge that they have read the AUP and accept its network-usage terms and conditions. Unlike guest access, where AUP enforcement is widely used, posture-triggered AUP enforcement is not a widely used or popular ISE feature, for two reasons: it interrupts the network login of the user and requires the user to accept the policy before they are granted network access, which impacts productivity, and it often is redundant, because most postured hosts are being used by users who have already accepted a corporate AUP as part of their employment contract.

When the feature is used, each AUP configuration must have a unique user identity group, or a unique combination of user identity groups. Cisco ISE finds the AUP for the first matched user identity group and communicates that to the client agent, which displays the AUP. These settings apply to AnyConnect ISE Posture and NAC Agents for Windows. This AUP does not apply to guest users; you must use guest portal settings instead. The configuration is group-based, like the posture reassessment. If AUP is enabled for a group, members of that group see a pop-up from their NAC Agent each time they log in. They have to click Accept before being allowed to log in. Because this happens at each login, it is typically enabled only where required, such as for high-risk user groups, non-employees, temporary workers, or other groups that haven't signed a contractual network AUP already. Another tactic is to enable the AUP for all network users once a year for a short period of time. This ensures that everyone is aware of your network AUP and accepts it yearly. To set up AUP enforcement, navigate to **Work Centers > Posture > Settings > Acceptable Use Policy.** Figure 15-13 depicts the AUP settings screen.

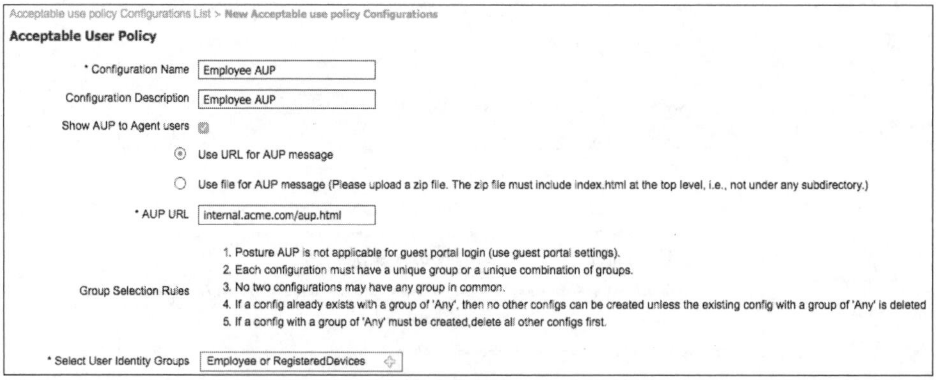

Figure 15-13 *Acceptable Use Policy Settings*

Configure the AnyConnect and NAC Client Provisioning Rules

ISE allows you to granularly control which client and client profiles are provisioned to a host. ISE has two agents: the AnyConnect Agent with the compliance module installed and the NAC Agent. Going forward, Cisco is migrating in favor of the AnyConnect Agent, so if you have a new deployment, you should opt to deploy the AnyConnect Agent.

AnyConnect Agent with ISE Compliance Module

This section walks you through configuring the AnyConnect Agent for use with ISE posture assessment. The AnyConnect client provisioning requires four different resources to be in place before it can be used in a client provisioning policy:

- AnyConnect Secure Mobility Client software

- AnyConnect Windows/OS X compliance module

- AnyConnect Posture Profile file

- AnyConnect configuration file

Cisco provides the first two resources. You need to create the last two resources inside of ISE (first the Posture Profile and then the configuration file). Figure 15-14 shows an example of the four required resources for AnyConnect.

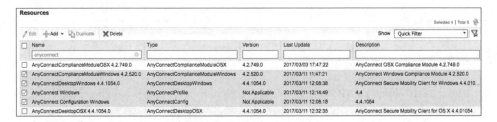

Figure 15-14 *AnyConnect Required Resources*

Note   As previously discussed, ISE, as of version 2.2, cannot download the AnyConnect client package directly from Cisco.com. Thus, it is necessary for you to download the AnyConnect Headend Deployment Package file to your computer and then upload it manually into the ISE client provisioning resources. Packages are available for Windows, OS X, and Linux. However, the Linux package does not support posture assessment.

AnyConnect Posture Profile Creation

The Posture Profile defines the AnyConnect Agent behaviors and is used in the AnyConnect configuration file. To configure it, go to **Work Centers > Posture > Client Provisioning > Resources**, click **Add**, and select **NAC Agent** or **AnyConnect Posture Profile**. Next, from the **Posture Agent Profile Settings** drop-down list, choose **AnyConnect**, as shown in Figure 15-15. Enter a descriptive name for your profile. The profile settings are broken into three sections:

- Agent Behavior
- IP Address Change
- Posture Protocol

Figure 15-15 shows the Agent Behavior section. Typically, the default values are fine for most deployments.

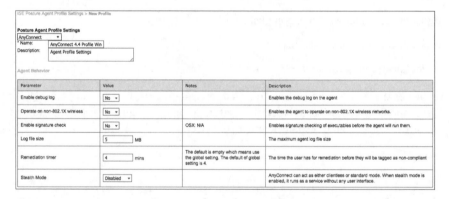

Figure 15-15   *Profile Settings: Agent Behavior Section*

Figure 15-16 shows the IP Address Change section. If you will be changing VLANs as part of your permission and remediation settings, then you need to tweak these settings. Figure 15-16 shows some example settings for this; however, if you are not changing the client's VLAN, the defaults will work fine for most deployments.

ISE Posture Agent Profile Settings > New Profile

Posture Agent Profile Settings

AnyConnect

* Name: AnyConnect 4.4 Profile Win
Description: Agent Profile Settings

IP Address Change

Parameter	Value		Notes	Description
Enable agent IP refresh	Yes		Enables VLAN change detection	Sets the Vlan change detection flag on the server, to transmit the configured dhcp release delay, and the dhcp renew delay values from the server to the client.
VLAN detection interval	5	secs	0 means VLAN detection is disabled	The interval at which the agent will check for a VLAN change
Ping or ARP	Ping ti		0=Ping, 1=ARP, 2=Ping then ARP	Method for detecting IP address change.
Maximum timeout for ping	1	secs		Ping timeout.
DHCP renew delay	1	secs		
DHCP release delay	4	secs		
Network transition delay	3	secs	The default is empty which means uses the global setting. The default of global setting is 3.	The period for which the agent suspends network monitoring so it can wait for a planned IP change to happen

Figure 15-16   *Profile Settings: IP Address Change Section*

Figure 15-17 shows the Posture Protocol section. You should set the discovery host, server name rules, and call home list.

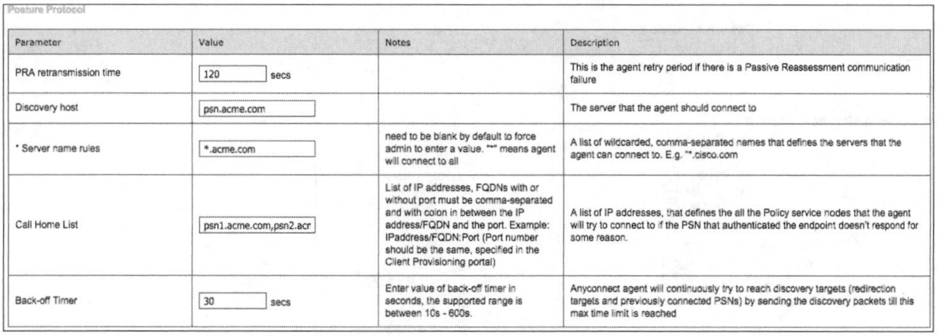

Posture Protocol			
Parameter	Value	Notes	Description
PRA retransmission time	120 secs		This is the agent retry period if there is a Passive Reassessment communication failure
Discovery host	psn.acme.com		The server that the agent should connect to
* Server name rules	*.acme.com	need to be blank by default to force admin to enter a value. "*" means agent will connect to all	A list of wildcarded, comma-separated names that defines the servers that the agent can connect to. E.g. "*.cisco.com
Call Home List	psn1.acme.com,psn2.acr	List of IP addresses, FQDNs with or without port must be comma-separated and with colon in between the IP address/FQDN and the port. Example: IPaddress/FQDN:Port (Port number should be the same, specified in the Client Provisioning portal)	A list of IP addresses, that defines the all the Policy service nodes that the agent will try to connect to if the PSN that authenticated the endpoint doesn't respond for some reason.
Back-off Timer	30 secs	Enter value of back-off timer in seconds, the supported range is between 10s - 600s.	Anyconnect agent will continuously try to reach discovery targets (redirection targets and previously connected PSNs) by sending the discovery packets till this max time limit is reached

Figure 15-17 *Profile Settings: Posture Protocol Section*

AnyConnect Configuration File Creation

The AnyConnect configuration file defines which AnyConnect software and its associated configuration files are used. This configuration can be used in the client provisioning policy that allows users to download and install AnyConnect resources on the clients.

Note   If you use both ISE and an ASA to deploy AnyConnect, then the configurations must match on both.

To create your configuration file, go to **Work Centers > Posture > Client Provisioning > Resources**. Click **Add** and select **AnyConnect Configuration**. The configuration is separated into five sections:

- AnyConnect Package Info
- AnyConnect Module Selection
- Profile Selection
- Deferred Update
- Installation Options

Fill out the first three sections with the values for your organization. Figure 15-18 shows some example values.

```
        * Select AnyConnect Package:  AnyConnectDesktopWindows 4.4.1054.0      ▼
           * Configuration Name:  AnyConnect Configuration Windows 4.4.1054
                  Description:  Windows 4.4.1054


                      DescriptionValue
           * Compliance Module  AnyConnectComplianceModuleWindows 4.2.520.0   ▼


  AnyConnect Module Selection
                     ISE Posture ☑
                          VPN ☑
          Network Access Manager ☐
                  Web Security ☐
                  AMP Enabler ☐
                   ASA Posture ☐
               Network Visibility ☐
        Umbrella Roaming Security ☐
              Start Before Logon ☐
      Diagnostic and Reporting Tool ☐


  Profile Selection
                   * ISE Posture  AnyConnect 4.4 Profile Windows      ▼
                          VPN                                          ▼
          Network Access Manager                                      ▼
                  Web Security                                         ▼
                  AMP Enabler                                          ▼
               Network Visibility                                      ▼
        Umbrella Roaming Security                                      ▼
              Customer Feedback                                        ▼
```

Figure 15-18 *AnyConnect Sample Configuration for First Three Sections*

The fourth section defines the settings for allowing or disallowing the end user to defer a client update. Figure 15-19 shows an example of allowing deferral of the agent software update but not allowing deferral of a compliance module update. Under Installation Options, the Uninstall Cisco NAC Agent check box will uninstall any existing NAC agents on the client after a successful AnyConnect posture module install. This should be checked; the AnyConnect posture module and the Cisco NAC agent should NOT both be installed on the same host.

```
  Customization Bundle                         AnyConnect can be customized to display your own corporate image in the software, scripts that can run during
                                               connection establishment and termination, transforms to alter the behavior of installers. Uploaded bundle must
                                               follow the guidelines specified in the documentation.
    Localization Bundle                        AnyConnect can be localized for different languages. Configure language translations the software uses to
                                               translate its messages. Uploaded bundle must follow the guidelines specified in the documentation.

  Deferred Update
  Allowed for AnyConnect Software  Yes         If set to 'Yes', the end user can defer the update as long as they already meet the minimum version in the setting
                                               below, for all required AnyConnect modules.
  Minimum Version Required for AnyConnect  4.4  Format is 'n.n.n'. '0.0.0' means no minimum version is required. '3' means minimum version is 3.0.0, '3.2' means
                 Software                      minimum is 3.2.0.
  Allowed for Compliance Module  No            If set to 'Yes', the end user can defer the update as long as they already meet the minimum version in the setting
                                               below.
  Minimum Version Required for Compliance  0.0.0.0  Format is 'n.n.n.n'. '0.0.0.0' means no minimum version is required. '3' means minimum version is 3.0.0.0, '3.6'
                 Module                        means minimum is 3.6.0.0, and so on.
  Prompt Auto Dismiss Timeout  5               The number of seconds that the deferred update prompt is displayed before being dismissed automatically. 'None'
                                               means the prompt can only be dismissed by the user. A '0' value and a 'defer' value for the response setting below
                                               will force a deferral of the software update.
  Prompt Auto Dismiss Default Response  Update  The action taken when the prompt is automatically dismissed.

  Installation Options
       Uninstall Cisco NAC Agent ☑            Uninstalls Cisco NAC Agent after successful installation of ISE Posture.
```

Figure 15-19 *AnyConnect Configuration: Deferred Update*

AnyConnect Client Provisioning Policy

Now that you have the four required resources for AnyConnect, you can create a provisioning policy. Client provisioning policy rules determine which users and endpoints receive which resources (agents, agent compliance modules, and/or agent customization packages/profiles) from Cisco ISE after authentication. Define the client provisioning policy to determine what users will receive upon login and user session initiation. For Agent configuration, this includes version of agent, agent profile, agent compliance module, and/or agent customization package.

Navigate to **Work Centers > Posture > Client Provisioning > Client Provisioning Policy**. Click the drop-down arrow at the right end of a policy row and choose **Insert New Policy**. There are two results per rule: Native supplicant and Agent configuration. We cover only the Agent rules here. Typically, you create at least one rule per operating system. An example is shown in Figure 15-20.

Figure 15-20 *AnyConnect Client Provisioning Rule*

Each rule has the following settings:

- **Status:** This is the green check box in Figure 15-20. Options are Enable, Disable, or Monitor. Monitor disables the policy and just "watches" and logs the client provisioning requests.

- **Rule Name:** Use a descriptive name that includes the key conditions you are matching, such as windows10-employees.

- **Identity Groups:** Not typically used.

- **Operating Systems:** This setting is a requirement for a proper rule base. You should at a minimum have a Windows policy and a Mac policy.

- **Other Conditions:** Includes AD group selection.

- **Results:** Agent and supplicant configuration selection.

Configure the Client Provisioning Portal

ISE posture assessment requires an agent to be installed on the endpoint. You can install that agent using ISE, ASA, or your own software provisioning system. If you use ISE, then you must configure the Client Provisioning Portal. After users successfully authenticate and request network access, ISE can route them to a Client Provisioning web portal to provide them with the posture agent for download. The posture agent downloads, installs, and runs and provides a posture verdict back to ISE.

To set up the portal, go to **Work Centers > Posture > Client Provisioning > Client Provisioning Portal**, select the **Default** portal, and click **Duplicate**. On the Portal Settings and Customization page, shown in Figure 15-21, give your new portal a descriptive name and, optionally, add a description. Click **Portal Settings**, and change the port and your interfaces as appropriate for your deployment. If you have multiple PSNs, the interfaces and ports chosen will be the same on all PSNs. At this point you are done unless you want to customize the page using the other sections shown in Figure 15-21.

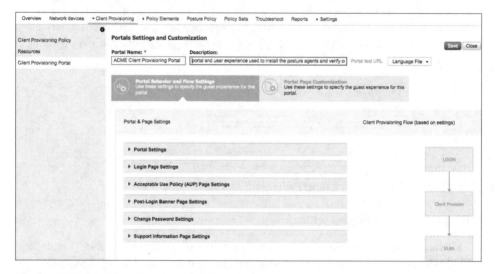

Figure 15-21   *Client Provisioning Portal*

Note   If users will access your portal page directly (not through the usual URL redirect mechanism), or if the redirect single sign-on (SSO) fails for any reason, you must configure the **Portal Settings > Authentication Method** section and authorized groups appropriately—for example, users accessing the portal page via an AnyConnect VPN session. In the authentication method section, change this to whichever user database should be used to authenticate users to the portal. Next, select **Authorized Groups**. The FQDN of the Client Provisioning Portal needs to be specified next. This FQDN should be resolvable to ISE PSN IPs. Caution: Make sure you don't specify the exact same FQDN of an ISE standalone admin login page; otherwise, you will lose your admin page. Users need to be instructed to enter the FQDN URL in the web browser to visit the portal during their first connection attempt.

Configure Posture Elements

Posture elements are the building blocks for your posture requirements. There are three major categories of posture policy elements you need to configure: Conditions, Remediations, and Requirements. Figure 15-22 shows these categories of elements, located at **Work Centers > Posture > Policy Elements**.

Figure 15-22 *Categories of Posture Elements*

Configure Posture Conditions

There are many types of posture conditions, as shown in Figure 15-23. To configure the conditions, go to posture **Work Centers > Posture > Policy Elements > Conditions**.

Figure 15-23 *Posture Condition Types*

The good news is that many of these condition types are prepopulated from the Cisco.com posture update process that you configured earlier. Updates continue to flow in as they are available, always keeping your conditions up to date. There are some condition types that, as of ISE 2.2, are not supported on Macs. The list seems to shrink with each AnyConnect release, so check the latest ISE release notes for details. Posture assessment is not supported at all on Linux.

ISE has many predefined conditions that help speed configuration and deployment. Cisco-defined simple conditions have pc_ as their prefixes and compound conditions have pr_ as their prefixes. You cannot delete or edit Cisco-defined posture conditions, but you can duplicate them and edit the duplicate. Figure 15-24 shows an example predefined compound condition. This condition checks to ensure that all Windows 7 x64 critical hotfixes are installed. As new hotfixes are released by Microsoft, this rule is auto-updated by Cisco ISE.

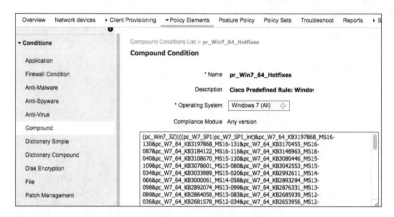

Figure 15-24   *Windows 7 Compound Condition*

Figures 15-25 through 15-30 provide example screenshots of some of the other condition types, in the following order: Registry, Application, Disk Encryption, Firewall, and Anti-Virus (both predefined and manual).

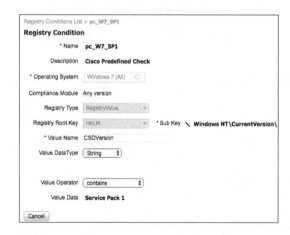

Figure 15-25   *Registry Condition Settings*

Figure 15-26 *Application Condition Settings*

> **Note**   You can use the command-line tool **tasklist** to find all running Windows applications.

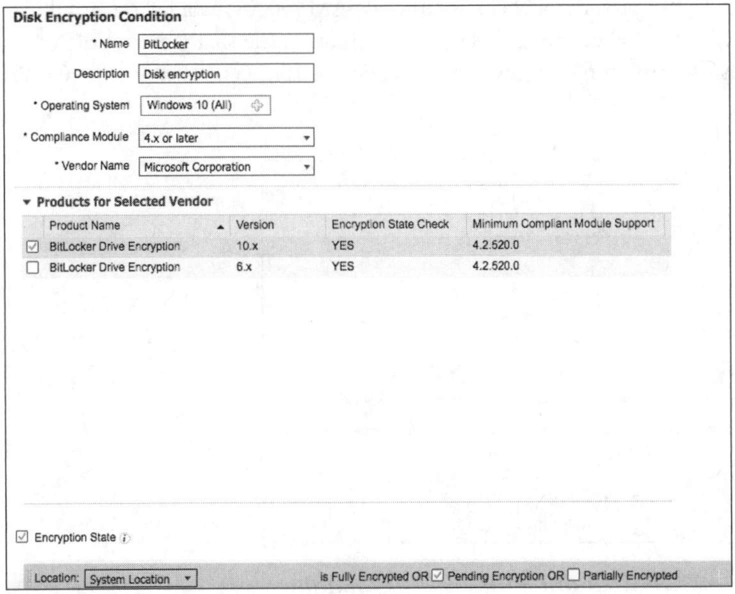

Disk Encryption Condition

* Name	BitLocker
Description	Disk encryption
* Operating System	Windows 10 (All)
* Compliance Module	4.x or later
* Vendor Name	Microsoft Corporation

▼ **Products for Selected Vendor**

	Product Name	▲ Version	Encryption State Check	Minimum Compliant Module Support
☑	BitLocker Drive Encryption	10.x	YES	4.2.520.0
☐	BitLocker Drive Encryption	6.x	YES	4.2.520.0

☑ Encryption State ⓘ

Location: System Location ▾   is Fully Encrypted OR ☑ Pending Encryption OR ☐ Partially Encrypted

Figure 15-27 *Disk Encryption Condition Settings*

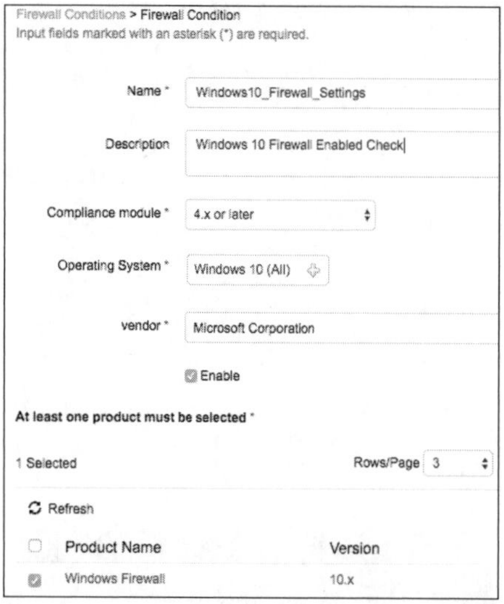

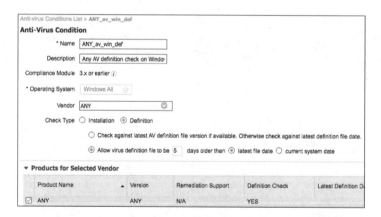

Figure 15-28   *Firewall Condition Settings*

The Anti-Virus (AV), Anti-Malware (AM), and Anti-Spyware (AS) compound conditions are similar. By default, ISE provides a check for any AV, AM, or AS installed on Windows and Mac. Also included is a check for any AV or AS definition file that is 5 days old or older than the latest file date for Windows and Mac. Figure 15-29 shows a predefined AV condition.

Figure 15-29   *Predefined AV Definition Up to Date Condition*

An ISE custom AV or AS condition can check for either the definition or the installation of the software. Use a compound condition to combine them into a single condition. Creating a custom AV rule is typically done when a corporation has standard AV software set up on its corporate PCs and Macs. Figure 15-30 shows an example of a custom

AV condition. This AV vendor also supports automatic remediation by ISE, allowing ISE to trigger an AV signature update action.

Anti-Virus Condition

* Name	Corp_mcafee_AV
Description	EST 10.x
Compliance Module	3.x or earlier
* Operating System	Windows 7 (All)
Vendor	McAfee, Inc.
Check Type	○ Installation ⊙ Definition
	⊙ Check against latest AV definition file version if available. Otherwise check against latest definition file date.
	○ Allow virus definition file to be 0 days older than ○ latest file date ○ current system date

Products for Selected Vendor

Product Name	▲ Version	Remediation Support	Definition Check	Latest Definition Date	Latest Definition Version	Minimum Compliance M	
						Installation	Definition Date
McAfee Endpoint Security Threat...	10.x	YES	YES	03/12/2017	2918.0	3.6.9038.2	3.6.9038.2

Figure 15-30 *Custom AV Definition Up to Date Condition*

Configure Posture Remediations

Now that you have created your various conditions, the next step is to configure client remediation actions. These are actions that the AnyConnect Agent, NAC Agent, and/or end user can perform to fix any failed conditions and thus come into posture compliance. For example, you could set up ISE to automatically update a host's antivirus definition file. Like the Conditions category, the Remediations category has various types in ISE, as shown in Figure 15-31.

Figure 15-31 *Remediation Types*

Table 15-1 outlines the available remediation actions, as of ISE version 2.2, listed by supported agent type.

Table 15-1 *ISE Version 2.2 Remediation Actions*

	Windows AnyConnect Posture Agent/ NAC Agent	Web Agent for Windows	Mac OS X AnyConnect Posture Agent/NAC Agent
Message Text (Local Check)	Supported	Supported	Supported
URL Link (Link Distribution)	Supported (manual and automatic)	Supported (manual)	Supported (manual)
Launch Program	Supported (manual and automatic)	Not Supported	Not supported
File Distribution	Supported	Supported	Not supported
Antivirus Definition Update	Supported (manual and automatic)	Not supported	Supported
Antispyware Definition Update	Supported (manual and automatic)	Not supported	Supported
Windows Update	Supported (manual and automatic)	Not supported	Not supported
WSUS	Supported (manual and automatic)	Not supported	Not supported
Patch Management	Supported (manual and automatic)	Not supported	Not supported
Host Firewall Enabled	Supported (manual and automatic)	Not supported	Supported (manual and automatic)
Block USB storage devices	Supported (automatic)	Not supported	Not supported
Application Uninstall or Kill	Supported (manual and automatic)	Not supported	Supported (manual and automatic)

If a remediation action is manual, the end user sees a NAC Agent popup with instructions to click it to perform the action. If the action is automatic, the end user doesn't have to perform any action. The NAC agent performs the action automatically.

To create or edit remediation actions, following these steps:

Step 1.   Navigate to **Work Centers > Posture > Policy Elements > Remediations**.

Step 2.   Select the type of remediation you want to create.

Step 3.   Fill in the fields.

Figure 15-32 provides an example of the Cisco predefined AV remediation action configured to occur automatically.

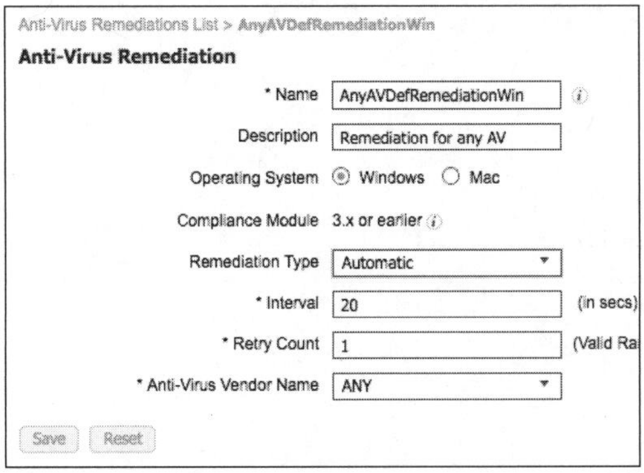

Figure 15-32   *AV Remediation Action*

In addition to creating a corporate AV remediation rule, it is also common to create a Patch Management rule. Patch management is only supported on Windows OSs. Figure 15-33 shows a typical Windows System Center Configuration Manager (SCCM) update rule example. ISE remediation natively supports over 20 patch management vendors.

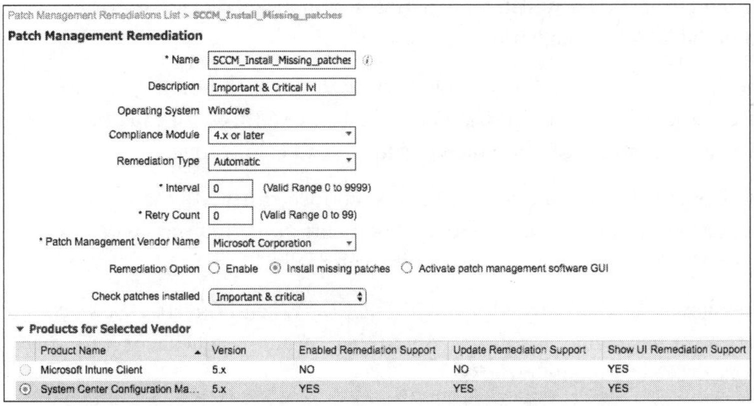

Figure 15-33   *Windows SCCM Patch Auto-Remediation*

Another very common Windows remediation rule is the Windows Server Update Services (WSUS) rule. This remediation action allows the AnyConnect or NAC Agent to talk with the client's WSUS agent to ensure the client is patched correctly. Figure 15-34 shows an example WSUS remediation action using severity level with a Microsoft Server. The Validate Windows Update Using option enables you to choose to trust the severity settings on your WSUS server (Severity Level radio button) or trust the Cisco rules that are downloaded to ISE. If you choose Cisco Rules, you can then select specific rules to check for in the corresponding posture requirement rule. These rules are ignored if you select the Severity Level option.

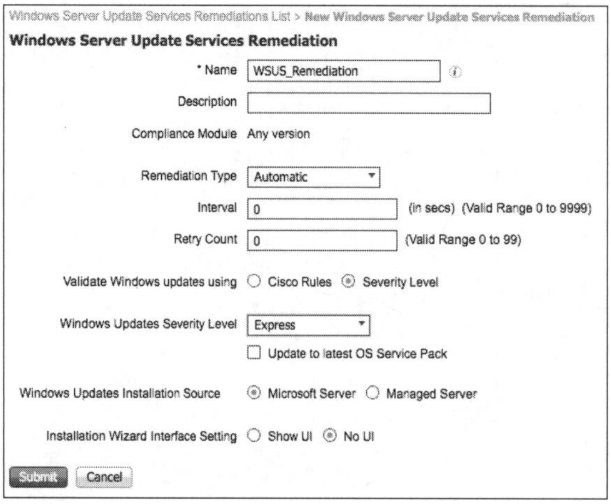

Figure 15-34   *WSUS Remediation Action*

When using the Severity Level option, you must choose the pr_WSUSRule compound condition in the corresponding posture requirement rule. When the posture requirement fails, the NAC Agent enforces the WSUS remediation action based on the severity level that you defined in the WSUS remediation action.

You also need to check the Update to Latest OS Service Pack check box if you want to force a Service Pack update on the client if one is available. Use this with care, because Windows Service Pack upgrades can be time-consuming and error-prone.

For the Windows Updates Installation Source setting, choose either Microsoft Server or Managed Server. A Microsoft server is hosted by Microsoft in the Internet, whereas a managed server is a WSUS server that you administer internally.

If you choose the Show UI radio button for the Installation Wizard Interface Setting option, your users must have administrator access to their Windows client for it to operate. The UI shows the WSUS update progress.

ISE can also uninstall or stop an application from running on Windows or Mac. Use an Application remediation rule to get this done. Say, for example, that you want to uninstall all versions of a vulnerable program, kill a malicious application running, or uninstall any prohibited applications. You can do this using ISE Application remediation rules. Figures 15-35 and 15-36 show an example of uninstalling BitTorrent on Mac OS X.

Figure 15-35 *Application Remediation Action*

Figure 15-36 *Application Remediation Action (Continued)*

Configure Posture Requirements

Now that you have configured or reviewed all of the pieces, the next step is to put them together in a series of posture requirements. A *posture requirement* is a set of compound conditions with an associated remediation action that can be linked with a role and an operating system. All the clients connecting to your network must meet mandatory requirements during posture evaluation to become compliant on the network. Several requirements come predefined in ISE and cover the AV, AM, USB, and AS use cases. In addition to these, you typically want to create a patch management or Windows update requirement. The requirements that you create are used as a part of your posture policies in the next section.

To create a posture requirement from the ISE GUI:

Step 1. Go to **Work Centers > Posture > Policy Elements > Requirements**.

Step 2. Click the drop-down arrow at the right end of a row and select **Insert New Requirement** or **Duplicate** to duplicate an existing one.

Figure 15-37 depicts an example requirement.

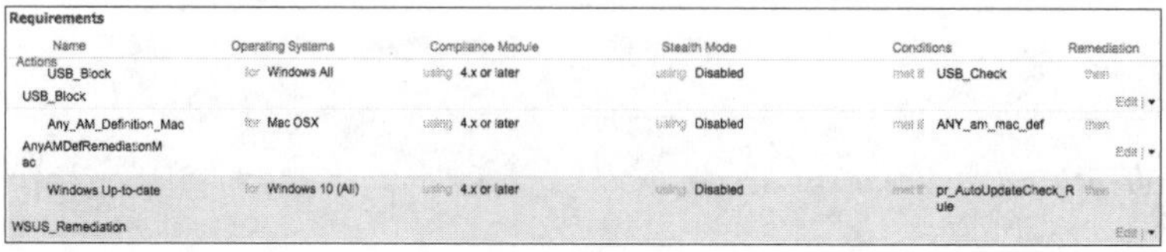

Requirements					
Name	Operating Systems	Compliance Module	Stealth Mode	Conditions	Remediation
Actions USB_Block USB_Block	for Windows All	using 4.x or later	using Disabled	met if USB_Check	then Edit | ▼
Any_AM_Definition_Mac AnyAMDefRemediationM ac	for Mac OSX	using 4.x or later	using Disabled	met if ANY_am_mac_def	then Edit | ▼
Windows Up-to-date WSUS_Remediation	for Windows 10 (All)	using 4.x or later	using Disabled	met if pr_AutoUpdateCheck_R ule	then Edit | ▼

Figure 15-37 *Windows Update Posture Requirement*

The requirement in Figure 15-37 called *Windows Up-to-date* applies to all Windows 10 endpoints and is met if the condition pr_AutoUpdateCheck_Rule is true. Otherwise, the remediation action of WSUS_Remediation is executed. Create the requirements that you need for your environment and host security policy.

You can deploy the AnyConnect 4.4+ Agent in stealth mode to monitor and enforce Cisco ISE posture policies. Stealth mode allows posture to be run as a service without any user agent or interaction allowed.

You can configure the following remediations in stealth mode (must be set to Automatic mode):

- Create Anti-Malware Remediation

- Create Launch Program Remediation

- Create Patch Management Remediation

- Create USB Remediation

- Create Windows Server Update Services Remediation

- Create Windows Update Remediation

You cannot configure the following remediations in stealth mode:

- Manual Remediation

- Link Remediation

- File Remediation

- Windows Server Update Services (WSUS) Remediation

- Patch Management Remediation—Activate Patch Management Software GUI (Remediation Option)

- AUP Policy

Configure Posture Policy

Up to now, you have configured items to support the policies you will create in this section. This section enacts the posture assessment process within ISE.

To configure posture policy, navigate to **Work Centers > Posture > Posture Policy**. A posture policy maps posture requirements to selection criteria such as operating system, identity or external group, or other conditions. This allows you to define different posture policy rules, which you can individually enable or disable, for the various client and user types. Each requirement listed within a posture policy rule has its own status setting of Mandatory, Optional, or Audit (Figure 15-38 shows the options). Mandatory means that the requirement must be met in order for the endpoint to be allowed on the network. Optional means that if the endpoint fails the requirement, it still passes onto the network but any automatic remediation actions are executed. Audit only logs the requirement result and does not affect the client's ability to access the network nor execute any automatic remediation actions. Audit requirements are transparent to the end user.

Figure 15-38 shows the posture policy table along with an example policy. No policies are configured by default. If you have created policies, to add a new one just click the drop-down arrow at the far right of a rule and select either **Duplicate** or **Insert**.

Figure 15-38 *Posture Policy Table*

The example policies shown in Figure 15-38 are in Audit mode. It is highly recommended that you use Audit first to test that your policies work as expected. The first example policy ensures that all Windows 10 endpoints with Domain Users logged in have an up-to-date antimalware program. If the requirement fails, then the assigned remediation action kicks off an AM client definition file that updates automatically. Let's step through the setup of this policy:

Step 1. Set the status to **Enabled** (default) or **Disabled**.

Step 2. Provide a name to the policy that describes its purpose.

Step 3.   Select the identity group that you want the policy to match against. You can set this to **Any** or to a specific group like **Employee** or **Contractor**. The example sets it to Any, which is typical.

Step 4.   Select the operating system to match this policy against. The example selects Windows 10, so any Windows 10 operating system will match it. You can select multiple operating systems within the same type but cannot mix operating systems of different types. For example, Windows 7 (All) or Windows 8 (All) is acceptable, but Windows 7 (All) or Mac OS X does not work.

Step 5.   Select the version of the AnyConnect or NAC Agent compliance module. New installs should use version 4.x or higher.

Step 6.   Set Stealth Mode to **Enabled** or **Disabled**.

Step 7.   Setting Other conditions is optional but useful. An Other condition to consider is an *initial posture* condition. This means the policy only matches if the endpoint is going through its initial posture assessment and not a period reassessment. In this example, the Other condition defined that the user had to be a member of AD domain users to match this rule.

Step 8.   Finally, define the requirement(s) when a rule is matched. Essentially, if all of the defined conditions are true, check the endpoint against certain posture requirements. In the example, there is just one requirement, Windows Up-to-date. This is a built-in ISE requirement you can use. What the policy doesn't show is the status of these requirements: Mandatory, Optional, or Audit. To edit or view the status, edit the policy and click the plus sign next to the requirements box. You can see the options in Figure 15-38.

It is highly recommended that, in a production environment, all requirements start with a status of either Audit or Optional. This lessens the impact on your user community, help-desk staff, and yourself. Because the posture reports in ISE provide you with a good idea of the impact your policies are having while in Audit or Optional status, you will know when the time is right to move them to Mandatory status. For example, you write a policy that requires AV to be installed and initially set it to Audit status. After a week, you check the ISE reports and determine that only 5% of your endpoints are failing the policy. At this time, you could move it to Optional status with automatic remediation. When you check back the following week, you see 99% of endpoints are passing, so you move the status to Mandatory to catch the last 1%.

Figure 15-38 depicts another common posture policy, for monitoring that the Windows Update Service is running and, if it is not, automatically turning it on. You can see the fine detail of a requirement by editing the policy rule, clicking in the requirements box, and clicking the target symbol next to a requirement. This opens up additional detailed dialog boxes as shown in Figure 15-39.

Figure 15-39   *Posture Policy Windows Update Detail*

The policy checks to ensure WSUS is running and is set to automatically enable updates if not. This policy affects AD Domain Users and Windows 10 (All) endpoints. The remediation action, in Audit mode, does not override the user's settings with the requirements settings of auto download and notify. The remediation action takes effect only after you move the policy to Optional or Mandatory status.

It is a best practice not to burden clients with an excessive amount of posture policy requirements. Doing so can adversely affect the user's network experience and login times. Keep it to a handful of your top security requirements per operating system.

Configure Host Application Visibility and Context Collection (Optional)

ISE with AnyConnect is capable of providing you with a running record of all the applications installed, version information, and running processes on your hosts. This works for both Windows and Mac operating systems. AnyConnect collects information about installed applications only with the 4.x (or later) compliance module. ISE populates this data in the **Context Visibility > Endpoints** dashboard. This data can then be used by you to better understand the various applications installed and running on your endpoints. Figure 15-40 shows an example.

Figure 15-40   *Endpoint Application Visibility and Context*

The Endpoint Applications list shows the following attributes:

- Application name.

- Application version.

- Vendor.

- Running processes for the application. If blank, that means the application was not running at the time of the audit. For each process, you are shown the Process Name, Hash, and Process ID.

- Category.

- Install path.

To set up ISE to start collecting endpoint application data, perform the following three steps:

Step 1.   Create an **Application Condition**. Typically, this condition is set to collect Everything, but you can set it to collect just certain applications or categories of applications. See Figure 15-41 for an example of collecting everything.

Figure 15-41   *Endpoint Application Visibility Condition*

Step 2.   Create a Posture Requirement for the condition in Step 1. Set the action to **Message Text Only** and input some text. This text is not displayed to your users. Figure 15-42 provides an example.

Figure 15-42   *Endpoint Application Visibility Posture Requirement*

Step 3.   Finally, create a Posture Policy Rule that executes your requirement on the hosts you want it to gather information from. Ensure that you set your rule requirement to **Audit** mode. Figure 15-43 provides an example.

Figure 15-43   *Endpoint Application Visibility Posture Policy Rule*

Enable Posture Client Provisioning and Assessment in Your ISE Authorization Policies

At this stage, all of the building blocks required to enable both posture client provisioning and authorization based on posture compliance are in place.

Posture Client Provisioning

This section walks you through an example of how to enable posture client provisioning to detect when a user does not have AnyConnect with the compliance module installed and redirect the user to the necessary files for download and installation. Here are the steps:

Step 1.   On the network device CLI or GUI, create an ACL named **redirect-acl**. You will enter this ACL name in the ISE authorization profile that you create in Step 3. This ACL defines what traffic type triggers a redirect action on the NAD. A redirect ACL should not trigger on traffic to and from ISE PSNs, DNS, and DHCP, at a minimum. You can set up your ACL to trigger on all other IP traffic or just on HTTP and HTTPS traffic.

Note   Cisco Wireless LAN Controllers and switches interpret their redirect ACLs oppositely. On a Cisco WLC, a permit ACL rule defines traffic that will not trigger a redirect and a deny rule match triggers a redirect. Conversely, on a Cisco switch, a permit ACL rule match triggers a redirect and a deny ACL rule defines traffic that will not trigger a redirect.

Step 2.   (Optional) Create a dACL in ISE to restrict users' access to your network during client provisioning. Ensure that you allow DNS plus HTTP/S and client access to all Cisco Provisioning Portal (CPP) pages' IP address and port.

Step 3.   Create an authorization profile for client provisioning. Go to **Work Centers > Posture > Policy Elements > Authorization Profiles**. Click **Add**. At a minimum, fill in the following profile form entries (also shown in Figure 15-44):

- In the Name text box, provide a meaningful name.

- From the Access Type drop-down list, choose **ACCESS_ACCEPT**.

- Expand **Common Tasks**, check the **Web Redirection** check box, and choose **Client Provisioning (Posture)** from the drop-down list. Enter the name of the ACL you created in Step 1 and set **Value** to the provisioning portal you created earlier.

- Optionally, check the **DACL Name** check box and enter a name for it.

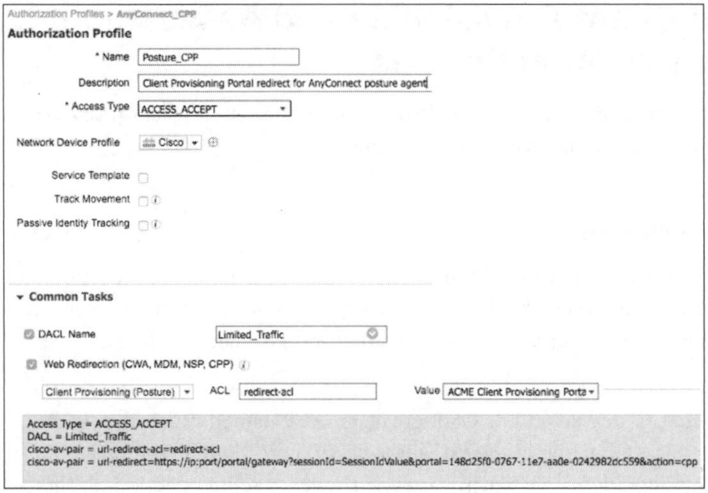

Figure 15-44   *Authorization Profile for Posture Client Provisioning*

Authorization Based On Posture Compliance

At this point, ISE is collecting posture information from your hosts and performing the remediation actions, if any, that you specified. Now you need to add authorization rules (at least two) that change a user's network permissions based on their posture compliance. You also must designate a posture agent for automatic installation if the client doesn't already have one. This will be done using the CPP set up previously.

> **Tip**   It is a good idea to initially set your posture authorization rules to Audit mode. Then set them to Mandatory or Optional after you have verified they function as expected.

Here are the steps to complete:

Step 1.   Create a Posture provisioning redirect authorization policy rule that matches when a host doesn't have a posture client to respond to ISE with. This rule redirects them to the Client Provisioning Portal page so that they can get the NAC Agent. Go to **Work Centers > Posture > Policy Sets** and select the relevant policy set. In the Authorization Rules section, select **Insert New Rule**. Figure 15-45 shows the result after selecting Insert New Rule and completing the task.

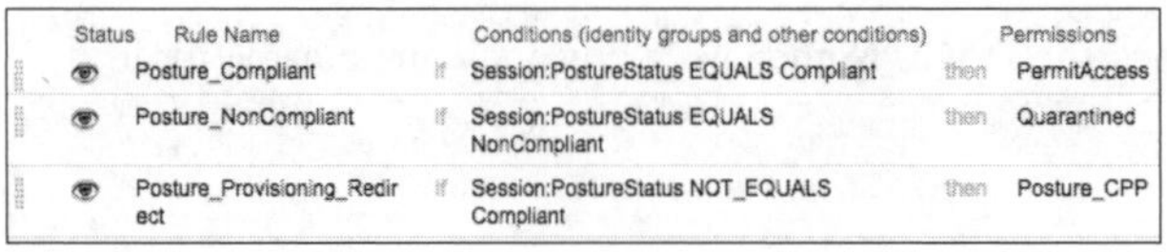

Figure 15-45   *Authorization Rules for Posture*

Step 2. Insert a Posture_Compliant authorization rule above the Posture_ Provisioning_Redirect rule in Step 1. This rule matches when a host returns posture status equals compliant, meaning the host passes all of your posture requirements. The permissions of this rule should match the network access permission you want to assign to your compliant hosts. Because the authorization rules are processed top down, first match, the redirect rule will never execute. See Figure 15-45 for an example.

Step 3. Finally, insert a Posture_NonCompliant authorization rule above the Posture_ Provisioning_Redirect rule in Step 1 that puts the host in *Quarantine* so that posture remediation can start. You need to define which permissions are allowed while in quarantine, but they should include access to any remediation resources that you want the client to access. See Figure 15-45 for an example.

Posture Reports and Troubleshooting

ISE has several reports for posture. To view the relevant reports available, go to **Work Centers > Posture > Reports**. The best reports for posture are Client Provisioning, Posture Assessment by Condition, Posture Assessment by Endpoint, and Current Active Sessions. You can schedule these reports or run them on demand.

For troubleshooting, ISE has a built-in Posture Troubleshooting tool, located at **Work Centers > Posture > Troubleshoot**. The Posture Troubleshooting tool helps you to find the cause of a posture-check failure by identifying the following:

- Which endpoints were successful in posture and which were not

- If an endpoint failed in posture, what steps failed in the posture process

- Which mandatory and optional checks passed and failed

ISE logs are also helpful for detailed posture troubleshooting. Go to **Administration > System > Logging > Debug Log Configuration**. For posture troubleshooting, the following ISE log components need to be in debug mode on the ISE nodes where the posture process happens:

- **client-webapp:** Component responsible for agent provisioning. Target log files guest.log and ise-psc.log.

- **guestaccess:** Component responsible for Client Provisioning Portal component and session owner lookup. Target log file guest.log.

- **provisioning:** Component responsible for client provisioning policy processing. Target log file guest.log.

- **posture:** All posture-related events. Target log file ise-psc.log.

For the AnyConnect compliance module (client side) troubleshooting, you can use

- **acisensa.log:** In case of a client provisioning failure on the client side, this file is created in the same folder from which the NAC Agent or AnyConnect software installation was run (the Downloads directory for Windows, normally).

- **AnyConnect_ISEPosture.txt:** This file can be found in the DART bundle in directory Cisco AnyConnect ISE Posture Module. All information about ISE PSN discovery and general steps of posture flow are logged into this file.

Enable Posture Assessment in the Network

You need to ensure that your endpoints are allowed the proper communication rights while in quarantine and performing posture assessment and remediation activities.

Ensure that the access switch pre-posture/limited access ACL allows HTTPS and SWISS communication between the Cisco ISE Policy Service Node(s) and the endpoint. Here is an example ACL showing the ports needed for posture assessment to work:

```
remark Allow DHCP
permit udp any eq bootpc any eq bootps
remark Allow DNS
permit udp any any eq domain
remark Allow ping to ISE PSN and any other devices necessary
permit icmp any host <ISE PSN IP>
! This is for URL redirect
permit tcp any host <ISE PSN IP> eq 443
! This is for URL redirect
permit tcp any host <ISE PSN IP> eq www
! This is for guest portal
permit tcp any host <ISE PSN IP> eq 8443
! This is for posture
! Communication between NAC agent and ISE (SWISS ports)
permit tcp any host <ISE PSN IP> eq 8905
! This is for posture
! Communication between NAC agent and ISE (SWISS ports)
permit udp any host <ISE PSN IP> eq 8905
deny ip any any
```

Ensure that you create a similar quarantine ACL for the posture-noncompliant endpoints with these rights plus rights to access the remediation IPs.

Finally, ensure that nothing in the traffic path—such as firewalls, ACLs, and so on—is preventing the traffic from flowing.

Note During posture assessment of a Windows endpoint using a login script, the endpoint user may encounter a delay in accessing the desktop. The reason might be that Windows is trying to restore the file server drive letter mappings before providing the user access to the desktop. The following are best practices to avoid the delay during posture:

■ Use Windows Group Policy Preference (GPP) drive mappings instead of a login script. GPP has a reconnect setting.

■ If you have to use login scripts, then set your drive mappings to nonpersistent, such as **net use S: \\server\share /persistent:no.**

■ Allow endpoints to reach the Active Directory server so the file server drive letter can be mapped properly. When posture (with AnyConnect ISE Posture Agent) triggers, it blocks access to AD, causing a delay in login. Use Posture Remediation ACLs to provide access to AD servers before posture is completed.

■ Set a delay for the login script until posture completes and set the drive mapping Persistence attribute to **NO.** Windows tries to reconnect all the network drives during login, and this cannot be done until the AnyConnect ISE Posture Agent gains full network access.

Summary

This chapter covered the details of configuring posture assessment on the Cisco ISE. Here are the high-level steps that were covered in this chapter:

1. Configure your network devices to connect users.

2. Configure client provisioning:

   a. Download to ISE the latest posture updates and the client provisioning packages.

   b. Verify the default global posture settings meet your needs.

   c. Configure the posture client provisioning policy.

   d. Configure the Client Provisioning Portal.

3. Configure posture elements:

   a. Configure posture conditions.

   b. Configure posture remediation.

   c. Configure posture requirements.

4. Configure posture policy.

5. Optionally, configure host application visibility and context collection.

6. Optionally, configure ISE posture integration with Microsoft SCCM.

7. Enable posture client provisioning and assessment in your ISE authorization policies.

8. Enable posture assessment in the network.

When used correctly, ISE posture assessment can greatly increase the host visibility and security throughout your organization. Plus, you'll sleep better knowing only security-compliant endpoints are allowed to attach to your network.

Chapter 16

Supplicant Configuration

This chapter covers the following topics:

- Comparison of popular supplicants

- Configuring common supplicants

The client 802.1X supplicant is a critical part of any Identity Services deployment. What is a supplicant? A client supplicant is simply the piece of software that the operating system uses to connect to networks, both wired and wireless. All of the major operating systems (such as Windows, Mac OS X, Android, iOS, Linux) and many network devices (such as Cisco IP Phones, IP cameras, and so on) include a built-in supplicant. The network access devices (NAD) interact with the client's supplicant upon connection to the wired or wireless network. The 802.1X transactions are performed between supplicant and the NAD. The NAD then talks RADIUS to Cisco ISE.

Cisco ISE has a very nice feature called native supplicant provisioning. This feature allows you to remove the burden from the end users of configuring their own supplicant; instead, it does it automatically for them via an ISE supplicant provisioning wizard. This feature is highly recommended because of its ability to simplify the deployment of ISE. It only works with the native built-in supplicants in the following operating systems:

- Android

- Mac OS X

- Apple iOS (for Apple iPhones and iPads)

- Microsoft Windows Vista, 7, 8/8.1, and 10

Note   If you are using one of these OSs, it is highly recommended that you skip this chapter and instead read Chapter 17, "BYOD: Self-Service Onboarding and Registration," which covers client provisioning in detail.

If you will not be using the native supplicants or would prefer not to use the ISE client provisioning wizards, this chapter is for you. It covers the configuration steps for the following client supplicants:

- Cisco AnyConnect Network Access Manager (NAM) for Windows

- Windows 7 Native Supplicant

- Mac OS X 10.8.2 Native Supplicant

The configuration steps focus solely on the wired network portion of their configuration. There is a lot of knowledge and readily available information for wireless configuration already out there, so including it here would be redundant.

Comparison of Popular Supplicants

There are only a handful of popular supplicants on the market today and a bunch of niche supplicants. The most popular ones for wired are the following:

- Windows Native Supplicant

- Mac OS X Native Supplicant

- Android/iOS Native Supplicants

- Cisco AnyConnect Secure Mobility NAM Client

- Linux Native Supplicants (wpa_supplicant)

When deciding on which supplicant to use, answer these basic questions:

1. What is the dominant OS going to be in my ISE deployment?

2. Are most of my clients members of Active Directory?

3. Which Extensible Authentication Protocol (EAP) type(s) will be required (PEAP, EAP-TLS, EAP-FAST, EAP-MSCHAPv2, etc.)?

4. Do I require an all-in-one client?

5. Will I be using the ISE native supplicant provisioning?

6. Is EAP-chaining required? EAP-chaining provides differentiated access based on enterprise and non-enterprise assets. It also has the ability to validate users and devices in a single EAP transaction and to perform both machine authentication and user authentication simultaneously.

You must consider several other deciding factors, depending on the complexity of your ISE deployment, but these are the most common ones. After you answer the preceding questions, you will be able to match your answers with the available supplicants and their requirements. It is space-prohibitive, and highly susceptible to becoming quickly outdated, to list all the supplicants and their supported features here. Instead, you should check the websites of the supplicant vendors for these details.

Note   In general, the native OS supplicants are sufficient for your ISE deployment. If you are using either Microsoft Active Directory Group Policy or Cisco ISE native client provisioning, you must choose the native supplicant.

Configuring Common Supplicants

This section deals with the manual configuration steps for some of the most common supplicants. Specifically, it covers Windows 7 Native, Mac OS X Native, and Cisco AnyConnect NAM. Only Wired 802.1X configuration is covered.

Mac OS X 10.8.2 Native Supplicant Configuration

In versions 10.8+ of OS X, Apple changed the wired 802.1X configuration steps. The good news is that the change made it a zero configuration setup for the vast majority of wired 802.1X ISE deployments. Upon connecting to the Ethernet network, the 802.1X authentication process is started automatically and the user is presented with a popup message to log in to the network.

Note   By default, during 802.1X authentication, OS X requires that the name in the server's certificate must match its DNS hostname. So, ensure that your ISE server-side certificate complies.

If the default setting for autoconnect, as shown in Figure 16-1, has been modified, you can reenable it by following these steps:

Step 1.   Click **System Preferences** and select **Network** under **Internet and Wireless**.

Figure 16-1   *Network—Ethernet*

Step 2.   Click **Ethernet** and click **Advanced**.

Step 3.   Click the **802.1X** tab.

Step 4.   Check the **Enable Automatic Connection** check box, as shown in Figure 16-2.

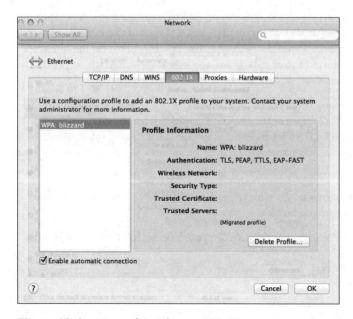

Figure 16-2   *Network—Ethernet 802.1X*

To access networks that cannot be joined with the method shown in Figure 16-2, or to use a login window mode or a system mode profile, you need to create and distribute a .mobileconfig file to clients that contains the correct network configuration information. You can create a .mobileconfig file by using the Profile Manager service provided in macOS Server. See Apple's support site for detailed information.

Windows GPO Configuration for Wired Supplicant

Windows 2008r2 or newer includes the capability to use Group Policy Objects (GPO) to configure clients' wired and wireless 802.1X settings. For complete instructions, go to https://technet.microsoft.com/en-us/library/cc733169.aspx.

Here are the common steps for configuring wired GPO 802.1X settings using EAP-TLS with certificates and single sign-on (SSO). This assumes you have already delivered the full certificate chain for your CA and machine and identity certificates to the client, hopefully using GPO for that as well.

Step 1.   Open the Group Policy Management console, as shown in Figure 16-3.

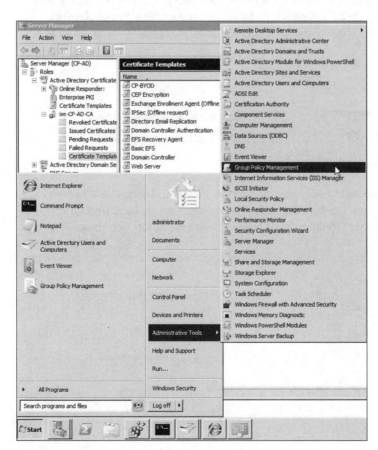

Figure 16-3 *GPO Management Console*

Step 2.   Select your domain. Either create a new Group Policy Object or select an existing one. Right-click and select **Edit**. This opens the Group Policy Management Editor, as shown in Figure 16-4.

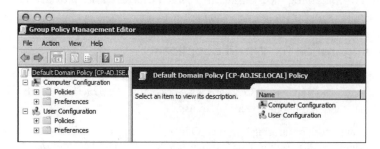

Figure 16-4   *GPO Management Editor*

Step 3.   Create a new wired network policy. To do this, go to **Computer Configuration > Policies > Windows Settings > Security Settings > Wired Network Policies**. Right-click and select **Create a New Wired Network Policy for Windows Vista and Later Releases**, as shown in Figure 16-5.

Figure 16-5   *Wired Network Policy Creation*

Step 4.   Fill in the policy name and description. Be sure to check **Use Windows Wired Auto Config Service for Clients**. Optionally, check **Don't Allow Shared User Credentials for Network Authentication**. See Figure 16-6 for an example.

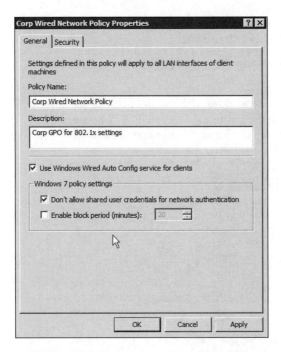

Figure 16-6 *Wired Network Policy—General Settings*

Step 5. Click the **Security** tab, shown in Figure 16-7. Check the **Enable Use of IEEE 802.1X Authentication for Network Access** check box.

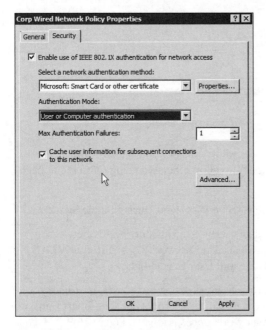

Figure 16-7 *Wired Network Policy—Security Settings*

Step 6.   From the Select a Network Authentication Method drop-down list, choose **Microsoft: Smart Card or Other Certificate**.

Step 7.   Check the **Cache User Information for Subsequent Connections to this Network** check box.

Step 8.   Click the **Advanced** button. In the Advanced Security Settings dialog box, shown in Figure 16-8, check the **Enforce Advanced 802.1X Settings** check box. You can leave the defaults or change for your environment.

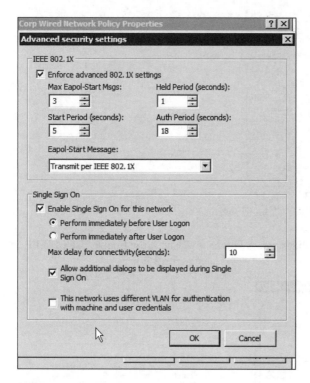

Figure 16-8   *Wired Network Policy—Advanced Security Settings*

Step 9.   Check **Enable Single Sign On**. The most common setting is Perform Immediately Before User Logon. This allows the user to log on to the domain and run logon scripts.

Step 10.   Check **Allow Additional Dialogs to Be Displayed During Single Sign On**.

Step 11.   If you will be using ISE to change the wired switchport VLAN between machine logon and user logon, check **This Network Uses Different VLAN for Authentication with Machine and User Credentials**.

Step 13.   Click **OK**. The Advanced Security Settings dialog box closes, returning you to the Security tab. On the Security tab, click **Properties**. The Smart Card or other Certificate Properties dialog box opens, shown in Figure 16-9.

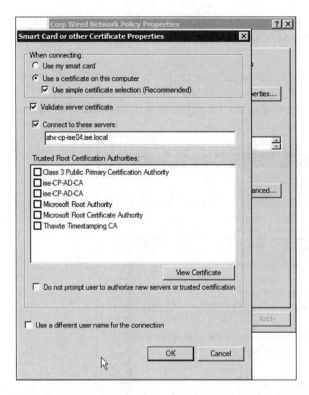

Figure 16-9 *Wired Network Policy—Certificate Settings*

Step 14. Click the **Use a Certificate on This Computer** radio button and check the **Use Simple Certificate Selection** check box.

Step 15. Check **Validate Server Certificate**.

Step 16. Check **Connect to These Servers** and type the name of each ISE policy server, exactly as it appears in the Subject field of the ISE server's certificate. Use semicolons to specify multiple ISE server names.

Step 17. Leave everything else disabled. For higher security settings, see the Microsoft documentation. Click **OK** and **OK** to close this all out.

Your new policy will be pushed out to your clients the next time they do a GPO update.

Windows 7, 8/8.1, and 10 Native Supplicant Configuration

Microsoft disables wired 802.1X by default on Windows 7, 8/8.1, and 10. The following steps show you how to enable and configure wired 802.1X on Windows 7. You must be logged in as an administrator to complete these steps.

Step 1.   Open Windows Services. Go to **Start > Search**, type in **services**, and click **Services** in the search results under Programs. This opens the Services Management Console.

Step 2.   Select and double-click **Wired AutoConfig**. In the dialog box that opens, from the Startup Type drop-down list, choose **Automatic**, as shown in Figure 16-10. Click **Start** to start the service. Click **OK**. The 802.1X service is now enabled by default.

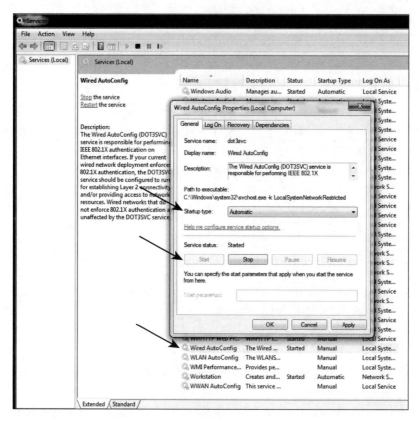

Figure 16-10   *Enable 802.1X Permanently*

Step 3.   Open the Control Panel and choose **Network and Internet > Network Connections**. Select your wired interface, right-click, and choose **Properties**. See Figure 16-11 for details.

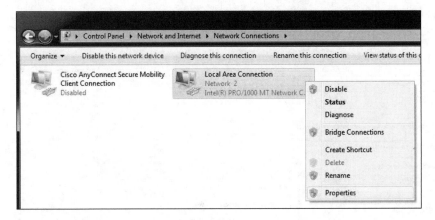

Figure 16-11 *Set Up Wired 802.1X*

Step 4.   Click the **Authentication** tab (this appears only if you have enabled the Wired
AutoConfig service). Check **Enable IEEE 802.1X authentication**. Choose
your authentication method; Protected EAP (PEAP) is the most popular,
because it uses your AD username and password by default. See Figure 16-12
for details.

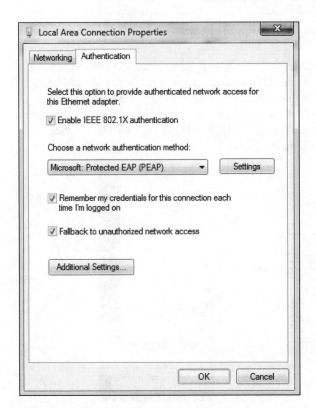

Figure 16-12 *Set Up Wired 802.1X Authentication*

Step 5. Click **Additional Settings**. In the Advanced Settings dialog box, shown in Figure 16-13, specify your authentication mode. Also, enable single sign-on. Click **OK**.

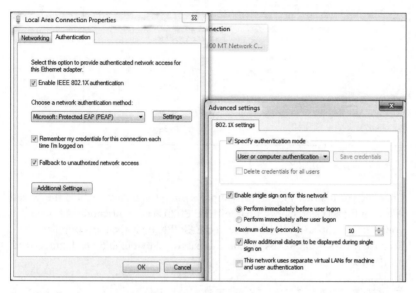

Figure 16-13 *Configure Wired 802.1X Advanced Settings*

Step 6. (Optional) Click **Settings**. Depending on the authentication method you chose, you may or may not have to configure settings. If you chose PEAP, the defaults are fine in most cases. If you want to use PEAP but not have it automatically use your Windows logon name and password, click **Configure** next to Secured Password (EAP-MSCHAPv2) and uncheck the box. See Figure 16-14 for an example.

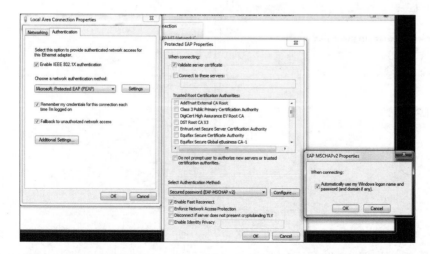

Figure 16-14 *Configure Wired 802.1X PEAP Properties*

Step 7. Click **OK** until you close out all the dialog boxes.

Your Windows 7 client is now ready to connect to a wired 802.1X protected network.

Cisco AnyConnect Secure Mobility Client NAM

This section walks through how to set up the Cisco AnyConnect client for wired PEAP 802.1X authentication. To start, you must download the standalone AnyConnect Profile Editor from Cisco.com or use the profile editor inside of Cisco Adaptive Security Device Manager (ASDM) or Cisco Security Manager (CSM). Once you have a profile editor installed, proceed with these steps:

Step 1. Open AnyConnect Profile Editor and select **Networks**. Click **Add** to launch the wizard shown in Figure 16-15. Provide a name. Change Group Membership to **In All Groups (Global)**. Select **Wired** under Choose Your Network Media. Click **Next**.

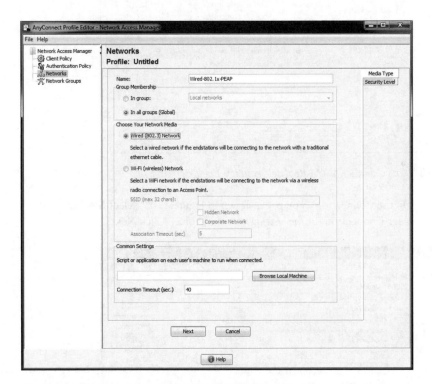

Figure 16-15 *AnyConnect NAM 802.1X Wired Profile*

Step 2. On the Security Level wizard page, shown in Figure 16-16, click the **Authenticating Network** radio button. If you are running in 802.1X open mode, do the following: check **Enable Port Exceptions**, click **Allow Data Traffic After Authentication Even If**, and check **EAP Fails**. In open mode, you want to ensure that your clients still access the network even if they have a failure, and this setting accomplishes that. Once you move away from open mode, you need to disable this setting. Click **Next**.

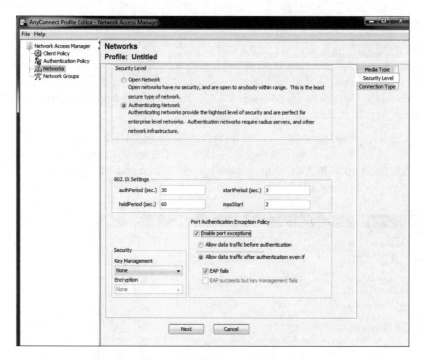

Figure 16-16 *AnyConnect NAM Profile Security Level*

Step 3. On the Connection Type page, shown in Figure 16-17, select **Machine and User Connection** (or the setting of your choice). Click **Next**.

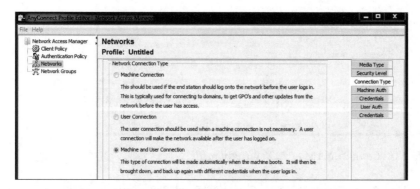

Figure 16-17 *AnyConnect NAM Profile Connection Type*

Step 4. On the Machine Auth page, enable **PEAP**, as shown in Figure 16-18. The default settings are usually not changed. Click **Next**.

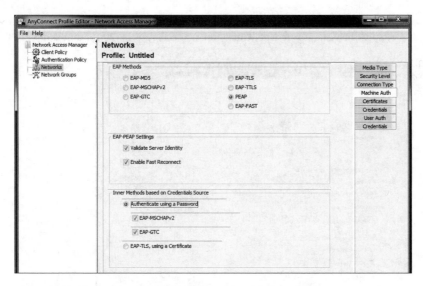

Figure 16-18   *AnyConnect NAM Profile Machine Auth*

Step 5.   On the Certificates page, you have the option to upload root certificates as part of the profile. If you need to do this (i.e., you are using your own CA server), add them here as shown in Figure 16-19. Click **Next**.

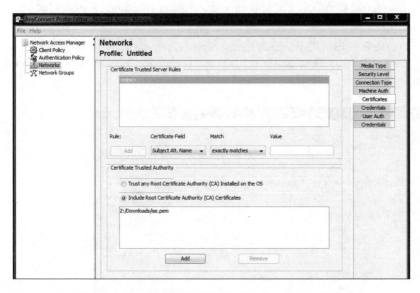

Figure 16-19   *AnyConnect NAM Profile Machine Auth Certificates*

Step 6.   Set the credentials that the machine should use. Normally, the defaults are fine. Click **Next**.

Step 7.   For User Auth, select **PEAP** or your choice of authentication methods. Normally, the defaults are fine. Click **Next**. See Figure 16-20 for an example.

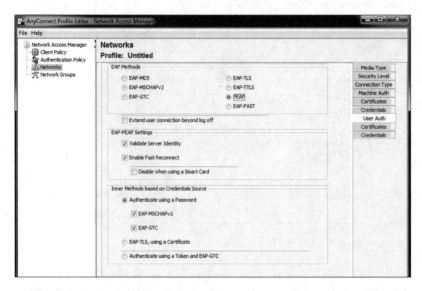

Figure 16-20   *AnyConnect NAM Profile User Auth*

Step 8.   The second Certificates page is for user certificate checking. Repeat what you did for machine certificates in Step 5. Click **Next**.

Step 9.   On the final page, Credentials for user authorization, click **Use Single Sign On Credentials** (or select the settings appropriate for your deployment). Click **Done**. See Figure 16-21.

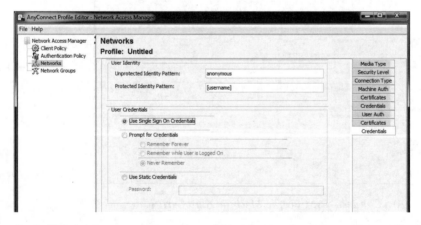

Figure 16-21   *AnyConnect NAM Profile User Credentials*

Step 10. On the AnyConnect Profile Editor screen, select **Network Groups** in the navigation pane on the left, as shown in Figure 16-22. Under Global Networks: Wired, make sure that your policy is at the top of the list. If it isn't, select it and click the **Up** button.

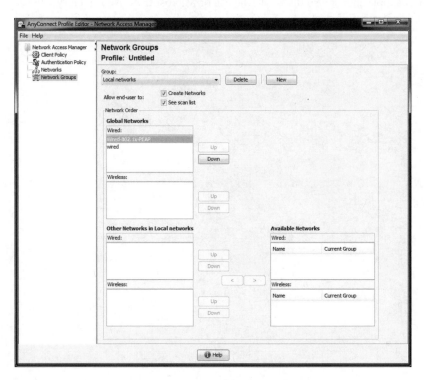

Figure 16-22   *AnyConnect NAM Profile Network Groups*

Step 11. Save the Profile file. On the top menu, click **File** and then **Save As**.

Step 12. You *must* save the configuration with the filename **configuration.xml** in the \ProgramData\Application Data\Cisco\Cisco AnyConnect Secure Mobility Client\Network Access Manager\newConfigFiles directory.

Step 13. To apply this new configuration, right-click the AnyConnect icon in the system tray and choose **Network Repair**. This forces the Cisco AnyConnect NAM to restart its services. A service restart causes NAM to search the newConfigFiles directory for a configuration.xml file.

Step 14. You're finished!

Summary

This chapter discussed 802.1X supplicants, with a particular focus on wired 802.1X supplicant configuration. It covered the setup of Windows 7, Mac OS X, and Cisco AnyConnect supplicants. It also discussed the use of Microsoft Active Directory GPO as a supplicant configuration tool.

Chapter 17

BYOD: Self-Service Onboarding and Registration

This chapter covers the following topics:

- BYOD challenges
- Onboarding process
- The opposite of BYOD: identify corporate systems

Back in January 2007, Steve Jobs introduced the iPhone and suggested that Apple was shooting for 1% of the mobile device market. The device had a revolutionary multi-touch screen interface, boasted a "real" browser instead of the cut-down versions on mobile devices to that point, and arguably "changed the game" for the experience that users expected from their mobile devices from that point on. In January 2010, the iPad was released. In June 2010, I was at Cisco Live in Las Vegas presenting a session on network access control (NAC).

In that session, I asked the audience if their company would allow users to bring in iPhones and iPad-type devices and connect to the corporate network for purposes of doing work from those devices. The few hundred people in my sample size responded with about 90% "no-way" responses and only 10% affirmative responses.

At that same conference, Cisco announced the Cius, which was designed to be a "corporate tablet," a device to provide that wonderful user experience along with the security and guarantees that IT departments required. Fast forward 18 months, and Cisco announced the end-of-sale of the Cius, due to lack of adoption. In June 2012, when asked the same question about allowing personal devices, the result was 90% affirmative and only 10% said their organizations would not allow personal devices. What a difference two years makes! Bring Your Own Device (BYOD) has become an absolute reality. In today's business world, it is no longer a question of if a company will allow the use of these devices, but a question of what level of support the end users will get with those devices.

As shown in Figure 17-1, we are moving into an era of BYOD, Choose Your Own Device (CYOD), and even a Bring Your Own App (BYOA) type of model. Employees are demanding the use of the devices that make them most productive, with native applications running on those platforms that provide the user experience they have become accustomed to. This introduces a new paradigm for security, especially the identification of the user, the device, the location of the user, and much more.

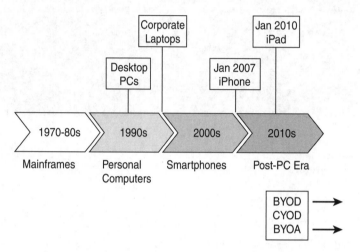

Figure 17-1   *BYOD Timeline*

BYOD Challenges

Because user identity is typically based on a single identity credential, IT does not possess the ability to create and enforce a rigorous secure access policy. Although the user might be authorized, the device, location, time, and access media can pose a company policy violation or even regulatory compliance violation that cannot be adequately detected or enforced.

This chapter focuses on the technical challenges of providing a secure BYOD access model. One of the most common challenges is referred to as *onboarding*. A user buys a new tablet or device and decides to connect it to the corporate Wi-Fi network and be productive on that consumer device. It has the challenge of identifying the device as a non-corporate device and providing a limited set of access to the device. This was originally what many companies used Cisco ISE to do. Figure 17-2 illustrates the flow of these original policies.

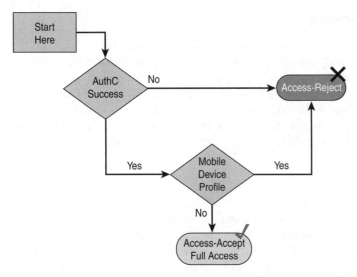

Figure 17-2 *Old-Style Policy*

Then, mobile device management (MDM) solutions came into play. They were able to manage these mobile platforms to some extent. MDM policies ensured that devices had security enabled, such as encryption, remote wipe capabilities, screen lock (pin lock), and so forth. The MDM could provision certificates down to the device and supplicant profiles to preconfigure the device to have network access. Then, ISE would provide the correct level of access for the devices based on the certificate the device had.

Figure 17-3 illustrates a policy that uses certificates to differentiate access.

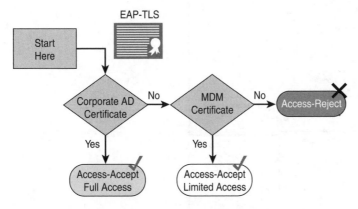

Figure 17-3 *Using Certificates to Differentiate Access*

MDM systems typically cost money per device, and many companies were only looking for a good way to provision certificates and configure the device supplicant to use that certificate with 802.1X. The MDM cost was often prohibitive. The main objective was to provision the certificate and get the device on the network. Cisco customers were looking for a much easier and cheaper way to accomplish the onboarding aspect of network access.

Onboarding Process

This chapter focuses on two types of onboarding. The first is what Cisco calls *BYOD onboarding*, which includes registering the device with ISE, provisioning the certificate to the device, and configuring the device's supplicant. BYOD onboarding uses the native supplicant within the operating system. It does not install a new supplicant. The second type is *MDM onboarding*, which is the process of registering the device with the MDM, installing the MDM client software, and enforcing the security policy on that device. The key to successful onboarding within a company is to make it self-service and not require involvement of IT.

BYOD Onboarding

ISE provides the My Devices Portal, which allows users to register devices and manage those devices that have been registered. A device may simply be registered, which may provide one level of authorization, such as Internet-only access. Or the device may go through the full-blown onboarding and provisioning process where the supplicant configuration is installed into the device along with the optional certificate used for EAP-TLS connectivity.

Regardless of your choice to use device registration only or to use the full onboarding process, you can choose a single-SSID approach or dual-SSID approach to the onboarding, plus wired access (of course).

Figure 17-4 depicts the dual-SSID approach, while Figure 17-5 depicts the single-SSID approach. A quick comparison of the approaches follows.

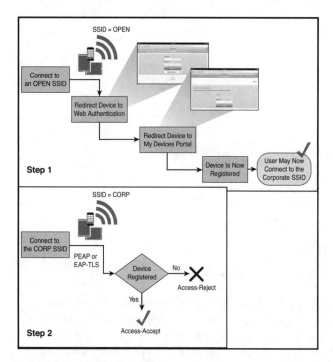

Figure 17-4 *Dual-SSID Flow*

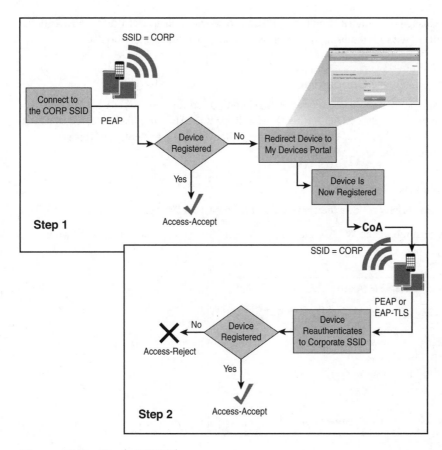

Figure 17-5 *Single-SSID Flow*

Dual SSID

The dual-SSID model of onboarding operates as follows (see Figure 17-4):

■ Employee does not need to configure the supplicant on the device.

■ Employee authenticates to a web form.

■ Employee connects to the open SSID before the provisioning process, and the employee must connect to the corporate SSID after the process.

Single SSID

The single-SSID model of onboarding operates as follows (see Figure 17-5):

■ Employee must configure the supplicant on the device to connect to the corporate SSID.

■ The authentication used to connect to the corporate SSID is used for single sign-on to the onboarding and provisioning process.

■ A Change of Authorization (CoA) is used to provide full access after the provisioning process without requiring the employee to reconnect to the network.

Configuring NADs for Onboarding

Dual-SSID onboarding uses an open WLAN configured for NAC RADIUS, CoA, and MAC filtering (wireless MAC Authentication Bypass [MAB]). You likely created this network already based on Chapter 14, "Guest Lifecycle Management," but this section briefly reviews the WLC settings.

Review of the WLC Configuration

This section briefly reviews the configuration for the Cisco Wireless LAN Controller (WLC).

The General tab of the WLAN should provide an SSID and profile name, as shown in Figure 17-6.

Figure 17-6 *Open WLAN General Tab Configuration for CiscoPress-Guest*

Under **Security > Layer 2**, the Layer 2 Security field should be set to **None** and the MAC Filtering check box should be checked, as displayed in Figure 17-7.

Note   Beginning with WLC version 8.4, the controller supports using WPA2-PSK on a guest network, but that's not what we are doing in this example.

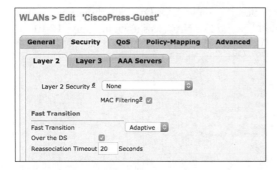

Figure 17-7 *Layer 2 Security Subtab Configuration for CiscoPress-Guest*

Under **Security > Layer 3**, the Layer 3 Security field should be set to **None**, as shown in Figure 17-8.

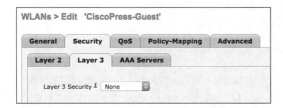

Figure 17-8 *Layer 3 Security Subtab Configuration for CiscoPress-Guest*

Under **Security > AAA Servers**, the ISE Policy Service Node(s) should be selected for authentication and accounting servers, as shown in Figure 17-9.

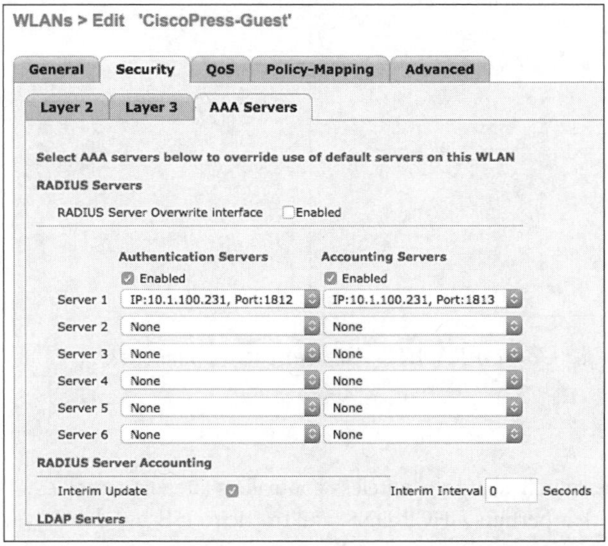

Figure 17-9 *AAA Servers Security Subtab Configuration for CiscoPress-Guest*

On the Advanced tab, the **Enabled** check box for Allow AAA Override should be checked, and the NAC State field should be set to **ISE NAC**, as shown in Figure 17-10.

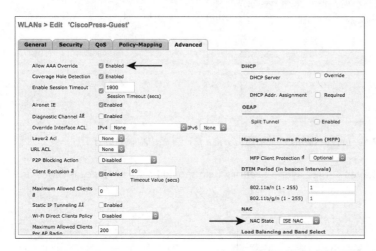

Figure 17-10 *Advanced Tab Configuration for CiscoPress-Guest*

Navigate to **Security > RADIUS > Authentication** and double-check that the RADIUS server definition is configured to allow CoA; the Support for CoA drop-down list box should be set to **Enabled**, as shown in Figure 17-11.

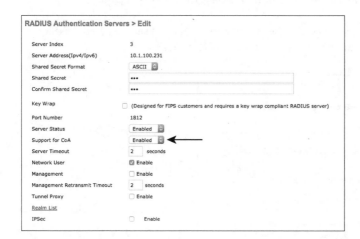

Figure 17-11 *Enabling Support for CoA on RADIUS Authentication Servers*

Required ACLs

You should have an ACL on the switches and the wireless controllers already named ACL_WEBAUTH_REDIRECT that permits DHCP, DNS, and traffic to ISE and denies most other traffic. This configuration was discussed and added in Chapter 14, and it also matches the preconfigured authorization policies within ISE 2.0 and newer.

When onboarding with iOS, Windows, and macOS, the endpoint need only communicate with ISE. Apple iOS uses its native Over the Air (OTA) provisioning process. Windows and macOS both use a native application that is downloaded from ISE through the device's browser. Because the communication is limited to just ISE, the ACL_WEBAUTH_REDIRECT ACL is sufficient to be repurposed for the onboarding ACL as well.

However, Android is a different story altogether. Android devices inherently do not trust apps being installed from an app store other than those trusted during the factory install, which includes Google Play. Therefore, ISE would not be allowed to host an app for Android devices by default. To keep the process simple for the end user, you have to either open the ACL to allow access to a range of addresses for Google Play or use the DNS ACL capabilities of the WLC.

The Google Play app store (https://play.google.com) is a cloud service, and the addresses it uses may change regularly. This presents a challenge to permit access to those address ranges. The current solution is to permit a series of blocks of addresses that are known to be used by Google Play, as shown here:

- 74.125.0.0/16
- 173.194.0.0/16
- 173.227.0.0/16
- 206.111.0.0/16

This ACL is used for both single- and dual-SSID onboarding. To read a Google support thread where Google discusses how to identify the current list of Google IP addresses, go to http://support.google.com/a/bin/answer.py?hl=en&answer=60764.

When adding the DNS names to the ACL, keep in mind there may be different URLs for different countries or regions. Additionally, there may be images or other ads that are displayed in Google Play that come from other places.

In our experience, the following two URLs will work in the United States and generally provide a good end-user experience:

- android.clients.google.com
- google.com

The DNS ACLs on the WLC are also known as URL Lists. When you add a URL, an implicit wildcard is added in front of whatever you enter. So, if you enter google.com, it is actually equal to *.google.com. Keep in mind that wildcards in FQDNs are specific to the level. So, for example, *.google.com would not include android.clients.google.com, which is why it is listed separately.

DNS ACLs work on the access points themselves, where they snoop DNS traffic, record the DNS results that match the URL list, and send those results to the controller to be appended as implicit permit entries in the ACL.

Add the URLs to ACL_WEBAUTH_REDIRECT

To add the URLs to ACL_WEBAUTH_REDIRECT, from the WLC GUI, navigate to **Security > Access Control Lists**, hover your mouse over the blue and white arrow icon next to ACL_WEBAUTH_REDIRECT, and then click **Add-Remove URL**, as shown in Figure 17-12.

Figure 17-12   *Add-Remove URL Pop-Up Option*

This takes you to the URL List, as shown in Figure 17-13, where you can add up to 20 URLs per ACL. To configure the list shown in Figure 17-13, if you are in the United States, type **google.com** and click **Add**, and then type **android.clients.google.com** and click **Add**. If you are based outside the United States, it might benefit you to use a wildcard after google in your entries: **google.*** and **android.clients.google.***.

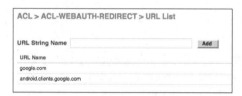

Figure 17-13   *URL List*

As with anything as dynamic as cloud services, you might need to alter these URLs for continued success. New URLs may become necessary and old URLs may become obsolete.

ISE Configuration for Onboarding

With the NADs prepared for the onboarding process, it's time to build the logic within the ISE authorization policy for both the dual- and single-SSID onboarding models.

The easier model to set up and understand first is the single-SSID model. It assumes that if a user or endpoint has been successfully admitted to the network, the user or endpoint must have authenticated with a certificate via EAP-TLS. If an authentication occurs with only a username and password (say, MsCHAPv2 inner method), you know the device must still need to be onboarded.

For example, suppose an employee shows up to work with his new mobile device. He decides to try and connect to the corporate Wi-Fi network and it prompts him for a username and password. The employee enters his Active Directory credentials (as would be expected), and when he opens the browser on the mobile device, he is redirected to the My Devices Portal, where he can begin the onboarding process. This process is simple, quick, and intuitive to most end users nowadays.

Beginning with ISE version 2.0, there is a preconfigured "smart-default" client provisioning policy. Aside from a single, small change, that default policy and its settings will be used in the following examples.

End-User Experience

To fully understand the configuration of ISE, it is best that you experience the end-user experience for both single- and dual-SSID onboarding. That will aid you in your understanding of each policy that is required, and each choice you will have to make. To demonstrate multiple user experiences, the following examples use Apple iOS for the first example, which demonstrates single-SSID onboarding, and Android for the second example, which demonstrates dual-SSID onboarding. However, each onboarding method could be used with any of the supported clients (iOS, Android, Mac OS X, and Windows).

For the examples, we will be leveraging a default, out-of-the-box policy set. The biggest difference is that we enabled the relevant rules for BYOD, as shown in Figure 17-14. Additionally, we changed the SSID in the default profile to be CiscoPress instead of the default one, which is named ISE.

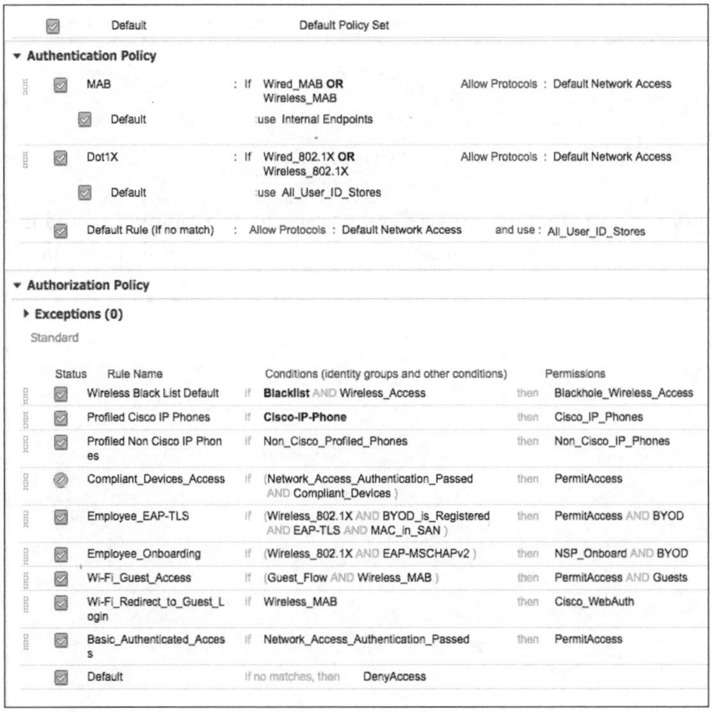

Figure 17-14 *Default Policy Set with Enabled BYOD Rules*

Beginning with ISE version 2.0, there are default policies commonly referred to as "smart defaults" to aid you in going from install to BYOD onboarding in 30 minutes or less. Don't worry too much about understanding this policy set just yet; we will go through it together after you focus on the end-user experience.

Single-SSID Onboarding with Apple iOS Example

The following steps are designed to follow the end-user experience with single-SSID onboarding using an Apple iOS device in a corporate setting:

Step 1. On your iOS device, choose **Settings > Wi-Fi**, enable Wi-Fi (as shown in Figure 17-15), and connect to the corporate Wi-Fi (CiscoPress in this example).

Figure 17-15 *Choosing a Wi-Fi Network on an iOS Device*

Step 2. You are prompted to input a username and password. An employee would use their Active Directory username and password, similar to what is shown in Figure 17-16.

Figure 17-16 *iOS: Enter Credentials*

Step 3. Because you are manually joining a secured network instead of joining a network that was provisioned to your device by an MDM, you are prompted to
accept (trust) ISE's EAP certificate, as shown in Figure 17-17.

Figure 17-17   *iOS: Trust ISE Certificate*

Step 4. After you are successfully connected to the corporate network, you see the
Wi-Fi symbol and can view your IP address, as shown in Figure 17-18. However,
you do not see anything indicating that your access is actually limited.

Figure 17-18   *iOS: Connected to Corporate Wi-Fi*

Step 5. Open a web browser, and you are redirected to the BYOD portal, where you
are stepped through entering some information about the device and then
beginning the OTA provisioning process. Figure 17-19 shows the welcome
screen for the BYOD portal.

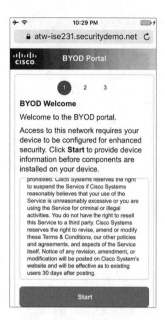

Figure 17-19   *iOS: BYOD Portal Welcome Screen*

Step 6.   Tap **Start**.

Step 7.   Step 2 within the BYOD portal is to provide a device name for the endpoint and, optionally, a description, as shown in Figure 17-20. Type in the requested information and tap **Continue**.

Figure 17-20   *iOS: BYOD Portal Device Information*

Step 8.   Tap the **Launch Apple Profile and Certificate Installers Now** button to launch the Apple OTA provisioning, as shown in Figure 17-21.

Figure 17-21   *iOS: BYOD Portal Install Screen*

Step 9.   For OTA to work correctly, the OTA profile must be signed by a trusted certificate authority (CA). This is often handled by an MDM; however, because this is a BYOD flow, you have to trust that CA manually. As part of the OTA process, ISE sends the public certificate of the CA that signed its admin certificate, as shown in Figure 17-22. You can tap **More Details** to see more about the usage of the certificate that you are installing, as shown in Figure 17-23. You are installing a profile that consists of a CA root certificate.

Figure 17-22   *iOS: Installing OTA Signing CA Certificate*

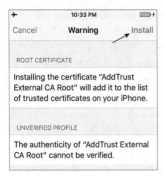

Figure 17-23   *iOS: Viewing More Details About the CA Certificate*

Step 10.   Tap **Install**. The root CA certificate is now marked as verified, as shown in Figure 17-24. Tap **Done**.

Figure 17-24   *iOS: OTA Signing CA Certificate Installed*

Step 11.   After you tap **Done**, the Install Profile screen changes a bit. It now shows that you are installing a Profile Service. It is signed by your ISE node's admin certificate, which is marked verified (it is trusted), as shown in Figure 17-25. The signed profile is trusted because you trusted the root CA in Step 10. Tap **Install**.

Figure 17-25   *iOS: Installing a Profile Service*

Step 12. The screen changes to the Installing Profile screen, as shown in Figure 17-26. Tap **Install**.

Figure 17-26 *iOS: Installing Profile*

Step 13. The screen updates itself several times without requiring any user interaction. You are notified that the OTA service is enrolling certificates and generating keys (see Figures 17-27 through 17-29), and then finally shown the end state with the profile installed, as shown in Figure 17-30.

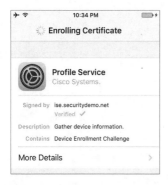

Figure 17-27 *iOS: Enrolling Certificate for Device*

Figure 17-28 *iOS: Generating Key*

Figure 17-29 *iOS: Enrolling Certificate for User*

Figure 17-30 *iOS: Profile Installed*

Step 14. When the profile is installed, tap **Done** and your web browser will refresh with the success message, as shown in Figure 17-31. It takes only a few minutes for the entire process if the end user is paying attention to the prompts.

Figure 17-31 *iOS: Success*

Step 15. You are now able to browse resources on the network. The IOS device authenticates using the certificate you just installed, and the device no longer remembers the username and password that were typed in when this device first joined the wireless SSID.

That concludes the onboarding process for iOS with a single SSID. Next, let's examine the user experience with dual SSID by using an Android example.

Dual-SSID Onboarding with Android Example

The user experience with dual SSIDs is a bit different from the single-SSID experience. In this type of onboarding, the user first joins an open SSID or a guest SSID and, after being logged in to the web authentication portal as an employee, then begins the onboarding process. The following steps are designed to follow the end-user experience with dual-SSID onboarding using an Android-based device in a corporate setting:

Step 1. On your Android device, choose **Settings > Wi-Fi** and connect to the guest Wi-Fi. In our example, we are connecting to an open WLAN named CiscoPress-Guest, as shown in Figure 17-32. Depending on your Android version, you may have to tap **Connect** after choosing the network, as shown in Figure 17-33. This is an extra precaution since you are joining an open (unsecured) SSID. If you aren't sure why open WLANs are a problem, just google "firesheep."

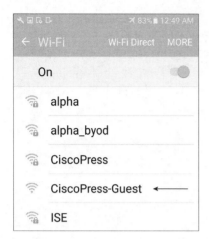

Figure 17-32 *Android: Choose a Wi-Fi Network*

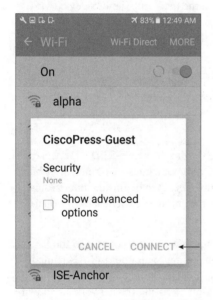

Figure 17-33 *Android: Tap Connect*

Step 2. Because you protected the guest Wi-Fi by requiring a login (Guest or Active Directory), you are redirected to the Web Authentication (WebAuth) portal, as shown in Figure 17-34. Keep in mind that these portals are fully customizable, so you can make it look any way you would like. Take note that the portal is a Guest portal: this is because ISE has no way of knowing if you are a guest or an employee until you provide your identity—in other words, until you log in.

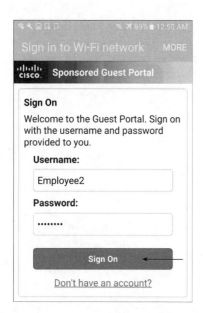

Figure 17-34   *Android: WebAuth Portal*

Step 3.   After you log in through the WebAuth portal, you are seamlessly redirected to the BYOD portal, as shown in Figure 17-35. The BYOD portal steps you through the onboarding process.

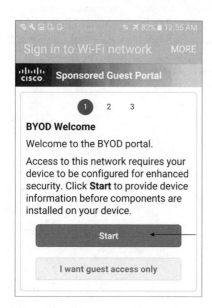

Figure 17-35   *Android: BYOD Portal Welcome Page*

Step 4.   Tap **Start**. You move to step 2 of the BYOD portal, which is where device information is captured. As you can see in Figure 17-36, you must enter a name that helps you to identify this device, and an optional description. The device ID (MAC address) is optionally displayed at the bottom.

Figure 17-36   *Android: Device Information*

Step 5.   Enter the required device name and then tap **Continue**. You are advanced to step 3 of the BYOD portal, where you must tap the button to reach out to Google Play and download the Cisco Network Setup Assistant app, as shown in Figure 17-37. Depending on your personal device settings, you may be given the choice between the Internet and the Google Play app.

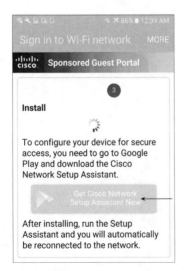

Figure 17-37   *Android: Connect to Google Play*

Step 6. Download or open the app from Google Play, as shown in Figure 17-38.

Figure 17-38 *Android: Download Cisco Network Setup Assistant*

Step 7. Run the app and tap **Start**, as shown in Figure 17-39.

Figure 17-39 *Android: Run the NSA App*

Step 8.   The NSA app downloads the profile from ISE, as shown in Figure 17-40.

Figure 17-40   *Android: NSA App Downloading Profile*

Step 9.   Name and save your certificate, as shown in Figure 17-41.

Figure 17-41   *Android: Name and Save the Certificate*

Step 10. Name and save the CA certificate, as shown in Figure 17-42.

Figure 17-42 *Android: Name and Save the CA Certificate*

Step 11. The NSA app automatically changes the network connection to the corporate SSID and authenticates with the new certificate using EAP-TLS, as shown in Figure 17-43 and Figure 17-44. Your Android device is now ready to be used regularly on the corporate network. The onboarding was a one-time thing.

Figure 17-43 *Android: Connect to the Corporate SSID*

Figure 17-44   *Android: Connected*

Configuring ISE for Onboarding

As you saw in the previous section, the end-user experience is designed to be straightforward and easy for a typical user to be able to follow without any interaction with the IT department. It is always advisable to keep the end-user experience as simple and easy as possible, and to put the administrative burden on yourself—the administrator—instead. To keep that end-user experience simple, you need to so some up-front work on the configuration side. A lot of it is completed for you out of the box in ISE version 2.0 and newer, but this section covers the entire configuration, default or not, so that you are familiar with it.

Configure the Native Supplicant Profile

The native supplicant profile (NSP) defines the network settings for the endpoints that will go through onboarding.

The native supplicant profile defines the following:

■ One or more wireless SSIDs

■ EAP type to use (PEAP or EAP-TLS)

■ Key size for certificates

■ Level of wireless security

■ If it applies to wired, wireless, or both

- Proxy configuration, if any

- Whether or not to connect to the SSID if not broadcasting

Beginning with ISE 2.0, ISE comes with the NSPs preinstalled. The following steps guide you through adding the latest client provisioning resources from the Cisco site (if necessary), and then editing the prebuilt native supplicant profile.

Step 1.   Navigate to **Work Centers > BYOD > Client Provisioning > Resources**. Examine the preinstalled resources, as shown in Figure 17-45.

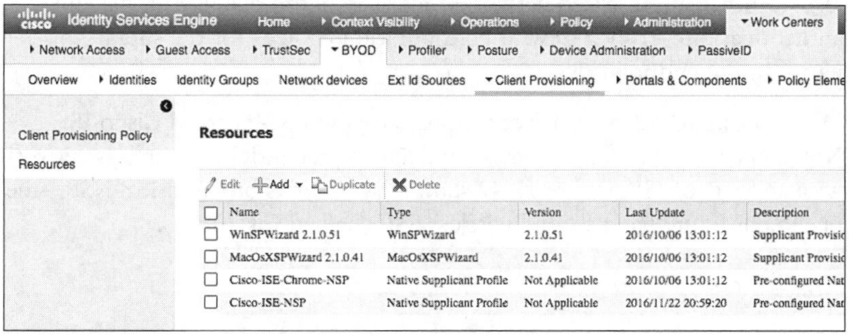

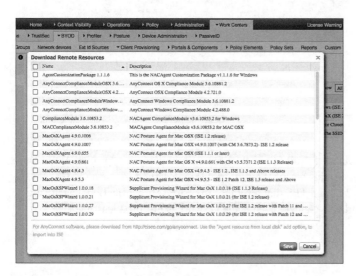

Figure 17-45   *Preinstalled Agent Resources*

Step 2.   To download newer or additional resources, choose **Add > Agent Resources from Cisco Site**. Note that this communication requires Internet access, which may require you to configure a proxy server to successfully communicate.

Step 3.   The list of all versions of the clients and wizards is displayed, as shown in Figure 17-46. Select any that you want to download and click **Save**.

Figure 17-46   *Agent Resources from Cisco Site*

Remember, with BYOD, you are not installing a network manager or a supplicant onto the device. Instead, you are configuring the endpoint for the end user. To help accomplish that, NSPs are used to configure the networking on the endpoints that are onboarded. In other words, the NSPs are the configuration instructions for the supplicants that exist in the endpoint operating systems.

An NSP contains configurations identifying which wireless SSID the client should connect to (if there is more than one wireless network), which security those wireless networks require to connect, whether the endpoint should also authenticate to wired networks, and whether to use user or machine authentication—truly a slew of configuration choices for the supplicant native to the endpoint OS.

Step 4.   On the Resources screen, select the preconfigured NSP named **Cisco-ISE-NSP** and click **Edit**. Your screen should have a preconfigured wireless network with an SSID of ISE. Figure 17-47 shows the contents of Cisco-ISE-NSP—the one in our figure has a second wireless SSID named CiscoPress.

Figure 17-47   *Cisco-ISE-NSP*

Step 5.   Select **ISE** and click **Edit** to see the preconfigured wireless profile. As shown in Figure 17-48, this out-of-the-box profile is designed to use an SSID named ISE with WPA2 and TLS that leverages the EAP_Authentication_Certificate_Template and will connect even if the network is not broadcasting.

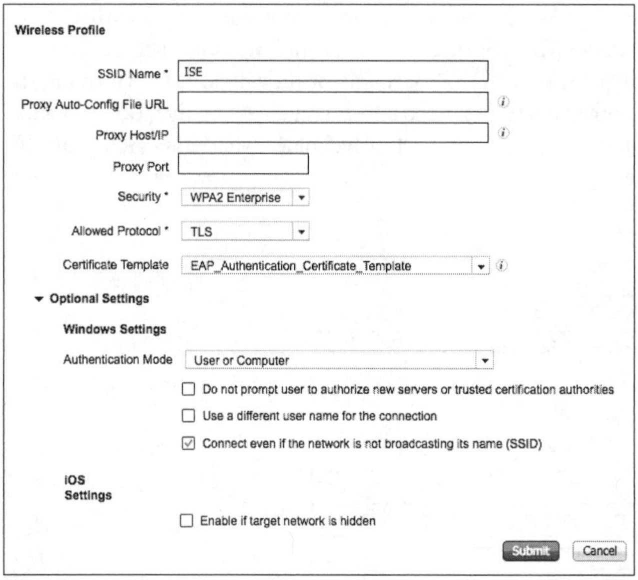

Figure 17-48 *ISE Wireless Profile*

Examine the Certificate Template

As you just learned, NSPs are the network configurations sent to the endpoints. EAP-TLS is the most common deployment, and when TLS is used, a certificate must be issued to the endpoint. The certificate template defines the content or fields of the certificate, the certificate strength, and even which CA should be used to issue the certificates.

Examine the default EAP_Authentication_Certificate_Template that is used in the default Cisco-ISE-NSP native supplicant profile by following these steps:

Step 1. Navigate to **Work Centers > BYOD > Portals & Components > Certificates > Certificate Templates** and select **EAP_Authentication_Certificate_Template**, as shown in Figure 17-49, and then click **Edit**.

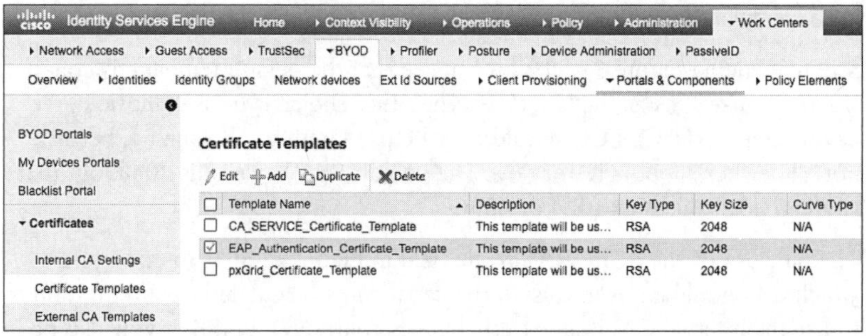

Figure 17-49 *Certificate Templates*

Step 2.   As shown in Figure 17-50, the certificate template is configured with a fixed common name (CN) set to the $UserName$ variable. This is automatically substituted with the username of the employee performing the onboarding. The other portions of the subject, such as organization (O) and organizational unit (OU), are filled with placeholders that you can modify to suit your own needs.

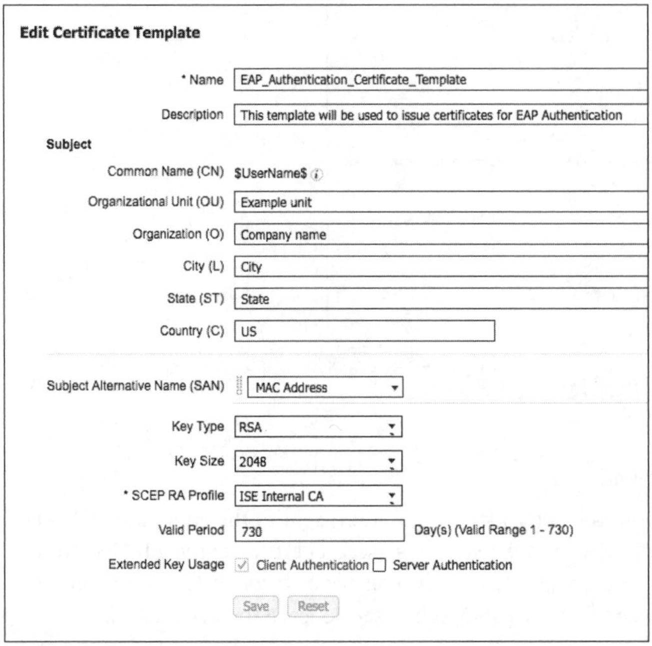

Edit Certificate Template	
* Name	EAP_Authentication_Certificate_Template
Description	This template will be used to issue certificates for EAP Authentication
Subject	
Common Name (CN)	$UserName$ ⓘ
Organizational Unit (OU)	Example unit
Organization (O)	Company name
City (L)	City
State (ST)	State
Country (C)	US
Subject Alternative Name (SAN)	MAC Address ▼
Key Type	RSA ▼
Key Size	2048 ▼
* SCEP RA Profile	ISE Internal CA ▼
Valid Period	730 Day(s) (Valid Range 1 - 730)
Extended Key Usage	☑ Client Authentication ☐ Server Authentication
	Save Reset

Figure 17-50   *EAP_Authentication_Certificate_Template*

Step 3.   Continuing with Figure 17-50, notice the Subject Alternative Name (SAN) field. The drop-down box has only one choice, which is MAC Address; because this cannot be changed or removed, it seems to be a bit of a UI mistake. The UI components are used to someday allow extending the template for other items in the template, but alas—those other options are not available yet.

Step 4.   Still referencing Figure 17-50, you can see that the default template is configured to use RSA as the key type. The other choice is to use elliptic curve cryptography (ECC). ECC should only be used with total planning, because not all devices support it, for now. The default RSA key size is 2048, but that size can be changed to 1024 or 4096.

Step 5.   The purpose of the SCEP RA Profile field in Figure 17-50 is to configure which CA should be used to sign the certificates. The default configuration is to use the internal CA; if an external CA is configured in ISE, it will also be in the drop-down list.

Step 6. The Valid Period setting determines how long the certificate is "warranted" by the CA, meaning how long the CA is responsible for publishing the revocation state of the certificate.

Step 7. The default setting for Extended Key Usage (EKU) of an endpoint certificate is Client Authentication only. Server authentication is available for you to configure if you need it, but it should not be required for a BYOD certificate.

Examine the Client Provisioning Policy

The NSPs are the network configurations sent to the endpoints, and they include the choice of which certificate template to use, which, in turn, decides which CA to use and which key sizes.

You still need a policy to determine which NSP to send to clients, which is completed in the client provisioning policy (CPP). The CPP dictates the software and profiles that should be downloaded and installed based on the operating system of the endpoint and a multitude of other possible attributes. For example, you might configure a policy for Android to be provisioned for the CORP-SSID wireless network when an employee is going through the provisioning process and configure another policy for Android to be provisioned for the CONTRACTOR-SSID wireless network for all vendors and contractors who are also working through the provisioning process.

Out of the box, there is one client provisioning policy per OS using the preinstalled native supplicant wizards, native supplicant profiles, and certificate templates. To examine these preconfigured policies, navigate to **Work Centers > BYOD > Client Provisioning**, as shown in Figure 17-51.

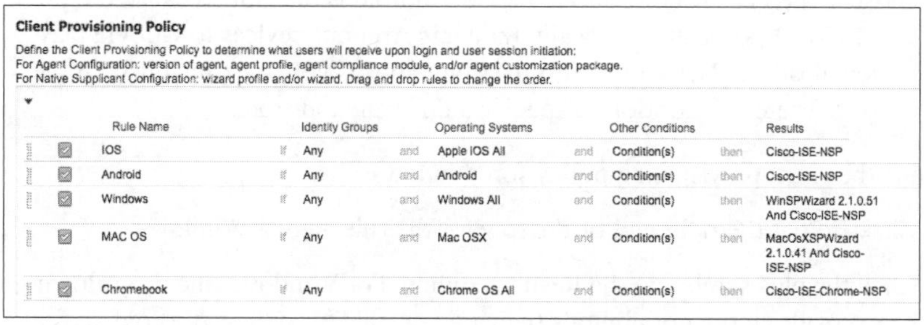

Client Provisioning Policy

Define the Client Provisioning Policy to determine what users will receive upon login and user session initiation:
For Agent Configuration: version of agent, agent profile, agent compliance module, and/or agent customization package.
For Native Supplicant Configuration: wizard profile and/or wizard. Drag and drop rules to change the order.

	Rule Name	Identity Groups	Operating Systems	Other Conditions	Results
☑	IOS	If Any and	Apple IOS All and	Condition(s) then	Cisco-ISE-NSP
☑	Android	If Any and	Android and	Condition(s) then	Cisco-ISE-NSP
☑	Windows	If Any and	Windows All and	Condition(s) then	WinSPWizard 2.1.0.51 And Cisco-ISE-NSP
☑	MAC OS	If Any and	Mac OSX and	Condition(s) then	MacOsXSPWizard 2.1.0.41 And Cisco-ISE-NSP
☑	Chromebook	If Any and	Chrome OS All and	Condition(s) then	Cisco-ISE-Chrome-NSP

Figure 17-51 *Client Provisioning Policy*

First, examine the client provisioning policy for Apple iOS:

Step 1.   Click **Edit** at the right end of the row for the rule named IOS.

Step 2.   Note that a rule can apply to specific user or endpoint identity groups, specific operating systems, and a slew of other conditions that are exposed to the CPP.

Step 3.   Click the plus symbol in the Results column. The result choices vary based on the OS chosen. For iOS, notice that only the profile is selectable, as shown in Figure 17-52. The ISE BYOD portal automatically uses the OTA provisioning process that is native to Apple iOS. There is no need to specify anything else here.

Figure 17-52 *Client Provisioning Policy for iOS*

Next, examine the client provisioning policy for Android:

Step 1.   Click **Edit** at the right end of the row for the rule named Android.

Step 2.   Click the plus symbol in the Results column to see the configuration options, as shown in Figure 17-53. Again, the result choices vary based on the OS chosen. The only selection available for Android is the NSP because the ISE client BYOD portal automatically redirects Android devices to Google Play to download the Network Setup Assistant app, as you saw previously in the chapter. There is no option to specify a different app store.

Next, examine the client provisioning policy for Windows:

Step 1.   Click **Edit** at the right end of the row for the rule named Windows.

Step 2.   Click the plus symbol in the Results column. For Windows, the drop-down box provides more possibilities than are available for iOS or Android, as shown in Figure 17-53. The upper portion of the results configuration is for posture, while the lower half is for BYOD provisioning. Focusing on BYOD, you see that it is preconfigured to use the preinstalled Windows program to implement the provisioning, and that must be specified here.

Figure 17-53 *Client Provisioning Policy for Windows and Android*

Next, examine the client provisioning policy for Mac OS X:

Step 1.   Click **Edit** at the right end of the row for the rule named MAC OS.

Step 2.   Click the plus symbol in the results column. Like Windows, the drop-down box for Mac OS X provides more possibilities than are available for iOS and Android, as shown in Figure 17-54. The upper portion of the results configuration is for posture, while the lower half is for BYOD provisioning. Focusing on BYOD, you see that it is preconfigured to use the preinstalled MAC OS program to implement the provisioning, and that must be specified here.

Figure 17-54 *Client Provisioning Policy for MAC OS*

Finally, examine the client provisioning policy for Chromebooks:

Step 1.   Click **Edit** at the right end of the row for the rule named Chromebook.

Step 2.   Click the plus symbol in the Results column. The result choices vary based on the OS chosen. Chrome OS onboarding is very different from the other BYOD platforms, and is actually a managed endpoint strategy, not a BYOD strategy at all. It gets its own NSP, separate from the other OSs, and requires that the devices be managed by Google domain registration and device licenses. The NSA must be pre-pushed to the device by the Google cloud.

BYOD and WebAuth Portals

Now that you have seen the client provisioning policies, you can take a look at the portals that the end users will see. You saw these portals yourself during the client experience review section and in figures such as Figure 17-19 and 17-34. The BYOD portal is used in single-SSID provisioning, while the WebAuth portal is used during the dual-SSID flow.

Let's start with the BYOD portal:

Step 1.   Navigate to **Work Centers > BYOD > Portals & Components > BYOD Portals.**

Step 2.   Edit the preconfigured **BYOD Portal (default),** as shown in Figure 17-55.

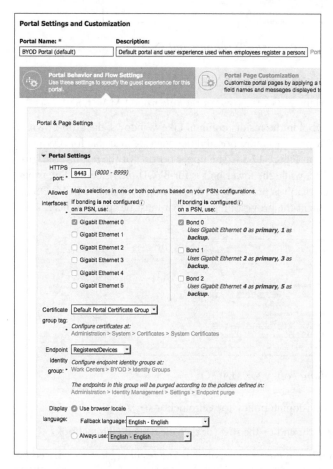

Figure 17-55   *BYOD Portal—Configuring Portal Settings*

Step 3.   Expand the **Portal Settings** section, which is used to configure the following:

- The TCP ports and interfaces for the portal to operate on. The default is to operate on the Gigabit Ethernet 0 interface or the Bond 0 interface for those Policy Service Nodes (PSN) configured with network interface card (NIC) bonding, and to operate on port 8443.

- The Certificate Group Tag drop-down list is used to pick which certificate should be used to identify the web service and secure the HTTPS connection. The default certificate group tag is used with an out-of-the-box configuration.

- The Endpoint Identity Group option is preconfigured to leverage the RegisteredDevices group. This means that any endpoints going through the BYOD process are added to this RegisteredDevices group. It is configurable per portal, so different users or endpoint types can be added to different endpoint identity groups.

Step 4.   Expand the **BYOD Settings** section, which is used to configure a few options, as shown in Figure 17-56:

- Whether to require the employee to agree to an acceptable use policy (AUP).

- Whether to display the Device ID (MAC Address) field during registration, which is very useful for an IT admin, but perhaps not so useful for the end user unless he or she needs to leverage the help desk.

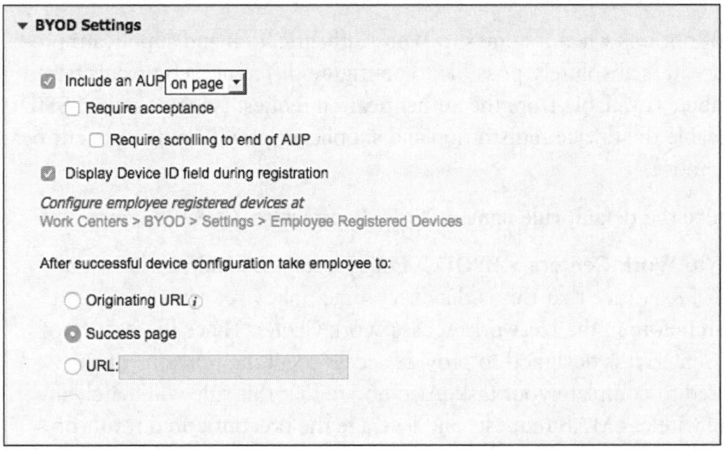

Figure 17-56   *BYOD Portal—Configuring BYOD Settings*

Step 5.   Expand the **Support Information Settings** section, which is used to display certain information to the employee that can aid the help desk, should a need arise to call them. Figure 17-57 shows the support information.

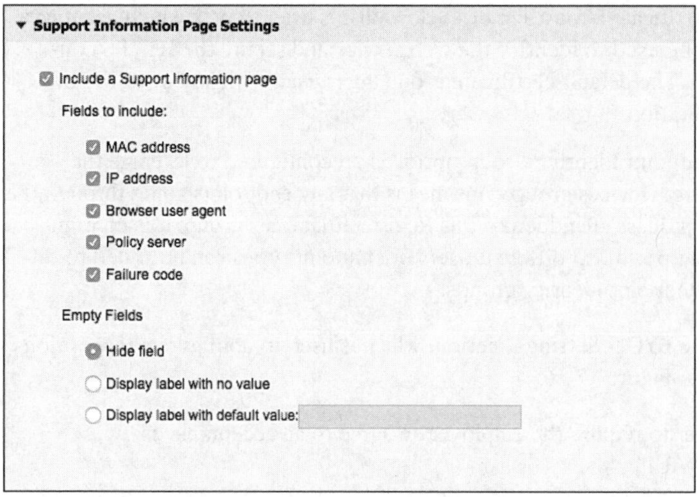

Figure 17-57   *BYOD Portal—Configuring Support Information Settings*

Now examine the WebAuth portal, which is the portal end users see in a dual-SSID onboarding flow.

There is a plethora of options when it comes to Web Authentication and supplicant provisioning. For instance, it is absolutely possible to configure different web portals based on a number of attributes available from the authentication request (such as source SSID). This way, you can enable the device registration and supplicant provisioning to occur per use case, if you so choose.

For simplicity, examine the default rule named Wi-Fi_Redirect_to_Guest_Login:

Step 1.   Navigate to **Work Centers > BYOD > Policy Sets > Default**, as shown in Figure 17-58. Notice that this is the exact same policy set screen that you have used before in the Network Access Work Center. That's the beauty of a Work Center: it is designed to provide access to all the portions of the UI required to complete your task. Also notice that this rule will match any incoming wireless MAB requests and leverage the preconfigured result of Cisco_WebAuth.

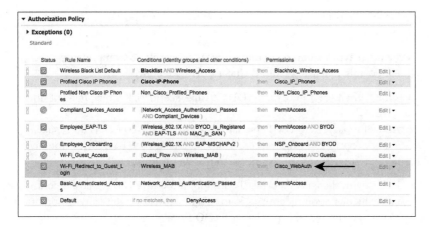

	Status	Rule Name		Conditions (identity groups and other conditions)		Permissions		
	☑	Wireless Black List Default	if	**Blacklist** AND Wireless_Access	then	Blackhole_Wireless_Access	Edit | ▾	
	☑	Profiled Cisco IP Phones		**Cisco-IP-Phone**	then	Cisco_IP_Phones	Edit | ▾	
	☑	Profiled Non Cisco IP Phones	if	Non_Cisco_Profiled_Phones	then	Non_Cisco_IP_Phones	Edit | ▾	
	◎	Compliant_Devices_Access	if	(Network_Access_Authentication_Passed AND Compliant_Devices)	then	PermitAccess	Edit | ▾	
	☑	Employee_EAP-TLS	if	(Wireless_802.1X AND BYOD_is_Registered AND EAP-TLS AND MAC_in_SAN)	then	PermitAccess AND BYOD	Edit | ▾	
	☑	Employee_Onboarding	if	(Wireless_802.1X AND EAP-MSCHAPv2)	then	NSP_Onboard AND BYOD	Edit | ▾	
	◎	Wi-Fi_Guest_Access	if	(Guest_Flow AND Wireless_MAB)	then	PermitAccess AND Guests	Edit | ▾	
	☑	Wi-Fi_Redirect_to_Guest_Login	if	Wireless_MAB	then	Cisco_WebAuth ←	Edit | ▾	
	☑	Basic_Authenticated_Access	if	Network_Access_Authentication_Passed	then	PermitAccess	Edit | ▾	
	☑	Default		if no matches, then		DenyAccess	Edit | ▾	

Figure 17-58 *Default Policy Set*

Step 2. Navigate to **Work Centers > BYOD > Policy Elements > Results > Authorization Profiles > Cisco_WebAuth**, as shown in Figure 17-59. Here you can see under the common tasks and the Attribute Details that Centralized Web Authentication has been preconfigured to use Self-Registered Guest Portal (default).

Authorization Profiles > Cisco_WebAuth
Authorization Profile

* Name   Cisco_WebAuth

Description   Default Profile used to redirect users to the CWA portal.

* Access Type   ACCESS_ACCEPT ▾

Network Device Profile   ⛁ Cisco ▾ ⊕

Service Template ☐

Track Movement ☐ ⓘ

Passive Identity Tracking ☐ ⓘ

▾ **Common Tasks**

☑ Web Redirection (CWA, MDM, NSP, CPP) ⓘ

　Centralized Web Auth ▾   ACL ACL_WEBAUTH_REDIRECT   Value
　　　　　　　　　　　　　　　　　　　　　　　　Self-Registered Guest Portal (de ▾

▾ **Attributes Details**

Access Type = ACCESS_ACCEPT
cisco-av-pair = url-redirect-acl=ACL_WEBAUTH_REDIRECT
cisco-av-pair = url-redirect=https://ip:port/portal/gateway?sessionId=SessionIdValue&portal=a03877d0-8c01-11e6-996c-525400b48521&action=cwa

Figure 17-59 *Cisco_WebAuth*

Now examine the Self-Registered Guest Portal to see how a guest portal ties into the BYOD flow:

Step 1.   Navigate to **Work Centers > Guest Access > Portals & Components > Guest Portals > Self-Registered Guest Portal (default).**

Step 2.   As shown in Figure 17-60, the BYOD Settings section has a few items of note:

   ■ Allow Employees to Use Personal Devices on the Network is the "make it work" option. In other words, it is what enables the BYOD flow for any non-guest users who authenticate to the WebAuth portal.

   ■ Just as with the BYOD portal, the Endpoint Identity Group setting configures which endpoint identity group to automatically assign any endpoints to who go through this particular BYOD flow.

   ■ Allow Employees to Choose to Guest Access Only provides an option for employees to click a button to choose guest-level access instead of going through the BYOD onboarding process. You saw this option back in Figure 17-35 in the example of the Android device going through the dual-SSID flow.

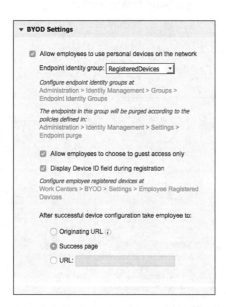

Figure 17-60   *Self-Registered Guest Portal (Default): BYOD Settings*

Verify Default Unavailable Client Provisioning Policy Action

ISE supports iOS, Android, Windows, Mac OS X, and Chrome OS; however, it is possible for an end user to attempt access with a client that is not supported by ISE native supplicant provisioning (such as attempting with a BlackBerry or Windows Mobile device).

To address such situations, navigate to **Work Centers > BYOD > Settings > Client Provisioning** and click the Native Supplicant Provisioning Policy Unavailable drop-down list, as shown in Figure 17-61. ISE offers two options:

- **Allow Network Access:** Users are allowed to register their device through the My Devices Portal and gain network access without having to install and launch a native supplicant wizard. This assumes the user will have to interact and configure the supplicant independently. This option is attractive if the end users are capable of requesting and installing their own certificates.

- **Apply Defined Authorization Policy:** Basically, this option leaves the client in the current state, which is a state of limited access. This is also the default setting.

Figure 17-61 *Default Unavailable Client Provisioning Policy Action*

Examine the Authorization Profiles

Although having the client provisioning policy is required, the authorization policy is still mission-critical. Without the properly configured authorization policy, there is no *call to action* that sends the endpoint over to the client provisioning portal. Of course, an authorization rule needs an authorization profile that includes that call to action.

Out of the box, there are two authorization profiles that contain the needed calls to action: NSP_Onboard for the single-SSID flow and Cisco_WebAuth for the dual-SSID flow. You have already examined the Cisco_WebAuth authorization profile in the "BYOD and WebAuth Portals" section (refer to Figure 17-59), so now examine NSP_Onboard:

Step 1. Navigate to **Work Centers > BYOD > Policy Elements > Results > Authorization > Authorization Profiles**.

Step 2. Edit the **NSP_Onboard** authorization profile, as shown in Figure 17-62. Note that this authorization profile is still using web authentication, but the portal is set to the BYOD Portal.

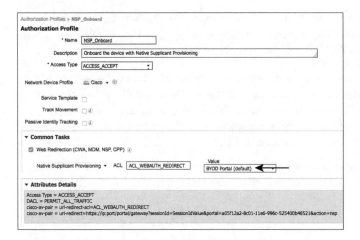

Figure 17-62 *NSP_Onboard Authorization Profile*

Examine the Authorization Policy Rules

Now that you have seen the authorization profiles, take a look at all the relevant authorization rules that use those profiles for results. Out of the box, you can leverage the following three rules in the default authorization policy, shown in Figure 17-63 and numbered for purposes of discussion:

Status	Rule Name		Conditions (identity groups and other conditions)		Permissions		
	Wireless Black List Default	if	**Blacklist** AND Wireless_Access	then	Blackhole_Wireless_Access		Edit | ▼
	Profiled Cisco IP Phones		**Cisco-IP-Phone**	then	Cisco_IP_Phones		Edit | ▼
	Profiled Non Cisco IP Phones		Non_Cisco_Profiled_Phones	then	Non_Cisco_IP_Phones		Edit | ▼
	Compliant_Devices_Access	if	(Network_Access_Authentication_Passed AND Compliant_Devices)	then	PermitAccess		Edit | ▼
③	Employee_EAP-TLS	if	(Wireless_802.1X AND BYOD_is_Registered AND EAP-TLS AND MAC_in_SAN)	then	PermitAccess AND BYOD		Edit | ▼
①	Employee_Onboarding	if	(Wireless_802.1X AND EAP-MSCHAPv2)	then	NSP_Onboard AND BYOD		Edit | ▼
	Wi-Fi_Guest_Access	if	(Guest_Flow AND Wireless_MAB)	then	PermitAccess AND Guests		Edit | ▼
②	Wi-Fi_Redirect_to_Guest_Login	if	Wireless_MAB	then	Cisco_WebAuth		Edit | ▼
	Basic_Authenticated_Access	if	Network_Access_Authentication_Passed	then	PermitAccess		Edit | ▼
	Default		If no matches, then	DenyAccess			Edit | ▼

Figure 17-63 *Default Authorization Policy*

- The Employee_Onboarding rule (1) is used for single-SSID onboarding. As shown in Figure 17-63, the rule takes any incoming authorization where the method is wireless 802.1X and EAP-MSCHAPv2 and then sends that user to the BYOD portal to be onboarded. Once the onboarding is complete, ISE sends a CoA to trigger a reauthentication, and the new authentication from the endpoint uses the certificate (EAP-TLS), thereby landing on the Employee_EAP-TLS rule (3), which provides full access.

- The Wi_Fi_Redirect_to_Guest_Login rule (2) is the rule for dual-SSID onboarding, as well as general guest access. As shown in Figure 17-63, the rule takes any incoming authorization where wireless MAB is used, and sends the user to the guest portal. If the user who logs into that WebAuth portal is an employee, that user is sent through the BYOD flow as described earlier in the chapter. Once the onboarding is complete, ISE sends a CoA to trigger a reauthentication, and the new authentication from the endpoint uses the certificate (EAP-TLS), thereby landing on the Employee_EAP-TLS rule (3), which provides full access.

- The Employee_EAP-TLS rule (3) is the final rule in the onboarding process. It is the end result of rules 1 and 2. As shown in Figure 17-63, the rule has conditions set to match authorizations where wireless 802.1X with EAP-TLS is used, where the endpoint object in ISE's database has the BYOD registered flag enabled, and the endpoint's MAC address is also in the subject alternative name (SAN) field of the certificate. Only if all those conditions are met is the employee granted full access.

BYOD Onboarding Process Detailed

Yes, this chapter is getting long, but there's a good chance you will find all of this information useful if you ever find yourself in a spot where you need to do troubleshooting of this process. You have seen that the user experience is simple and straightforward; the process behind the scenes, however, is complex.

iOS Onboarding Flow

To examine, in detail, the experience with iOS devices and onboarding, the following onboarding flow focuses on a single SSID onboarding experience. The end user should have to complete only a few actions, as noted in Figure 17-64, but all the items that occur behind the scenes are included to give you the full scope of the process.

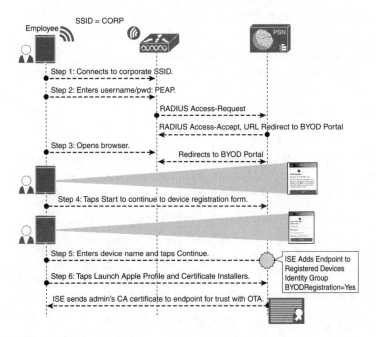

Figure 17-64 *iOS Phase 1: Device Registration*

Phase 1: Device Registration

1. A user joins the corporate SSID via his iOS device, and the iOS device prompts the user for credentials.

2. The user enters his AD username and password.

3. The EAP login request is sent to the wireless controller, which wraps the request in a RADIUS access-request packet to ISE.

4. The authorization result from ISE includes a URL redirection to the BYOD portal.

5. The user opens his web browser, which is redirected to the BYOD portal on ISE. The end user must tap Start to begin the onboarding process.

6. On the device registration page, the user completes the Device Name field and, optionally, the Description field. The user taps Continue, which causes ISE to do the following:

   ■ Set the BYODRegistration flag for the endpoint identity to Yes

   ■ Add the endpoint to the RegisteredDevices identity group

   ■ Send the admin's root CA certificate to the IOS device for it to trust for OTA provisioning

7. The user taps Launch Apple Profile and Certificate Installers Now.

Phase 2: Device Enrollment and Provisioning

1. The device registration flag is set on the endpoint record in ISE's database.

2. ISE sends a profile to the iOS endpoint via OTA.

3. The profile instructs iOS to generate a certificate signing request (CSR) using the employee's credentials (given to iOS by ISE via the OTA service) as the certificate's common name in the subject, and the endpoint's MAC address as the Subject Alternative Name (SAN) field:

   ■ CN=Username

   ■ SAN=MAC-Address

4. The CSR is sent to ISE via SCEP, which is received by the registration authority (RA) function of the PSN. Since the request is for the internal CA, the RA uses an internal API to pass the certificate enrollment request to the endpoint CA function of the PSN.

5. The internal endpoint CA automatically issues the certificate.

6. The certificate is sent back to ISE, which sends it to the device through the OTA service. Included in that OTA profile is the Wi-Fi configuration, which details the SSID and to use EAP-TLS.

7. ISE sends a CoA to the NAD of the type ReAuth, which causes a new authentication.

8. The endpoint authenticates to the corporate SSID using the certificate via EAP-TLS.

Figure 17-65 illustrates the transactions in Phase 2.

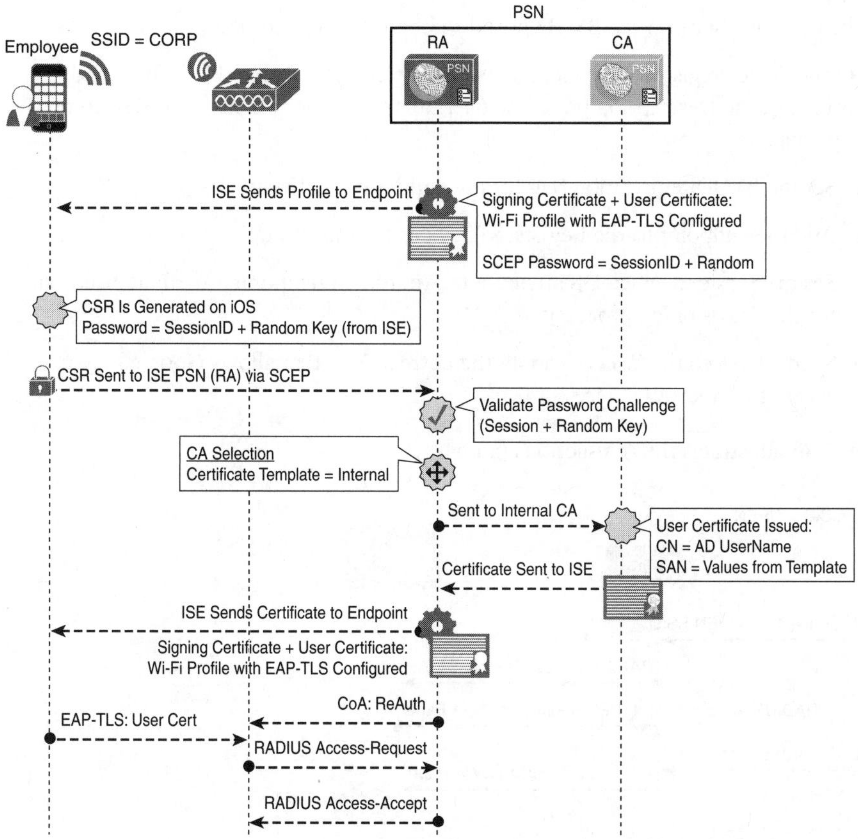

Figure 17-65 *iOS Phase 2: Device Enrollment*

Android Flow

To detail the flow of onboarding with Android, the following onboarding flow uses the dual-SSID approach. Android is certainly capable of doing a single-SSID approach as well. The end user should have to complete only a few actions, as noted in Figure 17-66, but all the items that occur behind the scenes are included to give you the full scope of the process.

Phase 1: Device Registration

1. A user joins the open SSID via her Android device, and the WLC sends a MAB request to ISE.

2. ISE sends a redirection to the Centralized Web Authentication portal.

3. The user opens a browser and is redirected to the CWA portal.

4. The user enters her AD username and password.

5. The successful WebAuth triggers a redirection, and the web page changes to the BYOD portal flow.

6. The user taps Start on the BYOD portal to begin the registration.

7. On the device registration page, the user completes the Device Name field and, optionally, the Description field. The user taps Continue, which causes ISE to do the following:

- Set the BYODRegistration flag for the endpoint identity to Yes

- Add the endpoint to the RegisteredDevices identity group

- Set the Session:Device-OS attribute to Android (a temporary attribute used only for the provisioning process)

- Send a CoA to the WLC to apply the correct ACL that allows Google Play to access the Android device

Figure 17-66 illustrates the transactions in Phase 1.

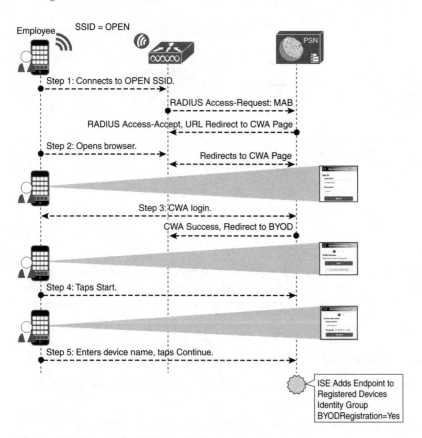

Figure 17-66 *Android Phase 1: Device Registration*

Phase 2: Download the NSA App

1. The CoA from phase 1 applied an ACL that permits traffic to Google Play.

2. The browser was automatically sent to Google Play and the Android device prompts the user to choose the Internet or Google Play to complete the request.

3. The user may be prompted to log in to Google Play.

4. The user taps a button to install and/or open the Cisco Network Setup Assistant app.

Figure 17-67 illustrates the transactions in Phase 2.

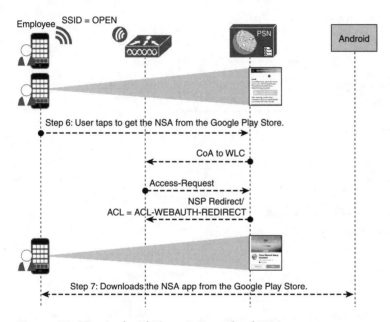

Figure 17-67 *Android Phase 2: Download NSA*

Phase 3: Device Provisioning

1. The Network Setup Assistant installs, and the user runs it.

2. The NSA sends a discovery message to http://*default-gateway*/auth/discovery.

3. The WLC redirects that HTTP message to the ISE native supplicant provisioning portal based on the URL-REDIRECT result within the authorization from ISE.

4. ISE sends the Android profile based on the native supplicant profile to the endpoint.

5. NSA generates the certificate signing request (CSR), using the employee's credentials as the certificate's subject, and the MAC address as the Subject Alternative Name (SAN) field:

   ■ CN=Username

   ■ SAN=MAC-Address

6. The CSR is sent to the ISE PSN's registration authority (RA) function, which in turn sends the certificate enrollment request to the endpoint CA function.

7. The CA automatically issues the certificate.

8. The certificate is sent back to ISE, which sends it to the NSA app. Included in the NSA profile is the Wi-Fi configuration, which details the SSID and to use EAP-TLS.

9. The NSA app connects the endpoint to the corporate SSID and ISE sends a CoA to the NAD of the type ReAuth, which also causes a new authentication.

10. The endpoint authenticates to the corporate SSID using the certificate via EAP-TLS.

Figure 17-68 illustrates the transactions in Phase 3.

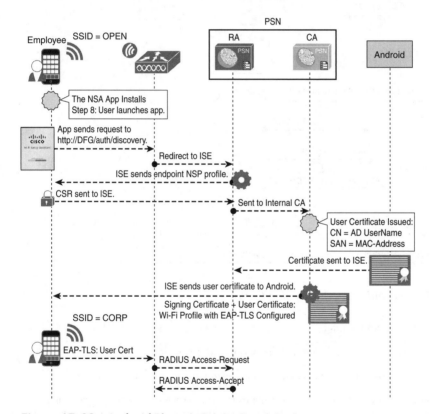

Figure 17-68 *Android Phase 3: Device Provisioning*

Windows and Mac OS X Flow

Mac OS X and Windows both use a wizard to accomplish the onboarding and provisioning. It is downloaded as a Microsoft Installer (.msi) file for Windows and a disk image (.dmg) file containing a native application for macOS. Both are named the Cisco native supplicant provisioning wizard. The wizard takes care of triggering the CSR from the OS and installing the supplicant profile, and it works very similarly to the way Android provisioning functions. One key difference is that the wizard downloads directly from ISE for Windows and macOS.

MDM Onboarding

Many organizations use mobile device management (MDM) solutions. These solutions provide endpoint management for a plethora of devices. They help enforce specific security requirements, such as endpoint encryption, PIN lock, jail-break detection, remote wipe capabilities, application whitelisting, application blacklisting, and more. Many MDMs even provision supplicants and certificates to devices as part of their management package.

In the past, the MDM solutions had some drawbacks. With a typical solution, a user who brought in a mobile device and wanted to gain access to the network had to call the help desk and receive instructions on how to onboard the device with the MDM solution. There were some significant downsides to this process, such as:

■ Users were required to manually connect to the MDM solution to begin the onboarding process.

■ It lacked enforcement to help "steer" the user toward that solution.

■ An MDM license was required for every device the organization would provision and allow to have network access, which often was cost-prohibitive.

Cisco and the MDM vendors recognized these drawbacks presented a beneficial and strategic opportunity. The MDM vendors possessed the mobile device-management capabilities, and Cisco had the onboarding, network access policy, and enforcement mechanisms. Since ISE 1.2, ISE has integrated with the industry's leading MDM vendors. Solutions include, but are not limited to

■ Cisco Meraki Systems Manager

■ VMware AirWatch

■ MobileIron

■ Citrix ZenMobile

■ Good Technology (acquired by BlackBerry in October 2016)

■ Jamf

■ SAP Afaria

All 20 or so supported vendors have implemented an API written by Cisco to enable scalable bidirectional communication between their solutions and ISE.

Integration Points

The API enables ISE to use MDM attributes in the authorization policies. The authorization can either use a macro-level attribute stating that the device is in compliance with the MDM policy or use micro-level attributes, such as jail break status, PIN lock, or even endpoint encryption.

Table 17-1 documents the possible MDM attribute values, provides a definition of each value, and lists the possible values for each attribute.

Table 17-1 *MDM Attributes*

MDM Attribute	Definition	Possible Values
DeviceRegisterStatus	Indicates whether the device is registered with the MDM.	Unregistered Registered
DeviceComplianceStatus	Macro-level attribute that indicates whether the device meets the security policy of the MDM.	NonCompliant Compliant
DiskEncryptionStatus	Indicates whether encryption is enabled on the storage of the device.	On Off
PinLockStatus	Specifies whether the device has an automatic lock, requiring a PIN or password to unlock the device.	On Off
JailBrokenStatus	Indicates whether the device been jail broken.	Unbroken Broken
Manufacturer	Identifies the manufacturer of the device.	Text field or can be compared to attribute from AD/LDAP
Model	Identifies the model of the device.	Text field or can be compared to attribute from AD/LDAP
IMEI	Identifies the unique ID of the device.	Text field or can be compared to attribute from AD/LDAP
SerialNumber	Identifies the serial number of the device.	Text field or can be compared to attribute from AD/LDAP
OSVersion	Identifies the version of the operating system.	Text field or can be compared to attribute from AD/LDAP
PhoneNumber	Identifies the phone number.	Text field or can be compared to attribute from AD/LDAP

MDM Attribute	Definition	Possible Values
DaysSinceLastCheckIn	Indicates how many days have passed since the endpoint has called home to the MDM.	Text field or can be compared to attribute from AD/LDAP
MDMServerReachable	Defines the MDM status which may be used as part of policy evaluation, so that endpoints may fall through to a rule if MDM is not reachable.	Drop-down selection, Reachable or Unreachable
MDMFailureReason	Identifies the reason that an MDM server might not be reached. The reason for the failure can be leveraged in a policy decision.	Text field or can be compared to attribute from AD/LDAP
MDMServerName	Identifies which MDM server was leveraged. Because ISE may connect to multiple MDMs simultaneously, this attribute can be used to uniquely identify a specific connection.	Drop-down list of configured MDMs

Configuring MDM Integration

Before you configure ISE to communicate with the MDM, ISE needs to trust the certificate of the MDM for the SSL-encrypted communications. You can accomplish this by using the following steps:

Step 1. Navigate to **Administration > System > Certificates**.

Step 2. Choose **Trusted Certificates**.

Step 3. Import the certificate of the MDM as a trusted certificate, as shown in Figure 17-69, and click **Submit**.

Figure 17-69   *Importing the MDM Certificate*

Now that the certificate is trusted, add the MDM server to ISE. You can configure and use multiple MDMs. For example, you may have an operation in Germany that requires its own MDM instance, separate from the ones that the rest of the company uses. To add an MDM to ISE:

Step 4.   Navigate to **Administration > Network Resources > External MDM**.

Step 5.   Click **Add**.

Step 6.   In the Name field, enter a name for the connection to the MDM.

Step 7.   From the Server Type drop-down list, choose **Mobile Device Management**.

Step 8.   From the Authentication Type drop-down list, choose **Basic**.

Step 9.   In the Host Name/IP Address field, enter the hostname of the server.

Step 10.   In the Port field, set the port to **443**, unless otherwise instructed by your MDM vendor.

Step 11.   (Optional) In the Instance Name field, if the vendor is multitenant-aware, enter the instance name.

Step 12.   In the Username and Password fields, enter the username and password for the MDM API authentication.

Step 13.   (Optional) Add a description.

Step 14.   Set the Polling Interval to **240** minutes.

Step 15.   Click **Test Connection** to test the connectivity.

Step 16.   Click **Save**.

Figure 17-70 shows the successful addition of the MDM.

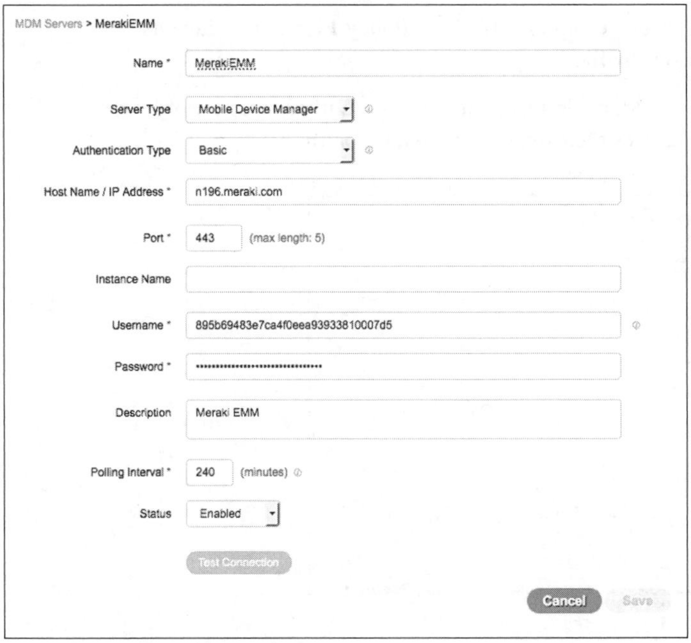

Figure 17-70 *Adding an MDM*

Configuring MDM Onboarding Policies

The MDM onboarding is configured much like the ISE BYOD onboarding. The authorization rules need to be configured to redirect the endpoint to MDM onboarding if it meets specific requirements.

One example of where to place an MDM onboarding policy is just below the BYOD onboarding rules but above the rule that would permit final access. Some organizations do not want to send all devices to the MDM, but prefer that specific devices be included. One way to achieve this is to maintain a separate list of MAC addresses belonging to corporate-owned assets and add that list to an endpoint identity group.

The example shown in Figure 17-71 does not use identity groups, but it represents a policy that has been used in production at a number of installs.

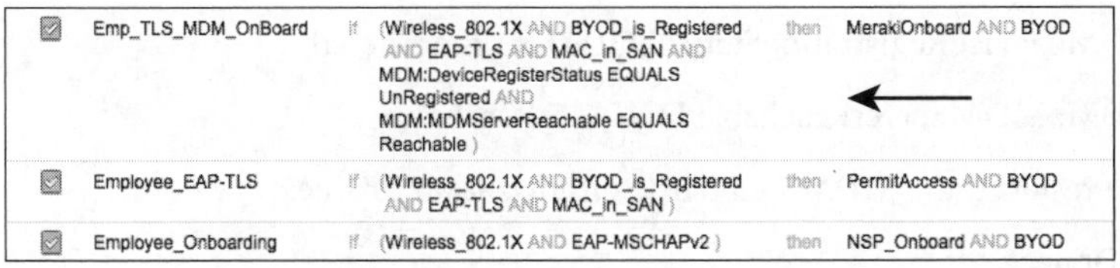

Figure 17-71 *MDM Authorization Rule Example*

The first step is to create the authorization profile that redirects the endpoint to the MDM for onboarding:

Step 1.   Navigate to **Work Centers > BYOD > Policy Elements > Results > Authorization Profiles.**

Step 2.   In the Name field, enter a name for the new authorization profile (Figure 17-72 uses the example MerakiOnboard).

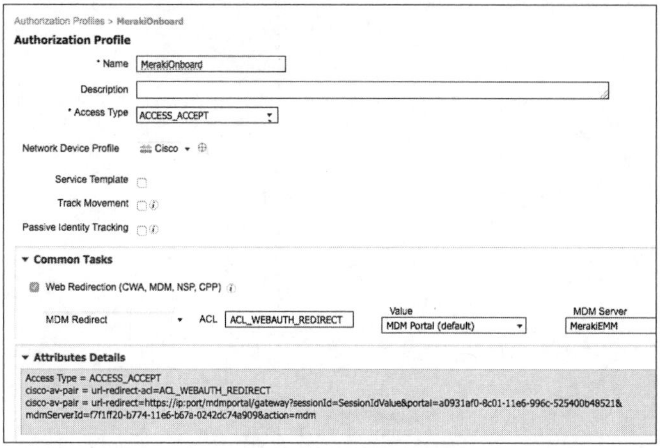

Figure 17-72   *MerakiOnboard Authorization Profile*

Step 3.   From the Access Type drop-down list, choose **Access-Accept.**

Step 4.   From the Web Redirection drop-down list, choose **MDM Redirect.**

Step 5.   For the Web Redirection ACL, reference an ACL that permits access to the MDM and ISE, but denies access to the rest of the Internet.

Step 6.   Click **Save.**

Now, create an authorization rule to send endpoints to the MDM for onboarding:

Step 1.   Navigate to **Work Centers > Network Access > Policy Sets.**

Step 2.   Duplicate the Employee_EAP-TLS rule above the original rule.

Step 3.   Name the rule (our example is named Emp_TLS_MDM_OnBoard).

Step 4.   Add the conditions, as follows:

■ MDM:DeviceRegistrationStatus EQUALS Unregistered

■ MDM: MDMServerReachable EQUALS Reachable

Step 5.   Set the result to the **MDM Onboard Authorization Profile.**

Step 6.   Click **Done.**

Duplicate the rule below so that it permits access to devices that are registered and meet the MDM compliance.

Step 7. Navigate to **Work Centers > Network Access > Policy Sets.**

Step 8. Duplicate the rule below it that permits access to devices that are registered and meet the MDM compliance.

Step 9. Name the rule **MDM Permit.**

Step 10. Modify the MDM:DeviceRegistrationStatus to be **Registered.**

Step 11. Add the condition MDM:DeviceComplianceStatus EQUALS Compliant.

Step 12. Set the Result to **Permit Access.**

Step 13. Click **Done.**

Step 14. Click **Save.** Figure 17-73 shows the final authorization policy.

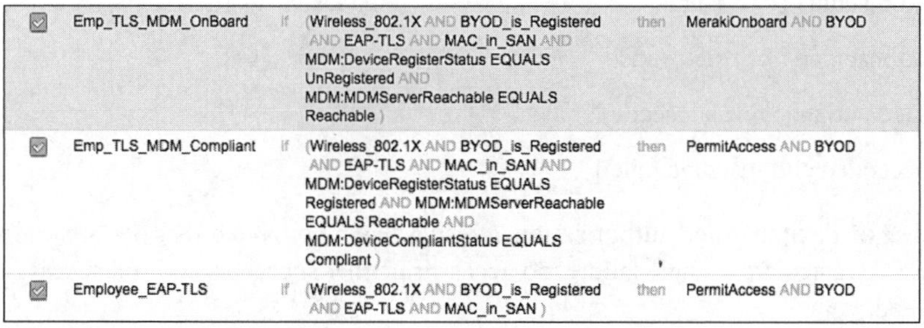

☑	Emp_TLS_MDM_OnBoard	If (Wireless_802.1X AND BYOD_is_Registered AND EAP-TLS AND MAC_in_SAN AND MDM:DeviceRegisterStatus EQUALS UnRegistered AND MDM:MDMServerReachable EQUALS Reachable)	then	MerakiOnboard AND BYOD
☑	Emp_TLS_MDM_Compliant	If (Wireless_802.1X AND BYOD_is_Registered AND EAP-TLS AND MAC_in_SAN AND MDM:DeviceRegisterStatus EQUALS Registered AND MDM:MDMServerReachable EQUALS Reachable AND MDM:DeviceCompliantStatus EQUALS Compliant)	then	PermitAccess AND BYOD
☑	Employee_EAP-TLS	If (Wireless_802.1X AND BYOD_is_Registered AND EAP-TLS AND MAC_in_SAN)	then	PermitAccess AND BYOD

Figure 17-73 *MDM Rules in the Authorization Policy*

The Opposite of BYOD: Identify Corporate Systems

For many years, customers have voiced their business need to identify the machine as an authorized asset, in addition to the user being an authorized user. Given that Microsoft Windows has both a user and a machine state, it allows the device to be authenticated to the network with what is commonly known as machine auth, as well as the ability to have the interactive user authenticated to the network.

The issue is that EAP was always designed to transport a single credential. The machine authentication occurs when there is no interactive user or if the supplicant profile is configured to only issue the machine's credentials. When the user logs into the system, it changes to a user state and issues the credentials associated to the user. With standard RADIUS and standard EAP, there was no way to join those authentications together.

To answer the issue, Cisco enhanced EAP-FAST with the capability to do EAP chaining. EAP chaining is the ability to authenticate both the machine and the user within the same authentication session. EAP-FASTv2 is being standardized on and should be known as EAP-TEAP when it finalizes standardization.

EAP Chaining

With EAP-FASTv2 and EAP chaining, both the machine and the user are issued a Protected Access Credential (PAC), similar to a secure cookie. So, ISE may request the machine PAC during the user authentication process, and the authorization policy is capable of using the results of either or both authentications.

The authorization condition is NetworkAccess:EAPChainingResult, and the options are as follows:

- No chaining
- User and machine both failed
- User and machine both succeeded
- User failed and machine succeeded
- User succeeded and machine failed

With that level of flexibility and authorization, a result may be provided that permits limited access to remediate a single failure, no access if neither succeeds, and full access if both succeed.

Figure 17-74 shows an example authorization rule that uses EAP chaining.

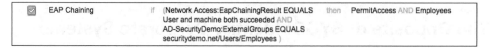

Figure 17-74 *EAP Chaining Authorization Rule Example*

A practical example from a customer was to use EAP chaining to identify corporate-owned and-managed devices. The authorization rule acted like this:

If

the device and user authentication both succeed

and the endpoint posture is compliant

and the user is a member of the PCI group in Active Directory

and the location of the endpoint is on a corporate campus

Then

permit full access

and assign the PCI Security Group Tag (SGT)

That authorization rule allows only those devices to communicate to the servers housing credit card data.

EAP chaining is part of RFC 7170 (TEAP) along with a slew of other secure networking enhancements. As of this writing, many vendors are in the process of incorporating TEAP into their products, but none were in production.

Summary

This chapter took an in-depth look at BYOD onboarding and MDM integration. It provided a brief look at identifying corporate assets and users with EAP chaining. The next chapter focuses on distributed ISE deployments.

Chapter 18

Setting Up and Maintaining a Distributed ISE Deployment

This chapter covers the following topics:

- Configuring ISE nodes in a distributed environment
- Understanding the HA options available
- Using load balancers
- IOS load balancing
- Maintaining ISE deployments

Chapter 5, "Making Sense of the ISE Deployment Design Options," discussed the many options within ISE design. At this point, you should have an idea of which type of deployment will be the best fit for your environment, based on the number of concurrent endpoints and the number of Policy Service Nodes (PSN) that will be used in the deployment. This chapter focuses on the configuration steps required to deploy ISE in a distributed design. It also covers the basics of using a load balancer and includes a special bonus section on a very cool high-availability (HA) configuration that uses Anycast routing, and covers patching distributed ISE deployments.

Configuring ISE Nodes in a Distributed Environment

All ISE nodes are installed in a standalone mode by default. When in a standalone mode, the ISE node is configured to run all personas by default. That means that the standalone node runs Administration, Monitoring, and Policy Service personas. Also, all ISE standalone nodes are configured as their own root certificate authority (CA).

It is up to you, the ISE administrator, to promote the first node to be a primary administration node and then join the additional nodes to this new deployment. At the time of joining, you also determine which services will run on which nodes; in other words, you determine which persona the node will have.

You can join more than one ISE node together to create a multinode deployment, known commonly in the field as an *ISE cube*. It is important to understand that before any ISE nodes can be joined together, they must trust each other's administrative certificate. Without that trust, you will receive a communication error stating that the "node was unreachable," but the root cause is the lack of trust.

Similar to a scenario of trying to connect to a secure website that is not using a trusted certificate, you would see an SSL error in your web browser. This is just like that, only it is based on Transport Layer Security (TLS).

If you are still using the default self-signed certificates in ISE, you'll be required to import the public certificate of each ISE node into each other ISE node's **Administration > System > Certificates > Trusted Certificates** screen, because they are all self-signed (untrusted) certificates and each ISE node needs to trust the primary node, and the primary node needs to trust each of the other nodes.

Instead of dealing with all this public key import for these self-signed certificates, the best practice is to always use certificates issued from the same trusted source. In that case, only the root certificates need to be added to the Trusted Certificates list.

Make the Policy Administration Node a Primary Device

Because all ISE nodes are standalone by default, you must first promote the ISE node that will become the Primary Policy Administration Node (PAN) to be a primary device instead of a standalone.

From the ISE GUI, perform the following steps:

Step 1.   Choose **Administration > System > Deployment**. Figure 18-1 shows an example of the Deployment screen.

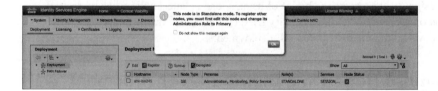

Figure 18-1   *Deployment Screen*

Step 2.   Select the ISE node (there should only be one at this point).

Step 3.   Click the **Make Primary** button, as shown in Figure 18-2.

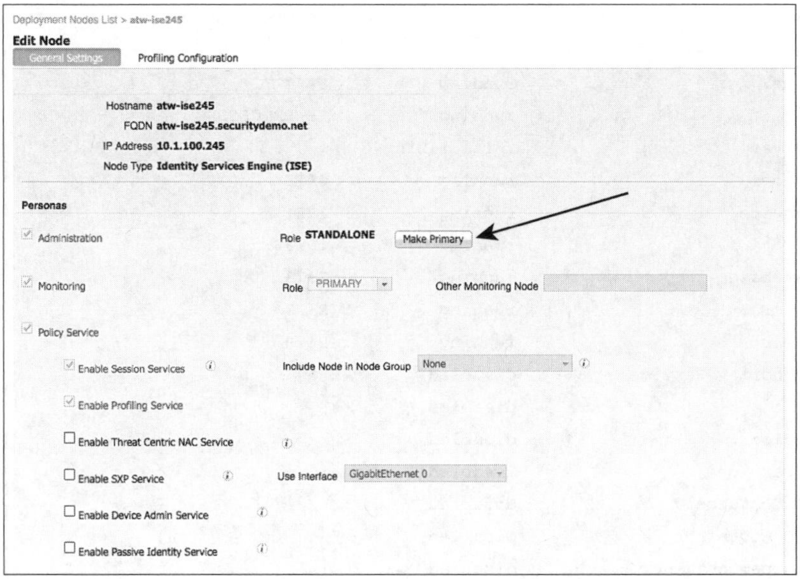

Figure 18-2   *Make Primary Button*

Step 4.   At this point, the Monitoring and Policy Service check boxes on the left have become selectable. If the primary node will not also be providing any of these services, uncheck them now. (You can always return later and make changes.)

Step 5.   Click **Save**.

After saving the changes, the ISE application restarts itself. This is a necessary process, as the sync services are started and the node prepares itself to handle all the responsibilities of the primary PAN persona. Once the application server has restarted, reconnect to the GUI, log in again, and proceed to the next section.

Note   You can monitor the status of the application server by using the **show application status ise** command from the command-line interface through either the console or a Secure Shell (SSH) session to the ISE node, as shown in Example 18-1. When the application server state changes from initializing to running, then ISE will be ready for you to log in to.

Example 18-1   show application status ise *Command Output*

```
atw-ise245/admin# show application status ise

ISE PROCESS NAME                    STATE            PROCESS ID
-----------------------------------------------------------------
Database Listener                   running          5851
Database Server                     running          75 PROCESSES
Application Server                  initializing
Profiler Database                   running          6975
ISE Indexing Engine                 running          1821
AD Connector                        running          10338
M&T Session Database                running          1373
M&T Log Collector                   running          2313
M&T Log Processor                   running          2219
Certificate Authority Service       disabled
EST Service                         disabled
SXP Engine Service                  disabled
TC-NAC Docker Service               disabled
TC-NAC MongoDB Container            disabled
TC-NAC RabbitMQ Container           disabled
TC-NAC Core Engine Container        disabled
VA Database                         disabled
VA Service                          disabled
pxGrid Infrastructure Service       disabled
pxGrid Publisher Subscriber Service disabled
pxGrid Connection Manager           disabled
pxGrid Controller                   disabled
PassiveID Service                   disabled
DHCP Server (dhcpd)                 disabled
DNS Server (named)                  disabled

atw-ise245/admin#
```

Register an ISE Node to the Deployment

Now that there is a primary PAN, you can implement a multinode deployment. From the GUI on the primary PAN, you will register and assign personas to all ISE nodes.

From the ISE GUI on the primary PAN, perform the following steps:

Step 1.   Choose **Administration > System > Deployment**.

Step 2.   Choose **Register > Register an ISE Node**, as shown in Figure 18-3.

Note   As with all other operations with ISE, DNS is a critical component.

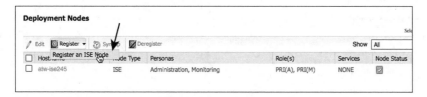

Figure 18-3   *Choosing to Register an ISE Node*

Step 3.   In the Host FQDN field, enter the IP address or DNS name of the first ISE node you will be joining to the deployment, as shown in Figure 18-4.

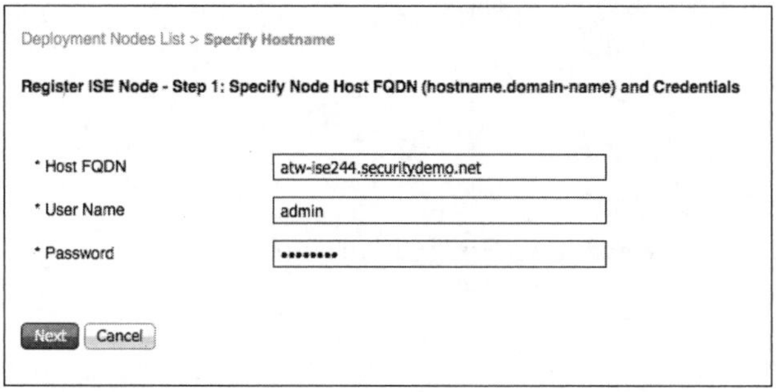

Deployment Nodes List > **Specify Hostname**

Register ISE Node - Step 1: Specify Node Host FQDN (hostname.domain-name) and Credentials

* Host FQDN	atw-ise244.securitydemo.net
* User Name	admin
* Password	••••••••

Next   Cancel

Figure 18-4   *Specifying Hostname and Credentials*

Step 4.   In the User Name and Password fields, enter the administrator name (admin by default) and password.

Step 5.   Click **Next**.

Note   If you have not installed valid certificates from a trusted root, you will receive an error. You'll be required to install the certificate of each ISE node as a trusted root, because they are all self-signed certificates. Best practice is to always use certificates issued from a trusted source.

Step 6.   On the Configure Node screen, shown in Figure 18-5, you can pick the main persona of the ISE node, including enabling of profiling services. You cannot, however, configure which probes to enable yet. Choose the persona for this node. Figure 18-5 shows adding a secondary Administration and Monitoring node, while Figure 18-6 shows adding a Policy Service Node.

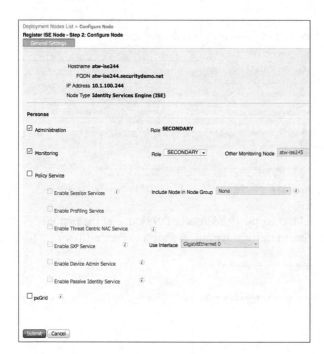

Figure 18-5 *Configure Node Screen Secondary Admin and MnT Addition*

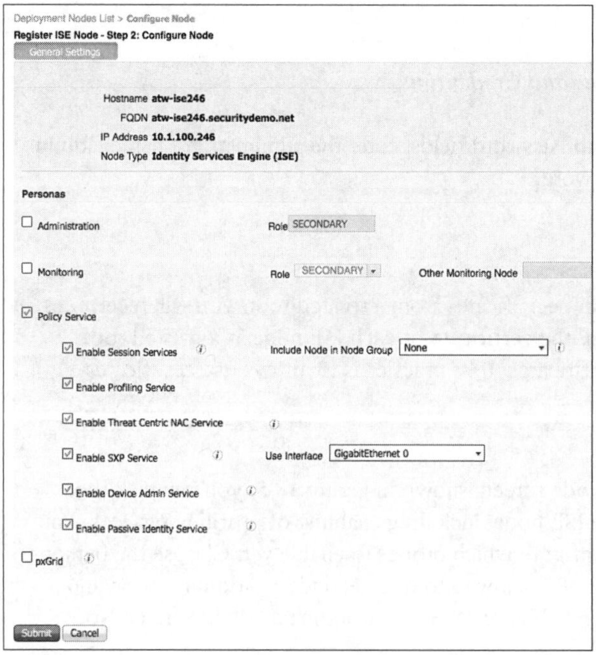

Figure 18-6 *Configure Node Screen Policy Service Node Addition*

Step 7.   Click **Submit**. At this point, the Policy Administration Node syncs the entire database to the newly joined ISE node, as you can see in Figure 18-7.

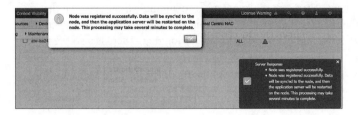

Figure 18-7   *Sync Initiated*

Step 8.   Repeat these steps for all the ISE nodes that should be joined to the same deployment.

Ensure the Persona of All Nodes Is Accurate

Now that all of your ISE nodes are joined to the deployment, you can ensure that the correct personas are assigned to the appropriate ISE nodes. Table 18-1 shows the ISE nodes in the sample deployment and the associated persona(s) that will be assigned. Figure 18-8 shows the final Deployment screen, after the synchronization has completed for all nodes (a check mark in the Node Status column indicates a node that is healthy and in sync).

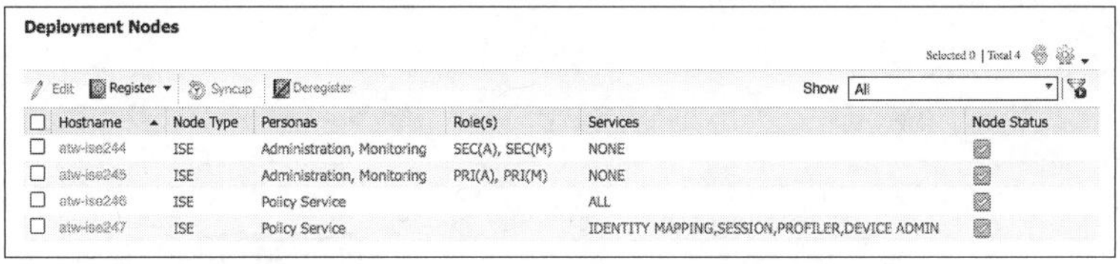

Figure 18-8   *Final Personas and Roles*

Note   This is also a good time to double-check that all the desired probes are enabled on the PSNs.

Table 18-1   *ISE Nodes and Personas*

ISE Node	Persona
atw-ise244	Administration, Monitoring
atw-ise245	Administration, Monitoring
atw-ise246	Policy Service
atw-ise247	Policy Service

Understanding the HA Options Available

There are many different items to note when it comes to high availability (HA) within a Secure Access deployment. There are the concerns of communication between the PANs and the other ISE nodes for database replications and synchronization, and communication between the PSNs and Monitoring nodes for logging. There is also the issue of authentication sessions from the network access devices (NAD) reaching the PSNs in the event of a WAN outage, as well as a NAD recognizing that a PSN may no longer be active, and sending authentication requests to the active PSN instead.

Primary and Secondary Nodes

PANs and Monitoring & Troubleshooting (MnT) nodes both employ the concept of primary and secondary nodes, but they operate very differently. Let's start with the easiest one first, the MnT node.

Monitoring & Troubleshooting Nodes

As you know, the MnT node is responsible for the logging and reporting functions of ISE. All PSNs will send their logging data to the MnT node as syslog messages (UDP port 20514).

When there are two monitoring nodes in an ISE deployment, all ISE nodes send their audit data to both monitoring nodes at the same time. Figure 18-9 displays this logging flow.

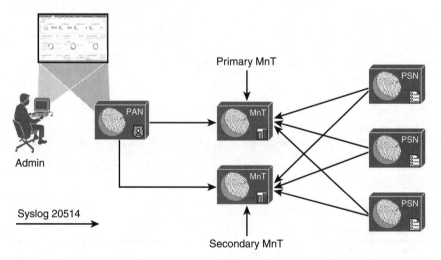

Figure 18-9   *Logging Flows*

The active/active nature of the MnT nodes can be viewed easily in the administrative console, as the two MnTs get defined as LogCollector and LogCollector2. Figures 18-10 and 18-11 display the log collector definitions and the logging categories, respectively.

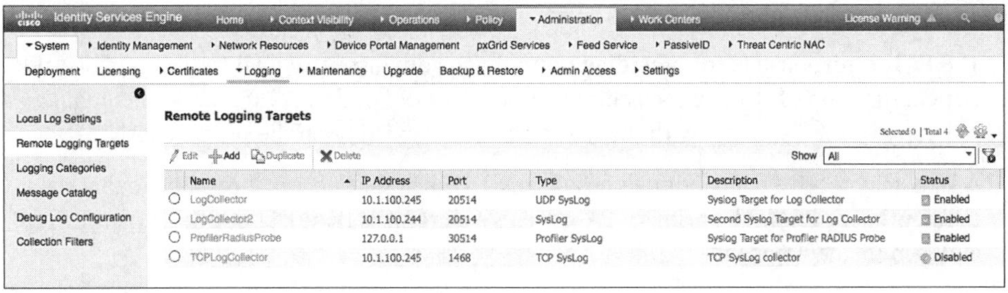

Figure 18-10 *Logging Targets*

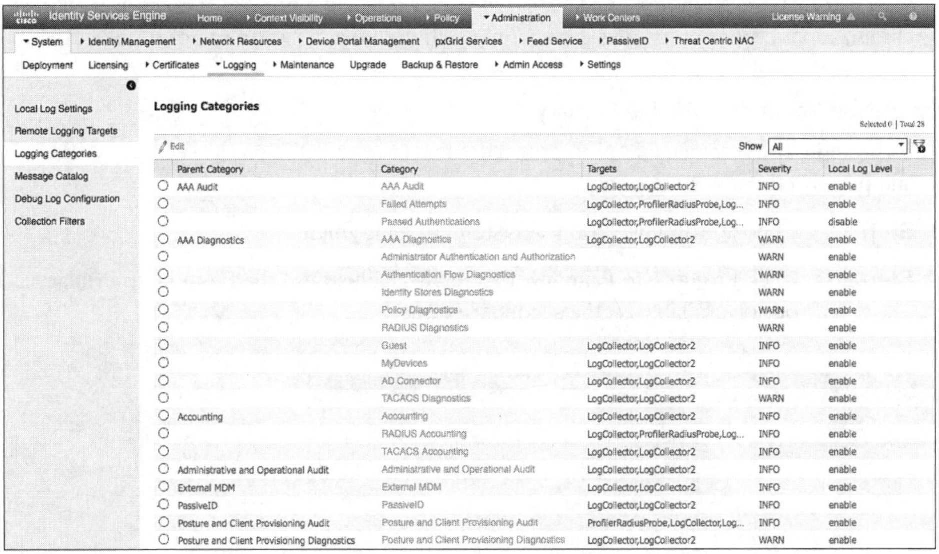

Figure 18-11 *Logging Categories*

Upon an MnT failure, all nodes continue to send logs to the remaining MnT node. Therefore, no logs are lost. The PAN retrieves all log and report data from the secondary MnT node, so there is no administrative function loss, either. However, the log database is not synchronized between the primary and secondary MnT nodes. Therefore, when the MnT node returns to service, a backup and restore of the monitoring node is required to keep the two MnT nodes in complete sync.

Note   The best practice for logging is to also send logging data to a security information and event manager (SIEM) tool, for long-term data archiving and reporting.

Policy Administration Nodes

The PAN is responsible for providing not only an administrative GUI for ISE but also the critical function of database synchronization of all ISE nodes. All ISE nodes maintain a full copy of the database, with the master database existing on the primary PAN.

A PSN may receive data about a guest user, and when that occurs it must sync that data to the primary PAN. The primary PAN then synchronizes that data out to all the ISE nodes in the deployment.

Because the functionality is so arduous, and having only a single source of truth for the data in the database is so critical, failing over to the secondary PAN is usually a manual process. In the event of the primary PAN going offline, no synchronizations occur until the secondary PAN is promoted to primary. Once it becomes the primary, it takes over all synchronization responsibility. This is sometimes referred to as a "warm spare" type of HA.

Promote the Secondary PAN to Primary

To promote the secondary PAN to primary, connect to the GUI on the secondary PAN and perform the following steps:

Step 1.   Choose **Administration > System > Deployment**.

Step 2.   Click **Promote to Primary**. Figure 18-12 illustrates the Promote to Primary option available on the secondary node.

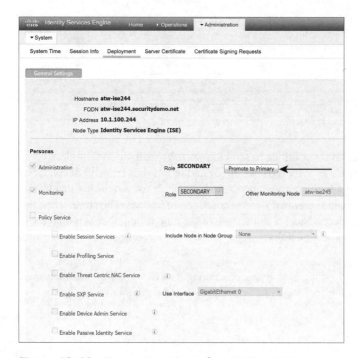

Figure 18-12   *Promoting a Secondary PAN to Primary*

Auto PAN Failover

An automated promotion function was added to ISE beginning with version 1.4. It requires there to be two admin nodes (obviously) and at least one other non-admin node in the deployment.

The non-admin node will act as a health check function for the admin node(s), probing the primary admin node at specified intervals. The Health Check Node will promote the secondary admin node when the primary fails a configurable number of probes. Once the original secondary node is promoted, it is probed. Figure 18-13 illustrates the process.

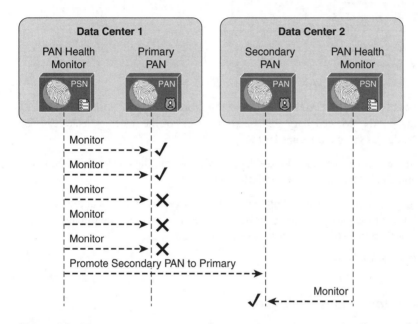

Figure 18-13 *Promoting a Secondary PAN to Primary with Automated Promotion*

As of ISE version 2.1, there is no ability to automatically sync the original primary PAN back into the ISE cube. That is still a manual process.

Configure Automatic Failover for the Primary PAN

For the configuration to be available, there must be two PANs and at least one non-PAN in the deployment.

From the ISE GUI, perform the following steps:

Step 1.   Navigate to **Administration > System > Deployment**.

Step 2.   Click **PAN Failover** in the left pane, as shown in Figure 18-14.

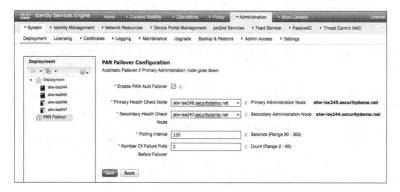

Figure 18-14 *PAN Failover*

Step 3. Check the **Enable PAN Auto Failover** check box.

Step 4. Select the **Health Check Nodes** from the drop-down lists. Notice the primary PAN and secondary are listed to the right of the selected Health Check Nodes, as shown in Figure 18-14.

Step 5. In the Polling Interval field, set the polling interval. The interval is in seconds and can be set between **30** and **300** (5 minutes).

Step 6. In the Number of Failure Polls Before Failover field, enter the number of failed probes that have to occur before failover is initiated. Valid range is anywhere from **2–60** consecutive failed probes.

Step 7. Click **Save**.

Policy Service Nodes and Node Groups

PSNs do not necessarily need to have an HA type of configuration. Every ISE node maintains a full copy of the database, and the NADs have their own detection of a "dead" RADIUS server, which triggers the NAD to send AAA communication to the next RADIUS server in the list.

However, ISE has the concept of a *node group*. Node groups are made up of PSNs, where the PSNs maintain a heartbeat with each other. Beginning with ISE 1.3, the PSNs can be in different subnets or can be Layer 2 adjacent. In older ISE versions, the PSNs required the use of multicast, but starting in version 1.3 they use direct encrypted TCP-based communication instead:

■ **TCP/7800:** Used for peer communication

■ **TCP/7802:** Used for failure detection

If a PSN goes down and orphans a URL-redirected session, one of the other PSNs in the node group sends a Change of Authorization (CoA) to the NAD so that the endpoint can restart the session establishment with a new PSN.

Node groups do have another function, which is entirely related to data replication. ISE used a serial replication model in ISE 1.0, 1.1, and 1.1.x, meaning that all data had to go through the primary PAN and it sent the data objects to every other node, waiting for an acknowledgement for each piece of data before sending the next one in line.

Beginning with ISE 1.2 and moving forward, ISE begins to use a common replication framework known as JGroups (http://bfy.tw/5vYC). One of the benefits of JGroups is the way it handles replications in a group or segmented fashion. JGroups enables replications with local peers directly without having to go back through a centralized master, and node groups are used to define those segments or groups of peers.

So, when a member of a node group learns endpoint attributes (profiling), it is able to send the information directly to the other members of the node group directly. However, when that data needs to be replicated globally (to all PSNs), then the JGroups communication must still go through the primary PAN, which in turn replicates it to all the other PSNs.

Node groups are most commonly used when deploying the PSNs behind a load balancer; however, there is no reason node groups could not be used with regionally located PSNs. You would not want to use a node group with PSNs that are geographically and logically separate.

Create a Node Group

To create a node group, from the ISE GUI, perform the following steps:

Step 1.   Choose **Administration > System > Deployment**.

Step 2.   In the Deployment pane on the left side of the screen, click the cog icon and choose **Create Node Group**, as shown in Figure 18-15.

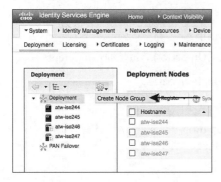

Figure 18-15   *Choosing to Create a Node Group*

Step 3.   On the Create Node Group screen, shown in Figure 18-16, enter in the Node Group Name field a name for the node group. Use a name that also helps describe the location of the group. In this example, SJCO was used to represent San Jose, Building O.

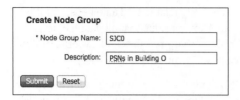

Figure 18-16   *Node Group Creation*

Step 4.   (Optional) In the Description field, enter a more detailed description that helps to identify exactly where the node group is (for example, PSNs in Building O). Click **Submit**.

Step 5.   Click **OK** in the success popup window, as shown in Figure 18-17. Also notice the appearance of the node group in the left pane.

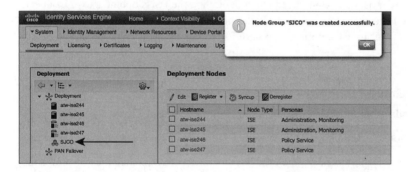

Figure 18-17   *Success Popup*

Add the Policy Service Nodes to the Node Group

To add the PSNs to the node group, from the ISE GUI, perform the following steps:

Step 1.   Choose **Administration > System > Deployment**.

Step 2.   Select one of the PSNs to add to the node group.

Step 3.   Click the **Include Node in Node Group** drop-down arrow and select the newly created group, as shown in Figure 18-18.

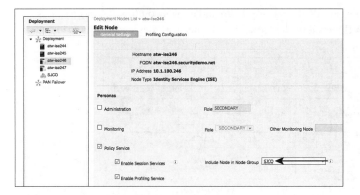

Figure 18-18 *Assigning a Node Group*

Step 4.   Click Save.

Step 5.   Repeat the preceding steps for each PSN that should be part of the node group.

Figure 18-19 shows the reorganization of the PSNs within the node group in the Deployment navigation pane on the left side.

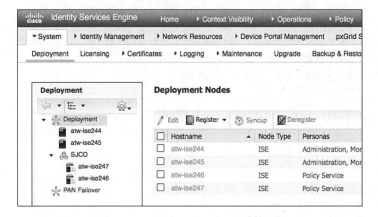

Figure 18-19 *Reorganized Deployment Navigation Pane*

Using Load Balancers

One high-availability option that is growing in popularity for Cisco ISE deployments is the use of load balancers. Load balancer adoption with ISE deployments has skyrocketed over the years because it can significantly simplify administration and designs in larger deployments. As Figure 18-20 illustrates, with load balancing, the NADs have to be con- figured with only one IP address per set of ISE PSNs, removing a lot of the complexity in the NAD configuration. The load balancer itself takes care of monitoring the ISE PSNs and removing them from service if they are down and allows you to scale more nodes behind the virtual IP (VIP) without ever touching the network device configuration again.

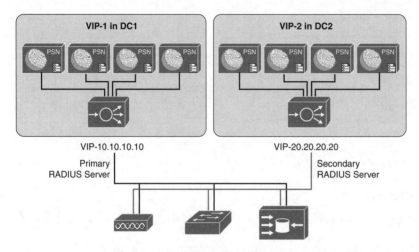

Figure 18-20   *Load-Balanced PSN Clusters*

Craig Hyps, a Principal Technical Marketing Engineer for ISE at Cisco, has written what is considered to be the definitive guide on load balancing with ISE, "How To: Cisco & F5 Deployment Guide: ISE Load Balancing Using BIG-IP." Craig wrote the guide based on using F5 load balancers, but the principles are identical regardless of which load balancer you choose to implement. You can find his guide here: https://communities.cisco.com/docs/DOC-68198.

Instead of replicating that entire large and detailed guide in this chapter, this section simply focuses on the basic principles that must be followed when using ISE with load balancers.

General Guidelines

When using a load balancer, you must ensure the following:

- Each PSN must be reachable by the PAN/MnT directly, without having to go through Network Address Translation (NAT). This sometimes is referred to as *routed mode* or *pass-through mode.*

- Each PSN must also be reachable directly from the endpoint.

  - When the PSN sends a URL-Redirection to the NAD, it uses the fully qualified domain name (FQDN) from the configuration, not the virtual IP (VIP) address.

  - You might want to use Subject Alternative Names (SAN) in the certificate to include the FQDN of the load-balancer VIP.

- The same PSN is used for the entire session. User persistence, sometimes called needs to be based on Calling-Station-ID.

- The VIP gets listed as the RADIUS server of each NAD for all 802.1X-related AAA.

  - Includes both authentication and accounting packets.

  - Some load balancers use a separate VIP for each protocol type.

- The list of RADIUS servers allowed to perform dynamic-authorizations (also known as Change of Authorization [CoA]) on the NAD should use the real IP addresses of the PSNs, not the VIP.

  The VIP could be used for the CoAs, if the load balancer is performing source NAT (SNAT) for the CoAs sent from the PSNs.

Note   ISE uses the device's Layer 3 address to identity the NAD, not the NAS-IP-Address in the RADIUS packet. This is another reason to avoid SNAT for the incoming RADIUS requests.

- Load balancers should be configured to use test probes to ensure the PSNs are still "alive and well."

  - A probe should be configured to ensure RADIUS is responding.

  - HTTPS should also be checked.

  - If either probe fails, the PSN should be taken out of service.

  - A PSN must be marked dead and taken out of service in the load balancer before the NAD's built-in failover occurs.

- Since the load balancer(s) should be configured to perform health checks of the RADIUS service on the PSN(s), the load balancer(s) must be configured as NADs in ISE so their test authentications may be answered correctly.

Failure Scenarios

If a single PSN fails, the load balancer takes that PSN out of service and spreads the load over the remaining PSNs. When the failed PSN is returned to service, the load balancer adds it back into the rotation. By using node groups along with a load balancer, another of the node group members issues a CoA-reauth for any sessions that were establishing. This CoA causes the session to begin again. At this point, the load balancer directs the new authentication to a different PSN.

NADs have some built-in capabilities to detect when the configured RADIUS server is "dead" and automatically fail over to the next RADIUS server configured. When using a load balancer, the RADIUS server IP address is actually the VIP address. So, if the entire VIP is unreachable (for example, the load balancer has died), the NAD should quickly fail over to the next RADIUS server in the list. That RADIUS server could be another VIP in a second data center or another backup RADIUS server.

Anycast HA for ISE PSNs

This section exists thanks to a friend of the author who is also one of the most talented and gifted technologists roaming the earth today. E. Pete Karelis, CCIE No. 8068, designed this high-availability solution for a small ISE deployment that had two data centers. Figure 18-21 illustrates the network architecture.

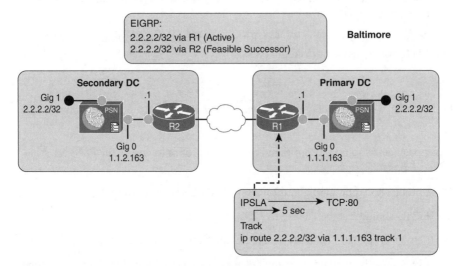

Figure 18-21 *Network Drawing and IPSLA*

Anycast is a networking technique where the same IP address exists in multiple places within the network. In this case, the same IP address (2.2.2.2) is assigned to the Gig1 interfaces on all the PSNs, which is connected to an isolated VLAN (or port group in VMware), so that the PSN sees the interface as "up" and connected with the assigned IP address (2.2.2.2). Each default gateway (router) in each data center is configured with a static route to 2.2.2.2/32 with the Gig0 IP address of the PSN as the next hop. Those static routes are redistributed into the routing protocol; in this case EIGRP is used. Anycast relies on the routing protocols to ensure that traffic destined to the Anycast address (2.2.2.2) is sent to the closest instance of that IP address.

After setting up Anycast to route 2.2.2.2 to the ISE PSN, Pete used EIGRP metrics to ensure that all routes preferred the primary data center, with the secondary data center route listed as the feasible successor (FS). With EIGRP, there is less than a 1-second delay when a route (the successor) is replaced with the backup route (the feasible successor).

Now, how do we make the successor route drop from the routing table when the ISE node goes down? Pete configured an IP service-level agreement (IPSLA) on the router that checked the status of the HTTP service on the ISE PSN in the data center every 5 seconds. If the HTTP service stops responding on the active ISE PSN, then the route is removed and the FS takes over, causing all the traffic for 2.2.2.2 to be sent to the PSN in the secondary data center. Figure 18-22 illustrates the IPSLA function, and when it occurs the only route left in the routing table is to the router at the secondary data center.

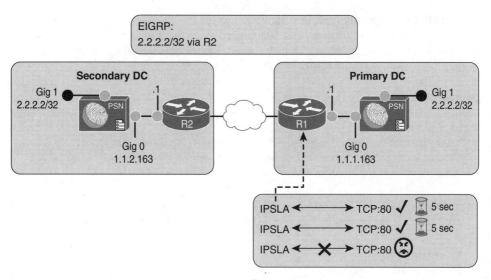

Figure 18-22 *IPSLA in Action*

All network devices are configured to use the Anycast address (2.2.2.2) as the only RADIUS server in their configuration. The RADIUS requests will always be sent to whichever ISE node is active and closest. Authentications originating within the secondary data center go to the local PSN.

Note The dynamic-authorization configuration of the NAD must still use the Gig0 interface IP addresses, as those will be the source when ISE sends a CoA to the switch.

Example 18-2 shows the interface configuration on the ISE PSN. The Gig0 interface is the actual routable IP address of the PSN, while Gig1 is in a VLAN to nowhere using the Anycast IP address.

Example 18-2 *ISE Interface Configuration*

```
interface gig 0
  !Actual  IP of Node
  ip address 1.1.1.163 255.255.255.0
interface gig 1
  !Anycast VIP assigned to all PSN nodes on G1
  ip address 2.2.2.2 255.255.255.255

ip default-gateway [Real Gateway for Gig0]
!note no static routes needed.
```

Example 18-3 shows the IPSLA configuration on the router, to test port 80 on the PSN every 5 seconds but to timeout after 1000 msec. When that timeout occurs, the IP SLA object will be marked as "down," which causes changed object tracking to remove the static route from the route table.

Example 18-3   *IPSLA Configuration*

```
ip sla 1
  !Test TCP to port 80 to the actual IP of the node.
  !"control disable" is necessary, since you are connecting to an
  !actual host instead of an SLA responder

  tcp-connect 1.1.1.163 80 control disable
  ! Consider the SLA as down if response takes longer than 1000msec

    threshold 1000
    ! Timeout after 1000 msec.
    timeout 1000
    !Test every 5 Seconds:
    frequency 5

ip sla schedule 1 life forever start-time now
track 1 ip sla 1
ip route 2.2.2.2 255.255.255.255 1.1.1.163 track 1
```

Example 18-4 shows the route redistribution configuration where the EIGRP metrics are applied. Pete was able to use the metrics that he chose specifically because he was very familiar with his network. His warning to others attempting the same thing is to be familiar with your network or to test thoroughly when identifying the metrics that would work for you.

Remember, you must avoid equal-cost, multiple-path routes, as this state could potentially introduce problems if RADIUS requests are not sticking to a single node. Furthermore, this technique is not limited to only two sites; Pete has since added a third location to the configuration and it works perfectly.

Note   There is an obvious, albeit rare, flaw in the design. With this design, we are using HTTP to validate the status of the node, rather than validating the state of the RADIUS service itself, since the status of the RADIUS service cannot be queried by IOS Changed Object Tracking. This works very well in most cases, but in the rare event that the HTTP service on a PSN is operational and the RADIUS service is not operational, it could theoretically cause issues.

Example 18-4   *Route Redistribution*

```
router eigrp [Autonomous-System-Number]
  redistribute static route-map STATIC-TO-EIGRP

route-map STATIC-TO-EIGRP permit 20
  match ip address prefix-list ISE_VIP
  !Set metrics correctly
  set metric 1000000 1 255 1 1500

ip prefix-list ISE_VIP seq 5 permit 2.2.2.2/32
```

Cisco IOS Load Balancing

Cisco network devices have a lot of intelligence built into them to aid in an intelligent access layer for policy and policy enforcement. One such intelligence level is the capability to perform local load balancing of RADIUS servers. This does not mean using a Cisco switch as a server load balancer instead of a dedicated appliance. Instead, it refers to the capability of the access layer switch to load-balance the outbound authentication requests for endpoints that are authenticated to the switch itself.

Enabling IOS RADIUS server load balancing only takes one additional command. After all the PSNs are defined as AAA servers in the switch, use the **radius-server load-balance** global configuration command to enable it.

Example 18-5 shows use of a **show** command to verify that multiple ISE servers are configured.

Example 18-5   *Verifying All ISE PSNs Are Configured on Switch*

```
3750-X# show aaa server | include host
RADIUS: id 4, priority 1, host 10.1.100.232, auth-port 1812, acct-port 1813
RADIUS: id 5, priority 2, host 10.1.100.233, auth-port 1812, acct-port 1813
RADIUS: id 6, priority 3, host 10.1.100.234, auth-port 1812, acct-port 1813
```

Example 18-6 shows how to enable IOS load balancing

Example 18-6   *Enabling IOS Load Balancing*

```
3750-X(config)# radius-server load-balance method least-outstanding
  batch-size 5
```

Maintaining ISE Deployments

Having a distributed deployment and load-balanced architecture are certainly critical items to scaling the deployment and ensuring it is highly available, but there are also critical basic maintenance items that should always be considered to ensure the most uptime and stability. That means having a patching strategy and a backup and restore strategy.

Patching ISE

Cisco releases ISE patches on a semi-regular basis. These patches contain bug fixes and, when necessary, security fixes. Think about the Heartbleed and Poodle vulnerabilities that were discovered with SSL. To ensure that bug fixes are applied, security vulnerabilities are plugged, and the solution works as seamlessly as possible, always have a planned patching strategy.

Patches are downloaded from Cisco.com, under **Downloads > Products > Security > Access Control and Policy > Identity Services Engine > Identity Services Engine Software**, as shown at the top of Figure 18-23.

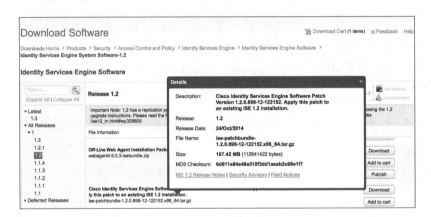

Figure 18-23 *ISE Downloads Page*

Search the list of software available for your specific version of ISE. Figure 18-24 illustrates the naming convention for ISE patches. Cisco ISE patches are normally cumulative, meaning that installing 1.2 patch 12 will include all the fixes in patches 1 through 11 as well.

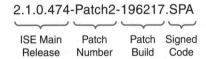

Figure 18-24 *Anatomy of ISE Patch Nomenclature*

After identifying the correct patch file, follow these steps:

Step 1.   Download the required patch.

Step 2.   From the ISE GUI, navigate to **Administration > System > Maintenance > Patch Management**.

Step 3.   Click the **Install** button, as shown in Figure 18-25.

Figure 18-25   *Patch Management Screen*

Step 4.   Click **Browse**, select the downloaded patch, and click **Install**, as shown in Figure 18-26.

Figure 18-26   *Installing the Selected Patch*

As the patch is installed on the PAN, you are logged out of the GUI and the patch is distributed from the PAN to all nodes in the ISE cube. After the patch is successfully installed on the PAN, it is applied to all nodes in the cube one at a time, in alphabetical order.

You can log back into the PAN when it's finished restarting services or rebooting. Click the **Show Node Status** button shown previously in Figure 18-25 to verify the progress of the patching. Figure 18-27 shows the resulting status of each node's progress for the patch installation.

Note   PAN Auto Failover must be disabled before upgrading, and can be re-enabled after the upgrade is completed.

Figure 18-27   *Node Status*

Backup and Restore

Another key strategy to assuring the availability of ISE in the environment is having a solid backup strategy. There are two types of ISE backups: configuration backup and operational backup. These two types are most easily related to backing up the product databases (configuration) and backing up the MnT data (operational).

Figure 18-28 shows the backup screen in ISE, located at **Administration > System > Backup & Restore**.

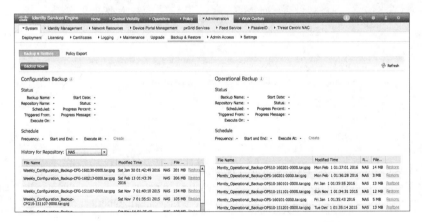

Figure 18-28   *Backup & Restore Screen*

As shown in Figure 18-28, the backups are stored in a repository, and can be restored from the same repository. You can schedule backups to run automatically or you can run them manually on demand. You can view the status of a backup from either the GUI or the CLI, but you can view the status of a restore only from the CLI.

Summary

This chapter reviewed the basic principles of deploying distributed ISE nodes, high availability for ISE Policy Administration and Monitoring & Troubleshooting nodes. It examined the pillars of successful load balancing with ISE Policy Service Nodes, failover selection on Cisco Catalyst switches, and IOS load balancing.

This chapter also emphasized the importance of having regular backups in addition to a highly available design, and described where to configure those backups in addition to patching an ISE deployment.

Chapter 19

Remote Access VPN and Cisco ISE

This chapter covers the following topics:

- Introduction to VPNs

- Client-Based remote access VPN

- Remote access VPN and posture

- Extending the ASA remote access VPN capabilities

You have read all about ISE and how it's a policy server for wired, wireless, and VPN; however, VPN has not been covered yet. While wired and wireless communicate in similar ways, remote-access VPN is vastly different; therefore, the way ISE integrates is also vastly different behind the scenes.

Introduction to VPNs

There are many different types of virtual private networks (VPN). A VPN can be used to connect two or more networks together, extending them almost like a wide-area network (WAN), except that a VPN uses an encrypted tunnel across public infrastructure (the Internet) to connect the networks instead of requiring the dedicated infrastructure of a WAN. This type of VPN is known as a *site-to-site VPN*, and is illustrated in Figure 19-1.

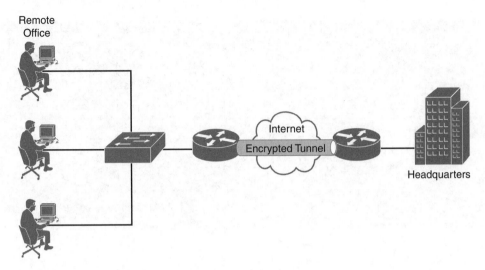

Figure 19-1   *Site-to-Site Virtual Private Network*

Because site-to-site VPNs simply join disparate networks into a single logical internetwork, ISE may still authenticate users and endpoints at the edge switch in the remote location. In other words, the site-to-site VPN is ultimately transparent to ISE, and the end users are treated the same as if they were connected to an access layer switch at the corporate headquarters.

Alternatively, virtual private networking also replaced dial-up networking in being the primary means of remote access to corporate networks directly from an endpoint. This type of VPN is known as a *remote access VPN* (RA-VPN).

To further classify VPN types, an RA-VPN can be clientless or client-based. A clientless RA-VPN is most commonly a method of providing access to internal data that uses a reverse-proxy mechanism, such that the endpoint never actually communicates directly to the corporate network. The VPN headend acts as a reverse proxy by publishing links to certain applications or data to the end user within an HTTPS secured portal that the user accesses through his or her web browser. When the end user attempts to access that published data, the VPN headend initiates the traffic and presents it to the end user through the secure web portal.

Figure 19-2 illustrates a clientless RA-VPN and demonstrates how it is a reverse proxy in nature.

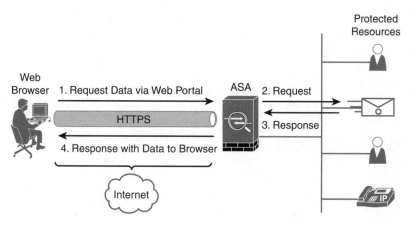

Figure 19-2 *Clientless Remote Access VPN*

Cisco Adaptive Security Appliances (ASA) and Cisco Firepower Threat Defense (FTD) Next-Generation Firewalls (NGFW) are common headends for clientless RA-VPNs. However, because the end user's endpoint never really communicates directly within the corporate network, traditional posture assessment is a technical improbability. Therefore, ISE integration is limited to traditional authentication, authorization, accounting (AAA) of the end-user logins; consequently, this chapter does not focus much on clientless VPNs.

The primary focus of this chapter is the client-based RA-VPN. It establishes the encrypted tunnel between software on the endpoint itself to the VPN headend, which could be located anywhere where there is a need to protect servers or data, such as the corporate headquarters or even in a cloud. Originally, this type of RA-VPN leveraged IP Security (IPsec) to provide the encrypted tunnel, but the industry moved quite hastily to using Secure Sockets Layer (SSL) as the encryption mechanism of choice. The primary reason for the move was ease of use—many environments do not allow IP protocols 50-51 and UDP port 500, which are required for the IPsec VPN to exit through their firewalls, but normally do not stop TCP/443 (SSL and TLS) or UDP/443 (dynamic TLS).

In truth, SSL has not really been used in years, and most of what you think is SSL is actually Transport Layer Security (TLS). Cisco AnyConnect uses TLS, and can use Datagram Transport Layer Security (DTLS) simultaneously for the VPN encryption. The overall VPN technology is still commonly referred to as "SSL-VPN," although it would be most accurate to refer to the client-based RA-VPN as "TLS-VPN" instead.

Figure 19-3 illustrates a client-based RA-VPN and demonstrates how the tunnel is formed between the VPN client and the VPN headend.

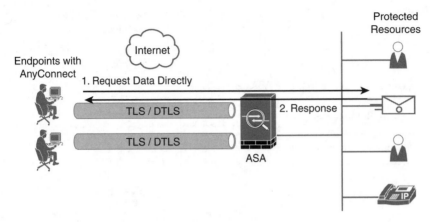

Figure 19-3   *Client-based Remote Access VPN*

An additional driver away from IPsec VPNs to SSL/TLS-based VPNs was the complexity and rigidity of the traditional IPsec configuration, key negotiation, and the static profiles for the endpoint client.

Now, let's add one more twist. IPsec uses Internet Key Exchange (IKE) for the exchange of encryption keys, and IKE version 2 (IKEv2) allows for a much more simplified VPN setup. The availability of the IKEv2 capabilities has revived the use of IPsec VPNs to some extent. In fact, Cisco AnyConnect Secure Mobility Client has support for IKEv2-based IPsec VPNs in addition to TLS VPNs.

Hopefully, this brief history and vocabulary lesson have been valuable to you. Virtual private networking is a broad topic that could easily fill its own book, and (as you know) this is an ISE book, not a VPN book.

Client-Based Remote Access VPN

As its name suggests, with this form of VPN, you must have a software client on the endpoint to establish the encrypted tunnel to a headend. The headend device could be located within your corporate data center, or even in the cloud—anywhere your organization has resources that need to be accessed and protected. For purposes of this discussion, the headend is a Cisco ASA or FTD NGFW. The endpoint software is the Cisco AnyConnect Secure Mobility Client (AnyConnect), which is deployed on more than 150 million endpoints around the world, making it far and away the number one RA-VPN client in the world.

At its core, AnyConnect is a VPN client, but it is also much more. The AnyConnect client is modular, allowing other Cisco security services modules to be fitted to the client. Many modules exist today, and more will be added in the future. Here are a few examples:

- **ISE Posture module:** Also referred to as the ISE compliance module, and also referred to as System Scan. This is the replacement for the older Cisco NAC Agent to provide posture. See Chapter 15, "Client Posture Assessment," for more details.

- **Umbrella Roaming module:** Connects endpoints to the Cisco Umbrella Secure Internet Gateway (SIG) service.

- **Network Access Manager (NAM) module:** An enterprise-class supplicant and network manager to handle wired and wireless connections along with the 802.1X authentications.

- **AMP Enabler module:** Reaches out to a distribution point and installs the Advanced Malware Protection (AMP) client.

So, how do you deploy AnyConnect onto the corporate endpoints? There are a number of installation options, but mostly they can be broken down into two installation models:

- **Pre-Deploy:** This mode enables enterprises to leverage their existing software distribution systems and push the client out to the managed assets before they need to connect to the VPN.

- **Web-Deploy:** This mode has the AnyConnect client staged on the headend. The end user can log in to the web portal on the ASA and have the client installed automatically through an ActiveX or Java applet, or the user can download from the web portal.

Note   In some cases, the Pre-Deploy package is used for the initial push, and Web-Deploy is used for updates going forward.

So, you need to install a client on the endpoint and set up a headend. In the typical fashion of this book, you'll learn as you configure.

Configuring a Client-Based RA-VPN on the Cisco ASA

You have several choices of tools to use to configure the ASA for a remote access VPN. You could use the command-line interface, the ASA Device Manager (ASDM) graphical user interface, or even Cisco Security Manager (CSM). This chapter shows you how to leverage ASDM for the configuration.

ASDM has several built-in wizards that you can use to configure the VPN. However, to learn the process, you need to step through the configuration manually. After that, you will understand what the wizards are doing behind the curtains. Here is an overview of the configuration steps:

Step 1.   Download the latest AnyConnect headend packages.

Step 2.   Prepare the headend.

Step 3.   Add an AnyConnect connection profile.

Step 4.   Add the ISE PSNs to the AAA server group.

Step 5.   Add a client address pool.

Step 6.   Perform network reachability tasks.

You *could* create each of the required items individually and then tie them together in the connection profile. However, ASDM brilliantly allows you to configure each of the items on the fly, which is what you are going to do in this section.

Download the Latest AnyConnect Headend Packages

Before focusing on ASDM and configuring the remote access VPN itself, download the latest AnyConnect packages from Cisco.com by navigating to **Support > All Downloads > Security > VPN and Endpoint Security Clients > Cisco VPN Clients > AnyConnect Secure Mobility Client > AnyConnect Secure Mobility Client v4.x**, as shown in Figure 19-4.

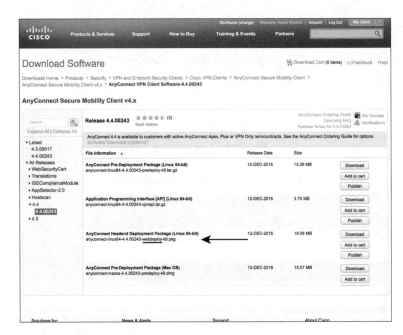

Figure 19-4   *Downloading AnyConnect from Cisco.com*

As you can see in Figure 19-4, locating the correct package is a bit daunting because there are so many folders listed and so many choices. With AnyConnect, you typically want to download the latest version (4.4.00243 at the time of this writing). When looking for the packages to load into the ASA, keep in mind that the names include the deployment method described previously in this chapter: Pre-Deploy packages are for downloading and installing manually or through a software management system, and the Web-Deploy packages are for loading into the ASA. The word *Headend* is also in the title, as indicated in Figure 19-4. Download all three Headend packages: Windows, Mac OS, and Linux. After you've downloaded the three AnyConnect packages, log in to ASDM; it is time to start configuring.

Prepare the Headend

After logging in to ASDM, follow these steps to prepare the headend:

Step 1.   Navigate to **Configuration > Remote Access VPN > Network (Client) Access > AnyConnect Connection Profiles**.

Step 2.   Check the **Enable Cisco AnyConnect VPN Client Access on the Interfaces Selected in the Table Below** check box.

If you do not have any AnyConnect packages loaded, you are prompted with "AnyConnect Client access cannot be enabled without a designated AnyConnect image. Would you like to designate an AnyConnect image?" (see Figure 19-5). If you do not receive this message, it means you already have AnyConnect packages installed on the ASA. In that case, navigate to **Configuration > Remote Access VPN > Network (Client) Access > AnyConnect Client Software** and click **Add** to follow along.

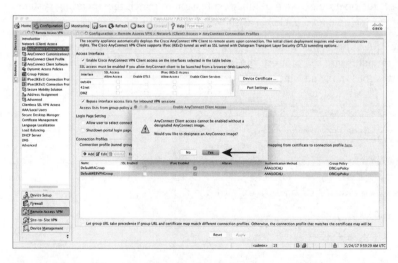

Figure 19-5   *Warning to Designate an AnyConnect Image*

Step 3. If you receive the prompt shown in Figure 19-5, click **Yes** to open the Add AnyConnect Client Image dialog box, shown in Figure 19-6.

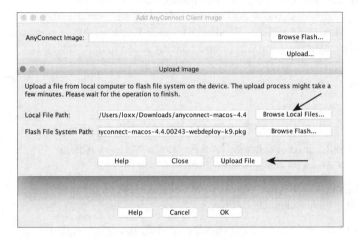

Figure 19-6 *Uploading an AnyConnect Package to the ASA*

Step 4. Click **Upload**, click **Browse Local Files**, and select one of the packages you downloaded, as shown in Figure 19-6.

Step 5. Click **Upload File**.

Step 6. Select the operating system regular expression to match the operating system type of the uploaded package, as shown in Figure 19-7.

The ASA expects the Windows client software to be the default, and therefore requires you to point out the operating system to match to the other images for Linux and Mac.

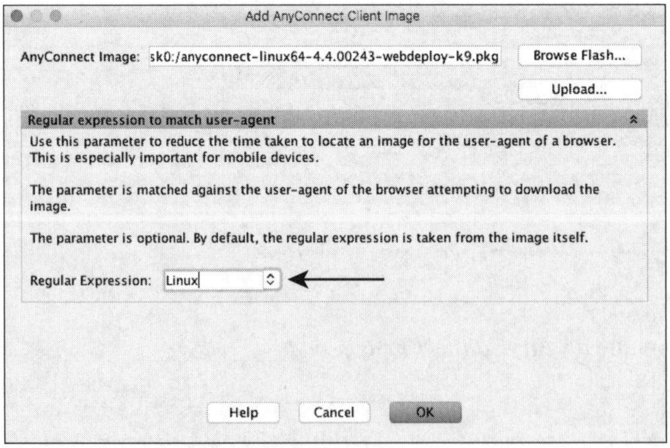

Figure 19-7 *Selecting the Operating System Regular Expression*

Step 7.   Click **OK** to complete the upload and mapping.

Step 8.   Repeat Steps 3 through 6 until Windows, Mac OS, and Linux are all uploaded. Skip Step 5 for Windows.

Step 9.   Click **Apply** to save the configuration changes to the running configuration.

Step 10.   Click **Save** to save the configuration to the startup configuration.

Figure 19-8 shows the final uploaded packages.

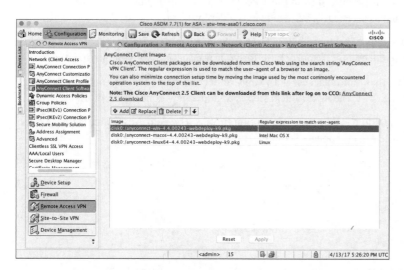

Figure 19-8   *Final Uploaded Packages*

Add an AnyConnect Connection Profile

Back on the AnyConnect Connection Profile screen, follow these steps to add an AnyConnect connection profile:

Step 1.   Check the **Enable Cisco AnyConnect VPN Client Access on the Interfaces Selected in the Table Below** check box.

Step 2.   In the interfaces table, choose the interface that you want to use for VPN access. Typically, the outside interface is used. In that case, check the **Allow Access** check boxes under SSL Access and IPsec (IKEv2) for the outside interface.

Step 3.   Check the **Enable DTLS** and **Enable Client Services** check boxes.

Note   Enabling DTLS allows AnyConnect to establish an SSL/TLS VPN using two tunnels simultaneously, a TLS tunnel and a DTLS tunnel. DTLS reduces the impact of latency on the VPN session and helps improve the performance of real-time applications, such as IP telephony, which are quite sensitive to delays.

Step 4.   Below the table, check the **Bypass Interface Access Lists for Inbound VPN Sessions** check box, which prevents the ACL from having to account for what traffic is permitted from the VPN users to the inside network. This is, of course, specific to your needs in the deployment.

Step 5.   (Optional) Check the **Allow User to Select Connection Profile on the Login Page** check box if appropriate for your production VPN deployment.

Now that remote access with AnyConnect is enabled on the outside interface of the ASA, the next logical step is to add a new connection profile.

Step 6.   Click **Add** to add a new connection profile. The Add AnyConnect Connection Profile screen appears, as shown in Figure 19-9.

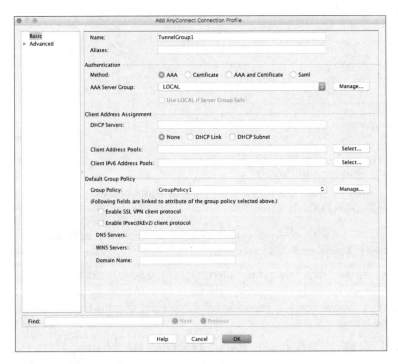

Figure 19-9   *Add AnyConnect Connection Profile Screen*

Step 7.   Rename the connection profile from TunnelGroup1 to something that makes sense to you and your users. For purposes of this example, use **ATW-ConnectionProfile**, as shown in Figure 19-10.

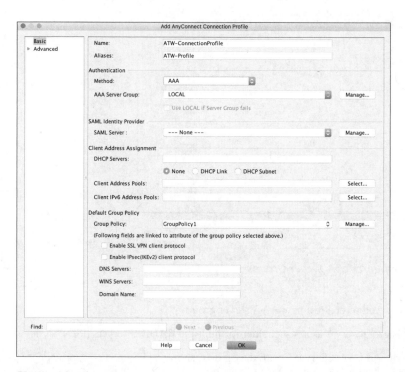

Figure 19-10   *Naming the AnyConnect Connection Profile and the Alias*

Step 8.   In the Aliases text box, provide an alias. This sometimes can be used by the end user to select from the drop-down list when connecting, and can be used for URL matching. For this example, use **ATW-Profile**, as shown in Figure 19-10.

Step 9.   In the Authentication Section, select **AAA** in the Method field and click **Manage**.

The VPN requires a mechanism to authenticate the users and authorize them to connect. (See Chapter 2, "Fundamentals of AAA," for a refresher on authentication, authorization, and accounting.) By default, the ASA uses a local user database. Obviously, this is a configuration *faux pas* that you must remedy immediately.

Figure 19-11 shows the Configure AAA Server Groups window.

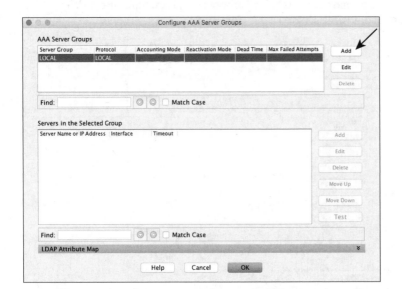

Figure 19-11 *Configure AAA Server Groups*

Step 10. Click **Add** to create a new AAA server group.

This group serves as a placeholder for multiple RADIUS servers (ISE PSNs).

Step 11. In the Add AAA Server Group dialog box, shown in Figure 19-12, provide a descriptive name that helps identify the servers that will be in this group. In the example, the group is named ISE231-232 because it will contain two ISE PSNs: atw-ise231 and atw-ise232. In retrospect, a better name would be SJC-ISE, describing the location (San Jose) and the server types (ISE), which considers the possibility of more PSNs being added in the future.

Step 12. From the Protocol drop-down list, choose **RADIUS**.

Step 13. Leave the Accounting Mode setting at the default, **Single**.

This is important. Single mode sends the accounting packet to the active RADIUS server only, whereas simultaneous mode sprays the accounting packets to all the RADIUS servers in the group. This is not a good idea, especially with RADIUS servers that track session state, like ISE does, and can have unwanted results.

Step 14. Leave the Reactivation Mode setting at the default, **Depletion**, the Dead Time at the default of **10** minutes, and the Max Failed attempts at the default of **3**.

With these settings, a RADIUS server will be marked unresponsive (dead) after three authentication attempts are not responded to. *Reactivation* refers to the method in which unresponsive (dead) RADIUS servers are brought back into service on the ASA. Depletion mode will not bring a dead server back until all the servers in the group have been depleted. Even so, it will wait 10 minutes by default (Dead Time).

Step 15. Check the **Enable Interim Accounting Update** check box.

Step 16. Check the **Update Interval** check box and leave the default value of **24** hours.

Interim accounting is important to ISE because it helps maintain that a user is still connected and the network session is still alive.

Step 17. In the ISE Policy Enforcement section, check the **Enable Dynamic Authorization** check box and leave the Dynamic Authorization Port setting at its default value of **1700**.

As you most likely know from reading the first 18 chapters of this book, *dynamic authorization* is the official name for Change of Authorization (CoA), which the ASA does a bit differently than the network devices that you have been configuring to this point in the book. For most of the use cases that you have seen within this book, a reauthentication CoA (CoA-ReAuth) is used.

Conversely, the ASA only uses a policy push type of CoA (CoA-Push). Here's the difference:

■ **CoA-ReAuth:** When a CoA is sent to the network access device (NAD), it in turn sends a request to the endpoint to authenticate again, in which case a full authentication and authorization process occurs again, with a new authorization result sent to the NAD.

■ **CoA-Push:** When a CoA is sent to the ASA, the CoA packet already contains the new authorization result. In the case of the ASA, that means a new ACL is being sent. More details on this method are provided later in the chapter.

Figure 19-12 shows the completed AAA server group.

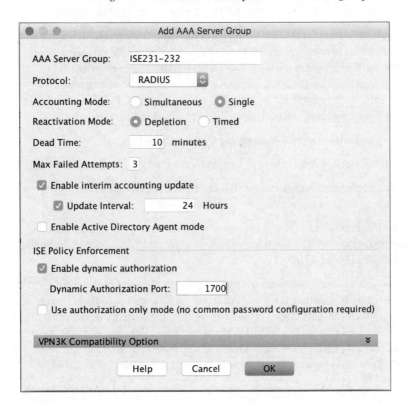

Figure 19-12 *Completed AAA Server Group*

Step 18. Click **OK**. Leave the Configure AAA Server Groups window open to proceed with the configuration in the next section.

Add the ISE PSNs to the AAA Server Group

Now that you have created an AAA server group, you are ready to add the PSNs to the group. With the newly created server group (ISE231-232 in the example) selected in the Configure AAA Server Groups window, as shown in Figure 19-13, follow these steps:

Step 1. To the right of the Servers in the Selected Group pane, click **Add** to create a RADIUS server object.

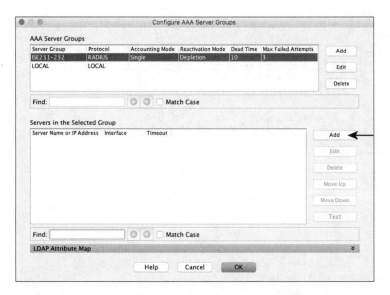

Figure 19-13 *Configure AAA Server Groups Window with New Server Group Selected*

Step 2.   In the Add AAA Server dialog box, shown in Figure 19-14, choose for the Interface Name the correct interface that is closest to the ISE PSNs. In the example, it is the **inside** interface.

Step 3.   In the Server Name or IP Address field, enter the first PSN's DNS name or IP address, and leave the Timeout value at the default **10** seconds.

Step 4.   Leave the Server Authentication Port and Server Accounting Port fields at their default values of **1645** and **1646**, respectfully.

Step 5.   Leave the Retry Interval at the default of **10** seconds.

Step 6.   In the Server Secret Key field, provide the RADIUS shared secret that is being used between the ASA and ISE. It must be the same as what is configured in the NAD object definition within ISE.

Step 7.   From the ACL Netmask Convert drop-down list, choose **Detect Automatically**.

This is an interesting setting. Whereas ACLs for Cisco Catalyst switches use a wildcard mask in the ACL instead of a standard netmask, the ASA uses a standard netmask for its ACL configuration. Because the ASA can accept the downloadable ACLs (dACL) that are sent from ISE, those dACLs could be configured for either the wildcard or the standard netmask method. The RADIUS server definition in the ASA can be configured for either, or to automatically detect which is being sent. Brilliant!

Figure 19-14 shows the final configuration for the RADIUS server.

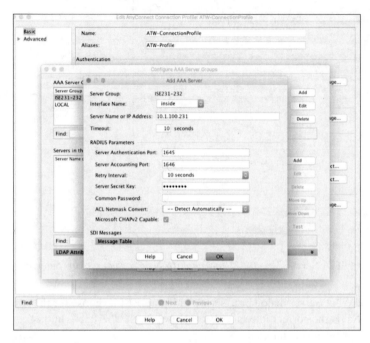

Figure 19-14   *Completed AAA Server Object*

Step 8.   Click **OK**.

Step 9.   Repeat Steps 1 through 8 for each of the PSNs.

Figure 19-15 shows the completed AAA server group.

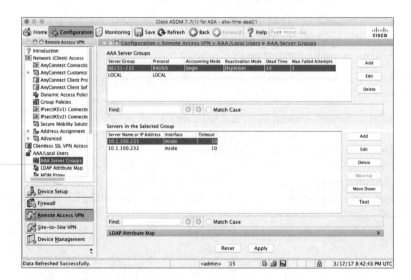

Figure 19-15   *Completed AAA Server Group*

Step 10.   Click **Apply**.

Step 11.   Click **Save**.

After clicking Save, you are returned to the AnyConnect Connection Profile window. You may choose to check the **Use LOCAL If Server Group Fails** check box if you prefer to fall back to the local user database if the ISE PSNs are unavailable, as shown in Figure 19-16.

The next step is to configure client address assignment.

Add a Client Address Pool

Figure 19-16 shows the connection profile after the AAA server group has been configured. The next item down in the configuration is the SAML Identity Provider section. This doesn't apply to the present ISE configuration example, so leave the SAML Server field set to None.

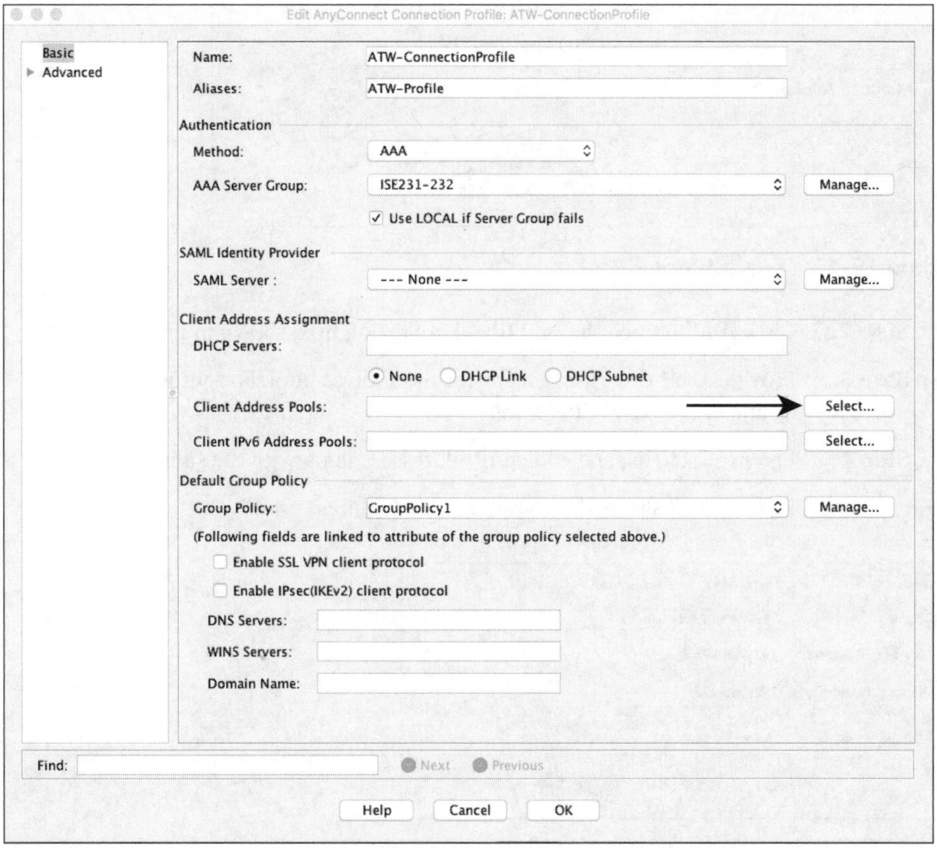

Figure 19-16   *Connection Profile in Progress After the AAA Server Group Configuration*

You do need to be able to assign an IP address to the clients when they connect to the VPN. As shown in the Client Address Assignment section of Figure 19-16, you can configure the connection profile to use an external DHCP server to assign IP addresses to the connecting endpoints, or you can use a pool of addresses configured locally on the ASA. This example uses the latter. The following steps demonstrate how to use a pool of addresses:

Step 1.   Click **Select** to the right of Client Address Pools, as pointed out in Figure 19-16, to open the Select Address Pools dialog box, shown in Figure 19-17.

Figure 19-17   *Select Address Pool*

Step 2.   Click **Add** to open the Add IPv4 Pool dialog box, shown in Figure 19-18.

Step 3.   Provide a self-descriptive name for the address pool. For purposes of the example, use **ATW-VPN-Pool**.

Step 4.   Enter the starting and ending IP addresses, along with the subnet mask.

Figure 19-18 shows the configured IPv4 address pool.

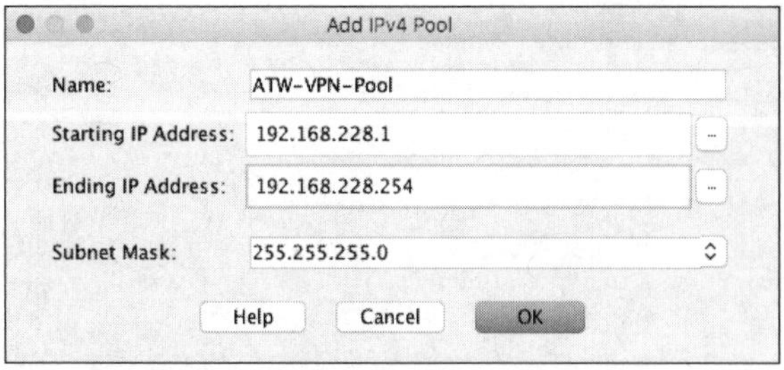

Figure 19-18   *Add IPv4 Pool*

Step 5.   Click **OK** to return to the Select Address Pools dialog box.

Step 6.   Select the newly created IPv4 address pool and click **Assign**, as shown in Figure 19-19.

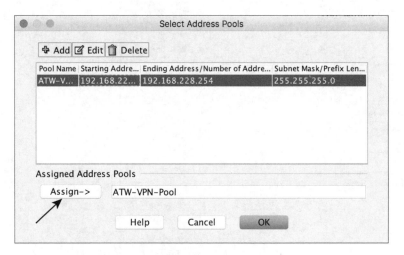

Figure 19-19   *Selecting the Address Pool*

Step 7.   Click **OK**. You are returned to the Connection Profile screen, with the address pool assigned.

The next logical step would be to configure a group policy, but that is not necessary for the goals of this chapter, so leave the default of **GroupPolicy1**, as shown in Figure 19-20.

Step 8.   Check the **Enable SSL VPN Client Protocol** check box.

Step 9.   Check the **Enable IPsec(IKEv2) Client Protocol** check box.

Step 10.   In the DNS Servers field, provide the DNS servers to be used for the connected clients.

Step 11.   In the Domain Name field, provide the DNS domain name to be assigned to the clients.

Figure 19-20 shows the configured connection profile.

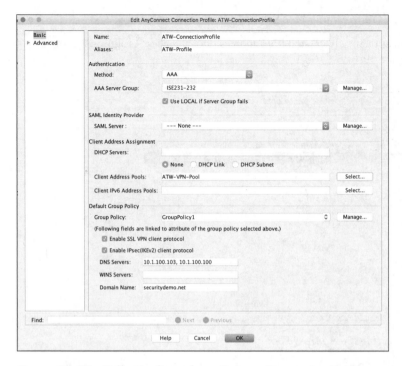

Figure 19-20   *Fully Configured AnyConnect Connection Profile*

Step 12.   Click **OK**.

Step 13.   Click **Apply**.

Step 14.   Click **Save**.

The AnyConnect connection profile now is fully configured, with an address pool from which to assign client IP addresses, ready to respond to SSL (TLS, actually) and IPsec(IKEv2) requests. However, you are not yet ready to have your clients join the VPN.

Perform Network Reachability Tasks

There are a few very important steps required to ensure that the VPN-connected endpoints can communicate to and from the other hosts in the network. These steps are often overlooked, leaving administrators scrambling to figure out why their VPN is not working. This section covers those steps.

Other hosts on the network need to know how to return traffic to addresses that are coming from the VPN pool. There are several ways to accomplish this task, the choice of which depends on the preference of your network team and whether you are running dynamic routing protocols on your ASA:

- If you are running a dynamic routing protocol, such as OSPF or EIGRP, you can redistribute the route for the address pool into that routing protocol.

> **Note** If you are running a dynamic routing protocol such as OSPF or EIGRP, you can also use reverse-route injection, as described in the Cisco document "ASA/PIX: Configure and Troubleshoot the Reverse Route Injection (RRI)" (http://www.cisco.com/c/en/us/support/docs/security/asa-5500-x-series-next-generation-firewalls/107596-asa-reverseroute.html).

■ You can add a static route in the network that sends all traffic for the VPN pool to the ASA.

■ Use the ASA as the default gateway. This option is common in smaller deployments, such as branch offices. In that scenario, the return traffic is already sent to the ASA.

The ASA in this example is the default gateway for this environment, and therefore the third option is used.

With the routing sorted out, the next step is to ensure that traffic to and from the VPN is exempted from network address translation (NAT). To accomplish this task, follow these steps:

Step 1.   Navigate to **Configuration > Firewall > NAT Rules**.

Step 2.   Click the drop-down arrow next to Add and choose **Add NAT Rule Before "Network Object" NAT Rules**, as shown in Figure 19-21. This ensures that the rule is processed correctly.

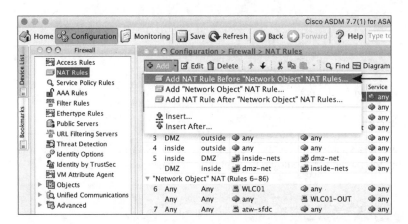

Figure 19-21   *Add NAT Rule Before "Network Object" NAT Rules*

Step 3.   In the Match Criteria: Original Packet section at the top of the Add NAT Rule dialog box, choose the **inside** interface of the Source Interface drop-down list, as shown in Figure 19-22.

Step 4.   Leave the Destination Interface field set to **Any**.

Step 5.   Change the Destination Address to be the addresses in your client address pool. You can use the network or create a network object.

Step 6. In the Action: Translated Packet section, leave the Source NAT Type field set to **Static** and the Source Address field set to **Original**.

Step 7. In the Options section, check the **Enable Rule** check box.

Step 8. Set the Direction field to **Both**, which ensures that the NAT rule is created for the return traffic as well.

Figure 19-22 shows the completed NAT rule configuration.

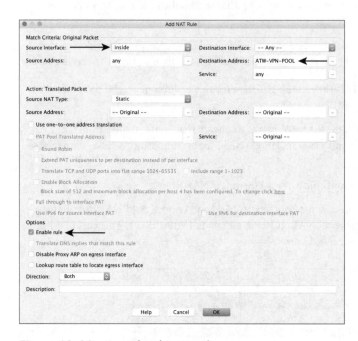

Figure 19-22 *Completed NAT Rule*

Step 9. Click **OK**.

Figure 19-23 shows the completed NAT rule in the NAT table. Ensure that it is at the top of the list, as shown by using the up and down arrows.

Figure 19-23 *Completed NAT Rule at Top of NAT Table*

Step 10. Click **Apply**.

Step 11. Click **Save**.

Configure ISE for the ASA VPN

At this point, all the required configuration in the ASA is complete, and it is time to move to the required configurations in ISE.

The ASA is an access-layer device when it acts as a VPN headend. Instead of an end user plugging in to a Catalyst switch port, or associating to the Wi-Fi SSID of the WLC, the user establishes a tunnel to the ASA.

Exactly like the switches and the WLCs, the ASA is the RADIUS client, and ISE is the RADIUS server. As such, you must ensure that ISE has a configured NAD object for the ASA under **Work Centers > Network Access > Network Resources > Network Devices**, and you must ensure that the RADIUS shared secret matches what was configured in the AAA server object in the ASA configuration. Figure 19-24 shows the configured NAD object in ISE.

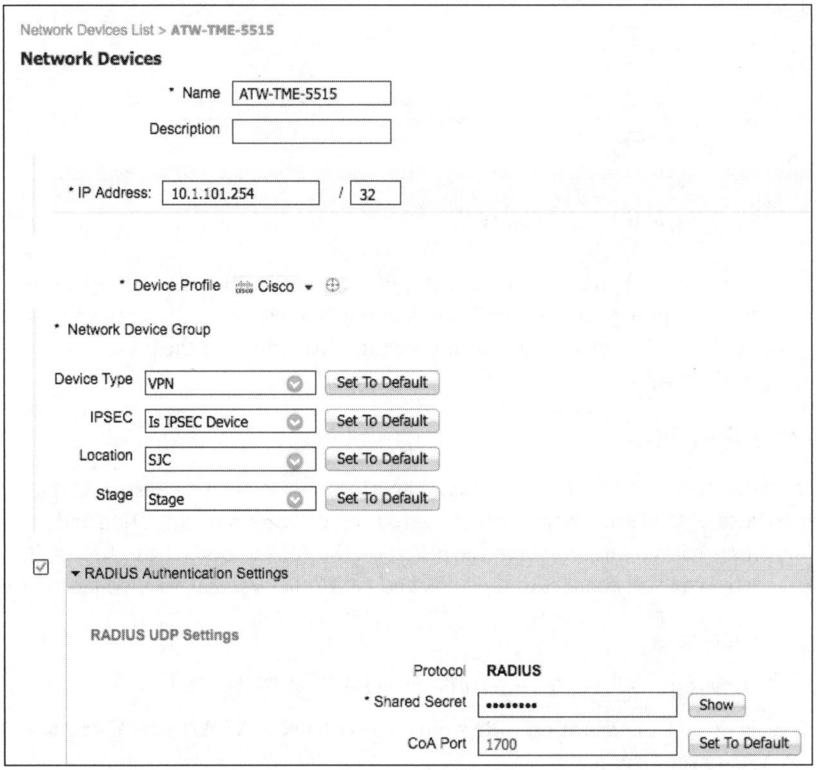

Figure 19-24 *ASA NAD Object in ISE*

Next, you need to configure the policy for remote access (go to **Work Centers > Network Access > Policy Sets**). The typical best practice is to dedicate a policy set for remote access policies, instead of blending them with a wired or wireless policy set. It makes it easier when troubleshooting, and avoids confusion when designing the policies.

Figure 19-25 shows an example policy set for VPN devices, with a generic authorization rule that sends a RADIUS Access-Accept if the user is a member of the Employees group in Active Directory.

> **Note** Always check with your company's security requirements, because a generic authorization rule might not be adequate in some cases. Many companies use an external identity store to authenticate against a two-factor authentication server.

Figure 19-25 *Sample Basic RA-VPN Policy Set*

This very simple policy is all you need to get the VPN authentication and authorization to work. Of course, the policy can be tuned and made much more specific to the needs of your organization. For instance, you can add posture assessment to the policy, as described later in the chapter.

Testing the Configuration

To test your configuration, the first test you should perform is a basic AAA test from the ASA to ISE, to ensure you have everything configured correctly for authentication and authorization. After that, you will log in to the portal on the ASA to download and install AnyConnect. Lastly, you will connect to the VPN and verify that you have full connectivity.

Perform a Basic AAA Test

The first test is to perform a basic AAA test. From the ASDM GUI:

Step 1.   Navigate to **Configuration > Remote Access VPN > AAA/Local Users > AAA Server Groups**.

Step 2.   Select the server group you configured earlier in the chapter.

Step 3. Select one of the PSNs you added to the AAA Server Group, as shown in Figure 19-26.

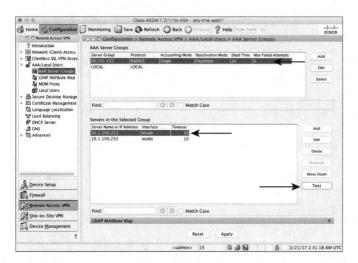

Figure 19-26 *Testing from the AAA Server Groups Window*

Step 4. Click **Test**.

Step 5. In the Test AAA Server dialog box, shown in Figure 19-27, choose **Authentication**, which actually tests both authentication and authorization because RADIUS performs both within a single transaction.

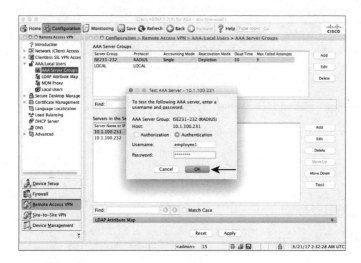

Figure 19-27 *Test AAA Server Window*

Step 6.   In the Username field, enter the username from Active Directory of the user who should receive an Access-Accept.

Step 7.   Enter the user's password.

Step 8.   Click **OK** to perform the test.

Step 9.   If all is configured correctly, you see a success message such as the one shown in Figure 19-28.

Figure 19-28   *Successful Test*

Log In to the ASA Web Portal

After confirming the AAA configuration in the ASA and in ISE is all correct, the next test is to log in to the web portal, where you can download and install AnyConnect.

From an endpoint that can access the outside of your ASA:

Step 1.   Open a web browser and navigate to the outside IP address of your ASA using HTTPS. For example: https://vpn.securitydemo.net/.

The URL automatically changes to /+CSCOE+/logon.html#.

Step 2.   In the portal, log in with a username and password, as shown in Figure 19-29. The username and password are sent to ISE via a RADIUS Access-Request.

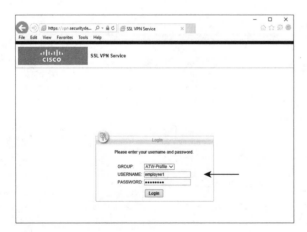

Figure 19-29   *ASA Web Portal*

Step 3.   Logging in to the portal automatically launches an ActiveX applet (Windows) or a Java applet (non-Windows) that installs AnyConnect.

■ If the applet fails to launch, you can download the manual installer directly from the portal.

■ If the endpoint already has AnyConnect installed, the applet connects the VPN using the credentials entered into the portal.

Step 4.   After AnyConnect installs or launches, you are logged in to the VPN with the tunnel established, as shown in Figure 19-30.

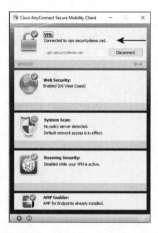

Figure 19-30   *AnyConnect Established VPN*

Also, don't forget to check the ISE RADIUS Live Logs to see the AAA from ISE's perspective, as illustrated in Figure 19-31.

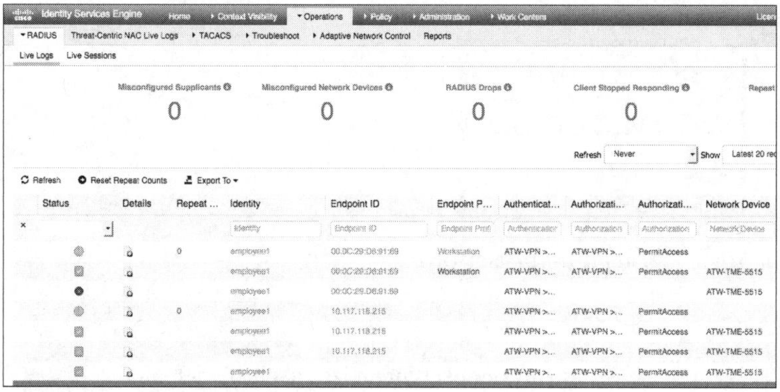

Figure 19-31   *Live Log*

Connect to the VPN via AnyConnect

The third and final test is to connect to the VPN directly from AnyConnect.

From the endpoint that can access the outside of your ASA, which now has AnyConnect installed:

Step 1.   Launch the AnyConnect Secure Mobility Client.

Step 2.   Enter the FQDN of the ASA's outside interface or the IP address itself into the VPN connection field, as shown in Figure 19-32.

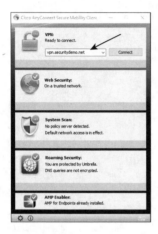

Figure 19-32   *Ready to Connect*

Step 3.   Click **Connect**.

Step 4.   Enter your username and password in the popup window, as shown in Figure 19-33.

Figure 19-33   *Enter Your Username and Password*

Step 5.   Click **OK**.

The VPN establishes and AnyConnect minimizes itself by default.

Step 6.   Click the AnyConnect icon in the system tray to bring the client user interface back up.

Step 7. Click the gear icon in the bottom-left corner of the AnyConnect client to bring up the status window, as shown in Figure 19-34.

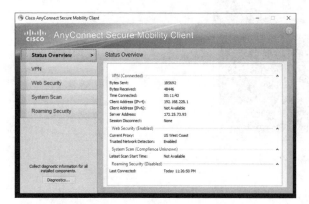

Figure 19-34 *Status Overview*

You can see in Figure 19-34 that AnyConnect was assigned an IPv4 address from the client pool configured earlier (192.168.228.1).

Step 8. Choose **VPN > Statistics** to see more connection information about the VPN, as shown in Figure 19-35.

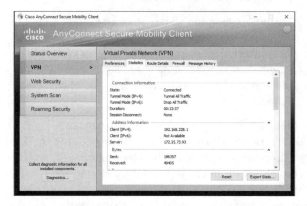

Figure 19-35 *VPN Statistics*

Finally, it's time to verify connectivity by trying to connect to a server in the corporate network.

Step 9. Using the web browser, connect to a server, as shown in Figure 19-36.

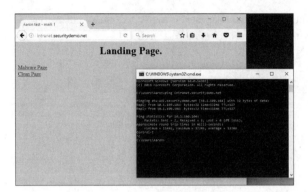

Figure 19-36 *Successful Connectivity to an Internal Server*

As you can see by the successful ping and successful web browsing to an internal server, the VPN connection is successful, and return traffic is also flowing back to the client.

Remote Access VPN and Posture

Thus far, we have focused on the ASA for remote access purposes only. However, as you well know, this is an ISE book! There is a lot more to network access nowadays than just basic authentication and authorization and the passing of traffic.

As you read in Chapter 15, "Client Posture Assessment," ISE posture assessment helps ensure that your endpoints are in compliance with your organization's host security policy. Posture assessment allows you to check the security "health" of your PC and Mac clients. This includes checking for the installation, running state, and last update for security software such as antivirus, antimalware, and personal firewall. With the ASA, there are two ways to perform this health check.

First, the ASA can use a function called HostScan, which is also available in the AnyConnect client as the VPN Posture (HostScan) module. This module performs the function of examining the endpoint software and patch installations, reporting the results back to the ASA. In this instance, the ASA is the policy server and the HostScan results are run through the Dynamic Access Policy (DAP), which will make changes to the endpoint's level of access. Examples of the changes are to apply ACLs, change settings in the web portal (clientless VPN), and quarantine the endpoint, among many other choices. However, all that fun you can have with DAP does nothing to tie into a single pane of glass for policy, or leverage the centralized control that you spent so much time creating throughout the many chapters of this book and beyond.

Therefore, the focus of this section is entirely on the other method to provide posture with the ASA: using the ISE compliance module in AnyConnect, also known as the System Scan module. This module is exactly the same as what you used in Chapter 15 to communicate with ISE and provide the security or "health" of the PC or Mac.

RA-VPN with Posture Flows

When using the AnyConnect ISE compliance module, the posture data is sent directly to ISE. This means the VPN tunnel must be established already; otherwise, the posture communication would never occur. Revisit Chapter 15 for more information on the posture discovery process; the focus here is on the basic flows as they relate to the RA-VPN.

Figure 19-37 shows the basic RA-VPN flows and their tie-in with posture.

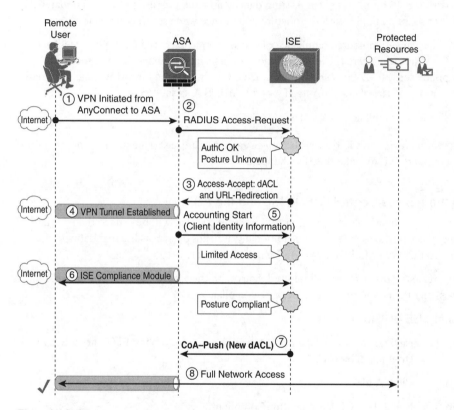

Figure 19-37 *Basic RA-VPN Flows with Posture*

Let's examine the steps that are in the flow:

1. The VPN is initiated from the AnyConnect VPN module to the ASA headend. Encryption is negotiated and then credentials are passed.

2. The ASA sends the user credentials to ISE within a RADIUS Access-Request packet. ISE processes the credentials and runs through the authorization policy. Assuming the user is allowed to connect, then Step 3 occurs and the user's session in ISE has the posture compliance value set to unknown.

3. ISE responds to the ASA with a RADIUS Access-Accept packet that includes the AV pairs for a URL redirection and a dACL. The dACL is applied to the user's session, limiting their access, and the redirection is for the ISE compliance module to be redirected to the ISE PSN.

4. The VPN tunnel is fully established and an IP address is assigned to the endpoint. At this point, the endpoint has limited access.

5. The ASA sends a RADIUS Accounting packet to the ISE PSN, which informs ISE of the assigned IP address.

6. With the access limited, and traffic redirected to the PSN, the ISE compliance module is able to communicate to the active ISE PSN and share the posture elements with ISE. ISE processes that posture data against the posture policy and updates the user's session in ISE with the posture compliance value set to compliant.

7. The change in posture compliance of the session triggers the CoA-Push. Unlike a CoA-ReAuth, where the authentication occurs again, running through the entire policy set, a CoA-Push sends down the new authorization (new dACL, no URL redirection) as part of the CoA itself, not a RADIUS Access-Accept.

8. The user has full network access.

This section reviewed the flow with the ASA and posture assessment. In the next section, you configure ISE to make this flow happen.

Adding the Access Control Lists to ISE and the ASA

ISE needs downloadable Access Control Lists (dACLs) that will be sent to the ASA at different stages of the user's session. Additionally, it needs an access list that defines what traffic to redirect to ISE and what traffic not to redirect.

First, create the dACLs that will be used. Start with the final dACL that will provide full access after the endpoint is found posture compliant.

From the ISE GUI, follow these steps:

Step 1. Navigate to **Work Centers > Network Access > Policy Elements > Results > Downloadable ACLS**.

Step 2. Click **Add**.

Step 3. Name the ACL **VPN-PostureCompliant**.

Step 4. Provide a description.

Step 5. Enter **permit ip any any** in the dACL Content field, or provide a more restrictive ACL if it suits your organizational needs.

Step 6. Click **Check DACL Syntax** to ensure there were not any typos.

Step 7. Click **Submit**.

Figure 19-38 shows the complete VPN-PostureCompliant dACL.

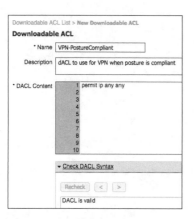

Figure 19-38 *VPN-PostureCompliant dACL*

Next, you need another dACL that limits traffic through the ASA for the endpoints that are posture-unknown or posture-noncompliant. This dACL should be set up to permit traffic destined to ISE nodes, the DNS server, and other critical infrastructure, just as you did in Chapter 15. It should permit access to the remediation server, and deny all other traffic.

Step 8. Click **Add**.

Step 9. Name the ACL **VPN-PostureNotCompliant**.

Step 10. Provide a description.

Step 11. In the dACL Content field, type **permit ip any host** *ISE_PSN*.

Step 12. Repeat Step 11 for each ISE PSN.

Step 13. Type **permit ip any host** *DNS_server*.

Step 14. Type **permit ip any host** *remediation_server*.

Step 15. Type **permit ip any** *internal network*.

Step 16. Type **deny ip any any**, or provide a more restrictive ACL if it suits your organizational needs.

Step 17. Click **Check DACL Syntax** to ensure there were not any typos.

Step 18. Click **Submit**.

Figure 19-39 shows the complete VPN-PostureNotCompliant dACL.

Figure 19-39   *VPN-PostureNotCompliant dACL*

The redirection ACL is configured locally on the ASA, not in ISE. It needs to be configured to deny any traffic that shouldn't be redirected, and permit any traffic that should be redirected.

Step 19.   From ASDM, navigate to **Configuration > Network (Client) Access > Advanced > ACL Manager.**

Step 20.   Click **Add > ACL.**

Step 21.   Name the ACL **POSTURE-REDIRECT**, as shown in Figure 19-40.

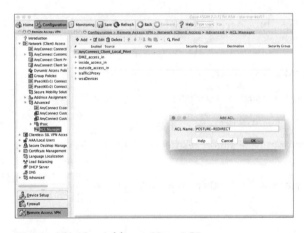

Figure 19-40   *Adding a New ACL*

Step 22.   Click **OK.**

Step 23.   With the newly created POSTURE-REDIRECT ACL selected, click **Add > ACE.**

Step 24. Add an ACE configured to deny traffic from any source to TCP port 8905 for posture discovery.

Step 25. Add an ACE configured to deny traffic from any source to UDP port 8905 for posture discovery.

Step 26. Add an ACE that denies traffic from any source to UDP port 53 for DNS.

Step 27. Add an ACE that denies traffic from any source to the remediation server.

Step 28. Add an ACE that permits traffic from any source to HTTP and HTTPS, to cause redirection.

Step 29. Add an ACE that denies all other traffic, which will *not* redirect any of the traffic that is not explicitly denied in the preceding steps.

Figure 19-41 shows the complete POSTURE-REDIRECT ACL.

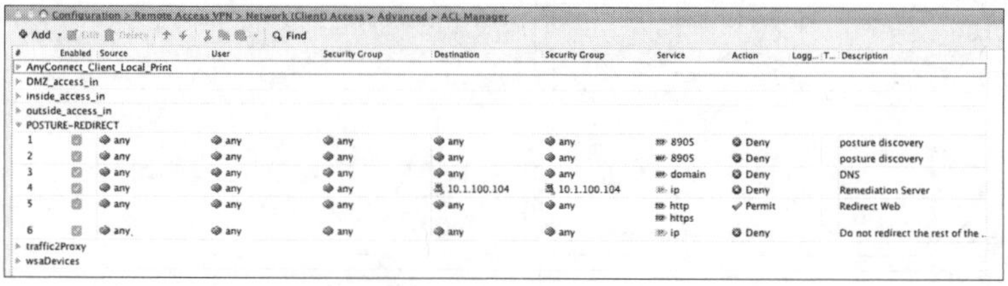

Figure 19-41 *POSTURE-REDIRECT ACL*

Step 30. Click **Apply**.

Step 31. Click **Save**.

Adding Posture Policies to the VPN Policy Set

You created posture checks, requirements, remediations, and policies in Chapter 15. Those same policies are used in this section, but are extended to the VPN policy set.

What remains in ISE is to create the authorization profiles that will use the dACLs you created previously, and then finally to create the authorization rules.

Create the Authorization Profiles

First, create the pre-posture authorization result. From the ISE GUI:

Step 1. Navigate to **Work Centers > Network Access > Policy Elements > Results > Authorization Profiles**.

Step 2. Click **Add**.

Step 3. Name the profile **VPN-Posture-Redirect**.

Step 4. Provide a description.

Step 5.   Ensure that the Access Type field is set to **ACCESS_ACCEPT**.

Step 6.   Under Common Tasks, check the **DACL Name** check box and choose the **VPN-PostureNonCompliant** dACL from the drop-down list.

Step 7.   Check the **Web Redirection** check box and choose **Client Provisioning (Posture)**.

Step 8.   For the ACL, type **POSTURE-REDIRECT**, which is the ACL you configured locally on the ASA.

Step 9.   From the Value drop-down list, choose **Client Provisioning Portal**.

Figure 19-42 shows the complete VPN-Posture-Redirect authorization profile.

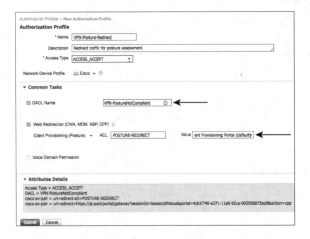

Figure 19-42   *VPN-Posture-Redirect Authorization Profile*

Step 10.   Click **Submit**.

Now, create the post-posture authorization result to be used after the endpoint is compliant.

From the ISE GUI:

Step 11.   Click **Add**.

Step 12.   Name the profile **VPN-Full-Access**.

Step 13.   Provide a description.

Step 14.   Ensure that Access Type field is set to **ACCESS_ACCEPT**.

Step 15.   Under Common Tasks, check the **DACL Name** check box and choose the **VPN-PostureCompliant** dACL from the drop-down list.

Step 16.   Click **Submit**.

Create the Authorization Policies

The authorization profiles are created, so now it's time to create the authorization policies.

Navigate to **Work Centers > Network Access > Policy Sets**. Choose the VPN Policy Set, and insert a rule at the top that looks for endpoints where Session:PostureStatus NOT_ EQUALS Compliant, and set the authorization result to be the **VPN-Posture-Redirect** profile, which limits access and redirects the posture traffic.

You also need to insert a rule below that one that looks for a condition where Session:PostureStatus EQUALS Compliant, and set the authorization result to be the **VPN-Full-Access** profile, which removes the redirection and replaces the traffic-limiting dACL with the less-restrictive dACL.

Figure 19-43 shows an example policy set leveraging a rule that redirects the endpoint to get posture, and another rule that permits full access.

Figure 19-43   *Example Modified VPN Policy Set*

Watching It Work

To see the fruits of your labor, connect to the VPN from an endpoint. Watching the AnyConnect client, the System Scan module should inform the end user about the posture checks occurring, as shown in Figure 19-44.

Figure 19-44   *AnyConnect System Scan Module in Progress*

From the ISE user interface, you can immediately focus on "old faithful," the ISE Live Log. As you can see in Figure 19-45, the Live Log allows you to watch the endpoint join the network, and watch all the activity that is happening related to the posture and CoA.

Status
Details
Identity
Endpoint ID
Endpoint Profile
Authentication P...
Authorization Policy
Authorization Profiles
Posture Status
5
#ACSACL#-IP-VPN-PostureCompliant...
4
10.117.11...
VPN-Full-Access
Compliant
3
employee1
00:0C:29:...
Windows7-Workst...
ATW-VPN >> Defa...
ATW-VPN >> Employee-PostureRedirect
VPN-Posture-Redirect
Compliant
2
#ACSACL#-IP-VPN-PostureNotCompl...
1
employee1
00:0C:29:...
Windows7-Workst...
ATW-VPN >> Defa...
ATW-VPN >> Employee-PostureRedirect
VPN-Posture-Redirect
Pending

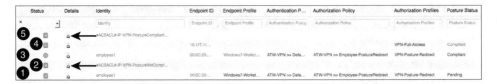

Figure 19-45 *Example Live Log*

Figure 19-45 shows an example policy set leveraging a rule that redirects the endpoint to get posture, and another rule that permits full access.

Let's examine what transpired in the Live Log snapshot in Figure 19-45:

1. The initial authentication and authorization. The posture was not known, and listed in Live Log as Pending, and therefore the resulting authorization rule is Employee-PostureRedirect.
2. The dACL was sent from ISE to the ASA, and the ASA has acknowledged the success. Click the Details icon for this entry to see the detailed report. Figure 19-46 shows a snippet of the details report of this Live Log entry. Notice in Figure 19-46 each line of the dACL is shown along with the success messages.

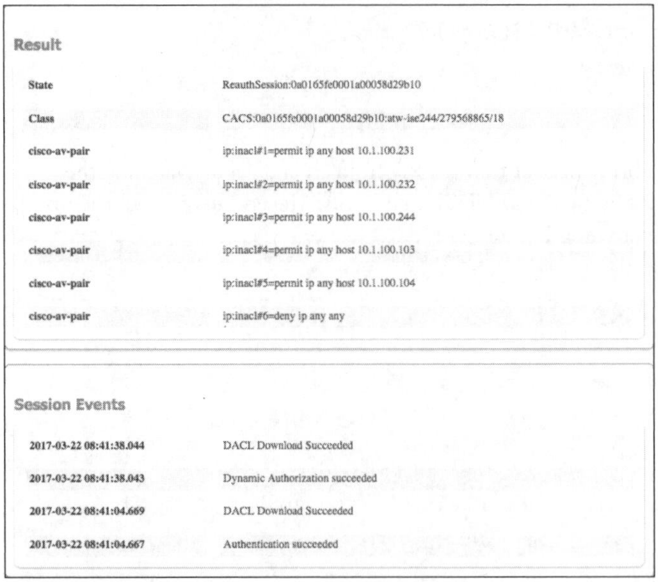
Result
State
ReauthSession:0a0165fe0001a00058d29b10
Class
CACS:0a0165fe0001a00058d29b10:atw-ise244/279568865/18
cisco-av-pair
ip:inacl#1=permit ip any host 10.1.100.231
cisco-av-pair
ip:inacl#2=permit ip any host 10.1.100.232
cisco-av-pair
ip:inacl#3=permit ip any host 10.1.100.244
cisco-av-pair
ip:inacl#4=permit ip any host 10.1.100.103
cisco-av-pair
ip:inacl#5=permit ip any host 10.1.100.104
cisco-av-pair
ip:inacl#6=deny ip any any
Session Events
2017-03-22 08:41:38.044
DACL Download Succeeded
2017-03-22 08:41:38.043
Dynamic Authorization succeeded
2017-03-22 08:41:04.669
DACL Download Succeeded
2017-03-22 08:41:04.667
Authentication succeeded

Figure 19-46 *Report Snippet for dACL Download*

3. The *i* in the Status column for this entry identifies it as an informational event, showing that the endpoint's posture status is now compliant.

4. This entry is the CoA initializing from ISE to the ASA.

5. This final entry is the success of the dACL. Click the Details icon for this entry to see the detailed report. Figure 19-47 shows a portion of the details report, where the session settled into its final state.

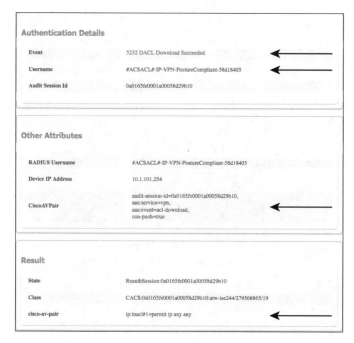

Figure 19-47   *Report Snippet for the Final dACL of the Session*

Finally, you can always look at the session from the ASA's perspective. You can use either the command-line interface or one of the graphical interfaces, such as ASDM. The CLI tends to be easier to view and understand in this context, so we'll switch to that to view the session.

The CLI command to view the session is **show vpn-sessiondb detail anyconnect**. Examples 19-1 and 19-2 show the output of the command in two different stages of the session. Example 19-1 shows the output of the command when the endpoint posture is unknown and the session is set to redirect traffic to ISE.

Example 19-1   show vpn-sessiondb detail anyconnect *Command Output*

```
atw-tme-5515# show vpn-sessiondb detail anyconnect


Session Type: AnyConnect Detailed


Username      : employee1              Index      : 26
Assigned IP   : 192.168.228.2          Public IP  : 10.117.118.215
Protocol      : AnyConnect-Parent SSL-Tunnel DTLS-Tunnel
License       : AnyConnect Premium
Encryption    : AnyConnect-Parent: (1)none  SSL-Tunnel: (1)AES-GCM-256  DTLS-Tunnel:
                (1)AES256
Hashing       : AnyConnect-Parent: (1)none  SSL-Tunnel: (1)SHA384  DTLS-Tunnel: (1)
                SHA1
Bytes Tx      : 24431                  Bytes Rx   : 13670
Pkts Tx       : 33                     Pkts Rx    : 67
Pkts Tx Drop  : 0                      Pkts Rx Drop : 0
Group Policy  : GroupPolicy1           Tunnel Group : ATW-ConnectionProfile
Login Time    : 15:41:04 UTC Wed Mar 22 2017
Duration      : 0h:00m:09s
Inactivity    : 0h:00m:00s
VLAN Mapping  : N/A                    VLAN       : none
Audt Sess ID  : 0a0165fe0001a00058d29b10
Security Grp  : none
AnyConnect-Parent Tunnels: 1
SSL-Tunnel Tunnels: 1
DTLS-Tunnel Tunnels: 1


< output removed for space >


SSL-Tunnel:
  Tunnel ID     : 26.2
  Assigned IP   : 192.168.228.2          Public IP   : 10.117.118.215
  Encryption    : AES-GCM-256            Hashing     : SHA384
  Ciphersuite   : ECDHE-RSA-AES256-GCM-SHA384
  Encapsulation : TLSv1.2                TCP Src Port : 58163
  TCP Dst Port  : 443                    Auth Mode    : userPassword
  Idle Time Out : 30 Minutes             Idle TO Left : 29 Minutes
  Client OS     : Windows
  Client Type   : SSL VPN Client
  Client Ver    : Cisco AnyConnect VPN Agent for Windows 4.4.01054
  Bytes Tx      : 7354                   Bytes Rx    : 816
  Pkts Tx       : 5                      Pkts Rx     : 12
  Pkts Tx Drop  : 0                      Pkts Rx Drop : 0
  Filter Name   : #ACSACL#-IP-VPN-PostureNotCompliant-58d1c6f2
```

```
< output removed for space >


ISE Posture:
  Redirect URL : https://atw-ise244.securitydemo.net:8443/portal/gateway?sessionId=0
                 a0165fe0001a00058d29b10&portal=4cb1...
  Redirect ACL : POSTURE-REDIRECT


atw-tme-5515#
```

Example 19-2 shows the output of the command when the endpoint posture is known to be compliant and the session is given full access.

Example 19-2   show vpn-sessiondb detail anyconnect *Command Output*

```
atw-tme-5515# show vpn-sessiondb detail anyconnect


Session Type: AnyConnect Detailed


Username    : employee1              Index      : 25
Assigned IP : 192.168.228.2          Public IP  : 10.117.118.215
Protocol    : AnyConnect-Parent SSL-Tunnel DTLS-Tunnel
License     : AnyConnect Premium
Encryption  : AnyConnect-Parent: (1)none  SSL-Tunnel: (1)AES-GCM-256  DTLS-Tunnel:
              (1)AES256
Hashing     : AnyConnect-Parent: (1)none  SSL-Tunnel: (1)SHA384  DTLS-Tunnel: (1)
              SHA1
Bytes Tx    : 101366                 Bytes Rx   : 92634
Pkts Tx     : 204                    Pkts Rx    : 511
Pkts Tx Drop : 0                     Pkts Rx Drop : 0
Group Policy : GroupPolicy1          Tunnel Group : ATW-ConnectionProfile
Login Time  : 15:31:17 UTC Wed Mar 22 2017
Duration    : 0h:05m:29s
Inactivity  : 0h:00m:00s
VLAN Mapping : N/A                   VLAN        : none
Audt Sess ID : 0a0165fe0001900058d298c5
Security Grp : none
AnyConnect-Parent Tunnels: 1
SSL-Tunnel Tunnels: 1
DTLS-Tunnel Tunnels: 1


< output removed for space >


SSL-Tunnel:
  Tunnel ID    : 25.2
  Assigned IP  : 192.168.228.2        Public IP    : 10.117.118.215
  Encryption   : AES-GCM-256          Hashing      : SHA384
```

```
Ciphersuite   : ECDHE-RSA-AES256-GCM-SHA384
Encapsulation: TLSv1.2                  TCP Src Port : 57916
TCP Dst Port : 443                      Auth Mode    : userPassword
Idle Time Out: 30 Minutes               Idle TO Left : 24 Minutes
Client OS    : Windows
Client Type  : SSL VPN Client
Client Ver   : Cisco AnyConnect VPN Agent for Windows 4.4.01054
Bytes Tx     : 7354                      Bytes Rx     : 216
Pkts Tx      : 5                         Pkts Rx      : 4
Pkts Tx Drop : 0                         Pkts Rx Drop : 0
Filter Name  : #ACSACL#-IP-VPN-PostureCompliant-58d18405

< output removed for space >

atw-tme-5515#
```

For completeness, Figure 19-48 shows a screenshot of viewing the same information
within ASDM. To view it in ASDM, navigate to **Monitoring > VPN > VPN Statistics
> Sessions**. Then, ensure that you are viewing remote access sessions, by selecting All
Remote Access from the **Filter By** dropbox. Figure 19-48 shows an example of the filtered results.

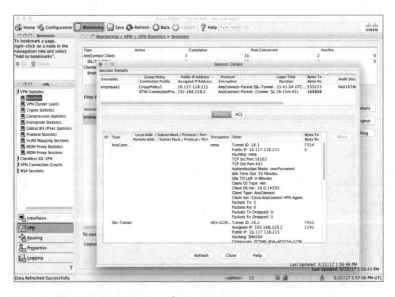

Figure 19-48 *Session Details in ASDM*

Extending the ASA Remote Access VPN Capabilities

One very interesting feature of the ASA is its ability to perform a double authentication (not to be confused with dual-factor authentication, which is a single authentication using two factors). The ASA can also authenticate VPNs using certificate-based authentication, in addition to using username and password authentications. Additionally, the ASA can help provision certificates to AnyConnect clients for VPN purposes, leveraging an external certificate authority such as ISE. These topics are covered in this section.

Double Authentication

As you might have noticed earlier in the chapter when configuring the AnyConnect connection profile, the navigation pane on the left also has an Advanced section. Click **Advanced**, and you see an option called Secondary Authentication, which is commonly referred to colloquially as double authentication. Whichever term is used, it refers to authenticating two completely different sets of credentials. Often, this is used to authenticate a machine certificate followed by the username and password, or a one-time password (OTP) followed by an Active Directory authentication. Only after passing both authentications is the end user authorized by the ASA to establish the full tunnel.

Note   At the time of writing, the ASA does not support doing a certificate-based authentication for both primary and secondary authentication.

Figure 19-49 shows the setting in ASDM. You select the AAA server group to use for the secondary authentication, and then configure some other options.

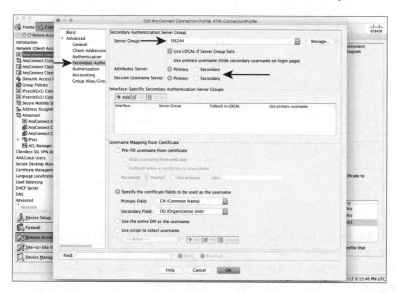

Figure 19-49   *AnyConnect Connection Profile: Secondary Authentication*

Figure 19-49 shows the ASA configuration screen, but what does double authentication look like to the end user? Figure 19-50 shows the AnyConnect user interface when double authentication is configured for two username/password-based authentications.

Figure 19-50   *Live Log of Double Authentication*

Where this becomes really interesting is how it looks when both authentications are sent to the same ISE PSN. You see both authentications and both authorizations, but only the second authorization is maintained as an active session. Figure 19-51 shows the Live Log, with the Identity column showing that both employee1 and doctor1 have entries. Click over to the Live Sessions screen, as shown in Figure 19-52, and you can see that only doctor1 has a session.

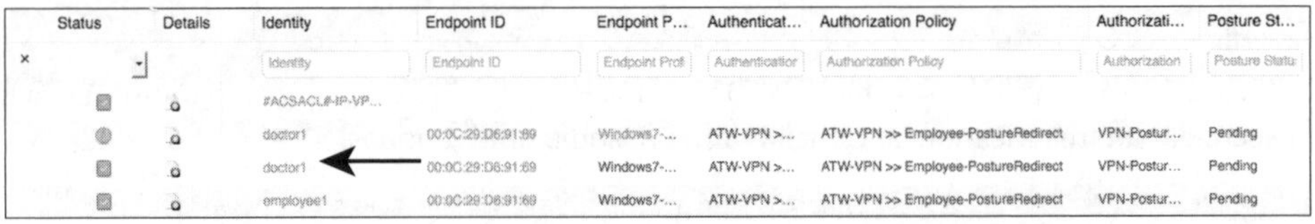

Status	Details	Identity	Endpoint ID	Endpoint P...	Authenticat...	Authorization Policy	Authorizati...	Posture St...
×	▾	Identity	Endpoint ID	Endpoint Prof	Authentication	Authorization Policy	Authorization	Posture Status
▣	â	#ACSACL#-IP-VP...						
◉	â	doctor1	00:0C:29:D6:91:69	Windows7-...	ATW-VPN >...	ATW-VPN >> Employee-PostureRedirect	VPN-Postur...	Pending
▣	â	doctor1 ←	00:0C:29:D6:91:69	Windows7-...	ATW-VPN >...	ATW-VPN >> Employee-PostureRedirect	VPN-Postur...	Pending
▣	â	employee1	00:0C:29:D6:91:69	Windows7-...	ATW-VPN >...	ATW-VPN >> Employee-PostureRedirect	VPN-Postur...	Pending

Figure 19-51   *Live Log of Double Authentication*

Updated	Session Status	Action	Endpoint ID	Identity	IP Address	Endpoint Profile	Posture Status	S
		▾	Endpoint ID	Identity	IP Address	▾ Endpoint Profile	Posture Status	
Mar 22 2017 11:38:53.170 AM	Authenticated	Show CoA Actions	00:0C:29:D6:91:69	doctor1 ←		Windows7-Workstation	Pending	

Last Updated: Wed Mar 22 2017 14:39:18 GMT-0400 (EDT)   Records

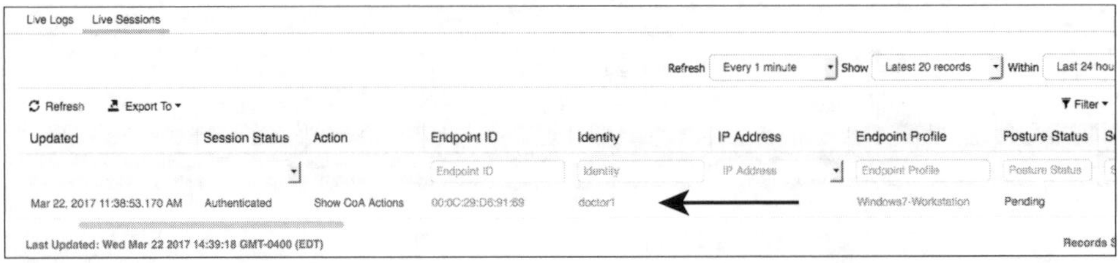

Figure 19-52   *Live Session Log of Double Authentication*

Double authentication makes sense when you are not using an intelligent centralized policy server, which ISE most certainly is. However, it also makes sense when you are performing two different types of authentications, such as a certificate-based authentication followed by a username/password-based authentication.

Certificate-Based Authentication

Now that your interest is fully piqued about certificate-based authentications, this section examines those certificate-based authentications with ASA RA-VPNs.

Provisioning Certificates

Before you can authenticate using a certificate, you have to be in possession of said certificate. So, we start our dive into this topic by looking at the function within AnyConnect and the ASA to provision certificates using Simple Certificate Enrollment Protocol (SCEP) from ISE's internal CA to the AnyConnect clients.

> **Note**   For more details on ISE's internal CA, revisit Chapter 17, "BYOD: Self Service Onboarding and Registration," but also take some time to read Appendix D, "The ISE CA and How Cert Based Auth Works."

The ASA can act as an SCEP proxy, taking the SCEP request from the AnyConnect client and passing it along to an external CA, such as ISE. ISE allows SCEP only from devices that are listed as NADs in the ISE configuration, so the ASA is perfect because it is already listed as a NAD for RA-VPN.

You first need to download the ISE CA certificates to be installed in the ASA as a trusted CA. From the ISE GUI:

Step 1.   Navigate to **Administration > System > Certificates > Certificate Authority > Certificate Authority Certificates,** as shown Figure 19-53.

Figure 19-53   *Certificate Authority Certificates*

Step 2.   Download the Root CA, all the Node CA, and all the Sub CA certificates by selecting them one at a time and clicking **Export.**

Step 3.   Save the downloaded files in a location where you can readily retrieve them later.

Now that you have the certificates from ISE, create an AnyConnect connection profile for the SCEP enrollment. From ASDM:

Step 4.   Navigate to **Configuration > Remote Access VPN > Network (Client) Access > AnyConnect Connection Profiles.**

Step 5.   Add a new connection profile named **Enroll.**

Step 6.   From the Method drop-down list under Authentication, choose **AAA and Certificate.**

Step 7.   From the AAA Server Group drop-down list, choose the ISE server group used previously (ISE244 in the example).

Step 8.   Click the **Select** button to the right of the Client Address Pools field and choose a client address pool.

Step 9.   Leave the Group Policy setting alone for now.

Step 10.   Enable the SSL VPN and IPsec client protocols by checking the corresponding check boxes.

Step 11.   Fill in the DNS Servers and Domain Name fields.

Figure 19-54 shows the configuration of the Enroll connection profile thus far.

Figure 19-54   *Enroll Connection Profile: Basic Configuration*

Step 12.   From the navigation pane on the left, choose **Advanced > General.**

Step 13.   Check the **Enable Simple Certificate Enrollment Protocol (SCEP) for this Connection Profile** check box, as shown in Figure 19-55.

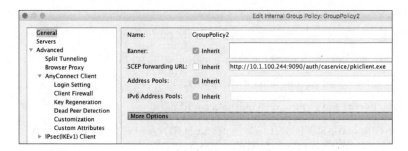

Figure 19-55 *Enroll Connection Profile: General Configuration*

Step 14. Click **OK**.

Step 15. Edit the newly created Enroll profile.

Step 16. Manage the Group Policy assigned to this profile.

Step 17. Set the SCEP Forwarding URL field to
http://<ISE>:9090/auth/caservice/pkiclient.exe.

Figure 19-56 shows the group policy with the SCEP forwarding URL configured.

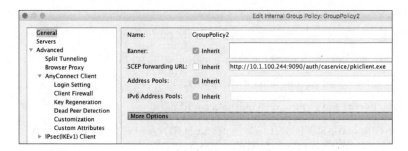

Figure 19-56 *Group Policy: General Configuration*

The connection profile and group policy now exist, which takes care of the ASA configuration for SCEP proxy. However, you still need to configure AnyConnect for SCEP, because the client must initiate the signing request. To accomplish that task, you need to create an AnyConnect client profile that will pass the configuration to AnyConnect after the client successfully connects to the ASA.

Step 18. Select **Network (Client) Access > AnyConnect Client Profile**.

Step 19.   Click **Add**.

Step 20.   Name the client profile **EnrollmentProfile**.

Step 21.   From the Profile Usage drop-down list, choose **AnyConnect VPN Profile**.

Step 22.   Ensure that the Group Policy field matches the group policy assigned to the connection profile that you edited in Step 16.

Figure 19-57 shows the addition of the client profile named EnrollmentProfile.

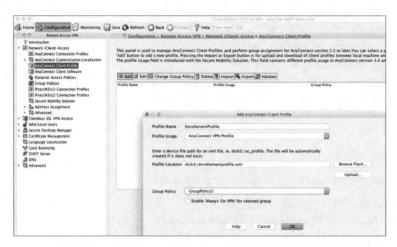

Figure 19-57   *Adding the EnrollmentProfile Client Profile*

Step 23.   Click **OK**.

Step 24.   Edit the newly created EnrollmentProfile client profile.

Step 25.   Select **Certificate Enrollment** in the navigation pane on the left side.

Step 26.   Check the **Certificate Enrollment** check box.

Step 27.   Set the Certificate Expiration Threshold to **30** days.

Step 28.   In the Automatic SCEP Host field, enter an FQDN for the SCEP host. From the Certificate Import drop-down list, choose **All**.

Step 29.   In the CA URL field, enter **http://<ISE>:9090/auth/caservice/pkiclient.exe**.

Step 30.   Type **%USER%** in the Name (CN) field.

Step 31.   Type **%MACHINEID%** in the Department (OU) field.

Step 32.   Set the Key Size field to **2048**.

Step 33.   Type **%USER%@<your domain>** in the Email (EA) field.

Figure 19-58 shows the Certificate Enrollment page of the EnrollmentProfile client profile.

Figure 19-58   *Certificate Enrollment Page*

Step 34.   Click **OK** to save the changes to the XML client profile.

Now that the ASA is configured for SCEP proxy and the AnyConnect client profile is configured to have the client initiate the certificate signing request, the ASA needs to be configured to trust certificates signed by the ISE CA.

Step 35.   Navigate to **Network (Client) Access > Certificate Management > CA Certificates**.

Step 36.   Click **Add** to import one of the ISE CA certificates that you exported and downloaded from ISE previously in Steps 1, 2, and 3.

Step 37.   Repeat Step 36 for each of the CA certificates. Figure 19-59 shows the certificates added to the ASA for trust.

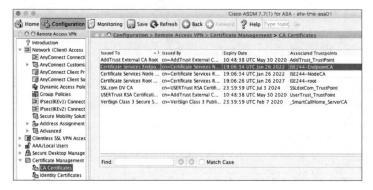

Figure 19-59   *CA Certificates*

That's it. You are all set and ready to connect to the ASA VPN and receive certificates.

When you connect to the Enroll profile, which is configured for AAA and certificate authentication, AnyConnect will look for the certificate, and when it doesn't find one, it will prompt for AAA authentication and perform the SCEP process to the ASA.

Figure 19-60 shows the user connecting the VPN headend.

Figure 19-60   *Connecting to the Enroll Profile*

Figure 19-61 shows AnyConnect after it has already processed the SCEP and is now storing the certificate. Figure 19-62 shows the Windows Certificates store with the employee1 certificate there.

Figure 19-61   *Storing the Certificate*

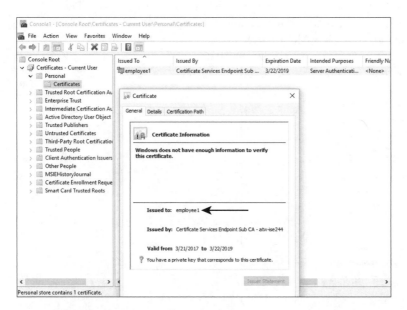

Figure 19-62   *Windows Certificates Store*

Now that the user and computer have a certificate, you can focus on the configuration of an AnyConnect connection profile that uses certificates for authentication.

Authenticating the VPN with Certificates

When authenticating a VPN with certificates, the ASA performs the certificate validation. This is in contrast to the way certificate-based authentication works with 802.1X on the wired and wireless LAN. When performing 802.1X with certificates, ISE receives the certificate and performs the authentication.

The ASA is handling the authentication, but it can still leverage ISE for the authorization process. This means configuring an AAA server group that is set up for authorize-only, configuring an AnyConnect connection profile set up for certificate-only authentication, and performing authorization against the AAA server group. It also means configuring some very different types of policies on the ISE side, because ISE would normally expect an authentication before processing an authorization.

To create an AnyConnect connection profile for the certificate-based authentication, from ASDM:

Step 1.   Navigate to **Configuration > Remote Access VPN > Network (Client) Access> AnyConnect Connection Profiles**.

Step 2.   Add a new connection profile named **CertProfile**.

Step 3.   From the method drop-down list, choose **Certificate Only**.

Step 4.   To the right of the AAA Server Group field, click **Manage**.

Step 5.   Add a new AAA server group configured normally, but check the **Use Authorization Only Mode** check box, as shown in Figure 19-63.

Figure 19-63   *AAA Server Group for Authorization Only*

Step 6.   Complete the remaining portions of the connection profile, as shown in Figure 19-64.

Figure 19-64   *CertProfile: Basic Configuration*

Step 7. Navigate to the **Advanced > Authorization** page of the connection profile, and select the AAA server group, as shown in Figure 19-65.

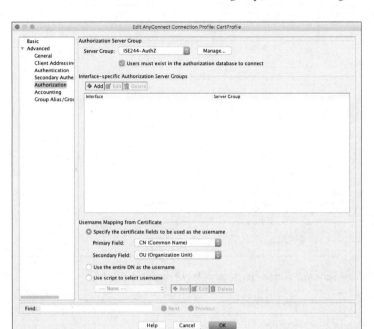

Figure 19-65 *CertProfile: Authorization*

Step 8. Check the **Users Must Exist in the Authorization Database to Connect** check box.

Step 9. Click **OK**.

The ASA configuration is complete. Ensure that you save the configuration before exiting ASDM. There is one last step, which is to configure ISE to allow the ASA to perform the authorizations.

In the ISE policy set for VPN, insert a new authorization rule with a condition of **RADIUS:Service-Type EQUALS Authorize Only**, and to use the **ALL_AD_Join_Points** identity source sequence. Ensure that the If Authentication Failed option is set to **Continue**.

You have created a special authentication rule that looks for authorize-only RADIUS requests. It is configured as a separate authentication rule, because the If Authentication Failed option is set to Continue. In theory, with this setting configured, you could inadvertently allow malicious users to gain access to the network, so it needs to be restricted as much as possible.

Figure 19-66 shows the VPN policy set with the new authentication rule configured.

Define the Policy Sets by configuring rules based on conditions. Drag and drop sets on the left hand side to change the order.
For Policy Export go to Administration > System > Backup & Restore > Policy Export Page

Status	Name	Description	Conditions	
☑	ATW-VPN	VPN Policy Set	DEVICE:Device Type STARTS WITH Device Type#All Device Types#VPN	Edit

▼ **Authentication Policy**

	Status					
⁝	☑	AuthZOnly	: If Radius:Service-Type EQUALS Authorize Only	Allow Protocols : Default Network Access	and	Edit I ▾
		☑ Default	:use All_AD_Join_Points			
	☑	Default Rule (If no match)	: Allow Protocols : Default Network Access	and use : All_User_ID_Stores		Edit I ▾

▼ **Authorization Policy**

▶ Exceptions (0)

Standard

	Status	Rule Name	Conditions (identity groups and other conditions)		Permissions	
⁝	☑	Employee-PostureRedirect	if (AD-Employees AND Session:PostureStatus NOT_EQUALS Compliant)	then	VPN-Posture-Redirect	Edit I ▾
⁝	☑	Employee-Permit	if (AD-Employees AND Session:PostureStatus EQUALS Compliant)	then	VPN-Full-Access	Edit I ▾
	☑	Default	if no matches, then DenyAccess			Edit I ▾

Figure 19-66 *VPN Policy Set with Authorize-Only Authentication Rule*

Connecting to the VPN via CertProfile

When connecting to the VPN through the new CertProfile connection profile, the user is not prompted for their username and password; instead, the connection occurs automatically using the certificate.

Figure 19-67 shows a connection attempt where the user chooses the CertProfile connection profile. Normally, you would not have the end user select their profile. All of this should happen in the background and be seamless to the end user.

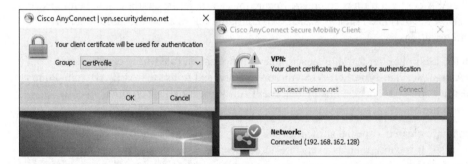

Figure 19-67 *Connecting to the VPN via CertProfile*

Figure 19-68 shows the Live Log, where you can see the connection establish, and the posture change from Pending to Compliant, all while the AuthZOnly authentication rule is being used. Whether certificate-based authentication or username/password-based authentication is being used doesn't matter; ISE is still able to perform its functions, such as performing the posture assessment.

Status	Details	Identity	Endpoint ID	Endpoint P...	Authentication Policy	Authorization Policy	Authorizati...	Posture St...	S
×	⬦	Identity	Endpoint ID	Endpoint Prof	Authentication Policy	Authorization Policy	Authorization	Posture Statu	
☑	⬦	#ACSACL#-IP-VP...							a
☑	⬦		10.117.118.215				VPN-Full-Ac...	Compliant	a
◉	⬦	employee1	00:0C:29:D6:91:69	Windows7-...	ATW-VPN >> AuthZOnly	ATW-VPN >> Employee-PostureRedirect	VPN-Postur...	Compliant	a
☑	⬦	#ACSACL#-IP-VP...							a
☑	⬦	employee1	00:0C:29:D6:91:69	Windows7-...	ATW-VPN >> AuthZOnly	ATW-VPN >> Employee-PostureRedirect	VPN-Postur...	Pending	a

Figure 19-68 *Live Log: Posture Compliance with Certificate-based Authentication*

Summary

Congratulations! You made it! This was a long chapter with a lot of configuration steps and technologies.

In this chapter, you learned about the different types of VPNs. The two types of remote access VPN are clientless and client-based, the latter of which was the focus of this chapter because it is relevant to ISE. Cisco AnyConnect is the VPN client used for the RA-VPN and the ASA, but it is also a very powerful endpoint client that has many different security modules, including HostScan, which is used for ASA-based posture assessment, and System Scan, which is used for ISE-based posture assessment.

You learned about the differences between the ASA and other NADs, especially with regard to the way CoA is used. The ASA uses CoA-Push, instead of CoA-Reauth. You also learned that the ASA has a lot of capabilities related to RA-VPNs, including double authentication. You discovered how to use the ASA as an SCEP proxy from AnyConnect to the ISE CA, for issuing certificates to AnyConnect that can then be used to perform certificate-based authentications.

You also examined how the certificate-based authentications leverage an authorize-only form of RADIUS request to ISE, and ISE never performs an authentication at all.

Keep in mind that the ASA VPN is capable of much more than we covered in this chapter. For more detailed information and knowledge, check out *Cisco ASA: All-in-One Next-Generation Firewall, IPS, and VPN Services, Third Edition* (Cisco Press, 2014).

Chapter 20

Deployment Phases

This chapter covers the following topics:

- Reasons to use a phased approach
- Monitor Mode
- Low-Impact Mode
- Closed Mode
- Transitioning from Monitor Mode to your end state
- Wireless networks

This book has already examined quite a bit of configuration detail about ISE and the network access devices. It has covered the technical merit of policy creation, guest lifecycle management, posture assessment, and much more. There is obviously a great deal to consider when you deploy a system such as this one. It is not something you should just enable overnight with the "flip of a switch."

This chapter focuses on the recommended approach to deploying the Secure Access system. It reviews some of the challenges that were encountered in the past, and why certain technologies were enhanced to provide a more prescriptive approach to deployment.

Why Use a Phased Approach?

Back in the early 2000s, a new technology was emerging that would revolutionize networking as we knew it. This technology was IEEE 802.1X, which enabled authentication of a network access port prior to allowing devices onto the network. The concept was simple, and some predicted that within 5 years there would not be any "hot ports" in the world that wouldn't first authenticate the user, and that unauthorized users would no longer be able to access networks.

802.1X was originally created to be very binary in nature. A device either is authenticated and gets access or fails authentication and is denied. Figure 20-1 graphically represents the logical process of 802.1X authentication.

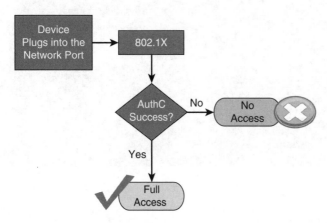

Figure 20-1   *802.1X Intended Behavior*

However, as you already know from reading the previous chapters in this book, this authentication process has many different moving parts that must all be aligned properly if you want to avoid causing denial of service (DoS) on your own user population. This can be accomplished with the following:

- Supplicants must be configured on devices.

- Lists of MAC addresses must be created in order to properly MAB devices.

- Profiling probes must be enabled and have the ability to collect data regarding endpoints to help build that list of MAC addresses.

- Certificates must be trusted.

- Guest accounts must be created.

If you were to just "flip the switch" and enable 802.1X on all access-layer switch ports all at once, you would most likely have a swarm of angry users converging on the IT department threatening to terminate their jobs. That is called a "career-limiting event," or CLE for short.

We're reminded of one implementation at a financial organization with 2000 switch ports in its campus building. Due to an audit requirement, the organization had to enable network authentication by a certain date to avoid being subject to fines. The mandate came down from management, the project received its funding, and away we went. We lab tested everything and proved it all would work using our Cisco Catalyst 6513 Switches and the native Windows XP (Service Pack 3) supplicant configured for EAP-TLS machine authentication with the Active Directory–issued machine certificate.

It was beautiful. Everything was working perfectly on our test systems in the lab, and the desktop team assured us that the Group Policy Object (GPO) was sent out properly and all the Windows XP systems were ready to authenticate. All we had to do was turn on the authentication on the switch ports (theoretically).

Our advice was still to deploy in Monitor Mode first, and then change over to Closed Mode (the end state). This meant that the **authentication open** command needed to be applied to the switch port, but Monitor Mode would allow us to validate that authentications would all be successful before we truly enforced access to the network.

The security oversight committee nixed the idea immediately, because the word "open" was in the command. We were simply not allowed to use it—ever. Never mind that all 2000 ports were currently wide open and that using the command would not make matters worse at all. We simply were not allowed to use that command.

So, the big day arrived. At 10 p.m. on a Sunday night, we had our change-control window to run our scripts and enable Closed Mode authentication across 2000 switch ports in a matter of minutes. Of those 2000 ports, only 10 were authenticating successfully, and we had accomplished exactly what I feared: a denial of service for all other systems.

Why did this occur? The policies were all correct. The certificates had all been pushed out to the desktops. The supplicants were configured. However, no one had realized that the supplicant configuration would not take effect prior to rebooting the Windows systems! We did not figure that out until the next afternoon, after the desktop team had researched the issue further; meanwhile, we had created a DoS problem for all the users that morning.

The story has a happy ending. After the desktop team pushed out a job to reboot all the systems, we re-enabled authentication at the next change-control window and were able to get 99 percent of the systems to authenticate successfully.

However, not all deployments are that lucky, or that well planned out in advance. This is why a phased approach to deploying identity solutions is always a good idea.

A Phased Approach

Using a phased deployment approach, you start off in Monitor Mode and gradually transition into your end state of either Low-Impact Mode or Closed Mode. By doing so, you can avoid DoS scenarios such as the one described in the previous section. With a monitoring phase, you have time to build your list of endpoints with profiling. You can manually import the MAC addresses that will be MAB'd without profiling and ensure that you know exactly what will happen, before it happens.

Then, you can gradually move into a final state of enforcement. Figure 20-2 shows how you logically start with Monitor Mode in Phase 1 and then move to either Low-Impact Mode or Closed Mode.

> **Note**   The end state of your deployment does not necessarily need to be either Low-Impact Mode or Closed Mode; you can blend the two. We have worked with a number of customers who use Low-Impact Mode in campus environments, and Closed Mode in their branches. It is up to you to determine what works best for your environment, and then deploy accordingly.

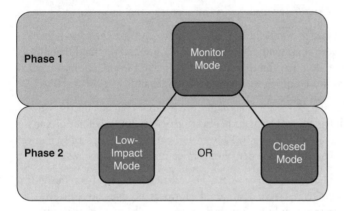

Figure 20-2   *Phased Deployments*

Authentication Open Versus Standard 802.1X

As previously described, a port that is protected with 802.1X will not allow network traffic to flow without a successful authentication. Figure 20-3 illustrates that an 802.1X-controlled port normally only allows Extensible Authentication Protocol (EAP), Cisco Discovery Protocol (CDP), and Link Layer Discovery Protocol (LLDP) traffic to enter the port (all three are Layer 2 protocols) and denies all other traffic. When 802.1X is enabled on a port, the port is said to be a *supplicant authenticator*. That is a fancy way of stating that the port will communicate with EAP at Layer 2; the switch will broker that authentication to the RADIUS server.

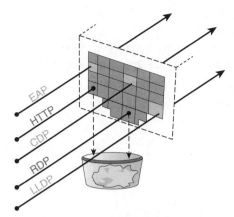

Figure 20-3 *Default Port Behavior with 802.1X*

Cisco created an enhancement to standard 802.1X ports that allows the port to be a supplicant authenticator. However, it permits all traffic to flow normally through the switch port even without an authentication occurring. This allows the supplicant to authenticate correctly if it is configured, but if the device does not have a supplicant configured or the switch receives an Access-Reject message from the RADIUS server, the Reject message is ignored.

Figure 20-4 illustrates that, regardless of authentication, the switch port allows all traffic to flow, but it also authenticates the supplicant and performs MAB just like a standard 802.1X-enabled switch port.

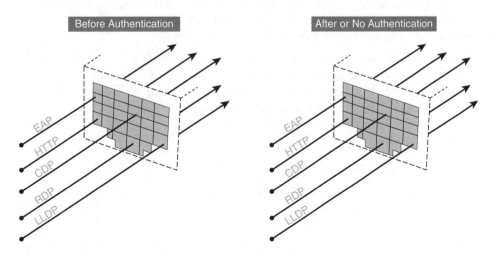

Figure 20-4 *Port Behavior with Open Authentication*

It is the creation of this authenticator enhancement that truly made Monitor Mode possible. It is, of course, not the only necessary component of Monitor Mode, but it is certainly the catalyst (pardon the pun).

Monitor Mode

Monitor Mode is a process, not just a command on a switch. The process is to enable authentication (with **authentication open**) to see exactly which devices fail and which ones succeed.

Figure 20-5 shows a high-level flow diagram describing Monitor Mode.

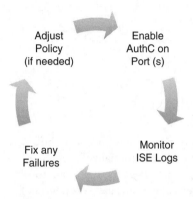

Figure 20-5   *Monitor Mode Operational Flow*

One key point to understand about Monitor Mode is that it is applicable to wired environments only. If you have ever configured a device to connect to a wireless network, you are familiar with the concept of a service set identifier (SSID). When using Wi-Fi, configuring a client (supplicant) is expected behavior. You must tell the Wi-Fi-capable endpoint which network to connect to by identifying its SSID, and then you provide credentials for that network. It's common, it's expected, and it's well known.

A wired network, however, does not have the concept of an SSID, so there is no popup window on the endpoint asking which network you would like to connect with. It's just assumed that your device is physically connected and therefore you are attached to the correct network. With wireless, if you don't have a supplicant, you cannot connect. Wired environments are expected to always work, supplicant or not. The wired port must be able to handle the following:

- A device that has a supplicant (802.1X)

- A corporate device that doesn't have a supplicant but belongs on the network (such as an IP phone or printer)

- Guest users

So, there is quite a bit to audit when in Monitor Mode.

Another very important thing to understand about Monitor Mode is that authorization results from the RADIUS server will absolutely be honored (Access-Reject is the only command that is ignored). So, if your authorization result from ISE includes dynamic

VLAN (dVLAN) assignment or downloadable ACLs (dACL), those will absolutely be honored and applied to the port.

For a phased deployment approach, it is highly recommended to use Network Device Groups (NDG) in ISE. Using these NDGs, you can build specific policies that only send the basic authorization results (Access-Accept and Access-Reject) to switches that are part of a Monitor Mode NDG.

Figure 20-6 shows a high-level flow diagram describing Monitor Mode.

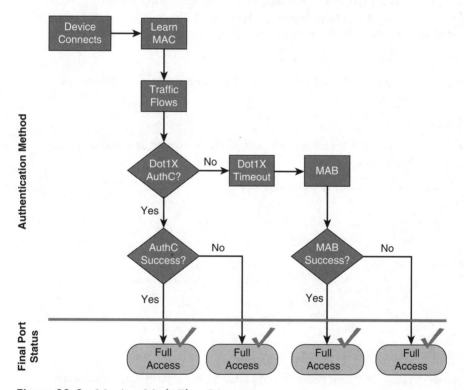

Figure 20-6 *Monitor Mode Flow Diagram*

Prepare ISE for a Staged Deployment

One of the primary ways to differentiate modes within your ISE policies is to use NDGs. In this section, you will configure the NDGs to have a top-level group of Stage, and then subgroups for Monitor Mode, Low-Impact Mode, and Closed Mode. With these NDGs, the authorization policies may look for the particular stage of deployment. For purposes of keeping the policies nice and clean, use separate policy sets for each stage of deployment.

> **Note**   The following exercises assume that policy sets have been enabled already under
> **Administration > System > Settings > Policy Sets.**

Create the Network Device Groups

A Network Device Group may be a top-level group, such as Location or Type. The NDG may also be created as a child (AKA subgroup) of an existing top-level group, such as Switch (which would be a subgroup of the Type NDG). The following steps guide you through the creation of both a new top-level group, named Stage, and subgroups.

From the ISE GUI, perform the following steps:

Step 1. Navigate to **Work Centers > Network Access > Network Resources > Device Groups.**

Step 2. Click **Add.**

Step 3. In the Name field, name the Network Device Group **Stage**, as shown in Figure 20-7.

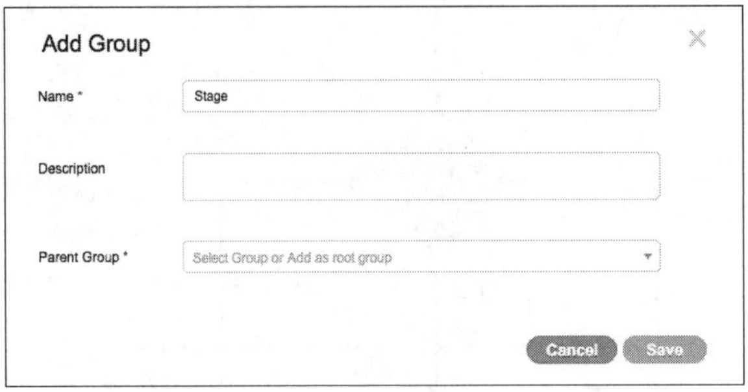

Figure 20-7   *Add a Stage NDG*

Step 4. Leave the Parent Group alone, so that Stage becomes a new root group.

Step 5. Click **Save.**

Step 6. Click **Add** to add another group named Monitor Mode, with Stage selected as the parent group.

Step 7. Repeat Step 6 and create a group for Low Impact Mode and Closed Mode. Figure 20-8 shows the final NDG configuration.

Figure 20-8 *Final Stage Network Device Groups*

Create the Policy Sets

Now that you have the NDGs configured for the different stages of the deployment, you can move on to creating the policies themselves. From the ISE GUI, perform the following steps:

Step 1.   Navigate to **Work Centers > Network Access > Policy Sets**.

Step 2.   Ensure that your default policy is selected on the left side (as shown in Figure 20-9) and click the **+** icon in the upper-left corner.

Figure 20-9 *Default Policy Set Selected*

Step 3.   Choose **Create Above**.

Step 4.   Name the new policy set **Monitor Mode**, as shown in Figure 20-10.

Figure 20-10   *Monitor Mode Policy Set*

Step 5.   Add a new condition of **DEVICE:Stage EQUALS Monitor Mode**.

Step 6.   Click **Done**.

At this point, any network device that is a member of the NDG named Monitor Mode will use this policy set. All authentications and authorizations occur with this set of policies.

It is up to you, the administrator of ISE policies, to ensure that any authorization results for Monitor Mode switches are only Access-Accept and Access-Reject. Always remember that other authorization results will be accepted and applied to the switch port, so you must ensure that web authentication, ACLs, and VLAN assignments do not occur for these switches.

Low-Impact Mode

As described previously in this chapter, Low-Impact Mode is one of the end-state choices for your deployment. Closed Mode is the other final stage. There is no specific best practice for which mode is better to deploy; it is entirely dependent on the organization and its needs.

For example, we have worked with a number of large organizations that use a variety of technologies to reimage desktop systems that make use of the Preboot Execution Environment (PXE) to boot into a pseudo OS and then connect to an imaging server that reimages the company desktop. Those PXEs were time sensitive and had no ability to authenticate to the network infrastructure. Yet they had to seamlessly be able to boot, connect to the reimaging server, and update the desktop to the latest corporate image, and do so without any additional user interaction. Low-Impact Mode was the only way to make this work feasibly in those environments.

Another example is a retail organization that uses thin clients in its retail stores. These thin clients must be able to boot using PXE, gain limited access to the network, download their OS from the local store server, and have that access before their local DHCP timers expire. Once that OS is loaded into memory and takes the system over, its supplicant sends an EAPoL-Start message into the network and authenticates with 802.1X. Low-Impact Mode allows the thin client to boot automatically and have the appropriate levels of access to the store server to download the OS.

Low-Impact Mode adds security on top of the framework that was built in Monitor Mode. It continues to use the **authentication open** capabilities of the switch port, which allows traffic to enter the switch prior to an authorization result. This permits the DHCP clients to be assigned an IP address before their DHCP timers run out (for example).

With Low-Impact Mode, you are adding security right from the start by putting a port-based ACL (pACL) on the switch port interface. This is a traffic-filtering ACL that gets applied to the port as part of the switch configuration and is then overridden by the dACL sent down from ISE.

Figure 20-11 shows the operational flow intended for Low-Impact Mode. As one of the two possible end states (Closed Mode being the second), it provides very specific access per user, per device, or other condition that you wish to use in the ISE authorization policies. Remember, the goal of Low-Impact Mode is to administer very limited network access to devices without authentication, and then provide very specific access to those that have been authorized. As with any other security solution, tuning the authorization results is something that can take a lot of operational man-hours. So, it is always recommended that you deploy authorization results in stages. For example, begin with a policy that permits full access to any device that has authenticated successfully. Ensure that the environment is fully functional, and then begin to "ratchet down" the security. Make the dACLs more specific, and so on.

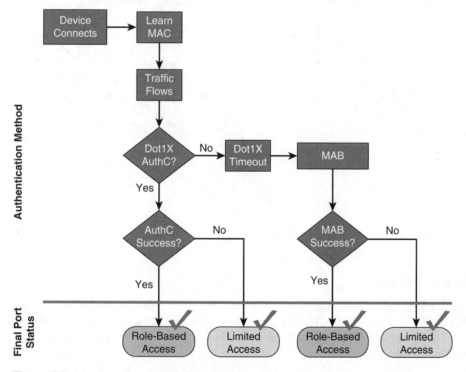

Figure 20-11 *Low-Impact Mode Operational Flow*

Figure 20-12 shows that the pACL is applied prior to authentication, which only allows specific traffic into the port. Once the authentication occurs, the authorization needs to include a dACL that selectively permits or denies traffic. Other authorization results may also be applied at the port, such as:

- URL redirection
- VLAN assignment
- Media Access Control Security (MACsec) encryption
- Security Group Tags

Note VLAN assignment should be used only on devices that use supplicants. Without a supplicant, the device will most likely not be able to identify the VLAN change, and may end up with the wrong IP address for its final VLAN assignment.

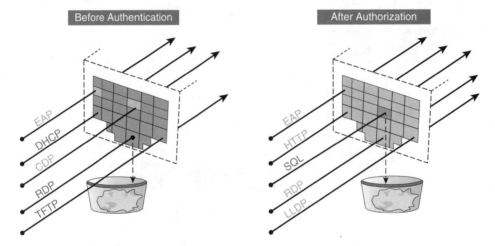

Figure 20-12 *Low-Impact Mode Port Behavior*

Closed Mode

Closed Mode is similar to the default behavior of 802.1X. As shown earlier in Figure 20-3, the port does not allow any traffic before the authentication (except for EAP, CDP, and LLDP), and then the port will be assigned to specific authorization results after the authentication.

Note Closed Mode was once called High-Security Mode. It was renamed to discourage the perception that it is more secure than Low-Impact Mode. In truth, both modes are equally protected. The security level of either end state is truly dependent on the configuration of the devices and the policies on ISE, not the mode of operation. In other words, an administrator can make Closed Mode very insecure or very secure, depending on their implementation.

As shown in Figure 20-1 earlier in the chapter, the operational model of 802.1X was always designed to deny access to any device that does not authenticate successfully. This is a perfectly understandable model for wireless network access, where a human is required to interact with the device and configure a wireless client (supplicant) to connect to a specific SSID with specific credentials.

However, in a wired world, there are many devices that require network access without any user interaction, such as IP cameras, IP phones, printers, fax machines, badge readers, and so much more. So, MAB had to be added to the process flow.

The concept of completely denying access to the network if authentication fails, or if a supplicant is not configured, proved to have operational difficulties. Some level of access was needed. Originally, the switch itself would have a "Failed Authentication VLAN," where the switch makes a local decision to authorize access to a specific VLAN when a device failed authentication. Additionally, if authentication were to time out (meaning there was no supplicant on the endpoint), then it would authorize access to a locally configured guest VLAN.

One of the problems with that original logic was the lack of centralized knowledge and control. As far as the policy server was concerned, the access was denied. Yet the device was still on the network because the NAD made a local decision in spite of what the policy server said.

Figure 20-13 shows the operational flow of Closed Mode. Notice that it is nearly exactly the same as Low-Impact Mode. All the same authorization results are available for use, but Closed Mode does not allow any of the PXE-type traffic into the port prior to the authorization result, unlike Low-Impact Mode.

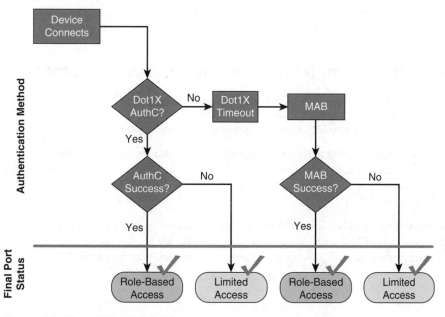

Figure 20-13 *Closed Mode Flow*

Figure 20-14 shows the port behavior in Closed Mode. Virtually zero traffic is allowed into the port before the authentication. Once the session is authorized, very specific authorization results may be applied to the port, such as:

■ VLAN assignment

■ dACL

■ URL redirection

■ MACSec encryption

■ Security Group Tags

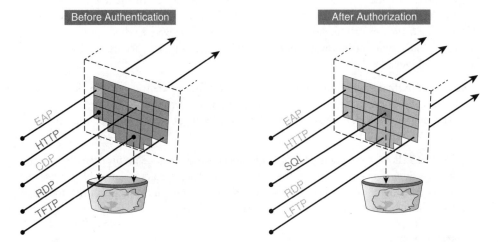

Figure 20-14 *Closed Mode Port Behavior*

Transitioning from Monitor Mode to Your End State

The key to using a phased deployment approach successfully is to understand how to transition from Monitor Mode to the end state chosen (Low-Impact Mode or Closed Mode). This is why you built out NDGs and policy sets previously in this chapter.

With Monitor Mode, you must ensure that only Access-Accept and Access-Reject authorizations are used. With Low-Impact Mode and Closed Mode, you are able to send the other authorization results, such as sending a URL redirection for Centralized Web Authentication (CWA).

The purpose of Monitor Mode is to ensure that the endpoints are all authenticating correctly, either via 802.1X with their supplicants or via MAB with profiling or even statically. You could get the first pilot switch ready, prepare all the devices for authentication, and, seeing that everything looks good, flip the switch and change the default authorization policy to send a CWA result instead of just the basic accept or reject message. That first switch will be fine, all the devices will work correctly, and life will look easy.

However, you wouldn't want to push the CWA result to the switch port if you have not fully prepared the supplicants and educated the users on a possible change of experience when logging in to the network. That would be another career-limiting event.

That is why you use NDGs. You ensure with the NAD's membership of the "Stage" NDG that you are sending the correct results to the correct network devices.

Imagine rolling out ISE to thousands of branch locations. You prepare a branch by putting it into Monitor Mode. When you are certain that that branch is fully ready and all the devices are recognized and authenticating successfully, you then can simply move the switch from the Monitor Mode NDG to the end-state NDG, and make a few command modifications to the switches.

Wireless Networks

Wireless networks behave differently than wired networks. With the creation of a WLAN, you must define the security for that WLAN. When using 802.1X, set the security to use WPA+WPA2 for key management. This setting cannot be mixed with an open authentication, and there are no "fallback" options.

For a guest authentication, the guest needs to connect to a different SSID. This is fundamentally a much different model from that used for a wired network.

Even though wireless behaves differently, the authorization results in ISE may be configured to send the responses to wired devices and wireless devices, providing a unified access strategy. This permits wireless networks to be managed as part of your Low-Impact Mode or Closed Mode deployments.

Summary

This chapter provided an overview of the phased deployment approach to deploying ISE and 802.1X. It covered the importance of Monitor Mode for wired environments, with an emphasis on using only basic authorization results while in Monitor Mode.

This chapter showed you how to configure policy sets differently for NADs based on their "Stage" NDG membership. It also discussed methods for how to use those NDG memberships to transition one switch at a time from Monitor Mode to the end-state mode of your choice.

Chapter 21

Advanced Profiling Configuration

This chapter covers the following topics:

- Profiler Work Center
- Creating custom profiles for unknown endpoints
- Advanced NetFlow probe configuration
- Profiler CoA and exceptions
- Profile monitoring and reporting

This chapter explores the intricacies of the Identity Services Engine profiling service. The profiling service is designed to help corporations correctly identify the various device types that are attaching to their network. Chapter 6, "Quick Setup of an ISE Proof of Concept," described how to quickly set up the ISE profiling service via the Visibility Setup Wizard, and Chapter 10, "Profiling Basics and Visibility," explained the basic configuration of the ISE profiling service and its different profiling probes. This chapter explains how to create basic and complex profiler policies, how to configure custom profiler rules, and how to use profiler data in authorization policies. By the end of this chapter, you will have a firm grasp of the advanced capabilities and configuration of the Cisco ISE profiling service.

Profiler Work Center

The Profiler Work Center was created to provide you with all of the steps necessary to configure profiling in ISE. Figure 21-1 shows an overview of the steps required, broken down into three sections: Prepare, Define, and Go Live & Monitor.

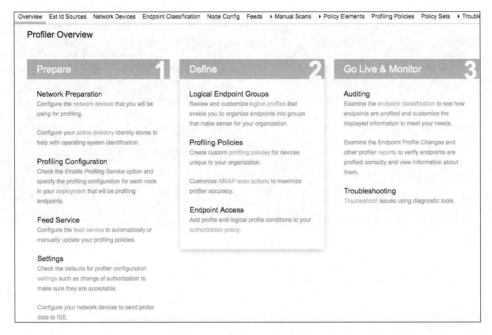

Figure 21-1 *Profiler Work Center*

Each of the steps in the three sections also aligns with one of the categories listed at the top of the Profiler Work Center. This menu bar remains visible as you step through the workflows, thus making it easy for you to navigate. By following the steps in the Work Center and using the Work Center as a go-to starting point for any profiling needs, you can quickly configure, operate, and troubleshoot the profiling service.

Creating Custom Profiles for Unknown Endpoints

Cisco ISE Profiler includes hundreds of device profiles out of the box. However, given the thousands of network device types available, it is inevitable that you will need to create a few custom profiles for your environment. When ISE cannot identify a device, it marks it as unknown and adds it to the Unknown Device Identity Group. ISE also saves all the attributes and their values it has collected on the device's behavior. You can then use these values to assist in creating your custom profile for this device type.

The key to creating a reliable custom device profile is to find profiler probe values that are unique to your custom device. If the values are too generic, you will have false-positive results matching your new device profile. Therefore, it is imperative that you choose unique profiler probe values or combination of values that become unique when combined into a profiler rule set. Refer to Chapter 10 for more information on the ISE profiling probes.

Identifying Unique Values for an Unknown Device

To identify the values that the ISE Profiler has collected on a device, go to **Context Visibility > Endpoints**. Filter under the Endpoint Profile column using the keyword **Unknown**, as shown in Figure 21-2. You can then use the other filter options to find your device.

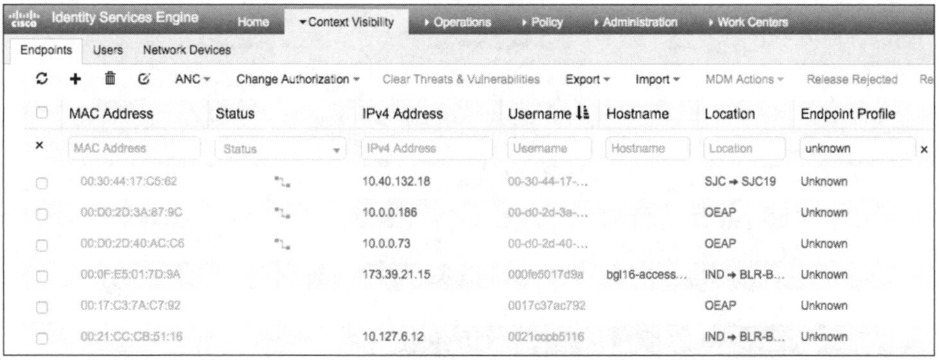

	MAC Address	Status	IPv4 Address	Username ↓↑	Hostname	Location	Endpoint Profile	
✕	MAC Address	Status ▾	IPv4 Address	Username	Hostname	Location	unknown	✕
☐	00:30:44:17:C5:62	ⁿ⌐◦	10.40.132.18	00-30-44-17-...		SJC → SJC19	Unknown	
☐	00:D0:2D:3A:87:9C	ⁿ⌐◦	10.0.0.186	00-d0-2d-3a-...		OEAP	Unknown	
☐	00:D0:2D:40:AC:C6	ⁿ⌐◦	10.0.0.73	00-d0-2d-40-...		OEAP	Unknown	
☐	00:0F:E5:01:7D:9A		173.39.21.15	000fe5017d9a	bgl16-access...	IND → BLR-B...	Unknown	
☐	00:17:C3:7A:C7:92			0017c37ac792		OEAP	Unknown	
☐	00:21:CC:C8:51:16		10.127.6.12	0021cccb5116		IND → BLR-B...	Unknown	

Figure 21-2   *Unknown Profile Endpoints in ISE*

Once you find your unknown device, click its MAC address. You are shown a list of all the attributes and their values that ISE has recognized from that device so far. Hopefully, this list is populated with enough unique information that you can now create your custom device profile. If this is not the case, you can do three things to gather more information:

- Create more traffic from this device

- Run a manual NMAP scan of the host

- Enable additional ISE profiler probes to capture more information types from this device

If all else fails, you could run an NMAP scan every time the device connects. This should be used with caution, however, because it drains ISE resources and performance.

By nature of the way profiling is used, make sure that the types of attributes and their values you use to create your device profile are

- Sent from the device every time it connects to the network

- Happen very, very early after the device is connected to the network

Figure 21-3 and Figure 21-4 depict an example device showing a manual NMAP scan and the host's various attributes/values that ISE has collected. You could then use any of these in the creation of your new custom device profile. To see the manual NMAP scan results, click on the link of the same name shown in Figure 21-3. You will be presented with data similar to that shown in Figure 21-4.

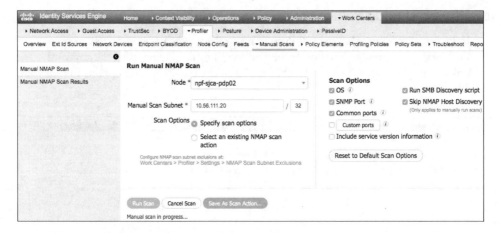

Figure 21-3   *Manual NMAP Scan*

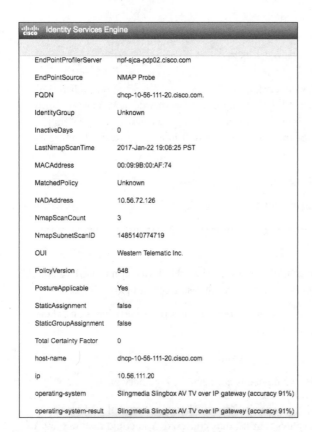

Figure 21-4   *Sample Endpoint Attributes*

Because not all attributes can be obtained from an NMAP scan, other attributes are typically gathered from multiple sources (such as DHCP helpers, NetFlow, and web redirects). In general, the more useful attributes to look for when creating custom device profilers include the following (shown with attributes from the example):

- **User-Agent:** Mozilla/4.0 (compatible; MSIE 6.0; Windows NT 5.1; SV1)

- **dhcp-class-identifier:** MSFT 5.0

- **host-name:** dhcp-10-56-111.20.cisco.com

- **ip:** 10.56.111.20

- **OUI:** Western Telematic Inc.

- **operating-system:** Slingmedia Slingbox AV TV over IP gateway

The User-Agent string is populated with information gathered from packets sent from a web browser. All web browsers send a User-Agent string in the HTML requests and responses to identity the type of browser and operating system being used.

The dhcp-class-identifier is populated either by the manufacturer of the device or by the operating system that is running on the device. In the case of embedded systems, it is almost always populated by the manufacturer and thus can be a helpful profiling attribute.

The host-name attribute can come in handy as a supporting attribute. For example, if the hostname contains a string such as "iPad," you can use that as part of a larger profiler policy with other rules. The other rules might be OUI vendor equaling "apple" and User-Agent string containing "iPad." Each rule adds something to the certainty value of the policy when matched. But alone, neither could add enough certainty to cause a match of the whole device profile policy. This helps to cut down on false positives with your custom profile policies.

Collecting Information for Custom Profiles

Table 21-1 depicts an example worksheet you could create to collect the information needed for your custom ISE device profiles.

Table 21-1   *Device Profile Information Worksheet*

Device Type	Attribute Type	Attribute Name	Condition Operator	Attribute Value	Collection Method
MRI Scanner	DHCP	host-name	Contains	TS34D	DHCP SPAN of corp. DHCP server ports
	MAC	OUI	Equals	Drier-ACME	Radius authentication
A/C Unit	DHCP	Vendor Class	Contains	GE	DHCP SPAN
	DHCP	host-name	Contains	GE	DHCP SPAN

ISE now includes hundreds of medical device profiles out of the box. Seeing as there are so many network-connected medical devices these days, let's walk through creating a theoretical profile policy to identify a medical device.

Here are the high-level steps:

Step 1.   (Optional) Create one or more profiler conditions using attributes and values collected by ISE.

Step 2.   Create an endpoint profiler policy using the conditions created.

Step 3.   (Optional) Create a logical profiler policy to group similar profiling policies under a single logical name. For example, IP Phones would include all IP Phone–related profiler policies.

Creating Custom Profiler Conditions

Creating a profiler condition is not a required step, but it is definitely a common one. Instead of creating a condition, you could just create the conditions within the profile policy ruleset. In most cases, though, you will want to create a condition for anything that you may use again, use in multiple policies, or have to change the value for periodically. Here are the steps to creating a profiler condition:

Step 1.   Connect the new device to your ISE Profiler–monitored network. Try to log on to the network with this device and then perform any typical startup activities that this device or operator would normally complete. This allows ISE to collect information about the device.

Step 2.   Look up the MAC address of your test device in the ISE endpoint classification list. Examine what was captured and look for values that either are unique by themselves or would be unique when combined. Write these down.

Step 3.   (Optional) Run a manual NMAP scan against the device. Note any useful findings of the scan.

Step 4.   Create a set of profiler conditions using the unique values that were captured. Go to **Policy > Policy Elements > Conditions > Profiling.** You should see a screen like Figure 21-5.

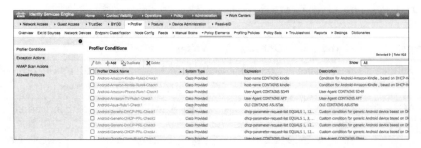

Figure 21-5   *Profiler Conditions List*

Step 5. To create a new condition, click **Add**.

Tip Each condition can only contain a single attribute and value. This makes it critical that your naming of the condition be descriptive not only of the device type but also the type of condition it is checking. Names are case sensitive and should usually start with a capital letter. A good name would be something like "Biomed-scanner-dhcp." The condition name communicates that it is a biomed device of type scanner that is keying off a DHCP attribute.

Step 6. Create your condition using the attributes and values you obtained from the endpoint's attributes list. Figure 21-6 depicts an example profiler condition for an MRI scanner.

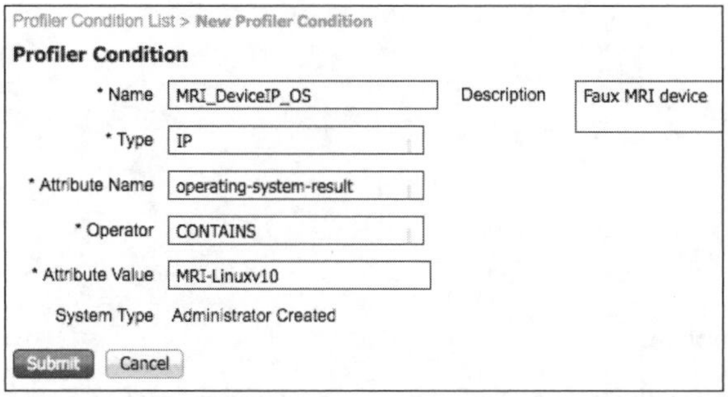

Figure 21-6 *Example Profiler Condition*

Step 7. Create as many additional profiler conditions as required for your device.

Creating Custom Profiler Policies

Even though ISE ships with hundreds of predefined profiler policies, it is inevitable that you will have a device on your network that isn't in the list. When that happens, follow these steps to create a custom profiler policy:

Step 1. Go to **Policy > Profiling > Profiling Policies**. Click **Add**.

Step 2. Fill in the policy information with a descriptive name and description.

Step 3. Fill in the Minimum Certainty Factor value for the policy; leave everything else at their default values.

Tip It is a best practice to start with a Minimum Certainty Factor value of at least 1,000 for all custom profiler policies. This ensures that they will not be undermined by current or future Cisco-provided policies.

If multiple profiler policies match a device, the one with the highest certainty value is used. Ties are handled through first alphabetical match of the policy name.

Step 4.   Add your rules. Insert a rule for each condition that you built previously for this device, as shown in the example in Figure 21-7. Ensure that when you add up your certainty values, they equal or exceed the minimum certainty value you set for the device policy.

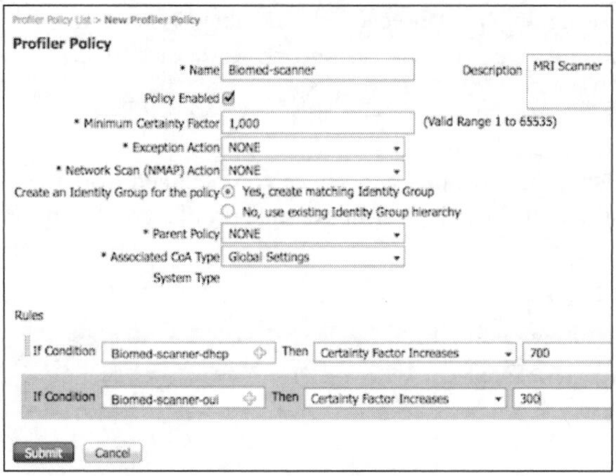

Figure 21-7   *Example Profiler Policy*

Step 5.   Click **Submit** when complete.

Step 6.   The Profiler now reprofiles all devices. Any matches to your new profile policy will take effect immediately.

Using these simple steps, you can create all sorts of custom profiles. You also might choose to group some of your policies into logical policies (see Chapter 10 for details). Some custom policies may be very simple; others might be extremely complex. Be sure to use a consistent naming scheme and always fill in the Description field on conditions and policies.

Advanced NetFlow Probe Configuration

Cisco NetFlow data for profiling comes in handy when the other ISE probes are not able to capture enough unique data from a device to be used in a custom device policy. In most cases, you will not need to enable the NetFlow probe. But if you do, this section provides some of the best practices for setting it up.

Note   The NetFlow probe should be used with caution, given its ability to overwhelm an ISE Policy Service Node (PSN) with millions of NetFlow records if not properly deployed.

Cisco NetFlow captures IP session data for network traffic flows. A NetFlow record can contain lots of useful information, but at a minimum, it contains the source/destination

(SRC/DST) IP address and port/protocol of a flow. NetFlow is supported on all Cisco router platforms and some Cisco switching and wireless platforms. NetFlow is collected from NetFlow-capable Cisco devices that export the flow data to an ISE PSN. The default port that Cisco ISE listens on for NetFlow is 9996.

NetFlow is a Cisco-proprietary messaging protocol that comes in several versions. The only version that is useful to ISE is NetFlow v9. Don't bother sending ISE the other versions; it's just not worth it. The following is a partial list of Cisco devices that support NetFlow:

- Cisco 7.4+ WLC

- Cisco ISR Router

- Cisco ISR G2

- Cisco 4500 Sup 8

- Cisco ASR1000

- Cisco ASR9000

- Cisco 3750X and 3560X

- Cisco 4500 and 4500X with Sup 7

- Cisco 6500 with SUP2T

- Cisco 6500 with Sup 32 and Sup 720

- Cisco 7600

- Cisco C3650/3850

- Cisco UCS Servers

- Cisco XR12000/12000 Series Routers

- Cisco CRS-1

- Cisco Nexus 7000

- Cisco Nexus 1000V

In addition to the NetFlow probe's ability to match a device to a device type based on its traffic flow characteristics, it can also identify a device that is sending anomalous traffic. Here is an example: A certain biomed device should only ever talk to two IP addresses and only on two TCP ports, 5454 and 4533. If NetFlow recognizes traffic other than that, the ISE Profiler can issue a Change of Authorization (CoA) or start an NMAP scan of the device to see if the device type for that MAC address has changed. Perhaps someone is trying to spoof the MAC address of a known device with his or her own device. Or perhaps the device itself has been compromised with malware and is being used as part of a botnet. Whatever the case might be for the anomalous traffic, NetFlow can detect it, and the ISE Profiler can take additional action because of it.

Commonly Used NetFlow Attributes

Cisco NetFlow offers a multitude of field types, called attributes by ISE. However, only a handful are commonly used for developing ISE device profiles. Here is a list and description of the most favored ISE NetFlow attributes:

- **IPv4_SRC_ADDR:** Source IP address of the flow

- **IPv4_DST_ADDR:** Destination IP address of the flow

- **L4_SRC_PORT:** TCP/UDP source port

- **L4_DST_PORT:** TCP/UDP destination port

- **DIRECTION:** Flow direction (0 - ingress flow, 1 - egress flow)

Example Profiler Policy Using NetFlow

Typically, NetFlow attributes would be used with other ISE probe data, such as OUI and DHCP rules. Figure 21-8 depicts a sample profiler policy that is just pure NetFlow rules.

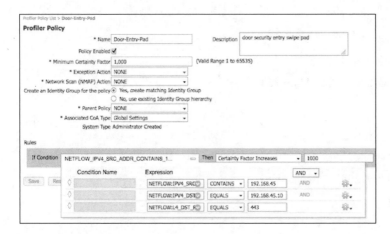

Figure 21-8   *NetFlow-Based Profiler Policy*

The policy shown in Figure 21-8 has one rule, but that rule is made up of three conditions that all must be true, as indicated by the AND operator between them:

- IPv4 source address contains 192.168.45. This effectively means the SRC addr needs to be in the 192.168.45.0/21 subnet.

- IPv4 destination address must be 192.168.45.10. The source must be talking to this destination.

- Layer 4 destination UDP/TCP port must equal 443.

Also notice that the policy does not use defined conditions but instead creates new conditions within the policy itself. To create new conditions, click the **Create New Condition** button, as show in Figure 21-9.

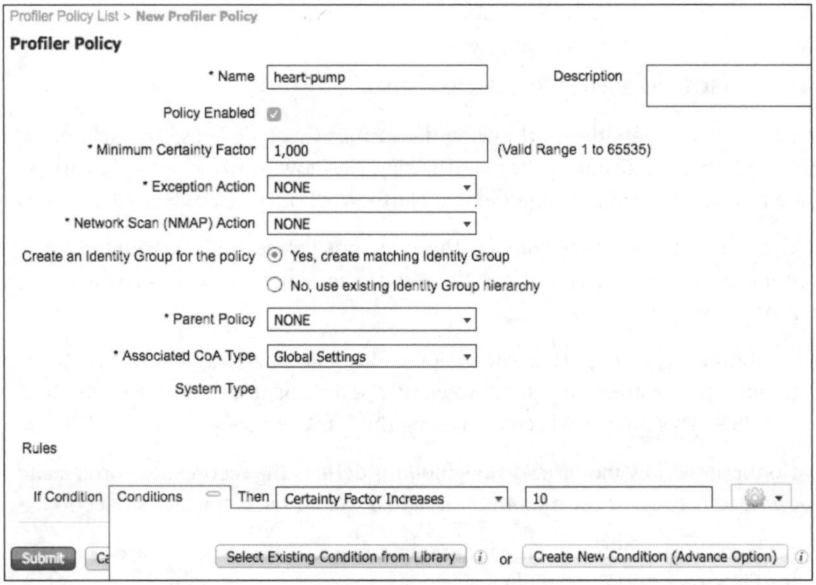

Figure 21-9   *NetFlow-Based Profiler Policy: Creating New Conditions*

Designing for Efficient Collection of NetFlow Data

As stated earlier, the collection of NetFlow data, if not done properly, can saturate ISE, causing a sort of denial-of-service condition. By using some best practices, you can alleviate much of that risk. Consider the following best practices in your deployment:

- Export an IP flow only once and from a single direction (ingress or egress) to ISE profiler.

- Use a dedicated ISE network interface for NetFlow collection. It will have its own IP address.

- Export flows to ISE only from parts of the network that are needed in ISE device profile policies.

- Position your PSNs as close to the NetFlow collectors as is practical. Avoid collection over a long-distance or low-speed WAN link.

- Use flexible NetFlow to reduce the amount of data that is exported to the ISE PSN profiler.

■ Implement a third-party NetFlow collector and forwarder that allows you to filter the exported NetFlow data to the bare minimum required for your ISE NetFlow policies.

■ Regularly monitor the health of your PSNs to ensure that NetFlow is not causing a problem.

Configuration of NetFlow on Cisco Devices

There are many ways to configure NetFlow on the various Cisco devices. This section focuses on the best practices and tips for configuring NetFlow to work properly with ISE. There are four steps to configuring flexible NetFlow v9 on a Cisco device:

Step 1. Create customized flow records. These records define which attributes you want to store for the flow. Keep these to the minimum needed for your profiler policies.

Step 2. Configure a flow exporter. The exporter destination is the closest ISE PSN running the Profiler. Remember to export to a dedicated IP/interface on the ISE PSN. This interface is created using the ISE CLI.

Step 3. Configure a flow monitor. A flow monitor defines the records, exporters, and cache to use. The flow monitor is assigned to interfaces for flow collection.

Step 4. Apply a flow monitor to one or more interfaces. This starts the flexible NetFlow process. Your done!

Example 21-1 through 21-4 outline some of the best practice configurations for each step.

Example 21-1 *Flexible NetFlow Record Configuration*

```
flow record ise-flows
 description export only flows needed by ise
 match datalink mac source-address
 match ipv4 protocol
 match ipv4 source address
 match ipv4 destination address
 match transport source-port
 match transport destination-port
 match transport tcp flags


Cswitch# show flow record
flow record ise-flows:
  Description:        export only flows needed by ise
  No. of users:      0
  Total field space: 20 bytes
  Fields:
    match datalink mac source-address
    match ipv4 protocol
```

```
    match ipv4 source address
    match ipv4 destination address
    match transport source-port
    match transport destination-port
    match transport tcp flags
```

Example 21-2 *Flexible NetFlow Exporter Configuration*

```
flow exporter ISE
 description Export to ISE PSN1
 destination 10.1.103.4
 source TenGigabitEthernet1/1/1
 transport udp 9996


Cswitch# show flow exporter
Flow Exporter ISE:
  Description:              Export to ISE PSN1
  Export protocol:         NetFlow Version 9
  Transport Configuration:
    Destination IP address: 10.1.103.4
    Source IP address:      10.1.48.2
    Source Interface:       TenGigabitEthernet1/1/1
    Transport Protocol:     UDP
    Destination Port:       9996
    Source Port:            49736
    DSCP:                   0x0
    TTL:                    255
    Output Features:        Not Used
```

Example 21-3 *Flexible NetFlow Monitor Configuration*

```
flow monitor ISE-Flows
 description Used for ISE Profiler
 record ise-flows
 exporter ISE
 cache timeout active 60


Cswitch# show flow monitor
Flow Monitor ISE-Flows:
  Description:       Used for ISE Profiler
  Flow Record:      ise-flows
  Flow Exporter:    ISE
```

```
Cache:
   Type:               normal
   Status:             not allocated
   Size:               128 entries / 0 bytes
Cache:
   Type:               normal (Platform cache)
   Status:             not allocated
   Size:               Unknown
 Timers:

                       Local       Global
   Inactive Timeout:   15 secs
   Active Timeout:     60 secs     1800 secs
   Update Timeout:     1800 secs
```

Example 21-4   *Flexible NetFlow Interface Configuration*

```
interface TenGigabitEthernet1/1/1
 description Cat6K Ten1/5
 no switchport
 ip flow monitor ISE-Flows input
 ip address 10.1.48.2 255.255.255.252
 ip authentication mode eigrp 1 md5
 ip authentication key-chain eigrp 1 EIGRP
 load-interval 60

Cswitch# show flow interface te1/1/1
Interface TenGigabitEthernet1/1/1
  FNF: monitor:         ISE-Flows
       direction:       Input
       traffic(ip):     on
```

Profiler CoA and Exceptions

If you want the ISE Profiler to take a more proactive action based on a device profile rule match or network activity, use the Profiler Change of Authorization (CoA) and exception rules. By default, the Profiler is passive and doesn't perform CoA actions. You may want to chance this default behavior globally and/or based on certain profiler conditions and exceptions. A profiler policy–based CoA action overrides the global CoA settings for the Profiler.

Here are some of the conditions for which the ISE Profiler issues a CoA request to a NAD:

■ An endpoint is deleted from the Endpoints page.

■ A profile policy exception is triggered.

■ An endpoint is profiled for the first time.

- There is any change in an endpoint identity group, and the endpoint identity group is used in the authorization policy for the following:

  - The endpoint identity group changes for endpoints when they are dynamically profiled.

  - The endpoint identity group changes when the static assignment flag is set to true for a dynamic endpoint.

- An endpoint profiler policy has changed, and the policy is used in an authorization policy.

- A profiler policy triggers a re-authentication based on anomalous device behavior.

- A device changes to a new profile that would result in a change to the endpoint's access rights. These access rights are defined in the authorization policies that use device identity groups.

It is also important to know which conditions do not produce a CoA event. Here are many of them:

- An endpoint disconnects from the network.

- A wired endpoint that is EAP capable connects to the network. For example, an 802.1X supplicant-enabled client.

- Multiple hosts are connected to a single port. A CoA with reauthorization will be issued even if you have configured port bounce (as described in the following section).

- For wireless clients, a packet-of-disconnect is sent to the WLC instead of a port bounce.

- CoA is disabled for any device going through the Guest Device Registration portal/ flow.

- If the global profiler CoA setting in ISE is set to No CoA, all profiler policy CoA actions are ignored. In effect, a global No CoA setting disables the ability of ISE profiler to issue any CoA.

Types of CoA

There are three types of CoA:

- No CoA (default)
- Port Bounce
- Reauth

To use CoA inside the Profiler, you have to enable it globally. Go to **Administration > System > Settings > Profiling**. In most cases, you will select the Reauth option, as shown in Figure 21-10. Best practice is to use Port Bounce for non-802.1X endpoints and Reauth for 802.1X endpoints.

Profiler Configuration

* CoA Type:	Reauth ▾
Current custom SNMP community strings:	●●●●●● [Show]
Change custom SNMP community strings:	[ ] (For NMAP,
Confirm changed custom SNMP community strings:	[ ] (For NMAP,
EndPoint Attribute Filter:	☑ Enabled ⓘ
Enable Anomalous Behaviour Detection:	☑ Enabled ⓘ
Enable Anomalous Behaviour Enforcement:	☑ Enabled

[Save] [Reset]

Figure 21-10 *Global Profiler CoA Setting*

Creating Exception Actions

A custom exception action does two things:

- Forces a CoA or prevents a CoA from happening

- Statically assigns the device to a profiler policy

To create an exception action, go to **Policy > Policy Elements > Results > Profiling > Exception Actions**. The CoA option either forces a CoA if checked or prevents a CoA if unchecked. See Figure 21-11 for an example.

Profiler Exception Action List > **New Profiler Exception Action**

Profiler Exception Action

* Name	[Force_COA_Unknown] Description [ ]
COA Action	☑ Force COA
* Policy Assignment	[Unknown ▾]
System Type	Administrator Created

[Submit] [Cancel]

Figure 21-11 *Exception Action*

The action shown in Figure 21-11 forces a CoA and assigns the Unknown profile to the device.

Configuring CoA and Exceptions in Profiler Policies

After you have created a few exception actions, you can use them in your profiler policies. It is also in the profile policy that you can change the CoA action from the global default. Changing the CoA action, known as the Associated CoA Type in the GUI, is trivial. As shown in Figure 21-12, use the Associated CoA Type drop-down list to select the type you want to use for this profiler profile.

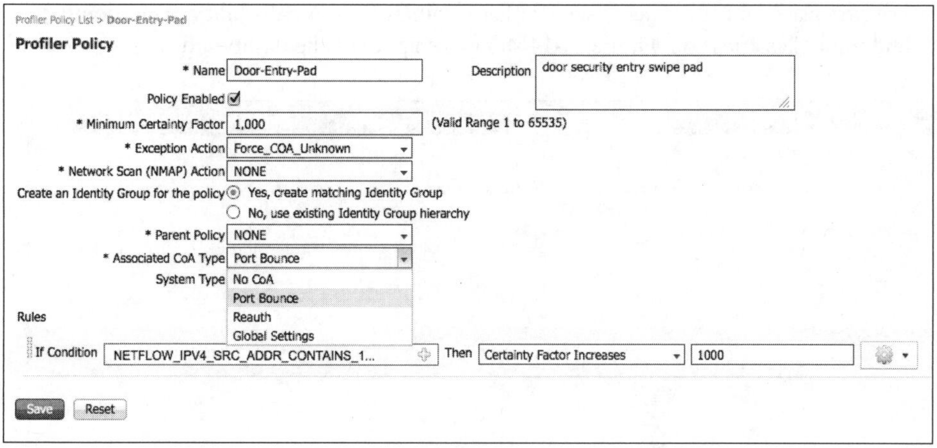

Figure 21-12 *Per-Profiler Policy CoA Action*

To configure an exception rule, you need to define which condition triggers an exception action. In Figure 21-13, the exception condition defined is this: If device communicates with any IP destination address except for 192.168.45.10, then issue the exception action.

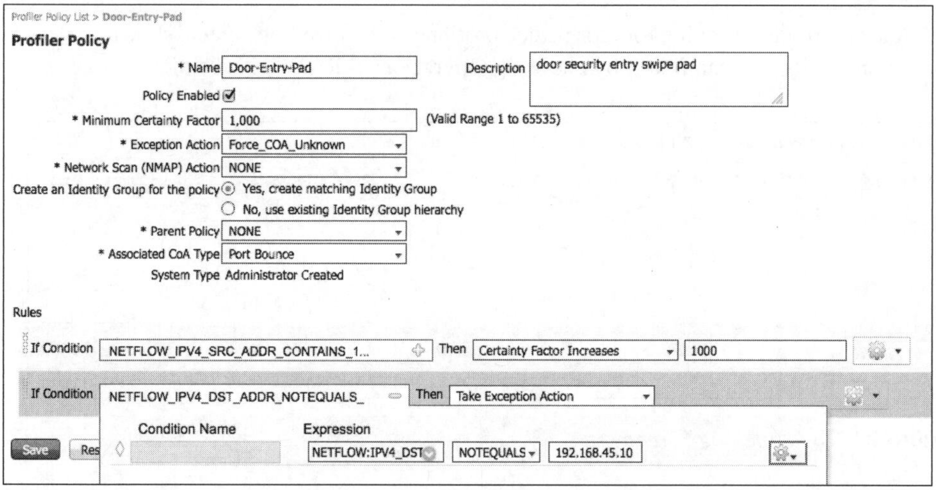

Figure 21-13 *Exception Profiler Policy Rule*

Profiler Monitoring and Reporting

Cisco ISE includes several reports that deal specifically with the Profiler function. These reports can be used to audit which devices are on your network, provide you with a device inventory, help you troubleshoot Profiler issues, and so on. This section covers the most useful reports and monitoring tools available in ISE.

The first place you can quickly see Profiler results is **Context Visibility > Endpoints > Endpoint Classification**. Figure 21-14 shows a snippet of the dashboard.

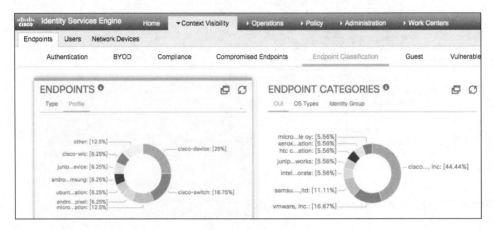

Figure 21-14   *Endpoint Classification Dashboard*

This dashboard provides you with a live snapshot of the profiled endpoints on the network and a detailed view of profiled endpoints.

A useful troubleshooting tool for device profiling is the Live Log screen, shown in Figure 21-15. You can find it by choosing **Operations > RADIUS Livelog**.

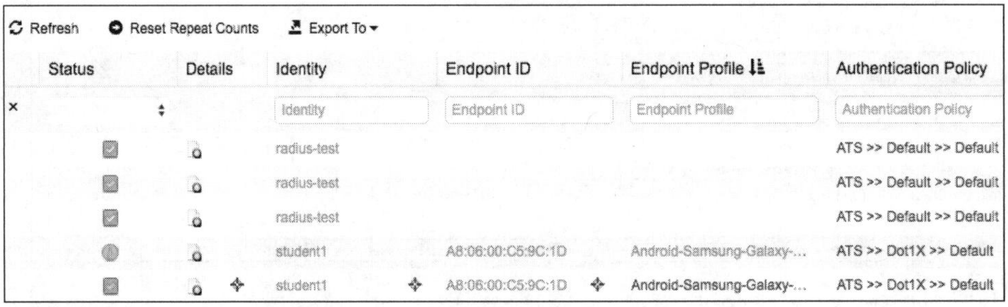

	Status		Details	Identity	Endpoint ID	Endpoint Profile ↓↑	Authentication Policy
×		↕		Identity	Endpoint ID	Endpoint Profile	Authentication Policy
	☑		ā	radius-test			ATS >> Default >> Default
	☑		ā	radius-test			ATS >> Default >> Default
	☑		ā	radius-test			ATS >> Default >> Default
	⊙		ā	student1	A8:06:00:C5:9C:1D	Android-Samsung-Galaxy-...	ATS >> Dot1X >> Default
	☑		ā ✦	student1 ✦	A8:06:00:C5:9C:1D ✦	Android-Samsung-Galaxy-...	ATS >> Dot1X >> Default

Figure 21-15   *Live Log Screen*

The Endpoint Profile column shows the profile group that the device matched. This value doesn't necessarily match the exact profile policy that was a match. It shows the closest identity group that is part of the profile policy hierarchy. To see the actual match profile for the device, click the **Details** icon in the row of the device. This opens the Details screen. As shown in Figure 21-16, if you scroll down you see the EndPoint Matched Policy attribute with a value. This value shows the exact profile policy matched.

Profiler Detail	
Logged At	2017-02-04 21:47:45.041
Server	atw-ise231
Endpoint MacAddress	D0:87:E2:12:B2:04
Day	
Endpoint Static Assignment	SNMPQuery Probe
Endpoint OUI	Samsung Electronics Co.,Ltd
Matched Rule	
Certainty Metric	70
Endpoint Matched Policy	Android-Samsung
Matched Rule	
Endpoint Identity Group	Android
Event	Profiler EndPoint profiling event occurred

Profiler History	
Day	Endpoint Profile
2017-02-04 21:47:45.041	Android-Samsung
2017-02-04 09:46:26.776	Android-Samsung

Figure 21-16   *Live Auth Details*

Under **Operations > Reports > Endpoints and Users,** you see several profiler reports. Figure 21-17 shows a list of them.

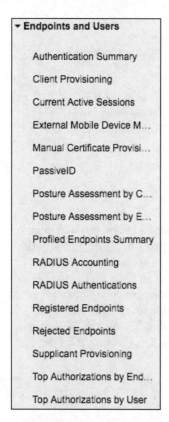

▼ **Endpoints and Users**

Authentication Summary

Client Provisioning

Current Active Sessions

External Mobile Device M…

Manual Certificate Provisi…

PassiveID

Posture Assessment by C…

Posture Assessment by E…

Profiled Endpoints Summary

RADIUS Accounting

RADIUS Authentications

Registered Endpoints

Rejected Endpoints

Supplicant Provisioning

Top Authorizations by End…

Top Authorizations by User

Figure 21-17   *Profiler Reports*

Two of the most helpful reports are

- **Posture Assessment by Condition:** This report shows endpoints that have changed from one profile match to a different profile match.

- **Profiled Endpoints Summary Report:** Clicking Details next to a device provides you all sorts of useful information for reporting and troubleshooting the Profiler. This screen also shows you the profile history of a particular device over time, as shown in Figure 21-18.

Profiler Detail	
Logged At	2017-02-04 21:47:45.041
Server	atw-ise231
Endpoint MacAddress	D0:87:E2:12:B2:04
Day	
Endpoint Static Assignment	SNMPQuery Probe
Endpoint OUI	Samsung Electronics Co.,Ltd
Matched Rule	
Certainity Metric	70
Endpoint Matched Policy	Android-Samsung
Matched Rule	
Endpoint Identity Group	Android
Event	Profiler EndPoint profiling event occurred

Profiler History	
Day	Endpoint Profile
2017-02-04 21:47:45.041	Android-Samsung
2017-02-04 09:46:26.776	Android-Samsung

Figure 21-18   *Profiler History*

Summary

This chapter covered several advanced profiler concepts, configurations, and best practices. These included creating custom profiles, advanced NetFlow, Change of Authorization (CoA), profiler exceptions, and profiler monitoring and reports. This chapter discussed that, when implemented correctly, NetFlow can be used as an effective profiler probe. It also discussed how to create your own custom and complex profile conditions and policies. Using the skills presented in this chapter, you will be able to correctly identify all of the devices on your network. As mentioned in the chapter introduction, the ISE Visibility Setup Wizard enables you to set up the Profiler very quickly. See Chapter 10 for details.

Chapter 22

Cisco TrustSec AKA Security Group Access

This chapter covers the following topics:

- Ingress access control challenges
- What Is TrustSec?
- Transport: Security Group Tag (SGT) eXchange Protocol (SXP)
- Transport: Platform eXchange Grid (pxGrid)
- Transport: native tagging
- Enforcement

Throughout this book, you have been exposed to many different ways of controlling network access based on the context of a user and device. There is VLAN assignment, in which Layer 2 segments are created and access is controlled at the Layer 3 edge, or by isolating that VLAN into a segmented virtual network (VRF). Additionally, there is ACL assignment, which can be a local ACL, called into action by a RADIUS attribute, or a downloadable ACL (dACL). These ACLs are applied ingress at the switch port or virtual port in the case of the Wireless LAN Controller (WLC).

These are all good access control methods, but regulating passage only at the point of network ingress can leave room for a more desirable and scalable solution. This chapter discusses one such Cisco enhancement to make access control more scalable and powerful: TrustSec (formerly known as Security Group Access [SGA]).

With TrustSec, controls are defined simply using endpoint roles, not IP addresses. By classifying systems using human-friendly logical groups, security rules can be defined using these groups, which are more flexible and much easier to manage than using IP address-based controls.

IP addresses do not indicate the role of a system, the type of application a server hosts, the purpose of an Internet of Things (IoT) device, or the threat state of a system, but a TrustSec security group can denote any of these roles. These security groups can be used to simplify firewall rules, web security appliance policies, and the access control lists (ACL) used in switches, WLAN controllers, and routers.

Ingress Access Control Challenges

VLAN assignment and dACLs are fantastic and classic ways of controlling access to a network; however, when a network grows, so do the challenges of keeping up with the ingress access controls. Let's look at each one of these standard use cases individually and discuss the challenges.

VLAN Assignment

VLAN assignment based on the context of a user or device is a common way to control access to the network. Let's use a hypothetical scenario of controlling access to servers that contain credit-card data, which falls under Payment Card Industry Data Security Standard (PCI DSS) compliance.

1. A user is a member of the Retail-Managers group in Active Directory.

2. The posture of the system is compliant.

3. Therefore, ISE assigns the user into the PCI-Allowed VLAN on the switch or WLC.

   Now, to use that VLAN assignment to control access to the servers that house that PCI data, an ACL must be applied somewhere. Let's assume the ACL is applied at a firewall between the campus/branch networks and the data center.

4. The ACL on the data center firewall must be updated to include the entire source IP address range of PCI-Allowed VLANs throughout the entire network infrastructure, as shown in Figure 22-1.

Source	Dest	Action
192.168.100.0/24	PCI	Permit
Any	PCI	Deny

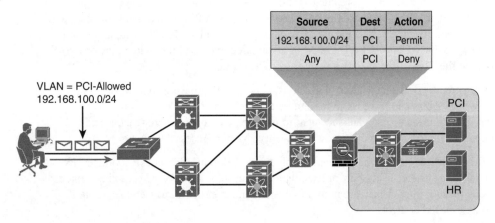

Figure 22-1   *Controlling Access with VLANs on Single Switch*

Next, the company decided to control access to the HR server, so that only members of the HR department may talk to HR servers. Another set of rules must be built that assign the HR VLAN, and another set of entries in the access list, as shown in Figure 22-2.

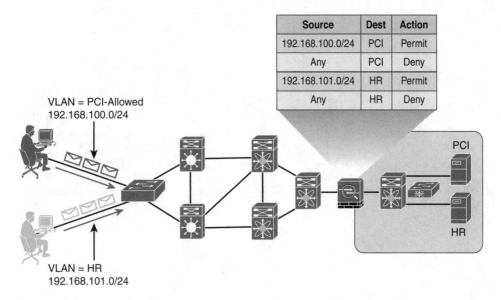

Source	Dest	Action
192.168.100.0/24	PCI	Permit
Any	PCI	Deny
192.168.101.0/24	HR	Permit
Any	HR	Deny

VLAN = PCI-Allowed
192.168.100.0/24

PCI

VLAN = HR
192.168.101.0/24

HR

Figure 22-2 *Controlling Access with Two VLANs on Single Switch*

Now, consider how this can scale as you continue to add VLANs and switches and WLCs to the equation. One of your large customers has over 50,000 switches in its access layer. That is a tremendous number of VLANs to create and addresses to maintain in an access list on a firewall. That same customer has 15 full-time employees managing the firewall rules. This customer needs to find some better mechanism to control access that would lower its operating expense (OPEX) tremendously.

What if you had 100 remote sites? That is 100 new IP subnets, which can easily modify your existing route summarization strategy. When that is the case, the route summarization alone can cause a network redesign, which will add even more operational cost, as shown in Figure 22-3.

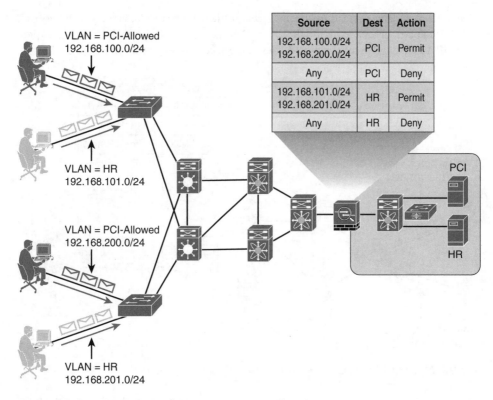

Source	Dest	Action
192.168.100.0/24 192.168.200.0/24	PCI	Permit
Any	PCI	Deny
192.168.101.0/24 192.168.201.0/24	HR	Permit
Any	HR	Deny

Figure 22-3 *VLAN Control Can Be Operationally Expensive*

There is a formula to determine the number of access control entries (ACE) in an access control list (ACL). The formula takes the number of sources multiplied by the number of destinations multiplied by the permissions of the ACL:

(# of sources) × (# of destinations) × permissions = # of ACEs

With the environment depicted in Figure 22-3, with only 4 sources × 2 destinations × 4 permissions, you would need 32 ACEs. We often refer to this as *ACE explosion*. This is obviously just a small example. This is examined more in the following sections.

Ingress Access Control Lists

Another way to control access is to use ACLs applied at ingress (inbound) at the port (or virtual port) that the user or device is using to access the network. This could be locally defined ACLs that are called by using the filter-ID RADIUS attribute, or they could be dACLs, where the entire ACL is defined on ISE and downloaded to the port.

Obviously, dACLs provide a better operational model, because there is only one place to update an ACL when a change needs to be made. Additionally, the number of ACEs required is lower when applying the ACL to a switch port than it would be to apply the ACL to a centralized location. Because the ACL is being applied at the point of ingress, there would only be a single source IP address (theoretically). Cisco switches perform source substitution on these ACLs to make it even easier. With source substitution, the **any** keyword in the source field of an ACL is replaced with the actual IP address of the host on the switch port.

Using the same formula for six destinations and four permissions, you would have

1 source × 6 destinations × 4 permissions = 24 ACEs

However, there are a few complications with using ACLs on access layer devices. Two major drawbacks that exist are the regular maintenance of the ACLs and the size of the ACLs.

If ACLs are being used to explicitly defend hosts, they must be updated regularly for all new destinations that get added to the network. This can cause an exorbitant amount of OPEX maintaining the lists and ensuring they get updated correctly. Additionally, there is a limited number of ACEs that a switch will be able to apply.

ACLs get loaded into and executed from Ternary Content Addressable Memory (TCAM). Access layer switches have a limited amount of TCAM, which is usually assigned per ASIC. Therefore, the number of ACEs that can be loaded depends on various factors, such as the number of hosts per ASIC and the amount of free TCAM space.

Because of that limited amount of TCAM, ACLs cannot be overly large, especially when the access layer may be a mixture of different switches, each switch having a different level of TCAM per ASIC. The best practice recommendation is to keep the ACEs less than 64 per dACL. This may need to be adjusted for your specific environment, but it is a good place to start.

Figure 22-4 shows ingress ACLs in the network.

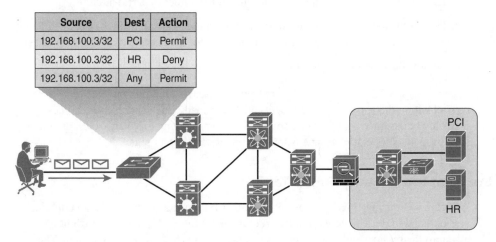

Source	Dest	Action
192.168.100.3/32	PCI	Permit
192.168.100.3/32	HR	Deny
192.168.100.3/32	Any	Permit

Figure 22-4 *Ingress ACLs*

What Is TrustSec?

TrustSec is a next-generation access control enforcement that was created to address the growing operational expenses with maintaining firewall rules and ACLs. TrustSec is a complementary enforcement technology that removes the concerns of TCAM space and ACE explosion.

The ultimate goal of TrustSec is to assign a tag (known as a Security Group Tag, or SGT) to the user/device's traffic at ingress (inbound into the network), and then enforce the access elsewhere in the infrastructure (in the data center, for example). So, TrustSec assigns an SGT at login and enforces that SGT elsewhere in the network (egress enforcement).

The SGT should be representative of some overarching roles within the company. For instance, an SGT may be assigned to a GUEST user, so that GUEST traffic may be isolated from non-GUEST traffic throughout the infrastructure. Here is a list of some common security groups:

- **Network Infrastructure:** This SGT gets assigned to all the switches, routers, WLCs, and firewalls within the organization.

- **Network Services:** This SGT is assigned to the servers providing common services that most everyone should be able to reach (DNS, DHCP, NTP, and so on).

- **Executive:** Many organizations may classify their executives into their own SGT, simply to ensure that executives will never be denied access to anything.

- **Sales:** This SGT would signify a member of the sales organization.

- **Finance:** This SGT would signify a member of the finance organization.

- **HR:** Used to signify a member of the Human Resources department.

- **Line-of-Business-1:** SGTs are used often when an umbrella company has many different lines of business, and those lines of business cannot have access to each other's data.

- **Line-of-Business-2:** *See previous.*

The trick with SGTs is to use them for bulk access control, and do your fine-grain access control within the application security itself. Additionally, each end user or end device may only be assigned a single SGT. You do not want to create too many roles, or you will spend too much operational time mapping users to the correct tags.

So, What Is a Security Group Tag?

A Security Group Tag (SGT) is a 16-bit value that ISE assigns to the user's or endpoint's session upon login. The network infrastructure views the SGT as another attribute to assign to the session, and inserts the Layer 2 tag into all traffic from that session. The SGT can represent the context of the user and device. Let's look at an example.

This is one of our favorite examples from a client that we worked with directly. It is a retail organization, and therefore, it accepts credit cards from customers, which places it under the domain of PCI DSS compliance. Access to any server housing credit-card data must be protected as strictly as any technology will allow.

In this client's case, we defined a rule in ISE that looked for machine and user authentication (EAP chaining) *and* verified the user was a member of a PCI group in Active Directory *and* the machine's posture was compliant. If the user and machine met all these conditions, an SGT named PCI was assigned. No access was granted to PCI servers without the PCI SGT.

So, as you can see, SGTs can be applied based on the full context of the authentication or simply based on a single condition, such as Guest.

> **Note**   The endpoint itself is not aware of the SGT. It is known in the network infrastructure. Figure 22-5 illustrates the SGT being assigned to an authentication session.

```
C3750X#sho authentication sess int g1/0/2
            Interface:  GigabitEthernet1/0/2
          MAC Address:  0050.5687.0004
           IP Address:  10.1.10.50
            User-Name:  employee1
               Status:  Authz Success
               Domain:  DATA
      Security Policy:  Should Secure
      Security Status:  Unsecure
       Oper host mode:  multi-auth
     Oper control dir:  both
        Authorized By:  Authentication Server
           Vlan Group:  N/A
             ACS ACL:   xACSACLx-IP-Employee-ACL-
                 SGT:   0002-0  ◄─────────
      Session timeout:  N/A
         Idle timeout:  N/A
    Common Session ID:  0A01300200000022DC6C328F
      Acct Session ID:  0x00000033
               Handle:  0xCC000022

Runnable methods list:
      Method    State
      dot1x     Authc Success
```

Figure 22-5   *SGT Applied to Session*

Defining the SGTs

One could say that ISE wears many hats. ISE serves as a TrustSec controller of sorts. In fact, there is even a dedicated TrustSec Work Center in ISE, and ISE can accurately be viewed as the single source of truth for what SGTs exist.

To view the TrustSec Work Center, navigate to **Work Centers > TrustSec**. Figure 22-6 shows an example TrustSec dashboard within the Work Center.

Figure 22-6   *TrustSec Dashboard*

ISE considers an SGT a policy result. Therefore, create one SGT result for each SGT you want to define in the environment. To help customers understand usages of SGTs, ISE also comes with a large number of preexisting SGTs with assigned icons, as shown in Figure 22-7.

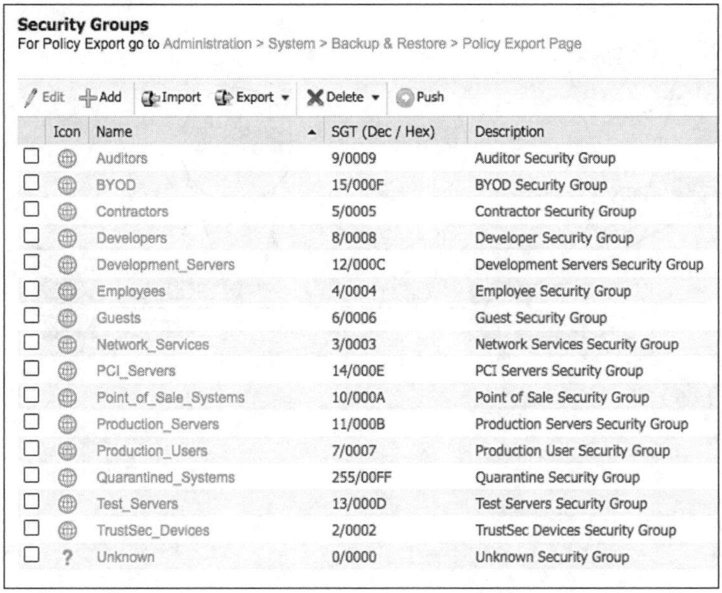

Security Groups
For Policy Export go to Administration > System > Backup & Restore > Policy Export Page

Icon	Name	SGT (Dec / Hex)	Description
⊕	Auditors	9/0009	Auditor Security Group
⊕	BYOD	15/000F	BYOD Security Group
⊕	Contractors	5/0005	Contractor Security Group
⊕	Developers	8/0008	Developer Security Group
⊕	Development_Servers	12/000C	Development Servers Security Group
⊕	Employees	4/0004	Employee Security Group
⊕	Guests	6/0006	Guest Security Group
⊕	Network_Services	3/0003	Network Services Security Group
⊕	PCI_Servers	14/000E	PCI Servers Security Group
⊕	Point_of_Sale_Systems	10/000A	Point of Sale Security Group
⊕	Production_Servers	11/000B	Production Servers Security Group
⊕	Production_Users	7/0007	Production User Security Group
⊕	Quarantined_Systems	255/00FF	Quarantine Security Group
⊕	Test_Servers	13/000D	Test Servers Security Group
⊕	TrustSec_Devices	2/0002	TrustSec Devices Security Group
?	Unknown	0/0000	Unknown Security Group

Figure 22-7 *Security Groups*

To view the preexisting SGTs or to create new ones within the ISE GUI, navigate to **Work Centers > TrustSec > Components > Security Groups**.

Notice in the last row of Figure 22-7 the default SGT of 0, Unknown. This SGT will be used if traffic arrives that is untagged. In other words, even the lack of an SGT can be used in the security policy.

Classification

This should not come as a surprise to you, but to use SGTs within your infrastructure, your devices should support SGTs. All supported Cisco switches and wireless controllers do support the assignment of the SGT. This is defined as *classification*. The process of communicating that assigned SGT upstream into the network can either occur via native tagging or via a peering protocol, and this process is defined as *transport*.

Figure 22-8 shows an example of one access switch that has native tagging, and the packets get tagged on the uplink port and through the infrastructure. It also shows a non-native-tagging capable switch, which uses a peering protocol to update the upstream switch. In both cases, the upstream switch continues to tag the traffic throughout the infrastructure.

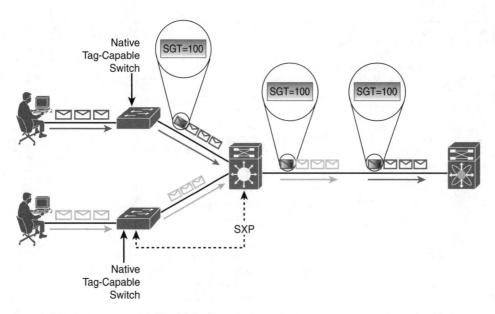

Figure 22-8   *Security Group Tagging*

To use the Security Group Tag, the tag needs to be assigned, which can happen in one of three ways: the SGT can be assigned dynamically, and be downloaded as the result of an ISE authorization; it can be assigned manually at the port level; or it can be mapped to IP addresses and downloaded to SGT-capable devices.

Note   For network devices that do not support SGT classification, ISE itself may still assign the tag as part of the authorization result. The network session within ISE's session directory will be updated and the IP address-to-SGT mapping may be shared via SXP or pxGrid for enforcement elsewhere.

Dynamically Assigning an SGT via 802.1X

Assigning an SGT is as simple as adding it as another permission or result of an authorization in an authorization policy. ISE comes with a few preconfigured examples of the TAG assignment, as highlighted in Figure 22-9. You can see these by navigating to **Work Centers > Network Access > Policy Sets > Default > Authorization**. The examples in Figure 22-9 show three different SGTs being assigned: BYOD, Employees, and Guests.

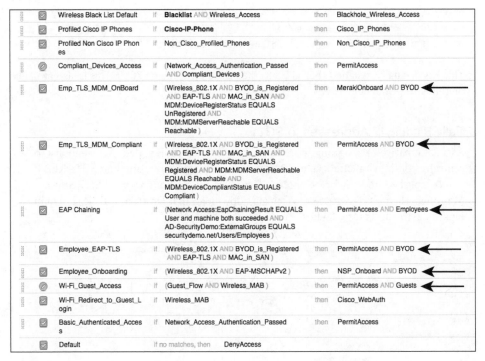

⬚	☑	Wireless Black List Default	if	**Blacklist** AND Wireless_Access	then	Blackhole_Wireless_Access
⬚	☑	Profiled Cisco IP Phones	if	**Cisco-IP-Phone**	then	Cisco_IP_Phones
⬚	☑	Profiled Non Cisco IP Phones	if	Non_Cisco_Profiled_Phones	then	Non_Cisco_IP_Phones
⬚	⊘	Compliant_Devices_Access	if	(Network_Access_Authentication_Passed AND Compliant_Devices)	then	PermitAccess
⬚	☑	Emp_TLS_MDM_OnBoard	if	(Wireless_802.1X AND BYOD_is_Registered AND EAP-TLS AND MAC_in_SAN AND MDM:DeviceRegisterStatus EQUALS UnRegistered AND MDM:MDMServerReachable EQUALS Reachable)	then	MerakiOnboard AND BYOD ←
⬚	☑	Emp_TLS_MDM_Compliant	if	(Wireless_802.1X AND BYOD_is_Registered AND EAP-TLS AND MAC_in_SAN AND MDM:DeviceRegisterStatus EQUALS Registered AND MDM:MDMServerReachable EQUALS Reachable AND MDM:DeviceCompliantStatus EQUALS Compliant)	then	PermitAccess AND BYOD ←
⬚	☑	EAP Chaining	if	(Network Access:EapChainingResult EQUALS User and machine both succeeded AND AD-SecurityDemo:ExternalGroups EQUALS securitydemo.net/Users/Employees)	then	PermitAccess AND Employees ←
⬚	☑	Employee_EAP-TLS	if	(Wireless_802.1X AND BYOD_is_Registered AND EAP-TLS AND MAC_in_SAN)	then	PermitAccess AND BYOD ←
⬚	☑	Employee_Onboarding	if	(Wireless_802.1X AND EAP-MSCHAPv2)	then	NSP_Onboard AND BYOD ←
⬚	⊘	Wi-Fi_Guest_Access	if	(Guest_Flow AND Wireless_MAB)	then	PermitAccess AND Guests ←
⬚	☑	Wi-Fi_Redirect_to_Guest_Login	if	Wireless_MAB	then	Cisco_WebAuth
⬚	☑	Basic_Authenticated_Access	if	Network_Access_Authentication_Passed	then	PermitAccess
	☑	Default	if no matches, then			DenyAccess

Figure 22-9   *Default Authorization Rules Showing SGT Assignment*

To add a Security Group Tag as an authorization result, perform the following steps:

Step 1.   Click **Edit** to edit your existing authorization rule.

Step 2.   Click the **+** sign under Permissions.

Step 3.   Click the **+** sign next to the authorization profile.

Step 4.   Choose **Security Group**.

Step 5.   Select the appropriate Security Group to apply.

Manually Assigning an SGT at the Port

In most cases, 802.1X is not used in the data center. Servers are not usually required to authenticate themselves to the data center switch, as the DC is normally considered physically secure, and there is no network access control applied there. However, the servers themselves will be the destination of traffic coming from the campus and from within the data center itself.

Because 802.1X is not typically used in the data center, you need a manual way to apply the SGT. This is configured at the interface level of the Nexus configuration and is manually applied to the port itself:

```
NX7K-DIST(config)# int eth1/3
NX7K-DIST(config-if)# cts manual
NX7K-DIST(config-if-cts-manual)# policy static sgt 0x3
```

This has manually assigned the SGT 3 to the port on the Nexus 7000. This is also available on the Nexus 5000 and 1000v.

Manually Binding IP Addresses to SGTs

As an alternative to assigning the SGT to the port itself, ISE added the capability to centrally configure a database of IP addresses and their corresponding SGTs. This is accomplished under **Work Centers > TrustSec > Components > IP SGT Static Mapping**. Then, SGT-capable devices may download that list from ISE, as shown in Figure 22-10 and Figure 22-11.

Figure 22-10   *Mapping an SGT to an IP Address in ISE*

Now that the mappings exist on ISE, you can download them to the other devices, such as a Nexus 7000 data center switch, or even a Cisco Firepower or Check Point firewall. Figure 22-11 shows multiple static mappings in the ISE GUI.

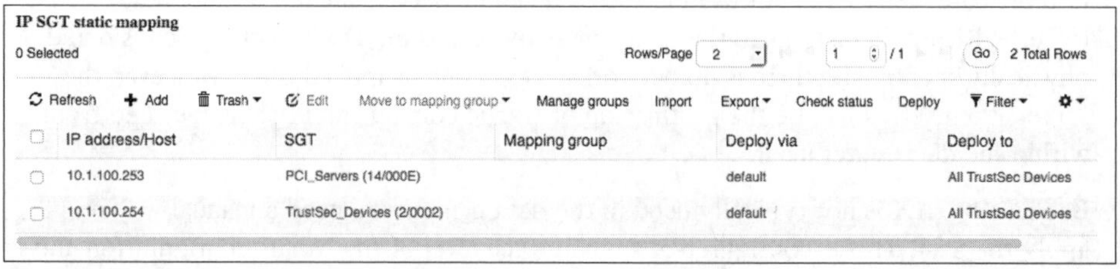

Figure 22-11   *IP SGT Static Mapping*

Access Layer Devices That Do Not Support SGTs

Because it isn't a perfect world, and not all the equipment on the network will be the latest and greatest, you need another way to classify the endpoint traffic. For example, you may still be using an older Cisco Wireless LAN Controller (like the 4400) that does not support version 7.2 or newer code and therefore cannot accept the SGT classification from ISE nor send the update via SXP.

Additionally, this could be a VPN Concentrator, or some third-party equipment that found its way into the deployment. Although that gear may not support the classification and transport natively, you may still use TrustSec in those environments. You can leverage ISE to maintain the list of bindings and share those via SXP or pxGrid; or that network device may be capable of assigning different VLANs or IP addresses per authorization result.

With the Catalyst 6500, you can map subnets and VLANs and assign all source IP addresses from the subnet or VLAN to a specific tag.

Mapping a Subnet to an SGT

Use the **cts role-based sgt-map** [*ipv4-subnet* | *ipv6-subnet*] **sgt** *tag-value* command to enable this binding. When used, the device-tracking feature in the Catalyst 6500 Supervisor 2T will be used to identify matches and assign the SGT. Here is an example of this mapping.

```
C6K-DIST(config)# cts role-based sgt-map 192.168.26.0/24 sgt 4
```

Mapping a VLAN to an SGT

Use the **cts role-based sgt-map vlan-list** *vlans* **sgt** *tag-value* command to enable this binding. When used, the device-tracking feature in the Catalyst 6500 Supervisor 2T will be used to identify matches and assign the SGT. Here is an example of this mapping.

```
C6K-DIST(config)# cts role-based sgt-map vlan-list 40 sgt 4
```

Transport: SGT eXchange Protocol (SXP)

In a perfect world, all of your access layer devices would support tagging the users' traffic natively. Yet in the world we live in, the reality is that not all devices support native tagging.

Cisco developed a peering protocol (similar to Border Gateway Protocol [BGP]) to allow devices to communicate their database of IP-address-to-SGT mappings to one another. This peering protocol is called SGT eXchange Protocol (SXP). Because this is a peering protocol, it is possible to be specific and deterministic as to which devices send updates and which ones receive updates.

An SXP peer may be defined as a speaker or as a listener. The definition of a *speaker* is a device that sends the IP-address-to-SGT bindings. The definition of a *listener* is a device that receives the IP-address-to-SGT bindings.

SXP Design

Because SXP uses TCP as its transport, the peer may be Layer 2 adjacent or multiple hops away. A network device may peer directly to the enforcement device (the data center switch or security group firewall). Figure 22-12 shows a rudimentary design to illustrate the point.

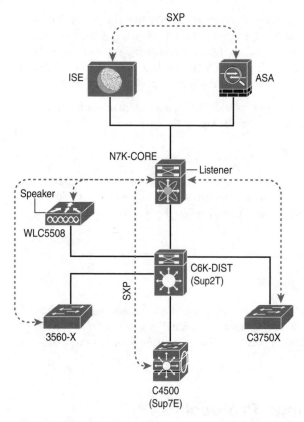

Figure 22-12   *SXP Peering*

Figure 22-12 shows some network access switches and a WLC. All of these NADs receive IP-address-to-SGT bindings as part of the user's authorization session. When users authenticate through these NADs, ISE authorizes them and sends back an SGT as part of the result (classification). The NAD in turn acts as an SXP speaker and updates any configured listeners. In Figure 22-12, each NAD is configured to send the updates to the Nexus 7000 in the data center, which is multiple hops away. Additionally, Figure 22-12 illustrates ISE updating a Cisco Adaptive Security Appliance (ASA) of all the bindings via SXP. The ASA could also peer directly to the Nexus 7000, or any of the NADs if that was your chosen design.

Remember that routing protocols have a limitation for the number of neighbors they can scale to, and so does SXP. Because of the limitations of scale for the number of peers, SXP design may be architected to be multihop, which allows for aggregation points, as shown in Figure 22-13. Devices like the Catalyst 6500 with a Supervisor 2T engine or the Aggregation Services Router (ASR) are solid choices for SXP aggregation.

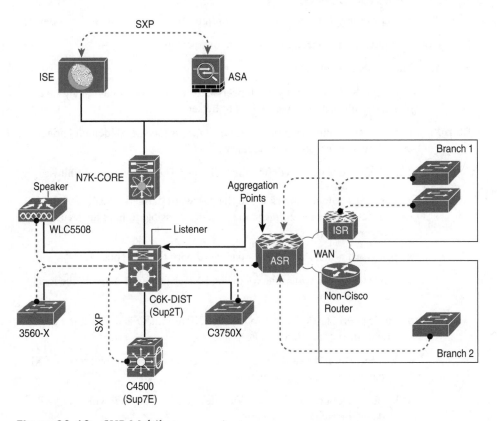

Figure 22-13 *SXP Multihop*

Figure 22-13 shows a design where multiple branch locations may have one or more switches, which aggregate their IP-address-to-SGT bindings at the gateway Integrated Services Router (ISR). Each gateway ISR sends those aggregated bindings to the WAN head-end, represented by an ASR, which in turn aggregates all those branch peers. The ASR sends the aggregated bindings to the Catalyst 6000 for further aggregation with all the other bindings from the campus access layer.

There are numerous benefits to this design. Mainly it provides a deterministic and scalable design; however, it also does not require SXP-aware infrastructure along every hop in the network path, because SXP peers do not need to be directly connected. For example, the switch in Branch 2 of Figure 22-13 bypasses the non-Cisco gateway router and is peering directly to the ASR.

Configuring SXP on IOS Devices

The following steps walk you through the SXP configuration on Cisco IOS–based devices.

From global configuration mode, perform the following steps:

Step 1.   Enter **cts sxp enable**.

This turns SXP on globally. Each peer needs to be added individually, and a global default SXP password needs to be set.

Step 2.   Enter **cts sxp connection peer** *peer-ip-address* **password [default | none] mode [local | peer] [listener | speaker]**.

This command is used to define the SXP peer. The options are as follows:

- **password default:** States to use the password defined globally for all SXP connections. At the current time, it is not possible to have different SXP passwords per peer.

- **password none:** Do not use a password with this SXP peer.

- **mode local:** States that the following SXP argument is defining the local side of the connection.

- **mode peer:** States that the following SXP argument is defining the peer's side of the connection.

- **listener:** Defines that the specified device (local or peer) will receive SXP updates through this connection.

- **speaker:** Defines that the specified device (local or peer) will send SXP updates through this connection.

Step 3.   (Optional) Enter **cts sxp default password** *password*.

This is an optional step for when your connections will use the globally defined password, instead of no password.

Example 22-1 and Example 22-2 display the steps for setting up the SXP connection between a Catalyst 4500 (access layer device that does not support native tagging) and a Catalyst 6500 with a Supervisor 2T (distribution layer device that supports native tagging) as previously shown in Figure 22-13.

Example 22-1 *Enabling SXP on the Catalyst 4500*

```
4503(config)# cts sxp enable
4503(config)#
*Aug  9 06:51:04.000: %CTS-5-SXP_STATE_CHANGE: CTS SXP enabled
4503(config)# cts sxp connection peer 10.1.40.1 password default mode peer listener
4503(config)#
*Aug 10 09:15:15.564: %CTS-6-SXP_TIMER_START: Connection <0.0.0.0, 0.0.0.0> retry
  open timer started.
*Aug 10 09:15:15.565: %CTS-6-SXP_CONN_STATE_CHG: Connection <10.1.40.1, 10.1.40.2>-1
  state changed from Off to Pending_On.
4503(config)#
*Aug 10 09:15:15.566: %CTS-3-SXP_CONN_STATE_CHG_OFF: Connection <10.1.40.1,
  10.1.40.2>-1 state changed from Pending_On to Off.
4503(config)# cts sxp default password TrustSec123
4503(config)#
*Aug 10 09:17:20.936: %CTS-5-SXP_DFT_PASSWORD_CHANGE: CTS SXP password changed.
```

Example 22-2 *Enabling SXP on the Catalyst 6500*

```
C6K-DIST(config)# cts sxp enable
C6K-DIST(config)#
Aug 10 16:16:25.719: %CTS-6-SXP_TIMER_START: Connection <0.0.0.0, 0.0.0.0> retry
  open timer started.
C6K-DIST(config)# cts sxp default password TrustSec123
C6K-DIST(config)# cts sxp connection peer 10.1.40.2 password default mode peer speaker
C6K-DIST(config)#
Aug 10 16:17:26.687: %CTS-6-SXP_CONN_STATE_CHG: Connection <10.1.40.2, 10.1.40.1>-1
  state changed from Off to Pending_On.
Aug 10 16:17:26.687: %CTS-6-SXP_CONN_STATE_CHG: Connection <10.1.40.2, 10.1.40.1>-1
  state changed from Pending_On to On.
```

Configuring SXP on Wireless LAN Controllers

The Cisco WLC added support for SGT classification and SXP transport in the 7.2 release.

From the WLC user interface, perform the following steps:

Step 1.   Using the top-menu navigation, select **Security**.

Step 2.   Along the left side, choose **TrustSec SXP**, as shown in Figure 22-14.

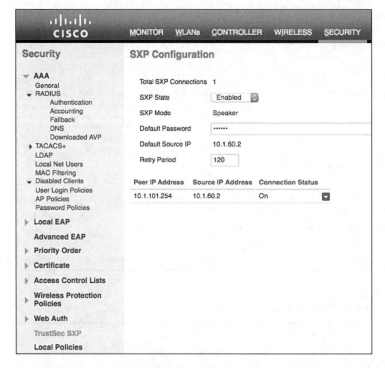

Figure 22-14   *SXP Connection on WLC*

Step 3.   From the SXP State drop-down list, choose **Enabled**.

Step 4.   In the Default Password field, enter the same default password you configured on the switches. All passwords in the SXP domain need to be the same.

This has turned SXP on globally. Each peer must be added individually. To add a new SXP peer (a listener), follow these steps:

Step 5.   Click **New** (in the upper-right corner).

Step 6.   Enter the IP address of the listener peer.

Step 7.   Click **Apply** (upper-right corner).

The added peers are displayed on the TrustSec SXP page. Their status is listed next to their IP address. Once the peer is configured on the other side, the status changes from **Off** to **On**, as shown in Figure 22-14.

It is also possible to verify the SXP connection from the other side, as shown in Figure 22-15 and demonstrated in Example 22-3.

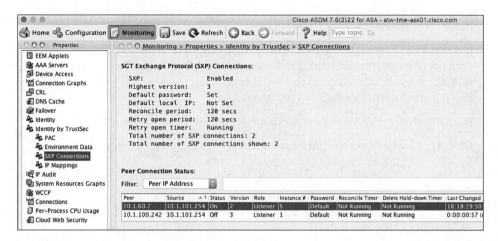

Figure 22-15 *SXP Connections on Cisco ASA*

Example 22-3 *Verifying the Connection Between the WLC and Catalyst 6500*

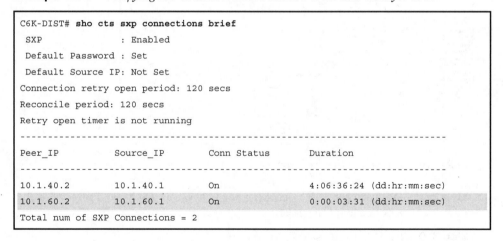

```
C6K-DIST# sho cts sxp connections brief
 SXP           : Enabled
 Default Password : Set
 Default Source IP: Not Set
Connection retry open period: 120 secs
Reconcile period: 120 secs
Retry open timer is not running
-----------------------------------------------------------------------
Peer_IP          Source_IP         Conn Status        Duration
-----------------------------------------------------------------------
10.1.40.2        10.1.40.1         On                 4:06:36:24 (dd:hr:mm:sec)
10.1.60.2        10.1.60.1         On                 0:00:03:31 (dd:hr:mm:sec)
Total num of SXP Connections = 2
```

Configuring SXP on Cisco ASA

Cisco ASA includes support for SGT enforcement (known commonly as SG-Firewall). Certain ASA models do support native tagging, and all ASA models support SXP for the transport of IP-address-to-SGT bindings.

It is important to note that the ASA has multiple functions. These functions include deep packet inspection firewalling and remote-access VPN (among many others). So, the ASA will enforce SGTs (enforcement) and receive SGTs (transport), as well as assign SGTs (classification) to Remote-Access VPN users.

From the ASA Device Manager (ASDM), perform the following steps:

Step 1. Navigate to **Configuration > Firewall > Identity by TrustSec**, as shown in Figure 22-16.

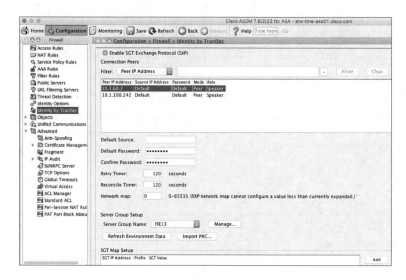

Figure 22-16 *ASDM Identity by TrustSec*

Step 2. Globally enable SXP by checking the **Enable SGT Exchange Protocol (SXP)** check box in the upper left.

Step 3. Click **Add** to add a new SXP peer.

Step 4. In the Add Connection Peer popup window, add the IP address of the remote peer.

Step 5. Choose **Default** for the Password (unless you will not be using passwords).

Step 6.   Set the mode to **Peer**.

Step 7.   Set the role to **Speaker**.

Step 8.   Click **OK**.

After clicking OK, you are returned to the main Identity by TrustSec page. At this point, you have SXP enabled and a single peer defined, but no default password yet.

Step 9.   (Optional) If you will be specifying the source IP address of the ASA, you may configure that source in the Default Source field.

Step 10.   In the Default Password field and Confirm Password field, enter the default password for your entire SXP deployment.

Figure 22-16 shows the Global Identity by TrustSec page in ASDM.

Step 11.   To verify the SXP connection in ASDM, navigate to **Monitoring > Properties > Identity by TrustSec > SXP Connections** to see the configured peers and their status, as shown previously in Figure 22-15.

Step 12.   Click **IP Mappings** to see any IP-address-to-SGT mappings that the ASA has learned about, as shown in Figure 22-17.

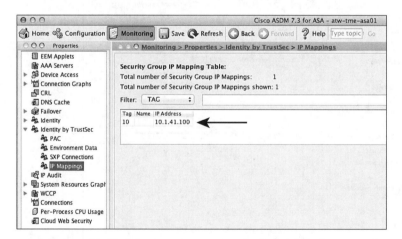

Figure 22-17   *ASDM Security Group IP Mapping Table*

Configuring SXP on ISE

As previously described, ISE acts as the TrustSec controller. So it only makes sense for ISE to be able to speak directly to enforcement devices, such as firewalls, and therefore SXP was added natively to ISE. This was illustrated previously in Figures 22-12 and 22-13.

You must enable SXP on at least one of the PSNs in the ISE cube. It is a simple matter of checking the **Enable SXP Service** check box at **Administration > System > Deployment**, as shown in Figure 22-18. After checking the check box, you must also specify the interface for SXP to operate on. The default is the GigabitEthernet 0 interface.

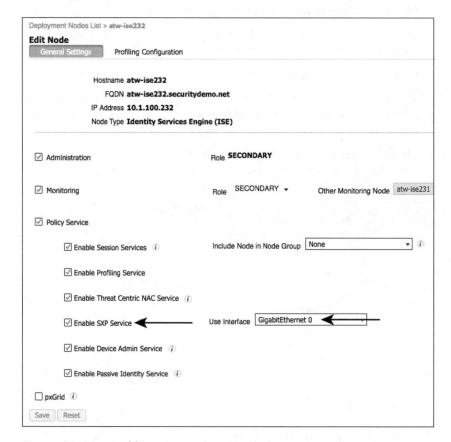

Figure 22-18 *Enabling SXP in the PSN Deployment Configuration*

After enabling SXP on one or more PSNs, navigate to **Work Centers > TrustSec > SXP > SXP Devices**, as shown in Figure 22-19. Here you configure the peers with which to share IP address-to-SGT bindings, as well as learn from. That's right, ISE can act as both a speaker and a listener.

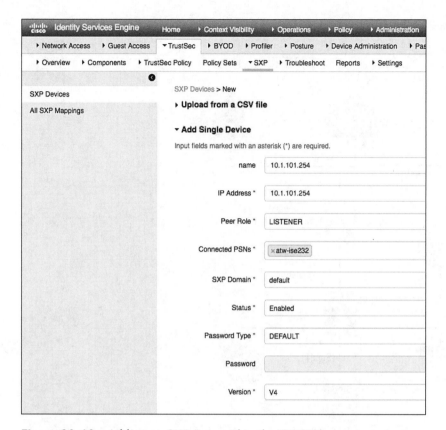

Figure 22-19 *Adding an SXP Peer within the ISE GUI*

Click **Add** to add an SXP peer. Figure 22-19 shows the ISE configuration of the ASA as a peer. ISE can operate with SXP versions 1 through 4, and will negotiate with the peer automatically.

Transport: pxGrid

SXP is not the only way that ISE can communicate the IP-address-to-SGT bindings. There are a number of devices that are also able to receive information via Cisco Platform Exchange Grid (pxGrid). pxGrid is a communication bus that is designed to share dynamic information at very large scale, and has a large number of security devices that use it to learn contextual information from ISE.

For example, the Cisco Firepower Next-Generation Firewall (NGFW) uses pxGrid to learn identities and SGT information from ISE, as does the Cisco Web Security Appliance (WSA) and Check Point firewalls.

pxGrid will be covered in more detail in Chapter 24, "ISE Ecosystems: The Platform Exchange Grid."

Figure 22-20 illustrates adding pxGrid receivers in addition to the SXP design.

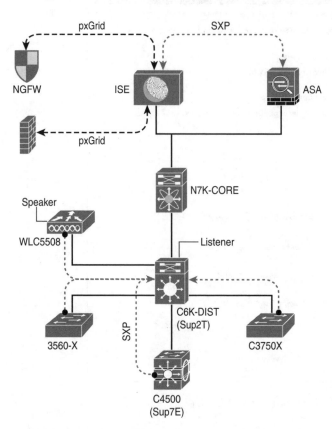

Figure 22-20   *SXP Design and pxGrid Consumers*

Transport: Native Tagging

Native tagging is the ultimate goal. With this approach, the access layer is capable of applying the SGT to the Layer 2 frame as it is sent across the wire to the upstream host. The upstream host continues that and ensures the SGT is applied. So, the SGT is always present throughout the entire infrastructure, as shown in Figure 22-21.

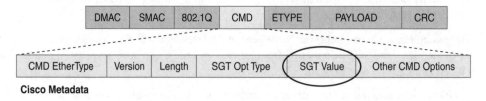

Figure 22-21   *Layer 2 Frame Format with SGT*

Native tagging allows the technology to scale virtually endlessly, and it remains completely independent of any Layer 3 protocol. In other words, architecturally speaking: If the traffic is IPv4 or IPv6, it does not matter. The SGT is completely independent.

As shown in Figure 22-22, when native tags are supported pervasively within the infrastructure, the SGT is communicated hop-by-hop. This provides for end-to-end segmentation and tremendous scale. With the SGT being applied to the traffic at every Layer 2 link, we are able to enforce policy at any point in the infrastructure, and there are no limitations to the size of an IP-address-to-SGT mapping database, because the database is not being used at all.

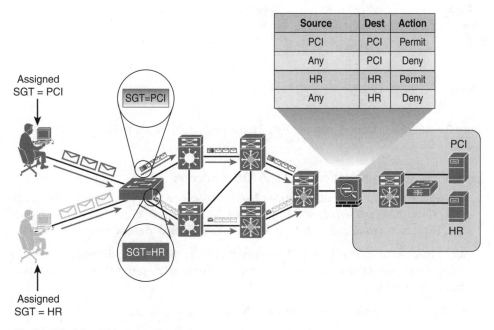

Source	Dest	Action
PCI	PCI	Permit
Any	PCI	Deny
HR	HR	Permit
Any	HR	Deny

Figure 22-22 *Pervasive Tagging*

For added security, the SGT may be encrypted with MACsec or IPsec, and the network infrastructure may be authenticated prior to sending or receiving tags, which is a solution known as Network Device Admission Control (NDAC).

Configuring Native SGT Propagation (Tagging)

The next few configuration exercises show the enabling of native security group tagging on three different types of switches: a Cisco Catalyst 3000 series access layer switch, a Cisco Catalyst 6500 series distribution layer switch, and Nexus 7000 data center switches. Figure 22-23 shows the logical network layout used in the configuration examples to follow.

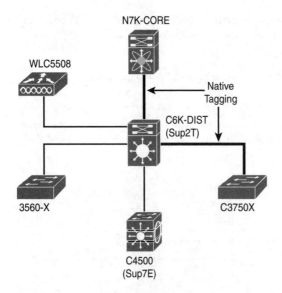

Figure 22-23   *SGTs from Access to Distribution and Distribution to Data Center*

Configuring SGT Propagation on Cisco IOS Switches

This section discusses the configuration of SGT propagation on access layer switches, such as the Cisco Catalyst 3560-X and Cisco Catalyst 3750-X, that have the ability to use native tags. The Catalyst 6500 and Nexus series switches are covered in subsequent sections.

When it comes to inserting the SGT into Layer 2 traffic, there is a fundamental choice to make: to use encryption or not to use encryption. For simplicity, this chapter focuses on the easy one: without encryption.

From global configuration mode, perform the following steps:

Step 1.   Enter **cts role-based enforcement**. This globally enables the tagging of SGTs. It also enables the ability to enforce Security Group ACLs (as discussed later, in the section "Traffic Enforcement with SGACLs"). However, without this command in the global configuration mode, the switch will not tag the Layer 2 traffic.

Step 2.   Enter into interface configuration mode of the tagging-capable port by typing **interface** *interface-name*.

Step 3.   Enter **cts manual**.

You are using **cts manual** because you are not utilizing NDAC at this point. The **cts manual** mode of operation allows you to apply the tag to the Layer 2 frame without having to negotiate encryption or requiring a fully trusted domain of Cisco switches (as you would need with NDAC).

Step 4.   Enter **policy static sgt** *sgt-value* **trusted**.

ISE has default security groups defined out of the box. One of those SGTs is a special group for network access devices named TrustSec_Devices, and the value of that group is 2 (0x02). That is the value you are applying here with this **policy static sgt 2 trusted** command. The **trusted** keyword in this command ensures that no changes are made to the incoming tags, as they are from a trusted source.

Example 22-4 displays the configuration to enable tagging, while Example 22-5 shows the monitoring output.

Example 22-4   *Enabling Tagging on a 3750-X Series Access Switch*

```
C3750X(config)# cts role-based enforcement
C3750X(config)# interface Ten 1/1/1
C3750X(config-if)# cts manual
C3750X(config-if-cts-manual)# policy static sgt 2 trusted
```

Example 22-5   *Verifying Tagging on a 3750-X Series Access Switch*

```
C3750X# sho cts interface Ten 1/1/1
Global Dot1x feature is Enabled
Interface TenGigabitEthernet1/1/1:
    CTS is enabled, mode:    MANUAL
     IFC state:              OPEN
     Authentication Status:  NOT APPLICABLE
         Peer identity:      "unknown"
         Peer's advertised capabilities: ""
     Authorization Status:   SUCCEEDED
         Peer SGT:           2
         Peer SGT assignment: Trusted
    SAP Status:              NOT APPLICABLE
         Configured pairwise ciphers:
             gcm-encrypt
             null
         Replay protection:      enabled
         Replay protection mode: STRICT
         Selected cipher:
    Propagate SGT:          Enabled
    Cache Info:
         Cache applied to link : NONE
    Statistics:
         authc success:         0
         authc reject:          0
         authc failure:         0
         authc no response:     0
         authc logoff:          0
```

```
      sap success:                0
      sap fail:                   0
      authz success:              3
      authz fail:                 0
      port auth fail:             0
L3 IPM:     disabled.
```

Configuring SGT Propagation on a Catalyst 6500

The Catalyst 6500 is a special case. This switch is sometimes used in the access layer, but it's most often used in the distribution layer or even in the data center. There are also a tremendous number of line cards possible for this chassis-based switch, some of which can support native tagging and others that cannot. Because of the possibility of multiple locations and multiple line-card possibilities, the Catalyst 6500 requires the administrator to set whether the switch should be used for egress (receiving the tag from other devices) or ingress (placing it at the access layer). These modes are referred to as *reflector modes*.

Note   This switch is unable to be configured for both ingress and egress mode simultaneously.

Ingress reflector mode should only be used in the access layer. This mode allows the use of non-TrustSec-capable line cards along with a TrustSec-capable supervisor. (An example of this would be a Catalyst 6504-E chassis populated with a Supervisor 2T and a 6148 series line card.) With this mode, all packet forwarding occurs on the Supervisor 2T PFC. Line cards that use distributed forwarding are not supported in ingress reflector mode (such as the 6748-GE-TX).

With this mode of operation, ISE is able to assign an SGT to a device entering the access layer via any supported line card, but that tag is only applied to network traffic leaving one of the ports physically on the Supervisor 2T. In other words, the switch applies the tag on an uplink port, but not on any of the downlink ports. Additionally, the switch cannot read the incoming tag on any ports except the ones physically on the Supervisor 2T module itself.

Note   Using a Supervisor 2T in the access layer is not normally recommended and is not part of Secure Access systems testing.

Egress reflector mode is normally associated with the Catalyst 6500 being deployed in the distribution layer or data center. With this mode, TrustSec propagation and encryption (MACsec) may be enabled on the Supervisor 2T and 6900 series line cards. These are the models of line card most often seen in the distribution layer, and as such, this provides for a nice TrustSec aggregation design. The switch can read all incoming SGT tagged packets and apply that tag to the traffic leaving the switch as well. This is the model of SGT that one normally thinks of when discussing the topic. Additionally, if the Catalyst 6500 is an SXP peer, it is capable of applying the SGT to Layer 2 traffic based on the IP-address-to-SGT bindings learned via SXP.

From global configuration mode on the Catalyst 6500, perform the following steps:

Step 1.   Choose the CTS reflector mode by typing **platform cts [egress | ingress]**.

Because this is a distribution layer deployment of the Catalyst 6500, choose egress mode. If this were an access layer deployment, where end users would be authenticated, you would choose ingress mode.

Step 2.   Enter **cts role-based enforcement**.

This globally enables the tagging of SGTs. It also has the capability to enforce SGACLs (discussed later in the section "Traffic Enforcement with SGACLs"). However, without this command in the global configuration mode, the switch will not tag the Layer 2 traffic.

Step 3.   Enter into interface configuration mode of the tagging-capable port by typing **interface** *interface-name*.

Step 4.   Enter **cts manual**.

You are using **cts manual** because you are not utilizing NDAC at this point. The **cts manual** mode of operation allows you to apply the tag to the Layer 2 frame without having to negotiate encryption or require a fully trusted domain of Cisco switches (as would be necessary with NDAC).

Step 5.   Enter **policy static sgt** *sgt-value* **trusted**.

ISE has default security groups defined out of the box. One of those SGTs is a special group for network access devices named TrustSec_Devices, and the value of that group is 2 (0x02). That is the value you are applying here with this **policy static sgt 2 trusted** command. The **trusted** keyword in this command ensures that no changes are made to the incoming tags, because they are from a trusted source.

Examples 22-6 and 22-7 display the enabling and verifying of tagging with the Catalyst 6500 Supervisor 2T.

Example 22-6   *Enabling Tagging on Catalyst 6500 Supervisor 2T*

```
C6K-DIST(config)# platform cts egress
C6K-DIST(config)# cts role-based enforcement
C6K-DIST(config)# interface Ten1/5
C6K-DIST(config-if)# cts manual
C6K-DIST(config-if-cts-manual)# policy static sgt 2 trusted
```

Example 22-7   *Verifying Tagging on the Catalyst 6500 Supervisor 2T*

```
C6K-DIST# show cts interface Ten1/5
Global Dot1x feature is Enabled
Interface TenGigabitEthernet1/5:
    CTS is enabled, mode:      MANUAL
    IFC state:                 OPEN
    Authentication Status:     NOT APPLICABLE
        Peer identity:         "unknown"
        Peer's advertised capabilities: ""
    Authorization Status:      SUCCEEDED
        Peer SGT:              2
        Peer SGT assignment:   Trusted
    SAP Status:                NOT APPLICABLE
        Configured pairwise ciphers:
            gcm-encrypt
            null
        Replay protection:        enabled
        Replay protection mode: STRICT
        Selected cipher:
    Propagate SGT:             Enabled
     Cache Info:
         Cache applied to link : NONE

    Statistics:
         authc success:             0
         authc reject:              0
         authc failure:             0
         authc no response:         0
         authc logoff:              0
         sap success:               0
         sap fail:                  0
         authz success:             1
         authz fail:                0
         port auth fail:            0
    L3 IPM:   disabled.
```

Configuring SGT Propagation on a Nexus Series Switch

The following steps guide you through the configuration of SGT propagation on the Nexus Series switch.

From global configuration mode on the Nexus Series switch, perform the following steps:

Step 1.   Type **feature dot1x** at global configuration mode.

The Nexus Series requires the feature dot1x to be enabled before enabling CTS features.

Step 2.   Type **cts enable** at global configuration mode.

This command enables TrustSec, MACsec, and NDAC features to be enabled and configured.

Step 3.   Enter **cts role-based enforcement**.

This globally enables the tagging of SGTs. It also provides the capability to enforce SGACLs (discussed later in the section, "Traffic Enforcement with SGACLs"). Without this command in the global configuration mode, however, the switch will not tag the Layer 2 traffic.

Step 4.   Enter into interface configuration mode of the tagging-capable port by typing **interface** *interface-name*.

Step 5.   Enter **cts manual**.

You are using **cts manual** because you are not utilizing NDAC at this point. The **cts manual** mode of operation allows you to apply the tag to the Layer 2 frame without having to negotiate encryption or requiring a fully trusted domain of Cisco switches (such as you would need with NDAC).

Step 6.   Enter **policy static sgt** *sgt-value* **trusted**.

ISE has default security groups defined out of the box. One of those SGTs is a special group for network access devices named TrustSec_Devices, and the value of that group is 2 (0x02). That is the value you are applying here with the **policy static sgt 2 trusted** command. The **trusted** keyword in this command ensures that no changes are made to the incoming tags, because they are from a trusted source.

Example 22-8 walks through the enabling of tagging on a Nexus 7000 series switch.

Example 22-8   *Enabling Tagging on Nexus 7000*

```
NX7K-CORE(config)# feature dot1x
NX7K-CORE(config)# cts enable
NX7K-CORE(config)# cts role-based enforcement
NX7K-CORE(config)# int eth1/26
NX7K-CORE(config-if)# cts manual
NX7K-CORE(config-if-cts-manual)# policy static sgt 0x2 trusted
```

Enforcement

Now that you have security groups being assigned (classification) and they are being transmitted across the network (transport), it is time to focus on the third staple of TrustSec: enforcement.

There are multiple ways to enforce traffic based on the tag, but they can ultimately be summarized into two major types:

■ Enforcement on a switch (SGACL)

■ Enforcement on a firewall (SG-FW)

Traffic Enforcement with SGACLs

Historically, enforcement with SGACLs was the only option available. It started with the Nexus 7000 Series and has expanded to the Nexus 5000 Series, Catalyst 6500 (Supervisor 2T), and the 3000-X Series switches. A major benefit to SGACL usage is the consolidation of ACEs and the operational savings involved with maintenance of those traditional ACLs.

An SGACL can be visualized in a format similar to a spreadsheet. It is always based on a source tag to a destination tag. Figure 22-24 shows an example SGACL policy on ISE, which represents the SGACLs in a columns and rows presentation, like a simple spreadsheet. The simple policy in Figure 22-24 shows that traffic from BYOD devices will be denied when attempting to communicate to PCI_Servers. It also shows that Developers will be permitted to contact Development_Servers, but those Development_Servers cannot communicate to each other.

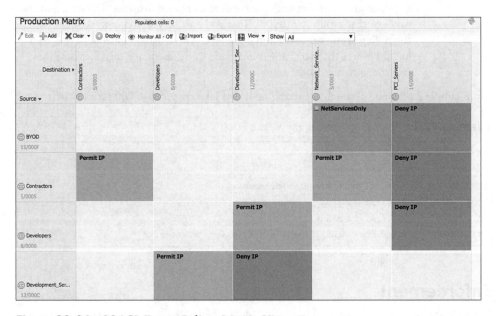

Figure 22-24 *SGACL Egress Policy: Matrix View*

In addition to blanket permit or deny SGACLs like Permit IP or Deny IP, an SGACL may be specific about the destination protocols and ports to permit or deny. NetServicesOnly is a more restrictive SGACL that is applied when BYOD devices attempt to reach Network_Services.

As you can see in Figure 22-25, the resulting ACL would be to permit only specific traffic and deny all the rest. This traffic is applied at egress of the switch where the SGACL is configured. In this case, it is applied at the Nexus 7000 in the data center, as traffic attempts to reach any Network_Services tagged devices.

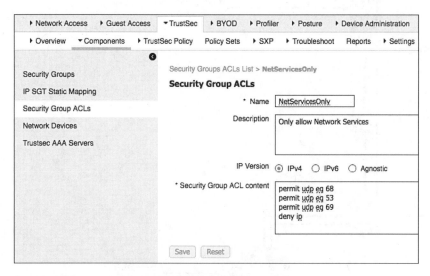

Figure 22-25 *NetServicesOnly SGACL Contents*

This form of traffic enforcement can provide a tremendous savings on the complexity and number of ACEs to maintain. There is a general formula to see the savings:

(# of sources) × (# of destinations) × permissions = # of ACEs

With a traditional ACL on a firewall:

4 VLANs (src) × 30 (dst) × 4 permission = 480 ACEs

Per source IP on a port using dACL:

1 group (source) × 30 (dst) × 4 permission = 120 ACEs

With SGACLs, the number of ACEs is a magnitude smaller:

4 SGT (src) × 3 SGT (dst) × 4 permission = 48 ACEs

There are two main ways to deploy SGACLs: North-South and East-West, as shown in Figure 22-26. North-South refers to the use case of a user or device being classified at the access layer, but enforcement with the SGACL occurring at the data center. For example, a guest entering the access layer is assigned a GUEST SGT. Traffic with a GUEST SGT is dropped if it tries to reach a server with financial data.

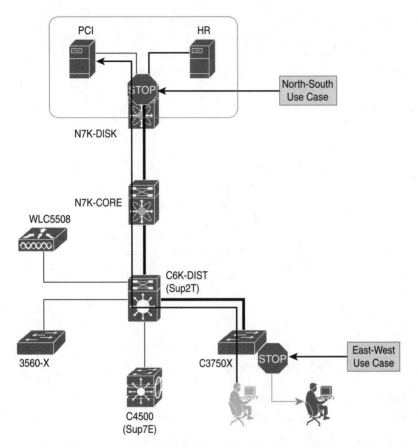

Figure 22-26 *North-South Versus East-West Visually Explained*

East-West refers to the use case of an SGACL protecting resources that exist on the same switch. For example, in a scenario with a development server and a production server on the same Nexus 5000 Series switch in the data center, an SGACL may be deployed to prevent the development server from ever communicating with the production server. Another East-West example is a guest and an employee both using the same access layer switch. Traffic may be filtered between these two devices so the guest cannot communicate to the employee who is in the same VLAN on the same switch.

Creating TrustSec Matrices in ISE

ISE provides three different views to create TrustSec policies and SGACLs: two tree views (Source Tree and Destination Tree), and a Matrix View. The Matrix View is the one that looks and acts more like a spreadsheet. Additionally, ISE allows you to have multiple matrices, so that you can test policy changes in limited environments before pushing those changes to production. The Matrix View is the view we focus on in this book.

From the ISE Administration GUI, perform the following steps:

Step 1.   Navigate to **Work Centers > TrustSec > TrustSec Policy > Matrix**.

Step 2.   Click the square that represents the intersection of a source SGT and a destination SGT.

Traffic Enforcement with Security Group Firewalls

Some organizations prefer to do the traffic enforcement on the switching infrastructure, on a device that was purpose-built to do traffic filtering: a firewall. Cisco has added the capability to enforce traffic on firewalls by including the source SGT and/or destination SGT in the firewall policy itself.

This section focuses on the Cisco ASA. The Cisco Firepower solution may also use source SGTs in its access policies, but that requires the use of pxGrid for context sharing and is part of the coverage in Chapter 24.

Security Group Firewall on the ASA

Beginning with ASA version 9.0, the ASA firewall gains SG-FW functionality. ASDM supports the full configuration, and therefore the ASA is the only SG-FW that has a GUI (as of this writing).

The SG-FW in the ASA is a simple concept. The powerful firewall policy in the firewall has been expanded to include source and destination security groups into the decision. As you can see in Figure 22-27, there is a new Security Group column in the Source Criteria and Destination Criteria sections.

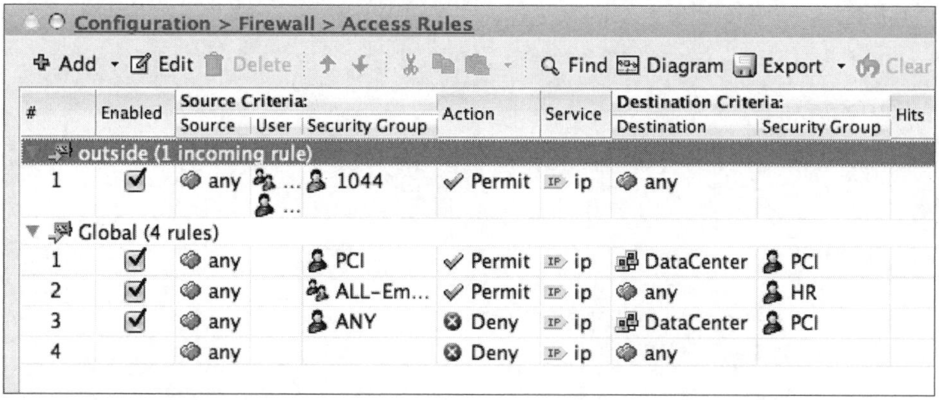

#	Enabled	Source Criteria: Source	Source Criteria: User	Source Criteria: Security Group	Action	Service	Destination Criteria: Destination	Destination Criteria: Security Group	Hits
outside (1 incoming rule)									
1	☑	⬡ any	⯐ ... ⯐	1044	✓ Permit	ᴵᴾ ip	⬡ any		
Global (4 rules)									
1	☑	⬡ any		⯐ PCI	✓ Permit	ᴵᴾ ip	▦ DataCenter	⯐ PCI	
2	☑	⬡ any		⯐ ALL–Em...	✓ Permit	ᴵᴾ ip	⬡ any	⯐ HR	
3	☑	⬡ any		⯐ ANY	✗ Deny	ᴵᴾ ip	▦ DataCenter	⯐ PCI	
4		⬡ any			✗ Deny	ᴵᴾ ip	⬡ any		

Figure 22-27 *ASDM Firewall Policy*

Security Group Firewall on the ISR and ASR

The ASA is not the only security group firewall on the market. Both the Cisco Integrated Services Router Generation 2 (ISR G2) and the Cisco Aggregation Services Router (ASR) have a powerful ZBF capability.

The Cisco ISR Gen2 (c3900, c3900e, c2900, c2901, c1941, c890) began support of SG-FW as of version 15.2(2)T. The Cisco ASR 1000 added support of the SG-FW as of IOS-XE version 3.4.

Summary

This chapter explained TrustSec, and at this point, you should be able to articulate why it is so valuable and how much OPEX it can save your organization.

You learned that there are three foundational pillars of security group access: classification, transport, and enforcement. Where classification is the ability to accept the tag for a particular network authentication session, transport is the ability to send that assigned tag to upstream neighbors either via native tagging, Security group eXchange Protocol (SXP), or the Platform eXchange Grid (pxGrid); and that enforcement may be on switches using Security Group ACLs (SGACL) or on a Security Group Firewall (SG-FW).

Chapter 23

Passive Identities, ISE-PIC, and EasyConnect

This chapter covers the following topics:

- Passive authentication
- Identity sharing
- ISE Passive Identity Connector (ISE-PIC)
- EasyConnect

One of the most common functions of secure network access is to identify who is attempting to access the network before granting them access. Throughout this book, you have learned about technologies such as supplicants, authenticators, authentication servers, 802.1X, WebAuth, MAB, and even Active Directory integration.

Up until this point, the identities have been presented directly to ISE, meaning the endpoint's supplicant was configured to pass the user's credentials inside of an EAP packet to ISE itself (802.1X) or the user's credentials were entered directly into a web page hosted on ISE (WebAuth). However, ISE isn't the only server or service on the network performing authentications day in and day out. The vast majority of organizations are using Microsoft Active Directory, so wouldn't it be neat if we could piggy-back off that for network access, even if only temporarily as 802.1X is being deployed across the organization?

The function of learning about identities that have been authenticated by another server or service is known as *passive authentication*, and the identities that have been learned are referred to as *passive identities*.

Most of this book is dedicated to the active authentication use cases. Conversely, this chapter remains focused on passive authentications.

Passive Authentication

Many security products on the market today use passive authentication to learn user identities and which IP addresses are assigned to those users. For example, most modern firewall and NGFW solutions use user identities within their firewall policies instead of constructing the policies with source IP addresses.

The Cisco ASA has used a solution known as Cisco Context Directory Agent (CDA) for years. The Cisco Sourcefire Firepower solution leveraged an Active Directory agent named Source Fire User Agent (SFUA). Both solutions would integrate with Active Directory using Windows Management Instrumentation (WMI) to learn about user authentications and their corresponding IP addresses, and then leverage that information within the firewall policies.

An active authentication learns the identity directly from the user, and a firewall usually only does this by sending the user through a web authentication process. By leveraging passive authentications, the firewall is able to transparently authenticate the user's IP address and apply the correct firewall rule to the traffic traversing the firewall.

For comparison, Figure 23-1 illustrates an active authentication and Figure 23-2 illustrates a passive authentication.

When it comes to ISE, identities could be used for its own policies and authorizing of network access. Of course, that is the main purpose of ISE, isn't it? Well the other major use case for ISE is sharing this information to other products. Chapter 24, "ISE Ecosystems: The Platform Exchange Grid (pxGrid)," is dedicated to this use case.

Figure 23-1 shows an EAP packet from the endpoint traversing the RADIUS connection to ISE. The following steps explain the active authentication process shown in Figure 23-1:

1. The identity is contained within the EAP packet and is sent from the supplicant to the network, which passes the packet to ISE within the RADIUS connection.

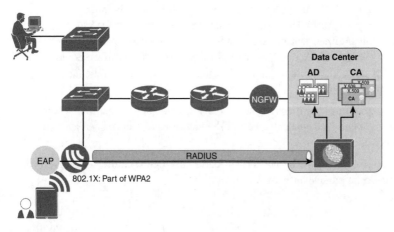

Figure 23-1   *Active Authentication Using 802.1X*

2. ISE validates the credentials against the correct ID store, ensuring the identity is valid. The identity may be in the form of a username and password, a certificate, or other credential.

3. As part of the authorization process, ISE learns the group membership and other attributes of the user's identity and adds this to ISE's session directory.

4. ISE provides the end result back to the network, authorizing the user to have the assigned level of access.

5. The session directory information can be shared with ecosystem partners, such as firewalls and web security appliances.

Figure 23-2 illustrates ISE learning about a user with a Windows workstation authenticating to Active Directory, which leverages Kerberos. The following steps explain the passive authentication process shown in Figure 23-2:

1. The identity is part of the Kerberos authentication that occurs as part of the normal Active Directory processes.

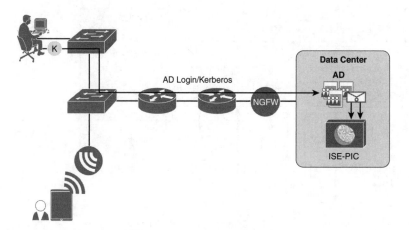

Figure 23-2 *Passive Authentication Using WMI*

2. The AD authentication triggers a notification through WMI.

3. ISE is subscribed to those WMI messages and learns about the authentication event, the user ID, and the source IP address of that authentication.

4. ISE performs an AD lookup and learns the user's group membership, adding the information to the session directory.

5. The session directory information can be shared with ecosystem partners, such as firewalls and web security appliances.

Most of this book is dedicated to the active authentication use cases. However, this chapter remains focused on passive authentications and the uses of that information for network access and for identity sharing.

Identity Sharing

Identity sharing is a key function of ISE. There are many solutions on the market that have their own identity sharing capabilities, designed for their firewall or for their web security appliance. ISE is architected to be the center of information sharing in a multivendor security ecosystem, including identities.

The vision for ISE is to provide these identities to all Cisco security products and more, through whichever means necessary. ISE version 2.2 moves the solution forward in a big way, but does not solve the entire problem yet. Because this book will most likely be referenced for many versions past version 2.2, Figure 23-3 illustrates ISE with some features that are not available in version 2.2. Specifically, it shows the CDA-RADIUS interface, which is not available at the time of writing.

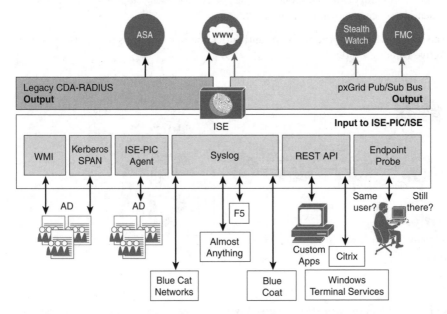

Figure 23-3   *ISE ID Sharing Inputs and Outputs*

Don't worry too much about Figure 23-3 just yet. We will dive into the different pieces of this design and solution throughout this chapter. For now, it's important that you understand a fundamental concept: identity sharing is a system with many moving parts, functions, and needs. To try and explain it, we will break all of it down to the four main pillars or tenets of a complete solution, as illustrated in Figure 23-4:

- Learn
- Share
- Use
- Update

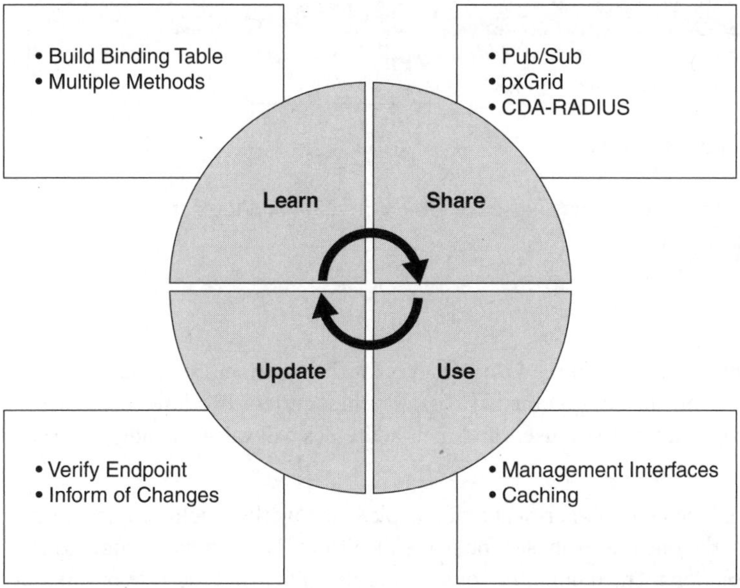

Figure 23-4 *Four Tenets of Identity Sharing*

The graphical user interface of ISE is organized in a way that also aligns well with these tenets. In ISE 2.2, passive identity functions have been consolidated into the PassiveID Work Center to make configuration and administration easier. Let's examine the PassiveID Work Center. Navigate to **Work Centers > PassiveID**.

As shown in Figure 23-5, the Work Center is organized into the following sections:

- **Overview:** This section includes a dashboard focused on passive identity functions, and the live sessions log.

- **Providers:** This section is focused on the sources of passive identity information such as Active Directory, syslog, and SPAN.

- **Subscribers:** This is where pxGrid and its related configuration exists, where the products and solutions that need to receive the username and IP bindings are configured in ISE.

- **Certificates:** There are a lot of certificate functions needed when leveraging pxGrid, and those configuration objects are in this section of the Work Center.

- **Troubleshoot:** In ISE 2.2, this section contains the TCP Dump tool. Expect more in future versions of ISE.

- **Reports:** Rather self-explanatory. This section provides the relevant reports for passive identity functions.

Figure 23-5 *PassiveID Work Center*

Now let's drill into those four tenets illustrated in Figure 23-4 and look at the configuration in the ISE GUI.

Tenet 1: Learn

The mission statement assigned to the Learn tenet is for the solution (ISE in our case) to build the bindings of the users on the network and their current IP addresses. The methods available to learn of these users and their addresses will vary depending on the source of the information.

Although all four of the tenets are critical to a complete and working solution, the Learn tenet is most likely the one that truly separates the men from the boys when comparing passive identity solutions. The number of sources, the flexibility, and the ease of integration to those sources all play a big role in the solution.

The next few sections drill into each of the different identity sources: Active Directory, syslog, and REST.

Active Directory

Active Directory is the main source of passive identities today. ISE can learn about the AD authentications through three main methods:

■ **Windows Management Instrumentation (WMI):** WMI is a publish/subscribe (pub/sub) messaging system within AD. ISE may remotely communicate with AD using WMI and subscribe to certain security events, like logins. When those events occur, ISE is notified by AD.

Note   At the time of writing, with ISE version 2.2, WMI is the only passive identity source that can be used with EasyConnect (covered in more detail later in this chapter).

■ **ISE-PIC agent:** The ISE Passive Identity Connector (ISE-PIC) agent is a native Windows application that can be loaded on an AD domain controller or an AD member server. The agent leverages native Windows APIs for WMI to learn about the authentications and sends the data to ISE over a secure channel.

■ **SPAN session:** You can leverage Cisco Switched Port Analyzer (SPAN) technology to allow ISE to examine Kerberos traffic to learn of the authentications by "sniffing the traffic on the wire" without having to install any agents or configure WMI.

Windows Management Instrumentation

As described previously, WMI is a core Windows management technology that allows you to manage Windows servers or workstations locally or remotely.

ISE can remotely communicate with AD using WMI and subscribe to certain security events, like logins. When those events occur, ISE is notified by AD.

The main benefits to using this WMI method to learn about the passive authentication is that it does not require installation of an agent on a domain controller or a member server. Before WMI can be used, connectivity requirements for successful WMI connections must be met. The good news is that the Config WMI function from the ISE GUI will perform that configuration for you, as demonstrated a bit later in this section.

This type of connection to AD has been around for a very long time. Cisco Context Directory Agent (CDA) used it, and it's been a part of ISE since version 1.3. In ISE, it was previously referred to as "pxGrid Identity Mapping" and was designed to bring the passive identity functionality of CDA into ISE for sharing with pxGrid subscribers.

This functionality was then extended to create the EasyConnect deployment method in ISE version 2.1 and then given a tremendous boost in capability and ease of use in ISE version 2.2.

The WMI connection allows ISE to remotely communicate to an AD domain controller as a subscriber of WMI security events. Specifically, ISE looks for new Kerberos tickets that are granted and when those tickets are renewed. The granting of a ticket shows that a new Windows authentication session has occurred; it could be a user or a machine authentication, but that is for ISE to sort through after it is notified. The renewing of Kerberos tickets shows that the session is still active and should not be timed out or purged.

Configuring WMI   To integrate ISE with Active Directory via WMI, from the ISE GUI, perform the following steps:

Step 1.   Navigate to **Administration > System > Deployment**. Ensure that at least one Policy Service Node (PSN) has the Passive Identity Service enabled, as shown in Figure 23-6.

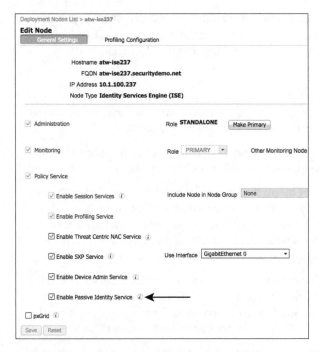

Figure 23-6 *Passive Identity Service*

Step 2.   Navigate to **Work Centers > PassiveID > Providers > Active Directory**.

Step 3.   Select your Active Directory join point. In the example used in this book, it is named AD-SecurityDemo.

Step 4.   Click the **PassiveID** tab, as shown in Figure 23-7.

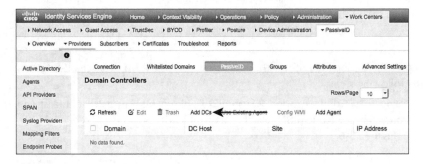

Figure 23-7 *PassiveID Tab*

Step 5. Click **Add DCs.** The list of domain controllers is displayed, as shown in Figure 23-8.

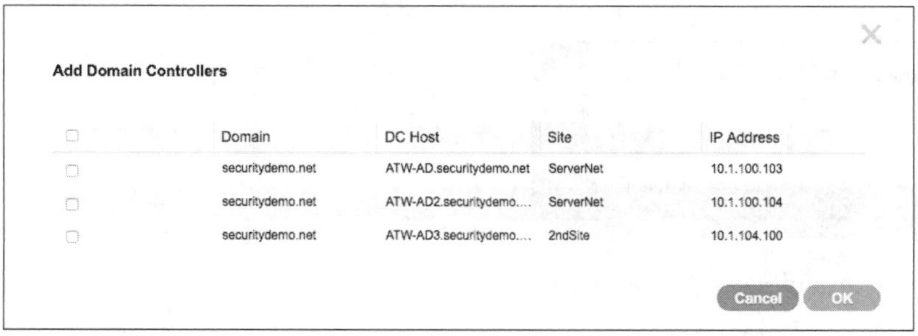

Add Domain Controllers

	Domain	DC Host	Site	IP Address
☐	securitydemo.net	ATW-AD.securitydemo.net	ServerNet	10.1.100.103
☐	securitydemo.net	ATW-AD2.securitydemo....	ServerNet	10.1.100.104
☐	securitydemo.net	ATW-AD3.securitydemo....	2ndSite	10.1.104.100

Cancel   OK

Figure 23-8 *Add Domain Controllers*

Step 6. Choose the domain controller(s) that you wish to monitor and click **OK**.

Step 7. The domain controllers are added to the list of PassiveID Domain Controllers. Select the DCs and click **Config WMI**, as highlighted in Figure 23-9.

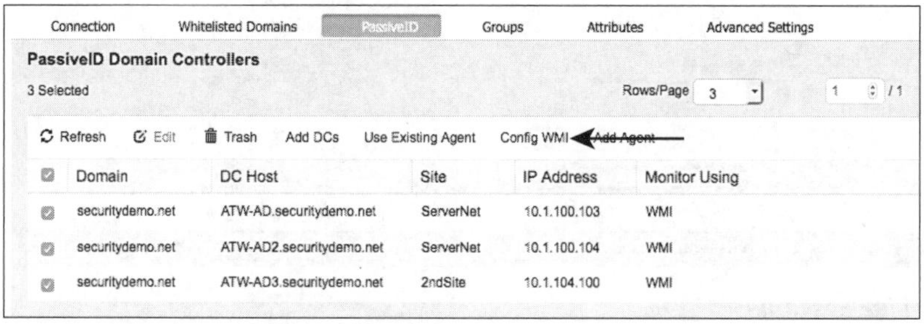

Connection	Whitelisted Domains	PassiveID	Groups	Attributes	Advanced Settings

PassiveID Domain Controllers

3 Selected   Rows/Page 3 ▾   1 ⬍ / 1

⟳ Refresh   ✑ Edit   🗑 Trash   Add DCs   Use Existing Agent   Config WMI ◀ Add Agent

	Domain	DC Host	Site	IP Address	Monitor Using
☑	securitydemo.net	ATW-AD.securitydemo.net	ServerNet	10.1.100.103	WMI
☑	securitydemo.net	ATW-AD2.securitydemo.net	ServerNet	10.1.100.104	WMI
☑	securitydemo.net	ATW-AD3.securitydemo.net	2ndSite	10.1.104.100	WMI

Figure 23-9 *Config WMI on Selected DCs*

Step 8. The Config WMI in Progress message is displayed, as shown in Figure 23-10.

⟳ Refresh ✑ Edit 🗑 Trash Add DCs Use Existing Agent Config WMI Add Agent				
☑ Domain	DC Host	Site	IP Address	Monitor Using
☑ securitydemo.net	AT			WMI
☑ securitydemo.net	AT			WMI
☑ securitydemo.net	AT			WMI

Config WMI in process...

Configuration of WMI has begun and will take some time. Status will be shown on completion. Run in background?

O.K

Figure 23-10 *Config WMI in Progress*

Step 9.   When the configuration process is complete, a success message is displayed, such as the one shown in Figure 23-11. The process performed by the Config WMI function is quite extensive and detailed after these configuration steps.

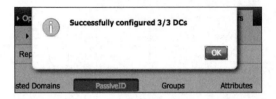

Figure 23-11   *Successfully Configured DCs*

Step 10.   ISE is now configured to subscribe to the WMI security events, and the AD controllers are configured to send those events to ISE. When AD authentications occur, those sessions are displayed in the Live Sessions screen, as shown in Figure 23-12.

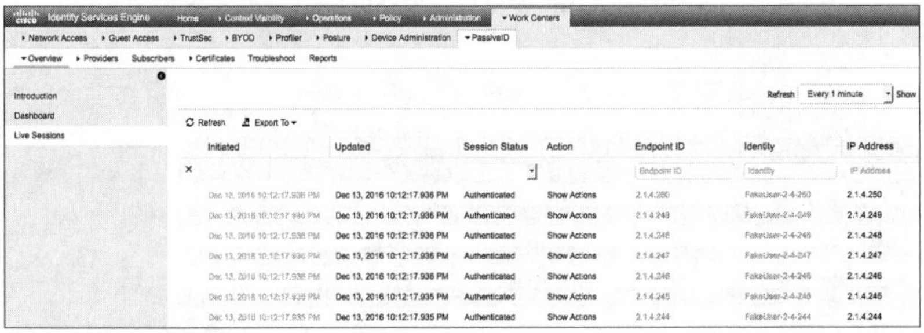

Figure 23-12   *Live Sessions*

What Does that Config WMI Button Do?   The Config WMI process performs an awful lot in the background. Prior to ISE version 2.2, everything detailed in this section needed to be performed manually. To see more of the painful process of the past, check out the *Cisco Identity Services Engine Administrator Guide* for ISE version 1.3 or 1.4 and its instructions for setting up the pxGrid Identity Mapping function.

There are five main things that Config WMI completes for you:

- **Registry changes:** ISE creates two registry keys that add the ID of the WMI client used by ISE. The key name is 76A64158-CB41-11D1-8B02-00600806D9B6 and it must be added in two locations:

  - HKEY_CLASSES_ROOT\CLSID\{76A64158-CB41-11D1-8B02-00600806D9B6}

  - HKLM\Software\Classes\Wow6432Node\CLSID\{76A64158-CB41-11D1-8B02-00600806D9B6}

These registry keys are used to list the ID as a valid application for the Distributed Component Object Model (DCOM).

■ **Permissions to use DCOM:** ISE communicates to the domain controllers using a Windows account, which needs to have local and remote access to DCOM. The **dcomcnfg** command could be used to configure DCOM permissions manually.

■ **Permissions to use WMI remotely:** By default, AD users do not have the Execute Methods and Remote Enable permissions by default. These can be granted manually by using the **wmimgmt.msc** command.

■ **Access to read the security event log of the AD domain controller:** To allow the AD user to read the security event log of the DC, the user must be added to two different security groups:

   ■ Event Log Readers group

   ■ Distributed COM Users group

■ **Configure the Windows firewall to allow traffic to and from ISE:** By default, the Windows firewall on the domain controller would block the communication, so a rule must be added to allow ISE to remotely access the server for DCOM/WMI.

ISE-PIC Agent

WMI is a very nice and popular option that is tried and true; however, not all organizations are keen on the idea of a non-Windows device like ISE remotely connecting and using DCOM. Those organizations prefer an agent-based approach, where software is installed on a Windows domain controller or a member server instead of connecting to an external system like ISE.

With ISE version 2.2 and newer, that option is a reality. The software that installs on an AD DC or on an AD Member server is named the ISE Passive Identity Connector Agent (aka the ISE-PIC agent).

The ISE-PIC agent comes preinstalled with ISE 2.2, but newer versions of the agent may be downloaded from Cisco.com and uploaded to ISE. The agent is a native 32-bit Windows application that you can install manually or, a much cooler option, have ISE push the install to the server! That's right, you can install the agent remotely, with the click of a button in ISE's user interface.

The ISE-PIC agent is located under **Work Centers > PassiveID > Providers > Agents**. From this screen, shown in Figure 23-13, you can manually register an agent, you can download the agent from ISE, you can upload a newer agent to ISE, and you can push the install of an agent to a server in the AD domain.

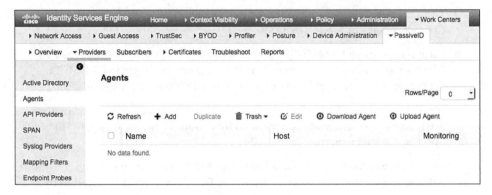

Figure 23-13   *ISE-PIC Agent Screen*

Deploying the Agent from ISE   Even though there is an Agents page in the ISE GUI for managing the existing agents and installing new ones, our experience has shown that it is a better experience to initiate the remote installation from the PassiveID tab within ISE's AD configuration itself. This way the configuration for the agent will be prepopulated and working immediately, not requiring you to log into the Windows server and add the list of domain controllers to be monitored.

To install the agent onto a Windows server remotely following this experience-based best practice:

Step 1.   Navigate to **Work Centers > Passive ID > Providers > Active Directory >** [*join point*] **> PassiveID** tab.

Step 2.   Select the Domain Controllers that you want to monitor.

Step 3.   Click **Add Agent**, as shown in Figure 23-14.

Figure 23-14   *PassiveID Tab, Servers Selected to Be Monitored*

Step 4.   In the Agents dialog box, click the **Deploy New Agent** radio button and enter a name for the agent. A good practice is to name the agent for the server that it will be installed on; however, keep in mind that a single agent may be installed on a single server but monitor many domain controllers.

Step 5.   (Optional) Enter a description, which is a good idea to remind you later why this agent exists.

Step 6.   In the Host text box, enter the fully qualified domain name (FQDN) for the domain controller or member server to install the agent onto.

Step 7.   Provide an AD username and password (not stored) for an account that has enough permissions to install the software onto the server. A Domain Admin account is preferable, to avoid chasing down odd permission issues. Figure 23-15 shows a completed new agent screen.

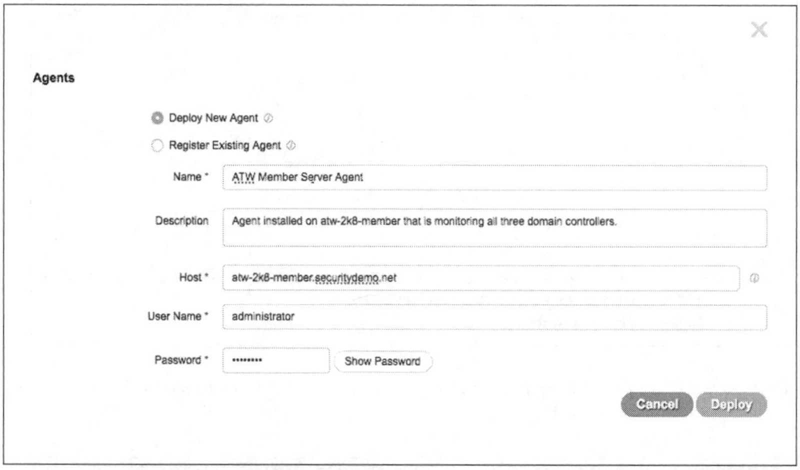

Figure 23-15   *Completed New Agent Screen*

Step 8.   Click **Deploy.**

At this point ISE logs in remotely to the server, copies the files to a temporary location, and installs the MSI package. All of this happens behind the scenes, without any interaction. To see if the installation completed successfully, leverage the Windows Programs and Features Control Panel applet, as shown in Figure 23-16. You can also see that the application is installed under the C:\Program Files (x86)\Cisco\Cisco ISE PassiveID Agent\ directory, as shown in Figure 23-17.

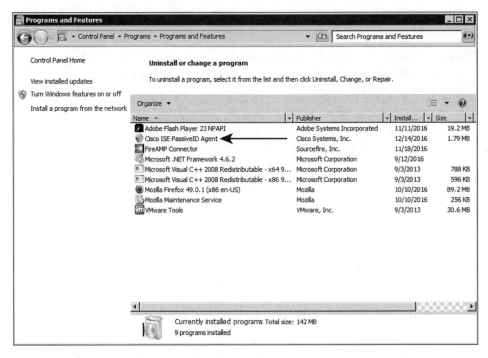

Figure 23-16   *Programs and Features: Cisco ISE PassiveID Agent Is Installed*

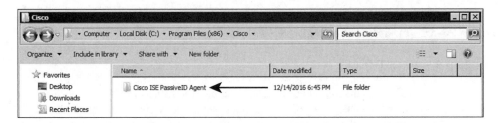

Figure 23-17   *Program Files on the Windows Server Hard Drive*

Additionally, you can view that the service was installed correctly and is running within the Services Control Panel applet. As shown in Figure 23-18, the service is named Cisco ISE Passive Identity Agent; it should be started and configured to start automatically.

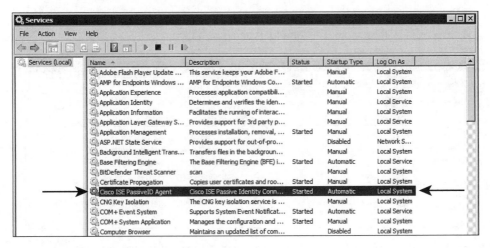

Figure 23-18   *Windows Services*

Back in the ISE GUI, the list of domain controllers will have changed from using WMI to using the recently added agent, as shown in Figure 23-19.

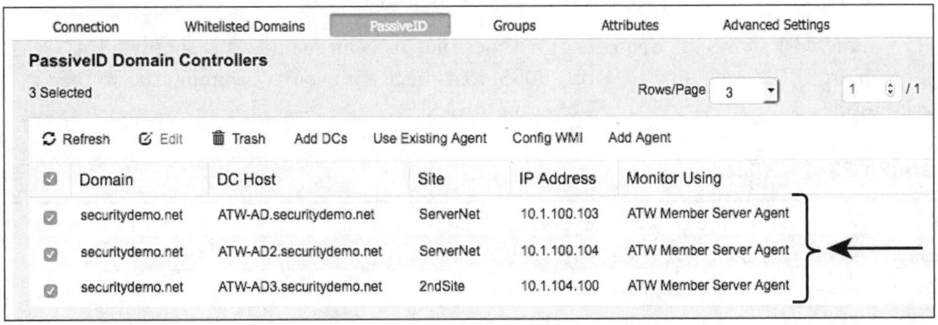

Figure 23-19   *PassiveID Tab, Servers Monitored by Agent*

There are some questions that must be burning in your mind right now: Is there a performance benefit to using the agent instead of WMI? Which method is better? Which approach should I use?

There is a bit of a performance benefit to using the native Windows application. Because it is a native process, running directly on the Windows server and leveraging local APIs for the WMI events, it does retrieve and consume those events more rapidly. However, at the time of writing, there are no official performance numbers to back up that statement.

Truthfully, there is no "better" solution; it is all a matter of preference and matching the needs of your environment. While the agent is very attractive, it does have one downside: EasyConnect only works with WMI in ISE version 2.2. So, any design leveraging the ISE-PIC agent with ISE version 2.2 will lose out on the capability to tie those passive identities into EasyConnect.

Nodes File   Figure 23-20 shows the contents of the agent's program files directory. There are a few files to pay attention to, starting with the *nodes* file.

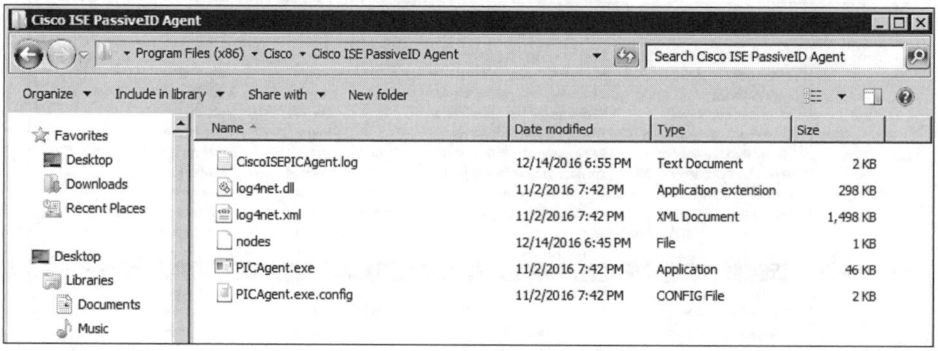

Figure 23-20   *Contents of the Cisco ISE Passive ID Agent Directory*

The nodes file is a text file that lists all the ISE nodes it could be sending data to. The agent processes the list one line at a time, and if the communication generates an error, it moves to the next line in the list. Put another way, the agent sends updates to only one ISE node, and it uses this list to provide backup nodes.

Example 23-1 shows the contents of a nodes file. You can see that it is simply a list of secure URLs, including the port (9095) that the agent uses to communicate to the ISE node.

Example 23-1   *Nodes File*

```
https://atw-ise237.securitydemo.net:9095
https://atw-ise231.securitydemo.net:9095
https://atw-ise232.securitydemo.net:9095
https://atw-ise233.securitydemo.net:9095
```

When the agent starts, it picks up the list of nodes from this file. Any changes to the nodes file will not be noticed until the next time the service starts. So if you make any changes, restart the service to have those changes picked up.

The communication is always from the agent to ISE, in a typical client-server architecture. The agent reaches out to the ISE node every 10 seconds. This 10-second polling interval acts as a keepalive, informing ISE that the agent is still alive and well. The agent configuration will be provided from ISE during that same polling interval.

The agent reports the status of its connection to the monitored domain controllers once per minute. However, when the agent learns of a new mapping, that information is sent immediately to the ISE node.

Note   When you deploy the agent from ISE as demonstrated previously in this chapter, the nodes file is preconfigured with the ISE nodes that have PassiveID enabled on them. However, if you perform a manual installation of the agent, you need to manually edit this nodes file and add the URLs for the applicable ISE nodes.

Agent Configuration File   The PICAgent.exe.config file defines the logging level for the agent, which is set to INFO by default. It defines the name and location of the log file and the configuration of its maximum size, and the rollover setting for when the log file reaches that maximum size.

Example 23-2 shows the default configuration of the agent.

Example 23-2   *PICAgent.exe.config*

```
<configuration>
  <configSections>
    <section name="log4net"
type="log4net.Config.Log4NetConfigurationSectionHandler, log4net"/>
  </configSections>

  <log4net>
    <root>
      <level value="INFO" />    <!--  Logging Levels: OFF,  FATAL, ERROR, WARN,
INFO, DEBUG, ALL    -->
      <appender-ref ref="RollingFileAppender" />
    </root>
    <appender name="RollingFileAppender"
type="log4net.Appender.RollingFileAppender">
      <file value="CiscoISEPICAgent.log" />
      <appendToFile value="true" />
      <rollingStyle value="Size" />
      <maxSizeRollBackups value="5" />
      <maximumFileSize value="10MB" />
      <staticLogFileName value="true" />
      <layout type="log4net.Layout.PatternLayout">
        <conversionPattern value="%date %level - %message%newline" />
      </layout>
    </appender>
  </log4net>

  <startup>
    <supportedRuntime version="v4.0"/>
    <supportedRuntime version="v2.0.50727"/>
  </startup>
  <configSections>
```

Design Fun   ISE version 2.2 supports monitoring events on 100 domain controllers. That is true of both WMI and the ISE-PIC agent. However, you should remember that a single agent can monitor more than one domain controller. This allows for a bit of fun when designing your passive identity deployment. Additionally, AD servers can be configured to forward event logs from one server to another, allowing consolidation. Figure 23-21 provides a crude sketch to illustrate this concept.

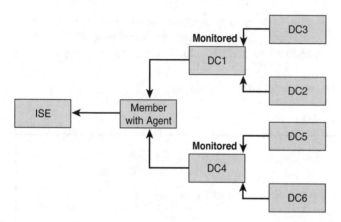

Figure 23-21   *Scaling Passive ID with Log Forwarding and Consolidation*

For more on log forwarding, see the TechNet article at https://blogs.technet.microsoft.com/wincat/2008/08/11/quick-and-dirty-large-scale-eventing-for-windows/.

Kerberos Sniffing via SPAN

The WMI approach is pretty darn cool. It's tried and true, and certainly works like a charm. The ISE-PIC agent is a very nice enhancement that comes with ISE 2.2 and will certainly help with certain customers who don't want to allow remote WMI from ISE to their Windows devices. However, both of these options require the help of your Active Directory team to set up. That fact makes doing a quick test or proof of concept a bit more challenging. That is why ISE added a SPAN option to learn about the passive identities. It allows for a quick and easy installation and very fast time to value.

Cisco SPAN is a technology that is sometimes referred to as port mirroring or port monitoring. It takes network traffic being transmitted through a switch port and sends a duplicate copy of that traffic to a configured destination port so that packet analyzing solutions such as intrusion prevention systems (IPS) and network monitors may examine that traffic.

Simply configure the SPAN on the switch to copy the AD traffic going to the domain controller (the source) and send that over to the configured SPAN port on ISE (the destination). This could result in an awful lot of traffic being sent over to ISE, and it only needs to see Kerberos traffic. A trick of the trade is to use a VLAN ACL (VACL) to filter the traffic that is being sent to the destination SPAN port so that it only receives Kerberos traffic to analyze.

Configuring the SPAN interface on the ISE node is fairly straightforward. Navigate to **Work Centers > PassiveID > Providers > SPAN**. Enable the SPAN provider, and then select the ISE node(s) that SPAN should be enabled for. Once you select the node, the list of possible interfaces is displayed and you must select one. Then click **Save** and you're done (on the ISE side).

Figure 23-22 shows the SPAN configuration in ISE.

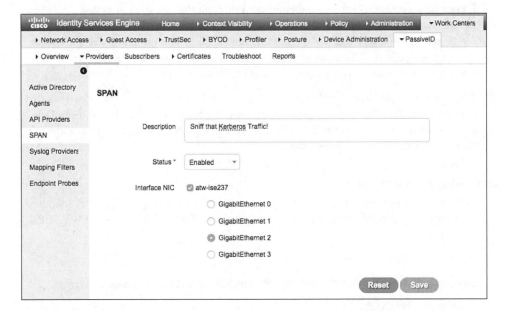

Figure 23-22   *SPAN Configuration*

Both SPAN and VACL configuration are covered in Chapter 10, "Profiling Basics and Visibility." For more detailed guidance on SPAN or VACLs, please check out the configuration guide for your Cisco switch at Cisco.com.

Syslog Sources

While Active Directory is the primary source for passive identities in the modern enterprise, AD and its use of Kerberos authentication for AD members is most certainly not the only game in town. There are many other authentications that can and do occur in a modern network. There could be other AAA servers, such as Cisco Secure Access Control System (ACS) or even FreeRADIUS, that are used to authenticate and authorize users accessing the network. Maybe VPN solutions are being used, such as Cisco ASA or F5 VPNs. Thinking more broadly, authentication could be occurring via web security appliances or web proxies that authenticate users through a web page or web prompt before allowing them to access the Internet.

Why not allow ISE to leverage the information from those systems to learn about users and their corresponding IP addresses, for the purposes of sharing that information?

That is where syslog comes in. You can configure those products to send their logs to ISE so ISE can learn about those users and add their information to the session directory for sharing. Beginning with ISE version 2.2, ISE has a generic syslog parser with some preconfigured templates for a variety of solutions on the market today.

It's not only user identities that can be learned through the ingestion of syslog. IP address management (IPAM) products such as Infoblox, BlueCat, and even Microsoft's DHCP server may provide very useful data that ISE can use to ensure the validity of the data in the session directory. When one of these solutions issues an IP address to a DHCP client, it logs the MAC address of the endpoint and the IP address that was assigned.

Those logs provide Layer 2 to Layer 3 bindings, so ISE can learn the MAC addresses that correspond to the IP addresses learned via passive ID methods. For instance, if the DHCP server assigns the IP address to a different MAC address, then ISE knows to invalidate the current passive authentication session.

Configuring a Syslog Provider

This section covers the ISE side of the configuration. Don't forget, you need to configure your individual product to send its syslog messages to ISE on UDP port 40514 or TCP port 11468.

From the ISE GUI, perform the following steps:

Step 1.   Navigate to **Work Centers > PassiveID > Providers > Syslog Providers.**

Step 2.   Click **Add.**

Step 3.   Enter a name for the provider.

Step 4.   (Optional) Provide a description of what you expect to get from this provider.

Step 5.   From the Status drop-down list, choose **Enabled.**

Step 6.   In the Host text box, enter the FQDN or IP address that the provider will source the logs from.

Note   This is a very important step. ISE uses reverse DNS to determine what hosts to allow through ISE's firewall to send the log messages. If there is a mismatch, the traffic will be dropped.

Step 7.   From the Connection Type drop-down list, choose **UDP** or **TCP.**

Step 8.   From the Template drop-down list, choose a syslog parsing template.

Step 9.   (Optional) Provide a default AD domain to map the identities to. This is used when the domain cannot be identified within the syslog message.

Figure 23-23 shows a completed example syslog provider.

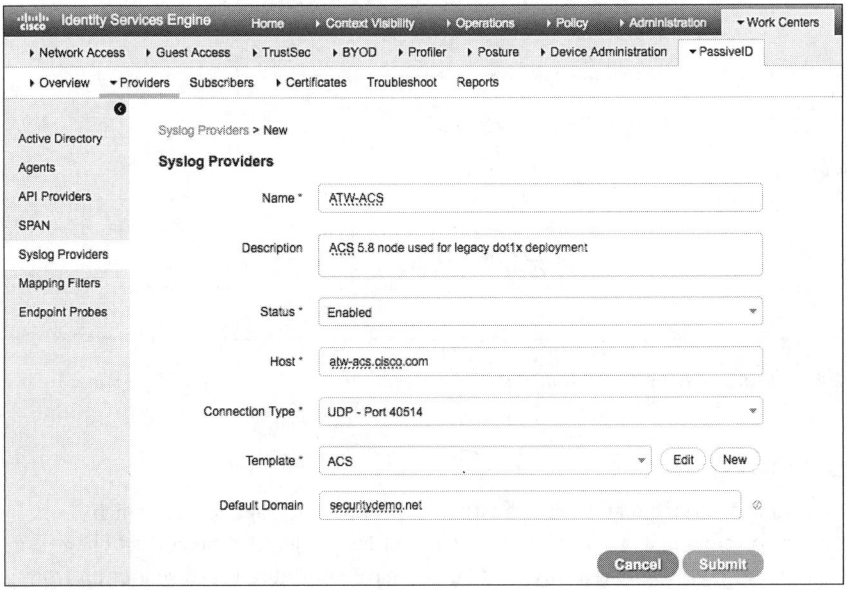

Figure 23-23   *Example Syslog Provider*

The template is critical to the success of your syslog provider. The template defines the regular expressions needed to identify the usernames and IP addresses from the log messages. You can edit or create a new template as needed. Figure 23-24 shows an example of a template for a Blue Coat gateway that is preconfigured during a default install of ISE 2.2. The template UI even provides a location on the right side to paste a raw syslog message and allow the UI to show you the identified information, as a way to test the template.

Figure 23-24   *Example Blue Coat Template*

More Tidbits on Syslog Providers

The syslog parsing service matches the hostname from the message to that which the administrator previously defined in the GUI in order to identify the correct client template. Therefore, you should always ensure you have configured reverse lookup from the syslog client's IP address to hostname for the relevant DNS server(s).

To achieve high availability with syslog providers, you need to set up redundancy. In other words, configure the source to send syslog to two different ISE nodes. However, that means double the logs and a lot of added noise, not to mention duplication of information. Another option is to use Anycast or a load-balancer to provide that redundancy.

For more on Anycast, take a look at an example solution designed by E. Peter Karelis and detailed on Aaron Woland's blog: http://www.networkworld.com/article/3074954/security/how-to-use-anycast-to-provide-high-availability-to-a-radius-server.html.

REST API Sources

The final identity source to discuss is the representational state transfer (REST) API that ISE implements to allow custom-built applications to update ISE with usernames and IP addresses. A simple use case might be a custom Guest solution in an enterprise. When a visitor arrives, she checks in with security and receives a visitor's badge and possibly guest credentials to access the Internet. When that guest user authenticates to that guest system, the user ID and IP address can be inserted into ISE's session directory via this REST API.

A more specific use case for the REST API is the Cisco Terminal Services (TS) Agent. This is a kernel-level agent that gets installed onto Microsoft or Citrix terminal servers and assigns each user a unique port range for all that user's network traffic. So now that allows a solution that normally has multiple users with the same IP address to have the users uniquely identified on the network. The TS Agent can be used directly with Cisco Firepower Management Center (FMC) or ISE, but obviously, FMC is out of scope for this book.

Learning More Is Critical

A major function of the Learn tenet is to get more than just the information included in the syslog or the WMI message, because that raw information might only include a simple username that hasn't been normalized in a way that every consumer requires to consume the data equally. It also does not include other pertinent information that is needed for the subscriber to apply the correct policy to the user. For example, most subscriber products such as firewalls and web security appliances want to use the group membership of a user within their policy constructs. The groups would not be included in the passive identity messaging (WMI, Kerberos, syslog). Therefore, ISE must take the learned identity and retrieve the user's applicable groups from Active Directory and add that information to the session directory to be shared to the subscribers. In addition to the group membership, ISE also retrieves the following attributes from AD for username normalization:

- **User principle name (UPN):** user@domain

- **Distinguished name (DN):** CN=Administrator,CN=Users,DC=securitydemo,DC=net

Remember, the goal of an identity sharing solution is to become the source of truth for its subscribers. Those productions shouldn't have to connect to AD separately to learn the groups of the user. If they did have to maintain that connection and do those lookups, then the identity sharing solution would be doing only partial work.

Tenet 2: Share

All that power of learning which users are on the network and which addresses correspond to them is all for naught if that information can't be used. EasyConnect is an example of ISE using the learned identity mappings within its own product.

Yet, this is not about EasyConnect, it's about identity sharing! There are a lot of products that require the knowledge of those identities to make using their solution easier and better. Firewalls, web proxies, behavioral analysis systems—you name it—can all use this information. Why should each product be required to code its own version of this capability?

Let's take Cisco's security portfolio as an example. It includes many different products, and each one may have a different identity solution with completely different capabilities. The long-term goal and vision is to consolidate those solutions into a single solution, all using ISE.

For ISE, there can be two mechanisms to share that data to the products that subscribe to the information. The main method is through the Cisco Platform Exchange Grid (pxGrid). However, there was an older solution called Cisco Context Directory Agent (CDA) that used a modified RADIUS interface, and a few Cisco products communicate with CDA leveraging that modified RADIUS interface already.

pxGrid

pxGrid is Cisco's premier publish/subscribe (pub/sub) communication bus that was designed from the ground up to be a scalable and secure data sharing system. pxGrid is covered in more detail in Chapter 24, so we won't look at how to configure it in this chapter.

pxGrid is the primary mechanism that ISE uses to share identities and other contextual data to those products and solutions that subscribe to that data. For convenience and completeness, Cisco has added the relevant pxGrid configuration UI to the PassiveID Work Center, as shown in Figure 23-25.

Figure 23-25 *pxGrid Configuration Interface*

Note   If you do not have pxGrid enabled yet, the UI will not display. You will need to come back to this part after performing the configuration in Chapter 24, or enable pxGrid on the desired ISE nodes under **Administration > System > Deployment**.

When a product such as Cisco Stealthwatch connects to ISE with pxGrid, it subscribes to the topics that it needs. A topic could be the session topic, where the shared information from ISE's session directory is published for consumption by the subscribed products and applications. The product or application joins pxGrid and subscribes to the session topic, and then the pxGrid controller (ISE) authorizes and directs the subscriber to download the bulk session data from the MnT node (the publisher). When new information is discovered, it is published to the session directory and sent to the subscribers of that topic. This is a very elegant way to share such dynamic data at large scale while being proactive about notifying the interested parties of interesting data.

ISE uses pxGrid to share those identities and the list of interesting groups that the identity is a member of. It's designed to be a one-stop shop for identity, providing all the possible tenets. Unlike the older CDA product, a product that uses ISE for identity sharing should not ever have to leverage its own connection to the source of identity truth (like AD). ISE should be able to provide all the information instead. Keep in mind that although this is how ISE is designed, it is not always how the integrated products are designed to integrate; and each integration may have different levels of integration. You will see that more clearly in the "Tenet 3: Use" section.

CDA-RADIUS

As previously mentioned, Cisco Context Directory Agent is an older solution that is used to provide passive identities to Cisco ASA, Cisco WSA, and a few other products. For ISE to be a drop-in replacement for CDA, ISE will have to support the same communication protocol used by CDA. CDA did not support pxGrid. Instead, CDA used a modified RADIUS interface, and any product that supported CDA would use that modified RADIUS protocol to pull the list of users and their IP addresses from the CDA appliance.

The CDA-RADIUS interface wasn't ready for release with ISE version 2.2, but is expected to be in the follow-on release. Since this book will not receive a third revision before that release is out, it is best to describe the CDA-RADIUS interface here.

Unlike ISE, when a product uses CDA for identity sharing, it must still have its own connection to the identity source to perform the additional lookups about the username that was shared. This means CDA will provide the username and IP address but won't have group membership (for example).

Tenet 3: Use

A product, such as a firewall or even a software-defined networking (SDN) controller, needs to know more than just which users exist on the network and which IP addresses they have assigned. That product needs a way to configure what level of access should be assigned to those users, and that policy creation must happen before users attempt to access the network.

Each product has some construct that permits this policy authoring. Perhaps it uses LDAP to query AD for which groups and users exist, and then builds the policy from that data. Then, once the information is received from pxGrid or CDA-RADIUS, the product can determine which level of access to assign through the firewall or the web gateway.

If an identity sharing product is to replace that integration, and prevent that product from having to have its own AD integration, then the identity sharing product requires APIs to provide that information. You may hear this type of API referred to as a *management API* or a *metadata AP* or even a *policy authoring API*. In this book, we refer to it as the metadata API.

ISE is able to provide that metadata API for AD user accounts and internal ISE accounts, including guest users. This information is provided through the External RESTful Services (ERS) set of APIs provided by ISE. ERS is enabled via **Administration > System > Settings > ERS Settings**, as shown in Figure 23-26. If you have more interest in understanding what is available with ERS, perhaps for your own custom integrations with ISE, the SDK is located on the ISE node itself, once you enable ERS itself, and is available at the following URL: https://[*ISE_IPaddress*]:9060/ers/sdk.

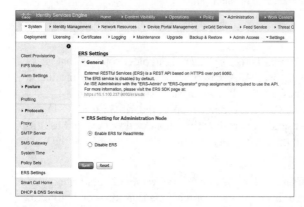

Figure 23-26   *Enabling the ERS APIs*

There are two key functions in this Use tenet: to get the information to build the policy, and to have ability to compare and match the information received from ISE via pxGrid or the CDA-RADIUS mechanisms with the information in their policies. In other words, they have to be able to bind the information received from the different sources to make it actionable. This might include the need to reach out to AD and get the list of groups that the user belongs to.

Integration Details

This section reviews some of the key identity consumers (AKA subscribers) and the way in which they integrate.

Stealthwatch

Stealthwatch has been a long-time partner of ISE, long before Cisco acquired its developer, Lancope. The initial integration only used pxGrid to initiate endpoint quarantine. The identities were gathered by parsing syslog messages from ISE and learning about the active authentications that ISE authorized for network access. Lancope also had its own identity appliance prior to Cisco's acquisition of the company. Beginning with Stealthwatch 6.9, ISE becomes the single source of identity. It could be either ISE or the ISE-PIC form factor, leveraging pxGrid as the communication mechanism.

When identities are sent to Stealthwatch, the session data is added to the user table and flow attribution. In other words, the identities are merged with all the identified network flows to provide usernames and context to those flows. Since Stealthwatch is a macro-analytical tool providing analysis of what has transpired and not a real-time traffic-regulating device like a firewall, there is no current need to have the metadata API for building policies prior to merging the live user data.

Figure 23-27 illustrates the passive identity flow with Stealthwatch, leveraging pxGrid. Configuration steps for integrating Stealthwatch and ISE are covered in Chapter 24.

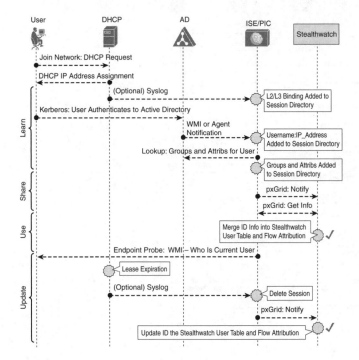

Figure 23-27 *Day in the Life of Passive ID: Cisco Stealthwatch*

Firepower Management Center

Firepower is an interesting solution when it comes to identity. There could probably be an entire chapter dedicated just to Firepower, because it had a fully functional identity sharing solution prior to the integration to ISE. That Active Directory identity sharing solution was named the Source Fire User Agent (SFUA).

Firepower Management Center (FMC) uses *realms* to provide the metadata for policy authoring. A realm configured for AD leverages LDAP to query for users, groups, and attributes. The policies are constructed using this data, and the passive identity and IP address bindings are sent from the SFUA to FMC, where the information gets added to the identity cache and sent to the Firepower appliances.

That was the old way. Starting with FMC version 6.2, the new way is to use ISE or the ISE-PIC form factor to replace the SFUA function.

The ISE integration is happening in phases. The first phase was to replace SFUA to provide the passive identities. However, the metadata is still coming from the realm configuration. At the time of writing, that is the state-of-the-art for ISE integration, and replacing the metadata API is a roadmapped item.

Figure 23-28 illustrates the passive identity flow with FMC, leveraging realms and pxGrid. Configuration steps for integrating Stealthwatch and ISE are covered in Chapter 24.

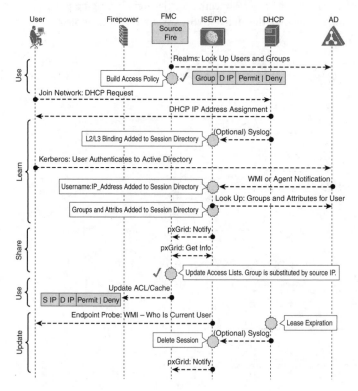

Figure 23-28 *Day in the Life of Passive ID: Firepower Management Center*

Web Security Appliance

The Web Security Appliance is an interesting consumer of identity. What makes it really intriguing is that it has support for both pxGrid and CDA-RADIUS, but as of WSA version 9.1.2, the capabilities are not equal.

The WSA can leverage CDA. In fact, CDA was the main option for passive identity. Similar to the way Firepower works, the metadata comes from the realm configuration, but the passive identity and IP address bindings come from CDA. The user identities are stored in the Auth Cache on the WSA.

Interestingly enough, the WSA can also leverage pxGrid, but not for passive identity. The WSA's pxGrid integration with ISE does not leverage AD groups at all. Instead, it is a TrustSec integration only, leveraging the assigned Security Group Tag (SGT) for the user session only. If the session does not have an SGT, it cannot be used with the WSA. The exception to this rule is when the WSA's policy uses individual user accounts instead of AD groups or SGTs.

The TrustSec integration makes life simple, clean, and easy. However, the ISE-PIC form factor doesn't have any authorization support, including TrustSec, and therefore cannot be used with the WSA. Full ISE does have TrustSec authorizations and therefore would work perfectly with the WSA for this type of integration.

When ISE releases the CDA-RADIUS interface, you should be able to drop in an ISE node to replace CDA without worry. The WSA would still use the realms for metadata used in policy authoring, and use the CDA-RADIUS interface for the real-time binding. Figure 23-29 illustrates the passive identity flow with WSA, leveraging realms and CDA-RADIUS. The configuration steps for integrating the WSA using pxGrid with ISE are covered in Chapter 24.

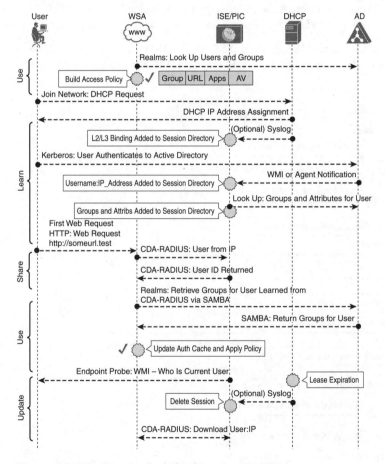

Figure 23-29   *Day in the Life of Passive ID: WSA*

Adaptive Security Appliance

The ASA is another interesting use case, particularly because it is entering another stage in its evolution. Most recently, the ASA is evolving into a Next-Generation Firewall platform, in the form of Firepower Threat Defense (FTD). So, the number of "classic ASA" being deployed has dropped off significantly.

If the ASA is an FTD appliance, the passive identity is integrated using Firepower Management Center, previously introduced. When the appliance is a classic ASA, then it requires the CDA-RADIUS interface.

The ASA is very similar to the WSA in how it integrates with an identity sharing solution. The ASA can and does leverage CDA. Similar to the way Firepower works, the metadata comes from an LDAP configuration, but the passive identity and IP address bindings come from CDA.

TrustSec integration is another option, but unlike FMC and WSA, the ASA does not learn about SGTs via pxGrid. The ASA can learn about TrustSec tags natively on the wire (in the Layer 2 frame) or through the Security group eXchange Protocol (SXP). Leveraging a tag is not passive identity and therefore is out of scope for this use case.

For passive identity sharing, the ASA requires the CDA-RADIUS interface. Figure 23-30 illustrates the passive identity flow with ASA, leveraging LDAP and CDA-RADIUS.

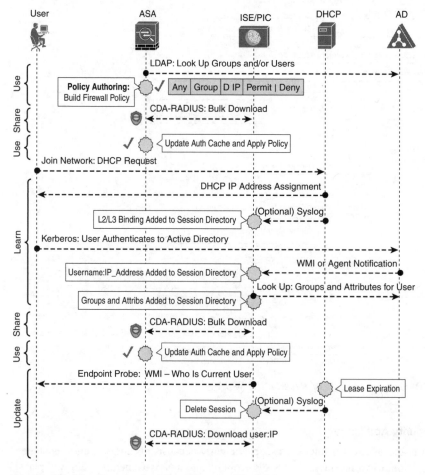

Figure 23-30 *Day in the Life of Passive ID: ASA*

Integration Summary

Stealthwatch, Firepower Management Center, WSA, and ASA are only four examples of integration. There are so many more that are expected within Cisco's product portfolio. Additionally, similar integrations exist within Cisco's security partner ecosystem, such as the integration between ISE and Infoblox, or ISE and Splunk.

Tenet 4: Update

This tenet is meant to keep the data up to date and as valid as possible. You wouldn't want a firewall working off stale information and allowing the wrong user through. One method to keep sessions up to date is to monitor the syslog messages from a DHCP server and see when the endpoint's lease expires or the IP address is assigned to a different MAC address. You saw this in the "Syslog Sources" section earlier in the chapter. Several other events and tools can be used to update the session data, including logoff detection, WMI updates, and session timeouts, all three of which are discussed in this section.

Logoff Detection with the Endpoint Probe

Users do not always log off from their computers before leaving the network. Often, they just close the lid on their laptop and pack up for the day. ISE 2.2 introduces an endpoint probe to aid with logoff detection. The probe is designed to answer the burning questions: Is the endpoint still there? If so, is the same user logged in?

The endpoint probe uses WMI to remotely communicate with the endpoint and check if the user is still there. If the endpoint is on the network but WMI is not responding, ISE tries to remotely log into the endpoint using the saved Domain Admin credentials and enable WMI. If you chose to not save the credential when joining AD, then the endpoint probe will not function. If the endpoint is not there or if a different user is logged in, the session will be cleared.

Keep in mind that the endpoint probe relies on reverse-DNS to map IP addresses to hostnames, and the probe runs every four hours. If the endpoint is online but is not responding to WMI, then ISE remotely logs in with the saved Domain Admin credentials and enables WMI. This behavior is not configurable—if it is not desirable for your organization, the only option is to disable the endpoint probe.

ISE also allows you to map subnets to PSNs for the endpoint probe. This way you can design and plan which PSN is responsible for specific areas of your network. If a subnet does not exist in the list, then the endpoint probe will not operate in that subnet.

To add a subnet to PSN mapping, from the ISE GUI:

Step 1.   Navigate to **Work Centers > PassiveID > Providers > Endpoint Probes.**

Step 2.   Click **Add.**

Step 3.   Name the endpoint probe and (optional) add a description.

Step 4.   From the Status drop-down list, choose **Enabled.**

Step 5.   From the Host Name drop-down list, choose the PSN.

Step 6.   In the Subnets text box, enter the subnets in Classless Interdomain Routing (CIDR) notation (x.x.x.x/y), with a comma separating multiple networks.

Step 7.   Click **Submit.**

Figure 23-31 shows the creation of an endpoint probe, while Figure 23-32 shows a completed list of multiple probes assigned to their respective PSN.

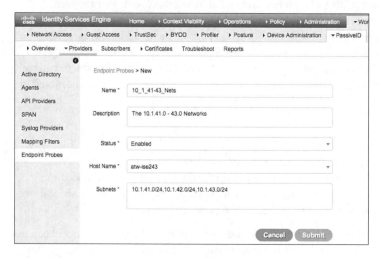

Figure 23-31   *Creating an Endpoint Probe*

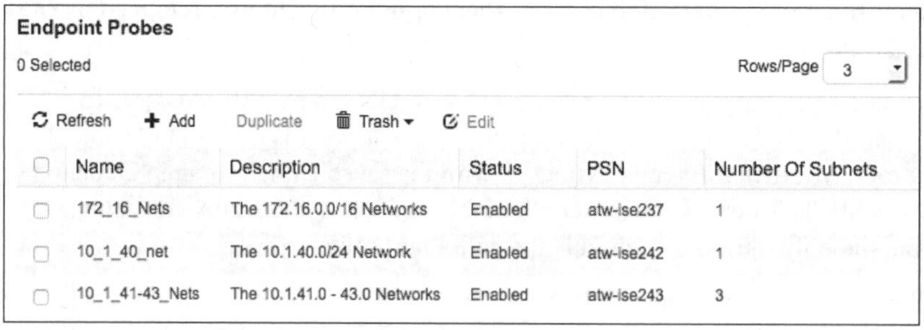

Endpoint Probes

0 Selected   Rows/Page 3

	Name	Description	Status	PSN	Number Of Subnets
	172_16_Nets	The 172.16.0.0/16 Networks	Enabled	atw-ise237	1
	10_1_40_net	The 10.1.40.0/24 Network	Enabled	atw-ise242	1
	10_1_41-43_Nets	The 10.1.41.0 - 43.0 Networks	Enabled	atw-ise243	3

Figure 23-32   *List of Endpoint Probes*

Note   The PSN to subnet mapping is only available with a full ISE install. When using the ISE-PIC form factor, configuration of the endpoint probe is limited to enabling and disabling only, as shown Figure 23-33. The ISE-PIC GUI shown in Figure 23-33 is discussed in the next section.

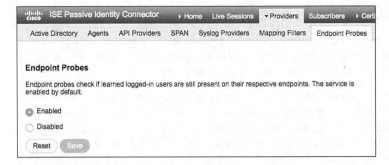

Figure 23-33 *Endpoint Probe in the ISE-PIC User Interface*

WMI Update Events

As described previously, Kerberos ticket renewals generate WMI events and keep the session alive. Other WMI events can also renew the session, show an actual user logoff, and expire the session when that logoff occurs.

Session Timeouts

All entries in the session directory will expire and be purged at a configured interval between 1 and 24 hours. If no qualifying events or activity has been seen, then ISE removes those inactive sessions. The session timeout is configurable under the Advanced Settings tab of your AD join point, as shown in Figure 23-34. The purge timer is called User Session Aging Time.

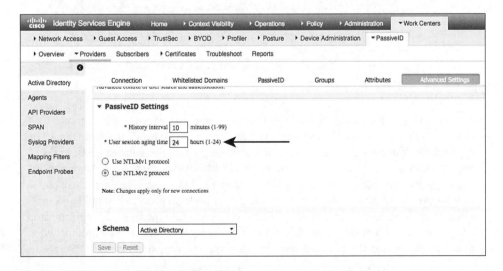

Figure 23-34 *User Session Aging Time*

ISE Passive Identity Connector

ISE version 2.2 introduces a new form factor to the world that is designed for passive identity sharing only. It's known as a form factor and not a persona because it's a stand-alone model known as the ISE Passive Identity Connector (ISE-PIC).

Cisco created ISE-PIC to provide a low-cost offering of the passive identity sharing capabilities within ISE for Cisco products to consume. Yes, it is still ISE, but the low-cost PIC license disables most of what comes with ISE, leaving only the services required for passive identity sharing enabled. Not only does it limit the services that run, it wraps this all up into a nice, simple, lightweight installation package and user interface. Figure 23-35 shows the ISE-PIC user interface.

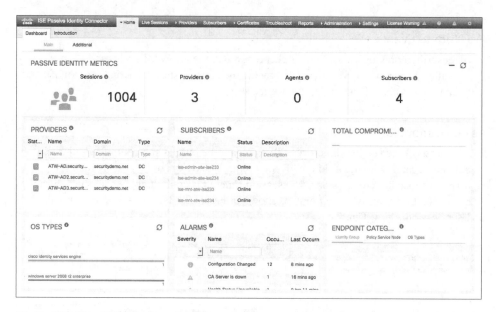

Figure 23-35   *ISE-PIC User Interface*

As you can see in Figure 23-35, the UI is basically just the PassiveID Work Center brought to the top level of the ISE menu system. Remember, ISE-PIC is a standalone deployment. It doesn't get added to an ISE cube. All the functions already exist in ISE and are enabled on a per-node basis. However, ISE-PIC does provide for redundancy by allowing for a secondary node to be added. Unlike a full ISE install, because there are so few options available to the administrator, the registration process is simplified even more. There is no need to import each node's certificates into the trusted certificate store like you must with full ISE. Instead, when joining the second node, the UI prompts you to accept the untrusted certificate, just like when you try to go to a new HTTPS website.

Figure 23-36 shows the deployment screen and the fields for adding a secondary node, but none of the options for selecting services are there because it is ISE-PIC. Figure 23-37 shows the UI prompting the admin to accept the secondary node's certificate.

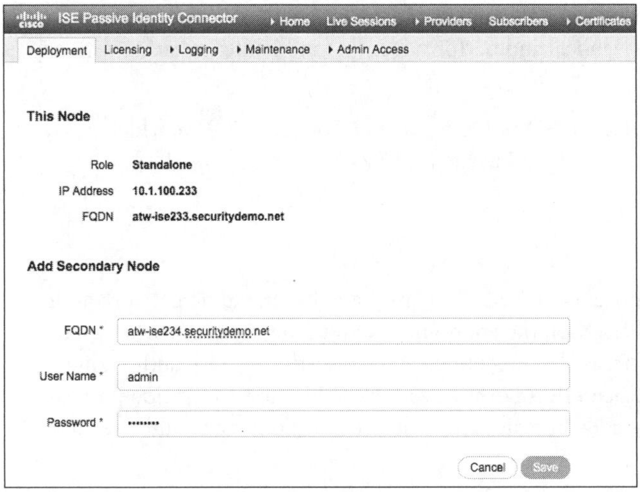

Figure 23-36 *Adding a Second ISE-PIC Node*

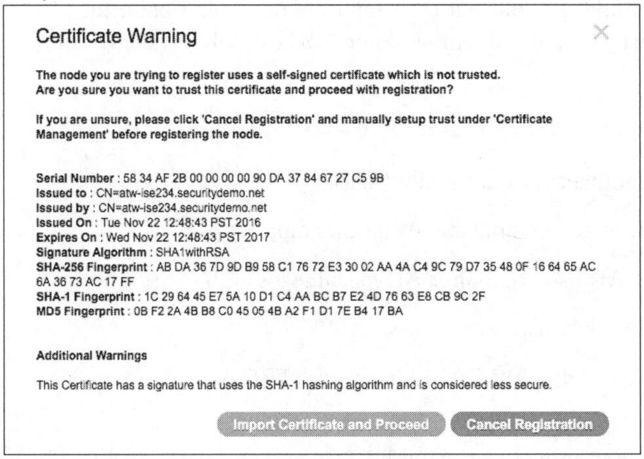

Figure 23-37 *Accepting a Certificate*

It's important to understand that, under the covers, ISE-PIC is still just ISE. Remember, it is a simpler and smaller install of ISE with only what is required for passive identity sharing enabled. It has no authentication, authorization, access control, device administration, or TrustSec. It still includes pxGrid, because it is required for sharing the identities. However, it only works for Cisco subscribers such as Stealthwatch and Firepower. Non-Cisco subscribers such as Splunk or Check Point would require Plus licenses to subscribe and integrate with pxGrid, which means you need a full ISE install.

Some good news: because ISE-PIC is still ISE under the covers, it is a simple license install to upgrade an ISE-PIC node to a full ISE node. Install the right license(s) and you can join a full ISE cube, separate out the functions and spread them across multiple nodes for scale and design elegance, and perform identity and context sharing with any pxGrid subscriber.

ISE-PIC has a separate installation ISO or Open Virtual Appliance (OVA), which exists to enable better tracking of downloads and usage for Cisco.

EasyConnect

EasyConnect extends the concepts of passive identity and by providing network authorization without requiring 802.1X on the endpoints. Active Directory logins are used to map user information to network connections, which is then used for authorizing users on the network even when ISE is not involved in the user authentication process. EasyConnect can be used as a backup authentication method or way to add a second level of identity.

Some customers use EasyConnect as a stepping stone toward a full 802.1X environment. They use EasyConnect in some locations to provide network access control before the supplicant is fully deployed on all endpoints. The deployment is capable of mixed authorizations, so as the desktop team rolls out the supplicant configuration to the managed endpoints, both dot1x-capable systems and non-dot1x-capable systems can coexist.

The following are some basic concepts about EasyConnect (EZC):

- EZC requires a network authentication, usually MAB.

- EZC is for Microsoft AD joined computers—Windows only.

- EZC identity is based on AD user login, *not* AD machine login.

- It is possible to combine authentications:

  - Combine MAB identity (endpoint MAC address) with EZC—this is the most common use of EZC.

  - Combine 802.1X machine authentication with EZC user information for a dual-factor authentication.

- EZC requires an AD login event to be processed from the endpoint to AD. If access to the domain controllers is not permitted at time of user login, EZC will fail.

- The network access devices (NADs) are not configured any differently:

  - They must still process network authentications (MAB and 802.1X).

  - ISE must still be configured as the RADIUS server.

When a machine joins the network, a MAB is processed. The authorization result must include the Passive Identity Tracking option, such as shown in Figure 23-38.

Figure 23-38 *Authorization Profile with Passive Identity Tracking Enabled*

When a network session is authorized with this flag, ISE monitors the session and looks for WMI events that leverage the same endpoint ID (MAC address), to stitch the passive identity together with the network session.

After the WMI event for that endpoint is stitched together, a CoA-Reauth is sent to the NAD and a new authorization result may be applied that is based on the combined authentication (MAB + EZC).

Figures 23-39 and 23-40 show the EasyConnect flow leveraging MAB for the network session.

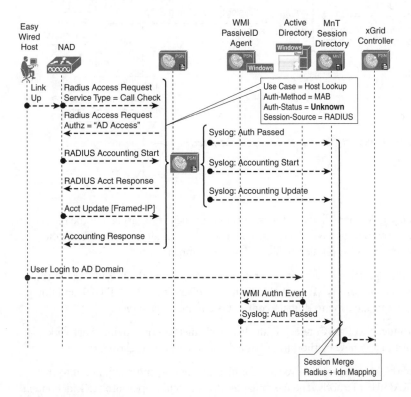

Figure 23-39 *EasyConnect Flow with MAB*

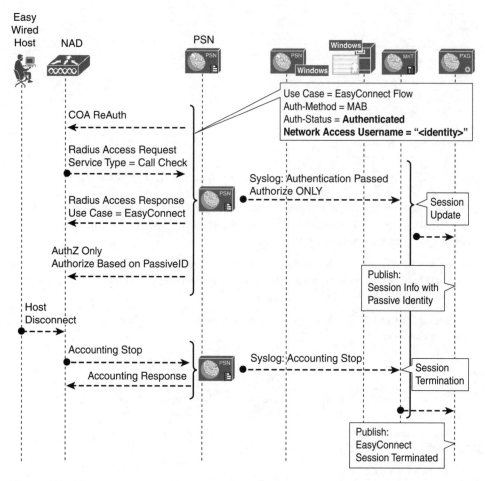

Figure 23-40   *EasyConnect Flow with MAB (Continued)*

Summary

In this chapter, you learned all about the importance of identity sharing and the difference between active and passive identities. You learned about all four tenets of a complete identity sharing solution: Learn, Share, Use, and Update.

You examined ISE's Active Directory integration with WMI and the ISE-PIC agent, saw how easy it is to configure WMI on the domain controllers from the ISE GUI, and how to push the agent installation to domain controllers and member servers.

You were introduced to EasyConnect as an alternative method of providing network access control and as a new method to provide dual-factor authentication.

You examined the basic premise of pxGrid for identity sharing and compared it to the legacy CDA-RADIUS methods. The next chapter dives much deeper into pxGrid, context sharing, and using ISE as the center of a security ecosystem.

Chapter 24

ISE Ecosystems: The Platform eXchange Grid (pxGrid)

This chapter covers the following topics:

■ The many integration types of the ecosystem

■ pxGrid in action

Because Cisco ISE is positioned to know exactly who and what is on the network at any given time, as well as assign different levels of access and context assignments with Security Group Tags (SGT), it is the perfect security tool to be at the center of a security ecosystem.

There are many tools that exist within your "security toolkit": firewalls, next-generation firewalls (NGFW), intrusion prevention systems (IPS), NG-IPSs, security information and event management (SIEM) systems, secure web gateways, threat defense tools, vulnerability assessment scanners, mobile device managers, and more.

Most of these tools do not know the identity of the user, only the identity of the endpoint. These other tools can be made even more valuable by integrating into a full security ecosystem with ISE. Wouldn't the reporting in the SIEM be more valuable if it showed which user was involved in the security event, instead of only the IP or MAC address? What about when your intrusion prevention tools or threat defense solutions identify malicious activity on the network? Wouldn't it be great if they could trigger something that would change the way the endpoint was treated on the network? With a single "trigger," the endpoint's level of network access can be changed, the endpoint's traffic can be inspected deeper as it passes through a Cisco Adaptive Security Appliance (ASA), the Cisco Web Security Appliance (WSA) can apply a different SSL decryption policy, and so much more.

You've already read about ISE integrating with mobile device managers (MDM), and how ISE can provide passive identities to ecosystem partners; it can also provide the single point of policy control for threat containment and context setting.

The Many Integration Types of the Ecosystem

An integration of ISE can take multiple forms, where data (referred to as context) may be received into ISE or shared out of ISE. Generally, the integrations can be classified in one of three ways:

■ **Context Sharing:** The endpoint and user attributes known to ISE are shared outbound to partner applications to consume.

■ **Context In:** ISE is learning new attributes about users and endpoints used to further enhance ISE's own authorization capabilities.

■ **Context Brokering:** ISE is being used as a transport medium to communicate security data from one system to another system.

MDM Integration

In Chapter 17, "BYOD: Self-Service Onboarding and Registration," you read all about BYOD and the integration between ISE and mobile device managers. That integration is two-fold. ISE provides the redirection to the MDM service for onboarding, but the MDM is also able to provide "context in" to ISE. In other words, the MDM tells ISE about the mobile endpoints, its compliance with the policies for the endpoint, the status of encryption or pin lock, and more.

This integration uses a specific bidirectional application programming interface (API) between ISE and the MDM (cloud service or appliance). This API is unique, and created just for MDM integration.

For more on MDM integration, refer to Chapter 17.

Rapid Threat Containment

MDM integration is one of the first and most common integration types for ISE. In true Cisco marketing fashion, Cisco Rapid Threat Containment has gone through many different names and marketing initiatives. This section describes the evolution of Rapid Threat Containment.

The roots of Rapid Threat Containment begin back in ISE 1.1, with the addition of a new feature called Endpoint Protection Services (EPS). EPS provided an API allowing other applications to initiate three actions against an endpoint based on IP address or MAC address:

■ **Quarantine:** Set the binary flag on the endpoint record to "true," added the endpoint to a list of quarantined endpoints, and allowed the administrator to create authorization policies that used that assignment to assign a different level of network access.

■ **Unquarantine:** Removed the endpoint from the list of quarantined endpoints and cleared the binary flag.

- **Shutdown:** Was supposed to send a CoA Terminate to the network and shut down the port on the network switch. Note: This option existed in the API, but it is not exposed to the policy and is therefore not usable.

Many of the first integrations with ISE used EPS, including the original integration with Lancope StealthWatch (now Cisco's Stealthwatch)—where an endpoint is quarantined from the StealthWatch user interface.

Figure 24-1 illustrates a flow with Stealthwatch initiating an EPS quarantine.

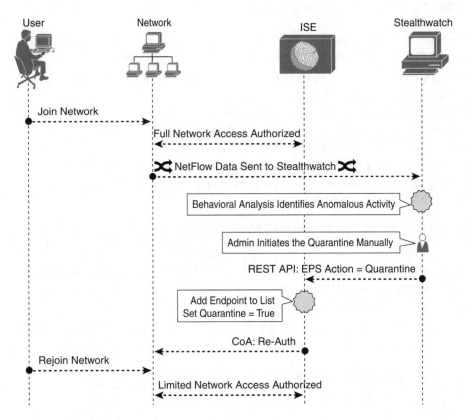

Figure 24-1 *Stealthwatch to ISE—EPS Quarantine*

The flow illustrated in Figure 24-1 shows an endpoint being admitted to the network with full access. The Stealthwatch admin initiates a quarantine, and Stealthwatch connects to ISE using the EPS REST API, telling ISE to quarantine the endpoint with the specific IP address. ISE then adds the endpoint to the EPS list and sets the flag on the endpoint object, and sends a CoA to the network.

When the new access request comes in, a rule created with the EPSStatus condition will be matched. Figure 24-2 shows that condition.

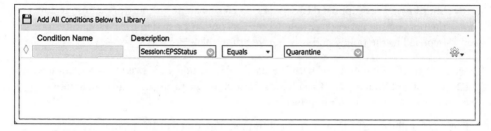

Figure 24-2   *EPSStatus Authorization Condition*

The resulting network authorization may provide for limited access, or even set a new SGT that can be acted upon differently at miscellaneous points in the network, such as the WSA.

Well, ultimately EPS was just too rigid. It only provided for a single actionable classification (quarantine). More flexibility was needed, not only to provide many different options, but also to integrate into the new-fangled context-sharing technology that Cisco was creating named the Platform eXchange Grid (pxGrid). So, EPS needed to evolve into EPS 2.0 or something like it.

In response, in ISE 1.3, Cisco introduced something new named Adaptive Network Control (ANC). A huge step forward? Alas, it amounted to simply renaming EPS to ANC. ISE 1.3 didn't improve anything.

ISE 1.4 actually added new functionality to ANC. It still supported the old EPS API calls for backward-compatibility purposes, but it also added a new API with different classifications available, including the ability to create your own classification. With ANC, each classification can correspond to a different action. Although you can add many different classifications, there are really only three choices for classification types: Quarantine, Shut Down, and Port Bounce.

To create an ANC policy (AKA classification), navigate to **Operations > Adaptive Network Control > Policy List**, and click **Add**, which opens the options shown in Figure 24-3.

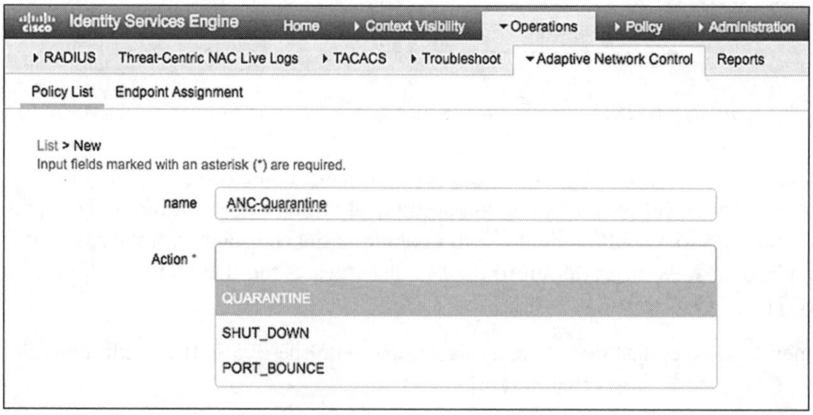

Figure 24-3   *Adding an ANC Policy*

You can create multiple ANC policies, and each policy can contain one or more actions. Each ANC policy can be associated to a different authorization. For example, you can end up with ANC policies such as

- Investigate

- Black Hole

- Eradicate

- Nuke from Orbit

In addition to a much more flexible approach to classification, or as Cisco's legendary Paul Forbes would call it, "flexible name spaces," ANC also integrates tightly with pxGrid, enabling pxGrid subscribers to trigger the ANC action within the pxGrid connection, not through the point API of the past.

So, Endpoint Protection Services was renamed to Adaptive Network Control. Then ANC got new functionality in ISE 1.4. Then Cisco security marketing got involved and came up with a new naming convention to refer to the entire integrated security system where any Cisco security product takes action through another Cisco security product. That name is *Rapid Threat Containment*. You now have solutions such as Rapid Threat Containment with Cisco Stealthwatch and the Identity Services Engine and Rapid Threat Containment with Cisco Firepower Management Center and Identity Services Engine.

Crystal clear, right?

Platform Exchange Grid

pxGrid is Cisco's premier publish and subscribe (pub/sub) communication bus that was designed from the ground up to be a scalable and secure data sharing system.

Like most other next-generation AAA solutions, ISE originally started sharing information through the use of APIs. It was quickly recognized that point APIs would not scale to the level of data that needed to be shared and the scale at which it was requested.

Cisco went down the path of a pub/sub bus, similar to the way Call Manager and Jabber work. There is a *controller* that keeps track of all the topics that exist. A topic is a list of information that is available. A topic might be session data of who and what is on the network, for example, or it might be a list of vulnerable endpoints and the list of those vulnerabilities.

pxGrid participants can subscribe to any topic of interest, after which they are notified when there is data for that topic to be retrieved. Those participants are known as *subscribers*. The true source of the data can be any other pxGrid participant, collectively known as *publishers*. A publisher registers the topic with the controller, who performs the authorization for each subscriber to retrieve the data from the many possible publishers.

Figure 24-4 shows the standard Cisco illustration that is often used to explain pxGrid. You can see the many different types of products, each one of which has different information to publish and needs information from one of the other products.

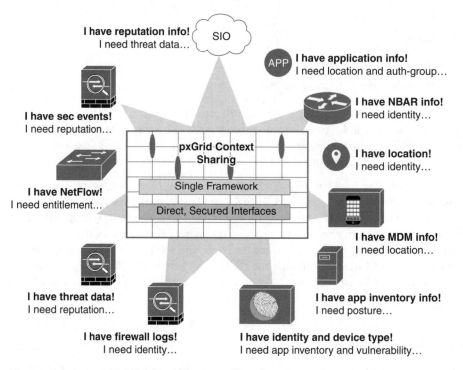

Figure 24-4   *Standard Cisco pxGrid Illustration*

pxGrid was initially added to ISE in version 1.3, so it's been around for a while now and has an ecosystem of partner applications that continues to grow at a very rapid pace.

ISE 2.2 makes great strides in enhancing pxGrid. Most of the pxGrid-related enhancements support ease of use, making it even easier to configure and maintain. ISE 2.2 also adds more information into ISE's pxGrid topics for consumption by the subscribers. It includes data such as the list of groups that each user is a member of, all shared within the same topics that were used in the past, which enables smooth backward compatibility.

pxGrid was designed by extending the Extensible Messaging and Presence Protocol (XMPP), which is also the communication protocol used by Jabber. In fact, the pxGrid controller is a modified Extensible Communication Platform (XCP). For more on XMPP, see https://www.xmpp.org.

Figure 24-5 depicts an example showing the three main components of pxGrid: a controller, publishers, and subscribers.

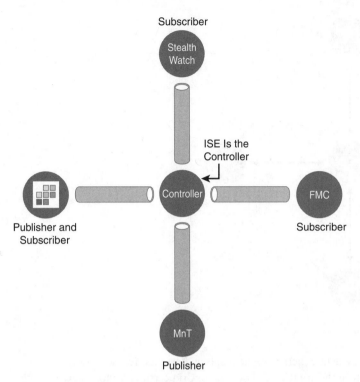

Figure 24-5   *Sample pxGrid Illustration*

pxGrid in Action

pxGrid uses secure communication between the participants, and therefore certificates are of great importance to the success and ease of your deployment. Every participant must trust the controller, and the controller must trust each of the participants.

Examining Figure 24-5 again, FMC needs to speak to the pxGrid controller to learn which topics exist, but then also needs to speak directly to the MnT node to perform bulk downloads of the published session data. If FMC were to trust the controllers' certificate but not the MnT's certificate, then the communication would ultimately fail.

Figure 24-6 illustrates this concept. You end up needing a full mesh of trust between pxGrid participants. Each participant must trust the controller as well as each other participant.

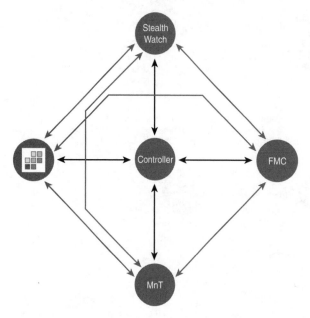

Figure 24-6   *Full Mesh of Trust*

Based on a lot of deployment experience, the resulting best practice is to always use the same certificate authority (CA) to issue the pxGrid certificates for each of the participants. To make that even easier, ISE's built-in CA was enhanced to issue pxGrid certificates in addition to endpoint certificates beginning with ISE version 2.1. Figure 24-7 illustrates a single CA issuing the certificates to all the participants.

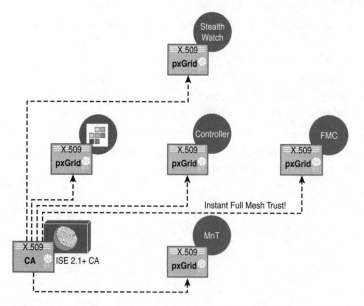

Figure 24-7   *ISE CA Issuing the pxGrid Certificates to All Participants*

Configuring ISE for pxGrid

The pxGrid user interface is located under **Administration > pxGrid Services**. Those services will not be enabled by default on any ISE node, as shown in Figure 24-8.

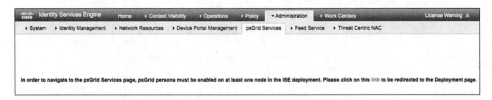

Figure 24-8 *pxGrid Services User Interface*

Before enabling pxGrid on any of the ISE nodes in the deployment, it's best to ensure that each node in the ISE cube has a pxGrid certificate signed by the same certificate authority.

Beginning in ISE 2.2, each node's pxGrid certificate will be signed automatically by the internal CA. Naturally, you can replace that certificate with one from an external CA of your choosing, but the default certificate will use the internal CA in an attempt to simplify the setup and follow best practices.

To check that each node has a pxGrid certificate signed by the same CA:

Step 1.   Navigate to **Administration > System > Certificates**.

Step 2.   Select the pxGrid certificate of one of the nodes, as shown in Figure 24-9.

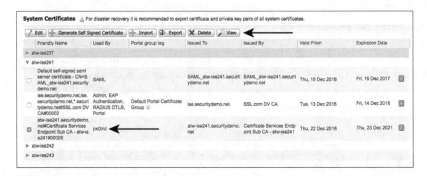

Figure 24-9 *Viewing System Certificates*

Step 3.   Click **View**.

Step 4.   Check that the root signer of the certificate is the primary Policy Administration Node (PAN) of the ISE cube (the root CA), as shown in Figure 24-10.

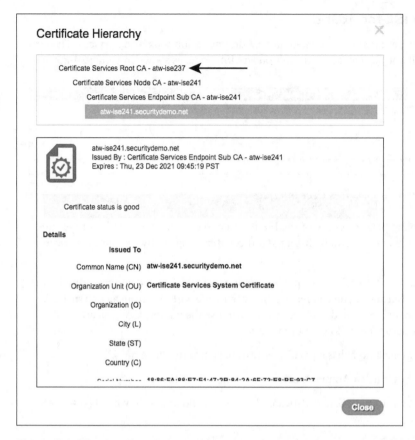

Figure 24-10 *Certificate Hierarchy*

Once you're sure the certificates in use are all issued by the same public key infrastructure (PKI), then it's time to enable them. It is an experienced-based recommendation to have a pxGrid certificate on every single node in the ISE deployment, even if the node will not run the pxGrid controller function.

Note Beginning in ISE version 2.2, all pxGrid communications occur within the secure pxGrid channel; in other words, all communication occurs leveraging the pxGrid certificate of the ISE node. In prior versions, all bulk downloads from the MnT node occurred using the Admin Certificate, not the pxGrid certificate. This caused many TAC cases and confusion, and needed to change. If you are implementing pxGrid on any ISE version prior to ISE 2.2, you must ensure the participant trusts the admin certificate issuing CA as well as the pxGrid certificate.

To enable the pxGrid controller function:

Step 1.   Navigate to **Administration > System > Deployment**.

Step 2.   The pxGrid controller function must run on a Policy Service Node (PSN). Select one of the PSNs from the list.

Step 3.   Check the **pxGrid** check box, as shown in Figure 24-11.

Step 4.   Click **Save**.

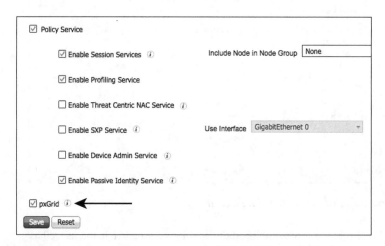

Figure 24-11   *Enabling the pxGrid Controller Function*

This enables the pxGrid controller function on the PSN. You may have up to two pxGrid controllers per ISE cube to provide redundancy.

Once the pxGrid services are all up and running, the PAN and MnT nodes automatically register and publish their respective topics into the grid, as shown in Figure 24-12. By default, only ISE nodes are registered; all others require approval, or require that you enable auto-registration.

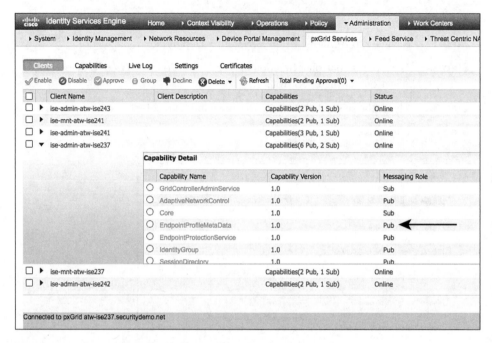

Figure 24-12   *pxGrid Capability (AKA Topic) Detail*

Notice in Figure 24-12 that the topics are listed under the pxGrid participant, as well as the role that node plays with the topic (Pub or Sub).

Configuring pxGrid Participants

Many different subscribers and publishers can participate in the ecosystem with pxGrid. Each one uses the information in its own way, and the integration UI is bound to be unique per product, but the basic requirements and configuration steps will always remain the same:

1. Trust the ISE certificate authority.

2. Install a pxGrid certificate for its own identity.

3. Configure the IP or FQDN of the pxGrid controller.

For the most part, that is all you need to do on each participant. Some will make things easier than others. Let's take a look configuring some of the main pxGrid participants: Cisco Firepower Management Center, Cisco Stealthwatch, and Cisco Web Security Appliance.

Configuring Firepower Management Center for pxGrid

Cisco FMC is the ultimate device manager and security monitoring tool for Cisco Firepower Threat Defense (FTD) NGFW, Firepower NGFW, and Firepower NGIPS devices.

FMC has had pxGrid integration for a while, but version 6.2 adds an even better integration, with the ability to use the TrustSec data independent of user identities. FMC can use context information provided by pxGrid, such as endpoint profiles, TrustSec tags, and both passive and active user identities.

Before configuring pxGrid on FMC, generate a pxGrid certificate for FMC to use. In versions past, you had to configure a certificate provisioning portal in ISE, but in ISE 2.2 you can generate certificates directly from the pxGrid services user interface.

To generate a pxGrid certificate for FMC:

Step 1. Navigate to **Administration > pxGrid Services > Certificates**, as shown in Figure 24-13.

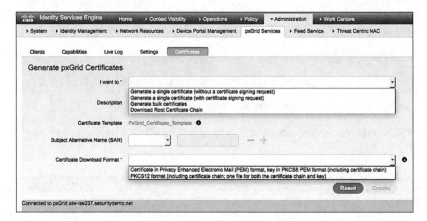

Figure 24-13 *Generating pxGrid Certificates*

Examining Figure 24-13, from this screen you can generate a single certificate, sign a certificate signing request (CSR), generate bulk certificates from a CSV file, or download the certificate authority chain for import into the trust store of the pxGrid participant. For FMC, you need to generate a certificate-key pair.

Step 2. From the I Want To drop-down list, choose **Generate a Single Certificate (Without a Certificate Signing Request)**.

Step 3. In the Common Name (CN) text box, enter a common name for the subject of your certificate.

The CN is normally the FQDN of the host (that is, atw-fmc.securitydemo. net); however, a common practice is to add a prefix to your CN, such as *pxGrid-* (as shown in Figure 24-14), which will help you avoid installation errors that can sometimes occur when you try to install more than one certificate with the same FQDN.

Step 4.   (Optional) In the Subject Alternative Name (SAN) field, add a SAN, if needed.

If you use anything other than the true FQDN for the device, then you need to complete this field. Per the RFC, anytime you use a SAN, it must also contain the CN. Add an entry for the FQDN of the host. Adding a SAN for the IP address is helpful, just in case one of the pxGrid peers is sent to the host via the IP address instead of the FQDN.

Step 5.   From the Certificate Download Format drop-down list, choose **Certificate in Privacy Enhanced Electronic Mail (PEM) Format, Key in PKCS8 PEM Format.**

All options include the internal CA's certificates, for the entire PKI hierarchy. There is also an option to download it as a PKCS12 chain file, where the public certificate + private key + signing chain are all in a single file. For FMC, the download format needs to be separate PEM files, not the PKCS12 chain.

Step 6.   Add a password for the private key.

ISE will never issue private keys without a password to encrypt the key.

Step 7.   Click **Create** and download the resulting ZIP file.

Figure 24-14 shows the completed certificate form, and Figure 24-15 shows the contents of the ZIP file.

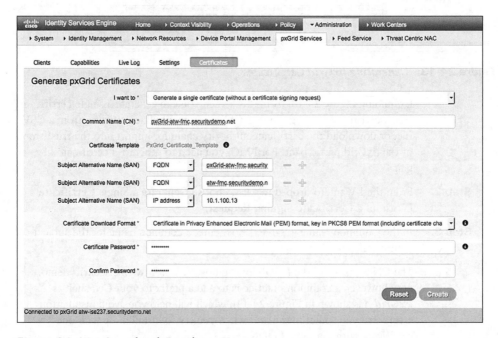

Figure 24-14 *Completed Certificate Form*

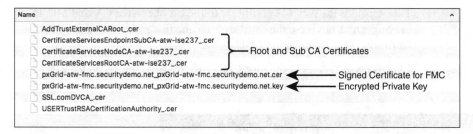

Figure 24-15 *Contents of the Resulting ZIP File*

Examining Figure 24-15, the ZIP file contains the signed certificate, the encrypted private key, and all the signing certificates in the PKI hierarchy for the issued certificate. Additionally, the signing certificates in the PKI hierarchy for the admin certificate are also included for good measure. Beginning with ISE 2.2, they should not be required.

Now you have all the required certificates and the private key for FMC. To configure pxGrid on FMC:

Step 1. Navigate to **System > Integration > Identity Sources**, as shown in Figure 24-16.

Figure 24-16 *Identity Sources*

Step 2. Click **Identity Services Engine**.

Figure 24-19, shown later in this process, shows the completed Identity Services Engine form.

Step 3. In the Primary Host Name/IP Address text box, enter the FQDN or IP address of the primary pxGrid controller.

Step 4. If there is a secondary controller, add its FQDN or IP address in the Secondary Host Name/IP Address text box.

Step 5. To add the ISE root CA certificate, click the green and white plus button to the right of the pxGrid Server CA field to open the Imported Trusted Certificate Authority dialog box.

This step adds the root CA certificate to the list of trusted CAs in FMC. In the Name text box, give the certificate a name that makes sense to you, similar to what you see in Figure 24-17.

Step 6.   Click **Browse** and select the root CA certificate from the expanded ZIP file you downloaded earlier, as shown in Figure 24-17.

Figure 24-17   *Import Trusted Certificate Authority: ISE Root CA*

Step 7.   Click **Save**.

Step 8.   Ensure that the newly imported root CA certificate is selected for both the pxGrid Server CA and the MNT Server CA fields, as shown later in Figure 24-19.

Step 9.   To add the signed certificate and private key for FMC, click the green and white plus button to the right of the FMC Server Certificate field to open the Add Known Internal Certificate dialog box.

This step adds the PEM encoded certificate that was signed by ISE's endpoint CA and the encrypted private key to FMC. In the Name text box, give the internal certificate a name that makes sense to you, similar to what you see in Figure 24-18.

Figure 24-18   *Adding the Internal Certificate*

Step 10. Click **Browse** to the right of Certificate Data and select the PEM certificate from the expanded ZIP file you downloaded earlier, as shown in Figure 24-18.

Step 11. Click **Browse** to the right of Key and select the PKCS8 key file from the expanded ZIP file you downloaded earlier, as shown in Figure 24-18.

Step 12. Check the **Encrypted, and the Password Is** check box.

Step 13. Enter the password used to encrypt the key file from the ISE certificate authority. Click **Save**.

Step 14. Click **Save** in the upper-right corner of the screen. Figure 24-19 shows the completed form.

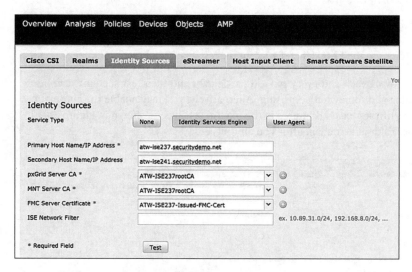

Figure 24-19 *Completed ISE Identity Source Form*

Step 15. Click **Test** to verify a successful connection.

The test will most likely fail the first time you try. Why? Because ISE is not configured to automatically approve new participants.

Step 16. In the ISE GUI, navigate to **Administration > pxGrid Services > Clients**.

Step 17. Check the box to the left of the iseagent client for FMC, as shown in Figure 24-20, and click **Approve**.

Figure 24-20 *pxGrid Clients*

Step 18.   Check the box to the left of the firesightisetest client and click **Approve**.

Step 19.   Return to the FMC UI and attempt the test again. This test should be successful.

Manually approving each and every pxGrid participant and their test accounts can be time consuming and somewhat confusing. Alternatively, you may enable the automatic approval of certificate-based accounts in the pxGrid settings, as shown in Figure 24-21. Just remember to disable it again after you are finished.

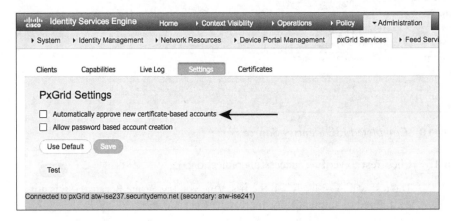

Figure 24-21 *pxGrid Settings*

Note   In the pxGrid settings is an option to allow password-based account creation. This is an alternative to the certificate-based accounts that you are seeing in this chapter, where a password is leveraged instead and then tokens are assigned for authorization. At the time of writing, there are not any pxGrid client applications leveraging this account method. Also in the settings screen is a Test button to verify that pxGrid is working as expected within ISE. It is very useful for checking that ISE trusts its own certificates.

Configuring the Web Security Appliance for pxGrid

Cisco WSA was one of the first pxGrid partner applications in the security ecosystem. The WSA may use pxGrid to ascertain both passive and active user identities, as well as TrustSec tags. However, at the time of writing, the WSA (version 9.1.2) is unable to combine Active Directory group membership with the identity information gathered from pxGrid, which means that TrustSec tagging is realistically the only scalable approach when using pxGrid.

Create a certificate for the WSA using the same procedure that you used for FMC, as shown in Figure 24-22.

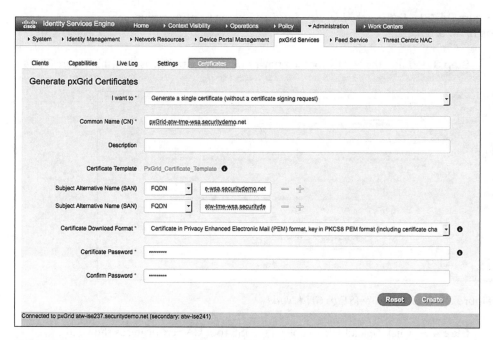

Figure 24-22 *Completed Certificate Form: WSA*

To configure pxGrid on the WSA:

Step 1. Navigate to **Network > Identification Services > Identity Services Engine.**

Step 2. Click **Enable and Edit Settings**, as shown in Figure 24-23.

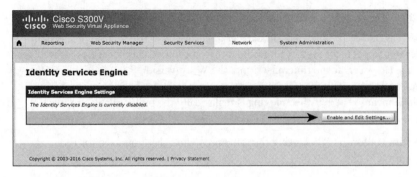

Figure 24-23 *Editing the Identity Services Engine Configuration on the WSA*

Step 3. Enter the FQDN for the primary pxGrid controller, as shown in Figure 24-24.

Figure 24-24 *Primary ISE pxGrid Node*

Step 4. Click **Upload File** to upload the ISE root CA certificate, as shown in Figure 24-24.

Step 5. Enter the FQDN for the optional secondary pxGrid controller.

Step 6. Upload the ISE root CA certificate.

> **Note** The WSA provides a location to upload the admin certificate for the primary and secondary Monitoring (MnT) nodes. This is left over from the days before ISE 2.2, when the admin certificate was used for the bulk downloads from the MnT nodes to the pxGrid subscribers. With ISE version 2.2 and newer, the same root CA certificate should be used.

Step 7. Click **Browse** to the right of Certificate and select the PEM certificate from the expanded ZIP file you downloaded earlier, as shown in Figure 24-25.

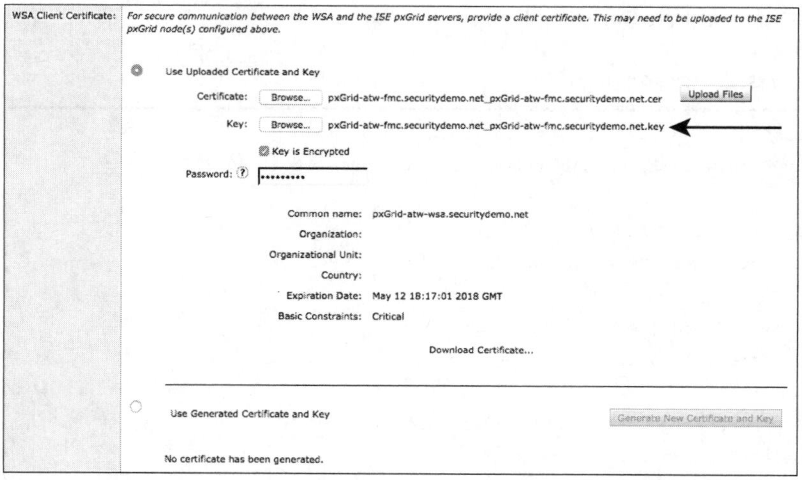

Figure 24-25 *WSA Client Certificate*

Step 8. Click **Browse** to the right of Key and select the PKCS8 key file from the expanded ZIP file you downloaded earlier, as shown in Figure 24-25.

Step 9. Check the **Key in Encrypted** check box. In the Password text box, enter the password to decrypt the key.

Step 10. Click **Upload Files**.

Step 11. Click **Submit** to complete the configuration.

Step 12. Click **Commit Changes** twice.

Step 13. To test the connection, click **Edit Settings**.

Step 14. Click **Start Test** at the bottom of the screen, as shown in Figure 24-26. If auto approval is enabled, then the test should be successful. If it is not enabled, the test will fail without manually approving the two WSA accounts on the pxGrid controller.

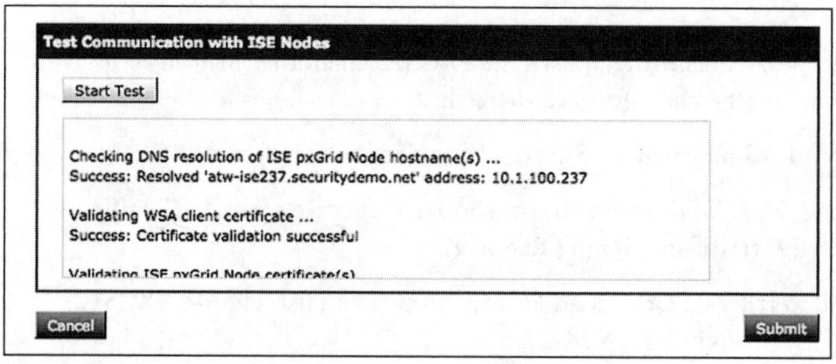

Figure 24-26 *Test Communication with ISE Nodes*

Example 24-1 demonstrates an example of the test output.

Example 24-1   *Test Execution on WSA*

```
Checking DNS resolution of ISE pxGrid Node hostname(s) ...
Success: Resolved 'atw-ise237.securitydemo.net' address: 10.1.100.237

Validating WSA client certificate ...
Success: Certificate validation successful

Validating ISE pxGrid Node certificate(s) ...
Success: Certificate validation successful

Validating ISE Monitorting Node Admin certificate(s) ...
Success: Certificate validation successful

Checking connection to ISE pxGrid Node(s) ...
Success: Connection to ISE pxGrid Node was successful.
Retrieved 17 SGTs from: atw-ise237.securitydemo.net

Checking connection to ISE Monitorting Node (REST server(s)) ...
Success: Connection to ISE Monitorting Node was successful.
REST Host contacted: atw-ise237.securitydemo.net

Test completed successfully.
```

Configuring Stealthwatch for pxGrid

Beginning with version 6.9, Cisco's Stealthwatch uses ISE as the primary source for learning passive and active user identities to merge into the flow records used for behavioral analysis. The mechanisms used are exactly the same, whether it is full ISE or the ISE Passive Identity Connector (ISE-PIC), which provides only passive identities (see Chapter 23, "Passive Identities, ISE PIC, and EZ Connect," for more information on ISE-PIC).

Unlike FMC and the WSA, Stealthwatch uses the PKCS12 chain files instead of individual certificates. To generate the chain for Stealthwatch:

Step 1.   Navigate to **Administration > pxGrid Services > Certificates**.

Step 2.   From the I Want To drop-down list, choose **Generate a Single Certificate (Without a Certificate Signing Request)**.

Step 3.   From the Certificate Download Format drop-down list, choose **PKCS12 Format**, as shown in Figure 24-27.

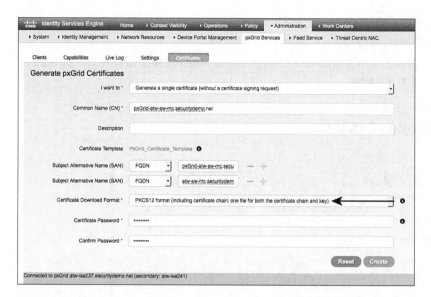

Figure 24-27 *Completed Certificate Form: Stealthwatch*

Step 4.   Click **Create** to download the certificate chain.

Next, download the root certificates in PEM format, as shown in
Figure 24-28.

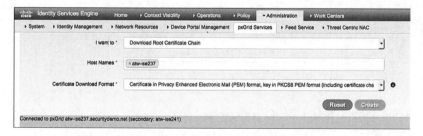

Figure 24-28 *Completed Certificate Form: Downloading the Root Chain*

Step 5.   From the I Want To drop-down list, choose **Download Root Certificate
Chain**.

Step 6.   From the Certificate Download Format drop-down list, choose **Certificate
in Privacy Enhanced Electronic Mail (PEM) Format, Key in PKCS8 PEM
Format**.

To configure Stealthwatch for pxGrid, first add the root certificate to the main list of trusted certificate authorities, as shown in Figure 24-29:

Step 1.   Navigate to **Administer Appliance > Configuration > Certificate Authority Certificates.**

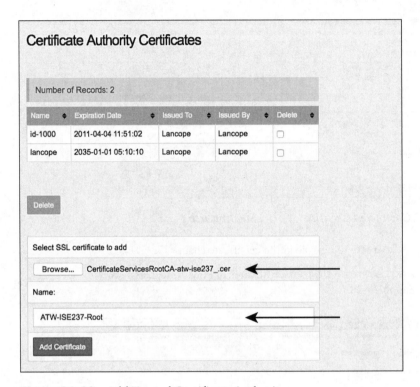

Figure 24-29 *Add Trusted Certificate Authority*

Step 2.   Scroll down to **Select SSL Certificate to Add.**

Step 3.   Click **Browse** and select the ISE root CA PEM file previously downloaded.

Step 4.   Click **Add Certificate.**

Next, add the PKCS12 chain file, as shown in Figure 24-30.

Step 5.   Navigate to **Configuration > SSL Certificate.**

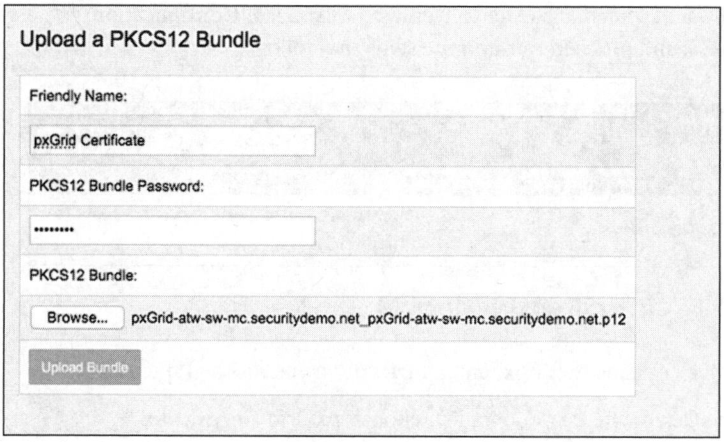

Figure 24-30   *Upload Bundle*

Step 6.   Scroll down to **Upload a PKCS12 Bundle**.

Step 7.   Provide a friendly name, such as **pxGrid Certificate**.

Step 8.   Enter the password for the encrypted PKCS12 file.

Step 9.   Click **Browse** and select the .p12 file previously downloaded.

Step 10. Click **Upload Bundle**.

The uploaded certificate identity is displayed in the SSL Client Identities section, as shown in Figure 24-31.

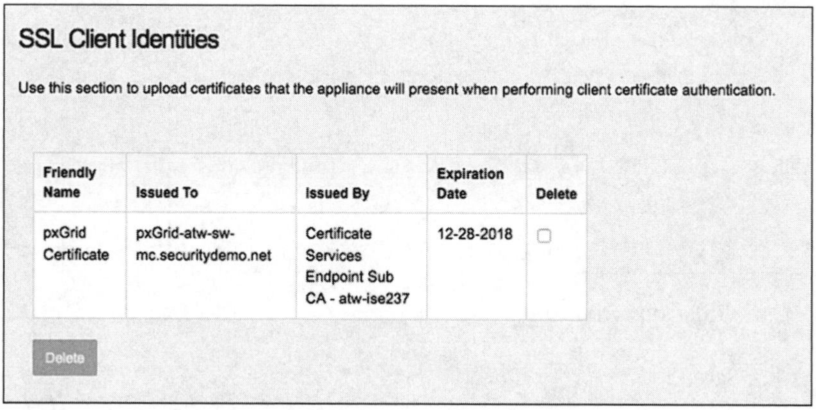

Figure 24-31   *SSL Client Identities*

Now that the CA is trusted, and the pxGrid identity has been installed into Stealthwatch, it is time to configure the ISE integration.

On the main Stealthwatch screen, navigate to **Deploy > Cisco ISE Configuration**, as shown in Figure 24-32, and proceed through the steps that follow:

Figure 24-32   *Deploying Cisco ISE Configuration*

Step 1.   In the Cluster Name text box, enter a friendly name for the ISE cube.

Step 2.   From the Certificate drop-down list, choose **pxGrid Certificate**.

Step 3.   Enter the IP addresses for the primary and secondary pxGrid controllers.

Step 4.   Create a username to uniquely identity Stealthwatch in the ISE pxGrid UI.

Figure 24-33 shows the completed Cisco ISE Configuration form.

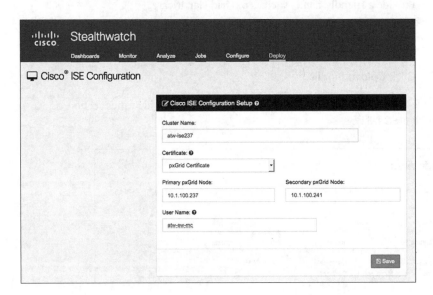

Figure 24-33   *Cisco ISE Configuration*

Step 5.   Click Save.

After saving the connection details, Stealthwatch will join the pxGrid connection and refresh the screen with the current connection status, as shown in Figure 24-34.

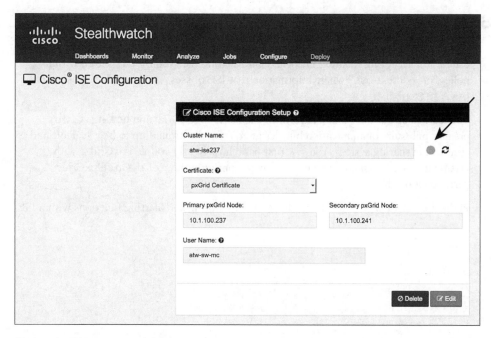

Figure 24-34 *Successful Connection*

Figure 24-35 shows the final pxGrid Clients screen, where you can see the FMC, WSA, and the Stealthwatch clients in the list.

	Client Name	Client Description	Capabilities	Status	Client Group(s)
☐ ▶	ise-mnt-atw-ise237		Capabilities(2 Pub, 1 Sub)	Online	Administrator
☐ ▶	ise-admin-atw-ise243		Capabilities(2 Pub, 1 Sub)	Online	Administrator
☐ ▶	ise-admin-atw-ise237		Capabilities(6 Pub, 2 Sub)	Online	Administrator
☐ ▶	ise-admin-atw-ise242		Capabilities(2 Pub, 1 Sub)	Online	Administrator
☐ ▶	ise-mnt-atw-ise241		Capabilities(2 Pub, 1 Sub)	Online	Administrator
☐ ▶	ise-admin-atw-ise241		Capabilities(3 Pub, 1 Sub)	Online	Administrator
☐ ▶	atw-tme-wsa.cisco.com-pxgrid_cl...	pxGrid Connection from WSA	Capabilities(0 Pub, 2 Sub)	Online	Session
☐ ▶	iseagent-sourcefire3d.securityde...		Capabilities(0 Pub, 6 Sub)	Online	ANC,EPS
☐ ▶	atw-sw-mc		Capabilities(0 Pub, 3 Sub)	Online	EPS
☐ ▶	ise_internal_test		Capabilities(0 Pub, 0 Sub)	Offline	Session
☐ ▶	atw-tme-wsa.cisco.com-test_client	pxGrid Connection from WSA	Capabilities(0 Pub, 0 Sub)	Offline	Session
☐ ▶	firesightisetest-sourcefire3d.secur...		Capabilities(0 Pub, 0 Sub)	Offline	ANC,EPS

Connected to pxGrid atw-ise237.securitydemo.net (secondary: atw-ise241)

Figure 24-35 *Final pxGrid Clients Screen*

Summary

In this chapter, you examined the many facets of the ISE ecosystem. Integration types can be ISE accepting "context-in," where information received by ISE is used within policy, or "context-out," where information that ISE possesses is shared to consumers (AKA subscribers).

You learned about the Cisco Platform Exchange Grid (pxGrid) and how it is Cisco's premier pub/sub communication bus designed from the ground up to be a scalable and secure data sharing system. You saw first-hand how tightly coupled pxGrid is with certificate-based communication and how to configure three of the main pxGrid participant products.

In the next chapter, you will learn about the monitoring and alerting functions within ISE.

Chapter 25

Understanding Monitoring, Reporting, and Alerting

This chapter covers the following topics:

- ISE monitoring
- ISE reporting
- ISE alarms

This chapter introduces you to the monitoring, reporting, and alerting functions of Cisco ISE.

Monitoring provides you with real-time or close-to-real-time data depicting the various activities, functions, and processes that ISE performs. Monitoring gives you an important operational tool for the daily usage of ISE and is key to the long-term success of an ISE deployment.

Reporting provides you with non-real-time information that is typically based on either a time frame or number of events. Examples of reports are top-client authentication, all authentications yesterday, administrator changes last month, and so on. The catalog of reports that ISE provides is meant to assist with analyzing trends, performance, and activities over time. Reports can also be run periodically or scheduled and then emailed and/or stored on completion.

ISE-alerting functions are handled by alarms. ISE alarms notify you when critical events occur or thresholds are met/crossed. Alarms are also sent when ISE completes some system functions, such as database purge, so you know they have been completed. ISE alarms are divided into multiple categories and are sent real-time when an alert is triggered.

ISE Monitoring

As discussed in Chapter 4, "The Building Blocks in an Identity Services Engine Design," the monitoring functions of ISE are separated into their own Monitoring persona. In a standalone ISE deployment, one node takes on the Administration, Monitoring, and Policy Service personas, but in a distributed deployment, you have a dedicated high availability (HA) pair of Monitoring nodes. Also recall that all of the monitoring data is viewed from the Admin node and never directly from the Monitoring node. A Cisco ISE node with the Monitoring persona functions as the log collector and stores log messages from all the Administration and Policy Service Nodes as well as from all the network access devices (NAD) in your network.

ISE displays monitoring information in many places:

- Cisco ISE Home page

- Context Visibility views

- RADIUS Live Logs and Live Sessions

- Global search

- Threat-Centric NAC Live Logs

- TACACS Live Logs

Most of these monitoring tools are explored in this chapter. TC-NAC and TACACS logs are beyond the scope of this book. Check the Cisco website for more information: www.cisco.com/go/ise.

Cisco ISE Home Page

The most prominent of the monitoring tools in ISE is the ISE Home page, which in the GUI is labeled *Home*. It includes multiple dashboards that display real-time consolidated and statistically correlated data that is most essential for effective ISE monitoring. ISE provides multiple dashboards by default (listed next) and allows you to create your own custom dashboards. Unless otherwise noted, the information shown in a dashboard is for a 24-hour period. Each dashboard is made up of several individual *dashlets* that you can manipulate.

Here is a description of the five default dashboards in ISE:

- **Summary:** This dashboard, shown in Figure 25-1, has a linear Metrics dashlet at the top to display noteworthy real-time ISE metrics, pie chart dashlets, and list dashlets. All but the Metrics dashlet are configurable.

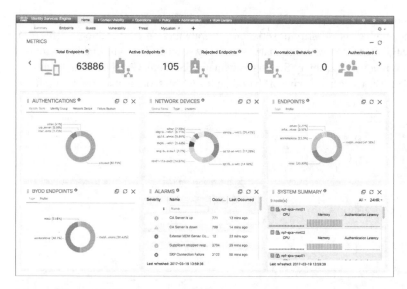

Figure 25-1 *ISE Summary Dashboard*

- **Endpoints:** Includes dashlets named Status, Endpoints, Endpoint Categories, and Network Devices.

- **Guests:** Displays information such as guest user type, logon failures, and location.

- **Vulnerability:** Displays information reported to ISE by vulnerability servers.

- **Threat:** Displays information reported to ISE by threat servers.

For more information on a dashlet, hover your mouse over it. Additionally, many of the elements are clickable and provide you with a drill-down view. You should explore the drill-down views of the dashboard elements and become familiar with them. Table 25-1 provides a description for each dashlet in the Summary dashboard.

Table 25-1 *ISE Summary Dashboard Dashlets*

Name	Description
Metrics	Summarizes the most important live information on the state of ISE.
Authentications	Passed/failed auths and a distribution of auths by type.
Network Devices	Authentications per network device.
Endpoints	Endpoint types recognized by ISE.
BYOD Endpoints	Endpoints profiled by network function.
Alarms	List of current alarms. Click each for more detail and a description of the alarm.
System Summary	Provides system-health information for each ISE node.

Figure 25-2 shows the Vulnerability dashboard in ISE. This dashboard is useful to quickly understand the number and severity of software vulnerabilities on your endpoints. This data comes from ISE's integration with external vulnerability scanner data. Vulnerabilities are classified by Common Vulnerability Scoring System (CVSS) score. CVSS uses the ratings shown in Table 25-2. You can quickly sort based on the CVSS score in many of the dashlets.

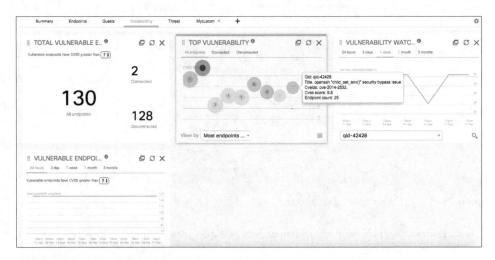

Figure 25-2   *ISE Vulnerability Dashboard*

Table 25-2   *CVSS Scoring*

Rating	CVSS Score
Low	0.1–3.9
Medium	4.0–6.9
High	7.0–8.9
Critical	9.0–10.0

The Vulnerability Watchlist dashlet enables you to track specific vulnerabilities. Figure 25-2 shows qid-42428 being tracked. Qid stands for Qualys ID; other vulnerability scanners have their own tracking IDs.

Figure 25-3 shows the Threat dashboard. This dashboard is useful for quickly seeing how many hosts are actively compromised and what indicators of compromise behaviors they are exhibiting. This data comes from ISE's integration with Cisco Advanced Malware Protection (AMP) for Endpoints and Cisco Cognitive Threat Analysis (CTA) software.

Figure 25-3   *ISE Threat Dashboard*

Context Visibility Views

Context Visibility views are a lot like dashboards except they are more customizable and provide you with a detailed results table that is actionable. There are three views available: Endpoints, Users, and Network Devices. Each view has multiple subviews to choose from. Context Visibility views are very useful when you need to get a live snapshot of what is happening, especially when you need the details. The most useful section of the views is the results table at the bottom of the page.

Figure 25-4 shows the Endpoints view with the Compliance subview. It shows you the state of posture compliance for your endpoints.

Figure 25-4   *Context Visibility Views: Endpoints*

The table at the bottom of Figure 25-4 is searchable, sortable, and allows you to take immediate actions on endpoints when needed. There are two drop-down menus available above the table to take an action on an endpoint:

- **ANC (Adaptive Network Control):** Enables you to shut down, port bounce, or quarantine a host

- **Change Authorization:** Enables you to select the CoA options shown in Figure 25-5

Figure 25-5   *Context Visibility Views: CoA Menu*

If ISE is connected to your mobile device management (MDM) system, you can take MDM actions from here as well, via the MDM Actions menu (grayed out as unavailable in Figure 25-4). ISE provides four actions it can send to your MDM vendor for execution: Corporate Wipe, Full Wipe, Pin Lock, and Refresh MDM Partner Endpoint.

Next, from this view you can also revoke a certificate from the endpoint if it was given a certificate from the built-in ISE CA.

Finally, from here you can clear threats and vulnerabilities, export and import the table data, and release rejected hosts.

The other Context Visibility views, Users and Network Devices, are shown in Figure 25-6 and Figure 25-7, respectively.

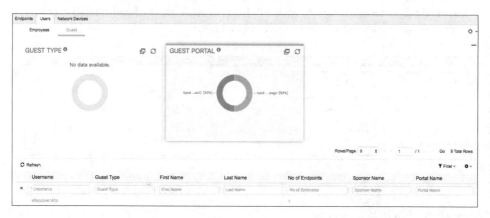

Figure 25-6   *Context Visibility Views: Users*

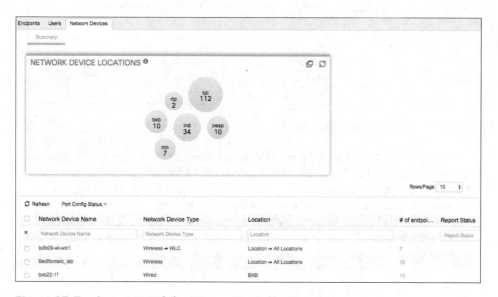

Figure 25-7   *Context Visibility Views: Network Devices*

RADIUS Live Logs and Live Sessions

The RADIUS Live Logs and Live Sessions views are perhaps the most useful monitoring and troubleshooting tools that ISE offers. These views are most useful for troubleshooting, which is covered in detail in Chapter 26, "Troubleshooting." This section covers just the monitoring aspects of the Live Logs page. To bring up a live log, go to **Operations > RADIUS > Live Logs**. Figure 25-8 displays the live log for RADIUS authentications, while Figure 25-9 shows the Live Sessions page. The sessions page only shows you hosts that have a live and fully established session with ISE. Hosts in other stages of authentication or in error states do not appear here but appear in Live Logs.

Figure 25-8   *RADIUS Live Logs*

Figure 25-9   *RADIUS Live Sessions*

Both the Live Logs and Live Sessions views have extensive filtering options. A filter box appears at the top of each column. This filter box allows for complete or partial matches but not compound conditions. For example, you could input 00:13 in the Endpoint ID column filter, and it shows you all devices with 00:13 anywhere in their MAC address. You can also sort by time or status by clicking the column headers. In the top right, notice a few additional fields you can change: refresh rate, show number of records, and within a timeframe. You can also export any of these tables from ISE.

The RADIUS Live Sessions page also allows you to take actions such as CoA or endpoint debugging, as shown in Figure 25-9. For both of these pages, the filtering feature is your friend and makes finding what you want easier.

Global Search

The global search box, positioned at the top of the ISE GUI, enables you to find endpoints. Here is a list of search criteria you can enter into the global search box:

- Username
- MAC address
- IP address
- Authorization profile
- Endpoint profile
- Failure reason
- Identity group
- Identity store
- Network device name
- Network device type
- Operating system
- Posture status
- Location
- Security group
- User type

With global search, the most popular search criteria are username, device name, IP address, and failure reason. After the RADIUS Live log and Live Sessions views, global search is perhaps the most useful tool for helpdesk personnel when troubleshooting an issue with a user. Just enter the user's IP or username and the search query quickly finds the user's session and status. Figure 25-10 shows the results of searching for an IP address.

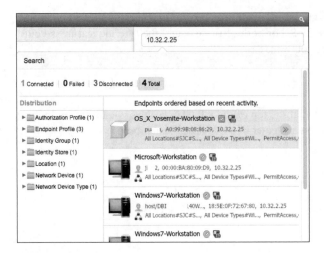

Figure 25-10   *ISE Global Search*

The search result shows a detailed current status of the device. At the top, notice live statistics on connection status. Clicking the arrows icon by a device shows you the latest session trace page, as shown in Figure 25-11. From there, click the **Endpoint Details** button or go back to the search results by clicking the **Search Results** button. Clicking Endpoint Details displays a wealth of information on the selected device, including authentication, accounting, posture, and profiler data. Figure 25-12 presents an example of authentication data. Notice that there are several other tabs (Result, Other Attributes, and Steps) to see more info. All this data can be exported too, using the export button at the bottom (not shown in Figure 25-12).

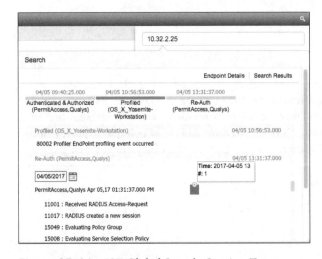

Figure 25-11   *ISE Global Search: Session Trace*

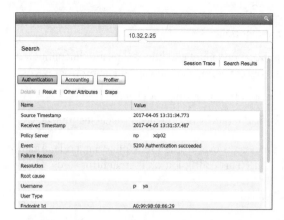

Search

Name	Value
Source Timestamp	2017-04-05 13:31:34.773
Received Timestamp	2017-04-05 13:31:37.487
Policy Server	np xdp02
Event	5200 Authentication succeeded
Failure Reason	
Resolution	
Root cause	
Username	p ya
User Type	
Endpoint Id	A0:99:9B:08:86:29

Figure 25-12   *ISE Global Search: Endpoint Details*

Monitoring Node in a Distributed Deployment

In larger deployments, it is required to set up a dedicated ISE Monitoring node. A Cisco ISE node with this persona functions as the log collector and stores log messages from all the ISE Administration and Policy Service Nodes in your network. At least one node in your distributed setup must assume the Monitoring persona. It is a best practice to not have the Monitoring and Policy Service personas enabled on the same Cisco ISE node. It is recommended that, in a larger ISE deployment, you dedicate a pair of nodes to be Monitoring nodes.

Device Configuration for Monitoring

For ISE to properly monitor your system, it must receive the appropriate information from network access devices. This requires that the NADs be configured properly. This section provides some examples of proper NAD configuration.

Cisco ISE monitoring requires that the logging source interface of a NAD be the same as the network access server (NAS) IP address configured in ISE. This allows ISE to correctly associate log messages with the proper NAD source. To accomplish this, configure the **source-interface** command on the NAD devices. The value of **source-interface** should be the same as the NAS IP address configured in ISE. The NAD CLI command **logging source-interface** should match the NAD CLI command **ip radius source-interface** and/or **ip tacacs source-interface**. Here is the command syntax for IOS:

```
logging source-interface type number
!sets the IP address associated with fastethernet 0/1 as the syslog message source.
logging source-interface fastethernet 0/1
```

The next command you want to have on your Cisco access switches is the global command **epm logging**. EPM is short for Enforcement Policy Module. EPM logging messages are displayed during the following switch events:

- **POLICY_APP_SUCCESS:** Policy application success events on named ACLs, proxy ACLs, service policies, and URL redirect policies

- **POLICY_APP_FAILURE:** Policy application failure conditions similar to unconfigured policies, wrong policies, download request failures, and download failures from AAA

- **IPEVENT:** IP assignment, IP release, and IP wait events for clients

- **AAA:** AAA events (similar to download requests or download successes from AAA)

Finally, you need to send switch syslog messages over to the ISE Monitoring node. Again, the source interface must be the ISE NAS IP. This configuration is straightforward:

```
logging monitor informational
logging origin-id ip
logging source-interface interface_id
logging host ISE Monitoring Node IP transport udp port 20514
```

For a complete list of the NAD syslogs that ISE collects, see the ISE user guide on cisco.com/go/ise.

ISE Reporting

The log data that ISE collects is organized and available in reports. The reports aggregate the data in useful ways so that you can get a longer-term view of ISE's operations. ISE provides a set of reports for you to use. Customization is possible in these reports. To see the ISE reports, go to **Operations > Reports**. As shown in Figure 25-13, the ISE reports are grouped into categories. Each category has several reports available. The My Reports category at the top of the list is where you save reports you customize or create. All reports are exportable, can be scheduled, and can be emailed.

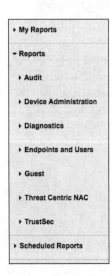

Figure 25-13 *ISE Report Categories*

Click any report to run it. You then use the report-specific filters to customize the contents of the report. Figure 25-14 shows an example report.

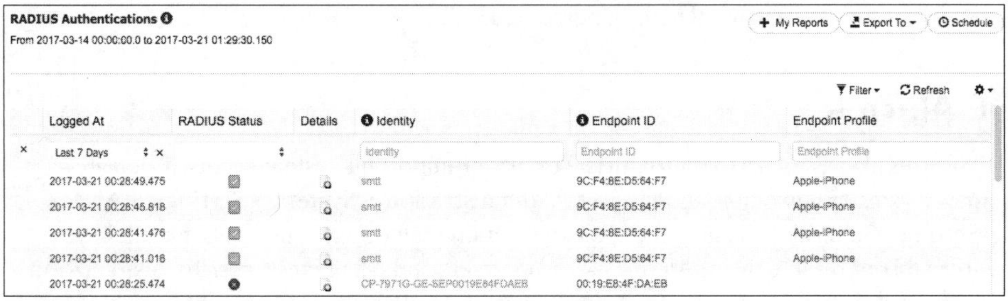

RADIUS Authentications ❶						+ My Reports ⬆ Export To ▾ 🕐 Schedule
From 2017-03-14 00:00:00.0 to 2017-03-21 01:29:30.150						
						▼ Filter ▾ ⟳ Refresh ⚙ ▾
Logged At	RADIUS Status	Details	❶ Identity	❶ Endpoint ID	Endpoint Profile	
✕ Last 7 Days ⇕ ✕	⇕		Identity	Endpoint ID	Endpoint Profile	
2017-03-21 00:28:49.475	☑	🔎	smtt	9C:F4:8E:D5:64:F7	Apple-iPhone	
2017-03-21 00:28:45.818	☑	🔎	smtt	9C:F4:8E:D5:64:F7	Apple-iPhone	
2017-03-21 00:28:41.476	☑	🔎	smtt	9C:F4:8E:D5:64:F7	Apple-iPhone	
2017-03-21 00:28:41.018	☑	🔎	smtt	9C:F4:8E:D5:64:F7	Apple-iPhone	
2017-03-21 00:28:25.474	⊗	🔎	CP-7971G-GE-SEP0019E84FDAEB	00:19:E8:4F:DA:EB		

Figure 25-14   *ISE Example Report*

In the upper right of the report screen, you see a few options:

■ **My Reports:** Click to put this report into your My Reports folder.

■ **Export To:** Click to export a version of the currently run report.

■ **Schedule:** Click to display any scheduled reports in the left category pane under Scheduled Reports, as shown in Figure 25-13.

Data Repository Setup

A data repository is a storage location that ISE can use to store non-system data such as reports, images, backup files, and so forth. If you don't already have a data repository set up or need to set up a new one, go to **Administration > System > Maintenance > Repository**. Click **Add**. Figure 25-15 shows the repository setup.

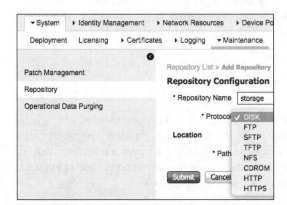

Figure 25-15   *Creating a Data Repository*

As you can see, there are many protocols you can use for data storage. Be careful when using DISK, as you may quickly run out of disk space on your ISE nodes. Any local repositories created on the Admin node are replicated to all other nodes. For more details on repositories, see Chapter 27, "Upgrading ISE."

ISE Alarms

ISE uses alarms to alert you to critical events or important system events. To create new alarms or customize alarms, go to **Administration > System > Settings > Alarm Settings**. Some alarms allow more customization than others, but all alarms allow you to enable or disable them. Alarms can send syslog and email messages. To customize an alarm, select the alarm and click **Edit**. Figure 25-16 shows the Alarm Settings screen.

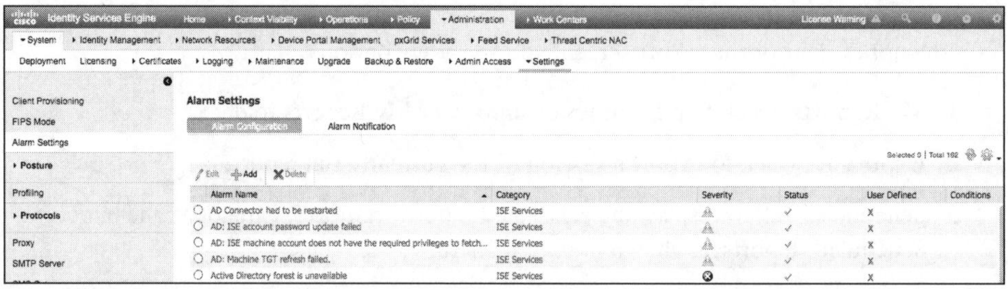

Figure 25-16   *Configuring ISE Alarms*

When an alarm fires, it shows up in a couple places in the ISE GUI. The first place is on the Summary dashboard's Alarms dashlet. Clicking an alarm brings up the alarm details. Click **Acknowledge** to remove the alarm from the active alarms. At any given point in time, only the latest 15,000 alarms are retained. If you want to send alarms to an email address or to a syslog server, you must configure these services first. For syslog setup, go to **Administration > System > Logging > Remote Logging Targets** and click **Add**. For email, go to **Administration > System > Settings > SMTP Server** and fill in the email server details.

Summary

This chapter explored the various monitoring, reporting, and alerting that ISE offers. It discussed key monitoring features, such as the ISE dashboards, dashlets, and the useful Live Log and Live Sessions views. Key reporting and alarm configuration settings and their usage were also reviewed. A firm understanding of the features and their operations will help ensure the successful operation of your ISE deployment.

Chapter 26

Troubleshooting

This chapter covers the following topics:

- Diagnostic tools
- Troubleshooting methodology

Troubleshooting a product can sometimes get fairly complex. Troubleshooting a solution made up of multiple products is bound to get down-right difficult. The biggest tip we can give you is this: always stay calm, take your time, and think through the flows. Once you are comfortable with the Secure Access solution and how the parts work together, troubleshooting it really is not bad at all.

This chapter attempts to provide you with a strong foundation by introducing proven troubleshooting methodologies for the Secure Access solution and examining some of the built-in tools and tricks that have assisted us in the field.

With each version of ISE, there are new serviceability enhancements and tools created to ease the administrative burden that comes with troubleshooting. Tools are created and updated to make your life easier, based on direct feedback from customers, partners, and Cisco TAC.

Regardless of the version of ISE that you are using, and which tools are available, the methodology for troubleshooting shall remain the same. Let's repeat that statement: the methodology for troubleshooting remains the same, regardless of the version of ISE that you are using; it is only some of the tooling that might be different.

We'll start off by introducing some of the tools that are provided within ISE.

Diagnostic Tools

Cisco ISE provides the following built-in tools to aid in your troubleshooting efforts:

■ RADIUS Authentication Troubleshooting

■ Evaluate Configuration Validator

■ TCP Dump

■ Endpoint Debug

■ Session Trace

We'll look at each in turn.

RADIUS Authentication Troubleshooting

The RADIUS Authentication Troubleshooting tool examines different aspects of a session and provides some additional details that may not have been available in the detailed authentication report. It also provides some suggestions for items to check next. To use this tool, follow these steps from the ISE GUI:

Step 1.   Navigate to **Operations > Troubleshoot > Diagnostic Tools > General Tools > RADIUS Authentication Troubleshooting**, as shown in Figure 26-1.

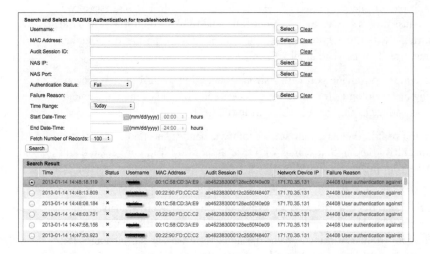

Figure 26-1   *RADIUS Authentication Troubleshooting Tool*

Step 2.   From here you may select any number of specifics to limit your search, such as a specific username, failed or passed authentication status, and more. Click **Search**.

Step 3.   Select one of the entries presented as the result of the search, scroll to the bottom, and click **Troubleshoot**.

ISE examines aspects of the session details, looks for possible causes of an issue, and offers suggestions on possible fixes, as shown in Figure 26-2.

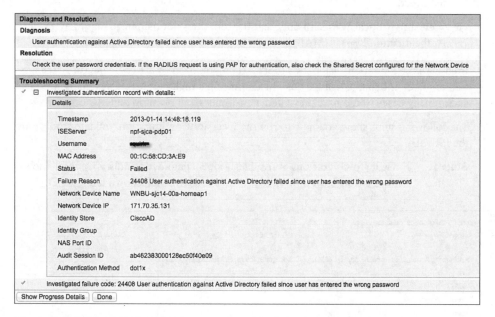

Figure 26-2   *RADIUS Authentication Troubleshooting Tool (Continued)*

In this simple example, either the user has mistyped their password or the shared secret is incorrect between the network access device (NAD) and ISE. Differentiating which is truly the cause is impossible because the shared secret is used to encrypt the password between the endpoint and the RADIUS server, and the result of a mismatched shared secret is the same as the result of an incorrect password.

Evaluate Configuration Validator

This is a great tool…with a terrible name. This tool connects to a switch via Telnet, Secure Shell (SSH), or even through a console server. It examines the configuration, compares it to a "template" configuration built into ISE, and then reports any differences between the configurations. At the time of writing, the tool was overdue for an update, as explained next, but it still may provide a lot of value.

The following list explains why Evaluate Configuration Validator may misdiagnose as missing or incorrect a few of the common configurations:

- Evaluate Configuration Validator does not currently understand Device Sensor, and expects the use of SNMP for the SNMP probe(s).

- Evaluate Configuration Validator does not recognize the active test options when defining a RADIUS server, and therefore may think the RADIUS server definition is incorrect.

- WebAuth is Local WebAuth only, and the tool does not recognize that MAC Authentication Bypass (MAB) is used for Centralized WebAuth instead.

Even with the limitations listed, this tool is still recognized by Cisco Technical Assistance Center (TAC) as being useful for quickly identifying a high number of misconfigurations, and in many cases would have prevented a customer from opening the TAC case.

The following steps show you how to run the Evaluate Configuration Validator tool from the ISE GUI:

Step 1. Navigate to **Operations > Troubleshoot > Diagnostic Tools > General Tools > Evaluate Configuration Validator** to access the tool, shown in Figure 26-3.

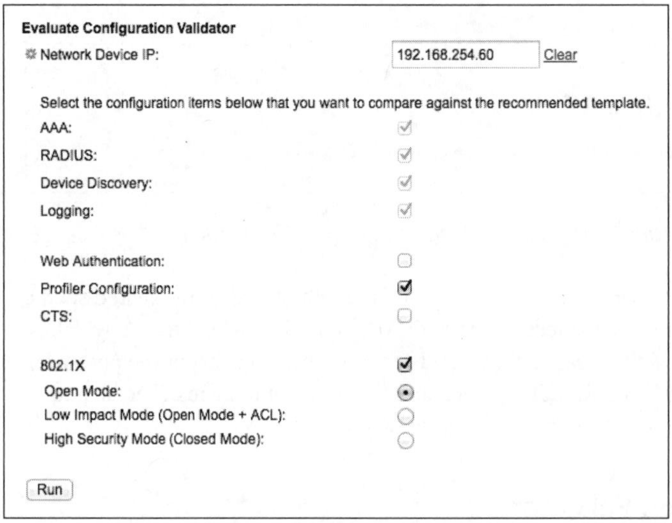

Evaluate Configuration Validator

Network Device IP: 192.168.254.60   Clear

Select the configuration items below that you want to compare against the recommended template.

AAA:	☑
RADIUS:	☑
Device Discovery:	☑
Logging:	☑
Web Authentication:	☐
Profiler Configuration:	☑
CTS:	☐
802.1X	☑
Open Mode:	◉
Low Impact Mode (Open Mode + ACL):	○
High Security Mode (Closed Mode):	○

Run

Figure 26-3 *Evaluate Configuration Validator*

Step 2. Enter the IP address of the NAD, and choose which options you would like the tool to examine.

In Figure 26-3, the check box for Web Authentication is unchecked because the tool is hard-coded to look for Local WebAuth (LWA), and not Centralized WebAuth (CWA).

Step 3. Click **Run** to begin the evaluation.

Step 4. ISE connects to the switch, and prompts for your interaction if the switch asks for user authentication or other interactive prompts, as shown in Figure 26-4. If prompted, click the **User Input Required** button, enter your credentials in the dialog box shown in Figure 26-5, and then click **Submit**.

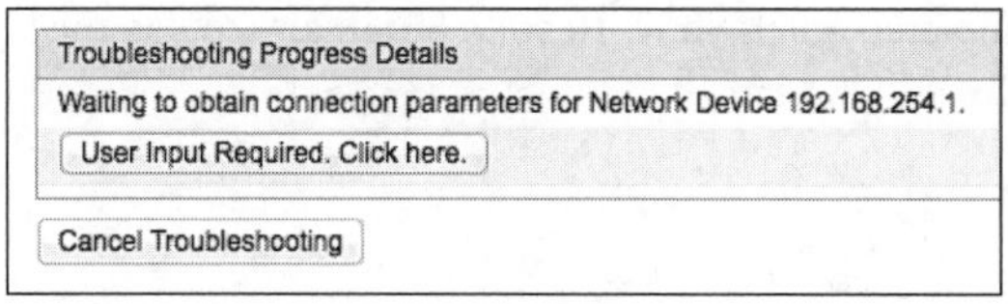

Figure 26-4 *User Input Required*

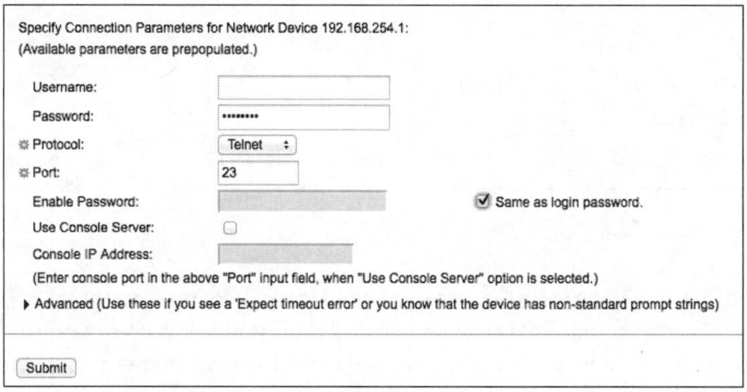

Figure 26-5 *Entering Credentials*

Step 5.   You should be prompted to select which interfaces you want to compare, as shown in Figure 26-6. If you have followed the guidelines set forth in this book, nearly every interface will have the exact same configuration, so you should only select one interface to compare, and then scroll to the bottom and click **Submit**.

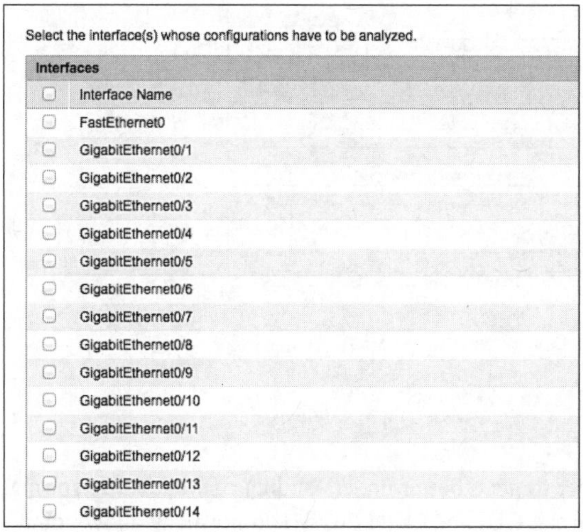

Figure 26-6 *Select an Interface*

Step 6.   After the comparison is completed, click **Show Results Summary** to see the results, as shown in Figure 26-7.

Troubleshooting Progress Details
Waiting to obtain connection parameters for Network Device 192.168.254.60.
User Input Obtained.
Connecting to Device...
CLI response retrieved from the Device.
Waiting to obtain interface names
User Input Obtained.
Analyzing the selected interfaces
Troubleshooting completed.
Click on Show Results Summary to view results.

`Show Results Summary`   `Done`

Figure 26-7   *Comparison Complete*

The report will be broken down into sections, as shown in Figure 26-8, and anything found to be missing or incorrect will be displayed in red. At this point, it is up to you to be familiar with your own deployment. For instance, you should know whether you truly need the SNMP community strings or are using Device Sensor instead.

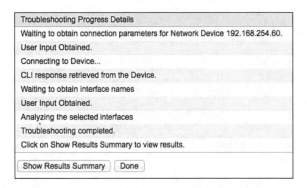

Figure 26-8   *Results Summary*

TCP Dump

When troubleshooting 802.1X, in order to get a better understanding of what is transpiring, it is often necessary to go deeper than the GUI and Live Logs would normally allow you to do. This is where packet captures come in very handy. We have personally used Wireshark more times than we can count to get a deep view of what is transpiring, such as whether ISE is even receiving the RADIUS message; what the certificate signing request (CSR) of the client actually looks like; and much more.

Cisco includes TCP Dump in ISE and even provides a fantastic way to grab TCP Dumps from any ISE node on the deployment, right from the main Admin GUI! TCP Dump also enables you to filter the capture, such as by specifying **ip host 10.1.40.60** (as shown in Figure 26-9). We use this filter all the time so that we can limit the traffic to just the NAD that we are troubleshooting with.

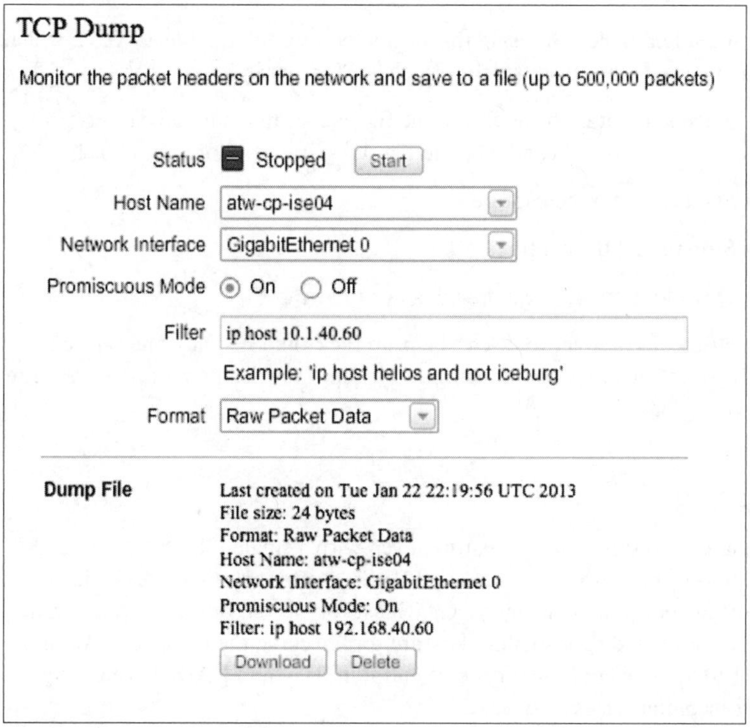

TCP Dump

Monitor the packet headers on the network and save to a file (up to 500,000 packets)

Status	▬ Stopped [Start]
Host Name	atw-cp-ise04 ▾
Network Interface	GigabitEthernet 0 ▾
Promiscuous Mode	⦿ On ◯ Off
Filter	ip host 10.1.40.60
	Example: 'ip host helios and not iceburg'
Format	Raw Packet Data ▾

Dump File   Last created on Tue Jan 22 22:19:56 UTC 2013
            File size: 24 bytes
            Format: Raw Packet Data
            Host Name: atw-cp-ise04
            Network Interface: GigabitEthernet 0
            Promiscuous Mode: On
            Filter: ip host 192.168.40.60
            [Download] [Delete]

Figure 26-9   *TCP Dump*

To set a TCP Dump capture, perform the following steps:

Step 1.   Navigate to **Operations > Troubleshoot > Diagnostic Tools > General Tools > TCP Dump.**

Step 2.   From the Host Name drop-down list, choose which ISE node to grab the TCP Dump from.

Step 3.   From the Network Interface drop-down list, choose which interface on that ISE node should be used.

Step 4.   Click the **On** radio button for Promiscuous Mode if you want to grab all traffic seen on the interface, even if it's not destined for ISE. So, if you have a Switched Port Analyzer (SPAN) set up for one of the ISE interfaces, you could capture all traffic seen on that SPAN interface.

Step 5.   In the Filter field, you can accept any standard TCP Dump filter, and limit the traffic captured.

Here is a link for TCP Dump filters: http://bit.ly/Va243S.

Step 6.   From the Format drop-down list, choose the file format:

- **Human Readable:** Choosing this option will format the file as XLM, which can be used when a sniffer tool (such as Wireshark) is unavailable.

- **Raw Packet Data:** This will save the file as a pcap (common packet capture format) and can be opened in the sniffer tool of your choice.

Step 7.   Click **Start** to begin the capture.

Step 8.   Click **Stop** to end the capture.

Step 9.   Click **Download** to initiate a download of the pcap file.

Step 10.   Click **Delete** if you want to delete the pcap file from ISE. Only one capture may be stored at a time, and starting a new capture will automatically overwrite the existing one.

Endpoint Debug

ISE can be quite large and distributed in nature. Even with a single ISE node, there are many different components within ISE that might be in use for any network session. These components include, among many others, Guest for all web portal traffic as well as guest account creation and sponsorship; Posture for checking the compliance of an endpoint; Profiler to help identify what type of endpoint it is; and RADIUS run times for the processing of incoming access requests.

As you go through the troubleshooting methodology within this chapter, there might come a time when you have to set the logging level of a particular component to debug and examine those debug logs within ISE. As you are likely to discover, there are so many logs and so many logging categories within ISE that searching through all those separate logs to find the entries that pertain to the endpoint, user, or session in question is often quite burdensome.

This is where Endpoint Debug comes into play. It was designed by Aaron Woland and a leader within Cisco TAC named Jesse Dubois. The purpose of this tool is to enable you, the ISE administrator, to easily and effectively troubleshoot an endpoint's activity with ISE in its entirety.

The Endpoint Debug tool provides a single debug file for all components of a specific endpoint across its entire session—across the entire deployment!

So, if an endpoint is getting profiled in the East-Coast Data Center and the West-Coast Data Center at the same time, all of that information will still show up in the single, consolidated debug file. It disburdens you from having to enable debug on the components themselves for all endpoints, and it focuses the debug on the specific endpoint and its related session activity instead. This is incredibly elegant, and it helps advanced admins and TAC engineers to greatly reduce time to resolution when experiencing an issue.

There are two ways to launch the Endpoint Debug tool. The first method (and the most cumbersome) is as follows:

Step 1.   Navigate directly to **Operations > Troubleshoot > Diagnostic Tools > EndPoint Debug**.

Step 2.   Click either the **MAC Address** radio button or **IP** radio button.

Step 3.   Enter the endpoint's address.

Step 4.   Click **Start**.

Figure 26-10 shows the Endpoint Debug screen.

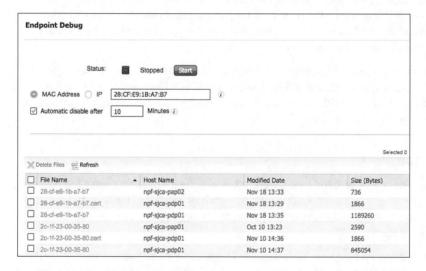

Figure 26-10   *Endpoint Debug*

The second (and easiest) method to launch Endpoint Debug is to navigate to **Operations > RADIUS > Live Logs**, click the Actions target icon for the endpoint you want to debug, and click **Endpoint Debug** from the list of available options, as shown in Figure 26-11.

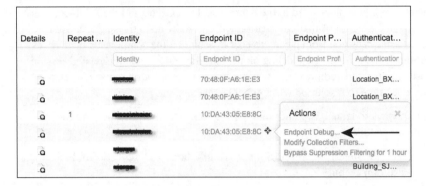

Figure 26-11 *Endpoint Debug from Live Logs*

When you use the option to launch Endpoint Debug from Live Logs, the tool automatically launches in a new window with the address for the endpoint displayed.

When you run Endpoint Debug, it creates a single file for the endpoint on each ISE node where that endpoint was active. All files are listed in the single GUI, as you can see in Figure 26-10. To view one of the files, click the filename and you will be prompted to download just the single file or to combine all the files from all the nodes into a single file for download and easier consumption.

If a certificate was used in the authentication, that captured certificate is listed with the same filename and a .cert extension. The certificate will be downloaded in Privacy Enhanced Electronic Mail (PEM) format so you can more easily examine it. Figure 26-10 also shows two examples of .cert files in the list.

Session Trace

The Session Trace tool is brand new for ISE 2.2, and is comparable to Packet Tracer, a feature in the ASA firewall and ASDM GUI that enables an administrator to test what the firewall would be expected to do with a packet matching certain traits. Session Trace is that tool for ISE.

The tool was designed by Aaron Woland, Jesse Dubois, and Vivek Santuka from TAC, along with a slew of developers at Cisco including Douglas Gash and Eyal Keren, among others. This is a tool that administrators, partners, and technical marketing engineers (TMEs) have been begging for since ISE 1.0, and it's so exciting to have it in the product now.

Just like the Endpoint Debug tool, there are two ways to launch Session Trace. You can navigate directly via **Operations > Troubleshoot > Diagnostic Tools > Session Trace Tests.** Much like using this method to launch the Endpoint Debug tool, you then have to create your test from scratch.

The easier option is to start with an existing session. You can launch the Session Trace tool, with the test prepopulated with all the attributes of an existing session, right from the Live Logs screen, as shown in Figure 26-12.

Figure 26-12 *Launching Session Trace Test from Live Logs Screen*

The Session Trace tool opens with the Test Setup tab displayed, as shown in Figure 26-13. The box labeled 1 is prepopulated with the attributes of the session you chose from Live Logs. You can add other attributes by using the Custom Attributes drop-down lists (identified as 2). The box labeled 3 is the summary of all attributes.

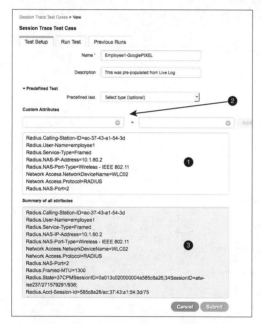

Figure 26-13 *Test Setup*

The Test Setup tab enables you to modify any of the attributes. For example, you could try a different username, or try changing the endpoint profile. This allows you to play with "what-if" scenarios to see what authentication and authorization rules would be used, in which policy sets, and what the end result would be.

Clicking **Submit** brings you to the Run Test tab of the tool, where you can select which ISE node to run the test against, as shown in Figure 26-14.

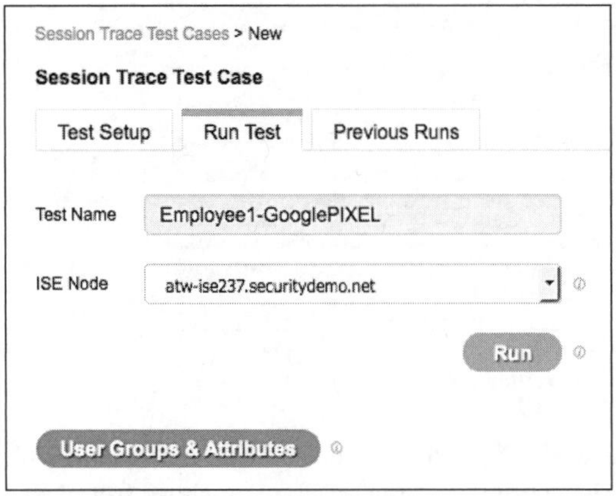

Figure 26-14   *Run Test*

Click **Run** to execute the test, and the results are displayed right on the same page, as shown in Figure 26-15.

Figure 26-15   *Executed Test Results*

The executed test is saved in the Previous Runs tab, as shown in Figure 26-16.

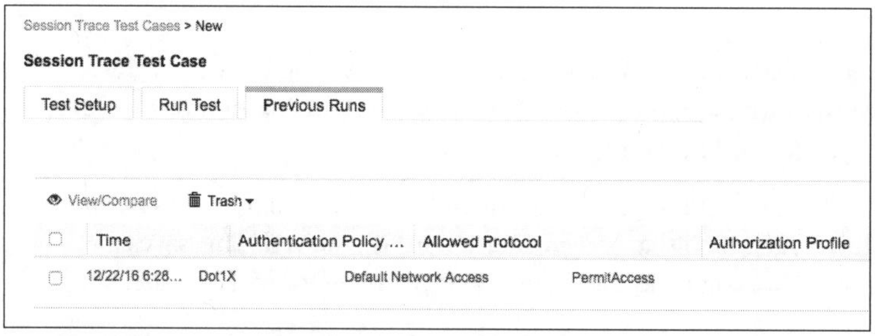

Session Trace Test Cases > New

Session Trace Test Case

| Test Setup | Run Test | Previous Runs |

👁 View/Compare   🗑 Trash ▾

☐	Time	Authentication Policy ...	Allowed Protocol	Authorization Profile
☐	12/22/16 6:26...	Dot1X	Default Network Access	PermitAccess	

Figure 26-16 *Previous Runs*

Troubleshooting Methodology

As you read this section, keep in mind the tip from the beginning of the chapter: always stay calm, take your time, and think through the flows. Taking your time may sound counterproductive, but when you rush to fix a problem, you often end up taking much longer. There have been many situations where we were asked to help when "it just isn't working," and by staying calm, taking our time, and thinking through the flows, we came to the solution very quickly.

This section examines some common troubleshooting exercises and how to resolve the problems.

Troubleshooting Authentication and Authorization

This section offers some possible options and solutions to a common complaint that a help desk or IT administrator may hear: "I plugged into the network, but my system is not granted access." As you read this section, your focus should be on understanding the methodology and the secure access flow. Always keep the authentication and authorization flows in mind, as shown in Figure 26-17.

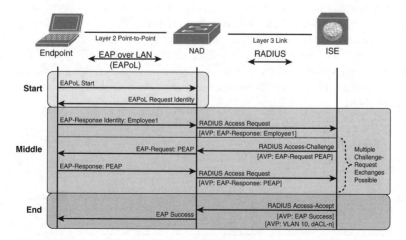

Figure 26-17 *Basic Authentication and Authorization Flows*

Log Deduplication

Prior to ISE 1.2, every authentication request created a 12-KB log record that was then stored. In a scenario where bad endpoint behavior was causing millions of failed authentications a day, a *lot* of log data was stored.

Beginning in ISE 1.2, ISE suppresses anomalous clients by default, only storing a single record and then logging each time that same exact record is received. This saves a tremendous amount of processing and log storage and provides for higher scale.

The deduplication feature is a very nice and welcome change, but it did leave a few gaps to be addressed. Live Logs is the first screen that you would use when troubleshooting a login problem; however, if the entries are not showing up in Live Logs because they are being suppressed, it leaves the admin in a very bad position with no visibility into what's going on.

So, ISE added key counters at the top of the Live Logs screen to help provide visibility. You can see those counters in Figure 26-18.

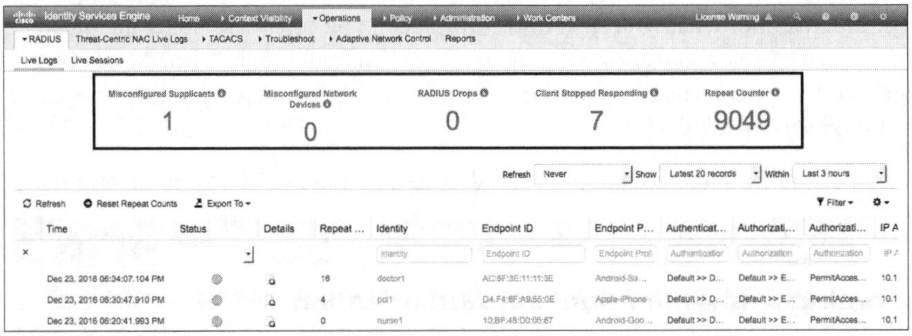

Figure 26-18   *Counters in Live Logs*

Although the counters improve quick visibility from the Live Logs screen, troubleshooting is still quite difficult when the log entries are not appearing in the tool. There are two main ways to disable deduplication so that the log entries appear in Live Logs and you can be more effective in troubleshooting. The main way is to click the **Actions** target icon from Live Logs and choose **Bypass Suppression Filtering for 1 Hour**, as shown in Figure 26-19. This automatically sets a collection filter for the endpoint that bypasses the deduplication for 60 minutes. After that hour, suppression is reenabled for that endpoint. Also shown in Figure 26-19 is the option **Modify Collection Filters**, which opens a screen that allows you to change an existing filter to extend the duration of time the filter is disabled (and more), as shown in Figure 26-20.

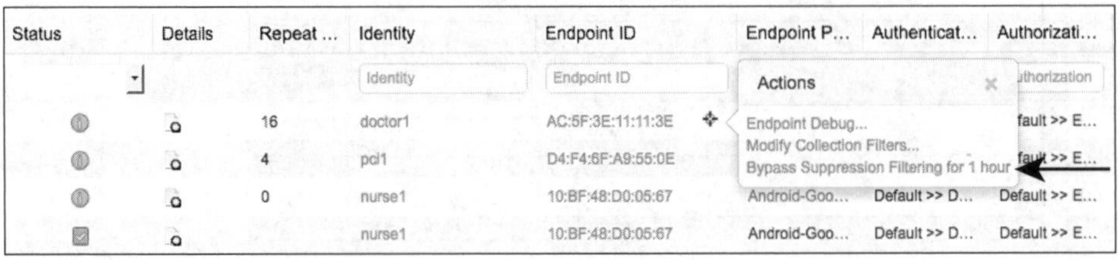

Figure 26-19   *Bypass Suppression Filtering for 1 Hour*

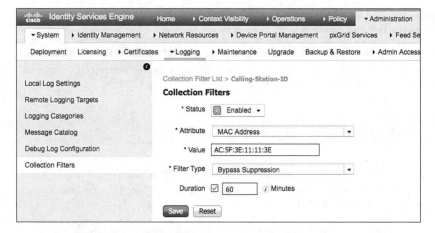

Figure 26-20   *Collection Filters*

The deduplication is a global setting that can be disabled; however, we do not recommend disabling the suppression in production networks without direction from Cisco TAC. The setting is found under **Administration > System > Settings > Protocols > RADIUS**, as shown in Figure 26-21.

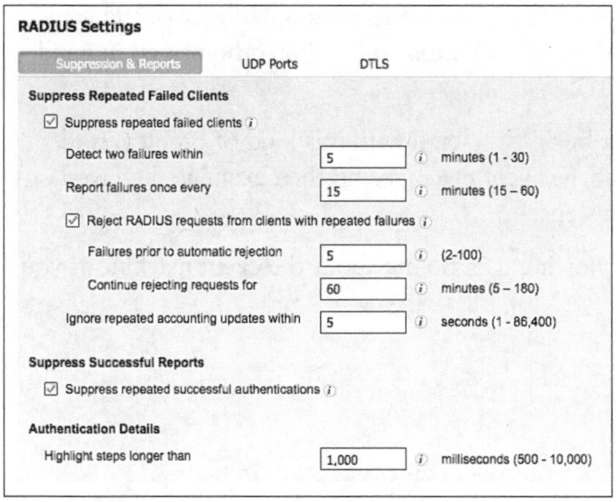

RADIUS Settings

| Suppression & Reports | UDP Ports | DTLS |

Suppress Repeated Failed Clients

☑ Suppress repeated failed clients ⓘ

Detect two failures within ____5____ ⓘ minutes (1 - 30)

Report failures once every ____15____ ⓘ minutes (15 – 60)

☑ Reject RADIUS requests from clients with repeated failures ⓘ

Failures prior to automatic rejection ____5____ ⓘ (2-100)

Continue rejecting requests for ____60____ ⓘ minutes (5 – 180)

Ignore repeated accounting updates within ____5____ ⓘ seconds (1 - 86,400)

Suppress Successful Reports

☑ Suppress repeated successful authentications ⓘ

Authentication Details

Highlight steps longer than ____1,000____ ⓘ milliseconds (500 - 10,000)

Figure 26-21   *RADIUS Settings*

Examining Figure 26-21 further, there are numerous settings:

- **Suppress repeated failed clients:** Globally enables or disables the suppression of logs from clients who repeatedly fail authentication.

- **Detect Two Failures Within** *interval* **Minutes:** Flags misbehaving supplicants when they fail authentication more than once per interval.

- **Report Failures Once Every** *interval* **Minutes:** Sends the alarm from the PSN to the MnT at the designated interval.

- **Reject RADIUS Requests from Clients With Repeated Failures:** Stops sending logs for repeat authentication failures for the same endpoint during the rejection interval set in the subfields (suppresses the logs).

Note   A successful authentication clears all flags.

Next, you will notice the ability to deduplicate successful authentications with the Suppress Repeated Successful Authentications settings. This applies the deduplication and suppresses the logs from MnT.

Finally, there is a setting to Highlight Steps Longer Than *Interval* Milliseconds. This relates to the step latency that is visible in the Authentication Detail report, to point out areas of possible trouble.

Active Troubleshooting

Now that you know about the deduplication feature and how to bypass it for trouble-shooting, it is time to get into that troubleshooting methodology for when you hear the complaint: "I plugged into the network, but my system is not granted access." Remember as you troubleshoot to always keep the authentication and authorization flows in mind, as previously illustrated in Figure 26-17.

The first action you should take after being contacted with this kind of problem is to gather as much data as you can about the client machine and then examine the Live Logs on ISE, as described in the following steps:

Step 1.   Collect as many of the following data points about the client machine as you can, if not all of them:

- Username (good)

- Machine name (good)

- Switch or Wireless LAN Controller name (better)

- Switch interface (even better)

- MAC address of the machine (best)

Step 2.   Go to the Live Logs by navigating to **Operations > RADIUS > Live Logs.**

Step 3.   Filter the log using the data that you gathered, until you find the attempted authentication. Figure 26-22 shows the Live Logs being filtered by Endpoint ID (MAC address).

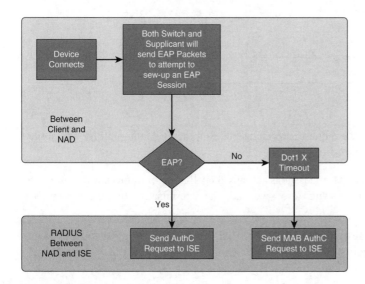

Figure 26-22 *Live Logs Filtered by MAC Address*

Step 4.   Your next action depends on what you find in the Live Logs:

■ If the log contains no entry at all for that MAC address, then you must determine whether ISE is even receiving an authentication request, as described in the following section.

■ If the log contains an entry for the MAC address, proceed as described in the subsequent section, "Option 2: An Entry Exists in the Live Logs."

Option 1: No Live Logs Entry Exists

If there is no entry at all in the Live Logs, you need to examine the communication between the NAD and ISE. Always keep the flows in mind, as shown in Figure 26-23.

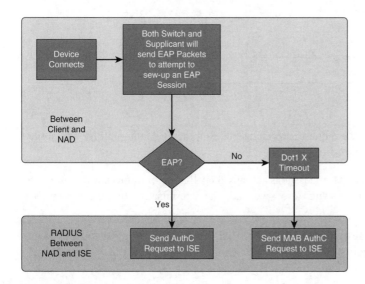

Figure 26-23 *Authentication Flow*

Remember that there must be an EAP communication occurring locally between the NAD and the endpoint first, which gets "wrapped" inside of RADIUS from the NAD to ISE. If EAP is not present (that is, no supplicant is present), then there should be a MAB request from the switch to ISE.

At this point, you need to verify that ISE is receiving the authentication requests. There are a few ways to accomplish this. Normally, either one of these methods would suffice, but for the purposes of completeness in this chapter, you will be shown both options in the steps that follow:

Step 1.   From the dashboard in ISE, check the Alarms section for any "Unknown NAD" alarms, as shown in Figure 26-24. If you see this alarm, there are two possible reasons:

   a. ISE does not have the switch configured as a network device.

   b. The switch is sending the request from an IP address that is not defined in the Network Device object within ISE.

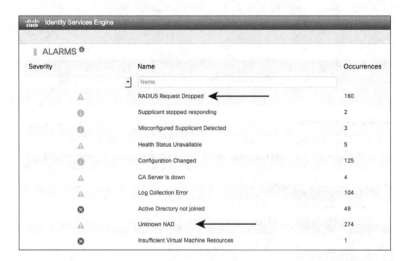

Figure 26-24   *Alarms*

Step 2.   Ensure that the request is reaching ISE. Run the TCP Dump utility with a filter of **ip host** *ip-address-of-nad*.

In this case, you will see that the issue is actually Step 1b. The **ip radius source-interface** command is missing on the switch. How we made the determination that it was Step 1b is described next.

The two alarms of interest in Figure 26-24 are RADIUS Request Dropped and Unknown NAD. Double-click the first alarm to drill into it, and you see the source of these alarms is 10.1.40.60, as shown in Figure 26-25.

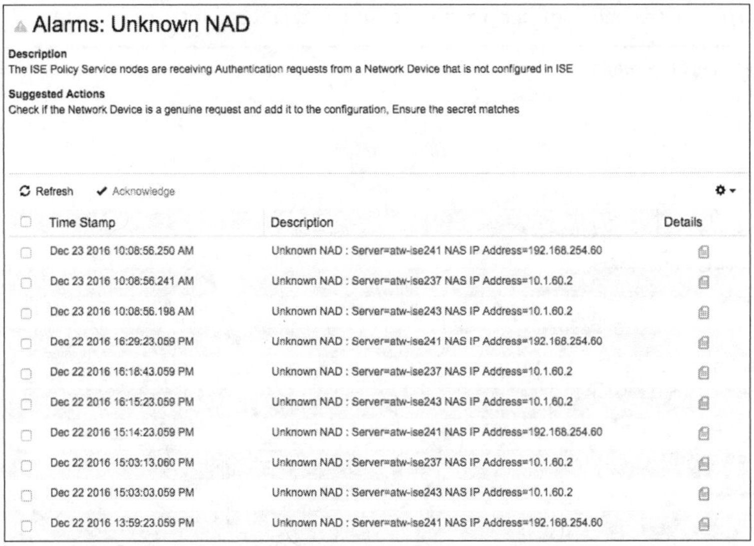

Figure 26-25 *Alarm Details*

The device with the IP address of 10.1.40.60 is the 3560-X switch, and you connect to it via SSH or the console. Upon doing so, notice immediately that authentication-related failures exist, as displayed in Example 26-1.

Example 26-1 *Failures Shown in the Switch Logs*

```
*Sep 13 19:26:39.634: %MAB-5-FAIL: Authentication failed for client
(0050.5687.0039) on Interface Gi0/1 AuditSessionID
0A01283C0000001517B7584B

*Sep 13 19:26:39.634: %AUTHMGR-7-RESULT: Authentication result
'server dead' from 'mab' for client (0050.5687.0039) on Interface
Gi0/1 AuditSessionID 0A01283C0000001517B7584B

*Sep 13 19:26:39.634: %AUTHMGR-5-FAIL: Authorization failed for
client (0050.5687.0039) on Interface Gi0/1 AuditSessionID
0A01283C0000001517B7584B
```

To see more details, issue the **show authentication session interface** *interface-name* command. This is one of the most commonly used commands when troubleshooting authentication with Cisco IOS Software. The output of this command shows that the switch is trying to do both MAB and 802.1X, and neither is successful. Example 26-2 displays that output.

Example 26-2   *Output of the* show authentication session interface *Command*

```
3560-X# sho authen sess int g0/1


            Interface:  GigabitEthernet0/1
          MAC Address:  0050.5687.0039
           IP Address:  10.1.41.102
            User-Name:  005056870039
               Status:  Running
               Domain:  UNKNOWN
      Security Policy:  Should Secure
      Security Status:  Unsecure
       Oper host mode:  multi-auth
      Oper control dir:  both
      Session timeout:  N/A
         Idle timeout:  N/A
    Common Session ID:  0A01283C00000018F595EC0B
      Acct Session ID:  0x00000049
               Handle:  0x41000018
Runnable methods list:
      Method    State
      mab       Failed over
      dot1x     Running
```

To verify which IP addresses the switch may be sending the RADIUS messages from, issue the **show ip interface brief** command, with the **| include up** option to limit your display, as shown in Example 26-3.

Example 26-3   *Output of the* show ip int brief | include up *Command*

```
3560-X# sho ip int brief | include up

Vlan1                  unassigned     YES NVRAM  up   up
Vlan40                 10.1.40.60     YES NVRAM  up   up
GigabitEthernet0/1     unassigned     YES unset  up   up
GigabitEthernet0/24    unassigned     YES unset  up   up
Loopback0              192.168.254.60 YES NVRAM  up   up
3560-X#
```

Next, verify the NAD definition in ISE by navigating to **Administration > Network Resources > Network Devices** and then editing the 3560-X object, as shown in Figure 26-26. Within this object, notice that the expected IP address is 192.168.254.60, which is the loopback interface.

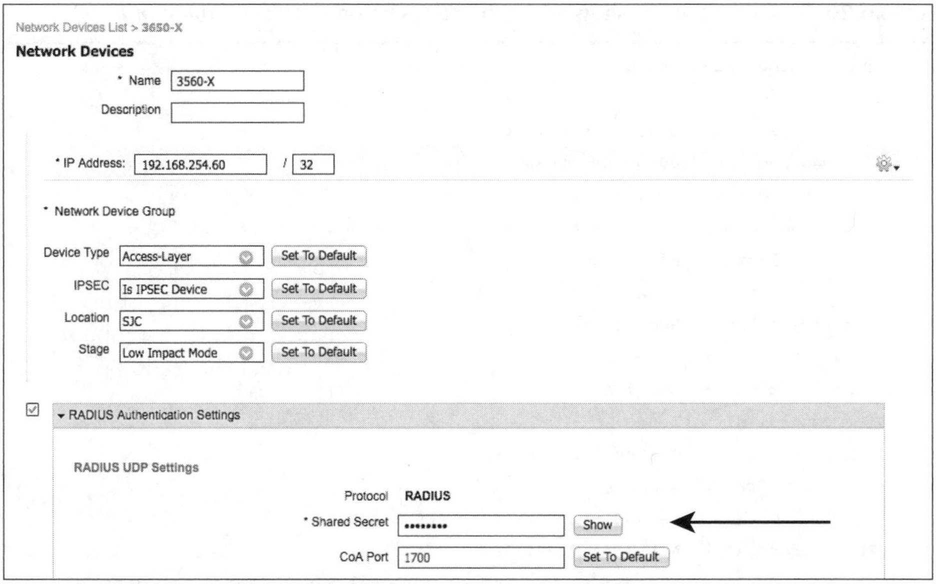

Figure 26-26 *NAD Object Definition*

To correct this, add the **ip radius source-interface** *interface-name* command into the configuration, as shown in Example 26-4.

This should have been part of your configuration already, but obviously something must have happened. This occurs quite often in customer environments; an admin might not fully know what the command was used for and could have removed it from the configuration, or the switch might have been added without the appropriate command. The reason behind the interface not being set is not the purpose of this exercise; the purpose is to enable the users to authenticate again.

Example 26-4 *Output of the* **ip radius source-interface** *Command*

```
3560-X(config)# ip radius source-interface Loopback0
3560-X(config)#
```

Verify that everything works now by reissuing the **show authentication session interface** *interface-name* command, or by checking the Live Logs on ISE.

Example 26-5 shows the working authentication on the switch, which happens to be a Centralized Web Authentication result.

Example 26-5   *Output of the* show authentication session interface *Command*

```
3560-X# sho authen sess int g0/1


            Interface:  GigabitEthernet0/1
          MAC Address:  0050.5687.0039
           IP Address:  10.1.41.102
            User-Name:  00-50-56-87-00-39
               Status:  Authz Success
               Domain:  DATA
      Security Policy:  Should Secure
      Security Status:  Unsecure
       Oper host mode:  multi-auth
      Oper control dir:  both
        Authorized By:  Authentication Server
            Vlan Group:  N/A
              ACS ACL:  xACSACLx-IP-Pre-Auth-ACL-50fc97ba
      URL Redirect ACL:  ACL-WEBAUTH-REDIRECT
         URL Redirect:  https://atw-cp-ise04.ise.local:8443/guestportal/gateway?
sessionId=0A01283C0000001AF59D671A&action=cwa
       Session timeout:  N/A
          Idle timeout:  N/A
      Common Session ID:  0A01283C0000001AF59D671A
       Acct Session ID:  0x0000004B
               Handle:  0xAC00001A
Runnable methods list:


      Method   State
        mab      Authc Success
        dot1x    Not run
3560-X#
```

Option 2: An Entry Exists in the Live Logs

If there is an entry for the MAC address in the Live Logs, you are in luck, because you can troubleshoot this almost entirely from the ISE GUI, as described in the following steps:

Step 1.   Starting with the Live Logs, as shown in Figure 26-27, in the Details column, click the icon (which looks like a magnifying glass on a piece of paper) to view the details of the failure. Figure 26-27 shows an older Live Logs screen, but the activity is the same regardless of the ISE version.

Figure 26-27 *Live Logs with a Failure*

Step 2.   Review the Authentication Details that open in the new window (shown in Figure 26-28), and you can see almost instantly that the authentication failed because the user's AD account is disabled.

Authentication Details

Source Timestamp	2013-01-25 09:29:14.457
Received Timestamp	2013-01-25 09:29:14.461
Policy Server	atw-cp-ise04
Event	5400 Authentication failed
Username	employee2
User Type	
Endpoint Id	00:50:56:87:00:39
IP Address	10.1.41.102
Identity Store	AD1
Identity Group	
Audit Session Id	0A01283C0000001AF59D671A
Authentication Method	dot1x
Authentication Protocol	PEAP (EAP-MSCHAPv2)
Service Type	Framed
Network Device	3560-X
Device Type	Switches#Access-Layer
Location	NorthAmerica#SJC
NAS IP Address	192.168.254.60
NAS Port Id	GigabitEthernet0/1
Authorization Profile	
Posture Status	
Security Group	
Failure Reason	24409 User authentication against Active Directory failed since the user's account is disabled

Figure 26-28 *Authentication Details*

Step 3.   Access your Active Directory management console and check the account; reenable the account if it really is disabled by checking the **Unlock Account** check box, as displayed in Figure 26-29.

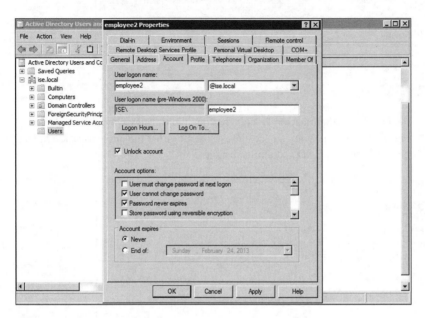

Figure 26-29   *Unlocking the Disabled Account*

Now, the authentications are succeeding for Employee2, as shown in Figure 26-30.

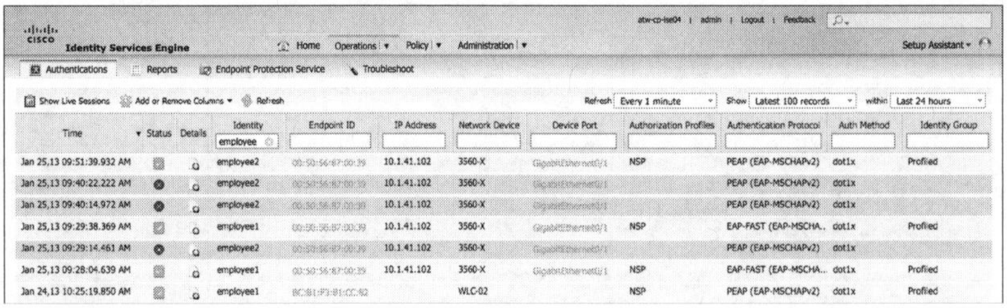

Figure 26-30   *Success*

General High-Level Troubleshooting Flowchart

One of our colleagues, Hosuk Won, put together the flowchart shown in Figure 26-31 to aid in the troubleshooting of the Secure Access system. This is an excellent flowchart to follow for general high-level troubleshooting.

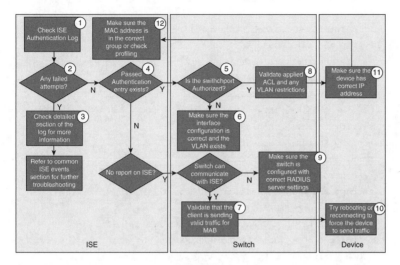

Figure 26-31   *High-Level Troubleshooting Flowchart*

Troubleshooting WebAuth and URL Redirection

The URL redirection employed by CWA—as well as by both BYOD and MDM onboarding—is one of those things that can be confusing to folks who are new to it. One of the most common troubleshooting exercises that our team(s) will get involved in is helping someone when they report "WebAuth isn't working." Of course, they will also report "nothing was missed" and "nothing has changed." You know, the normal cliché statements that you hear from someone who is asking for assistance. Ninety-nine times out of a hundred, staying calm and remembering to always "follow the flows" is what enabled us to solve their problem.

The following is an example series of steps to follow:

Step 1.   Check the Live Logs. Ensure that the authorization result includes the URL redirection, as displayed in Figure 26-32. If so, make note of the url-redirect-acl name.

```
▼ Attributes Details
  Access Type = ACCESS_ACCEPT
  DACL = Pre-Auth-ACL
  cisco-av-pair = url-redirect-acl=ACL-WEBAUTH-REDIRECT
  cisco-av-pair = url-redirect=https://ip:port/guestportal/gateway?sessionId=SessionIdValue&action=cwa
```

Figure 26-32   *Attribute Details from the Authorization Result*

Step 2.   Gather information about the client session.

a. For wired URL redirection, execute the **show authentication session interface** *interface-name* command:

```
3560-X# sho authen sess int g0/1

                 Interface:  GigabitEthernet0/1
               MAC Address:  0050.5687.0039
                IP Address:  10.1.41.102
                 User-Name:  00-50-56-87-00-39
                    Status:  Authz Success
                    Domain:  DATA
           Security Policy:  Should Secure
           Security Status:  Unsecure
            Oper host mode:  multi-auth
           Oper control dir:  both
              Authorized By:  Authentication Server
                Vlan Group:  N/A
                   ACS ACL:  xACSACLx-IP-Pre-Auth-ACL-50fc97ba
          URL Redirect ACL:  ACL-WEBAUTH-REDIRECT
              URL Redirect:  https://atw-cp-ise04.ise.local:8443/
     guestportal/gateway?sessionId=0A01283C0000001D059317CE&action=cwa
           Session timeout:  N/A
              Idle timeout:  N/A
          Common Session ID:  0A01283C0000001D059317CE
           Acct Session ID:  0x00000055
                    Handle:  0x7500001D
    Runnable methods list:

        Method    State
        dot1x     Failed over
        mab       Authc Success
```

The preceding output highlights the most important fields for this exercise. The ACS-ACL field is displaying the downloadable ACL (dACL) name that was downloaded from ISE and applied to the sessions' IP traffic. This ACL is examined further in Step 4.

The URL Redirect ACL describes the name of a local ACL that must pre-exist on the switch for it to be used. That ACL determines which traffic is redirected and which is not. This ACL is examined further in Step 4.

Finally, the session ID from ISE will be present in the URL Redirect field, and it must match the Common Session ID displayed below it. If by chance these IDs do not match, you should open a TAC case to receive further assistance.

b. For wireless URL redirection, choose **Monitor > Clients**, as shown in Figure 26-33.

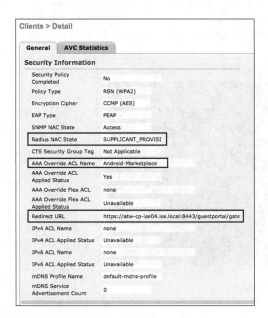

Figure 26-33 *Client > Details Showing the AAA Override and Redirect URL*

Figure 26-33 points out the most important fields for this exercise. If the Radius NAC State field shows RUN, then the RADIUS NAC setting was never enabled on the WLAN. This is a pretty common oversight. The fix is to enable RADIUS NAC in the controller.

The AAA Override ACL Name field must list the exact name that was noted in Step 1 and Figure 26-32.

The Redirect URL field should contain the URL pointing to ISE. Make note of the hostname.

Step 3.   Verify that DNS resolution is working from the client.

The URL redirect is automatically sent to the fully qualified domain name as configured in ADE-OS, such as https://atw-cp-ise04.ise.local—which is visible in Figure 26-32 and Figure 26-33, as well as in the output in Step 2a. The client must be able to resolve this name with DNS. This is another common error, and easily correctable.

Sometimes, the issue may be that the entry was never made on the DNS server that the client is using, or that the ACL is not permitting DNS traffic. The ACLs are examined in Step 4.

To verify DNS from the client, you would normally use **ping** or **nslookup**, as shown in Figure 26-34. The **ping** may fail, depending on the ACL. However, you are looking for DNS resolution, not successful ICMP. Figure 26-34 demonstrates a successful DNS lookup, using both **ping** and **nslookup**.

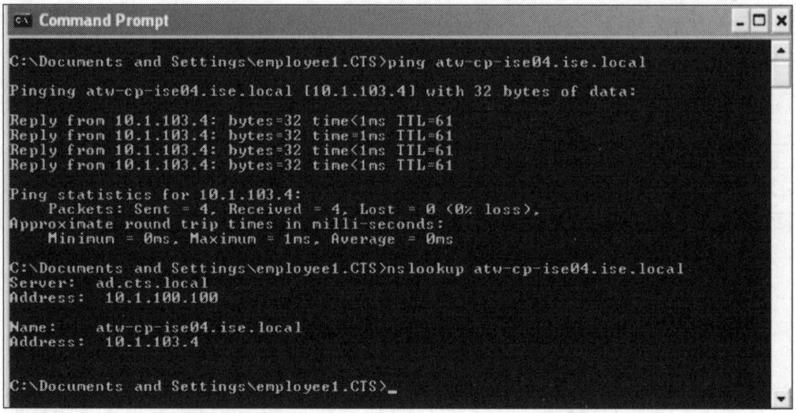

Figure 26-34   *Verifying DNS from the Client*

Step 4.   Examine the ACLs.

a. For wired devices, execute the **show ip access-list interface** *interface-name* command:

```
3560-X# sho ip access-list int g0/1

      permit udp host 10.1.41.102 any eq bootps
      permit udp host 10.1.41.102 any eq domain (4 matches)
      permit icmp host 10.1.41.102 any
      permit tcp host 10.1.41.102 host 10.1.100.232 eq 8443
      permit tcp host 10.1.41.102 host 10.1.100.232 eq 8905
      permit tcp host 10.1.41.102 host 10.1.100.232 eq 8909
      permit udp host 10.1.41.102 host 10.1.100.232 range 8905 8906
      permit udp host 10.1.41.102 host 10.1.100.232 eq 8909
```

As you see, the output of this **show** command displays the effective ACL that is applied to the interface, after applying the downloadable ACL.

b. Also for wired devices, you have to ensure that the redirection ACL is correct with the **show ip access-list** *access-list-name* command, as shown in the output that follows. This ACL will redirect only traffic that is permitted. Any traffic that is denied will bypass redirection.

```
3560-X# sho ip access-list ACL-WEBAUTH-REDIRECT

Extended IP access list ACL-WEBAUTH-REDIRECT
    10 deny udp any any eq domain (58523 matches)
    20 permit tcp any any eq www (7978448 matches)
    30 permit tcp any any eq 443 (416 matches)
```

Ensure that traffic is being redirected by looking for the matches for TCP ports 80 and 443.

c. With wireless access, only a single ACL is in effect. To examine the contents of the ACL and ensure it is named correctly, choose **Security > Access-Control-Lists.**

Ensure the name matches exactly what is sent in the authorization result noted in Step 1. If it does, edit the ACL to examine the individual rules, as shown in Figure 26-35.

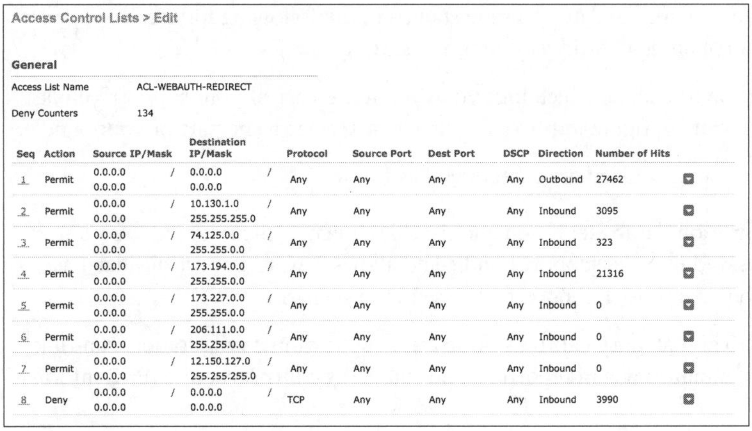
Access Control Lists > Edit

General

Access List Name: ACL-WEBAUTH-REDIRECT

Deny Counters: 134

Seq	Action	Source IP/Mask	Destination IP/Mask	Protocol	Source Port	Dest Port	DSCP	Direction	Number of Hits
1	Permit	0.0.0.0 / 0.0.0.0	0.0.0.0 / 0.0.0.0	Any	Any	Any	Any	Outbound	27462
2	Permit	0.0.0.0 / 0.0.0.0	10.130.1.0 / 255.255.255.0	Any	Any	Any	Any	Inbound	3095
3	Permit	0.0.0.0 / 0.0.0.0	74.125.0.0 / 255.255.0.0	Any	Any	Any	Any	Inbound	323
4	Permit	0.0.0.0 / 0.0.0.0	173.194.0.0 / 255.255.0.0	Any	Any	Any	Any	Inbound	21316
5	Permit	0.0.0.0 / 0.0.0.0	173.227.0.0 / 255.255.0.0	Any	Any	Any	Any	Inbound	0
6	Permit	0.0.0.0 / 0.0.0.0	206.111.0.0 / 255.255.0.0	Any	Any	Any	Any	Inbound	0
7	Permit	0.0.0.0 / 0.0.0.0	12.150.127.0 / 255.255.255.0	Any	Any	Any	Any	Inbound	0
8	Deny	0.0.0.0 / 0.0.0.0	0.0.0.0 / 0.0.0.0	TCP	Any	Any	Any	Inbound	3990

Figure 26-35 *Verifying Airespace ACL*

Debug Situations: ISE Logs

If you are unable to isolate a root cause via the ISE GUI, it may be necessary to look into the log files. ISE maintains very detailed logging, and enables you to set the logging levels. If it becomes necessary to start debugging, perform the following steps:

Step 1. Navigate to **Administration > System > Logging > Debug Log Configuration.**

Step 2. Choose the appropriate ISE Policy Service Node (PSN).

Step 3. Set the appropriate logs to debug level.

Step 4. Reproduce the problem and gather relevant seed information to aid in searching the logs, such as MAC Address, IP Address, sessionID, and so forth.

Step 5.   Navigate to **Operations > Troubleshoot > Download Logs** and choose the appropriate ISE node.

Step 6.   On the Debug Logs tab, download the logs.

Step 7.   Use an intelligent editor such as Notepad++ (Windows) or TextWrangler (Mac) to parse the log files.

Step 8.   Once the issue has been isolated, return the log levels to their default levels.

The Support Bundle

Cisco TAC may ask for the support bundle, which contains the full ISE configuration and all logs. You can think of it as an equivalent of the **show tech-support** command on a Cisco IOS device. It allows the support engineer to re-create the environment in a lab, if necessary.

The bundle will save as a simple tar.gpg (GPG encrypted) file. The support bundle is automatically named with the date and time stamps in the following format: ise-support-bundle_ise-support-bundle-mm-dd-yyyy-hh-mm.tar.gpg.

You have the option to choose which logs you want to be part of your support bundle. For example, you can configure logs from a particular service to be part of your bundle.

The logs that you can download are categorized as follows:

■ **Full configuration database:** If you choose this category, the ISE configuration database is saved into the support bundle and allows TAC to import this database configuration in another ISE node to re-create the scenario.

■ **Debug logs:** This category captures bootstrap, application configuration, run-time, deployment, monitoring and reporting, and Public Key Infrastructure (PKI) information.

■ **Local logs:** This category contains log messages from the various processes that run but are not collected by the MnT node.

■ **Core files:** This category contains critical information that would help identify the cause of a crash. These logs are created if the application crashed and includes core dumps.

■ **Monitoring and reporting logs:** This category contains information about the alarms and reports from the MnT node.

■ **System logs:** This category contains the underlying OS (Application Deployment Engine [ADE-OS]) logs. These logs are not directly part of the ISE application itself.

There are two ways to create and download the support bundle: from the ISE GUI and from the command-line interface (CLI).

From the ISE GUI, perform the following steps:

Step 1.   Navigate to **Operations > Troubleshoot > Download Logs**.

Step 2.   Select the ISE node in the left pane.

Step 3.   Choose which categories of logs you want to include, which were described in the previous list.

Step 4.   Enter a password to use for encrypting the bundle, or select to use **Public Key Encryption**. The Public Key Encryption option uses Cisco's PKI to encrypt the bundle where only Cisco can decrypt it, and helps with TAC case automation tooling.

Step 5.   Click **Create Support Bundle**, such as what is displayed in Figure 26-36.

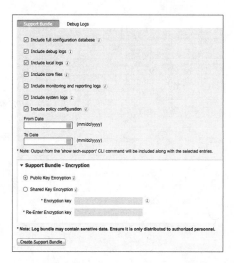

Figure 26-36   *Creating a Support Bundle from the GUI*

Summary

If you have gained nothing else from this chapter, you should at least take away the following lesson: when troubleshooting, always stay calm, take your time, and follow the flows.

If you can do that, you will be an expert troubleshooter in no time, and your understanding of the solution will grow exponentially. Cisco has also provided you with a number of tools to help solve common problems, so don't hesitate to use those tools.

For more on serviceability in ISE and troubleshooting, take a look at Aaron Woland's blog: http://www.networkworld.com/article/3053669/security/troubleshooting-ciscos-ise-without-tac.html

Chapter 27

Upgrading ISE

This chapter covers the following topics:

- The upgrade process
- Repositories
- Performing the upgrade
- Command-line upgrade

As with many feature and functions in ISE, upgrades have improved with each release as ISE has evolved over the years. Prior to version 1.2, you had to make every ISE node a standalone before upgrading it. Beginning in version 1.2, the process improved by eliminating the requirement to remove each node from the deployment and make it standalone. It also removed a number of erroneous reboots, speeding the process up even more.

The Upgrade Process

If you are going to upgrade a multinode ISE cube, the upgrade model is known as the Secondary PAN First (SPF) flow. This means that you should upgrade the Secondary PAN First and then upgrade all other nodes sequentially or in parallel. This section provides an overview of the upgrade process. The specific steps that you follow to perform the upgrade are presented later in the chapter, both for a GUI-based upgrade for a command-line upgrade.

The Secondary PAN First flow works in this manner:

1. The upgrade always starts with the Secondary PAN (S-PAN). When the upgrade begins on the Secondary PAN, it automatically becomes the Primary PAN for the upgraded deployment. The PANs no longer sync with one another, because their versioning is different, as shown in Figure 27-1.

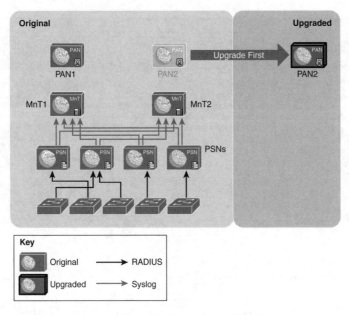

Figure 27-1   *Upgrading the Secondary PAN First*

Because this newly upgraded PAN is the first node in the new deployment, it is automatically configured to run both the Admin and Monitoring personas, and to be the primary role for those personas.

After the S-PAN has been successfully upgraded, you can upgrade the PSNs and MnT nodes one at a time or a few simultaneously. Always leave enough PSNs active to handle the authentication load of the entire deployment.

2. Upgrade one of the MnT nodes, so that a full logging target exists in the new deployment.

3. Ensure that each PSN is taken out of service before beginning the upgrade process on that node.

If your deployment is using a load balancer, all you need to do is mark the server as down to remove it from the virtual IP (VIP). If the NADs are pointing directly to the PSNs, you must go into the NAD configuration and remove the server from the configuration, or leverage a network ACL to stop RADIUS traffic from reaching the out-of-service PSN that is going through the upgrade.

Why? The PSNs will go through a number of changes and restarts. The entire database gets wiped out. During that process, the RADIUS runtime (the RADIUS engine) goes up and down, and possibly responds to RADIUS requests with an invalid configuration, which can cause an accidental denial of service (DoS).

4. When each of the PSNs is finished upgrading, it automatically joins the new PAN, which synchronizes its database to the PSN. This saves a tremendous amount of time per PSN, because it does not need to upgrade the entire database, like the process for the PAN. The MnT nodes take the longest amount of time, followed by the PAN, and the PSNs are fastest.

5. All logging is sent to the configured MnT node(s) of the new deployment, as shown in Figure 27-2, and the PSN is ready to be reinstated to active duty once it's fully in sync with the PAN.

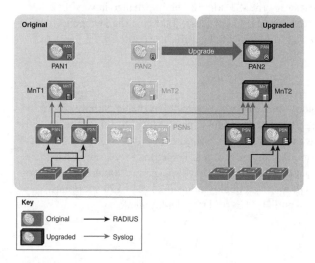

Figure 27-2   *Staged Upgrade*

6. Remember to take the PSNs out of service before upgrading them to ensure that you have limited the risk of end-user downtime, as shown in Figure 27-3.

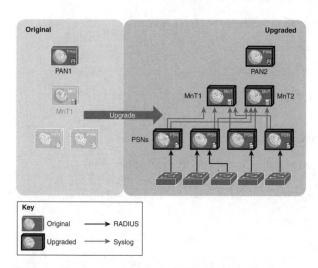

Figure 27-3   *Staged Upgrade: Primary PAN Is Last*

7. The last node to be upgraded should be the original Primary PAN. It also receives a complete database dump from the Secondary PAN.

If you want the original primary PAN to be primary in the upgraded model, you need to manually promote it back to the primary role.

In all ISE versions prior to 2.0, this is a very manual process to be performed by you, the ISE administrator, through the CLI of each node in the ISE cube.

Beginning with ISE 2.0, the product took a major step forward with regard to usability of upgrades and making it much easier for the ISE admin. The big change in version 2.0 is a graphical tool to automate most of the upgrade process, following the Secondary PAN First (SPF) approach. We review that tool in detail later in this chapter.

Repositories

The upgrade cannot occur without one or more repositories available. Simply put, a *repository* is a location to store files. The repository may be local to ISE or positioned on a remote server. You may have more than one configured, but you certainly need at least one before you can perform upgrade procedures. The repository stores all application upgrade bundles, support bundles, and system backups. It is recommended that you have a repository of at least 10 GB for small deployments (less than 100 endpoints), 100 GB for medium deployments, and 200 GB for large deployments.

Configuring a Repository

You add repositories via the Maintenance tab of the System Properties of ISE. Technically, you can add a repository within the CLI, but all repositories are always overwritten by the ones added within the ISE GUI.

To add a repository, perform the following steps from the ISE GUI:

Step 1.   Navigate to **Administration > System > Maintenance**.

Step 2.   Choose **Repository** on the left side.

Step 3.   Click **Add** to add a new repository.

Step 4.   Give the repository a name and choose the type.

Repository Types and Configuration

Multiple types of repositories are available. When adding a repository in the GUI, the GUI automatically displays the necessary fields. For example, you need to enter a username and password for an FTP repository, but not for a CD-ROM. Repository types include

- Disk
- FTP

- SFTP

- TFTP

- NFS

- CDROM

- HTTP

- HTTPS

The disk repository type is used to provide a repository on the local hard disk. This type of repository is not used often, but sometimes, it can be helpful when Cisco TAC needs to export a support bundle quickly or for other reactive needs. This type of repository needs a name and a path (such as /tac/helpme/), as shown in Figure 27-4.

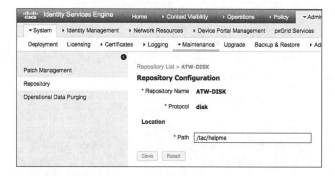

Figure 27-4 *Disk Repository*

FTP is the most common repository type. It uses File Transfer Protocol (FTP) and requires a server address or DNS name, along with the path, username, and password, as shown in Figure 27-5.

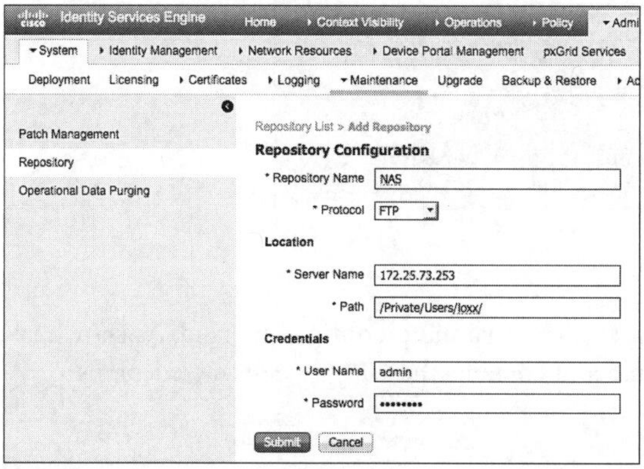

Figure 27-5 *FTP Repository*

The SFTP repository uses Secure File Transfer Protocol (SFTP). It also requires a server address or DNS name along with the path, username, and password, as shown in Figure 27-6.

Figure 27-6   *SFTP Repository*

> **Note**   Before this type of repository works, you must trust the certificate of the SFTP server with the **host-key** command, as shown in Figure 27-7.

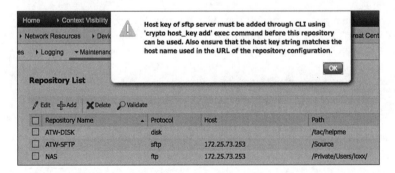

Figure 27-7   *Host-Key Required Popup*

Example 27-1 shows truncated output of a **show running-config** command. As shown in the example, the repository was created and contains the URL as well as credentials.

Example 27-1 *Repository Output from* **show running-config**

```
atw-cp-ise02/admin# show run
! - Displaying only necessary information
repository ATW-SFTP
  url sftp://172.25.73.252/array1/FTPROOT/
  user admin password hash b5558b4ef1742747cc50723474f842818642df47
```

Next, to support SFTP, you need to enter repository configuration mode to add the host key to the repository, as shown in Example 27-2.

Example 27-2 *Adding the Host Key to the Repository*

```
atw-cp-ise02/admin# conf t
atw-cp-ise02/admin(config)# repository ATW-SFTP
% Warning: Host key of the server must be added using 'crypto host_key add' exec
  command before sftp repository can be used.
atw-cp-ise02/admin(config-Repository)# exit
atw-ise245/admin# crypto host_key add host 172.25.73.253
host key fingerprint added
# Host 172.25.73.253 found: line 1 type RSA
2048 fa:0c:a4:b4:28:78:fd:0f:b7:91:1a:a5:8f:72:4a:1c 172.25.73.253 (RSA)
```

TFTP is not a common repository type for ISE. TFTP servers often have drawbacks related to file sizes, and ISE packages usually exceed those file-size limitations. No credentials are necessary because TFTP is connectionless and does not use authentication credentials, as shown in Figure 27-8.

Note TFTP is significantly slower than FTP because it uses 512-byte packets, and each packet must be acknowledged (ACK'd). Therefore, on high-latency links, TFTP can be hundreds of times slower. Even on low-latency links, TFTP is much slower than FTP.

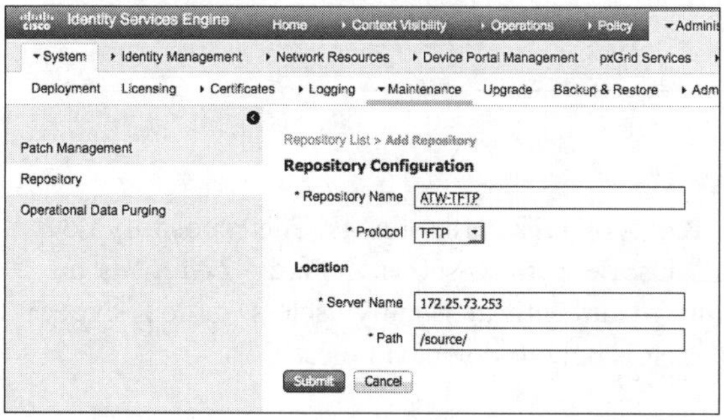

Figure 27-8 *TFTP Repository*

The Network File System (NFS) repository is fairly common, especially in environments with a network-attached storage (NAS) system. NFS is usually a responsive and reliable transport mechanism for storage. This repository requires the NFS server, IP address or FQDN, and path and credentials, as shown in Figure 27-9.

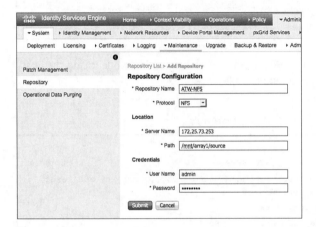

Figure 27-9   *NFS Repository*

CD-ROM is a repository that is used with the physical CD-ROM/DVD-ROM drive of the Cisco SNS 3315, 3355, and 3395 appliances (SNS 3415, 3495, 3515, and 3595 appliances have no drive) or the virtual CD drive with VMware, as shown in Figure 27-10.

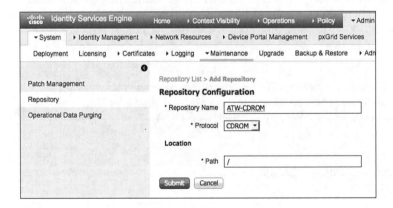

Figure 27-10   *CD-ROM Repository*

HTTP is used for Hypertext Transfer Protocol (HTTP) file storage. This repository does not support authentication credentials, just the path, as shown in Figure 27-11. Yes, an HTTP repository without the capability to authenticate is fairly useless, so don't expect this one to get much usage today unless it is only to download files.

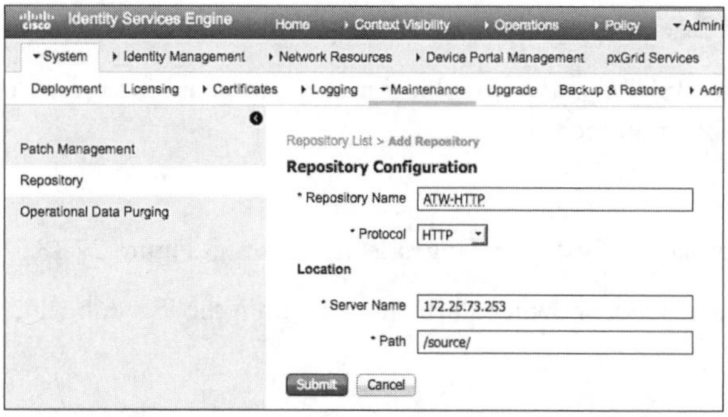

Figure 27-11   *HTTP Repository*

HTTPS is used for HTTP Secure file storage. This repository does not provide authentication credentials, just the path, as shown in Figure 27-12. Yes, an HTTPS-encrypted repository type that does not provide enough security to authenticate the user is again pretty useless. So, don't expect this one to get too much usage today, either.

Figure 27-12   *HTTPS Repository*

You may validate the repository at any time from the command line by using the **show repository** *repository-name* command, as shown in Example 27-3.

Example 27-3   *Output of* **show repository** *Command*

```
atw-cp-ise02/admin# show repository ATW-CDROM
FILE NAME                             SIZE   MODIFIED TIME
================================================================================
.discinfo                        102 Bytes  Tue Nov 13 18:38:10 2012
Server                              72 KB   Mon Nov 19 02:26:26 2012
TRANS.TBL                            1 KB   Mon Nov 19 02:26:26 2012
images                               2 KB   Mon Nov 19 02:25:36 2012
isolinux                             2 KB   Mon Nov 19 02:25:36 2012
ks.cfg                              24 KB   Mon Nov 19 02:25:36 2012
```

Performing the Upgrade

As mentioned earlier in the chapter, ISE 2.0 adds a graphical tool to automate the upgrade process and the tool follows the SPF approach.

To perform the upgrade:

Step 1.   Navigate to **Administration > System > Upgrade,** as shown in Figure 27-13.

The Overview tab is displayed, showing all the nodes within the ISE cube and their role.

Figure 27-13   *Upgrade Overview*

Step 2.   Click the **Upgrade** tab.

As you can see in Figure 27-14, you are presented with a checklist that you must acknowledge before proceeding with the upgrade.

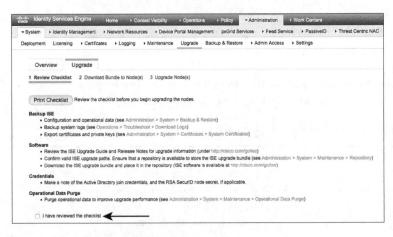

Figure 27-14   *Upgrade Checklist*

Step 3.   Review and perform the items in the checklist prior to upgrading, check the **I Have Reviewed the Checklist** check box, and click **Continue.**

Step 4. Check the check boxes on the left to select the first nodes to download the bundle to.

Step 2 in the tool is to download the upgrade bundle from a repository to each node in the cube, as shown in Figure 27-15. You are selecting nodes that will use the same repository. For instance, if there are two data centers, select the nodes that are all in the same data center together.

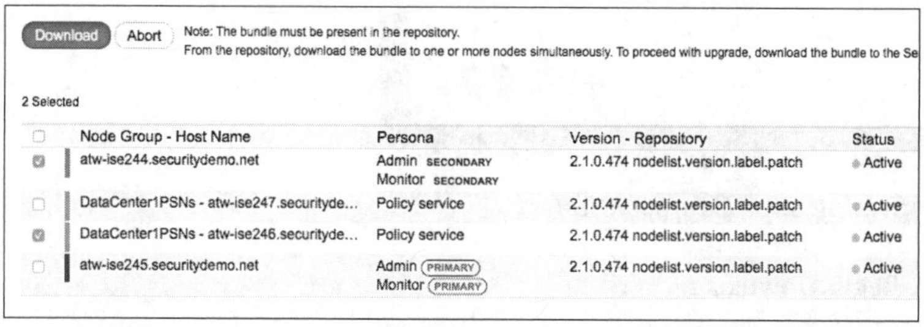

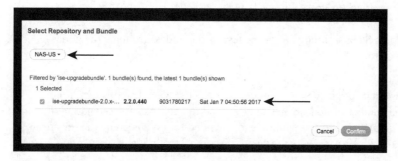

Figure 27-15 *Selecting First Nodes*

Step 5. Click **Download**.

Step 6. Select the repository from the drop-down list.

Any properly named upgrade bundles that exist in that repository are listed in the UI automatically, as shown in Figure 27-16. Select the correct upgrade bundle.

Figure 27-16 *Choosing a Repository for Nodes*

Step 7. Click **Confirm**. Another confirmation box appears, as shown in Figure 27-17.

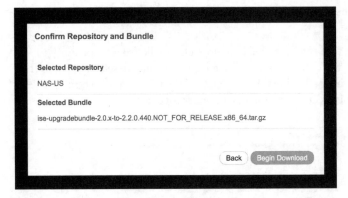

Figure 27-17 *Confirming Your Confirmation*

Step 8.   Click **Begin Download**.

The selected nodes start downloading the bundle from the repository and a progress bar for the download is displayed, as shown in Figure 27-18.

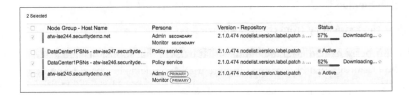

Figure 27-18 *Download Progress*

Step 9.   Repeat Steps 4 through 8 for the rest of the nodes, grouping the nodes by repository.

Note   There is no limit to the number of nodes that can use a single repository, nor is there a limit to the number of nodes you can download to at a time. The separating of nodes and grouping by repository is simply recommended for downloading the files from the closest and most performant repository with respect to that node.

After all the nodes have the upgrade bundle downloaded, it is unbundled onto the local disk. After that succeeds, the node status changes to Ready for Upgrade and the Continue button enables itself, as shown in Figure 27-19.

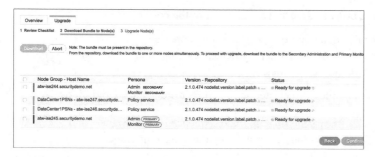

Figure 27-19   *Ready for Upgrade*

Step 10.   Click **Continue**.

Now you are presented with a screen where you can choose the upgrade order of the nodes, as shown in Figure 27-20.

Figure 27-20   *Upgrade Nodes Screen*

Step 11.   Select the secondary admin node and click the arrow icon to move it from the left to the right.

Step 12.   Click **Continue**, as seen in Figure 27-21.

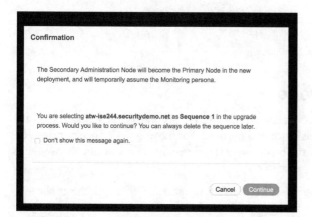

Figure 27-21   *Confirming Your Choice*

Step 13. Select the other node(s) and assign them to the correct order.

It's recommended that you never upgrade more than two nodes simultaneously. In smaller deployments, never upgrade more than one at a time, in order to be cautious.

Step 14. After all the nodes are selected in the correct order, click **Upgrade**.

Figure 27-22 shows the final upgrade sequence being assigned, and Figure 27-23 shows the nodes all being queued for upgrade.

Figure 27-22   *Upgrade Sequence Assigned*

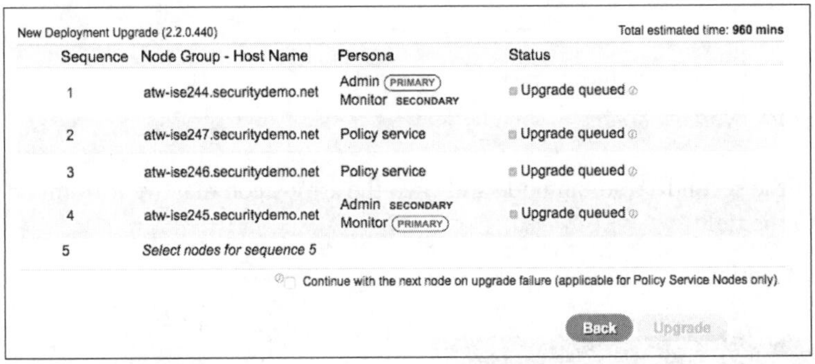

	New Deployment Upgrade (2.2.0.440)			Total estimated time: **960 mins**
Sequence	Node Group - Host Name	Persona	Status	
1	atw-ise244.securitydemo.net	Admin PRIMARY Monitor SECONDARY	⊞ Upgrade queued ⊘	
2	atw-ise247.securitydemo.net	Policy service	⊞ Upgrade queued ⊙	
3	atw-ise246.securitydemo.net	Policy service	⊞ Upgrade queued ⊘	
4	atw-ise245.securitydemo.net	Admin SECONDARY Monitor PRIMARY	⊞ Upgrade queued ⊘	
5	Select nodes for sequence 5			

⊘ Continue with the next node on upgrade failure (applicable for Policy Service Nodes only)

Back   Upgrade

Figure 27-23   *Upgrade Queued*

Command-Line Upgrade

For smaller deployments, such as standalone systems, the Secondary PAN First graphical upgrade process does not hold as much of a purpose. For those types of deployments, or if you just want more control of the process in a larger deployment, you can choose the CLI option.

The command is **application upgrade**, and it has a few options. Begin with the **application upgrade prepare** command, as shown in Example 27-4. This downloads the upgrade bundle to the local disk, unpacks the bundle, and verifies it is valid and usable.

The node waits for the ISE administrator to continue or cancel the upgrade, so the admin can choose when the upgrade occurs, such as during a change control window.

Example 27-4   *Output of* application upgrade prepare *Command*

```
atw-ise245/admin# application upgrade prepare ise-upgradebundle-2.0.x-to-2.2.0.440.
  NOT_FOR_RELEASE.x86_64.tar.gz NAS-US
Getting bundle to local machine...
Unbundling Application Package...
Verifying Application Signature...
Application upgrade preparation successful
```

If you need to cancel the upgrade, use the **application upgrade cleanup** command, as shown in Example 27-5. This deletes all the unpacked upgrade files created during the prepare phase.

Example 27-5   *Output of* application upgrade cleanup *Command*

```
atw-ise245/admin# application upgrade cleanup
Application upgrade preparation directory cleanup successful
```

To continue the upgrade, use the **application upgrade proceed** command, as shown in Example 27-6. This begins the upgrade process. If it's a multinode deployment, remember to do the Secondary PAN First.

Example 27-6   *Output of* application upgrade proceed *Command*

```
atw-ise244/admin# application upgrade proceed
Initiating Application Upgrade...
% Warning: Do not use Ctrl-C or close this terminal window until upgrade completes.
-Checking VM for minimum hardware requirements
STEP 1: Stopping ISE application...
STEP 2: Verifying files in bundle...
-Internal hash verification passed for bundle
STEP 3: Validating data before upgrade...
STEP 4: De-registering node from current deployment...
STEP 5: Taking backup of the configuration data...
- Running db sanity check to fix index corruption, if any...
- Auto Upgrading Schema for UPS Model...
- Upgrading Schema completed for UPS Model.

ISE database schema upgrade completed.
STEP 7: Running ISE configuration data upgrade...
- Data upgrade step 1/48, NSFUpgradeService(2.1.101.145)... Done in 33 seconds.
- Data upgrade step 2/48, ProfilerUpgradeService(2.1.101.145)... Done in 1 seconds.
<SNIP>
```

```
- Data upgrade step 48/48, GuestAccessUpgradeService(2.2.0.440)... Done in 5
  seconds.
STEP 8: Running ISE configuration data upgrade for node specific data...
STEP 9: Making this node PRIMARY of the new deployment. When other nodes are
  upgraded it will be added to this deployment.
STEP 10: Running ISE M&T database upgrade...
ISE M&T Log Processor is not running
ISE database M&T schema upgrade completed.
% Warning: Some warnings encountered during MNT sanity check
Gathering Config schema(CEPM) stats .....
Gathering Operational schema(MNT) stats .......
% NOTICE: Upgrading ADEOS. Appliance will be rebooted after upgrade completes
  successfully.
<SNIP>

% This application Install or Upgrade requires reboot, rebooting now...
Broadcast message from root@atw-ise244 (pts/1) (Sat Jan  7 18:12:13 2017):
The system is going down for reboot NOW
```

Summary

This chapter discussed the importance of repositories and the types of repositories available. It reviewed the Secondary PAN First upgrade process, and stepped through examples of using the GUI-based upgrade tool and the command-line upgrade commands.

Chapter 28

Device Administration Fundamentals

This chapter covers the following topics:

- Device administration in ISE

- Enabling TACACS+ in ISE

- Network devices

In Chapter 2, "Fundamentals of AAA," you were introduced to the concepts of network access AAA and device administration AAA. Although both are focused on identifying "who" is allowed to perform "what" action, they are vastly different in their ultimate purpose. The purposes are so different, in fact, that a few years ago Aaron Woland wrote an article for *Network World* about why both types shouldn't be in ISE; that ISE should stick to network access AAA and leave device admin AAA for Cisco Access Control Server (ACS) to handle. You can read that opinion piece here: http://www.networkworld.com/article/2838882/radius-versus-tacacs.html.

As described in Chapter 2, device administration AAA exists to control access to network device consoles, Telnet sessions, Secure Shell (SSH) sessions, or other method of gaining administrative control over a network device. The purpose is not only to control the access, but also to provide centralized visibility of all those actions. For example, if an administrator makes a change that causes a network outage, then the organization will need an audit trail (proof) of who caused it and what they did.

Figure 28-1 illustrates device administration graphically.

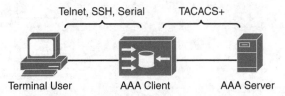

Figure 28-1   *Device Administration AAA*

Device administration AAA is very interactive in nature, or at least it can be. An administrator could write a policy that authorizes the user's entire CLI session, or a policy that requires authorization of each and every command the user enters (authenticate once, authorize many). Due to the extremely interactive nature of command authorization, TACACS+ lends itself to be the perfect AAA protocol for device administration.

Figure 28-2 illustrates how TACACS+ can perform the authenticate once, authorize many. This is key for device administration. Think about it: You can authenticate the user, then authorize them to access the CLI of a router, but you may still have to authorize each of the commands entered from that CLI for granular control.

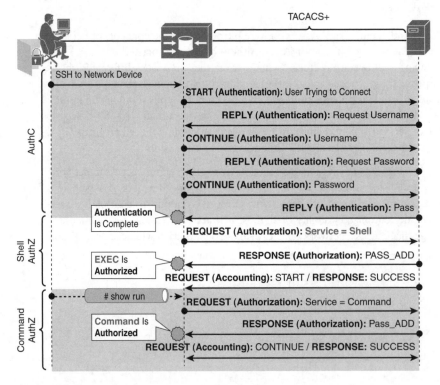

Figure 28-2   *Authenticate Once, Authorize Many*

Please review Chapter 2 for more information on what device administration AAA is and for a detailed look at TACACS+.

Device Administration in ISE

When it comes to the Identity Services Engine, device administration is synonymous with TACACS+. Everything to do with TACACS+ exists within the Device Administration Work Center. In fact, to enable TACACS+, there is a single license, named Device Admin, as shown in Figure 28-3. Unlike Base, Plus, and Apex licenses, the Device Admin license does not have a per-device count. It's a single license that applies for the entire ISE cube, and is valid for the maximum number of network devices. This differs a bit from what you may be used to with the predecessor to ISE, Cisco ACS, which had a base license and a large deployment license. ISE only has the latter.

Figure 28-3   *Device Admin License Enabled*

If the device admin license is not enabled, the corresponding Work Center is not displayed.

There are a few schools of thought when it comes to designing ISE for device administration. As previously mentioned, Aaron Woland has publically stated his belief that device administration AAA has no business being in a network access AAA product. There is too much disparity in the uses of the two AAA types, their traffic patterns, and the load level they put on the AAA and monitoring servers.

There are a few different design options:

- Separate ISE cubes, with one for RADIUS and another for TACACS+. Provides dedicated PSNs and dedicated MnT nodes for each function.

- Mixed ISE cube with separate PSNs, which provides dedicated PSNs for each AAA protocol but shares a single MnT node for logging and reporting.

- Mixed ISE cube where the PSNs are not dedicated to any protocol.

Figure 28-4 presents a table created by the father of TACACS+ at Cisco, Douglas Gash. Doug is the brilliant chief architect of TACACS+ for ACS and ISE at Cisco, as well as a major contributor to the TACACS+ standard within the IETF. This table helps you to decide which deployment model to follow, based on what is most important to your organization. Is it scale of TACACS+ and RADIUS services? Are the audit trail and log retention most important? Perhaps it is a political separation of duties within your organization?

Priorities According to Policy		Separate Deployment TACACS RADIUS	Separate PSN Mode RADIUS TACACS	Mixed PSN Mode RADIUS/TACACS
Separation of Configuration	Yes: Specialization for TACACS+	✓		
	No: Avoid Duplication of Shared Items Avoid Cost of Duplicate PAN/PSN		✓	✓
Separation of Logging Store	Yes: Optimize Log Retention VM	✓		
	No: Centralized Monitoring		✓	✓
Independent Scaling of Services	Yes: Scale as Needed Avoid NAC/Device Admin Load	✓	✓	
	No: Avoid Underutilized PSNs			✓

Figure 28-4 *Doug Gash's Options for Deploying Device Admin*

For simplicity, in this chapter we separate the deployment recommendations into categories based on deployment size: large, medium, and small.

Large Deployments

For a large deployment, it is best to have separate ISE cubes for network access and device administration. That ensures one will never affect the other. After all, you would never want to accidently prevent your CEO from getting on the wireless network, just because a script was actively making a lot of changes across your network infrastructure. Nor would you want the audit logs for network device changes to be kept for less time because the limited MnT disk space was shared between network access and device admin.

MnT is one of the key items of concern. The MnT node plays a key role with network access functions beyond just logging and reporting. As of ISE 2.2, MnT is still the holder of critical functions such as the centralized session directory; the pxGrid topic publishing for session data; merging of passiveID and active authentication data into the session directory; and much more.

If the MnT node must also process tremendous amounts of logging for all the command authorization accounting—logging entries for every single command entered on every single network device in the entire organization—you can begin to see why this becomes a point of concern.

Figure 28-5 illustrates two different ISE cubes. Cube 1 is dedicated to TACACS+ and Cube 2 is dedicated to RADIUS. Therefore, the PAN and MnT nodes are also dedicated, not just the PSNs. Although the illustration does include a virtual IP (VIP) for the PSNs, a load balancer is not required. It's only illustrated this way to show a common practice.

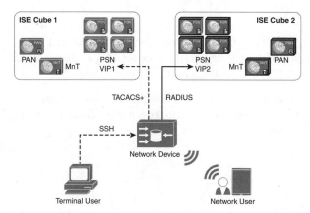

Figure 28-5 *Large Deployments: Separate ISE Cubes for TACACS+ and RADIUS*

Medium Deployments

With medium-size deployments, you may want to have a single ISE cube, but it is best to have separate PSNs for network access and device administration. That ensures one will never affect the other, without having to maintain separate cubes.

One set of PSNs would primarily be responsible for all the RADIUS traffic, while another set of PSNs would be primarily responsible for the TACACS+ traffic. For redundancy, you may choose to send the RADIUS traffic to the TACACS+ PSNs, but only in the case of a disaster. The primary purpose of the PSNs is still dedicated to either RADIUS or TACACS+.

Figure 28-6 illustrates a single ISE cube, with dedicated PSNs per function. As with a large deployment, although the illustration shows a VIP for the PSNs, a load balancer is not required. It's only illustrated this way to show a common practice.

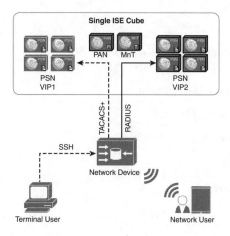

Figure 28-6 *Medium Deployments: One ISE Cube, Separate PSNs for TACACS+ and RADIUS*

Small Deployments

A small deployment could certainly be just a single ISE cube, or even a standalone ISE node that is performing all functions. In these instances, there are no dedicated nodes—all PSNs handle equal amounts of TACACS+ and RADIUS traffic.

Figure 28-7 illustrates a single ISE cube with dedicated PSNs per function. Again, the illustration shows a VIP for the PSNs, but a load balancer is not required. It's only illustrated this way to show a common practice.

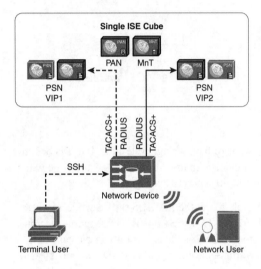

Figure 28-7   *Small Deployments: One ISE Cube, No Separation of TACACS+ and RADIUS*

Enabling TACACS+ in ISE

Installing the Device Admin license is not enough to start accepting TACACS+ communications. You also must enable it in the Deployment settings:

Step 1.   Navigate to **Administration > System > Deployment**.

Step 2.   Select the PSN where you wish to enable TACACS+.

Step 3.   Check the **Enable Device Admin Service** check box.

Step 4.   Click **Save**.

Figure 28-8 shows the deployment screen for a PSN.

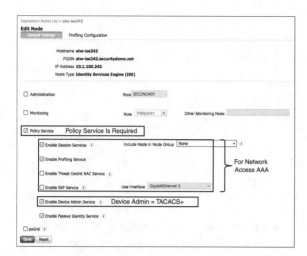

Figure 28-8 *Deployment Screen*

Know your intended design before enabling the TACACS+ functionality, and only enable the Device Admin service on the PSNs that will handle TACACS+; leave it disabled on any PSNs that are supposed to be dedicated for RADIUS, and vice versa. Keep the remainder of the session services disabled on the dedicated TACACS+ PSNs.

A more practical and easier-to-use method for enabling the TACACS+ run time on an ISE PSN is shown later in the chapter, in the section "Device Administration Work Center."

Network Devices

We can design ISE cubes and TACACS+ or RADIUS PSNs all day long. Yet, none of it will matter if the network access device (NAD) is not set up correctly. Just like RADIUS, the NAD object within ISE must be configured with the TACACS+ shared secret, and the connection type.

The same Network Device Group (NDG) guidelines for network access apply for device administration as well. The more applicable the NDG design is for your organization, the more it aids in your policy creation. Device type, location, and line of business are all very useful types of NAD groupings.

Figure 28-9 shows the TACACS+ portion of the NAD definition in the ISE UI.

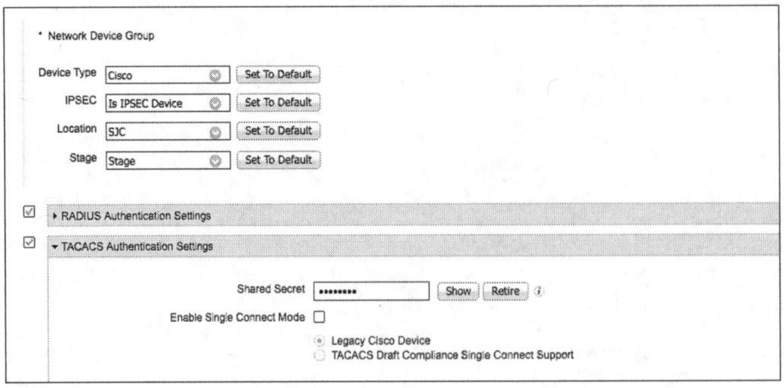

Figure 28-9   *NAD TACACS+ and NDG Configuration*

In Figure 28-9 you can see the NDG assignments, such as Device Type. In this instance, the Device Type assignment is leveraged to identify this switch as a Cisco access layer switch, so we effectively use that assignment to point the TACACS+ requests to a policy set that is created for IOS devices.

Figure 28-9 also shows how the TACACS+ shared secret gets configured, just like with RADIUS. That shared secret is the password used between the NAD and ISE to validate the source of the TACACS+ communication and to provide a seed value for the encryption.

There is also an option to Enable Single Connect Mode. The normal communication mode for TACACS+ is to open a new TCP session for each and every TACACS communication, which means each authentication request, each authorization request, and each accounting request. Enabling this setting allows the NAD to maintain a single open connection between itself and the TACACS+ service on ISE. This type of connection is more efficient because it allows the service to handle a higher number of TACACS operations, but it does require the NAD to also be configured for Single Connect.

Next, note the Retire button. This allows the administrator to retire the existing shared secret and configure a new one. During the retirement period, ISE accepts both the old and new shared secrets for the device, allowing the administrator some buffer time, making the updating of shared secrets more operationally feasible. The retirement time leverages the timer configured under Work Centers > Device Administration > Settings > Connection Settings, as shown in Figure 28-10 in the next section.

Device Administration Global Settings

The retire option for shared secrets is just one of the many global settings for TACACS+ within ISE. To see the globally applicable settings, navigate to **Work Centers > Device Administration > Settings**, as shown in Figure 28-10.

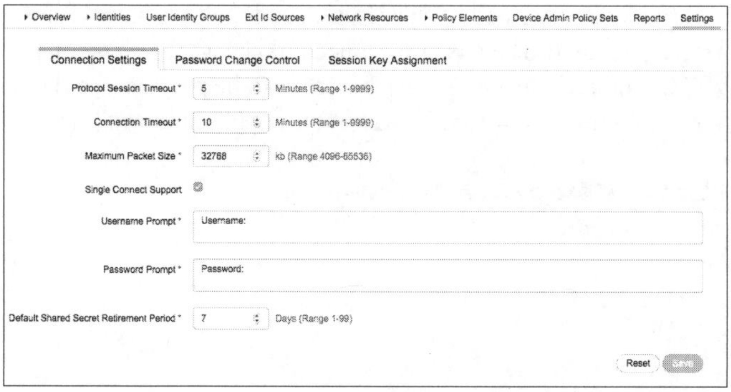

Figure 28-10 *Device Administration Work Center Settings*

Connection Settings

Figure 28-10 shows that the tab displayed by default is Connection Settings. The shared secret retirement period is configured on this tab, and can range from 1 to 99 days. The connection and session timers are also configured on this tab, as well as the string used for username and password prompts and a check box for indicating whether Single Connect Mode should be enabled.

Password Change Control

Click the **Password Change Control** tab, shown in Figure 28-11, where you can globally enable or disable the ability to change passwords through the TACACS+ session, and enter the strings to be used in the prompts.

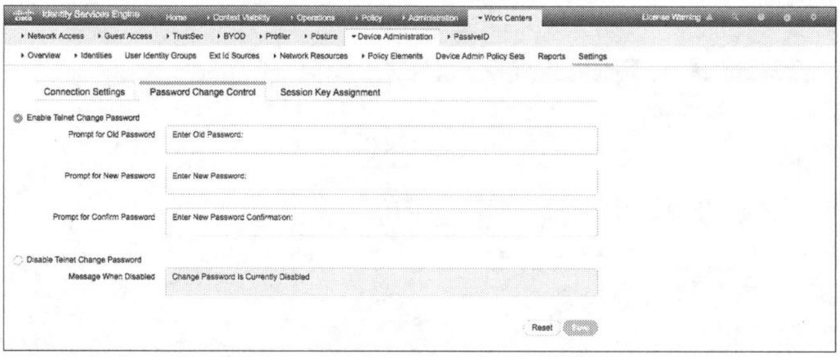

Figure 28-11 *Password Change Control Tab*

Session Key Assignment

Click the **Session Key Assignment** tab, shown in Figure 28-12, to access the remaining global settings. On this tab, you see the different values from the TACACS packets that are available for use in identifying when the packets are part of the same session. This enables

ISE to track the full session throughout the single authentication and multiple authorization and accounting requests that may come in. There is rarely a need to change anything on this tab, unless directed by TAC. The real purpose of this setting is to help determine the number of sessions when you configure a limit for the maximum sessions allowed.

Figure 28-12   *Session Key Assignment Tab*

Device Administration Work Center

Now that you have been introduced to the Settings screen of the Device Administration Work Center, this section walks you through the remaining eight screens. As with the other Work Centers in ISE, Device Administration is designed to provide you with access to just about everything you need to accomplish a complete set of tasks, in this case the administrative tasks associated with device administration AAA. Also, as is the user experience typical of ISE Work Centers, the flow when starting from no configuration is to go from left to right, starting with the Overview screen.

Overview

Figure 28-13 shows the ISE GUI navigation for the Overview screen of the Device Administration Work Center.

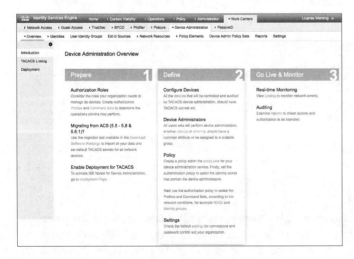

Figure 28-13   *Navigation UI and Introduction Page*

You first see the standard Work Center Introduction page, which provides a very broad review of the activities within the Work Center, as well as some helpful links. In this particular introduction page, there is a link to the ACS-to-ISE migration tool.

Next in the Overview navigation menu on the left is TACACS Livelog, a dedicated, near-real-time log screen, but for TACACS only. Much the same as the original Live Log (renamed to RADIUS Live Log), this will become your go-to page when looking for an overview of operations and for troubleshooting. We will come back to this page in the next few chapters.

Finally in the Overview navigation menu is the Deployment page (designed by Aaron Woland and Doug Gash), shown in Figure 28-14. It is a TACACS deployment page designed to allow you to quickly enable TACACS+ on any number of PSNs from a single screen, instead of having to enable it on each PSN one at a time, as demonstrated previously in Figure 28-8.

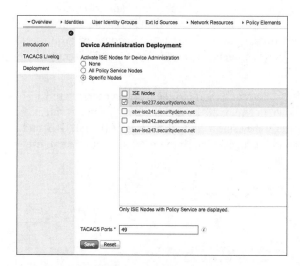

Figure 28-14   *TACACS Deployment Page*

Examining Figure 28-14, you have three options to enable TACACS: on None of the PSNs, on All of the PSNs, or on Specific Nodes. This page alone saves countless amounts of time and aggravation when setting up ISE for device administration.

Finally, this is the page where you configure the TCP port(s) for TACACS+. By default, only port 49 is leveraged for TACACS. You can add more ports by separating the values with a comma.

Identities

Moving to the right through the Device Administration Work Center navigation, the next three screens are related to user identities: Identities, User Identity Groups, and Ext Id Sources. However, these user identities are not unique to the Device Administration Work

Center at all. In fact, they are the same as the identities you find in the other Work Centers. The Identities screen (see Figure 28-15) houses the internal users created within ISE's internal user database. The Users page is titled Network Access Users, but that is simply a legacy name, as these user accounts can be leveraged for device administration as well.

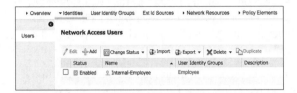

Figure 28-15   *User Identities*

Remember, internal users can be configured to leverage internal passwords, or they can be local accounts with the same names as AD user accounts and leverage the AD passwords. This is commonly used with device administration as an additional authorization condition—in other words, not only leverage an account or group membership from AD, but also rely on the need for the TACACS+ administrator to create that local account within ISE.

Just as the Identities screen is simply a shortcut of sorts to the existing users, so too are the User Identity Groups screen, shown in Figure 28-16, and the Ext Id Sources screen, shown in Figure 28-17. These are exactly the same as the other areas of the ISE GUI, and are simply shortcuts to those configuration areas to make the Work Center easier to use and more complete.

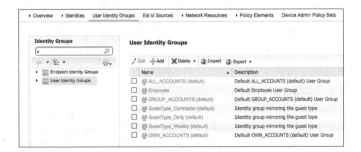

Figure 28-16   *User Identity Groups*

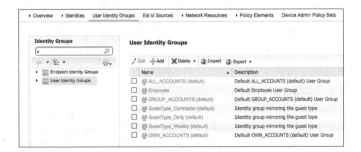

Figure 28-17   *Ext Id Sources*

Network Resources

Again, similar to the three screens to its left, the Network Resources screen of the Device Administration Work Center is a shortcut to the same network resources available all throughout the ISE GUI and within other Work Centers. A very noticeable difference is the inclusion of TACACS External Servers and TACACS Server Sequence pages, as shown in Figure 28-18.

Figure 28-18   *Network Resources*

Just like with external RADIUS servers and RADIUS server sequences, there are many reasons why you may need to forward TACACS+ requests to other servers. It could be a requirement for proof of concept or a phase in migrating away from another solution. The external TACACS servers that you add are then added to one or more TACACS Server Sequences, which are leveraged in a proxy sequence instead of a standard authentication within the policy set.

Policy Elements

The Policy Elements screen of the Work Center is a shortcut to the conditions and results. Let's focus on the results. The two main results that are used with device administration are TACACS command sets and TACACS profiles.

TACACS Command Sets

You will dive deeper into command sets in the following chapter when you actually configure device administration with TACACS+. The purpose is to limit which commands a user can or cannot use, and to assign those permissions to a session as one of the authorization results.

Navigate to **Work Centers > Device Administration > Policy Elements > Results > TACACS Command Sets**, as shown in Figure 28-19.

Figure 28-19   *TACACS Command Sets*

The command sets are groups of commands that should be permitted, commands that should be denied, or any combination thereof. The command set provides you with the ability to use simple or complex combinations of permit and deny statements.

Click **Add** to see the available choices with a command set, as shown in Figure 28-20.

Figure 28-20   *A Look at a Command Set*

Figure 28-20 keeps things very simple to illustrate a point about command sets. This particular command set has the check box for Permit Any Command That Is Not Listed Below checked, with **configure** the only command listed below, set to Deny Always.

The choices per command are Permit, Deny, or Deny Always. The difference between Deny and Deny Always has to do with stacking command sets—in other words, combining multiple command sets together in an authorization result. A Permit always trumps a Deny, but a Deny Always wins every time.

You will work more with command sets in the following chapters as you configure device administration with TACACS+.

TACACS Profiles

TACACS profiles are most aptly compared to authorization profiles with network access (RADIUS). They are the basic form of authorization result for device administration, similar to allowing access or denying access—a result that is more bulk and uniform than the granular command sets that you looked at previously.

TACACS profiles are located under **Work Centers > Device Administration > Policy Elements > Results > TACACS Profiles,** as shown in Figure 28-21. There are some predefined profiles out of the box, and there are different profile types: Shell (IOS), WLC, Nexus, and Generic. Those types are provided to help make it even easier to work with well-known devices.

Figure 28-21 *Default TACACS Profiles*

Figure 28-22 shows an example TACACS profile for the type of Shell, in other words for an IOS device. Figure 28-23 shows the exact same profile, but it shows the Raw View tab, which is live. You can make changes in either the Task Attribute View tab or the Raw View tab. The Task Attribute View tab is just a friendly view of the raw data.

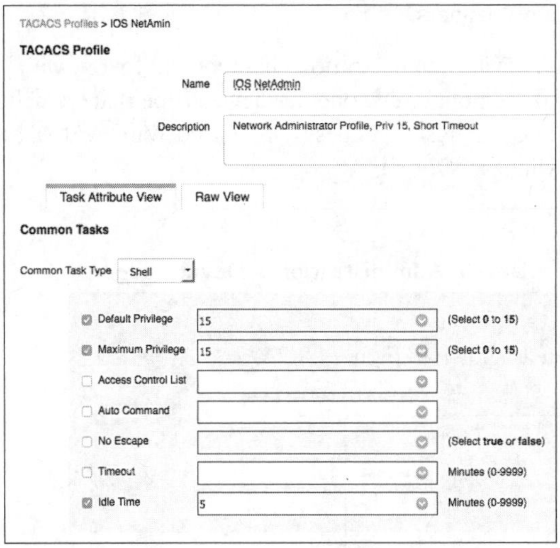

TACACS Profiles > IOS NetAmin

TACACS Profile

Name   IOS NetAdmin

Description   Network Administrator Profile, Priv 15, Short Timeout

| Task Attribute View | Raw View |

Common Tasks

Common Task Type   Shell

☑	Default Privilege	15	(Select 0 to 15)
☑	Maximum Privilege	15	(Select 0 to 15)
☐	Access Control List		
☐	Auto Command		
☐	No Escape		(Select **true** or **false**)
☐	Timeout		Minutes (0-9999)
☑	Idle Time	5	Minutes (0-9999)

Figure 28-22 *TACACS Profile: Shell, Task Attribute View*

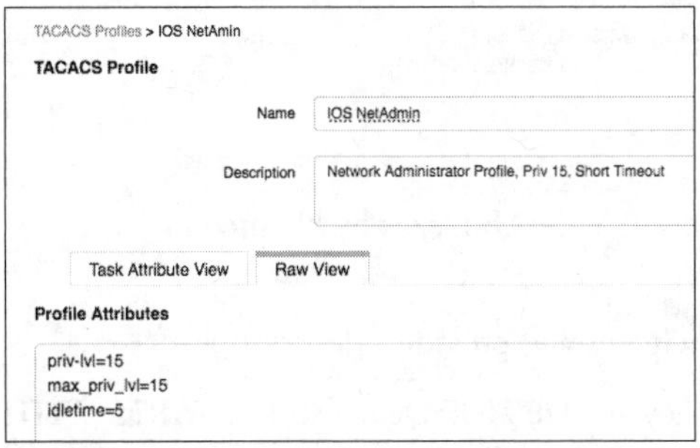

TACACS Profiles > IOS NetAmin

TACACS Profile

Name   IOS NetAdmin

Description   Network Administrator Profile, Priv 15, Short Timeout

| Task Attribute View | Raw View |

Profile Attributes

```
priv-lvl=15
max_priv_lvl=15
idletime=5
```

Figure 28-23 *TACACS Profile: Shell, Raw View*

You will see the different profile types in the subsequent chapters when you configure TACACS+ for Cisco Catalyst Switches (IOS), Cisco Wireless LAN Controller (WLC), and Cisco Nexus Switches (NX-OS).

Device Admin Policy Sets

As my old guitar instructor, Jamie Hoover, used to say: we are now at the "crux of the biscuit." In more familiar terms, it means we are at the heart of the matter, or the most important part.

As described in Chapter 13, "Authentication and Authorization Policies," policy sets for network access policies should have been included in the first version of ISE. Instead, they weren't added to ISE until version 1.2, and are not on by default (yet). That is different for Device Administration Policies, which have policy sets turned on by default, and that's a great thing.

You can and should create policy sets that work with your organization's need: perhaps based on location, job role, or even line of business.

For the purposes of this chapter and the device administration chapters that follow, we will walk through the configuration of three policy sets, one per device type that we will work with in the following chapters: Cisco Catalyst Switches (IOS), Cisco Wireless LAN Controller (WLC), and Cisco Nexus Switches (NX-OS).

To create the Catalyst policy set:

Step 1.   Navigate to **Work Centers > Device Administration > Device Admin Policy Sets.**

Step 2.   Click the **Default** policy set, as shown in Figure 28-24.

Figure 28-24   *Default Device Admin Policy Set*

Step 3.   Click the plus symbol, and choose **Create Above**, as highlighted in Figure 28-24.

Step 4.   Name the policy set **Catalyst Switches** and provide a description.

Step 5.   Choose the condition for the policy set: **DEVICE:Device Type STARTS WITH All Device Types#Switches#Access-Layer#Cisco**, as shown in Figure 28-25.

Figure 28-25 *Catalyst Switches Policy Set*

Note   The policy sets in the figures are using the NDGs created in the earlier chapters.

Step 6.   Click **Submit**

Next, create the WLC policy set:

Step 1.   Navigate to **Work Centers > Device Administration > Device Admin Policy Sets**.

Step 2.   Click the **Default** policy set, as shown in Figure 28-24.

Step 3.   Click the plus symbol, and choose **Create Above**, as highlighted in Figure 28-24.

Step 4.   Name the policy set **Wireless Controllers** and provide a description.

Step 5.   Choose the condition for the policy set: **DEVICE:Device Type STARTS WITH Device Type#All Device Types#WiFi#Cisco**, as shown in Figure 28-26 (the resulting summary of policies).

Figure 28-26 *Summary of Policies*

Step 6.   Click **Submit**.

Next, create the Nexus policy set:

Step 1.   Navigate to **Work Centers > Device Administration > Device Admin Policy Sets**.

Step 2.   Click the **Default** policy set, as shown in Figure 28-24.

Step 3. Click the plus symbol, and choose **Create Above**, as highlighted in Figure 28-24.

Step 4. Name the policy set **Nexus Switches** and provide a description.

Step 5. Choose the condition for the policy set: **DEVICE:Device Type EQUALS Device Type#All Device Types#Switches#DC**, as shown in Figure 28-26 (the resulting summary of policies).

Step 6. Click **Submit**.

The policy sets are now ready for Chapters 29 through 31, where you will configure device administration policies.

It is important to note that TACACS+ is not the only protocol that could be used for device administration. Some devices may use RADIUS, even though RADIUS is better suited for network access AAA. If you need a device administration AAA policy set for RADIUS, that set cannot exist within the Device Administration Work Center; you would need to create it in the Network Access Work Center, because ISE logically separates them based on the AAA protocol.

Reports

The reports related to device administration are packaged up quite neatly within the Device Administration Work Center, so that you don't have to leave the Work Center. Navigating to **Work Centers > Device Administration > Reports** will show you the four default reports: TACACS Accounting, TACACS Authentication, TACACS Authorization, and TACACS Command Accounting—as seen in Figure 28-27.

Figure 28-27 *Reports*

Summary

This chapter reviewed the purpose of device administration AAA and how it fits into the ISE administrative user experience. You learned about ISE cube design with separate cubes, or cubes that mix RADIUS and TACACS+ together.

You walked through the entire Device Administration Work Center, and created policy sets for use in the next three chapters where you will dive deeper into configuring device admin for IOS, WLC, and NX-OS.

Chapter 29

Configuring Device Admin AAA with Cisco IOS

This chapter covers the following topics:

- Preparing ISE for incoming AAA requests

- Time to test

Much of what you are about to read and do in this chapter should feel rather familiar. There is quite a bit of overlap and similarity between configuring IOS for network access AAA and configuring IOS for device administration AAA. Because the features are so similar, you will certainly see overlap with Chapter 11, "Bootstrapping Network Devices."

Preparing ISE for Incoming AAA Requests

Before configuring the Cisco IOS device, you should ensure that the AAA server (ISE) is ready for the incoming authentication and authorization requests. If the network device is configured to authenticate users before granting them access to the IOS shell, and the AAA server is not responding with an authorization, you could create an accidental denial of service (DoS) incident.

You need to prepare the TACACS profiles and TACACS command sets that will be used as authorization results. You also need to ensure that the Network Device object in ISE is configured for TACACS and is in the correct Network Device Groups (NDG).

Preparing the Policy Results

For the purposes of this chapter, we will design the policies to support the following groups of people who require command-line access to the organization's Catalyst switches:

- **NetAdmin:** Network administrators who receive full control of the network device.

- **NetOps:** Network operators who receive full control of the network device but are not permitted to erase the configuration.

- **SecAdmin:** Security administrators who receive read-only access to view the configuration but not change anything.

- **Helpdesk:** Personnel who need to be able to see the status of certain **show** commands, to aid in their assistance of employees and guests.

In this section, you will create a TACACS profile and a command set for each of the four role types. It is best to preface each result object with its type: IOS for the Catalyst switches, WLC for the wireless controllers, and NXOS for the Nexus switches. This will help you greatly when creating policies and will ensure that you don't get confused when building the policies later.

Create the Authorization Results for Network Administrators

First create the TACACS profile:

Step 1. Navigate to **Work Centers > Device Administration > Policy Elements > Results > TACACS Profiles.**

Step 2. Click **Add.**

Step 3. Name the profile **IOS NetAdmin**, as shown in Figure 29-1.

Figure 29-1 *IOS NetAdmin TACACS Profile*

Step 4. Leave the Common Task Type field at its default value, **Shell.**

Step 5. Check the **Default Privilege** check box and set the value to **15.**

Cisco IOS offers 16 different levels of access to the shell, level 0 through 15, with 15 being the highest level of access, known as privileged EXEC mode. Because the network administrator must receive full control of the device, set the privilege level to 15.

> **Note**   When using the Task Attribute View tab to set the timeout values and the privilege levels, you can select the predefined options from the drop-down, or you can use an attribute or value that was stored in Active Directory.

Step 6.   Check the **Maximum Privilege** check box and set the value to **15**.

The default privilege is the assigned privilege level provided to the logged-in user. Although it is the assigned privilege, it is not the maximum privilege that a user could use within IOS. By typing the **enable** command, the user could use a second authorization to gain escalated privilege. The Maximum Privilege setting provides that limit.

Step 7.   Check the **Idle Time** check box and set the value to **5** minutes.

Because this user has elevated privilege, you may want to provide a relatively short timeout to the EXEC session, kind of like an automatic lock on your laptop screen or mobile device.

Step 8.   Click **Submit**.

Figure 29-1 shows the final configuration of the TACACS profile.

After the TACACS profile is complete, create the TACACS command set for network administrators:

Step 1.   Navigate to **Work Centers > Device Administration > Policy Elements > Results > TACACS Command Sets**.

Step 2.   Click **Add**.

Step 3.   Name the profile **IOS NetAdmin Command Set**.

Step 4.   Provide a description.

Step 5.   Check the box for **Permit Any Command That Is Not Listed Below**.

Step 6.   Click **Submit**.

You have just created a command set that permits all commands, no exceptions. Figure 29-2 shows the final configuration of the TACACS command set.

Figure 29-2   *IOS NetAdmin TACACS Command Set*

Create the Authorization Results for Network Operators

First create the TACACS profile:

Step 1.   Navigate to **Work Centers > Device Administration > Policy Elements > Results > TACACS Profiles**.

Step 2.   Click **Add**.

Step 3.   Name the profile **IOS NetOps**.

Step 4.   Leave the Common Task Type field at its default value, **Shell**.

Step 5.   Check the **Default Privilege** check box and set the value to 7.

Step 6.   Check the **Maximum Privilege** check box and set the value to **15**.

Step 7.   Click **Submit**.

Figure 29-3 shows the final configuration of the TACACS profile.

Figure 29-3   *IOS NetOps TACACS Profile*

Create the TACACS command set for network operators:

Step 1. Navigate to **Work Centers > Device Administration > Policy Elements > Results > TACACS Command Sets**.

Step 2. Click **Add**.

Step 3. Name the profile **IOS NetOps Command Set**.

Step 4. Provide a description.

Step 5. Check the box for **Permit Any Command That Is Not Listed Below**.

Step 6. In the Commands section, click **Add**.

Step 7. Set to **DENY_ALWAYS** the **reload** and **shutdown** commands, as shown in Figure 29-4.

Figure 29-4 *IOS NetOps TACACS Command Set*

Step 8. Click **Submit**.

You have just created a command set that permits all commands, except **reload** and **shutdown**.

Create the Authorization Results for Security Administrators

First create the TACACS profile:

Step 1. Navigate to **Work Centers > Device Administration > Policy Elements > Results > TACACS Profiles**.

Step 2. Click **Add**.

Step 3. Name the profile **IOS SecAdmin**.

Step 4. Leave the Common Task Type drop-down at its default value, **Shell**.

Step 5. Check the **Default Privilege** check box and set the value to **15**.

Step 6. Check the **Maximum Privilege** check box and set the value to **15**.

Step 7. Check the **Timeout** check box and set the value to **5** minutes.

Step 8. Check the **Idle Time** check box and set the value to **5** minutes.

Step 9. Click **Submit**.

Figure 29-5 shows the final configuration of the TACACS profile.

Figure 29-5 *IOS SecAdmin TACACS Profile*

Create the TACACS command set for security administrators:

Step 1. Navigate to **Work Centers > Device Administration > Policy Elements > Results > TACACS Command Sets**.

Step 2. Click **Add**.

Step 3. Name the profile **IOS SecAdmin Command Set**.

Step 4. Provide a description.

Step 5. Check the box for **Permit Any Command That Is Not Listed Below**.

Step 6. In the Commands section, click **Add**.

Step 7. Set to **DENY_ALWAYS** the **configure** command, as shown in Figure 29-6.

Figure 29-6 *IOS SecAdmin TACACS Command Set*

Step 8.   Click **Submit**.

You have just created a command set that permits all commands, except **configure**.

Create the Authorization Results for the Helpdesk

First, create the TACACS profile:

Step 1.   Navigate to **Work Centers > Device Administration > Policy Elements > Results > TACACS Profiles**.

Step 2.   Click **Add**.

Step 3.   Name the profile **IOS Helpdesk**.

Step 4.   Leave the Common Task Type field at its default value, **Shell**.

Step 5.   Check the **Default Privilege** check box and set the value to **2**.

Step 6.   Check the **Maximum Privilege** check box and set the value to **2**.

Step 7.   Click **Submit**.

Figure 29-7 shows the final configuration of the TACACS profile.

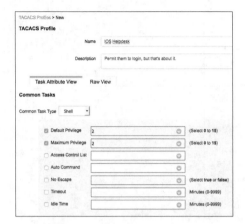

Figure 29-7   *IOS Helpdesk TACACS Profile*

Create the TACACS command set for the helpdesk users:

Step 1.   Navigate to **Work Centers > Device Administration > Policy Elements > Results > TACACS Command Sets.**

Step 2.   Click **Add.**

Step 3.   Name the profile **IOS Helpdesk Command Set.**

Step 4.   Provide a description.

Step 5.   In the Commands section, click **Add.**

Step 6.   Set to **PERMIT** the **show**, **exit**, and **quit** commands, as shown in Figure 29-8.

Figure 29-8   *IOS Helpdesk TACACS Command Set*

Step 7.   Click **Submit.**

You have just created a command set that only allows **show** commands, and the ability to type **exit** and **quit**.

Preparing the Policy Set

Now it's time to use the policy sets that you prepared in Chapter 28. Navigate to **Work Centers > Device Administration > Device Admin Policy Sets**. Here you'll see the three policy sets you created along with the Default set. Choose the **Catalyst Switches** policy set.

Figure 29-9 shows the policy set that you created for IOS-based Catalyst switches. There is a default authentication rule with a result of All_User_ID_Stores, just like in the network access policies. This identity sequence attempts to authenticate incoming TACACS+ requests against all the internal and external identity stores in order.

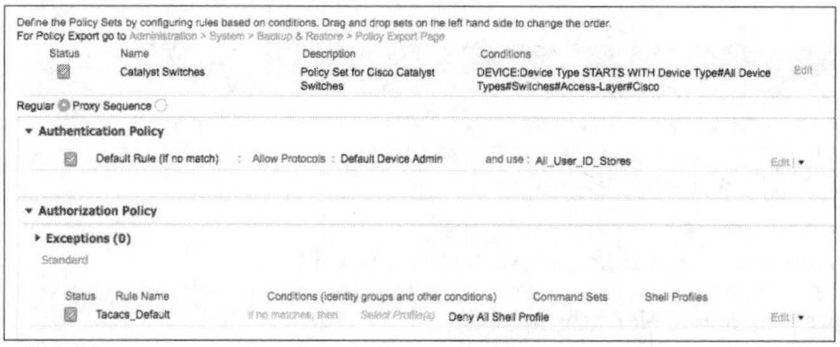

Figure 29-9   *Catalyst Switches Policy Set*

There is also a default authorization rule at the end of the policy set, named Tacacs_Default. This rule is a last resort in a top-down, first-match policy set. It has a special authorization result, the Deny All Shell Profile, which will send a TACACS+ fail result even though the authentication passed. In other words, if you are not authorized, you will be denied access.

I know this probably seems silly to point out, because that is how authorization is supposed to work. However, in ISE 2.0 there was no way to do this, and the Deny All Shell Profile was added into ISE in version 2.1.

It's your job to ensure that valid traffic never meets this default rule and suffers the ultimate fate of service denial. So, let's begin creating the authorization rules, shall we?

Add the authorization rule for network administrators:

Step 1.   Insert a rule above the Tacacs_Default rule.

Step 2.   Name the rule **NetAdmin IOS**.

Step 3.   Set the condition to be an external group from AD, like you see in Figure 29-10.

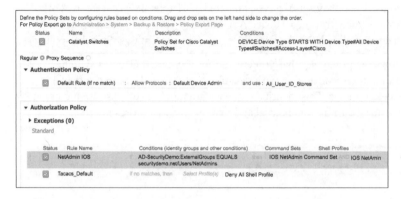

Figure 29-10   *NetAdmin IOS Authorization Rule*

Step 4.   For the command set, select **IOS NetAmin Command Set**.

Step 5.   For the shell profile, select **NetAdmin IOS**.

Step 6.   Click **Done**.

Step 7.   Click **Save**.

Figure 29-10 shows the completed NetAdmin IOS authorization rule.

Add the authorization rule for network operators:

Step 1.   Insert a rule above the Tacacs_Default rule.

Step 2.   Name the rule **NetOps IOS**.

Step 3.   Set the condition to be an external group from AD, like you see in Figure 29-11.

Figure 29-11   *Finished Catalyst Switches Policy Set*

Step 4. For the command set, select **IOS NetOps Command Set.**

Step 5. For the shell profile, select **IOS NetOps.**

Add the authorization rule for security administrators:

Step 1. Insert a rule above the Tacacs_Default rule.

Step 2. Name the rule **SecAdmin IOS.**

Step 3. Set the condition to be an external group from AD, like you see in Figure 29-11.

Step 4. For the command set, select **IOS SecAdmin Command Set.**

Step 5. For the shell profile, select **IOS SecAdmin.**

Finally, add the authorization rule for helpdesk users:

Step 1. Insert a rule above the Tacacs_Default rule.

Step 2. Name the rule **Helpdesk IOS.**

Step 3. Set the condition to be an external group from AD, like you see in Figure 29-11.

Step 4. For the command set, select **IOS Helpdesk Command Set.**

Step 5. For the shell profile, select **IOS Helpdesk.**

Figure 29-11 shows the completed Catalyst Switches policy set.

Configuring the Network Access Device

Now that the policy set is ready, it's time to start configuring the network devices to authenticate the interactive logins and authorize the commands executed in their shell:

Step 1. Enable Authentication, Authorization, and Accounting on the access switch(es).

By default, the AAA subsystem of the Cisco switch is disabled. Prior to enabling the AAA subsystem, none of the required commands will be available in the configuration. You likely have configured this already, back in Chapter 11, but if not, here is the command:

```
3750-X(config)# aaa new-model
```

Step 2. Define the TACACS+ servers.

Just as with RADIUS in Chapter 11, you have to define the TACACS AAA servers:

```
3750-X(config)# tacacs server atw-ise237
3750-X(config-server-tacacs)# address ipv4 10.1.100.237
3750-X(config-server-tacacs)# key Cisco123

3750-X(config)# tacacs server atw-ise241
3750-X(config-server-tacacs)# address ipv4 10.1.100.241
3750-X(config-server-tacacs)# key Cisco123
```

Step 3. Create a TACACS+ server group, named ISE-Group, and add the AAA servers to the group:

```
3750-X(config)# aaa group server tacacs+ ISE-Group
3750-X(config-sg-tacacs+)# server name atw-ise237
3750-X(config-sg-tacacs+)# server name atw-ise241
```

Step 4. Just like you did for RADIUS traffic, configure all TACACS+ communication to be sourced from the loopback interface that matches what is configured in the ISE NAD object:

```
3750-X(config)# ip tacacs source-interface Loopback0
```

Step 5. Create an AAA method that disables authentication, and apply it to the console during your configuration.

This action helps to ensure that you do not accidently lock yourself out of the switch while you are creating the authentication and authorization methods. You will come back and apply the correct authentication to the console after you are certain the authentications and authorizations are built correctly. Here is the command:

```
3750-X(config)# aaa authentication login failsafe none
```

The word *failsafe* is the name of the method you just created. It could be called anything, but it's always a good practice to name the method something that helps describe what it does. The **none** keyword in the method configures it to not perform any authentication.

Method lists are used to define an order for IOS to leverage for AAA. At this point, you should be very familiar with these, but Figure 29-12 illustrates the method lists and a breakdown of each portion.

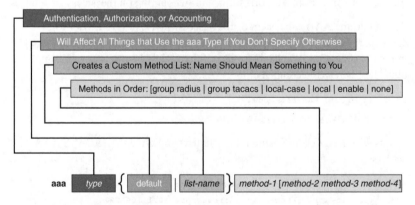

Figure 29-12 *Method Lists Breakdown*

Step 6. Apply the new failsafe authentication method to the console:

```
3750-X(config)# line con 0
3750-X(config-line)# login authentication failsafe
```

Assuming you are configuring the switch through the console port, you have now protected yourself during this configuration, ensuring that you cannot accidently lock yourself out of the switch. It's a trick many of us used in the CCIE lab to ensure seamless configuration, and we have brought that practice forward into the field.

Step 7. Create an authentication method using the TACACS+ server group you created in Step 3.

Field deployment experience dictates that we should always create a local user or two for an additional failsafe in case the TACACS+ servers are unavailable.

```
3750-X(config)# aaa authentication login ISE-TAC+ group ISE-Group local
```

Note If you do not have a local user created with the **username** global-configuration command, then the fallback option of using local users will certainly not help you.

Step 8. Create authorization methods using the same TACACS+ server group.

Hopefully at this point, you understand that authentication alone does nothing. You must configure authorizations to provide or restrict access. There are different locations within the shell to enforce authorization. Here you create methods for the shell itself (exec), configuration mode, and commands at four different levels (0, 1, 7 and 15):

```
3750-X(config)# aaa authorization exec ISE-TAC+ group ISE-Group local
3750-X(config)# aaa authorization config-commands
3750-X(config)# aaa authorization commands 0 ISE-TAC+ group ISE-Group
  local
3750-X(config)# aaa authorization commands 1 ISE-TAC+ group ISE-Group
  local
3750-X(config)# aaa authorization commands 7 ISE-TAC+ group ISE-Group
  local
3750-X(config)# aaa authorization commands 15 ISE-TAC+ group ISE-Group
  local
```

Note Without the **aaa authorization config-commands** option, the IOS device will only authorize commands in the exec mode, and not in configuration mode. In other words, no configuration changes will be authorized.

Step 9. Create accounting methods using the same TACACS+ server group.

At this point the IOS device is ready to authenticate users and authorize their activity. Now it is important to set up accounting, so you have an audit trail of the activities:

```
3750-X(config)# aaa accounting exec default start-stop group ISE-Group
3750-X(config)# aaa accounting commands 0 default start-stop group
    ISE-Group
3750-X(config)# aaa accounting commands 1 default start-stop group
    ISE-Group
3750-X(config)# aaa accounting commands 7 default start-stop group
    ISE-Group
3750-X(config)# aaa accounting commands 15 default start-stop group
    ISE-Group
```

Step 10. Apply the methods to the lines for Telnet and SSH.

Now that all the methods are defined, it's time to apply the methods to the access type (Telnet, SSH, HTTP, etc.). Remember, your console is currently exempt from authentication, until you're certain everything is working.

```
3750-X(config)# line vty 0 4
3750-X(config-line)# login authentication ISE-TAC+
3750-X(config-line)# authorization exec ISE-TAC+
3750-X(config-line)# authorization commands 0 ISE-TAC+
3750-X(config-line)# authorization commands 1 ISE-TAC+
3750-X(config-line)# authorization commands 7 ISE-TAC+
3750-X(config-line)# authorization commands 15 ISE-TAC+
```

Time to Test

You have configured policy sets, authorization results, network devices, and all the authentication and authorization methods in the switch, applying those methods to the virtual terminal lines for Telnet, SSH, and HTTP. Now we'll ensure that it all works.

From the command-line interface:

Step 1. Issue the **test aaa** command to ensure the NAD is communicating successfully with ISE:

```
3750-X# test aaa group tacacs+ employee1 xxxxxxx legacy
Attempting authentication test to server-group tacacs+ using tacacs+
User authentication request was rejected by server.
```

The authentication request was rejected by the server? Don't worry, we did this on purpose—to show you the default Deny All Shell Profile, and how it appears to fail authentication.

Step 2. Examine the TACACS Live Log at **Work Centers > Device Administration > Overview > TACACS Live Log**, as shown in Figure 29-13.

Figure 29-13 *Live Log: Failed Test Authentication*

> Notice in Figure 29-13 that the authentication policy is Catalyst Switches >> Default >> Default. This shows us the policy set selection worked. But why did the authentication fail? I'm certain that I put in the correct username and password.

Step 3. To find out, click the icon under **Details**, as highlighted in Figure 29-13, which opens another window with the details report. The details report contains a tremendous amount of detail. However, the Overview section in the upper-left portion of the report contains everything you need to understand why this attempt failed. Figure 29-14 shows the Overview section of the report.

Figure 29-14 *Live Log: Failed Test Authentication Details Overview*

In the Overview section, you see the message text of "Failed-Attempt: Authentication failed", and that the Selected Authorization Profile is "Deny All Shell Profile". Wait a second…if it failed authentication, then how did it land on a shell profile at all? Shell profiles are part of authorization, and a failed authentication would mean the request should have dropped before getting to the authorization portion of the policy set!

The answer is right there in the details report, but may not be obvious. Take a look at the right side of the report, where all the steps are listed. You will see an Authentication Passed step, shown in Figure 29-15, which is showing you that the username and password were good. You *did* have a successful authentication.

24343	RPC Logon request succeeded - Employee1@securitydemo.net
24402	User authentication against Active Directory succeeded - All_AD_Join_Points
22037	Authentication Passed
15036	Evaluating Authorization Policy
24432	Looking up user in Active Directory
24325	Resolving identity
24313	Search for matching accounts at join point
24319	Single matching account found in forest
24323	Identity resolution detected single matching account
24355	LDAP fetch succeeded
24416	User's Groups retrieval from Active Directory succeeded
15048	Queried PIP - AD-SecurityDemo.ExternalGroups
13036	Selected Shell Profile is DenyAccess
13015	Returned TACACS+ Authentication Reply

Figure 29-15 *Live Log: Failed Test Authentication Details Steps*

Because of the way that TACACS+ works, with the separation of authentication and authorization, ISE has to take a "peek" at the authorization policy before sending the authentication request. It has to look ahead and be sure the authorization is not going to be rejected before sending the authentication pass message back to the NAD.

Examining Figure 29-15, you see the successful authentication followed by a selected shell profile of Deny Access, and a returned authentication message. ISE cannot send the authentication success to the NAD if the user will end up being denied access to the shell. This is exactly what was wrong in ISE 2.0, before the Deny All Shell Profile was created. Any successful authentication resulted in access, regardless of the authorization.

Step 1.   Test again, but with an account that should receive access to the IOS exec:

```
3750-X# test aaa group tacacs+ netadmin1 xxxxxxx legacy
Attempting authentication test to server-group tacacs+ using tacacs+
User was successfully authenticated.
```

This time the result was successful. Figure 29-16 shows the TACACS Live Log showing the successful authentication attempt.

Figure 29-16 *Live Log: Successful Test*

Step 2. SSH or Telnet into the switch to verify the authentication and authorization aspects.

We have just proven that the communication between the NAD and ISE is working correctly using TACACS+. Now it's time to try to log in remotely to the CLI of the device and test all aspects of the device administration configuration:

```
loxx@atw-ubuntu:~$ telnet 10.1.48.2
Trying 10.1.48.2...
Connected to 10.1.48.2.
Escape character is '^]'.

Username:netadmin1
Password:

3750-X# show privilege
Current privilege level is 15
3750-X# exit
Connection closed by foreign host.
```

We just used **telnet** to remotely log in as a user named netadmin1 to the switch via one of its IP addresses. The login was successful, and the **show privilege** command shows us that we were assigned privilege level 15 (privileged EXEC).

Step 3. Examine the TACACS Live Log at **Work Centers > Device Administration > Overview > TACACS Live Log,** as shown in Figure 29-17.

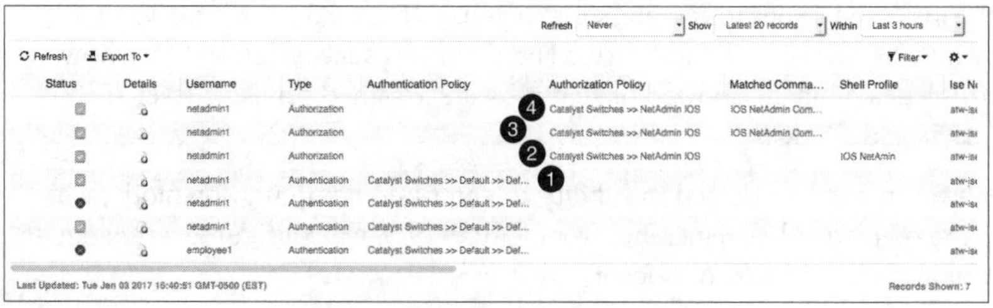

Figure 29-17 *Live Log: netadmin1 Successes*

Notice the four highlighted lines in Figure 29-17:

1. The successful authentication

2. Successful authorization to the shell, with IOS NetAdmin as the shell profile

3. Successful authorization of the **show privilege** command

4. Successful authorization of the **exit** command

Step 4.   Log in as a user from the SecAdmin group:

```
loxx@atw-ubuntu:~$ telnet 10.1.48.2
Trying 10.1.48.2...
Connected to 10.1.48.2.
Escape character is '^]'.

Username:secadmin1
Password:

3750-X# show privilege
Current privilege level is 15
3750-X# show run
Building configuration...

<SNIP>

3750-X# conf t
Command authorization failed.
3750-X#
*
*
* Line timeout expired
*
*
3750-X#Connection closed by foreign host.
loxx@atw-ubuntu:~$
```

We just used **telnet** to remotely log in as a user named secadmin1 to the switch via one of its IP addresses. The login was successful, and the **show privilege** command showed us that we were assigned privilege level 15 (privileged EXEC).

However, we were denied the ability to enter into configuration mode, which was expected. Also, remember from Figure 29-5, we configured a timeout. You just saw that timeout occur.

Step 5.   Examine the TACACS Live Log, as shown in Figure 29-18.

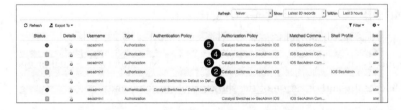

Figure 29-18   *Live Log: secadmin1 Successes*

Notice the five highlighted lines in Figure 29-18:

1. The successful authentication

2. Successful authorization to the shell, with IOS SecAdmin as the shell profile

3. Successful authorization of the **show privilege** command

4. Successful authorization of the **show run** command

5. Failed authorization of the **conf t** command

Step 6. Navigate to **Work Centers > Device Administration > Reports > Device Administration Reports > TACACS Command Accounting**, as shown in Figure 29-19.

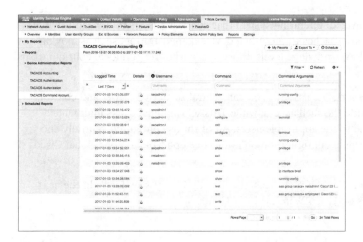

Figure 29-19 *TACACS Command Accounting Report*

The TACACS Command Accounting report provides the detailed command-level audit trail of who typed what and when. It's incredibly useful when you need to identify who it was that broke a configuration of sorts, and auditors will truly love the details of this report. However, think about all the interactive communication between all the devices on your network and ISE, and then all those logs going from the PSNs to the MnT node of your ISE cube. If your organization uses scripts or other automation tools to make configuration changes, there could be a tremendous amount of activity that ISE has to maintain records of. This brings us back to the design discussion earlier in Chapter 28, and why some of us still prefer to maintain separate ISE cubes for device administration.

Step 7.   Before you move on, don't forget to set the authentication on the console. Remember, we currently have it disabled to ensure we don't get locked out.

```
3750-X(config)# line con 0
3750-X(config-line)# login authentication ISE-TAC+
3750-X(config-line)# authorization exec ISE-TAC+
3750-X(config-line)# authorization commands 0 ISE-TAC+
3750-X(config-line)# authorization commands 1 ISE-TAC+
3750-X(config-line)# authorization commands 7 ISE-TAC+
3750-X(config-line)# authorization commands 15 ISE-TAC+
```

Summary

Cisco IOS is a very powerful operating system that controls Cisco's routers and switches. While there are many approaches to providing device administration, such as moving certain commands to lower privilege levels, those approaches rely on local configurations of the switch.

By leveraging AAA servers, such as ISE, you can centralize all that power and control. TACACS profiles provide the shell access, while TACACS command sets limit which commands are available to the applicable users. All of this is configured centrally and therefore allows for a single configuration on ISE to be applicable to your global Cisco network.

This chapter focused on Cisco IOS devices, specifically Catalyst switches. In the next chapter, you will focus on Cisco Wireless LAN Controllers.

Chapter 30

Configuring Device Admin AAA with Cisco WLC

This chapter covers the following topics:

- Overview of WLC device admin AAA
- Configuring ISE and the WLC for device admin AAA
- Testing and troubleshooting

In Chapter 29, "Configuring Device Admin AAA with Cisco IOS," you focused on a network device that has very granular control all the way down to individual commands. Keep in mind that not all network devices have the capability to control access at a per-command level. Many provide a more broad-stroke access control, such as the assignment of roles.

The Cisco Wireless LAN Controller (WLC) provides a broad-level approach to role-based access control by controlling access at a menu level.

Overview of WLC Device Admin AAA

The WLC provides role-based access control (RBAC) on a per-menu basis. However, the WLC does not prevent access to those sections of the GUI, but instead prevents changes from being saved when inside a menu section that is not authorized.

Figure 30-1 shows the WLC user interface. The top-level menus are where the RBAC occurs.

Figure 30-1   *Cisco WLC Top-Level Menus*

The WLC expects the authorization results from ISE to include a list of the menus that the user is authorized to make changes within. The WLC refers to those results as *roles*. The AAA server can send back a single role, or multiple roles that will be additive, as long as each role is designated with a unique role#. For example, to allow a user to make changes only within the WLANs, Wireless, and Security menus, the TACACS+ authorization result should include the following text: role1=WLANS role2=SECURITY role3=WIRELESS. The good news is that the order does not matter.

There are six different roles that exist that correspond directly to the menu system in the WLC user interface:

- **WLAN:** Permits write access to the WLAN menu structure.

- **CONTROLLER:** Permits write access to the CONTROLLER menu structure.

- **WIRELESS:** Permits write access to the WIRELESS menu structure.

- **SECURITY:** Permits write access to the SECURITY menu structure.

- **MANAGEMENT:** Permits write access to the MANAGEMENT menu structure.

- **COMMANDS:** Permits write access to the COMMANDS menu structure.

Additionally, there are three special roles that cannot be mixed with any other roles:

- **LOBBY:** Permits access to the Lobby Ambassador functions, which remain from when the WLC performed its own guest lifecycle management. Lobby Ambassador on the WLC has since been superseded by the Guest capabilities in ISE.

- **MONITOR:** Provides a read-only style of access to the WLC. All pages are visible to the user, but no changes are authorized.

- **ALL:** Just like it sounds, it permits access to all menus.

Configuring ISE and the WLC for Device Admin AAA

The requisite steps for configuring device administration AAA are very similar regardless of what the actual network device is. You perform some configuration on ISE, to ensure that ISE is ready to receive the TACACS+ requests from the network access device (NAD), and then you configure the NAD to send those TACACS+ requests to ISE.

Preparing ISE for WLC Device Admin AAA

Within the ISE GUI, you need to ensure that the Network Device object is configured correctly and assigned to appropriate Network Device Groups (NDG). Then you create the authorization results and configure the Wireless LAN Controllers policy set that you created in Chapter 28.

Prepare the Network Device

In the ISE GUI, navigate to **Work Centers > Device Administration > Network Resources > Network Device Groups.**

You should already have a detailed set of hierarchical NDGs, similar to what you see in Figure 30-2. Ensure that you have the appropriate groups to go along with the policies you want to create.

Figure 30-2 *Example NDG Hierarchy*

At the very least, ensure that these Cisco WLCs have their own group for a device type. With that group, you can ensure that a device administration policy set is built just for these devices and their unique way of doing device administration.

Next, you should ensure that your Cisco WLC itself has a Network Device object in ISE with the TACACS+ shared secret configured:

Step 1.   Navigate to **Work Centers > Device Administration > Network Resources > Network Devices.**

Step 2.   Click the WLC or click **Add** to create a new object.

Step 3.   Ensure that the NDGs are assigned properly and the TACACS+ shared secret is configured correctly. Figure 30-3 shows the NAD settings.

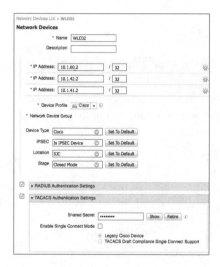

Figure 30-3   *WLC Network Device Object*

Prepare the Policy Results

Device administration AAA is ready on ISE, but you have no policies and no authorizations to send down to the WLC yet. Now you're going to add one TACACS profile for each role that you plan to use with the WLC.

Following suit with Chapter 29, you will create three different roles for the WLC: NetAdmin, SecAdmin, and Helpdesk. Finally, you will create a LobbyAmbassador result to apply for any other employee who attempts to log in.

Navigate to **Work Centers > Device Administration > Policy Elements > Results > TACACS Profiles.** Notice the predefined TACACS profiles, WLC ALL and WLC MONITOR, as shown in Figure 30-4.

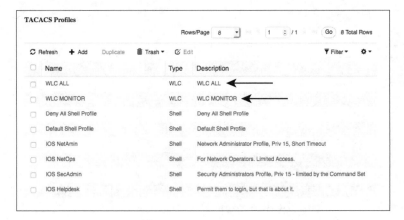

Figure 30-4 *Predefined TACACS Profiles for the WLC*

Create the NetAdmin Profile

To create the NetAdmin profile, from the TACACS Profiles screen:

Step 1.   Click **Add**.

Step 2.   Name the profile **WLC NetAdmin**.

It is always best to prefix the profile name on the device that will use it, such as WLC *[role type]*. That makes it easy to know which result is for the WLC and which result is for IOS devices.

Step 3.   From the Common Task Type drop-down list, choose **WLC**.

Notice the UI changes to one that aligns with the UI of the WLC menu structure. You have a choice to select from the three special roles (All, Monitor, Lobby) or to select the individual menus. Thank you Doug Gash for this very cool UI enhancement, making the experience of configuring the WLC TACACS profiles intuitive to anyone who is familiar with the WLC!

Step 4.   Click the **All** radio button.

Notice in Figure 30-5 the text "The configured options give a mgmtRole Debug value of: **0xfffffffff8**." This is calling out a mngtRole field that will appear in debug logs on the WLC, to help you troubleshoot if and when the time arises. Again, this is another wonderful user experience that we can thank Doug Gash for thinking of.

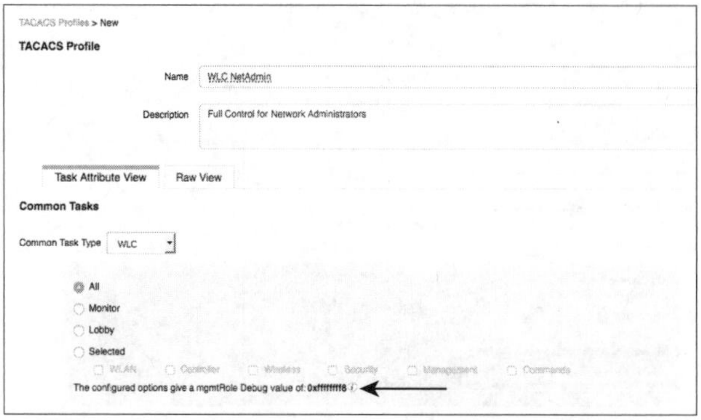

Figure 30-5   *Completed NetAdmin TACACS Profile*

Step 5.   Click **Submit**.

Figure 30-5 shows the completed WLC NetAdmin profile.

Create the SecAdmin Profile

From the TACACS Profiles screen, create the profile for the SecAdmin users:

Step 1.   Click **Add**.

Step 2.   Name the profile **WLC SecAdmin**.

Step 3.   From the Common Task Type drop-down list, choose **WLC**.

Step 4.   Click the **Selected** radio button and check the **WLAN** check box.

Step 5.   Check the **Security** check box.

Step 6.   Click **Submit**.

Figure 30-6 shows the completed WLC SecAdmin profile.

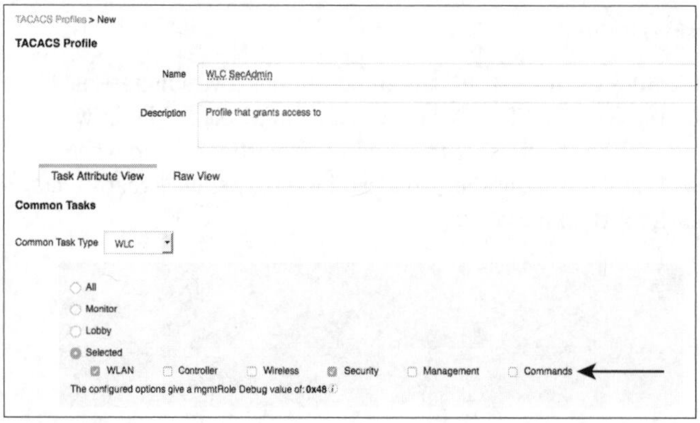

Figure 30-6   *Completed SecAdmin TACACS Profile*

Create the Helpdesk Profile

From the TACACS Profiles screen, create the profile for the helpdesk users:

Step 1.   Click **Add**.

Step 2.   Name the profile **WLC Helpdesk**.

Step 3.   From the Common Task Type drop-down list, choose **WLC**.

Step 4.   Click the **Monitor** radio button.

Step 5.   Click **Submit**.

Figure 30-7 shows the completed WLC Helpdesk profile.

Figure 30-7   *Completed Helpdesk TACACS Profile*

Create the Employee Profile

The last profile to create is for the rest of the employees. From the TACACS Profiles screen:

Step 1.   Click **Add**.

Step 2.   Name the profile **WLC Employees**.

Step 3.   From the Common Task Type drop-down list, choose **WLC**.

Step 4.   Click the **Lobby** radio button.

Step 5.   Click **Submit**.

Figure 30-8 shows the completed WLC Employees profile.

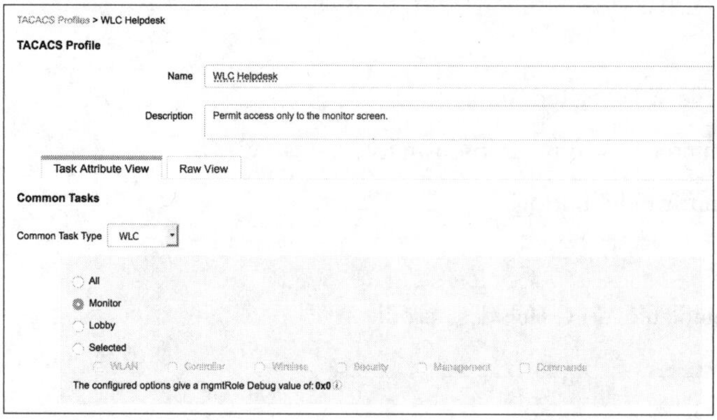

Figure 30-8 *Completed Employees TACACS Profile*

Configure the Policy Set

Now that you have all the role types that you need, it's time to configure the device administration policy set for the WLCs.

Add the authorization rule for network administrators:

Step 1. Navigate to **Work Centers > Device Administration > Device Admin Policy Sets.**

Step 2. Click the previously created **Wireless Controllers** policy set.

Step 3. Insert a new authorization rule above the Tacacs_Default rule.

Step 4. Name the rule **NetAdmin WLC.**

Step 5. Set the condition to be an external group from AD, like you see in Figure 30-9.

Step 6. There are no command sets for the WLC, so you can ignore that option.

Step 7. For the shell profile, select **WLC NetAdmin.**

Step 8. Click **Done.**

Step 9. Click **Save.**

Figure 30-9 shows the completed NetAdmin WLC authorization rule.

▼ Authorization Policy

▶ Exceptions (0)

Standard

	Status	Rule Name		Conditions (identity groups and other conditions)		Command Sets	Shell Profiles
	☑	NetAdmin WLC	if	AD-SecurityDemo:ExternalGroups EQUALS securitydemo.net/Users/NetAdmins	then	*Select Profile(s)*	WLC NetAdmin
	☑	Tacacs_Default	if no matches, then			*Select Profile(s)*	Deny All Shell Profile

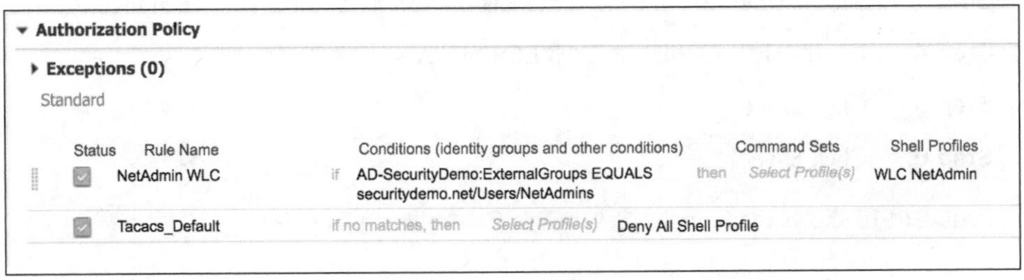

Figure 30-9 *NetAdmin WLC Authorization Rule*

Add the authorization rule for the security administrators:

Step 1. Insert a rule above the Tacacs_Default rule.

Step 2. Name the rule **SecAdmin WLC.**

Step 3. Set the condition to be an external group from AD, like you see in Figure 30-10.

Step 4. For the shell profile, select **WLC SecAdmin.**

Add the authorization rule for the helpdesk:

Step 1. Insert a rule above the Tacacs_Default rule.

Step 2. Name the rule **Helpdesk WLC.**

Step 3. Set the condition to be an external group from AD, like you see in Figure 30-10.

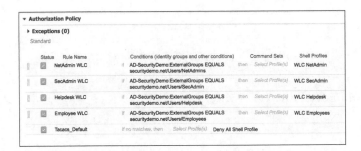

Figure 30-10 *Complete Wireless Controllers Policy Set*

Step 4. For the shell profile, select **WLC Helpdesk.**

Add the authorization rule for the rest of the employees to get LobbyAmbassador access:

Step 1. Insert a rule above the Tacacs_Default rule.

Step 2.   Name the rule **Employees WLC.**

Step 3.   Set the condition to be an external group from AD, like you see in Figure 30-10.

Step 4.   For the shell profile, select **WLC Employees.**

Step 5.   Click **Done.**

Step 6.   Click **Save.**

Figure 30-10 shows the completed Wireless Controllers policy set.

Adding ISE to the WLC TACACS+ Servers

Now that the policy set is ready, it's time to start configuring the WLC to authenticate and authorize interactive users. ISE needs to be added to the WLC as a TACACS+ Authentication Server, an Authorization Server, and an Accounting Server.

Configure the TACACS+ servers from the WLC GUI as follows:

Step 1.   Navigate to **Security > AAA > TACACS+ > Authentication.**

Step 2.   Click **New.**

Step 3.   Complete the Server IP Address and Shared Secret/Confirm Shared Secret text boxes, as shown in Figure 30-11.

Figure 30-11   *Authentication Server Entry*

Step 4.   Click **Apply.**

Step 5.   Navigate to **Security > AAA > TACACS+ > Accounting.**

Step 6.   Click **New.**

Step 7.   Complete the Server IP Address and Shared Secret/Confirm Shared Secret text boxes, as shown in Figure 30-12.

Figure 30-12 *Accounting Server Entry*

Step 8.   Click **Apply**.

Step 9.   Navigate to **Security > AAA > TACACS+ > Authorization**.

Step 10.   Click **New**.

Step 11.   Complete the Server IP Address and Shared Secret/Confirm Shared Secret text boxes, as shown in Figure 30-13.

Figure 30-13 *Authorization Server Entry*

Step 12.   Click **Apply**.

Repeat this process for each of the ISE PSNs running TACACS+.

Now that you have added the ISE PSN(s) to the WLC for use with TACACS+, built the authorization policy, and the defined the TACACS+ servers in the WLC, the next step is to configure the WLC to use TACACS+ for administrative access.

Step 13.   Navigate to **Security > Priority Order > Management User**.

Step 14.   Ensure that TACACS+ is at the top of the Order Used for Authentication list, as shown in Figure 30-14.

Figure 30-14 *Management Order*

Step 15. Click **Apply**.

By putting TACACS+ at the top of the list, and leaving LOCAL below it, you are providing yourself with a failsafe mechanism. The WLC will use the local accounts (such as the built-in admin account) in the case that the TACACS+ servers are not reachable.

The WLC is now configured to use TACACS+ for its logins. Let's test it.

Testing and Troubleshooting

It should be very easy to test the logins from the WLC—just try to log in from a browser.

Step 1. Log in as **admin**.

Figure 30-15 shows an attempted login using the same admin account that was used to configure the WLC up to this point.

Figure 30-15 *Logging In to the WLC*

The authentication fails. So, where do you look first to identify why an authentication has failed? That's right, the TACACS Live Log.

Step 2.   Navigate to **Work Centers > Device Administration > Overview > TACACS Live Log**.

Figure 30-16 shows the failed admin login.

Figure 30-16   *TACACS Live Log: Failed admin Login*

Click the icon under Details to view the authentication details report, which explains the failure reason as **22056 Subject not found in the applicable identity store(s)**, as shown in Figure 30-17.

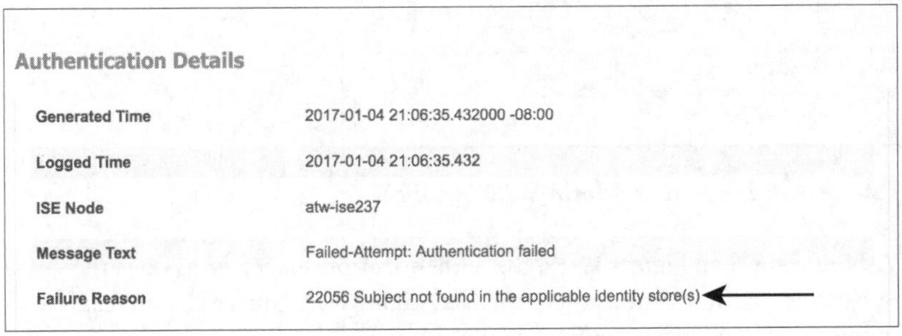

Authentication Details	
Generated Time	2017-01-04 21:06:35.432000 -08:00
Logged Time	2017-01-04 21:06:35.432
ISE Node	atw-ise237
Message Text	Failed-Attempt: Authentication failed
Failure Reason	22056 Subject not found in the applicable identity store(s) ◄────

Figure 30-17   *Failure Reason*

This makes sense. ISE is configured to check with the backend identity stores, such as its own internal user database and Active Directory. The admin account is a local account that only exists on the WLC. The WLC will not attempt to authenticate local accounts while the TACACS+ server responds.

Step 3.   Log in again, but this time as the **NetAdmin1** user, as shown in Figure 30-18.

Figure 30-18 *Logging In as NetAdmin1*

This time the authentication succeeds.

Step 4.   Examine the Live Log, as shown in Figure 30-19.

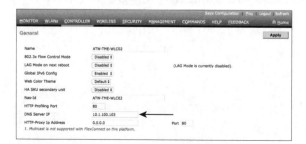

Figure 30-19 *Successful Login, NetAdmin WLC Result*

As you can see in Figure 30-19, the authentication succeeds, as does the subsequent authorization where the NetAdmin WLC authorization result is applied. Test making a configuration change.

Step 5.   Navigate to a WLC menu that the other roles do not have access to, such as **CONTROLLER**.

Step 6.   Make a change to that configuration page, such as adding a DNS server, like what you see in Figure 30-20.

Figure 30-20 *Controller > General Settings*

Step 7. Click **Apply**.

Step 8. Click **Save Configuration**.

As you can see in Figure 30-21, the change is applied successfully, and the configuration is saved successfully.

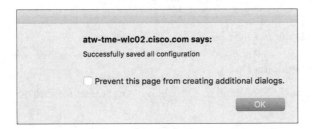

atw-tme-wlc02.cisco.com says:

Successfully saved all configuration

☐ Prevent this page from creating additional dialogs.

OK

Figure 30-21 *Successful Configuration Save*

Step 9. SSH into the WLC.

Step 10. Log in as **admin**, and it will fail.

Step 11. Log in as **NetAdmin1**, and it will succeed.

Now you can see that the CLI is being controlled by the same RBAC as the GUI. Figure 30-22 shows the login attempts from the CLI.

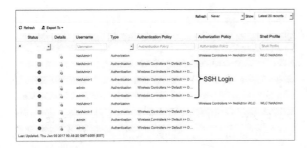

Figure 30-22 *CLI Login Attempts in Live Log*

Step 12. In the WLC CLI, type **debug aaa tacacs enable**.

Step 13. Log out of the GUI.

Step 14. Log in to the GUI as **SecAdmin1**.

The login as SecAdmin1 succeeds. Figure 30-23 shows the success and the assigned SecAdmin WLC profile in Live Log. Additionally, in the CLI there is a tremendous amount of debug activity happening. One of the messages in the debug reads **User has the following mgmtRole 48**. That number matches the value shown in the ISE GUI for the SecAdmin WLC TACACS profile.

Figure 30-23   *SecAdmin1 Login Shown in Live Log*

Test by making a configuration change.

Step 15.   Navigate to a menu that the SecAdmin role should not have access to, such as **CONTROLLER**.

Step 16.   Make a change to that configuration page, such as adding a DNS server. The change is accepted.

Step 17.   Click **Apply**.

As you can see in Figure 30-24, the user's attempt to apply the change fails due to insufficient privileges.

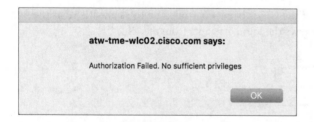

Figure 30-24   *Authorization Failed*

This is more proof of how RBAC works with the WLC. The menus are available to everyone, but only authorized changes will be applied.

Step 18.   Navigate to a menu that the SecAdmin role does have access to, such as **SECURITY**.

Step 19.   Make a change to that configuration page, such as adding a new ACL. The change is accepted.

Step 20.   Click **Apply**.

Step 21.   Click **Save Configuration**.

The change is applied successfully, and the configuration is saved successfully.

Step 22.   Log out of the GUI.

Step 23.   Log in to the GUI as **Helpdesk1**.

Step 24. The login as Helpdesk1 succeeds.

All of the UI pages are available, but no changes will be applied. The Helpdesk users are assigned the MONITOR role, which is basically equivalent to "read everything, write nothing."

Step 25. Log out of the GUI.

Step 26. Log in to the GUI as **Employee1**.

Step 27. The login as Employee1 succeeds.

As you see in Figure 30-25, it's a different GUI. The LOBBY role that is assigned to any employee not matching one of the more specific groups in the configuration provides access to a guest management user interface only.

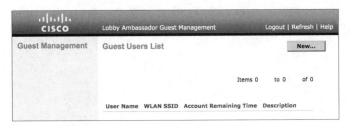

Figure 30-25 *Lobby Ambassador UI*

Summary

In this chapter you saw how a Cisco Wireless LAN Controller is designed to handle role-based access control (RBAC) with device administration AAA. Unlike Cisco IOS-based systems, which provide granular command-level controls, the WLC provides a more broad-stroke role-based approach.

The roles are tied to top-level menu items. While most users will see all menu items and configuration pages, they cannot apply changes in any page where they are not authorized by their role.

ISE has a very easy-to-use WLC-specific shell profile, which is even organized just like the actual WLC user interface to make things even easier.

The next chapter looks at another role-based device administration model with the Nexus NX-OS platforms.

Chapter 31

Configuring Device Admin AAA with Cisco Nexus Switches

This chapter covers the following topics:

■ Overview of NX-OS device admin AAA

■ Configuring ISE and the Nexus switch for device admin AAA

In Chapter 29, "Configuring Device Admin AAA with Cisco IOS," you focused on a network device that has very granular control all the way down to individual commands. In Chapter 30, "Configuring Device Admin AAA with Cisco WLC," you saw how the WLC provides a broad-level approach to role-based access control by controlling access at a menu level.

The NX-OS provides a combination of the granular command-level approach and the easier-to-use role-based approach.

Overview of NX-OS Device Admin AAA

The Cisco NX-OS software leverages user roles. Each role contains one or more rules, and each user can have more than one role. The roles are additive in nature, to allow this.

NX-OS provides two default user roles:

■ **network-admin (superuser):** Full read/write access to entire switch

■ **network-operator:** Complete read access to entire switch

Additionally, for the NX-OS platforms that support virtual device contexts (VDC), there are two more default user roles:

■ **vdc-admin (superuser):** Full access to the management VDC that is used to create individual VDCs

■ **vdc-operator:** Read-only access to the management VDC

NX-OS also provides built-in roles for each of the privilege levels, but assigns all the features and commands to Priv-1 and Priv-15, to behave similarly to IOS.

A role is made up of rules, which are the most basic element of the role. They state which operation the user role is allowed to perform. Each rule has parameters:

- **Command:** Command or group of commands defined with regular expressions (regex)

- **Feature:** Commands that apply to a function of the NX-OS switch (**show role feature** command)

- **Feature group:** Default or user-defined group of features (**show role feature-group** command)

For the purposes of this chapter, we will stick with the built-in network-admin and network-operator roles.

Configuring ISE and the Nexus for Device Admin AAA

The requisite steps for configuring device administration AAA are very similar regardless of what the actual network device is. You perform some configuration on ISE, to ensure ISE is ready to receive the TACACS+ requests from the network access device (NAD), and then you configure the NAD to send those TACACS+ requests to ISE.

Preparing ISE for Nexus Device Admin AAA

Before configuring the Nexus switch, you should ensure that the AAA server (ISE) is ready for the incoming TACACS+ requests. If the network device is configured to authenticate users before granting them access to the IOS shell, and the AAA server is not responding with an authorization, you could create an accidental denial of service (DoS) incident.

You need to prepare the TACACS profiles that will be used as authorization results. There are no command sets needed with NX-OS. You also need to ensure that the Network Device object in ISE is configured for TACACS and is in the correct Network Device Groups (NDG).

Prepare the Network Device

Ensure the Nexus switch has a Network Device object in ISE with the TACACS+ shared secret configured. From the ISE GUI:

Step 1.   Navigate to **Work Centers > Device Administration > Network Resources > Network Devices.**

Step 2.   Click the Nexus or click **Add** to create a new object.

Step 3.   Ensure that the NDGs are assigned properly and the TACACS+ shared secret is configured correctly. Figure 31-1 shows the NAD settings.

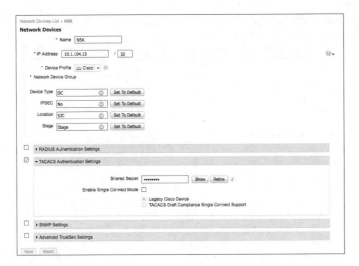

Figure 31-1 *Nexus Network Device Object*

Prepare the Policy Results

For the purposes of this chapter, we will design the policies to support the following groups of people who each require command-line access to the organization's Nexus switches:

- **NetAdmin:** Network administrators who receive full read-write access to the switch.

- **NetOps:** Network operators who receive read-only access to the switch.

- **SecAdmin:** Security administrators who receive read-only access to the switch.

- **Helpdesk:** Personnel who receive read-only access to the switch.

In this section, you will create a TACACS profile for each of the four role types. It is best to preface each result object with its type: IOS for the Catalyst switches, WLC for the wireless controllers, and NXOS for the Nexus switches. This will help you greatly when creating policies and will ensure that you don't get confused when building the policies later.

Create the NetAdmin Profile

The steps to create the NetAdmin profile are as follows:

Step 1.   Navigate to **Work Centers > Device Administration > Policy Elements > Results > TACACS Profiles**.

Step 2.   Click **Add**.

Step 3.   Name the profile **NXOS NetAdmin**.

Step 4.   From the Common Task Type drop-down list, choose **Nexus**.

The UI immediately changes to allow you to configure the Network role and VDC role directly, as shown in Figure 31-2.

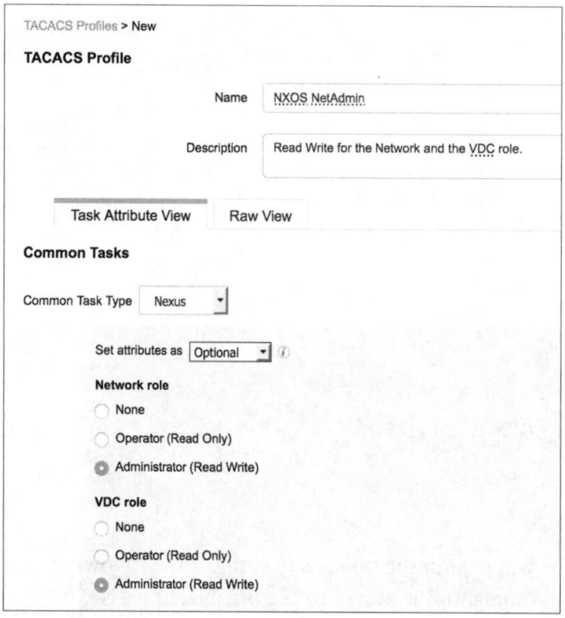

Figure 31-2   *NXOS NetAdmin TACACS Profile*

Step 5.   Set the Network role to **Administrator (Read Write)**.

Step 6.   Set the VDC role to **Administrator (Read Write)**.

Step 7.   Click **Submit**.

Figure 31-2 shows the final configuration of the TACACS profile.

Create the NetOps Profile

The steps to create the NetOps profile are as follows:

Step 1.   Navigate to **Work Centers > Device Administration > Policy Elements > Results > TACACS Profiles**.

Step 2.   Click **Add**.

Step 3.   Name the profile **NXOS NetOps**.

Step 4.   From the Common Task Type drop-down list, choose **Nexus**.

Step 5.   Set the Network role to **Operator (Read Only)**.

Step 6.   Set the VDC role to **Operator (Read Only)**.

Step 7.   Click **Submit**.

Figure 31-3 shows the final configuration of the TACACS profile.

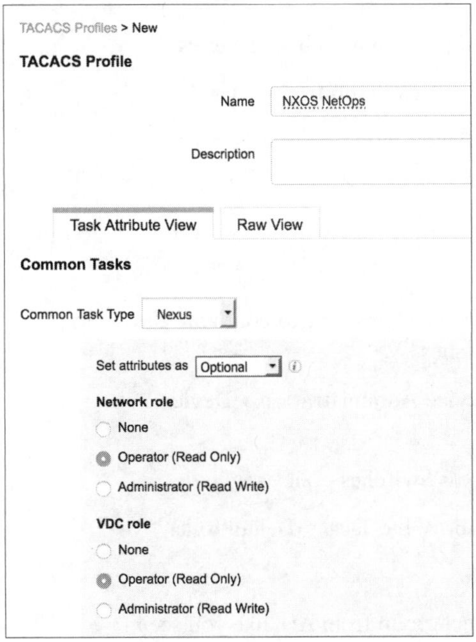

TACACS Profiles > New
TACACS Profile

Name: NXOS NetOps

Description:

Task Attribute View   Raw View

Common Tasks

Common Task Type: Nexus

Set attributes as: Optional

Network role
- None
- Operator (Read Only)
- Administrator (Read Write)

VDC role
- None
- Operator (Read Only)
- Administrator (Read Write)

Figure 31-3   *NXOS NetOps TACACS Profile*

Create the SecAdmin Profile

The steps to create the SecAdmin profile are as follows:

Step 1. Navigate to **Work Centers > Device Administration > Policy Elements > Results > TACACS Profiles.**

Step 2. Click **Add.**

Step 3. Name the profile **NXOS SecAdmin.**

Step 4. From the Common Task Type drop-down list, choose **Nexus.**

Step 5. Set the Network role to **Operator (Read Only).**

Step 6. Set the VDC role to **Operator (Read Only).**

Step 7. Click **Submit.**

Create the Helpdesk Profile

The steps to create the Helpdesk profile are as follows:

Step 1. Navigate to **Work Centers > Device Administration > Policy Elements > Results > TACACS Profiles.**

Step 2.   Click **Add.**

Step 3.   Name the profile **NXOS SecAdmin.**

Step 4.   From the Common Task Type drop-down list, choose **Nexus.**

Step 5.   Set the Network role to **Operator (Read Only).**

Step 6.   Set the VDC role to **Operator (Read Only).**

Step 7.   Click **Submit.**

Configure the Policy Set

Now that you have all the role types that you need, it's time to configure the device administration policy set for the Nexus switches.

Step 1.   Navigate to **Work Centers > Device Administration > Device Admin Policy Sets.**

Step 2.   Click the previously created **Nexus Switches** policy set.

Step 3.   Insert a new authorization rule above the Tacacs_Default rule.

Step 4.   Name the rule **NetAdmin NXOS.**

Step 5.   Set the condition to be an external group from AD, like you see in Figure 31-4.

Step 6.   There are no command sets for the NXOS device, so you can ignore that option.

Step 7.   For the shell profile, select **NXOS NetAdmin.**

Step 8.   Click **Done.**

Step 9.   Click **Save.**

Figure 31-4 shows the completed NetAdmin NXOS authorization rule.

Figure 31-4   *NetAdmin NXOS Authorization Rule*

Add the authorization rule for the network operators:

Step 1.   Insert a rule above the Tacacs_Default rule.

Step 2.   Name the rule **NetOps NXOS.**

Step 3.   Set the condition to be an external group from AD, like you see in Figure 31-5.

Step 4.   For the shell profile, select **NXOS NetOps.**

Add the authorization rule for the security administrators:

Step 1.   Insert a rule above the Tacacs_Default rule.

Step 2.   Name the rule **SecAdmin NXOS.**

Step 3.   Set the condition to be an external group from AD, like you see in Figure 31-5.

Step 4.   For the shell profile, select **NXOS SecAdmin.**

Add the authorization rule for the helpdesk personnel:

Step 1.   Insert a rule above the Tacacs_Default rule.

Step 2.   Name the rule **Helpdesk NXOS.**

Step 3.   Set the condition to be an external group from AD, like you see in Figure 31-5.

Step 4.   For the shell profile, select **NXOS Helpdesk.**

Step 5.   Click **Done.**

Step 6.   Click **Save.**

Figure 31-5 shows the completed Nexus Switches policy set.

Figure 31-5   *Complete Nexus Switches Policy Set*

Preparing the Nexus Switch for TACACS+ with ISE

Now that the policy set is ready, it's time to start configuring the Nexus switch to authenticate and authorize interactive users. You need to add ISE to the Nexus switch as a TACACS+ Authentication Server, configure a shared secret, and add the authentication method.

Enable TACACS+ and Add ISE to NX-OS

To configure the network devices to authenticate the interactive logins and authorize the commands executed in their shell, follow these steps.

Step 1. Enable TACACS+ on the switch.

By default, the tacacs+ feature of the Nexus switch is disabled. Enable TACACS+ with the **feature** command:

```
n5k(config)# feature tacacs+
```

Step 2. Define the TACACS+ AAA servers in the configuration:

```
n5k(config)# tacacs-server host 10.1.100.237 key xxxxxxxx
n5k(config)# tacacs-server host 10.1.100.241 key xxxxxxxx
```

Step 3. Configure the automated tester for the TACACS servers:

```
n5k(config)# tacacs-server host 10.1.100.237 test username tacacs-test
password xxxxxxxx idle-time 5
n5k(config)# tacacs-server host 10.1.100.241 test username tacacs-test
password xxxxxxxx idle-time 5
n5k(config)# tacacs-server timeout 5
```

Step 4. Create a TACACS+ server group, named ISE-TAC+, and add the PSNs to the group:

```
n5k(config)# aaa group server tacacs+ ISE-TAC+
n5k(config-tacacs+)# server 10.1.100.237
n5k(config-tacacs+)# deadtime 5
n5k(config-tacacs+)# server 10.1.100.241
n5k(config-tacacs+)# deadtime 5
```

Step 5. Enable TACACS with the **directed-request** command:

```
n5k(config)# tacacs-server directed-request
```

Step 6. Set the AAA authentication and accounting methods to use the ISE-TAC+ group:

```
n5k(config)# aaa authentication login default group ISE-TAC+
n5k(config)# aaa accounting default group ISE-TAC+
```

Summary

There are a few ways to provide device administration AAA and role-based access control. IOS provides a very granular control all the way down to individual commands. The Cisco WLC provides a broad-level approach to role-based access control by controlling access at a menu level. The NX-OS provides a combination of the granular command-level approach and the easier-to-use role-based approach. There are two main role types out of the box: networkadmin, which gives administrators read-write access, and network-operator, which gives operators read-only access.

Sample User Community Deployment Messaging Material

This appendix provides sample messaging for you to use to inform your user population about what Identity Services Engine is, how to use it, and where to get help. This messaging is primarily tailored for the education environment but can be easily tailored for use in other environments. This appendix contains the following information and materials:

- Sample Identity Services Engine requirement change notification email

- Sample Identity Services Engine notice for a bulletin board or poster

- Sample Identity Services Engine letter to students

Feel free to modify and adapt these samples to your needs.

Sample Identity Services Engine Requirement Change Notification Email

The following email sample is meant to be sent out to the user community prior to the enforcement of a new posture assessment requirement or check in ISE. It is recommended that you first roll out all new requirements as Audit only, so that you can review the possible impact on your organization without actually causing any outage in the production environment. Then, after a set amount of time, make the new requirement Optional. The sending of this email should coincide with the implementation of the Optional requirement, to provide ample warning to the user community prior to the Mandatory enforcement date. It should then be sent again immediately prior to the requirement being made Mandatory.

To: Students and Faculty

From: ITD

Subject: NEW PC security updates required

Faculty and Students,

Starting tomorrow, September 23rd, there will be two new security requirements for all **Windows** *PCs connected to the residential network. You may see the NAC Agent prompt you to install these new security updates on your PC. Please follow the instructions given to install these updates. You have a two-week discretionary period within which to install the new updates before enforcement begins.*

In order to ensure uninterrupted network access, it is **strongly recommended** *that you install the new updates during this discretionary period. Please keep in mind that these updates can take from 5 to 30 minutes to install depending on the performance of your PC.*

Starting October 8th, *the NAC system will initiate the enforcement of the new security updates. Once enforcement begins, any PC not running the required security updates will be forced to install them before being allowed full network access.*

If you have any questions or need technical assistance, please go to the ITD ISE support page at www.univ.com/nac/support *or call the help desk at x4000.*

Sample Identity Services Engine Notice for a Bulletin Board or Poster

The following announcement can be posted on internal websites, posted on bulletin boards, or handed out as a flyer. Your implementation may differ, so please use this only as a guideline. The objectives of this announcement are as follows:

- To inform the user community that the ISE solution is in place, and to explain why
- To inform users how to employ the system
- To set expectations on its use
- To give references for obtaining more information

Connecting to the Campus Network

In an effort to reduce the threat posed by viruses and worms to the campus network, the University has implemented the Cisco Identity Services Engine network admission control solution.

Here's what students need to know:

- All students living in the residence halls will be required to go through the new network policy controls to gain access to any campus network.

- Students with Windows PCs and Mac computers are required to install the Cisco NAC Agent and Cisco AnyConnect security software. This will be delivered to you automatically through the student web portal page.

- Students are required to authenticate to the network using their campus username and password.

- The PC being used will be checked to make sure it has the necessary security software and system patches installed before being allowed onto the network.

- Any PC that does not meet the security requirements will dynamically be placed into network quarantine and provided the necessary instructions and security software. Once the PC is certified, full network access will be restored.

- The Cisco Identity Services Engine solution does NOT access your personal files, block any applications, or monitor your network traffic.

Why is Cisco Identity Services Engine necessary?

Nearly all network outages or brown-outs experienced on the campus network are the result of virus-infected or severely compromised student PCs accessing the network. As a result, it has become necessary for the University to implement a network security system in order to minimize the risk posed by students who connect infected PCs to the campus network. This security solution will keep your computers much more secure, allowing them to resist the infection of viruses that may destroy your documents or render your PC unusable.

How to obtain the Cisco NAC Agent:

1. Plug in to the campus network.

2. Open your web browser of choice. You will be redirected to the University login page.

3. Log in using your campus username and password.

4. You will be directed to install the Cisco NAC Agent and Cisco AnyConnect software.

5. Click the **Download** button and follow the installation wizard's instructions to install the software. Installation may require a reboot.

How to log in to the network:

1. Login is done using the Cisco AnyConnect Agent.

2. The agent login will happen automatically whenever your computer attempts to access the campus network.

3. If required, enter your username and password and click **Login**.

4. Follow the instructions given to remediate any failed security checks on your PC.

5. Once your PC is compliant, you will gain full network access.

Who to contact for help:

- Help desk at x4000

- www.university.com/nac/support

- Email: Support@university.com

Additional information can be found at www.university.com/nac/support.

Sample Identity Services Engine Letter to Students

The following sample letter is intended to be added to the university's student handbook, which is typically sent to students before the beginning of the new school year. The letter serves two purposes: to inform students about the ISE solution, and to instruct students on how to obtain the NAC Agent prior to arriving on campus.

Dear Student,

This letter is to inform you that the university's campus network is protected using a system called Cisco Identity Services Engine. This security solution was put in place in an effort to decrease the threat posed by viruses and worms on the university's network. The vast majority of previous network outages or slowness could be attributed directly to the outbreak of a computer virus or worm. These outbreaks also resulted in the widespread damage or loss of data on student PCs. An effective method of combating these outbreaks is to ensure that every PC connecting to the network is running an up-to-date antivirus software package and also has all of the latest Windows security patches installed. The Cisco Identity Services Engine security solution provides this capability to the University.

In order to be ready for the school year, you will need to download and install the NAC Agent on your Windows or Mac-based computer. Please make every effort to install the agent prior to arriving on campus. This will help make your arrival go that much smoother. The agent download can be found at www.university.com/agent. Just follow the instructions provided to complete the simple install. Should you have any questions or need technical assistance, please call the University help desk at 800-333-3333.

Thank you,

The ITD Staff

Sample ISE Deployment Questionnaire

This appendix provides a series of questions meant to help you determine the scope of your proposed ISE deployment. Most of this content comes from the *Cisco ISE High-level Design Guide* that is used by the Cisco ISE Certified Partners. Once you have answered the questions in each given table, you can then proceed to determine your Bill of Materials for Cisco ISE and your approximate project scope to plan for.

State Your Business Goals for ISE

Services	Wire (Yes or No)	Wireless (Yes or No)
Guest Services		
Device Profiling		
Host Posture Assessment		
TC-NAC		
BYOD		

Estimated Timelines

Phase	Number of Endpoints	Begin	End	Comments
Lab testing and qualification				
Final Design Review call with Cisco SME	—			
Production phase 1 (pilot)				
Production phase 2				
Production phase 3				

Customer Environment Summary

Deployment Summary	Response
Use cases in scope for design	
Wired?	
Wireless?	
VPN?	
Guest?	
Endpoint count	
Total endpoint count for entire deployment (endpoint count equals the sum of user and non-user devices)	
Total user endpoints (laptops, PCs, mobile devices, etc.)	
Total non-user endpoints that support 802.1X (i.e., IP phones, printers, BioMed, etc.)	
Total non-user endpoints that do not support 802.1X (i.e., IP cameras, badge readers, etc.)	
Concurrent endpoint count	
Max. number of endpoints online with ISE at any given time	
ISE is licensed based on max. concurrent online users and devices.	
Total physical locations	
How many physical buildings/locations will you protect with ISE?	
Is your deployment geographically disperse?	
How many ISE Policy Service Node locations do you anticipate?	
Total number of network infrastructure devices	
Switches	
Wireless controllers	
VPN gateways	
Wireless Access Points	
IP phones (do they support dot1x?)	
Routers	
Other	

Topology Specifics

Required Information	Response
Network Access Devices	
Provide the general switch/controller model numbers/ platforms deployed and Cisco IOS Software versions to be deployed to support ISE design.	
Client OS and Supplicant Types	
List all non-mobile client OS types and versions that will be used by non-guest users.	
Which 802.1X supplicant is used (native OS, AnyConnect NAM, other)?	
Number (general count for each type)?	
*Please provide service pack details for Windows and OS types for Mac OS X.	
Mobile Devices (smartphones, tablets)	
List all vendor types and mobile OS versions deployed by non-guest users.	
Are mobile devices corporate- or employee-owned assets?	
Will you use a mobile device management system? If so, list the details.	
802.1X Authentication	
Will you be deploying 802.1X for wired, wireless, or both?	
Will you be using machine authentication, user authentication, or both?	
What percentage of your devices will not support 802.1X?	
Extensible Authentication Protocol (EAP) Types	
EAP types for users	
EAP types for machines	
Examples:	
PEAP (Username/password-based auth.)	
EAP-TLS (Certificate-based auth.)	
EAP-FAST	

Required Information	Response
ID Stores	
[EAP and ID Store Compatibility Reference]	
List the ID store to be used by each Auth. Type:	
802.1X machine auth.	
802.1X user auth.	
802.1X cert-based auth.	
MAB	
Web Authentication/Guests	
For Active Directory:	
Are there multiple domains?	
Are there multiple forests?	
Authorization	
Which enforcement types will be used? List wired/wireless.	
VLANs	
Downloadable ACLs	
Security Group Tags (SGTs/SGACLs)	
SmartPort macros	
Posture	
Will you be using host posture assessment?	
If so, which operating systems are in scope?	
Profiling	
List the primary device types to be profiled.	
Which probes will be deployed to collect the required data?	
If RSPAN or NetFlow is to be used, is there sufficient bandwidth between source SPAN/NetFlow exporter and ISE Policy Service Node used for profiling?	
Is profiling for visibility only or for use in Authorization Policy?	
ISE Nodes/Personas	
Will high availability be deployed for ISE?	
Number and type of each ISE appliance (node).	
Define the personas assigned to each node (e.g., Administration, Monitoring, Policy Service, Inline Posture).	

Sample Switch Configurations

This appendix includes some full sample configurations of various device types with multiple Cisco IOS versions, all designed to follow the guidelines and practices laid out in Chapter 11, "Bootstrapping Network Access Devices."

Catalyst 3000 Series, 12.2(55)SE

```
3560-X# sho run
Building configuration...
Current configuration : 22928 bytes
!
version 12.2
hostname 3560-X
logging monitor informational
username radius-test password 0 Cisco123
!
aaa new-model
!
!
aaa authentication dot1x default group radius
aaa authorization network default group radius
aaa accounting dot1x default start-stop group radius
!
!
aaa server radius dynamic-author
client 10.1.103.231 server-key Cisco123
client 10.1.103.4 server-key Cisco123
!
aaa session-id common
authentication mac-move permit
```

```
ip routing
!
ip domain-name cts.local
ip name-server 10.1.100.100
ip device tracking
!
!
crypto pki trustpoint TP-self-signed-4076357888
enrollment selfsigned
subject-name cn=IOS-Self-Signed-Certificate-4076357888
revocation-check none
rsakeypair TP-self-signed-4076357888
!
!
crypto pki certificate chain TP-self-signed-4076357888
certificate self-signed 01
quit
!
dot1x system-auth-control
!
interface Loopback0
ip address 192.168.254.60 255.255.255.255
!
interface <ALL EDGE PORTS>
switchport access vlan 41
switchport mode access
switchport voice vlan 99
ip access-group ACL-ALLOW in
authentication event fail action next-method
authentication event server dead action authorize vlan 41
authentication event server dead action authorize voice
authentication event server alive action reinitialize
authentication host-mode multi-auth
authentication open
authentication order dot1x mab
authentication priority dot1x mab
authentication port-control auto
authentication violation restrict
mab
dot1x pae authenticator
dot1x timeout tx-period 10
spanning-tree portfast
!
interface Vlan1
```

```
no ip address
!
interface Vlan40
ip address 10.1.40.60 255.255.255.0
!
!
ip http server
ip http secure-server
!
ip access-list extended ACL-AGENT-REDIRECT
remark explicitly prevent DNS from being redirected to address a bug
deny udp any any eq domain
remark redirect HTTP traffic only
permit tcp any any eq www
remark all other traffic will be implicitly denied from the redirection
ip access-list extended ACL-ALLOW
permit ip any any
ip access-list extended ACL-DEFAULT
remark DHCP
permit udp any eq bootpc any eq bootps
remark DNS
permit udp any any eq domain
remark Ping
permit icmp any any
remark PXE / TFTP
permit udp any any eq tftp
remark Drop all the rest
deny ip any any log
ip access-list extended ACL-WEBAUTH-REDIRECT
remark explicitly prevent DNS from being redirected to accommodate
certain switches
deny udp any any eq domain
remark redirect all applicable traffic to the ISE Server
permit tcp any any eq www
permit tcp any any eq 443
remark all other traffic will be implicitly denied from the redirection
!
ip radius source-interface Loopback0
logging origin-id ip
logging source-interface Loopback0
logging host 10.1.103.4 transport udp port 20514
!
snmp-server community CiscoPressRO RO
snmp-server trap-source Loopback0
snmp-server source-interface informs Loopback0
```

```
snmp-server host 10.1.103.231 version 2c CiscoPressRO
radius-server attribute 6 on-for-login-auth
radius-server attribute 8 include-in-access-req
radius-server attribute 25 access-request include
radius-server dead-criteria time 5 tries 3
radius-server host 10.1.103.231 auth-port 1812 acct-port 1813 key Cisco123
radius-server host 10.1.103.4 auth-port 1812 acct-port 1813 key Cisco123
radius-server vsa send accounting
radius-server vsa send authentication
!
end
```

Catalyst 3000 Series, 15.0(2)SE

```
C3750X# sho run brief

Building configuration...

Current configuration : 18936 bytes
!
version 15.0
no service pad
service timestamps debug datetime msec
service timestamps log datetime msec
no service password-encryption
!
hostname C3750X
!
boot-start-marker
boot-end-marker
!
logging monitor informational
!
username radius-test password 0 Cisco123
aaa new-model
!
!
aaa authentication dot1x default group radius
aaa authorization network default group radius
aaa accounting dot1x default start-stop group radius
!
!
aaa server radius dynamic-author
client 10.1.103.231 server-key Cisco123
```

```
client 10.1.103.4 server-key Cisco123
!
aaa session-id common
clock timezone EDT -1 0
authentication mac-move permit
ip routing
!
!
ip dhcp snooping vlan 10-13
ip dhcp snooping
ip domain-name cts.local
ip device tracking
!
!
device-sensor filter-list cdp list my_cdp_list
tlv name device-name
tlv name platform-type
!
device-sensor filter-list lldp list my_lldp_list
tlv name port-id
tlv name system-name
tlv name system-description
!
device-sensor filter-list dhcp list my_dhcp_list
option name host-name
option name class-identifier
option name client-identifier
device-sensor filter-spec dhcp include list my_dhcp_list
device-sensor filter-spec lldp include list my_lldp_list
device-sensor filter-spec cdp include list my_cdp_list
device-sensor accounting
device-sensor notify all-changes
!
epm logging
!
crypto pki trustpoint TP-self-signed-254914560
enrollment selfsigned
subject-name cn=IOS-Self-Signed-Certificate-254914560
revocation-check none
rsakeypair TP-self-signed-254914560
!
!
crypto pki certificate chain TP-self-signed-254914560
certificate self-signed 01
cts role-based enforcement
```

```
!
dot1x system-auth-control
!
interface Loopback0
ip address 192.168.254.1 255.255.255.255
!
interface <ALL EDGE PORTS>
switchport access vlan 10
switchport mode access
switchport voice vlan 99
ip access-group ACL-ALLOW in
authentication event fail action next-method
authentication event server dead action authorize vlan 10
authentication event server dead action authorize voice
authentication event server alive action reinitialize
authentication host-mode multi-auth
authentication open
authentication order dot1x mab
authentication priority dot1x mab
authentication port-control auto
authentication violation restrict
mab
dot1x pae authenticator
dot1x timeout tx-period 10
spanning-tree portfast
ip dhcp snooping information option allow-untrusted
!
!
interface Vlan1
no ip address
shutdown
!
interface Vlan10
ip address 10.1.10.1 255.255.255.0
!
interface Vlan20
ip address 10.1.20.1 255.255.255.0
!
interface Vlan30
ip address 10.1.30.1 255.255.255.0
!
interface Vlan99
ip address 10.1.99.1 255.255.255.0
!
!
```

```
ip http server
ip http secure-server
!
!
ip access-list extended ACL-AGENT-REDIRECT
remark explicitly prevent DNS from being redirected
deny udp any any eq domain
remark redirect HTTP traffic only
permit tcp any any eq www
remark all other traffic will be implicitly denied from the redirection
ip access-list extended ACL-ALLOW
permit ip any any
ip access-list extended ACL-DEFAULT
remark DHCP
permit udp any eq bootpc any eq bootps
remark DNS
permit udp any any eq domain
remark Ping
permit icmp any any
remark PXE / TFTP
permit udp any any eq tftp
remark Drop all the rest
deny ip any any log
ip access-list extended ACL-WEBAUTH-REDIRECT
remark explicitly prevent DNS from being redirected to address
deny udp any any eq domain
remark redirect all applicable traffic to the ISE Server
permit tcp any any eq www
permit tcp any any eq 443
remark all other traffic will be implicitly denied from the redirection
ip access-list extended AGENT-REDIRECT
remark explicitly prevent DNS from being redirected to address
deny udp any any eq domain
remark redirect HTTP traffic only
permit tcp any any eq www
remark all other traffic will be implicitly denied from the redirection
!
ip radius source-interface Loopback0
ip sla enable reaction-alerts
logging origin-id ip
logging source-interface Loopback0
logging host 10.1.103.4 transport udp port 20514
!
snmp-server community Cisco123 RO
snmp-server community TrustSecRO RO
```

```
snmp-server trap-source Loopback0
snmp-server source-interface informs Loopback0
snmp-server host 10.1.103.4 version 2c Cisco123 mac-notification
!
radius-server attribute 6 on-for-login-auth
radius-server attribute 8 include-in-access-req
radius-server attribute 25 access-request include
radius-server dead-criteria time 5 tries 3
radius-server vsa send accounting
radius-server vsa send authentication
!
radius server CP-VIP
address ipv4 10.1.103.231 auth-port 1812 acct-port 1813
automate-tester username radius-test
key Cisco123
!
radius server CP-04
address ipv4 10.1.103.4 auth-port 1812 acct-port 1813
automate-tester username radius-test
key Cisco123
!
end
```

Catalyst 4500 Series, IOS-XE 3.3.0 / 15.1(1)SG

```
4503# show run brief

Building configuration...
Current configuration : 35699 bytes
!
!
version 15.1
!
hostname 4503
!
!
username radius-test password 0 Cisco123
aaa new-model
!
!
aaa authentication dot1x default group radius
aaa authorization network default group radius
aaa accounting dot1x default start-stop group radius
!
```

```
!
aaa server radius dynamic-author
client 10.1.103.231 server-key Cisco123
client 10.1.103.4 server-key Cisco123
!
aaa session-id common
clock timezone EDT -1 0
!
ip domain-name cts.local
!
ip device tracking
!
device-sensor filter-list cdp list my_cdp_list
tlv name device-name
tlv name platform-type
!
device-sensor filter-list lldp list my_lldp_list
tlv name port-id
tlv name system-name
tlv name system-description
!
device-sensor filter-list dhcp list my_dhcp_list
option name host-name
option name class-identifier
option name client-identifier
device-sensor filter-spec dhcp include list my_dhcp_list
device-sensor filter-spec lldp include list my_lldp_list
device-sensor filter-spec cdp include list my_cdp_list
device-sensor accounting
device-sensor notify all-changes
epm logging
!
!
crypto pki trustpoint CISCO_IDEVID_SUDI
revocation-check none
rsakeypair CISCO_IDEVID_SUDI
!
crypto pki trustpoint CISCO_IDEVID_SUDI0
revocation-check none
!
!
crypto pki certificate chain CISCO_IDEVID_SUDI
certificate 238FC0E90000002BFCA1
certificate ca 6A6967B3000000000003
crypto pki certificate chain CISCO_IDEVID_SUDI0
```

```
certificate ca 5FF87B282B54DC8D42A315B568C9ADFF
!
dot1x system-auth-control
!
!
vlan 40
name jump
!
vlan 41
name data
!
vlan 99
name voice
!
interface <ALL EDGE PORTS>
switchport access vlan 41
switchport mode access
switchport voice vlan 99
ip access-group ACL-ALLOW in
authentication event fail action next-method
authentication event server dead action authorize vlan 41
authentication event server dead action authorize voice
authentication event server alive action reinitialize
authentication host-mode multi-auth
authentication open
authentication order dot1x mab
authentication priority dot1x mab
authentication port-control auto
authentication violation restrict
mab
dot1x pae authenticator
dot1x timeout tx-period 10
spanning-tree portfast
ip dhcp snooping information option allow-untrusted
!
interface Vlan1
no ip address
!
interface Vlan40
ip address 10.1.40.2 255.255.255.0
!
ip http server
ip http secure-server
ip route 0.0.0.0 0.0.0.0 10.1.40.1
```

```
!
ip access-list extended ACL-AGENT-REDIRECT
remark explicitly prevent DNS from being redirected to address
deny udp any any eq domain
remark redirect HTTP traffic only
permit tcp any any eq www
remark all other traffic will be implicitly denied from the redirection
ip access-list extended ACL-ALLOW
permit ip any any
ip access-list extended ACL-DEFAULT
remark DHCP
permit udp any eq bootpc any eq bootps
remark DNS
permit udp any any eq domain
remark Ping
permit icmp any any
remark PXE / TFTP
permit udp any any eq tftp
remark Drop all the rest
deny ip any any log
ip access-list extended ACL-WEBAUTH-REDIRECT
remark explicitly prevent DNS from being redirected to address
deny udp any any eq domain
remark redirect all applicable traffic to the ISE Server
permit tcp any any eq www
permit tcp any any eq 443
remark all other traffic will be implicitly denied from the redirection
!
logging 10.1.103.4
!
snmp-server community Cisco123 RO
radius-server attribute 6 on-for-login-auth
radius-server attribute 8 include-in-access-req
radius-server attribute 25 access-request include
radius-server dead-criteria time 5 tries 3
radius-server host 10.1.103.231 auth-port 1812 acct-port 1813 test username radi-
ustest
key Cisco123
radius-server host 10.1.103.4 auth-port 1812 acct-port 1813 test username radiust-
est
key Cisco123
radius-server vsa send accounting
radius-server vsa send authentication
!
end
```

Catalyst 6500 Series, 12.2(33)SXJ

```
hostname 6503
logging monitor informational
username radius-test password 0 Cisco123
!
aaa new-model
!
!
aaa authentication dot1x default group radius
aaa authorization network default group radius
aaa accounting dot1x default start-stop group radius
!
!
aaa server radius dynamic-author
client 10.1.103.231 server-key Cisco123
client 10.1.103.4 server-key Cisco123
!
aaa session-id common
authentication mac-move permit
ip routing
!
ip domain-name cts.local
ip name-server 10.1.100.100
ip device tracking
!
!
crypto pki trustpoint TP-self-signed-4076357888
enrollment selfsigned
subject-name cn=IOS-Self-Signed-Certificate-4076357888
revocation-check none
rsakeypair TP-self-signed-4076357888
!
!
crypto pki certificate chain TP-self-signed-4076357888
certificate self-signed 01
quit
!
dot1x system-auth-control
!
interface Loopback0
ip address 192.168.254.1 255.255.255.255
!
interface <ALL EDGE PORTS>
switchport access vlan 10
```

```
switchport mode access
switchport voice vlan 99
ip access-group ACL-ALLOW in
authentication event fail action next-method
authentication event server dead action authorize vlan 10
authentication event server alive action reinitialize
authentication host-mode multi-auth
authentication open
authentication order dot1x mab
authentication priority dot1x mab
authentication port-control auto
authentication violation restrict
mab
dot1x pae authenticator
dot1x timeout tx-period 10
spanning-tree portfast
!
interface Vlan1
no ip address
!
interface Vlan40
ip address 10.1.40.1 255.255.255.0
!
!
ip http server
ip http secure-server
!
ip access-list extended ACL-AGENT-REDIRECT
remark explicitly prevent DNS from being redirected to address a bug
deny udp any any eq domain
remark redirect HTTP traffic only
permit tcp any any eq www
remark all other traffic will be implicitly denied from the redirection
deny ip any any
ip access-list extended ACL-ALLOW
permit ip any any
ip access-list extended ACL-DEFAULT
remark DHCP
permit udp any eq bootpc any eq bootps
remark DNS
permit udp any any eq domain
remark Ping
permit icmp any any
remark PXE / TFTP
permit udp any any eq tftp
```

```
    remark Drop all the rest
    deny ip any any log
    ip access-list extended ACL-WEBAUTH-REDIRECT
    remark explicitly prevent DNS from being redirected
    deny udp any any eq domain
    remark redirect all applicable traffic to the ISE Server
    permit tcp any any eq www
    permit tcp any any eq 443
    deny ip any any
    !
    ip radius source-interface Loopback0
    logging origin-id ip
    logging source-interface Loopback0
    logging host 10.1.103.4 transport udp port 20514
    !
    snmp-server community CiscoPressRO RO
    snmp-server trap-source Loopback0
    snmp-server source-interface informs Loopback0
    radius-server attribute 6 on-for-login-auth
    radius-server attribute 8 include-in-access-req
    radius-server attribute 25 access-request include
    radius-server dead-criteria time 5 tries 3
    radius-server host 10.1.103.231 auth-port 1812 acct-port 1813 key Cisco123
    radius-server host 10.1.103.4 auth-port 1812 acct-port 1813 key Cisco123
    radius-server vsa send accounting
    radius-server vsa send authentication
    !
    end
```

The ISE CA and How Cert-Based Auth Works

This appendix provides a primer on certificate-based authentications as described by Aaron Woland.

I find a few universal truths when mentioning certificates to IT professionals. Almost without fail, most people I speak with consider certificates and public key cryptography (PKI) to be a very secure concept. However, upon mentioning to someone that I want to talk about certificates or PKI, that person's face turns a slightly lighter shade, their eyes get a bit wider, and they have this immediate fight-or-flight instinct kick in.

This is a subject that does not have to be scary; there are just a few misunderstandings. One example of a common misunderstanding is the notion that a certificate is the same as two-factor authentication. Another common misconception is: "Since the certificate was issued by Active Directory's certificate authority, then authenticating that certificate is the same as an Active Directory authentication." I realize how and why that assumption is made. It does get awfully confusing to try to separate out Active Directory from a certificate authority (CA) when they are so tightly integrated. However, let me assure you, standard certificate-based authentication is the same regardless of which vendor has created the CA you are using.

Before moving on, a quick shout out to Max Pritkin. Max is one of the unsung heroes working behind the scenes in the standards bodies, like the IETF, to build standards around PKI and other technologies. Max is a flat-out, uncontested genius with PKI and yet can somehow still explain it in simple terms. I call him out because he has taught me so much about PKI that I can no longer remember what it was like working with PKI without the knowledge he bestowed upon me. I now transfer a portion of that wisdom to you.

Certificate-Based Authentication

Let's take some time and review how certificate-based authentications actually work. When presented with a certificate, an authentication server checks the following (at a minimum):

1. Has the digital certificate been issued (signed) by a trusted CA?

2. Is the certificate expired? This check examines both the start and end dates.

3. Has the certificate been revoked? Revocation could be identified using the Online Certificate Status Protocol (OCSP) or a certificate revocation list CRL to verify.

4. Has the client provided proof of possession?

Let's examine these four items one at a time.

Has the Digital Certificate Been Signed by a Trusted CA?

This first check is something you are most likely very familiar with, whether you know it or not. To describe it, let's focus on a hypothetical real-world situation.

Suppose you are a bartender and have to check the ID of a patron who is asking for an alcoholic beverage. That person hands you a napkin with the name Bob Smith written on it, a date of birth over 21 years ago written below the name, and has signed that napkin. Would you trust that it is a valid ID? Of course not! In the same situation, if Bob Smith hands you a state-issued driver's license, that would be much more trustworthy, right? In this hypothetical scenario, the state is the authority that signed the credential (the driver's license). A digital certificate works the same way. A trustworthy authority must sign the certificate.

The signing of the certificate has two parts. First, the certificate must be signed correctly (following the correct format, etc.). If it is not, it will be discarded immediately. Second, the signing CA's public key must be in a Trusted Certificates store, and that certificate must be trusted for purposes of authentication. Using Cisco ISE as an example, the trusted certificate needs to have the "Trust for client authentication" use case selected, as shown in Figures D-1 and D-2. Figure D-1 shows a certificate that is trusted by ISE, while Figure D-2 shows a certificate trusted on an Apple Mac device.

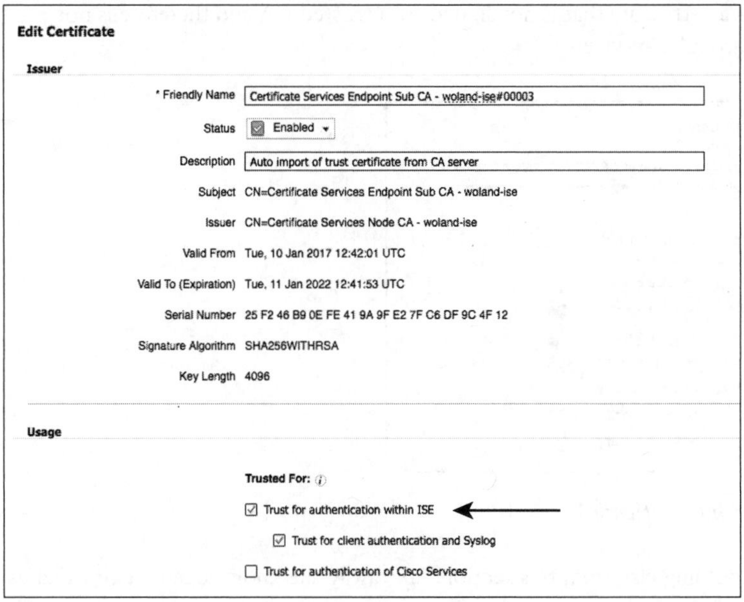

Edit Certificate

Issuer

* Friendly Name   Certificate Services Endpoint Sub CA - woland-ise#00003

Status   ☑ Enabled ▾

Description   Auto import of trust certificate from CA server

Subject   CN=Certificate Services Endpoint Sub CA - woland-ise

Issuer   CN=Certificate Services Node CA - woland-ise

Valid From   Tue, 10 Jan 2017 12:42:01 UTC

Valid To (Expiration)   Tue, 11 Jan 2022 12:41:53 UTC

Serial Number   25 F2 46 B9 0E FE 41 9A 9F E2 7F C6 DF 9C 4F 12

Signature Algorithm   SHA256WITHRSA

Key Length   4096

Usage

Trusted For: ⓘ

☑ Trust for authentication within ISE ◀——————

☑ Trust for client authentication and Syslog

☐ Trust for authentication of Cisco Services

Figure D-1   *Cisco ISE Trusting a Certificate*

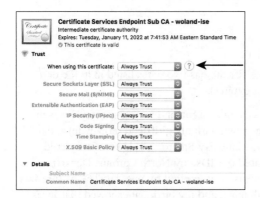

Figure D-2   *Apple Mac OS Trusting a Certificate*

So not only does ISE trust certificates that have been signed by this CA, it trusts those for a specific use-case (client authentication). If a client presents a certificate, and that certificate has not been signed by a CA that is trusted for client authentication, *the authentication will fail*. It's exactly like someone entering in the wrong password.

With the Apple example in Figure D-2, that system has even more purposes or uses to trust the certificate for, including Secure Sockets Layer (SSL), Secure Mail (S/MIME), and Extensible Authentication (EAP), among others.

Figure D-3 shows a certificate that is not signed by a trusted CA and therefore is not trusted for any particular service.

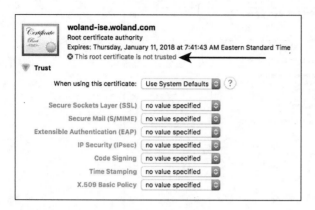

Figure D-3   *Untrusted Certificate*

If you take away nothing else from this section, take away the knowledge that certificates are signed by certificate authorities. Authenticators are configured to trust certain authorities. If the certificate is signed by a trusted certificate authority, it is considered a valid certificate, and the authenticator will proceed to the next check: has the certificate expired?

Has the Certificate Expired?

Just like a driver's license or a passport, a certificate has two dates listed in it: the date issued, and the date it is valid until (when it expires).

To relate that back to a driver's license, let's examine a fun and very true story. I was in Las Vegas for a conference. I was out on the town with my girlfriend (now wife) and a few friends and we went into the ICE bar at Mandalay Bay to sample some very cold vodka in a unique setting. When we presented our IDs, my North Carolina Department of Motor Vehicles (DMV)-issued driver's license was expired by one day. The picture was still a valid picture of me, the name was still mine, and my birth date showed that I was of legal drinking age and it was (in fact) the day after my birthday—yet I was refused service because the license expired and was therefore no longer a valid source of identity. In RADIUS terms: Access-Reject.

An authenticator does the same sort of check. Is the certificate valid for the date and time that the authentication request comes in? This is one reason why Network Time Protocol (NTP) is so important when working with certificates. Many of us have seen problems where time was out of sync. For example, a certificate was presented on January 10, 2014 at 11:11 a.m., but its "valid-from" value started on January 10, 2014 at 11:30 a.m. This discrepancy occurred because of a time sync issue that caused the CA to think it was 20 minutes later than the authentication server, and the brand-new certificate was not valid yet! This is so common you would laugh, or maybe even cry.

Notice in Figure D-4 that the certificate has a Valid From attribute and a Valid To (Expiration) attribute.

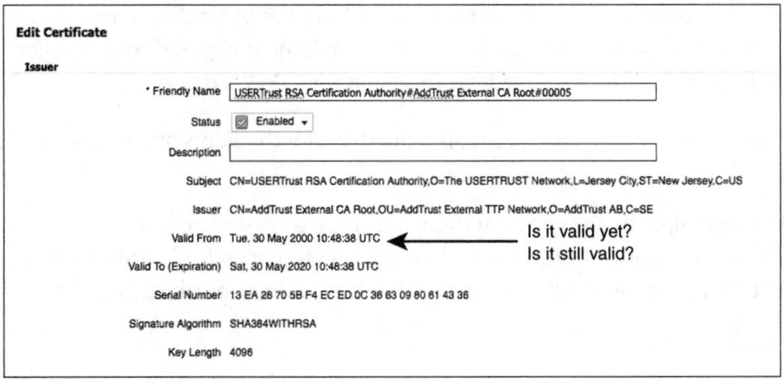

Edit Certificate

Issuer

* Friendly Name   USERTrust RSA Certification Authority#AddTrust External CA Root#00005

Status   ☑ Enabled ▾

Description

Subject   CN=USERTrust RSA Certification Authority,O=The USERTRUST Network,L=Jersey City,ST=New Jersey,C=US

Issuer   CN=AddTrust External CA Root,OU=AddTrust External TTP Network,O=AddTrust AB,C=SE

Valid From   Tue, 30 May 2000 10:48:38 UTC ◄——— Is it valid yet?
Is it still valid?

Valid To (Expiration)   Sat, 30 May 2020 10:48:38 UTC

Serial Number   13 EA 28 70 5B F4 EC ED 0C 36 63 09 80 61 43 36

Signature Algorithm   SHA384WITHRSA

Key Length   4096

Figure D-4   *Validity Period*

Has the Certificate Been Revoked?

Let's examine another hypothetical real-world situation. You are driving down the road, and are pulled over by a police officer. The officer asks for your driver's license and proof of insurance. You hand your driver's license to the officer, who immediately checks for evidence of authenticity; that is, does it look like a valid driver's license or a forgery? The officer determines that it's not fake. Check. Next, the officer inspects the expiration: it is not expired. Check. Now the officer asks you to wait while he goes back to his squad car.

While in the squad car, the officer performs some authorization checks (whether you are a registered owner of the car you are driving, etc.). Those are not important for this hypothetical situation, though. What is important is that the police officer must make sure your valid driver's license has not been revoked by the DMV. A quick lookup on the computer into the DMV records shows that your driver's license was revoked for too many unpaid speeding tickets. The cold steel of the handcuffs and the rough shove into the back seat of the squad car as you are hauled off to jail make you re-evaluate your life choices.

Certificate authentication has the same capability. No, not the handcuffs. It has the same capability to perform a lookup to verify the revocation status. Every certificate authority should also have a service to publish a list of certificates that have been revoked. There are two main ways to do this today:

- **Certificate revocation list (CRL):** This is basically a signed list that the CA publishes on a website that can be read by authentication servers. The file is periodically downloaded and stored locally on the authentication server, and when a certificate is being authenticated, the server examines the CRL to see if the client's certificate was revoked already. A CRL could be compared to the police officer having a printed list of suspended driver's licenses in his squad car.

■ **Online Certificate Status Protocol (OCSP):** This is the preferred method for revocation checks in most environments today, because it provides near-real-time updates. OCSP allows the authentication server to send a real-time request (similar to an HTTP web request) to the service running on the CA or another device to check the status of the certificate in near real time. OCSP could be compared to the police officer using the computer in the squad car to search the DMV's database.

If the certificate has been revoked, then access is denied. Enjoy the lights and sirens on the way to jail.

Figure D-5 shows an example of the configuration screen for a trusted certificate authority in Cisco ISE. You have options to configure where to check for OCSP and/or the CRL, when a certificate is signed by this particular root (or its subordinates).

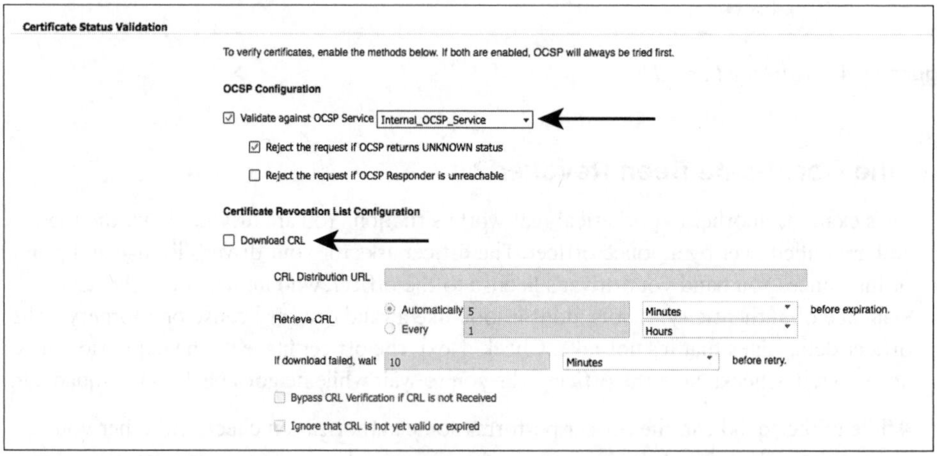

Figure D-5   *Revocation Checking Settings*

It is very important for you to understand that checking for certificate revocation is an option. When you initially trust a certificate, neither CRL nor OCSP is on by default; they require the administrator to configure the URL or the service location. It is also critical to understand what behavior will happen if the service is not available or the status of the certificate is unknown. This determines how the authentication policy will handle exceptions. It could be configured to fail-open or fail-closed.

The client's certificate itself will have a field (known as an extension) named CRL Distribution Points, which can be populated with the URI where the authentication server may locate the CRL. Figure D-6 shows an example of the CRL Distribution Points extension in a certificate and the defined URI.

Figure D-6 *CRL Distribution Points Certificate Extension*

Here is another interesting piece of trivia about managing revocation lists that may help you win a bet someday: In the earlier discussion of certificate expiration, Figure D-4 displayed the Valid From and Valid To fields in the certificate. These fields form the *validity period*, the time range during which the signing CA will warrant that it will maintain revocation information regarding that certificate. This helps keep CRL and OCSP lists at manageable sizes. In other words, an expired certificate should be no less valid than one that has not expired, except for the fact that the issuing CA will no longer guarantee the revocation list for that certificate. That's all.

Has the Client Provided Proof of Possession?

Proof of possession is a way for an authentication server to be sure the client truly owns the certificate and private key pair, and isn't just presenting someone else's public certificate. Returning to our scenario, you are pulled over by a police officer for speeding and you hand your driver's license to the police officer, who confirms the following:

- It is a valid driver's license, issued by a trusted root (the state DMV).

- It has not expired yet.

- The DMV has not revoked the driver's license.

All of the checks have passed, but the picture on the driver's license is of a woman with long flowing brown hair and hazel eyes, whereas you are a bald elderly man. Oops! This "valid" driver's license was not issued to you—the proof of possession has failed! Again, proceed directly to jail!

Certificate authentications do something similar. There will be some throwaway piece of data that must be encrypted and decrypted. Successfully encrypting and decrypting that data ensures that the client has both the public and private keys, and therefore it is the proof of possession. This ensures that someone did not just grab the client's public key and try to present that as being their own. If the client cannot provide proof of possession, then the authentication will fail: Access-Reject.

So, What Does Any of This Have to Do with Active Directory?

What can often confuse people with regard to AAA is the difference between authentication and authorization. They often blend so much. A certificate issued by Active Directory Certificate Services (the CA built into AD) is still just an X.509 digital certificate. It will go through all the authentication validation discussed in this appendix regardless of the fact that the CA is integrated into AD.

What is possible with certificates and Active Directory is to examine a field of the certificate and then do a separate lookup into AD based on that field during the authorization phase. For example, a certificate with a subject of Aaron is sent to the authentication server using EAP-TLS. The certificate is validated through the four functions described previously and it passed. So the authentication was successful.

Now it's time for the authorization. The RADIUS server (ISE) will take the certificate subject (Aaron) and do a lookup into AD for that username. This is where group membership and other policy conditions will be examined, and the specific authorization result will be issued.

Cisco ISE uses something called a certificate authentication profile (CAP) to examine a specific field and map it to a username for authorization. Figure D-7 shows an example CAP.

Note   Cisco ISE will also do a courtesy check to validate whether the machine or account has been disabled in AD. If the account has been disabled in AD, then the authorization will be to deny access.

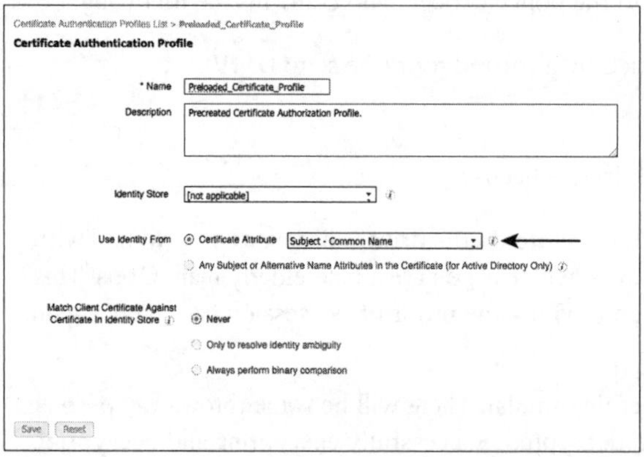

Figure D-7   *Certificate Authentication Profile (CAP)*

This is a very different process than an Active Directory authentication, which uses Kerberos, and therefore AD logs will be recorded differently. As covered in Chapter 24, there are solutions on the market that examine AD log files and use that information to help tie together usernames and IP addresses for single sign-on to web proxy servers, identity-enabled firewalls, and other services.

If the authentication was a certificate-based authentication (EAP-TLS) but the user was authorized from an AD lookup, that process will not provide the right types of logging for those identity-enabled firewalls, web proxies, and so forth.

ISE's Internal Certificate Authority

Now that you are an emergent expert on certificate-based authentication, let's review the internal CA added to ISE beginning in version 1.3.

Why Put a CA into ISE?

The first edition of this book, which covered ISE version 1.2, included an appendix covering the configuration of the Microsoft CA and another appendix for using the Cisco IOS CA. These appendixes were included because ISE did not have its own CA in version 1.2, and CAs are a key function of any complete BYOD solution. At that time, the most common CA in a BYOD deployment, and the only CA fully tested by the ISE quality assurance team, was the Microsoft enterprise CA. That presented many challenges: organizational, political, financial, and sometimes technical. One team could be controlling Active Directory while another team controlled the Microsoft CA, and the two teams (network and AD) did not necessarily communicate or collaborate well. Perhaps the organization didn't need to pay for the Enterprise version of Windows Server, yet the functionality required for that CA was only available in the Enterprise edition. (Once upon a time, I created a 54-slide step-by-step PowerPoint on configuring the Microsoft CA for use in the BYOD solution.)

So, Cisco needed to simplify the ISE BYOD deployment, and integrating an internal certificate authority simplifies BYOD exponentially. Among others, Avinash Kumar, Victor Ashe, Mohammad Zayed, and Rajesh Thattakath deserve major kudos for truly developing a rock-solid CA.

You no longer need to rely on integrating ISE to your existing PKI, providing ISE with a closed-loop BYOD solution—although you can absolutely make ISE's CA a subordinate CA to an existing PKI if you choose.

ISE CA PKI Hierarchy

While ISE can join an existing PKI, it is a PKI hierarchy unto itself. Every ISE cube from version 1.3 on has a root CA (on the initial Primary PAN by default), as well as subordinate CAs and other roles within a PKI. Figure D-8 illustrates a basic PKI hierarchy. There is a single root CA, and there can be numerous subordinate CAs that are allowed to sign certificates on behalf of that root CA. As shown, there can be additional layers of CAs that are authorized to sign on behalf of their parent CA in the tree.

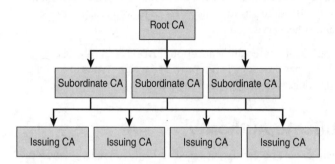

Figure D-8   *Generic PKI Hierarchy*

PKI design is quite basic. The root is only used to sign the certificates of its subordinate CAs, and then it sits idle. In fact, the best practice for PKI is to take the root offline and only bring it back online whenever a new subordinate CA needs to be added. As an example of that behavior, the certificates for the common root CAs on the public Internet are kept locked up in safes and an actual key ceremony occurs for the extraction of those keys from the safe for the signing of a new subordinate CA. Google the term "key ceremony" for more information. If you are a geek, like me, it is a fun thing to watch when it happens.

Figure D-9 illustrates the basic PKI hierarchy of a distributed ISE cube. You can see that the Primary PAN (P-PAN) is also the Root CA. Each PSN is a subordinate CA, and also has additional functionalities related to PKI.

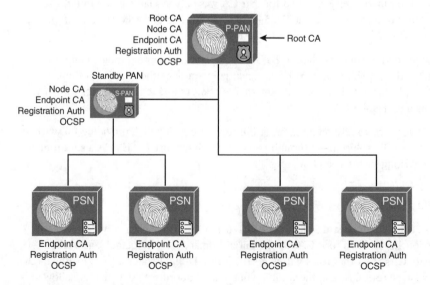

Figure D-9   *Basic ISE PKI Hierarchy*

The important thing to understand is that the first PAN in an ISE cube, the P-PAN, is always the root of an ISE PKI, and the PSNs are automatically joined to that root without any intervention from you, the ISE administrator.

The actual PKI design of ISE is a little more complicated than the simple one displayed in Figure D-9. Figure D-10 illustrates the complete PKI tree for an ISE cube, with the roles called out explicitly.

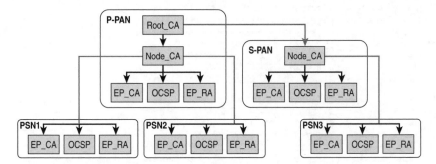

Figure D-10 *Detailed ISE PKI Hierarchy*

Let's dive into those detailed PKI roles:

- **Root CA:** The root of the PKI tree. There can be only one, and it is always the first PAN in the ISE cube: the P-PAN. Promoting the secondary PAN (S-PAN) to primary will not change the root, as the S-PAN does not have the root certificate.

> **Note** The root CA is only used to sign the node CA certificates. Once that is completed, the root certificate has no active function.

- **Node CA:** This tier of CA exists on both administrative nodes, and is used to sign the endpoint CA of each node in the ISE cube.

- **Endpoint CA:** The final tier in the PKI tree. This is the CA function that performs the signing of the endpoint certificates themselves. Both PANs and all PSNs have the endpoint CA function.

- **Endpoint registration authority (RA):** The function used to broker certificate requests from the endpoint to external CAs. Both PANs and all PSNs have the RA function.

- **Online Certificate Status Protocol (OCSP):** The function used for certificate revocation checking. All nodes in the ISE cube maintain a copy of the certificate database, and the OCSP service runs on both PANs and all PSNs to allow the checking of those certificates.

Each function in the PKI has a corresponding certificate to go along with it, used to uniquely identify the node and the individual function in the PKI tree. Figure D-11 shows an example list of certificates for the internal CA of a distributed ISE cube, located under **Administration > System > Certificates > Certificate Authority > Certificate Authority Certificates**.

CA Certificates

Edit | Import | Export | Delete | View | Refresh

Friendly Name	Status	Trusted For	Serial Number	Issued To	Issued By	Valid From
▼ atw-ise237						
Certificate Services Root CA - atw-ise237#00001	Enabled	Endpoints,Infrastructure	39 54 DA F9 A3 E6 48 5C BE F0 9C 60 0F FF 7D AB	Certificate Services Root CA - atw-ise237	Certificate Services Root CA - atw-ise237	Mon, 12 Dec 2016
Certificate Services Endpoint Sub CA - atw-ise237#00003	Enabled	Infrastructure,Endpoints	5B 7F 94 B6 5E C8 4C BC 8B 33 9A 29 7E BB F8 D2	Certificate Services Endpoint Sub CA - atw-ise237	Certificate Services Root CA - atw-ise237	Mon, 12 Dec 2016
Certificate Services OCSP Responder - atw-ise237#00004	Enabled	Infrastructure,Endpoints	3D 0C EA A2 22 11 42 9A 93 3E 9B 5D C2 5B E6 64	Certificate Services OCSP Responder - atw-ise237	Certificate Services Node CA - atw-ise237	Mon, 12 Dec 2016
Certificate Services Node CA - atw-ise237#00002	Enabled	Endpoints,Infrastructure	5D 62 EA A5 BB 05 47 2D BF 88 81 82 73 90 D7 FE	Certificate Services Node CA - atw-ise237	Certificate Services Root CA - atw-ise237	Mon, 12 Dec 2016
Certificate Services Root CA - atw-ise237#0001B	Enabled	Infrastructure,Endpoints	21 CA 5B 62 3B 6F 42 CB 8E 8B 90 75 B4 0E FD D6	Certificate Services Root CA - atw-ise237	Certificate Services Root CA - atw-ise237	Thu, 22 Dec 2016
Certificate Services Node CA - atw-ise237#00019	Enabled	Infrastructure,Endpoints	4E 3E FA 0A CC D0 4A 1F BF DA AE 22 04 F0 8F 66	Certificate Services Node CA - atw-ise237	Certificate Services Root CA - atw-ise237	Thu, 22 Dec 2016
Certificate Services Endpoint Sub CA - atw-ise237#00020	Enabled	Infrastructure,Endpoints	20 90 3E 3A BB C9 4F 08 A0 C4 DD 23 28 4C 0E 8B	Certificate Services Endpoint Sub CA - atw-ise237	Certificate Services Node CA - atw-ise237	Thu, 22 Dec 2016
Certificate Services OCSP Responder - atw-ise237#00021	Enabled	Infrastructure,Endpoints	09 DD EF B3 18 10 45 55 94 13 19 D9 89 44 0B CF	Certificate Services OCSP Responder - atw-ise237	Certificate Services Node CA - atw-ise237	Thu, 22 Dec 2016
▼ atw-ise241						
Certificate Services Node CA - atw-ise241#00015	Enabled	Infrastructure,Endpoints	6B 64 30 D7 AB B5 4D A3 9B 8D 8F 73 87 F1 E9 C4	Certificate Services Node CA - atw-ise241	Certificate Services Root CA - atw-ise237	Sun, 18 Dec 2016
Certificate Services Endpoint Sub CA - atw-ise241#00018	Enabled	Infrastructure,Endpoints	3B 02 D0 03 9E 7F 41 23 A9 39 09 52 82 8E 3F 5C	Certificate Services Endpoint Sub CA - atw-ise241	Certificate Services Node CA - atw-ise241	Sun, 18 Dec 2016
Certificate Services OCSP Responder - atw-ise241#00017	Enabled	Infrastructure,Endpoints	2F C8 45 B2 40 0A 4B 23 B4 46 A6 BC 09 43 00 CE	Certificate Services OCSP Responder - atw-ise241	Certificate Services Node CA - atw-ise241	Sun, 18 Dec 2016
Certificate Services Node CA - atw-ise241#00026	Enabled	Infrastructure,Endpoints	09 45 E7 79 DD 82 4D B5 99 9B 0C A7 FD C6 FC 59	Certificate Services Node CA - atw-ise241	Certificate Services Root CA - atw-ise237	Thu, 22 Dec 2016
Certificate Services Endpoint Sub CA - atw-ise241#00027	Enabled	Infrastructure,Endpoints	49 1E F8 39 A2 A0 48 F6 89 B2 A9 F7 D0 80 8A C2	Certificate Services Endpoint Sub CA - atw-ise241	Certificate Services Node CA - atw-ise241	Thu, 22 Dec 2016
Certificate Services OCSP Responder - atw-ise241#00028	Enabled	Infrastructure,Endpoints	56 84 49 02 BF 5F 47 49 A8 C5 89 D0 F6 26 4C 7F	Certificate Services OCSP Responder - atw-ise241	Certificate Services Node CA - atw-ise241	Thu, 22 Dec 2016
▼ atw-ise242						
Certificate Services OCSP Responder - atw-ise242#00024	Enabled	Infrastructure,Endpoints	37 60 3A FF 07 2D 45 A3 90 C5 CA 98 60 32 A6 FA	Certificate Services OCSP Responder - atw-ise242	Certificate Services Node CA - atw-ise237	Thu, 22 Dec 2016

Figure D-11   *Example Certificate Authority Certificates*

The Endpoint CA

When a PSN joins the ISE cube, the PAN instructs the PSN to generate three certificate signing requests (CSR). The PSN is requesting the node CA to sign a certificate for the endpoint CA, another certificate for the OCSP function, and a third certificate for the RA role. There is no administrative action needed; it all happens automatically, unless you have disabled the internal CA. Figure D-12 illustrates this behavior.

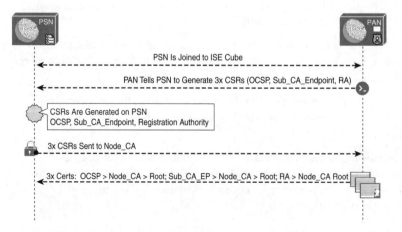

Figure D-12   *Example Certificate Authority Certificates*

Reissuing CA Certificates

There may come a time when you have to start over with your certificate authority's certificates. Perhaps you didn't back things up (securely) and you lost the original root CA certificate. There could be a number of reasons.

Reissuing CA certificates is fairly easy to do (some consider it too easy, considering the importance of the task). From the ISE GUI, perform the following steps:

Step 1. Navigate to **Administration > System > Certificates > Certificate Management > Certificate Signing Requests**.

Step 2. Click **Generate Certificate Signing Requests (CSR)**.

Step 3. From the Usage drop-down list, choose **ISE Root CA**, as shown in Figure D-13.

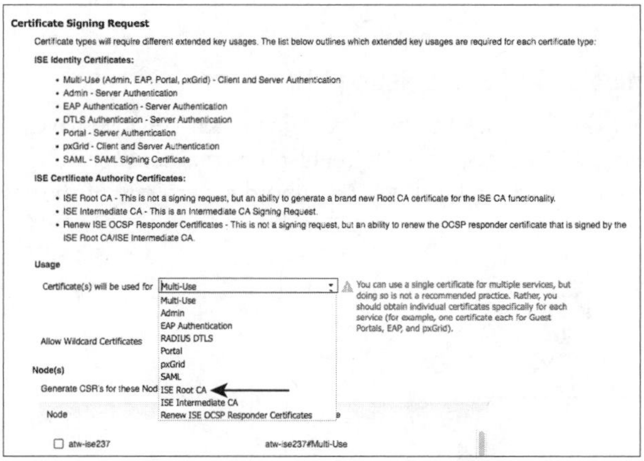

Figure D-13 *Certificate Signing Request*

Step 4. Click **Replace ISE Root CA Certificate chain**, as shown in Figure D-14.

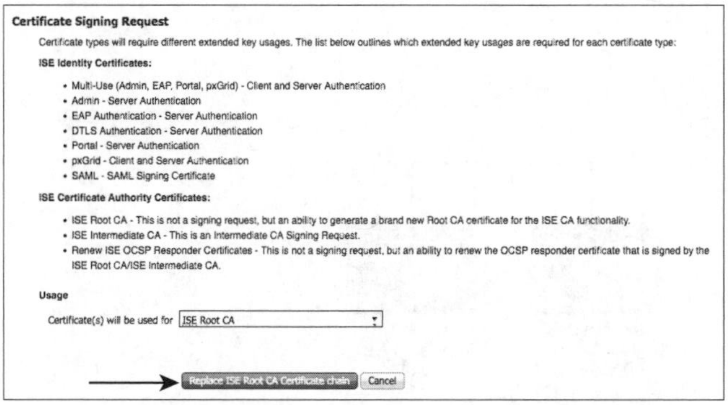

Figure D-14 *Replace ISE Root CA Certificate Chain*

That's it. You've just replaced all the CA certificates on all the ISE nodes. Don't worry, you did not invalidate all the existing endpoints that have already gotten certificates. Those certificates are still in the database and still warranted by the CA until their expiration date. ISE still trusts any certificate that was signed by the older PKI chain, as the old and new certificates are now listed in **Administration > System > Certificates > Certificate Authority > Certificate Authority Certificates.** You also continue to have the power to revoke any certificates that were previously issued.

> **Warning**   Do not ever delete the certificates from **Administration > System > Certificates > Certificate Authority > Certificate Authority Certificates,** unless you are certain and directed by Cisco TAC. Doing so will result in the CA revoking every certificate issued under that PKI chain, and could result in your denying access to all those endpoints. There is no way to undo this action.

Configuring ISE to be a Subordinate CA to an Existing PKI

ISE's internal certificate authority does not need to be a standalone PKI. You also have the option to "join" it to an existing hierarchy. Figure D-15 illustrates this concept, where the root CA is a Microsoft CA, and the ISE P-PAN is subordinate to one of the Microsoft issuing CAs.

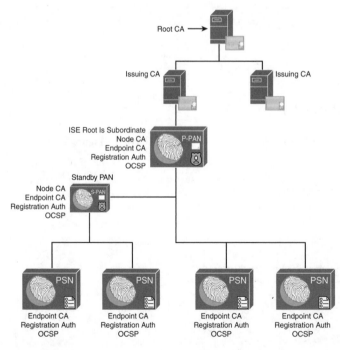

Figure D-15   *ISE CA as Subordinate to Existing PKI*

In the illustration shown in Figure D-15, it is possible that the endpoint CA that issues the certificate to the BYOD endpoints is actually five levels deep in the PKI hierarchy. Note that this is not a best practice, just an illustration.

When considering the depths of a PKI tree (also known as branches), you must remember that ISE's CA by itself is three branches deep on its own. Many enterprise CAs allow the administrator to limit the depth of the PKI tree, so an adjustment to the policy may be required before you can sign ISE's certificate with the existing PKI.

To help illustrate the tree depth, Figure D-16 shows the logical tree of the illustration in D-15.

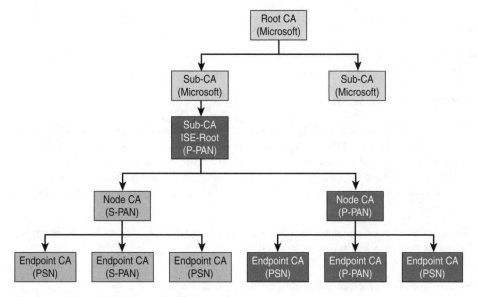

Figure D-16   *PKI Hierarchy Illustrated*

Notice in Figure D-16 that the P-PAN may be a single physical ISE node, but it acts as three separate CAs: root, node, and endpoint CA. The secondary PAN is a single physical node, but it acts as two separate CAs: node and endpoint. All nodes descend from a single root of the PKI tree.

Although the PKI design may look complex, ISE truly simplifies the configuration. To configure ISE to be a subordinate CA to an existing PKI, follow these steps:

Step 1.   Navigate to **Administration > System > Certificates > Certificate Management > Certificate Signing Requests**.

Step 2.   Click **Generate Certificate Signing Requests (CSR)**.

Step 3.   From the Usage drop-down list, choose **ISE Intermediate CA**, as shown in Figure D-17.

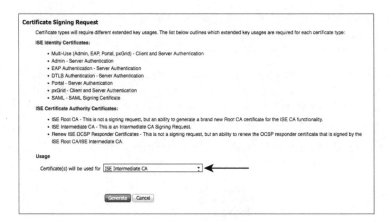

Figure D-17   *Generating the Intermediate CA Certificate Signing Request*

Step 4.   Click **Generate**.

The CSR that is generated is requesting a certificate with permissions to sign certificates (a CA certificate), not an end-entity certificate like the BYOD. You will take the CSR to whichever CA you wish to become subordinate to. If the example in Figure D-17 were real, you would take the CSR to the certificate portal on the subordinate Microsoft CA, not the root. It all depends on what level of the existing PKI tree you want the ISE branch to start at.

Figure D-18 shows an example certificate portal on a Microsoft CA signing the intermediate CA CSR that was exported from ISE.

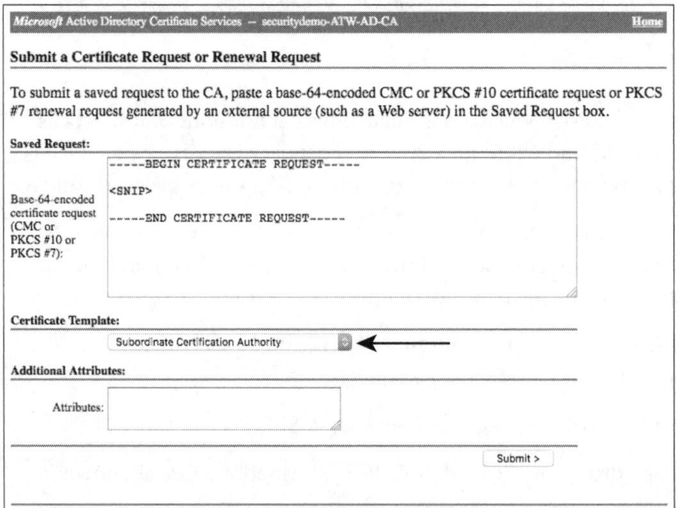

Figure D-18   *Signing the Intermediate CA Certificate Signing Request*

Now that you know how to make ISE subordinate to an existing PKI, ask yourself: "Why do I want to?" One reason is that any client that already trusts the root certificate authority of the existing PKI will now trust the certificates signed by one of its subordinates. Therefore, ISE issued certificates are automagically trusted. However, as you read in Chapter 17, that is not how it works with trust chains for EAP. The network client on the endpoint has to explicitly trust the certificates of the EAP servers before an EAP exchange will occur, unless that list of trusted certificates was provided by an MDM or similar management solution.

Being part of the same PKI hierarchy does not mean that the CAs share their issued certificate databases, or revocation status. The ISE database will remain separate from the Microsoft one, and any Microsoft CRL or OCSP databases will not get the list of certificates that ISE has issued or revoked. There are no APIs in existence today to make CAs of different vendors share the data.

Due to the separate certificate databases and because the ISE CA is very specific to BYOD, network authentication, and pxGrid, it is a more common practice to leave the ISE PKI hierarchy as standalone, and not join it to the existing PKI.

Backing Up the Certificates

Backing up certificates is a very controversial topic in the PKI community. The general security guideline would frown on any situation where a private key is exposed. Public certificates are designed to be passed around, and it shouldn't matter who has a copy of them, but the private key must remain private.

Within the certificate authority, the signing keys should always be stored in an encrypted database, perhaps even within a hardware security module (HSM). The use of HSMs is deemed the ultimate method of securing your private keys, and HSMs are used for the Internet roots as well as many enterprises. An HSM is a piece of hardware that stores digital keys in a nonreversible encrypted storage.

Although the ISE CA stores the private keys within a key storage database that leverages very strong encryption, it does not yet make use of HSMs. Therefore, it is not possible to simply detach the HSM housing the root key and store it in a safe.

The keys used by the ISE CA to sign certificates are not backed up as part of the normal ISE backup process. What ISE does provide is a separate mechanism to extract the certificate and private key pairs for the CA in an encrypted bundle, which can then be imported back into a restored ISE node.

It is up to you, the administrator, to ensure those private keys remain secure once they are outside of ISE's secured storage. One idea is to use an encrypted USB drive that is locked away in a physical vault.

To back up the certificate authority key pairs:

Step 1.   Connect to the ISE console, or SSH to the ISE node.

Step 2.   Issue the **application configure ise** command.

Step 3.   Choose [7]Export Internal CA Store.

Step 4.   Type the name of the ISE repository to export the encrypted bundle to.

Step 5.   Provide an encryption key (passphrase) for encrypting and decrypting the bundle.

Example D-1 shows the exporting of keys from an ISE node.

Example D-1   *Exporting Keys from an ISE Node*

```
woland-ise/admin# application configure ise

Selection ISE configuration option
[1]Reset M&T Session Database
[2]Rebuild M&T Unusable Indexes
[3]Purge M&T Operational Data
[4]Reset M&T Database
[5]Refresh Database Statistics
[6]Display Profiler Statistics
[7]Export Internal CA Store
[8]Import Internal CA Store
[9]Create Missing Config Indexes
[10]Create Missing M&T Indexes
[11]Enable/Disable ACS Migration
[12]Generate Daily KPM Stats
[13]Generate KPM Stats for last 8 Weeks
[14]Enable/Disable Counter Attribute Collection
[15]View Admin Users
[16]Get all Endpoints
[17]Exit


7

Export Repository Name: Synology
Enter encryption-key for export: [redacted]
log4j:WARN No appenders could be found for logger
   (org.springframework.core.env.StandardEnvironment).
log4j:WARN Please initialize the log4j system properly.
log4j:WARN See http://logging.apache.org/log4j/1.2/faq.html#noconfig for more info.
Integritycheck Openssl digest output from verification with Swims release key:
   Verified OK
Integritycheck Output: Verified signature of integritycheck program with Swims
   release key
Integritycheck Output: Verified signature of integritycheck.sums file with Swims
   release key
```

```
Integritycheck PASSED
Inside Session facade init
node-config.rc has been modified - rebuilding active properties file
PlatformProperties whoami: root

PlatformProperties show inventory: Process Output:

Getting profile properties for profile 'ibmLarge' and persona 'standalone'
In the init method of PDPFacade
Time taken for NSFAdminServiceFactory to load4158
Export in progress...




The following 5 CA key pairs were exported to repository 'Synology' at
 'ise_ca_key_pairs_of_woland-ise':
        Subject:CN=Certificate Services Root CA - woland-ise
        Issuer:CN=Certificate Services Root CA - woland-ise
        Serial#:0x769a465c-342c4a7b-a529bf09-f3e5720c

        Subject:CN=Certificate Services Node CA - woland-ise
        Issuer:CN=Certificate Services Root CA - woland-ise
        Serial#:0x4bfc93d9-e0b147a7-a1955f9e-e2041967

        Subject:CN=Certificate Services Endpoint Sub CA - woland-ise
        Issuer:CN=Certificate Services Node CA - woland-ise
        Serial#:0x25f246b9-0efe419a-9fe27fc6-df9c4f12

        Subject:CN=Certificate Services Endpoint RA - woland-ise
        Issuer:CN=Certificate Services Endpoint Sub CA - woland-ise
        Serial#:0x6e1d8208-3c2647fa-9fbdbcb4-2f732ba0

        Subject:CN=Certificate Services OCSP Responder - woland-ise
        Issuer:CN=Certificate Services Node CA - woland-ise
        Serial#:0x2f5ba187-4eb4452f-8a35c3b7-fa6d9548

ISE CA keys export completed successfully

Selection ISE configuration option
[1]Reset M&T Session Database
[2]Rebuild M&T Unusable Indexes
[3]Purge M&T Operational Data
[4]Reset M&T Database
[5]Refresh Database Statistics
```

```
[6]Display Profiler Statistics

[7]Export Internal CA Store

[8]Import Internal CA Store

[9]Create Missing Config Indexes

[10]Create Missing M&T Indexes

[11]Enable/Disable ACS Migration

[12]Generate Daily KPM Stats

[13]Generate KPM Stats for last 8 Weeks

[14]Enable/Disable Counter Attribute Collection

[15]View Admin Users

[16]Get all Endpoints

[17]Exit


17
woland-ise/admin#
```

Note   The keys exported and backed up through this process are the CA key pairs, not the certificates that have been signed and issued to endpoints. Those public certificates are backed up as part of the normal ISE backup process.

Issuing Certificates from the ISE CA

As you saw in Chapter 17, the ISE CA is capable of delivering certificates directly to the BYOD endpoints during the onboarding phase. In fact, there are default out-of-the-box rules and certificate templates within ISE that leverage the internal CA without your having to configure much of anything.

You saw in Chapter 25 that the ISE CA is also capable of providing certificates to pxGrid participants using the pxGrid user interface, as shown in Figure D-19. ISE also automatically issues those pxGrid certificates to ISE nodes in the cube.

Figure D-19   *Issuing pxGrid Certificates from the pxGrid Admin UI*

In addition to the methods already listed, ISE is also able to provide certificates through a web-based portal, for those devices that cannot participate in the BYOD onboarding flows (such as Windows Mobile and IoT devices).

The portal can be configured for any network user to provision themselves a certificate, or for an ISE SuperAdmin to provision certificates for anyone at all. To configure the portal:

Step 1. Navigate to **Administration > Device Portal Management > Certificate Provisioning.**

Step 2. Edit the **Certificate Provisioning Portal (default)** or create a new one.

The Certificate Provisioning Portal leverages the same portal framework as all the other client-facing portals within ISE. Therefore, it is fully customizable. The port, interfaces, and certificate used are all configurable. You can change out the look and feel to brand the portal as you wish for your organization.

By default, there are no groups permitted to access the portal.

Step 3. Within the Portal Settings section, under Configure Authorized Groups, select from the list on the left each group that should be able to access this portal, and move that group to the right side of the widget by clicking the right-facing arrow, as shown in Figure D-20.

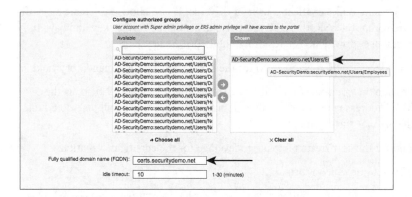

Figure D-20 *Authorizing Groups to Access the Portal*

Step 4. Provide a friendly name for the FQDN, also shown in Figure D-20, which is required to access the portal.

Step 5. Expand the Certificate Portal Settings section, and select one or more certificate templates to allow users of this portal to issue certificates for, as shown in Figure D-21.

For example, perhaps this portal is for pxGrid certificates only, or this portal was added for endpoint certificates only.

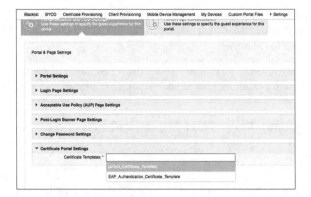

Figure D-21   *Selecting the Certificate Templates for the Portal*

Step 6.   Click **Save**.

To issue or sign certificates from the portal:

Step 7.   Navigate to the friendly FQDN that you defined previously in Step 4.

Step 8.   Log in to the portal.

Step 9.   Select the action you wish to pursue.

The portal allows you to create a single certificate with and without a CSR, or to generate bulk certificates using a CSV file. If you choose to create a certificate without a CSR, then ISE must also generate the private key and have the portal user download the resulting public/private key pair.

Step 10.   Provide a Common Name (CN) for the certificate. This is a mandatory field.

Step 11.   Provide the endpoint MAC address. This is also a mandatory field, as the MAC address is required for all endpoint certificates, and will be entered into the SAN of the certificate.

Step 12.   Choose the certificate template to leverage for the certificate creation.

Step 13.   Pick your download format.

Different endpoints will be able to work with different formats. The ISE CA tries to be as flexible as possible.

Step 14.   Because this request will include a private key, a password to use for the encryption is required. Enter the password in the Password field.

Step 15.   Click **Generate**.

Figure D-22 illustrates the portal login screen, and Figure D-23 shows an example portal being filled out.

Figure D-22 *Portal Login Screen*

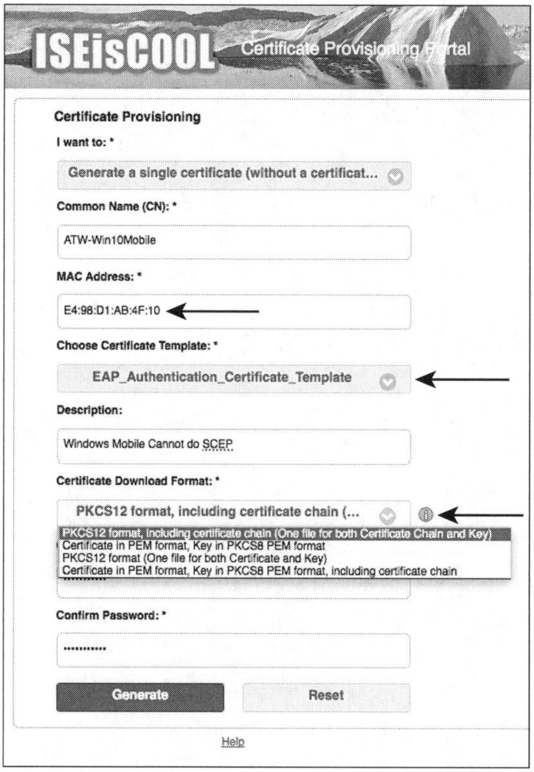

Figure D-23 *Selecting the Certificate Templates for the Portal*

Index

Numbers

D

J–K

L

M

Q–R

S

T

U

X–Y–Z